Strategic Management

6BM028

Instructor:
Jim Milligan

University of Derby

McGraw-Hill/Irwin

A Division of The McGraw·Hill Companies

McGraw–Hill Primis

ISBN: 0–390–72895–0

Text:

Strategic Management: Text and Cases,
Third Edition
Dess–Lumpkin–Eisner

International Business: Competing in the
Global Marketplace, Sixth Edition
Hill

Taking Sides: Issues in Business Ethics and
Society, Ninth Edition
Newton–Ford

Crafting and Executing Strategy, Text and
Readings, 14/e
Thompson et al

Strategy: Analysis and Practice, Text and
Cases
McGee–Thomas–Wilson

Handwritten notes:

1) P.33 (MANIFEST, DRIVERS, etc)

2) P.73 THE PROCESS OF CRAFTING AND EXECUTING STRATEGY (Planned vs Approaches)

3) P.101 Competitive Strategy – Strategic position P163 & Capability (Markets and Resources)

4) P.204 No (Corporate Parenting / Synergy etc)

5) 244 (Alliances / Mergers / Acquisitions) (networking Strategies)

6) 384 Knowledge, information, innovation

This book was printed on recycled paper.

Strategic Management

http://www.mhhe.com/primis/online/

111   STMGGEN   ISBN: 0-390-72895-0

Strategic Management

Contents

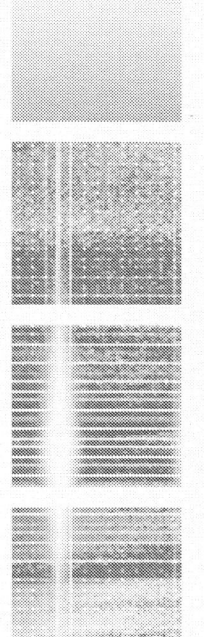

Part 1

An introduction to strategy

Part contents

In this part you will find the following chapters:

Introduction

This section forms the key introductory theme music both to the concepts of strategy and to the orientation of this book. In the opening two chapters we try to cover both the basics of strategy – what it is and how we might conceive of it analytically – and how strategy and organization can interact, mutually influencing what happens in practice. This section also presents our own theoretical model (depicted in Figure 1.6 and Figure 2.2) which attempts to show how quite often disparate perspectives on strategy (for example planning, performance, execution and feedback) can be seen as a coherent system. In this respect, these opening chapters form the essential foundation of the book and help inform all the sections and chapters that follow. Each section discusses elements of the overall framework (Figure 1.6). You will see that at the beginning of each section of the book we have depicted which parts of the systemic framework are being emphasized and addressed. The final chapter of the book then attempts to reassemble these component parts into our overall view of strategy and the strategy process.

Chapter 1 points out the contested terrain of strategy, in particular its various definitions and descriptions. Showing how different perspectives on strategy developed, the chapter then provides examples and techniques for assessing strategy. Beginning with planning, the chapter outlines the basics of the planning process and shows the basic analytical tools which can help underpin future plans and trajectories. Taking the perspective that a large proportion of strategy researchers have viewed it largely as a question of alignment (or fit) of the organization with its environment, the chapter covers the various positioning tools and perspectives that can help determine future actions (strategies). Knowing where the organization is positioned in relation to its operating environment allows strategists to plan either for achieving a better (more competitive) position or to try to make it more difficult for others to enter the market and compete. The chapter concludes its analysis of planning by looking at the public face of strategic planning for many organizations. This public face is captured in the notions of goals and mission. A few examples of mission statements shows how such goal-oriented statements can be the overall guide of strategic decisions taken in the organization. Such guiding can take the form of a statement about future economic positioning (we want to be number one in the industry) or can take the form of expressed values (we want to be seen as environmentally friendly and socially responsible).

Nevertheless, we know some curious things can happen when planned strategies are implemented. As the popular expression has it, there can be many a slip between cup and lip. The rest of Chapter 1 and all of Chapter 2 then deal with these questions of what happens when we view strategy as embedded in a particular organizational context. For example, viewing an organization as a constellation of resources (people, knowledge, financial and so on) reveals that some organizations are better endowed with such resources than others. They have more people with more skills and knowledge and are able to resource strategic decisions to a greater extent than other organizations. Taking this perspective leads us to the resource-based view of the organization and we discuss this in some detail.

Similarly, we know that strategy is not always a linear process. By this we mean that strategy is not necessarily a long period of thinking (planning) followed by a long period of acting (implementation). In many cases, strategists implement decisions without much (or, sometimes, any) planning. Decisions emerge from an organization, driven by a wide range of influences such as history (what strategists have done in the past), organizational values (the way we do things around here) and knee-jerk reactions to external threats. Planning, if it exists at all, is then retro-fitted to the process. This debate over whether strategic decisions are planned or emerge is covered in detail in Part 1.

Chapter 2 hinges around what many researchers have termed the more 'process' views of strategy. Taking the view that planning a trajectory is necessary but not sufficient to ensure strategic decisions follow automatically, the chapter shows how animation is as important as orientation for strategists. Animation examines the interplay between strategic intention and how managers interpret the environment, providing a context in which organizational members can become enthused and committed to a particular set of tasks.

The chapter also examines in detail debates over the appropriate levels of analysis we might adopt to understand strategy. In particular, recent work has stressed the importance of relatively micro approaches (what managers think, do and say) over the more macro approaches (level of competition, industry characteristics). Taking the individual as pivotal, the chapter shows how we can conceive of strategy as being essentially a process of individual *interpretation* of events and actions. This view has gathered momentum over recent years and it draws on classic work in the 1950s and 60s about behavioural theories of the firm as well as classic work on strategic decision making in the 1970s and 80s. The point of such debates is that, ultimately, strategists have to make a choice between the extremes of voluntarism and determinism. Determinism implies that all managerial action is shaped and, in the extreme, pre-determined by the context in which they operate. Voluntarism is the opposite view, arguing that strategists can act freely and without environmental constraints. Depending on which perspective you take (or what mixture of each), your view of how strategy processes actually work will be completely different.

Finally, Chapter 2 emphasizes the important role of history. Where an organization and its members have been in the past will have an influence upon its present activities. The longer an organization has been in operation, the longer will be its history of strategic decisions and it is likely to have built up a substantial repertoire of standard responses and actions to particular situations. Organizations can easily become programmed to the degree that they are more accurately described as a collection of ready-made solutions looking for new problems, rather than there being any proactive approach towards taking strategic decisions. Having read both chapters, you should then re-visit Figure 1.6 and 2.2. Here you will recognize both the detail and the bigger pictures of strategy. We have tried to show these as a dynamic and self-reinforcing model that also acts as a frame and as a lens to the rest of the book. The Online Learning Centre (www.mcgraw-hill.co.uk/textbooks/mcgee) shows how we simplify these two figures to create the two maps that we use in the Introductions to Parts 2, 3, 4 and 5. Figure 1.6 becomes the Strategy Resources Concepts map and Figure 2.2 becomes the Strategy Process Concepts map.

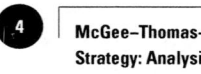

Chapter 1

The concept of strategy

Introduction

Why another book on strategy? Given the huge number of books on the subject, an initial conclusion might be that all that needs to be communicated has already been written. There is some truth in this statement if one assumes that the nature and definitions of strategy are pretty well aligned no matter which authors are consulted, or if one assumes that the theoretical and practical aspects of understanding strategy are uncontested. However, congruence in any of these areas is very difficult to find. Strategy remains one of the most contested and ill-defined concepts in management theory. As Magretta (2003) states:

> . . . of all the concepts in management, strategy is the one that attracts the most attention and generates the most controversy. Almost everyone agrees that it is important. Almost no-one agrees on what it is.

Chapter contents

This book will acknowledge some of the key debates concerning how scholars and practitioners have viewed and practised strategy, but it will not dwell in great detail on either the historical development of the field or on the intense debates which have emerged from five or so decades of theoretical and empirical work. This has indeed been achieved in many textbooks on strategy already (see, for example, Hussey 1998 for a conventional history of strategy, and Cummings and Wilson 2003 for a relatively less conventional mapping of the field). Our intention here is to review briefly some of the key shapers and characteristics of the field and then to see to what extent it is possible both to acknowledge and to combine competing perspectives to create a more holistic approach to understanding strategy. This book analyses the meaning of strategy by breaking it down into its component parts, namely: its *external logic* – how the organization positions itself relative to its external context; its *internal logic* – the levels of the organization at which strategy has different meanings and what distinctive resources and competences it must acquire; its *performance over time* – distinguishing between achievement of long-term objectives, meeting milestones along the way, and preserving short-term stability; and, finally, its *managerial requirements* – the role of general managers and how strategy is planned, managed, monitored and maintained. The next section tries to clarify what we mean by strategy in this book by building upon and trying to synthesize the approaches of key works in the field.

1.1 Key definitions of strategy

In a conference at Harvard Business School in 1963, Cook (reported in Bower 1982) argued that 'the charter of business policy is to focus on the life and death issues of central interest to top management . . . to help top management to deal with these issues effectively, profitably and morally'. Legge (2003), in her chapter on strategy as organizing, points out when discussing Henry Mintzberg's (1994) work that, in general, 'if you ask someone to define strategy, you will likely be told that strategy is a plan or something equivalent – a direction, a guide, a course of action into the future, a path to get from here to there'. Of course, Mintzberg *et al.* (1998) argue that this definition of intended strategy fails to recognize strategy as an emergent process, which is best seen as a pattern in a stream of decisions. Strategy, for Mintzberg, is what emerges from actions rather than something planned in advance or in anticipation of future contexts. We explore this planned versus emergent aspect of strategy in later sections of this chapter.

Prahalad and Hamel (1990), have also been very instrumental in influencing how we view strategy. They conceptualized strategy in terms of strategic intent, which they define as providing an overarching strategic direction. Strategic intent is, in essence, about winning in a competitive game. This leads to a focus on strategy as a process for reinforcing intent by developing the core competences of a corporation, and leading and managing change.

They also propose the viewpoint of 'strategy as stretch and leverage', in which the strategist sees the advantage of breaking the strategic frame and leveraging the critical core competences in an innovative and distinctive manner. Indeed, the concept of strategy as innovation is dominant in their current thinking and they stress the need for strategists to embrace radical innovation and innovate to stay in front of the competitive game. Their thinking in this respect mirrors that of Christensen (1997) who has discussed the role of the disruptive innovation and the new economy in shaping strategy in the evolving competitive landscape.

Perhaps the definition of strategy that is most common in the field is that attributed to the renowned Harvard business historian Alfred D. Chandler in his landmark book *Strategy and Structure*. The Chandler (1963) definition characterizes strategy as:

> *the determination of the basic long-term goals and objective of an enterprise and the adoption of courses of action and the allocation of resources necessary for carrying out these goals.*

This is the classical view of strategy, very much rational in analysis and following militaristic traditions, including those specified in the Japanese strategy book authored by Sun Tzu entitled *The Art of War* (1990). Quinn (1980), in an equally famous book entitled *Strategies for Change: Logical Incrementalism*, follows Chandler's case study tradition and talks about strategy in a more process-oriented way. Quinn's definition is:

> *the pattern or plan that integrates an organization's major goals, policies and action sequences into a cohesive whole. A well-formulated strategy helps to marshal and allocate an organization's resources into a unique and viable posture based on its relative internal competences and shortcomings, anticipated changes in the environment and contingent moves by intelligent opponents.*

Porter (1987), the Harvard Business School strategy professor, who has also had a tremendous influence on the field of strategic management and competitive strategy, picks up the themes of being different and achieving strategic coherence in organizational strategy. He argues, therefore, that competitive strategy is about being different (i.e. effective strategic positioning). It means deliberately choosing a different set of activities to deliver a unique mix of value. However, a strategic position is not sustainable unless there are trade-offs with other positions. Trade-offs create the need for choice (making strategic decisions) and protect against repositioners and straddlers. Strategy is about combining activities that are complementary and reinforcing. This strategic 'coherence' among many activities is fundamental not only to achieving competitive advantage, but also to the sustainability of that advantage. It is harder for a rival to match an array of interlocked activities than it is merely to match a particular sales force approach, match a process technology or replicate a set of product features. Positions built on a series of coherent activities are far more sustainable than those built on individual activities.

McGee–Thomas–Wilson:
Strategy: Analysis and
Practice, Text and Cases

1. The concept of strategy

Text

© The McGraw–Hill
Companies, 2006

8   CHAPTER 1 THE CONCEPT OF STRATEGY

Although the previous definitions might seem at odds with one another (even mutually exclusive in some cases, for example between planned and emergent strategies) there are some common elements which we can identify to help us clarify the analysis a little. Common elements in these viewpoints include the following:

- Strategy as a means of establishing organizational purpose.
- Strategy as a definition of the competitive domains of the firm and the organizational context.
- Strategy as a response to the complexity of external opportunities and threats and internal strengths and weaknesses in order to achieve sustainable competitive advantage.
- Strategy as a way to define managerial tasks and processes with corporate, business and functional perspectives.
- Strategy as a system involving a coherent, unifying and integrative systematic pattern of decisions.
- Strategy as a definition of the economic and non-economic contributions which the firm intends to make to its stakeholders.
- Strategy as an architecture to develop the distinctive competences of an organization.
- Strategy as a vehicle for determining investments in tangible and intangible resources to develop the core capabilities which lead to sustainable advantages.
- Strategy as an expression of strategic intent; stretching the organization to innovate, leverage resources and develop new skills.

These common elements form the backbone of this book. They include the economic analysis of strategy to help plan and inform strategic decisions (Part 2); the analysis of strategy as both a feature of organizational positioning and capabilities, especially in a changing context of globalization and the new economy (Part 3); the analysis of strategy as a series of processes in which decisions have to be implemented and put into practice and which require an understanding of how organizations and individuals change and develop (Part 4); and a view of strategy as monitoring, improving and developing, helping data feedback into the next wave of strategy formulation (Part 5). Complex though all these factors are, the basics of strategy are relatively easily summarized and described. We examine these in the next section.

1.2 The basics of strategy

Figure 1.1 depicts the main basic dynamics and key factors to be taken into consideration when we begin to examine what we mean by strategy. At the most basic level, we mean that actions and decisions need to be analysed and taken in order for the organization to survive and thrive as conditions develop and change around it. These conditions (the external

McGee–Thomas–Wilson:
Strategy: Analysis and
Practice, Text and Cases

1. The concept of strategy

Text

© The McGraw–Hill
Companies, 2006

9

environment in Figure 1.1) comprise a wide range of factors. They include characteristics of the industry (for example the typewriter industry is today completely different from when electronic typewriters were state of the art); characteristics of the market (this may change from being benign to highly competitive and back again); sustainable development is now something all strategists have to consider and political conditions may change the context of business and government markedly (the impact of global terrorism, for example). We take each of the key factors and examine them in more detail in the following sections.

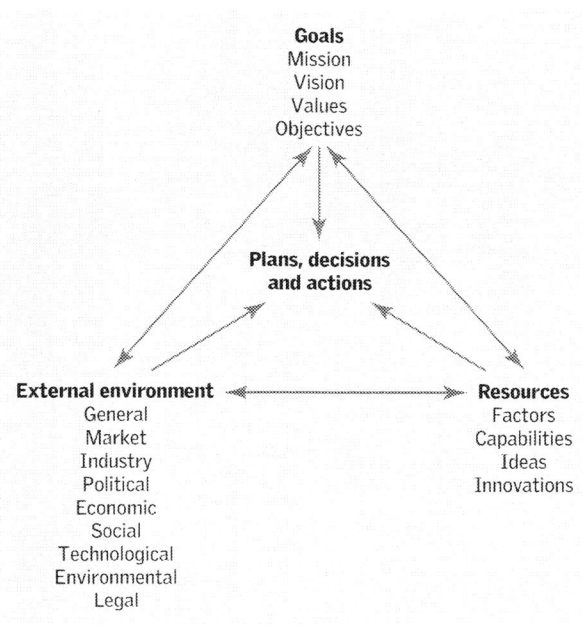

Figure 1.1 The basic dynamics of strategy

1.2.1 Plans, decisions and actions

The notion of planning heralds the beginnings of strategy. Many authors, such as Quinn (1980) and Cummings and Wilson (2003), have traced the military genesis of the term strategy from the Greeks and the Macedonians. The word 'strategos' began as a term describing a commanding role in the army (a general, for example) and by the time of Alexander the Great (330 BC) had become the word which described the successful deployment of troops to overcome the enemy and to the system of governance which facilitated this planning. It is this combined notion of planned deployment and governance which pervades the planning schools of strategy. Authors such as Ansoff (1965; 1972), building on the earlier work of the Stanford Research Institute, epitomize the translation of this planning orientation to the strategic conduct of business and the view of the general manager as a 'strategist' (coining the phrase 'strategic management' in 1972).

Most of today's organizations have some form of corporate plan or strategic plan and some form of planning process. In terms of Figure 1.1, strategic planning is the process by which the firm organizes its resources and actions in relation to an external environment in order to achieve its goals or objectives. This is usually a formal rather than an informal process, the key elements of which are outlined in Figure 1.2.

Planning is conducted in a very hierarchical and formal manner. It is typically top down with the direction and energy being supplied by top management. The process is iterative and the cycle is repeated (typically) on an annual basis. Planning horizons are in practice about three years in Western companies but this does depend on the length of product life cycles and the life of capital equipment.

Formal analysis would go through a number of stages in sequence. The first is typically the statement of the mission of the business. This would then be followed by a review of the external environment in which, for example, the economics of the industry would be assessed, the nature of markets and customers analysed, and broader political and social trends identified. In parallel there would be a review of the internal environment of the organization. This covers basic strengths and weaknesses, core competences and capability assessments. Based on these, views of the strengths and weaknesses and opportunities and threats (the well-known SWOT analysis which covers the reviews of the internal and external environments) are used as a starting point for formulating the

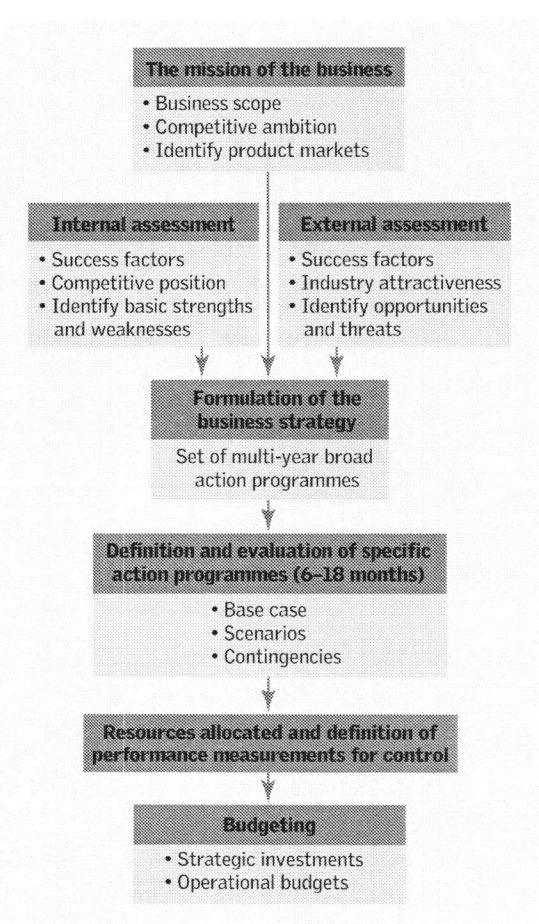

Figure 1.2 A typical planned, formal process of strategy formulation

strategy. From the basic business strategy will come a definition of the specific action programmes required to put the strategy into practice. This is what is usually called the business plan although the way in which this term is used varies widely between firms. This business plan is then submitted to an investment committee (this also goes under a variety of names) for resource allocation along with definition of performance milestones. After the investment expenditures are agreed, budgets are specified and agreed throughout the organization.

However, any person who has had experience of the above process in action in any organization may well have a wry smile on their face as they read the above seemingly rational and militaristic procedure. Great in theory, but never happens in practice might summarize their feelings. According to Mintzberg and Waters (1985) some strategies

McGee–Thomas–Wilson: | 1. The concept of strategy | Text
Strategy: Analysis and
Practice, Text and Cases

© The McGraw–Hill
Companies, 2006

11

1.2 THE BASICS OF STRATEGY 11

may be planned, at least in their first stages, but many more just simply *emerge* in an organization without being consciously intended or being deliberate acts. We might make sense of the *pattern* of these actions later and call them a strategy, but we do so with the luxury of hindsight. We construct a logic which was never intended in the first place. Emergent strategies can be seen as responses to unexpected opportunities and problems and are usually developed from the locations at which

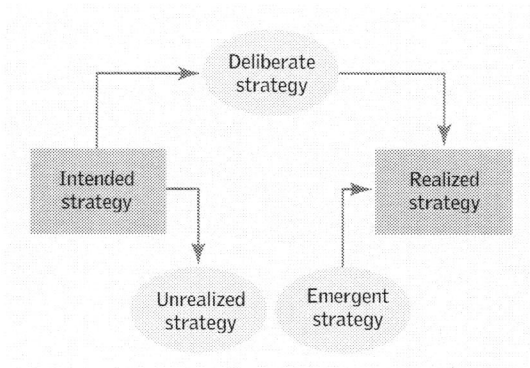

Figure 1.3 Intended and emergent strategies

business-level strategies are usually implemented, i.e. within business units and not at corporate headquarters. The pure definition of emergence requires the absence of any intentions. This is too strong for most occasions but, as Mintzberg and Waters (1985) observe, organizations come close to pure emergent strategies when an environment directly imposes a pattern of actions on them.

Quinn (1980) developed logical incrementalism as a way of explaining the combination of longer-term plans and targets with evolutionary, learning-based patterns of movement on the way (patterns of decisions which emerge). This is an attractive explanation because it seems to combine rational resource allocation thinking with practical learning by doing. Quinn argues that 'properly managed, it is a conscious, purposeful, pro-active, executive practice'.

The twin lenses of intentions and emergence are useful tools with which to analyse strategy since neither as a pure form is likely to be observable. Instead there is a continuum on which different blends can be seen. Figure 1.3 illustrates intentions being formulated as deliberate strategies, some of which come to fruition. But we also see a simultaneous pressure from circumstances producing a stream of emergent (but purposeful) thinking. Realized strategy is a blend of intentions and emergence which can be interpreted by reference to the strength of pressure from the external environment – a kind of environmental determinism.

1.2.2 The external environment

The external context of strategic decisions is very broad ranging. In principle, it can include anything and everything that might have an effect on decisions. We could include governments, international trade organizations, buyer and supplier markets, competitors, trade associations, civil servants, and the impersonal progression of science and technology. In order to provide some structure to this variety of influences, we can think of three regions of impact upon firm A (*see* Figure 1.4). These are market structure, industry structure, and the institutional/social context.

Market structure includes the intimate competition for the customers' attention between rivals in the marketplace. This is the competitive battleground within which the firm's long-term objectives are gained or lost and which provides the basis for assessing the distinctiveness of rival offerings to customers. It is here that competitive advantage (which we will define in Part 2) is won or lost.

The broader industry structure provides inputs of traded goods, knowledge and technical rules and procedures that condition the conduct of firms. Thus, pharmaceutical firms will hire scientists trained at universities. Car assemblers such as Ford and GM buy from components manufacturers such as GKN and Valeo. Industry trade associations stipulate rules of conduct and may conduct joint research. Distribution channels act across the board as intermediate customers and sometimes as powerful buyers in their own right. This industry structure has a deep impact on the underlying economic possibilities open to the participants in the market structure.

The broader institutional and social structure sets out the rules of the game in terms of what is morally, legally and ethically possible as well as setting the political terms of reference within which firms are obliged to operate.

These regions represent zones of influence for firms. Most influence is exercised within the market structure and least within the broad institutional context – at least as a general rule. However, firms see it as at least possible that they might shape the rules of the game by seeking to promote changes at various levels. But firms might also see their sphere of

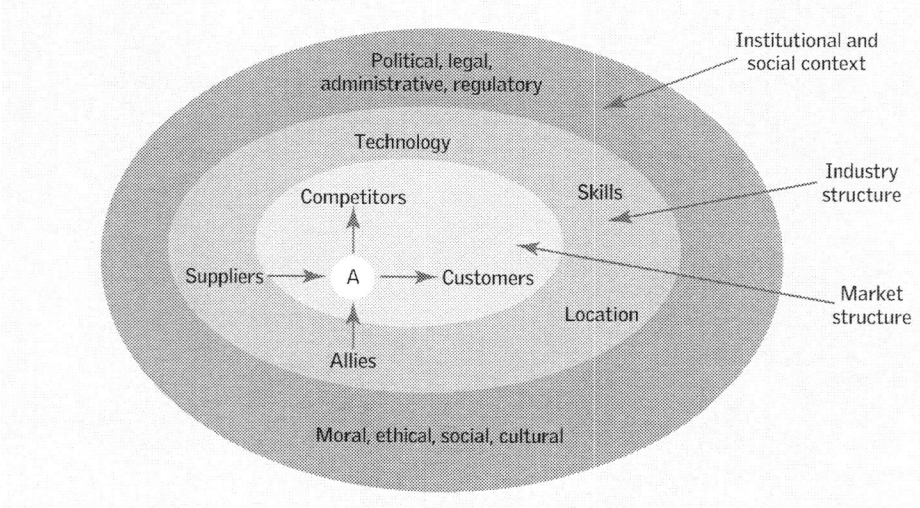

Figure 1.4 The external environment

influence as tightly focused within their market environment and subject, without any recourse, to powerful forces from elsewhere. One way for firms to assess exposure to forces within this broad context is through a PEST analysis. This is an analysis of political, economic, social and technological forces. Occasionally, specific aspects of dealing in particular national legal systems (for example) can be added to this analysis, but for simplicity they are excluded in the following description. Figure 1.5 provides an illustration of the variety of forces that can be identified via a PEST analysis.

In order to make sense of this 'shopping list' some analysis is needed to identify the really significant influences. This involves assigning probabilities and possible outcomes to each event and calculating an 'expected value' (technically the probability multiplied by the outcome). In practice this requires considerable judgement because many of the events can only be described in qualitative terms and because managers may have little, or very partial, information on each factor. We need also to identify ways in which the probabilities of the events and the outcomes of the events might be moderated by management action.

Political future	**Economic future**
• Political parties and alignment at local, national and European or regional trading-bloc level • Legislation, for example on taxation or employment law • Relations between government and the organization • Government ownership of industry and attitude to monopolies and to competition	• Total GDP, and GDP per head • Inflation • Disposable income and consumer expenditure • Interest rates • Currency fluctuations and exchange rates • Investment: by the state, by private firms and by foreign companies (FCI) • Business cycles • Unemployment • Key unit costs: for example energy, transport, telecommunications, raw materials
Socio-cultural future	**Technological future**
• Shifts in values and culture • Changes in lifestyle • Attitudes to work and leisure • 'Green' environmental issues • Education and health • Demographic changes • Distribution of income	• Government and EU investment policy • Identified new research initiatives • New patents and products • Rate of adoption of new technologies • Expenditure on research and development by rivals • 'Significant' developments in normally unrelated industries

Figure 1.5 An example of a PEST Analysis

1.2.3 Goals

As Quinn (1980) observes, goals (or objectives) are statements about 'what is to be achieved and when results are to be accomplished'. Goals do not address the question of *how* these objectives are to be achieved. They are basic statements of desired future objectives.

To communicate goals, organizations typically provide detailed statements of their strategic intent and their major goals in the form of mission statements. These are often criticized for their vacuity – indeed, one test of a good mission statement is said to be if employees can recite it without ironic laughter breaking out. It is possible to characterize two approaches to mission statements. One expresses mission in terms of *philosophy* and *ethics*, thereby widening the band of actors that are relevant to the long-term future of the company and capturing the notion of stakeholders. It also captures those forms of corporate behaviour that have implications for the social good and which are not reflected in the pricing mechanisms in marketplaces. The second approach expresses mission as *strategy*, an intellectual discourse that defines the firm's commercial *rationale* and *target markets*. Overall, mission is supposed to answer the question, What is our business and what should it be?

A selection of approaches to mission statements is provided by Collins and Porras (2000). The box below lists a number of well-known mission statements.

Some examples of goals expressed through mission statements

General Electric (rationale)

The first step is for the company to define its destiny in broad but clear terms. You need an overarching message, something big, but simple and understandable. (Jack Welch)

To become No. 1 or No. 2 in every market we serve and revolutionize this company to have the speed and agility of a small enterprise. (Jack Welch)

Sony (business philosophy and ethics)

The difference between our efforts and those of other Japanese companies lies not in the level of technology, or the quality of the engineers, or even in the amount of money budgeted for development (about 5 per cent of sales). The main difference lies in ... the establishment of mission-oriented research and proper **targets**. *Many other companies give their researchers full freedom. We don't; we find an aim, a very real and clear* **target** *and then establish the* *necessary task forces to get the job done ... once the commitment to go ahead is made, **never** give up. This pervades all the research and development work at Sony.*

Mission as business objectives

To build a car for the great multitude ... (Ford, Henry Ford 1907)

To change the image around the world of Japanese products as poor in quality. (Sony, Akio Morita 1950)

To make my little Newport store the best, most profitable variety store in Arkansas within five years. (Walmart, Sam Walton 1945)

To become a $1 billion company in four years. (Walmart, Sam Walton 1977)

To double the number of stores and increase the dollar volume per square foot by 60 per cent by year 2000. (Walmart, Sam Walton 1990)

To build the airplane (the 747) even if it takes the entire resources of the company. (Boeing 1969)

Less well-known mission statements also reflect and try to tap into the values of potential customers. Consider the mission statement from Don Hewitson.

Don Hewitson's wine bar: The Cork & Bottle

A MISSION STATEMENT
'LIFE'S TOO SHORT TO DRINK BORING WINE'

Nowadays most wine can be relied upon to be an agreeable tipple. None of the gut-searing acidic whites or over-ripe, jammy oxidised reds which were all I could afford when I arrived in Blighty in 1972. Elton John was on Top Of The Pops with 'Rocket Man' that very day ... and the charts have gone down the tubes ever since!

BUT ... and it is a 'big' BUT. In the desire for squeaky clean wines at as cheap as possible prices, have we thrown the baby out with the bathwater? I didn't develop a passion for wine in order to drink virtually the same taste sensation every time ... I love the bewildering variety of styles and flavours.

STUART WALTON, in his excellent book 'YOU HEARD IT THROUGH THE GRAPEVINE' (Aurum Press £9.99) sums up the desire for conformity brilliantly by blaming the High Street.

> *'What has happened in the last few years . . . is the wholesale mediocratisation of wine in the UK . . . As monotony begins to set in, there is the Safebury' wine-buyer at the door, cheque-book in hand and ready to spread this monotony all over the UK high street.'*
>
> *These wines can be avoided, especially when you are a small operator in a business striving for globalisation. There are thousands of wine producers out there, in all countries, with no interest in producing bland, boring wines. Even if they make wines in sufficient quantities to satisfy the High Street chains, they are not prepared to shave their costs to fit supermarket price points. These days supermarkets invariably require a major financial contribution (a fee to be on their shelves, although they do put it a little less like the Kray twins, it's basically the same approach to business).*
>
> *My suppliers wouldn't recognise a 'marketing budget' if they fell over one! They are my mates. I trust them implicitly. They are a disparate bunch of individuals dedicated to producing the best wines possible . . . I'll drink to that!*
>
> Salut Don

This is a 'Mission Statement' written on the inside page of an eight-page pamphlet entitled *Wines To Go* – an order form for customers. The Cork & Bottle is a very well-known wine bar in Leicester Square, London, founded by an Australian whose original mission was to bring Australian and New Zealand wines to the British drinking public. It represents an approach to mission statements which is very different from those illustrated earlier. For one thing it is included in a selling/marketing document which is to be read by potential customers. But the main difference lies in the style and content of the narrative. It sets out clear values which are intended to engage with potential customers who share the same values (the charts have gone down the tubes since Elton John's 'Rocket Man') and the statement also acts as both an assessment of the competition (supermarket wines) and as an ethical comment upon them ('like the Kray twins'). Finally, the statement tells the consumer something about the way in which the supply chain is managed (trust – 'they are my mates'). It is also considerably longer than most mission statements, making it suitable for inclusion in a leaflet, but not as useful as a single-sentence strap line to describe the whole organization.

1.2.4 Resources

During the 1980s, the view that organizational resources were important became known as the resource-based view (RBV). Its arguments are deceptively simple. An organization has, develops or acquires a range of competences which can then be mobilized by strategists to gain an advantage on the competition. The origins of this way of thinking about strategy can be traced back to Penrose (1959). She adopted what was then something of a unique stance against the conception of the firm by her fellow economists, who had concentrated on conditions external to the firm (such as demand) as drivers of strategy and growth. Penrose took the opposite view, arguing that an organization can be viewed as a collection of resources (in her case she focused particularly on the entrepreneurial resource) which are the drivers of strategy and growth rather than external factors.

In the late 1950s, this was a radical view, but by the time Andrews (1980) had talked about identifying corporate competence and Prahalad and Hamel (1990) had published their article on the core competence of the organization, the RBV had become established. The argument is that strategists can build and mobilize resources which, if unique enough, can bring huge rewards to the organization. One of the most famous examples of this is the 3M Corporation. This organization valued the capacity of its staff to innovate, allowing them up to 25 per cent of company time in which to experiment, regardless of whether the outcome was successful or not. The result of one of these experiments was the Post-It note. Born from an adhesive which did not stick very well (in an organization dedicated to finding better and stronger adhesives) the idea looked initially doomed. But a use for this low-grade adhesive was found by attaching it to small pieces of paper. It could be stuck to paper and other delicate products as a marker, or with a note scribbled on it, and could be removed years later without damaging the paper.

Curiously, no customers were begging 3M or any other organization to produce such sticky notes. In terms of pure economics, there was no *demand* to drive creation of the product. Rather, 3M had produced something that customers did not even know they needed (yet). Here is a core competence according to Prahalad and Hamel (1990). It is the ability to produce something customers need but have never imagined. Conceiving of the firm as a collection of competences allows strategies to be planned 'inside–out'. That is, from the inside of the organization, out to its external environment (markets and industries). In turn, feedback from customers and demand could identify additional competences which might be needed (and may indicate which current core competences might be redundant).

Prahalad and Hamel (1990) define core competences as:

> the collective learning in the organization, especially how to co-ordinate diverse production skills and integrate multiple streams of technologies . . .

For example, Honda's core competence in engine and power trains gives it a clear advantage in car, motorcycle, lawnmower and generator businesses. There are three characteristics of a core competence. Competences should:

* provide potential access to a wide variety of markets;
* make a significant contribution to the perceived customer benefits of the end product;
* be difficult for competitors to imitate.

Prahalad and Hamel (1990) argue that very few organizations are likely to build world leadership in more than five or six competences. Firms may have many capabilities (more than 20 or 30) but they have not aggregated these into the key four or five competences needed for success and growth. Not knowing what are an organization's core competences can create difficulties for strategists. For example, they may outsource a function or operation not realizing that they have saved some costs at the expense of losing a core competence. Prahalad and Hamel (1990) cite the example of Honda, which would never outsource its manufacturing or design to an outside company, versus Chrysler, which has done so. Honda has preserved its core competence in engine and power trains while Chrysler has not. Of course, it is difficult to devise an effective outsourcing strategy if the core competences of the organization have not previously been identified. The crown jewels of the company could easily be outsourced this way in what might seem like a simple (and rational) cost-saving exercise.

So Figure 1.1 provides the basic factors in understanding strategy. Core competences (resources) allow strategists to have strategic intent (goals). These are orientated toward the external environment (market or socio-economic conditions) and these become organizational goals which are often communicated to stakeholders by means of mission statements. However, conceptualizing strategy is a little more complicated than these three factors (important thought they are). The next sections show how we can build upon Figure 1.1 to understand strategy a little more fully.

1.3 Towards a systemic concept of strategy

In this section, we will develop a concept of strategy that builds on Figure 1.1 and which guides the rest of this book. Strategy, as a topic of study, concentrates very much on the situational problems of the general manager (or top management team or CEO). Strategy is different, then, from a more general theory of organizations. It is more specific and more focused than general organizational theories. The general manager's job is to diagnose what is critical in complex business situations and to find realistic solutions to strategic and organizational problems. To solve problems, the general manager must be capable of understanding and using the knowledge from each of the organization's functional areas to provide a holistic 'total business' (systems) perspective on issues pertaining to strategic management. In addition, the general manager must be able to analyse competitive situations within industries in order to understand the sources of the firm's competitive advantage. We see strategy as determined and constrained by the underlying economic and political conditions which prevail in an industry or country, as well as by the resources available to management.

In consequence, we believe that a strategist (or the strategic team) must focus on understanding the specific *context* of the strategic problem. He or she must have an intuitive feel for defining the boundaries of the problem and the issues to include in any analysis. A strategist must also recognize the interrelationships between all the organizational functions, activities and processes, and be able to frame the problem by recognizing the influence not only of history but also of the future on the problem context. The strategist must be willing to act, must have a bias for action and be equally willing to accept the consequences – be they success or failure of the strategies he or she chooses. Therefore, unashamedly, we present in this book a conception of strategy which focuses on the role and the perspective of the general manager.

That said, it is important to develop a discussion about strategy around an appreciation of some of the theories which contribute to current strategic thinking and which help to outline managers' cognitive frames and interpretations of strategy. It is important to understand how these theories develop, how they have evolved and what problems they either seek to solve or begin to explain. What follows, therefore, is a very brief review of the main theories in the strategy field as a basis for showing how they are reflected in the development of the strategic framework and strategic systems model which are the basis for this book.

As noted earlier, the Chandler definition of strategy is the guiding principle underlying the so-called classical or rational view of strategy. A range of other eminent academics, including March and Simon (1958), Cyert and March (1963), Mintzberg (1994), Alchian (1950), Henderson (1973), Williamson (1975), Pascale (1984) and others, personify the main viewpoints in the field of strategy. The so-called evolutionary view emphasizes competitive processes of natural selection and environmental determination; survival is everything and nature is the optimiser. In this world, strategy can be a delusion and 'economy is the best strategy'. On the other hand, the so-called strategy processual or organizational process view of strategy expresses a more agnostic view about a market's ability to produce satisfactory outcomes, which we explain more fully in Chapter 2. In this view, both organizations and markets are sticky and messy, and strategies emerge slowly with much confusion and in small steps. Strategic behaviour is embedded and entrenched in cultures, routines and standard operating procedures. In this view, strategy is programmed by the DNA of organizations. An alternative and more recent viewpoint, focusing on the strategy-as-systems perspective, has room for managers and organizations to look forward and make effective plans, in contrast with the agnostic and even nihilistic stance of the evolutionary and strategy process perspectives. The systemic view is drawn principally from the work of organizational sociologists such as Granovetter (1985) and rests on notions of social embeddedness. Embeddedness maintains that people's economic behaviour is embedded in a network of social relations that may involve their families, the state, their professional and educational backgrounds, even their religion and ethnicity. Such influences are absent from the restricted environment of the classical and processual approaches but may find some expression in the evolutionary view.

These viewpoints are largely mutually exclusive but practising strategists in organizations would recognize their presence in strategy as practised. However, there is a new approach which has gained recent significant support. This is the resource-based view attributed to economist Edith Penrose. In this view, the emphasis is on those resources and competences that are distinctive to the organization and are the fundamental underpinning of their marketplace positioning. In this world, competition is a contest for the acquisition of skills and competences and other intangible assets. This represents a theory of core competences (to use the words popularized by gurus Gary Hamel and C.K. Prahalad) that provides linkages between the classical, processual and systemic views. By virtue of its focus on tacit and intangible resources, it links directly with new theories of knowledge management and is the basis for a new knowledge-based view of strategy advanced by Nelson and Winter (1982) and others, in which superior knowledge is likely to be the most valuable resource of all.

Our observation of many of these writers is that they err on the side of conventional rationality, the classical model, and provide the reader with little guidance about how to interpret the changing world of technology and globalization in which we live and the way in which organizations form strategic positions in this world. We observe also that strategizing in the real world is something of a caricature in conventional writing with little attention paid to providing realistic appreciations of the forces at work. It is obvious that the drivers of change have been new structures of scientific knowledge, the internationalization of experience in a time of rapid media access to diverse cultures and the acceleration of technological change in post-industrial society. Thus, we see strategy as marked increasingly by an eclecticism and multicultural nature and a post-industrial, high-tech, internationalistic context. For example, the US and the UK are essentially post-industrial service economies; Asia is entering the industrial stage with specialized industries but markets that are almost entirely international. Structural change is endemic in the world economy and even the largest corporations are caught up in the ebb and flow of outsourcing, refocusing new technologies and intangible, human capital. This is in sharp contrast to the world of the rationalist, where strategy is the preserve of top management and the approach is strategy-as-planning, where organizations are efficient, rational resource-allocation mechanisms designed to achieve competitive advantage and economic rents.

What we propose in our conceptual strategic model is a much more blended, balanced and systemic view of the world. It is a treatment of strategy that builds on the roots provided by the classical model (after all, there is still virtue in rationality) that reflects the modern resource-based and knowledge-based view but uses all the available lenses and viewpoints of strategy and strategic thinking to interpret, make sense and provide a basis for strategic decisions.

As a motivating example to illustrate of the use of multiple viewpoints in framing strategy, we attempt to make sense of Honda's strategic behaviour in the celebrated case of its entry into the US motorcycle marketplace. This has been extensively discussed in the strategy literature but its very familiarity enables us to make the point convincingly. The classical view held that Honda's successful entry was a masterpiece of rational economic calculation, so much so that Boston Consulting Group, in a celebrated report, laid out their view about

McGee–Thomas–Wilson:
Strategy: Analysis and
Practice, Text and Cases

1. The concept of strategy

Text

© The McGraw–Hill
Companies, 2006

21

the importance of market share objectives and economies of scale and experience in the motorcycle industry. They used this argument as a benchmark in providing advice to the British government in its own attempts to revitalize the failing British motorcycle industry in the mid 1970s. The opposing explanation of Honda's success was the processual view advanced powerfully by Richard Pascale. He maintained that Honda's successful entry was, indeed, a masterpiece of strategic thinking but rather of flexible, quick incremental adjustment to the marketplace realities and emergent thinking in framing their ongoing strategy. Honda management did not know what they were taking on but learned very quickly. The broader, all-encompassing systemic view holds that it is not the Japanese management of Honda that determines the strategy, nor is it simply a version of 'muddling through', but it is the local US management of Honda that works out how the game has to be played. Indeed, Honda USA becomes embedded in the network of American social and business relationships, albeit with a very distinctive Japanese flavour. In particular, Honda, like all auto/motorcycle companies, worked out that they face the same industry conditions of scale economies, access, capacity, persistent entry by newly industrializing countries and trends towards commoditization. Although, while Honda may have found short-term distinctiveness in the US market, in the end it will find that this will erode and the only strategy available to it over the long term will be to 'economize', i.e. keep its costs low and its options open.

This commentary on Honda exemplifies the need for contemporary strategic thinking to move away from the purely rational or planned view towards a more eclectic view that embraces the emergent, incremental or processual approaches with a stronger respect for the power or markets and institutions – primarily governments – to shape the behaviour of corporations. Corporate behaviour is neither simply rational nor simply determined by its various environments. Any strategic model has to capture the increasing complexity of modern corporate life by, first, providing alternative lenses (perspectives, theories and rules of thumb) through which to see the world and, second, by articulating a way of telling the strategy story so that the reader can see how organizations frame their strategic positioning in their drive for long-term strategic successes. Thus, the centrepiece – our strategy story – is the juxtaposition of intangible resources at the firm level with imperfectly competitive markets in the context of ever more dynamic and intrusive environments involving globalization and rapid, disruptive technological change. We now move on to a discussion of the strategy systems framework which defines the structure and context of this book.

1.3.1 The strategy systems framework

Figure 1.6 shows the conceptual framework and the logic underlying the approach taken to understanding strategy in this book. It argues that the various models, definitions of strategy and frameworks provided in the book are vehicles for thinking about strategy and policy and carrying out a dialogue about strategic options. In essence, our strategy story is conceptualized in terms of a strategy map, which motivates the strategy team and leads to a discussion of strategy options in a broad, systemic fashion. We believe, following Cummings and Wilson (2003), that:

> *strategy frameworks, images or maps help people to do their own mapping, thereby kick-starting an oscillating thinking/acting or strategising process, which instills a momentum that brings other choices and possibilities to the fore. It may not get people 'down the mountain' in a straight line but it gets things moving and, when things move, other things come into view.*

In short, the interaction between the general map and the mapping of a particular course of action orientates and animates, and no course is likely to be taken effectively without a measure of each of these things. Cumming and Wilson (2003) go on to propose that strategy is an art in the following terms:

> *It is argued that the art of strategy lies both in the combination of frameworks, images or maps and the choice of their focus (e.g. big picture versus certain detail) toward mapping an organization's particular course.*

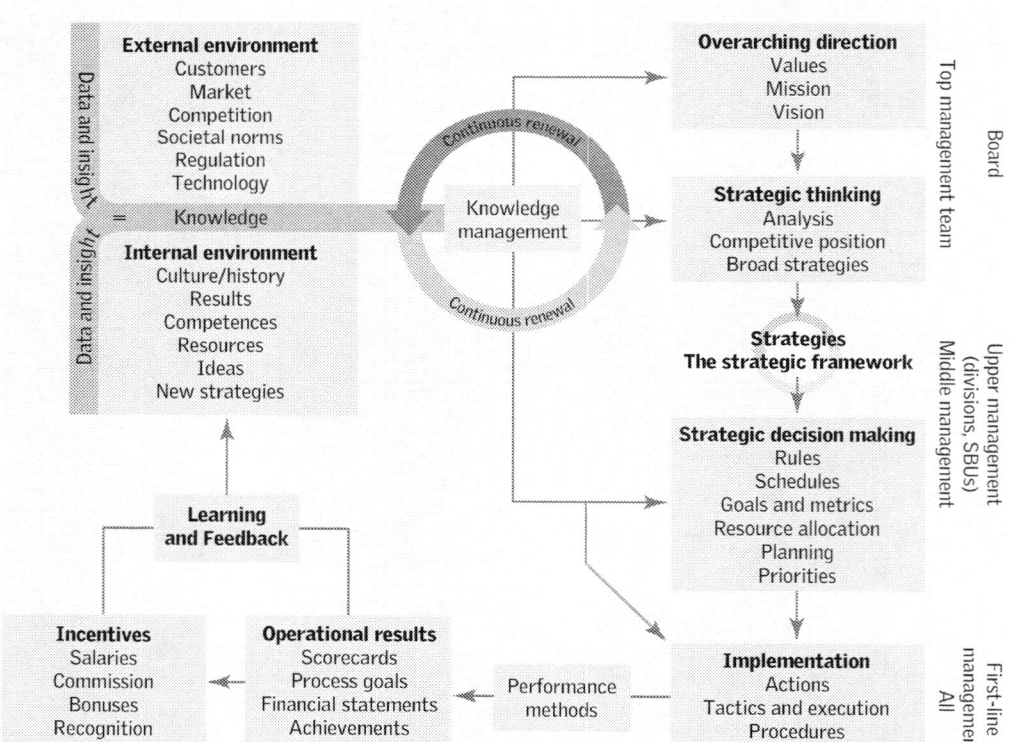

Figure 1.6 A systemic model of strategy

As we shall see, our framework in Figure 1.6 interacts as an organizing framework with strategic processes of animation and orientation (see our introduction in Chapter 2) to produce a preferred strategy for an organization.

What follows now, therefore, is an articulation of the elements of Figure 1.6, recognizing that it is a map and a system model. It 'animates and orientates' the problem of strategy and invites debate and dialogue among those strategists taking part in the strategy process. Note that each of the elements in the diagram (e.g. overarching direction or strategic thinking) encompasses a set of issues and generally poses a specific question. For example, the notion of the overarching direction of an organization begs the question, What do we want to be?

Let us follow through with each of these elements and describe what is going on in each of the boxes.

Overarching direction

Understanding the firm's overarching direction is critical. The general question being asked here is What does the organization want to be? The organization must develop a long-term vision of what it wants to be and take into account the company's culture, reputation, competences and resources in addressing that question. The vision is the core ideology of the organization, which provides the glue that binds the organization together. It encompasses a set of core values that address questions such as why the company exists and what it believes in. The core values may include such things as honesty and integrity, hard work and continuous self-improvement, strong customer service, creativity and imagination. On the other hand, the core purpose is to do with the company's reason for being – in Walt Disney's case, it is simply stated as being to make people happy or, in Hewlett Packard's case, to make a technological contribution to the advancement and welfare of humanity. Purpose, in this sense, is very close to the mission of the organization and, as stated earlier, the vision is the core ideology that binds the organization together. Collins and Porras (2000) argue that what they describe as 'big, hairy, audacious goals' improve long-term vision – for example, Stanford University's statement in the 1940s that they wanted to become 'the Harvard of the West' or Boeing's vision in the 1950s of becoming the 'dominant player in aviation and bringing the world into the jet age'. Thus, a vision breaks down into a more flexible set of aspirations, perhaps sub-goals, which are defined in both qualitative and quantitative terms (e.g. long-term growth or profit), and these aspirations tend to be refreshed more frequently than the overall vision.

Strategic thinking

This element of the strategic concept advances a holistic and integrated view of the business. It asks the question of how, through analysis and strategic positioning, the firm will answer the question, Together, how will we do that?

What we seek to understand here is the relationship between the firm's positioning, resources and capabilities, and organization. We seek to ensure here that the firm's strategy is such that the elements complement and reinforce each other, i.e. the strategies are cohesive. In other words, a co-ordinated framework of high-level enterprise strategies is developed to achieve the vision. This brings together the best strategic thinking and analysis and widely communicates one strategic viewpoint to get everyone pulling in the same direction and to discourage unproductive behaviour.

The agreed enterprise strategy is then broken down into a range of strategies that position the organization in its markets and in its various functional activities (e.g. product strategies, distribution strategies, etc.). They emphasize strategic options and positions, and highlight them in a framework such that they work together. Obviously, strategic thinking requires a whole range of techniques and tools. These include a determination of the broad goals of the organization, thus answering the question, What is most important? Analysts and strategists also have to understand the sources of value creation through revenue drivers, cost drivers and risk drivers.

In other words, strategic thinking begins with a good business model that analyses the economic relationships central to achieving the organization's purpose. These include value creation and analysing industry dynamics – perhaps using the 'five forces' framework developed by Porter (1980). The firm must also recognize the distinctiveness of its own resources and capabilities, because these core capabilities are often long-lasting and provide the linkage with a firm sustaining superior performance over the long run. Porter's (1980) framework is shown in Figure 1.7.

In terms of new entrants, there can be threats from, for example, low barriers to entry, where it is fairly easy for an organization to start trading and enter the market. Equally, if brand identity is weak (say in a commodity product) then the threat of new entrants is likely to be high. Barriers against these threats can be high capital cost of entry (for example, it is very costly to set up a new pharmaceutical manufacturing and R&D organization from scratch) or the development of economies of scale (where bigger and older companies will always benefit from economies of scale and new entrants will not). Substitutes can present a threat if, for example, the cost of a customer switching from one product to that of the substitute is low. Not surprisingly, these are known as switching costs. The lower the switching costs, the greater are the threats from substitution. Substitution can also occur via price. A substitute product at a much lower price (and a

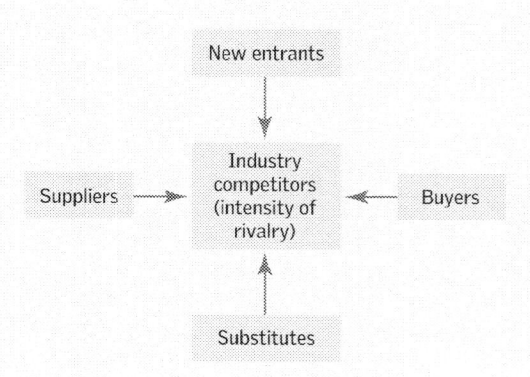

Figure 1.7 Porter's five forces: the elements of industry structure

product which customers will value just as much) will pose a large threat to the company charging higher prices for similar products. Commodity products, such as washing powders, and white consumer goods are examples where customers will switch relatively easily to a lower price product.

Buyers can exert power. If a small number of suppliers serve a large number of firms, then the concentration of supplier power is relatively high. If the reverse situation holds, and there are many suppliers for a few firms, then supplier power is low. In the former case, buyer power is low; in the latter, buyer power is high. An example of the latter case can be found among the large supermarkets worldwide, which exert so much power over their suppliers that they can sometimes charge a premium for stocking and displaying items on their shelves (wine is an example).

Supplier power is really the opposite of buyer power. Where the switching costs of firms in the industry are high, they will not decide lightly to change suppliers. In this case, suppliers have relatively high levels of power over those organizations. However, new suppliers entering the market will have a potential substitution effect and reduce existing levels of supplier power. The relative threat of forward and backward integration will also affect supplier (and buyer) power. For example, if a firm decides it can manufacture its own raw materials (rather than buy from a supplier) then the balance of power between supplier and firm will be changed radically in favour of the firm and to the disadvantage of the supplier.

This kind of framework is useful for picturing the dynamics of an industry but such frameworks do not tell the whole story. They are relatively static frameworks which make a number of assumptions, not least that all players will have perfect knowledge (everyone is aware of the extent of their power or the threat they pose) and will always exercise the power they have. To inject a more dynamic perspective, these frameworks should be seen as one part of a greater process. The strategist has to recognize the source of the power balances or imbalances, but having done that he or she needs to drill deeper into the analysis to analyse not only the sources of such threats and power but also the impact of each on the strategy process. This explains why the five forces model, central to many scholars' strategy frameworks, is only a part of the systemic model presented here. We will be referring to Porter's model again in Chapter 5, where we will use it to explore competitive advantage in more detail.

Strategies: the strategic framework and product goals

In its simplest terms, a strategy consists of a set of goals and a set of policies or actions to achieve those goals. Goals answer the question of what is most important for the organization. The strategy and process also encompass the strategic planning process, which varies from organization to organization in levels of familiarity. However, the most important element in strategic planning is to link the strategic framework and broad goals as guides and allow each of the divisions or sub-units of the organization to develop their own strategies in a co-ordinated fashion. That is, responsibility for strategy formulation should be devolved to the sub-units or entities within the business which have responsibility for products and services. The individual managers running those units are the ones who know the products and services, the product markets and the presence of other competitors in the marketplace. They can then develop a statement of what strategic positioning the organization should reasonably adopt at that level. The role of top management is to co-ordinate those strategies in an enterprise sense, so that it fits the overall strategic framework defined by the vision and the overarching direction of the organization.

Strategic programming

This focuses on the answers to questions such as Who, when and how much? In other words, assuming broad strategies are agreed, an operating plan must be developed to attack such issues as day-to-day priorities, organizational roles and responsibilities, and resource allocation with regard to budgets and systems development. Obviously, this leads to the development of a clearer, tactical plan.

Tactics and execution

This phase of the strategy process answers the tasks of 'Let's get organized and let's do it, and do it right!' In other words, the tactical part of the operating plan fills in the gaps about division plans, unit plans and individual goals, and develops performance metrics at each level, so that monitoring of those plans can be undertaken. The executive focuses not only on the monitoring of performance and targets but the ability to adjust plans quickly and rapidly as new ideas and challenges are developed within the organization.

Performance measurement and purpose

In any organization, there must be a linkage to performance. The feedback that is necessary for any organization in re-framing its strategy in a sensible way is the answer to the question, How do we do a check of performance against targets and cost? Performance metrics are extremely important – they highlight issues such as progress towards goals and, more importantly, how certain tasks and certain strategies can be adjusted better and faster and how change can be incorporated most effectively within the context of the organization.

Information and analysis: the internal and external environment

Obviously, changing the organization through performance monitoring and strategy adjustment is but one process in a series of feedbacks and feedback loops which are absolutely necessary in analysing information about both internal and external environments. In the external environment, we have to question what is happening around us; there must be a process of data gathering and development of insight and knowledge about such issues as new technology and its impact on the business, and the potential impact of regulation and legislation on the activities of the company. The underlying national economic and macroeconomic conditions are also important in setting the global economic context for the organization and, at a more micro level, framing intelligence and analysis about competition, the nature and changing shape of markets and customer needs and opinions. Obviously, key success factors in this external environment enable the firm to focus on appropriate product renewal and generate knowledge and insight about new products and ideas. In the context of the internal environment, the firm needs to analyse and identify its key resources and capabilities and evaluate their impact on competitive advantage. For example, a company's culture and the history of its development can provide a source of competitive strength as in the case of Johnson & Johnson (J&J), which is regarded by many as an extremely ethical and well-run pharmaceutical company. That perception is a result of J&J's strong culture, its history and the strength of its financial resources over a long period of time. Internal analysis also requires a process of continual investigation, discovery and criticism, leading to new ideas, new product concepts, updated financial results and updated metrics. Information about organizational strengths and weaknesses can, in turn, lead to the continual renewal of the strategy process.

Feedback of results and incentives

Kaplan and Norton (1992) have developed processes known as a balanced scorecard for monitoring operational financial results within the organization. Figure 1.8 depicts this scorecard in its simplest form (it is used elsewhere in this book in greater detail; *see*, for example, Chapter 14).

The balanced scorecard attempts to answer questions about progress towards goals and identifies any operational results which can be fed back to continually improve organizational processes. The balanced scorecard also contains an incentive structure which answers the question, What's in it for me? Clearly, if incentives such as salaries, commission and bonuses can be co-aligned with strategic objectives, the employee recognition will lead

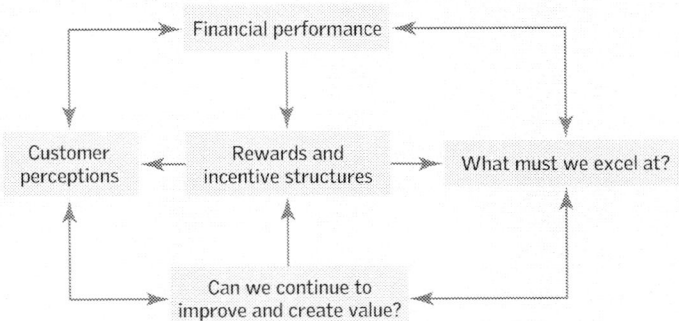

Figure 1.8 The balanced scorecard
Source: adapted from Kaplan and Norton (1992).

to employee loyalty and a strong alignment between individual objectives, organizational objectives and organizational strategy.

In summary, the strategy concept presented here in Figure 1.6 is a map, a framework and a virtuous circle, at the core of which is a process of knowledge management which trades upon analysis of the external and internal environment, analysis of performance, analysis of strategies and competitive updating of values and mission in order to achieve a process whereby the organization is engaged in a continual debate about how it can improve and how it can frame its strategy so that the organization itself fits in a dynamic sense with its current and future strategic position.

1.4 Summary

This chapter has outlined the contested terrain of strategy. The field is full of competing definitions. In order to move beyond a battle of definitions, we have attempted to build a framework which helps show how strategy 'works' rather than debating exactly what it 'is'. Complex though this model might appear at first sight, it provides a framework which the following chapters of this book outline in greater detail.

For example, a solely economics-based perspective would examine the dynamics of *matching the internal environment* of the firm *with its external environment*. As Figure 1.6 makes clear, this is only part of the process – but is an important part. Strategists who do not consider the implications of internal and external do so at their peril. Thus, Part 2 of this book describes in detail the essential elements of this process. In order for strategists to make decisions, they need a detailed appreciation of both the micro- and the macro-economic characteristics of the firm and its environment. But such analysis cannot stand alone. We have already seen in this chapter how values, mission and vision communicate an organization's strategic stance to its wider audience, most importantly its customers. Getting this wrong (as when Gerald Ratner famously called his company's jewellery products 'crap') can seal the demise of the firm no matter how sophisticated the economic analysis has been. In one sentence, Ratner's was doomed.

This chapter has also highlighted the importance of analysis. Strategists are faced with a range of options and rarely are faced with simple go or no-go decisions. Therefore, the skill of *thinking strategically* cannot be overemphasized. Strategists need to be aware not only of the options they face, but also the trade-offs they make, for example, by choosing one course of action over another. This can be a problem for many organizations. Consider Volkswagen's decision to position the Skoda (which it acquired) as a quality mid-range car available in medium to high performance ranges as well as diesel, petrol and dual fuel. What seemed initially like a good decision – to beef up the brand and reputational image of Skoda (Skoda jokes were legendary: what do you call an open-top Skoda? Answer – a skip!) – backfired on Volkswagen since the trade-off this decision produced was to reduce demand for the equivalent Volkswagen products (the Golf and Passat). Skodas were selling at the expense of the firm's existing products. Part 3 of this book examines these sorts of analysis and thinking problems both from the domestic viewpoint (what is our strategic position?) and in the global context (how do we take strategic decisions in an international environment?).

Strategies do not exist independently of organizations, however. The notion of a small number of policy makers sitting in a darkened room formulating key decisions which they then unleash on an unsuspecting organization is a fond and inaccurate character-ization. First of all, making strategic decisions involves a wide range of stakeholders and interests which are both internal and external to the organization. Their influences shape and often control what happens. Second, strategies have to be put into practice. They have to be implemented. Moreover, they have to be implemented in often large and complex social environments, which have the convenient label 'organizations' or 'firms' but which contain very high levels of social, individual, elite and irrational behaviours. Organizations are social environments and not solely economic machines. What man-agers do and how people behave matters. Hence, Part 4 of this book examines in detail the question of strategic acting. It looks at how strategic decisions can be formulated relatively easily but can run into difficulties once managers start to try to implement strategic decisions. The ways in which they organize, oversee and govern decisions matter. Putting decisions into practice means organizations and people are faced with often significant levels of change and new learning. Managers neglect these aspects of strategy (which have often been dismissed as the softer, intangible aspects of strategy) at their peril. Resistance to change and an inability to learn will ensure the death of an organization independently of whether or not it is in a fierce or benign environment. Internal barriers to strategy are just as important as external competitive threats, for example.

Finally, strategies (and organizations) need continuous renewal. Putting decisions into practice is one thing. Knowing and measuring how they have performed and knowing why are completely different skills and processes. Part 5 of this book examines the important questions of performance. How do decision makers know they made the right, or the wrong, decision? This part discusses such topics as performance, quality and process improvements as well as operational results such as financial statements, achievement of stated objectives and process goals. In turn, we view these performance metrics as helping the feedback process into the next set of strategic decisions which managers will take in the future. In this sense, performance metrics also help the learning process and the development of new capabilities as well as the abandonment of old capa-bilities which might no longer be useful for future strategies.

Before looking at the next parts of the book, it is important to place some of the above arguments in their organizational contexts. The following chapter raises some questions about what happens when 'strategies meet organizations' and provides more detail about the contextual aspects of organization. We would view Chapter 2 as essential pre-reading to Part 4 of this book.

Key terms

Emergent strategy *11*

Evolutionary view *19*

External environment *9*

Goals *9*

Intended strategy *6*

Internal environment *10, 14*

Mission/mission statement *10*

Objectives *see* Goals

Organizational process view *19*

Realized strategy *11*

Resource-based view *16*

Strategic intent *see* Intended strategy

Strategy-as-systems perspective *19*

Strategy processual view *19*

Organizational process view *19*

Online Learning Centre

When you have read this chapter, log on to the Online Learning Centre website at www.mcgraw-hill.co.uk/textbooks/mcgee to explore chapter-by-chapter test questions, further reading and more online study tools for strategy.

Further reading and references

Alchian, AA (1950) 'Uncertainty, evolution and economic theory', *Journal of Political Economy*, **58**, pp. 211–21.

Andrews, KR (1980) *The Concept of Corporate Strategy*, Irwin, Homewood, Il.

Ansoff, HI (1965) *Corporate Strategy*, Penguin, Harmondsworth.

Ansoff, HI (1972) 'The concept of strategic management', *Journal of Business Policy*, **2**, **4**, Summer.

Bower, JL (1982) 'Business policy in the 1980s', *Academy of Management Review*, vol. 7, no. 4, 630–8.

Bower, JL (1986) *Managing the Resource Allocation Process*, Harvard Business School Press, Boston, MA.

Chandler, AD (1963) *Strategy and Structure: Chapters in the History of the Industrial Enterprise*, MIT Press, Cambridge, MA.

Christensen, C (1997) *The Innovator's Dilemma: When New Technologies Cause Great Firms to Fail*, Harvard Business School Press, Cambridge, MA.

Collins, JC and Porras, JI (2000) *Built to Last: Sucessful Habits of Visionary Companies*, Random House, New York.

Cummings S, and Wilson, DC (eds) (2003) *Images of Strategy*, Blackwell, Oxford.

Cyert, RM and March, JG (1963) *A Behavioral Theory of the Firm*, Blackwell, Oxford.

Granovetter, M (1985) 'Economic action and social culture: the problem of embeddedness', *American Journal of Sociology*, **91**, **3**, pp. 481–510.

Henderson, BD (1973) *The Experience Curve Reviewed*, Boston Consulting Group, Boston, MA.

Hussey, D (1998) *Strategic Management: From Theory to Implementation*, 4th edition, Butterworth-Heinemann, Oxford.

Kaplan, RS and Norton, DP (1992) 'The Balanced Scorecard: Measures that Drive Performance', *Harvard Business Review*, Jan–Feb.

Legge, K (2003) 'Strategy as organising', in S Cummings and DC Wilson (eds) *Images of Strategy*, Blackwell, Oxford.

Magretta, J (2003) *What Management is*, Profile Books, London.

March, JG and Simon, HA (1958) *Organizations*, Blackwell, Cambridge, MA.

Mintzberg, H (1994) *The Rise and Fall of Strategic Planning*, Prentice-Hall, Englewood Cliffs, NJ.

Mintzberg, H and Waters, J (1985) 'Of strategies, deliberate and emergent', *Strategic Management Journal*, **6**, pp. 257–72.

Mintzberg, H, Lampel, J and Ahlstrand, P (1998) *The Strategy Safari: A Guided Tour Through the Jungle of Strategic Management*, Prentice-Hall, Englewood Cliffs, NJ.

Nelson, RR and Winter, SG (1982) *An Evolutionary Theory of Economic Change*, Harvard University Press, Cambridge, MA.

Pascale, R (1984) 'Perspectives on strategy: the real story behind Honda's success', *California Management Review*, **14**, **3**, pp. 47–72.

Penrose, E (1959) *The Theory of the Growth of the Firm*, Blackwell, Oxford.

Porter, M (1980) *Competitive Strategy*, Free Press, New York.

Porter, ME (1985) *Competitive Advantage*, Free Press, New York.

Porter, ME (1987) 'From competitive advantage to corporate strategy', *Harvard Business Review*, May–June, pp. 2–21.

Prahalad, CK and Hamel, G (1990) 'The core competence of the organization', *Harvard Business Review*, May–June.

Quinn, JB (1980) *Strategies for Change: Logical Incrementalism*, Irwin, Homewood, Il.

Sun Tzu (1990) *The Art of War*, Sterling Publishing, New York.

Williamson, OE (1975) *Markets and Hierarchies: Analysis and Antitrust Implications*, Free Press, New York.

Hill: International
Business: Competing in the
Global Marketplace, Sixth
Edition

I. Introduction and
Overview

1. Globalization

© The McGraw–Hill
Companies, 2007

33

Introduction
and Overview Part 1

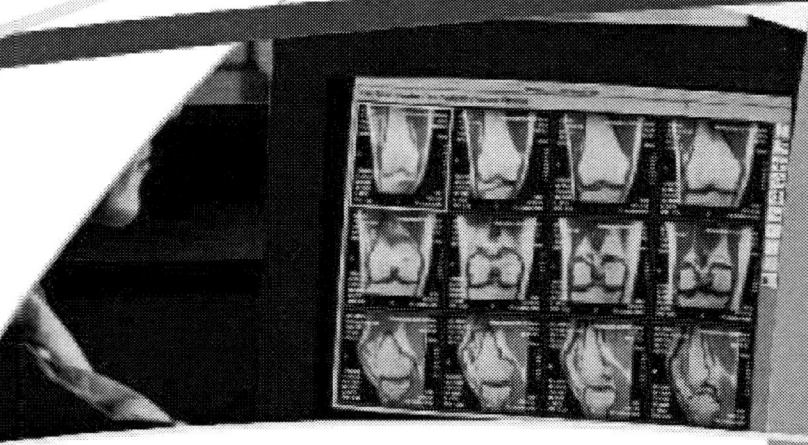

1

Globalization

The Globalization of Health Care

Conventional wisdom holds that health care is one of the industries least vulnerable to dislocation from globalization. After all, like many service businesses, health care is delivered where it is purchased, right? If an American goes to a hospital for an MRI scan, won't that scan be read by a local radiologist? And if the MRI scan shows that surgery is required, surely the surgery will be done at a local hospital in the United States. Until recently, this was true, but we are now witnessing the beginnings of globalization in this traditionally most local of industries.

Consider the MRI scan: The United States has a shortage of radiologists, the doctors who specialize in reading and interpreting diagnostic medical images including X-rays, CT scans, MRI scans, and ultrasound. Demand for radiologists is reportedly growing twice as fast as the rate at which medical schools are graduating radiologists with the skills and qualifications required to read medical images. This imbalance between supply and demand means that radiologists are expensive; an American radiologist can earn as much as $350,000 a year. In 2002, an Indian radiologist working at the prestigious Massachusetts General Hospital, Dr. Sanjay Saini, thought he had found a clever way to deal with the shortage and expense—beam images over the Internet to India where they could be interpreted by radiologists. This would reduce the workload on America's radiologists and also cut costs. A radiologist in India might earn one-tenth of his or her U.S. counterpart. Plus, because India is on the opposite side of the globe, the images could be interpreted while it was nighttime in the United States, and be ready for the attending physician when he or she arrived for work the following morning.

As for the surgery, here too we are witnessing the beginnings of an outsourcing trend. In October 2004, for example, Howard Staab, a 53-year-old uninsured self-employed carpenter from North Carolina had surgery to repair a leaking heart valve—in India! Mr. Staab flew to New Delhi, had the operation, and afterward toured the Taj Mahal, the price of which was bundled with that of the surgery. The cost, including airfare, totaled $10,000. If Mr. Staab's surgery had been performed in the United States, the cost would have been $60,000 and there would have been no visit to the Taj Mahal.

Howard Staab is not alone. Some 170,000 foreigners visited India in 2004 for medical treatments. That number is projected to rise by 15 percent a year for the next several years. According to the management consultancy McKinsey & Co., medical tourism (overseas trips to have medical procedures performed) could be a $2.3 billion industry in India by 2012. In another example, after years of living in pain, Robert Beeney, a 64-year-old from San Francisco, was advised to get his hip joint replaced, but after doing some research on the Internet, Mr. Beeney elected instead for joint resurfacing, which was not covered by his insurance. Instead of going to a nearby hospital, he flew to Hyderabad in southern India and had the surgery done for $6,600, a fraction of the $25,000 the procedure would have cost in the United States.

Mr. Beeney had his surgery performed at a branch of the Apollo hospital chain. Apollo, which was founded by Dr. Prathap C. Reddy, a surgeon trained at Massachusetts General Hospital, runs a chain of 18 state-of-the-art hospitals throughout Asia. Between 2001 and 2004, Apollo treated 43,000 foreigners, mainly from nations in Southeast Asia and the Persian Gulf, although a growing number are from Western Europe and North America. In 2004, 7 percent of its revenue came from foreigners. With 200 U.S.-trained doctors on his staff, Dr. Reddy reckons that he can offer medical care equivalent to that in the United States, but at a fraction of the cost. Nor is he alone; Mr. Staab's surgery was performed by Dr. Naresh Trehan, a cardiac surgeon who was trained at New York University School of Medicine and worked there for a decade. Dr. Trehan returned home to India and opened his own cardiac hospital, which now conducts 4,000 heart surgeries a year, with a 0.8 percent mortality rate and 0.3 percent infection rate, on par with the best of the world's hospitals.

So will demand for American health services soon collapse as work moves offshore to places like India? Hardly! Regulations, personal preferences, and practical considerations mean that the majority of health services will always be performed in the country where the patient resides. Consider the MRI scan—to safeguard patient care, U.S. regulations require that a radiologist be licensed in the state where the image was made and that he or she be certified by the hospital where care is being given. Given that not many radiologists in India have these qualifications, no more than a small fraction of images can be interpreted overseas. Another complication is that the U.S. government-sponsored medical insurance program, Medicare, will not pay for services done outside of the country. Nor will many private insurance plans, or not yet anyway. Moreover, most people would prefer to have care delivered close to home, and only in exceptional cases, such as when the procedure is not covered by their medical plan, are they likely to consider the foreign option. Still, most experts believe that the trends now in place will continue, and that a small but significant percentage of medical service will be performed in a country that is different from the one where the patient resides.

Sources: G. Colvin, "Think Your Job Can't Be Sent to India?" *Fortune*, December 13, 2004, p. 80; A. Pollack, "Who's Reading Your X-Ray," *The New York Times*, November 16, 2003, pp. 1, 9; S. Rai, "Low Costs Lure Foreigners to India for Medical Care," *The New York Times*, April 7, 2005, p. C6; J. Solomon, "Traveling Cure: India's New Coup in Outsourcing," *The Wall Street Journal*, April 26, 2004, p. A1; and J. Slater, "Increasing Doses in India," *Far Eastern Economic Review*, February 19, 2004, pp. 32–35.

4   **Part 1**   Introduction and Overview

A fundamental shift is occurring in the world economy. We are moving away from a world in which national economies were relatively self-contained entities, isolated from each other by barriers to cross-border trade and investment; by distance, time zones, and language; and by national differences in government regulation, culture, and business systems. And we are moving toward a world in which barriers to cross-border trade and investment are declining; perceived distance is shrinking due to advances in transportation and telecommunications technology; material culture is starting to look similar the world over; and national economies are merging into an interdependent, integrated global economic system. The process by which this is occurring is commonly referred to as globalization.

In this interdependent global economy, an American might drive to work in a car designed in Germany that was assembled in Mexico by DaimlerChrysler from components made in the United States and Japan that were fabricated from Korean steel and Malaysian rubber. She may have filled the car with gasoline at a BP service station owned by a British multinational company. The gasoline could have been made from oil pumped out of a well off the coast of Africa by a French oil company that transported it to the United States in a ship owned by a Greek shipping line. While driving to work, the American might talk to her stockbroker on a Nokia cell phone that was designed in Finland and assembled in Texas using chip sets produced in Taiwan that were designed by Indian engineers working for Texas Instruments. She could tell the stockbroker to purchase shares in Deutsche Telekom, a German telecommunications firm that was transformed from a former state-owned monopoly into a global company by an energetic Israeli CEO. She may turn on the car radio, which was made in Malaysia by a Japanese firm, to hear a popular hip-hop song composed by a Swede and sung by a group of Danes in English who signed a record contract with a French music company to promote their record in America. The driver might pull into a drive-through coffee stall run by a Korean immigrant and order a "single-tall-non-fat latte" and chocolate-covered biscotti. The coffee beans come from Brazil and the chocolate from Peru, while the biscotti was made locally using an old Italian recipe. After the song ends, a news announcer might inform the American listener that antiglobalization protests at a meeting of heads of state in Davos, Switzerland, have turned violent. One protester has been killed. The announcer then turns to the next item, a story about how fear of interest rate hikes in the United States has sent Japan's Nikkei stock market index down to new lows for the year.

This is the world we live in. It is a world where the volume of goods, services, and investment crossing national borders has expanded faster than world output consistently for more than half a century. It is a world where more than $1.2 billion in foreign exchange transactions are made every day, where $8.88 trillion of goods and $2.10 trillion of services were sold across national borders in 2004.[1] It is a world in which international institutions such as the World Trade Organization and gatherings of leaders from the world's most powerful economies have called for even lower barriers to cross-border trade and investment. It is a world where the symbols of material and popular culture are increasingly global: from Coca-Cola and Starbucks to Sony PlayStations, Nokia cell phones, MTV shows, and Disney films. It is a world in which products are made from inputs that come from all over the world. It is a world in which an economic crisis in Asia can cause a recession in the United States, and the threat of higher interest rates in the United States really did help drive Japan's Nikkei index down in the spring of 2004. It is also a world in which vigorous and vocal groups protest against globalization, which they blame for a list of ills, from unemployment in developed nations to environmental degradation and the Americanization of popular culture. And yes, these protests really have turned violent.

For businesses, this process has produced many opportunities. Firms can expand their revenues by selling around the world and reduce their costs by producing in nations where key inputs, including labor, are cheap. Since the collapse of communism at the end of the 1980s, the pendulum of public policy in nation after nation has swung toward the free market end of the economic spectrum. Regulatory and administrative barriers to doing business in foreign nations have come down, while those nations have often transformed their economies, privatizing state-owned enterprises, deregulating markets, increasing competition, and welcoming investment by foreign businesses. This has allowed businesses both large and small, from both advanced nations and developing nations, to expand internationally.

At the same time, globalization has created new threats for businesses accustomed to dominating their domestic markets. Foreign companies have entered many formerly protected industries in developing nations, increasing competition and driving down prices. For three decades, U.S. automobile companies have been battling foreign enterprises, as Japanese, European, and now Korean companies have taken business from them. General Motors has seen its market share decline from more than 50 percent to about 28 percent, while Japan's Toyota has passed Chrysler, now DaimlerChrysler, to become the third largest automobile company in America behind Ford and GM.

As globalization unfolds, it is transforming industries and creating anxiety among those who believed their jobs were protected from foreign competition. Historically, while many workers in manufacturing industries worried about the impact foreign competition might have on their jobs, workers in service industries felt more secure. Now this too is changing. Advances in technology, lower transportation costs, and the rise of skilled workers in developing countries imply that many services no longer need to be performed where they are delivered. As illustrated by the opening case, the outsourcing trend is even hitting health services. An MRI scan might now be interpreted by a radiologist living in Bangalore, and a North Carolina man might elect to have surgery in Hyderabad, India, rather than his local hospital. Similar trends can be seen in many other service industries. Accounting work is being outsourced from America to India. In 2003, some 25,000 U.S. individual tax returns were done in India; in 2005 the number was expected to be closer to 400,000. Indian accountants, trained in U.S. tax rules, perform work for U.S. accounting firms.[2] They access individual tax returns stored on computers in the United States, perform routine calculations, and save their work so that it can be inspected by a U.S. accountant, who then bills clients. As the best-selling author Thomas Friedman has recently argued, the world is becoming flat.[3] People living in developed nations no longer have the playing field tilted in their favor. Increasingly, enterprising individuals based in India, China, or Brazil have the same opportunities to better themselves as those living in Western Europe, the United States, or Canada.

In this book we will take a close look at the issues introduced here, and at many more besides. We will explore how changes in regulations governing international trade and investment, when coupled with changes in political systems and technology, have dramatically altered the competitive playing field confronting many businesses. We will discuss the resulting opportunities and threats, and review the different strategies that managers can pursue to exploit the opportunities and counter the threats. We will consider whether globalization benefits or harms national economies. We will look at what economic theory has to say about the outsourcing of manufacturing and service jobs to places such as India and China, and at the benefits and costs of outsourcing, not just to business firms and their employees, but also to entire economies. First, though, we need to get a better overview of the nature and process of globalization, and that is the function of the current chapter.

What is Globalization?

As used in this book, **globalization** refers to the shift toward a more integrated and interdependent world economy. Globalization has several facets, including the globalization of markets and the globalization of production.

BEIJING, CHINA: Chinese shoppers walk through Beijing's main downtown shopping promenade past a Kentucky Fried Chicken (KFC) franchise. KFC is one of the most successful international businesses in China due to its adaptation and appeal to the Chinese market.

THE GLOBALIZATION OF MARKETS

The **globalization of markets** refers to the merging of historically distinct and separate national markets into one huge global marketplace. Falling barriers to cross-border trade have made it easier to sell internationally. It has been argued for some time that the tastes and preferences of consumers in different nations are beginning to converge on some global norm, thereby helping to create a global market.[4] Consumer products such as Citigroup credit cards, Coca-Cola soft drinks, Sony PlayStation video games, McDonald's hamburgers, and Starbucks coffee are frequently held up as prototypical examples of this trend. Firms such as Citigroup, Coca-Cola, McDonald's, Starbucks, and Sony are more than just benefactors of this trend; they are also facilitators of it. By offering the same basic product worldwide, they help to create a global market.

A company does not have to be the size of these multinational giants to facilitate, and benefit from, the globalization of markets. In the United States, for example, nearly 90 percent of firms that export are small businesses that employ less than 100 people, and their share of total U.S. exports has grown steadily over the last decade and now exceeds 20 percent.[5] Firms with less than 500 employees accounted for 97 percent of all U.S. exporters and almost 30 percent of all exports by value.[6] Typical of these is Hytech, a New York–based manufacturer of solar panels that generates 40 percent of its $3 million in annual sales from exports to five countries, or B&S Aircraft Alloys, another New York company whose exports account for 40 percent of its $8 million annual revenues.[7] The situation is similar in several other nations. In Germany, for example, companies with less than 500 employees account for about 30 percent of that nation's exports.[8]

Despite the global prevalence of Citigroup credit cards, McDonald's hamburgers, and Starbucks coffee, it is important not to push too far the view that national markets are giving way to the global market. As we shall see in later chapters, very significant differences still exist among national markets along many relevant dimensions, including consumer tastes and preferences, distribution channels, culturally embedded value systems, business systems, and legal regulations. These differences frequently require that marketing strategies, product features, and operating practices be customized to best match conditions in a country. For example, automobile companies will promote different car models depending on a range of factors such as local fuel costs, income levels, traffic congestion, and cultural values. Similarly, many companies need to vary aspects of their product mix and operations from country to country depending on local tastes and preferences.

The most global markets currently are not markets for consumer products—where national differences in tastes and preferences are still often important enough to act as a brake on globalization—but markets for industrial goods and materials that serve a universal need the world over. These include the markets for commodities such as aluminum, oil, and wheat; the markets for industrial products such as microprocessors, DRAMs (computer memory chips), and commercial jet aircraft; the markets for computer software; and the markets for financial assets from U.S. Treasury bills to eurobonds and futures on the Nikkei index or the Mexican peso.

In many global markets, the same firms frequently confront each other as competitors in nation after nation. Coca-Cola's rivalry with PepsiCo is a global one, as are the rivalries between Ford and Toyota, Boeing and Airbus, Caterpillar and Komatsu in earthmoving equipment, and Sony, Nintendo, and Microsoft in video games. If one firm moves into a nation that is not currently served by its rivals, those rivals are sure to follow to prevent their competitor from gaining an advantage.[9] As firms follow each

other around the world, they bring with them many of the assets that served them well in other national markets—including their products, operating strategies, marketing strategies, and brand names—creating some homogeneity across markets. Thus, greater uniformity replaces diversity. In an increasing number of industries, it is no longer meaningful to talk about "the German market," "the American market," "the Brazilian market," or "the Japanese market"; for many firms there is only the global market.

THE GLOBALIZATION OF PRODUCTION

The **globalization of production** refers to the sourcing of goods and services from locations around the globe to take advantage of national differences in the cost and quality of **factors of production** (such as labor, energy, land, and capital). By doing this, companies hope to lower their overall cost structure and/or improve the quality or functionality of their product offering, thereby allowing them to compete more effectively. Consider the Boeing Company's commercial jet airliner, the 777. Eight Japanese suppliers make parts for the fuselage, doors, and wings; a supplier in Singapore makes the doors for the nose landing gear; three suppliers in Italy manufacture wing flaps; and so on.[10] In total, some 30 percent of the 777, by value, is built by foreign companies. For its next jet airliner, the 787, Boeing is pushing this trend even further, with some 65 percent of the total value of the aircraft scheduled to be outsourced to foreign companies, 35 percent of which will go to three major Japanese companies.[11]

Part of Boeing's rationale for outsourcing so much production to foreign suppliers is that these suppliers are the best in the world at their particular activity. A global web of suppliers yields a better final product, which enhances the chances of Boeing winning a greater share of total orders for aircraft than its global rival, Airbus Industrie. Boeing also outsources some production to foreign countries to increase the chance that it will win significant orders from airlines based in that country.

For another example of a global web of activities, consider the IBM ThinkPad X31 laptop computer.[12] This product was designed in the United States by IBM engineers because IBM believed that was the best location in the world to do the basic design work. The case, keyboard, and hard drive were made in Thailand; the display screen and memory were made in South Korea; the built-in wireless card was made in Malaysia; and the microprocessor was manufactured in the United States. In each case, these components were manufactured in the optimal location given an assessment of production costs and transportation costs. These components were shipped to an IBM operation in Mexico, where the product was assembled, before being shipped to the United States for final sale. IBM assembled the ThinkPad in Mexico because IBM's managers calculated that due to low labor costs, the costs of assembly could be minimized there. The marketing and sales strategy for North America was developed by IBM personnel in the United States, primarily because IBM believed that due to their knowledge of the local marketplace, U.S. personnel would add more value to the product through their marketing efforts than personnel based elsewhere. (Interestingly, in another comment on the nature of globalization, in 2005, IBM's personal computer business, including the ThinkPad, was purchased by the Chinese company Lenovo, which promptly moved its headquarters to the United States because it believed that was the best location from which to run this business. See the Management Focus later in this chapter on Lenovo.)

While historically significant outsourcing has been primarily confined to manufacturing enterprises such as Boeing and IBM, increasingly companies take advantage of modern communications technology, particularly the Internet, to outsource service activities to low-cost producers in other nations. As we saw in the opening case, the Internet has allowed hospitals to outsource some radiology work to India, where images from MRI scans and the like are read at night while U.S. physicians sleep and the results are ready for them in the morning. Similarly, in December 2003, IBM

The ThinkPad X31 is ultra-global—its components come from various locations worldwide, but the assembly occurs in Mexico.

announced it would move the work of some 4,300 software engineers from the United States to India and China (software production is counted as a service activity).[13] Many software companies now use Indian engineers to perform maintenance functions on software designed in the United States. Due to the time difference, Indian engineers can run debugging tests on software written in the United States when U.S. engineers sleep, transmitting the corrected code back to the United States over secure Internet connections so it is ready for U.S. engineers to work on the following day. Dispersing value creation activities in this way can compress the time and lower the costs required to develop new software programs. Other companies from computer makers to banks are outsourcing customer service functions, such as customer call centers, to developing nations where labor is cheaper.

Robert Reich, who served as secretary of labor in the Clinton administration, has argued that as a consequence of the trend exemplified by companies such as Boeing, Microsoft, and IBM, in many cases it is becoming irrelevant to talk about American products, Japanese products, German products, or Korean products. Increasingly, according to Reich, the outsourcing of productive activities to different suppliers results in the creation of products that are global in nature; that is, "global products."[14] But as with the globalization of markets, one must be careful not to push the globalization of production too far. As we will see in later chapters, substantial impediments still make it difficult for firms to achieve the optimal dispersion of their productive activities to locations around the globe. These impediments include formal and informal barriers to trade between countries, barriers to foreign direct investment, transportation costs, and issues associated with economic and political risk. For example, government regulations ultimately limit the ability of hospitals to outsource the process of interpreting MRI scans to developing nations where radiologists are cheaper (see the opening case).

Nevertheless, we are traveling down the road toward a future characterized by the increased globalization of markets and production. Modern firms are important actors in this drama, by their very actions fostering increased globalization. These firms, however, are merely responding in an efficient manner to changing conditions in their operating environment—as well they should.

The Emergence of Global Institutions

As markets globalize and an increasing proportion of business activity transcends national borders, institutions are needed to help manage, regulate, and police the global marketplace, and to promote the establishment of multinational treaties to govern the global business system. Over the past half century, a number of important global institutions have been created to help perform these functions. These institutions include the **General Agreement on Tariffs and Trade (the GATT)** and its successor, the World Trade Organization (WTO); the International Monetary Fund (IMF) and its sister institution, the World Bank; and the United Nations (UN). All these institutions were created by voluntary agreement between individual nation-states, and their functions are enshrined in international treaties.

The **World Trade Organization** (like the GATT before it) is primarily responsible for policing the world trading system and making sure nation-states adhere to the rules laid down in trade treaties signed by WTO member states. As of May 2005, 148 nations that collectively accounted for 97 percent of world trade were WTO members, thereby giving the organization enormous scope and influence. The WTO is also responsible for facilitating the establishment of additional multinational agreements between WTO member states. Over its entire history, and that of the GATT before it, the WTO has promoted the lowering of barriers to cross-border trade and investment.

The United Nations has the important goal of improving the well-being of people around the world.

In doing so, the WTO has been the instrument of its member states, which have sought to create a more open global business system unencumbered by barriers to trade and investment between countries. Without an institution such as the WTO, the globalization of markets and production is unlikely to have proceeded as far as it has. However, as we shall see in this chapter and in Chapter 6 when we look closely at the WTO, critics charge that the WTO is usurping the national sovereignty of individual nation-states.

The **International Monetary Fund (IMF)** and the **World Bank** were both created in 1944 by 44 nations that met at **Bretton Woods,** New Hampshire. The task of the IMF was to maintain order in the international monetary system, and that of the World Bank was to promote economic development. In the 60 years since their creation, both institutions have emerged as significant players in the global economy. The World Bank is the less controversial of the two sister institutions. It has focused on making low-interest loans to cash-strapped governments in poor nations that wish to undertake significant infrastructure investments (such as building dams or roads).

The IMF is often seen as the lender of last resort to nation-states whose economies are in turmoil and currencies are losing value against those of other nations. Repeatedly during the past decade, for example, the IMF has lent money to the governments of troubled states, including Argentina, Indonesia, Mexico, Russia, South Korea, Thailand, and Turkey. The IMF loans come with strings attached; in return for loans, the IMF requires nation-states to adopt specific economic policies aimed at returning their troubled economies to stability and growth. These "strings" have generated the most debate, for some critics charge that the IMF's policy recommendations are often inappropriate, while others maintain that by telling national governments what economic policies they must adopt, the IMF, like the WTO, is usurping the sovereignty of nation-states. We shall look at the debate over the role of the IMF in Chapter 11.

The **United Nations** was established October 24, 1945, by 51 countries committed to preserving peace through international cooperation and collective security. Today nearly every nation in the world belongs to the United Nations; membership now totals 191 countries. When states become members of the United Nations, they agree to accept the obligations of the UN Charter, an international treaty that establishes basic principles of international relations. According to the charter, the United Nations has four purposes: to maintain international peace and security, to develop friendly relations among nations, to cooperate in solving international problems and in promoting respect for human rights, and to be a center for harmonizing the actions of nations. Although the UN is perhaps best known for its peacekeeping role, one of the organization's central mandates is the promotion of higher standards of living, full employment, and conditions of economic and social progress and development—all issues that are central to the creation of a vibrant global economy. As much as 70 percent of the work of the UN system is devoted to accomplishing this mandate. To do so, the United Nations works closely with other international institutions such as the World Bank. Guiding the work is the belief that eradicating poverty and improving the well-being of people everywhere are necessary steps in creating conditions for lasting world peace.[15]

Drivers of Globalization

Two macro factors seem to underlie the trend toward greater globalization.[16] The first is the decline in barriers to the free flow of goods, services, and capital that has occurred since the end of World War II. The second factor is technological change, particularly the dramatic developments in recent years in communication, information processing, and transportation technologies.

DECLINING TRADE AND INVESTMENT BARRIERS

During the 1920s and 30s, many of the world's nation-states erected formidable barriers to international trade and foreign direct investment. **International trade** occurs when a firm exports goods or services to consumers in another country. **Foreign direct investment (FDI)** occurs when a firm invests resources in business activities outside its home country. Many of the barriers to international trade took the form of high tariffs on imports of manufactured goods. The typical aim of such tariffs was to protect domestic industries from foreign competition. One consequence, however, was "beggar thy neighbor" retaliatory trade policies with countries progressively raising trade barriers against each other. Ultimately, this depressed world demand and contributed to the Great Depression of the 1930s.

Having learned from this experience, the advanced industrial nations of the West committed themselves after World War II to removing barriers to the free flow of goods, services, and capital between nations.[17] This goal was enshrined in the General Agreement on Tariffs and Trade (GATT). Under the umbrella of GATT, eight rounds of negotiations among member states (now numbering 148) have worked to lower barriers to the free flow of goods and services. The most recent round of negotiations, known as the Uruguay Round, was completed in December 1993. The Uruguay Round further reduced trade barriers; extended GATT to cover services as well as manufactured goods; provided enhanced protection for patents, trademarks, and copyrights; and established the World Trade Organization (WTO) to police the international trading system.[18] Table 1.1 summarizes the impact of GATT agreements on average tariff rates for manufactured goods. As can be seen, average tariff rates have fallen significantly since 1950 and now stand at about 4 percent.

In late 2001, the WTO launched a new round of talks aimed at further liberalizing the global trade and investment framework. For this meeting, it picked the remote location of Doha in the Persian Gulf state of Qatar. At Doha, the member states of the WTO staked out an agenda. The talks were scheduled to last three years, although it now looks as if they may go on significantly longer. The agenda includes cutting tariffs on industrial goods, services, and agricultural products; phasing out subsidies to agricultural producers; reducing barriers to cross-border investment; and limiting the use of antidumping laws.

	1913	**1950**	**1990**	**2003**
France	21%	18%	5.9%	4.0%
Germany	20	26	5.9	4.0
Italy	18	25	5.9	4.0
Japan	30	—	5.3	3.8
Holland	5	11	5.9	4.0
Sweden	20	9	4.4	4.0
Great Britain	—	23	5.9	4.0
United States	44	14	4.8	4.0

TABLE 1.1

Average Tariff Rates on Manufactured Products as Percent of Value

Sources: 1913–1990 data from "Who Wants to Be a Giant?" *The Economist: A Survey of the Multinationals,* June 24, 1995, pp. 3–4. Copyright © The Economist Books, Ltd. The 2003 data are from World Trade Organization, *2004 Annual Report* (Geneva: WTO, 2005).

The biggest gain may come from discussion on agricultural products; average agricultural tariff rates are still about 40 percent, and rich nations spend some $300 billion a year in subsidies to support their farm sectors. The world's poorer nations have the most to gain from any reduction in agricultural tariffs and subsidies; such reforms would give them access to the markets of the developed world.[19]

In addition to reducing trade barriers, many countries have also been progressively removing restrictions to foreign direct investment (FDI). According to the United Nations, some 94 percent of the 1,885 changes made worldwide between 1991 and 2003 in the laws governing foreign direct investment created a more favorable environment for FDI.[20] Governments' desire to facilitate FDI also has been reflected in a dramatic increase in the number of bilateral investment treaties designed to protect and promote investment between two countries. As of 2003, 2,265 such treaties in the world involved more than 160 countries, a 12-fold increase from the 181 treaties that existed in 1980.[21]

Such trends have been driving both the globalization of markets and the globalization of production. The lowering of barriers to international trade enables firms to view the world, rather than a single country, as their market. The lowering of trade and investment barriers also allows firms to base production at the optimal location for that activity. Thus, a firm might design a product in one country, produce component parts in two other countries, assemble the product in yet another country, and then export the finished product around the world.

According to data from the World Trade Organization, the volume of world merchandise trade has grown faster than the world economy since 1950 (see Figure 1.1).[22] From 1970 to 2004, the volume of world merchandise trade expanded almost 26-fold, outstripping the expansion of world production, which grew about 7.5 times in real terms. (World merchandise trade includes trade in manufactured goods, agricultural goods and mining products, but *not* services. World production and trade are measured in real, or inflation-adjusted, dollars.) As suggested by Figure 1.1, due to falling barriers to cross-border trade and investment, the growth in world trade seems to have accelerated since the early 1980s.

The data summarized in Figure 1.1 imply several things. First, more firms are doing what Boeing does with the 777 and 787 and IBM with the ThinkPad: dispersing parts of their production process to different locations around the globe to drive down production costs and increase product quality. Second, the economies of the world's nation-states are becoming more intertwined. As trade expands, nations are becoming increasingly dependent on each other for important goods and services. Third, the world

12   **Part 1**   Introduction and Overview

FIGURE 1.1

Growth in World Trade and World Production, 1950–2004

Source: Calculated by the author from World Trade Organization data accessed May 2005 at www.wto.org/english/res_e/statis_e/statis_e.htm

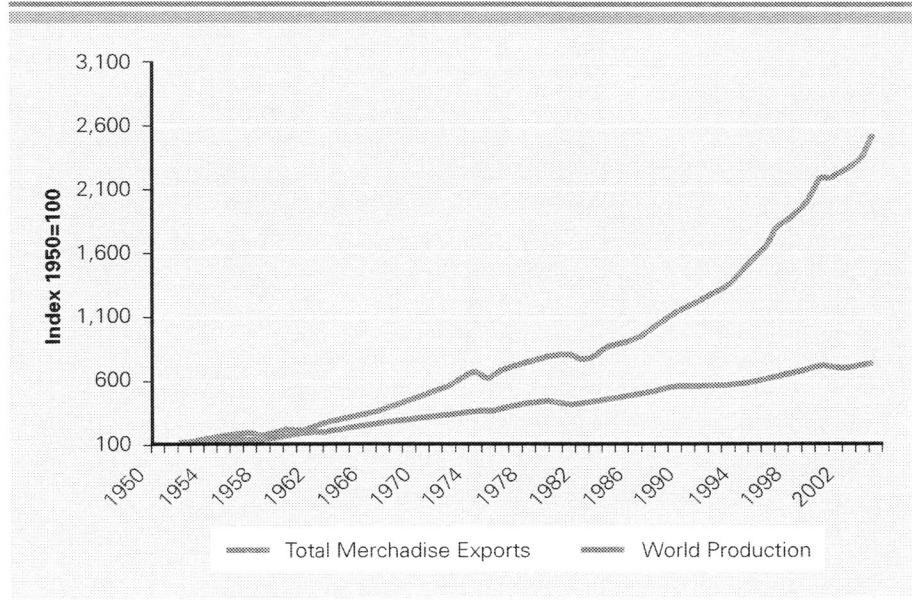

has become significantly wealthier since 1950, and the implication is that rising trade is the engine that has helped to pull the global economy along.

What Figure 1.1 does not show is that since the mid-1980s the value of international trade in services grew robustly. Trade in services now accounts for almost 20 percent of the value of all international trade. Increasingly, international trade in services has been driven by advances in communications, which allow corporations to outsource service activities to different locations around the globe (see the opening case). Thus, as noted earlier, many corporations in the developed world outsource customer service functions, from software maintenance activities to customer call centers, to developing nations where labor costs are lower.

The evidence also suggests that foreign direct investment (FDI) is playing an increasing role in the global economy as firms increase their cross-border investments. The average yearly outflow of FDI increased from $25 billion in 1975 to a record $1.3 trillion in 2000, before falling back to $620 billion in 2004.[23] Despite the slowdown in 2001–04, the flow of FDI not only accelerated over the past quarter century, but also accelerated faster than the growth in world trade. As shown in Figure 1.2, between 1992 and 2004 the total flow of FDI from all countries increased by about 360 percent, while world trade doubled and world output grew by 35 percent.[24] As a result of the strong FDI flow, by 2003 the global stock of FDI exceeded $8.1 trillion. In total, at least 61,000 parent companies had 900,000 affiliates in foreign markets that collectively employed some 54 million people abroad and generated value accounting for about one-tenth of global GDP. The foreign affiliates of multinationals had an estimated $17.6 trillion in global sales, nearly twice as high as the value of global exports of goods and service combined, which stood at $9.2 trillion.[25]

The globalization of markets and production and the resulting growth of world trade, foreign direct investment, and imports all imply that firms are finding their home markets under attack from foreign competitors. This is true in Japan, where U.S. companies such as Kodak, Procter & Gamble, and Merrill Lynch are expanding their presence. It is true in the United States, where Japanese automobile firms have taken market share away from General Motors and Ford. And it is true in Europe, where the once-dominant Dutch company Philips has seen its market share in the consumer electronics industry taken by

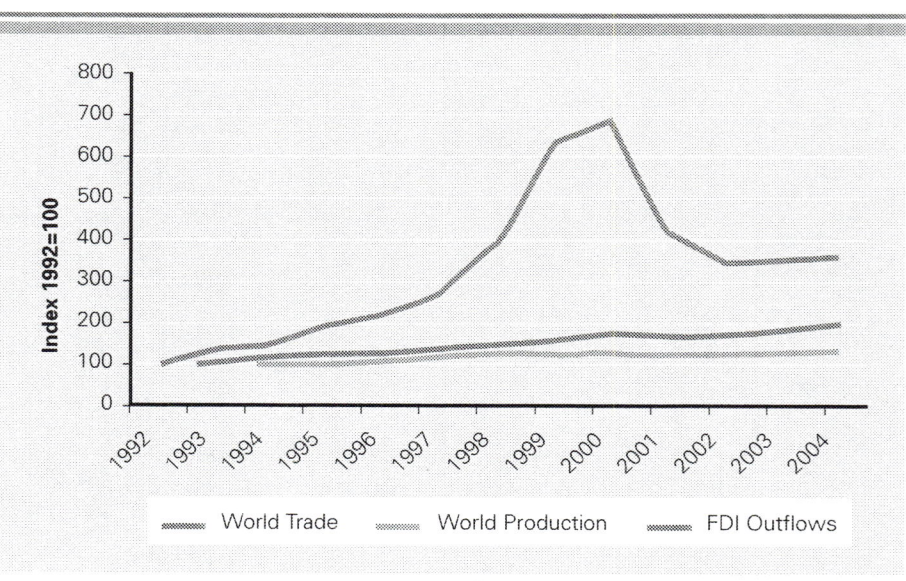

FIGURE 1.2

Growth of World Trade, Production, and FDI, 1992–2004

Sources: Calculated by the author from World Trade Organization data accessed May 2005 at www.wto.org/english/res_e/statis_e/statis_e.htm, and from United Nations, *World Investment Report*, 2004 (New York and Geneva: United Nations, 2004), and United Nations Conference on Trade and Development, "World FDI Flows Grew and Estimated 6% in 2004," UNCTAD Press Release, January 11, 2005.

Japan's JVC, Matsushita, and Sony. The growing integration of the world economy into a single, huge marketplace is increasing the intensity of competition in a range of manufacturing and service industries.

However, declining barriers to cross-border trade and investment cannot be taken for granted. As we shall see in subsequent chapters, demands for "protection" from foreign competitors are still often heard in countries around the world, including the United States. Although a return to the restrictive trade policies of the 1920s and 30s is unlikely, it is not clear whether the political majority in the industrialized world favors further reductions in trade barriers. If trade barriers decline no further, at least for the time being, this will put a brake upon the globalization of both markets and production.

THE ROLE OF TECHNOLOGICAL CHANGE

The lowering of trade barriers made globalization of markets and production a theoretical possibility. Technological change has made it a tangible reality. Since the end of World War II, the world has seen major advances in communication, information processing, and transportation technology, including the explosive emergence of the Internet and World Wide Web. Telecommunications is creating a global audience. Transportation is creating a global village. From Buenos Aires to Boston, and from Birmingham to Beijing, ordinary people are watching MTV, they're wearing blue jeans, and they're listening to iPods as they commute to work.

Microprocessors and Telecommunications

Perhaps the single most important innovation has been development of the microprocessor, which enabled the explosive growth of high-power, low-cost computing, vastly increasing the amount of information that can be processed by individuals and firms. The microprocessor also underlies many recent advances in telecommunications technology. Over the past 30 years, global communications have been revolutionized by developments in satellite, optical fiber, and wireless technologies, and now the Internet and the World Wide Web. These technologies rely on the microprocessor to encode, transmit, and decode the vast amount of information that flows along these electronic highways. The cost of microprocessors continues to fall, while their power increases (a phenomenon known as **Moore's Law,** which predicts that the power of microprocessor technology doubles and its cost of production falls in half every 18 months).[26] As this happens, the cost of global communications plummets, which lowers the costs of coordinating and controlling a global organization. Thus, between 1930 and 1990, the cost of a three-minute phone call between New York and London fell from $244.65 to $3.32.[27] By 1998 it had plunged to just 36 cents for consumers, and much lower rates were available for businesses.[28]

The Internet and World Wide Web

The rapid growth of the Internet and the associated World Wide Web (which utilizes the Internet to communicate between World Wide Web sites) is the latest expression of this development. In 1990, fewer than 1 million users were connected to the Internet. By 1995 the figure had risen to 50 million. In 2004 it grew to about 945 million. By 2007, forecasts suggest the Internet may have more than 1.47 billion users, or about 25 percent of the world's population.[29] In July 1993, some 1.8 million host computers were connected to the Internet (host computers host the Web pages of local users). By January 2005, the number of host computers had increased to 317 million, and the number is still growing rapidly.[30] In the United States, where Internet usage is most advanced, almost 60 percent of the population was using the Internet by 2003 (see Figure 1.3). Worldwide the figure was 15 percent and growing fast. The Internet and World Wide Web (WWW) promise to develop into the information backbone of the global economy. According to Forrester Research, the value of Web-based transactions hit $657 billion in 2000, up from virtually nothing in 1994, and was predicted to hit $6.8 trillion in 2004, with the United States accounting for 47 percent of all Web-based transactions.[31] Many of these transactions are not business-to-consumer transactions (e-commerce), but business-to-business (or e-business) transactions. The greatest current potential of the Web seems to be in the business-to-business arena.

Included in the expanding volume of Web-based traffic is a growing percentage of cross-border trade. Viewed globally, the Web is emerging as an equalizer. It rolls back some of the constraints of location, scale, and time zones.[32] The Web makes it much easier for buyers and sellers to find each other, wherever they may be located and whatever their size. The Web allows businesses, both small and large, to expand their global presence at a lower cost than ever before. One example is a small California-based start-up, Cardiac Science, which makes defibrillators and heart monitors. In 1996, Cardiac Science was itching to break into international markets but had little idea of how to establish an international presence. By 1998, the company was selling to customers in 46 countries and foreign sales accounted for $1.02 million of its $1.2 million revenues. By 2002 revenues had surged on the back of product introductions to $50 million, some $17.5 million of which came from sales to customers in 50 countries. Although some of this business was developed through conventional export channels, a good percentage of it came from hits to the company's Web site, which, according to the company's CEO, "attracts international business people like bees to honey."[33] Similarly, 10 years ago no one would have thought that a small British company based in Stafford could have built a global market for its products by utilizing the Internet, but that is exactly what Bridgewater Pottery has done.[34] Bridgewater traditionally sold premium pottery through exclusive distribution channels, but the company found it difficult and laborious to identify new retail outlets. Since establishing an Internet presence in 1997, Bridgewater has conducted a significant amount of business with consumers in other countries who could not be reached through existing distribution channels or could not be reached cost effectively.

Transportation Technology

In addition to developments in communication technology, several major innovations in transportation technology have occurred since World War II. In economic terms, the most important are probably the development of commercial jet aircraft and super-freighters

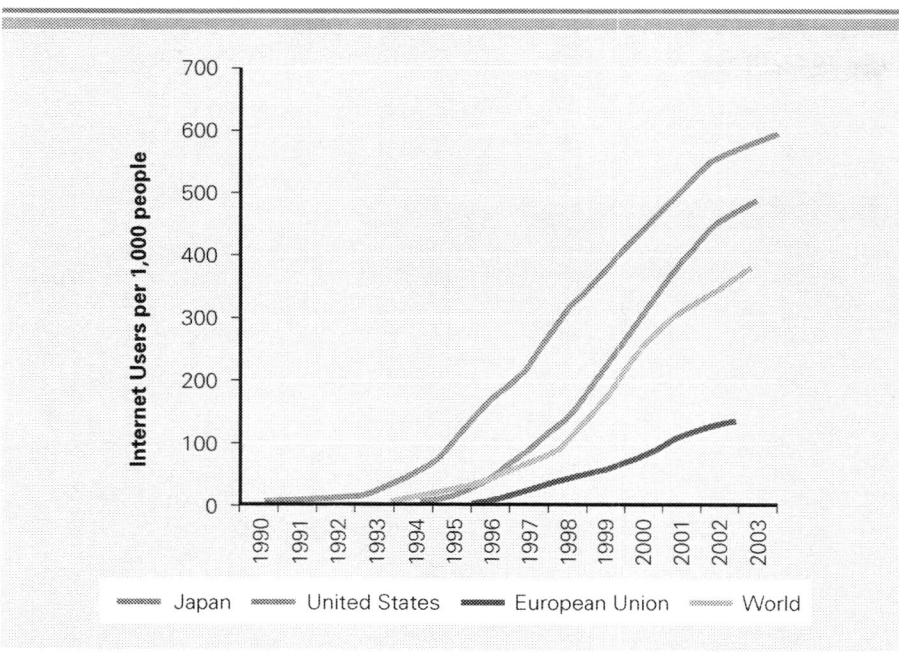

FIGURE 1.3

Internet Users per 1,000 People, 1990–2003

Source: Constructed by the author from World Bank, *World Development Indicators*, 2005.

and the introduction of containerization, which simplifies transshipment from one mode of transport to another. The advent of commercial jet travel, by reducing the time needed to get from one location to another, has effectively shrunk the globe. In terms of travel time, New York is now "closer" to Tokyo than it was to Philadelphia in the Colonial days.

Containerization has revolutionized the transportation business, significantly lowering the costs of shipping goods over long distances. Before the advent of containerization, moving goods from one mode of transport to another was very labor intensive, lengthy, and costly. It could take days and several hundred longshoremen to unload a ship and reload goods onto trucks and trains. With the advent of widespread containerization in the 1970s and 1980s, the whole process can be executed by a handful of longshoremen in a couple of days. Since 1980, the world's containership fleet has more than quadrupled, reflecting in part the growing volume of international trade and in part the switch to this mode of transportation. As a result of the efficiency gains associated with containerization, transportation costs have plummeted, making it much more economical to ship goods around the globe, thereby helping to drive the globalization of markets and production. Between 1920 and 1990, the average ocean freight and port charges per ton of U.S. export and import cargo fell from $95 to $29 (in 1990 dollars).[35] The cost of shipping freight per ton-mile on railroads in the United States fell from 3.04 cents in 1985 to 2.3 cents in 2000, largely as a result of efficiency gains from the widespread use of containers.[36] An increased share of cargo now goes by air. Between 1955 and 1999, average air transportation revenue per ton-kilometer fell by more than 80 percent.[37] Reflecting the falling cost of airfreight, by the early 2000s air shipments accounted for 28 percent of the value of U.S. trade, up from 7 percent in 1965.[38]

Implications for the Globalization of Production

As transportation costs associated with the globalization of production declined, dispersal of production to geographically separate locations became more economical. As a result of the technological innovations discussed above, the real costs of information processing and communication have fallen dramatically in the past two decades. These

developments make it possible for a firm to create and then manage a globally dispersed production system, further facilitating the globalization of production. A worldwide communications network has become essential for many international businesses. For example, Dell uses the Internet to coordinate and control a globally dispersed production system to such an extent that it holds only three days' worth of inventory at its assembly locations. Dell's Internet-based system records orders for computer equipment as they are submitted by customers via the company's Web site, then immediately transmits the resulting orders for components to various suppliers around the world, which have a real-time look at Dell's order flow and can adjust their production schedules accordingly. Given the low cost of airfreight, Dell can use air transportation to speed up the delivery of critical components to meet unanticipated demand shifts without delaying the shipment of final product to consumers. Dell also has used modern communications technology to outsource its customer service operations to India. When U.S. customers call Dell with a service inquiry, they are routed to Bangalore in India, where English-speaking service personnel handle the call.

The Internet has been a major force facilitating international trade in services. It is the Web that allows hospitals in Chicago to send MRI scans to India for analysis, accounting offices in San Francisco to outsource routine tax preparation work to accountants living in the Philippines, and software testers in India to debug code written by developers in Redmond, Washington, the headquarters of Microsoft. We are probably still in the early stages of this development. As Moore's Law continues to advance and telecommunications bandwidth continues to increase, almost any work processes that can be digitalized will be, and this will allow that work to be performed wherever in the world it is most efficient and effective to do so.

The development of commercial jet aircraft has also helped knit together the worldwide operations of many international businesses. Using jet travel, an American manager need spend a day at most traveling to her firm's European or Asian operations. This enables her to oversee a globally dispersed production system.

Implications for the Globalization of Markets

In addition to the globalization of production, technological innovations have also facilitated the globalization of markets. Low-cost global communications networks such as the World Wide Web are helping to create electronic global marketplaces. As noted above, low-cost transportation has made it more economical to ship products around the world, thereby helping to create global markets. For example, due to the tumbling costs of shipping goods by air, roses grown in Ecuador can be cut and sold in New York two days later while they are still fresh. This has given rise to an industry in Ecuador that did not exist 20 years ago and now supplies a global market for roses (see the accompanying Country Focus). In addition, low-cost jet travel has resulted in the mass movement of people between countries. This has reduced the cultural distance between countries and is bringing about some convergence of consumer tastes and preferences. At the same time, global communication networks and global media are creating a worldwide culture. U.S. television networks such as CNN, MTV, and HBO are now received in many countries, and Hollywood films are shown the world over. In any society, the media are primary conveyors of culture; as global media develop, we must expect the evolution of something akin to a global culture. A logical result of this evolution is the emergence of global markets for consumer products. The first signs of this are already apparent. It is now as easy to find a McDonald's restaurant in Tokyo as it is in New York, to buy an iPod in Rio as it is in Berlin, and to buy Gap jeans in Paris as it is in San Francisco.

Despite these trends, we must be careful not to overemphasize their importance. While modern communication and transportation technologies are ushering in the "global village," very significant national differences remain in culture, consumer preferences, and business practices. A firm that ignores differences between countries does so at its peril. We shall stress this point repeatedly throughout this book and elaborate on it in later chapters.

Ecuadorean Valentine Roses

COUNTRY FOCUS It is 6:20 A.M. February 7, in the Ecuadorean town of Cayambe, and Maria Pacheco has just been dropped off for work by the company bus. She pulls on thick rubber gloves, wraps an apron over her white, traditional embroidered dress, and grabs her clippers, ready for another long day. Any other time of year, Maria would work until 2 P.M., but it's a week before Valentine's Day, and Maria along with her 84 coworkers at the farm are likely to be busy until 5 P.M. By then, Maria will have cut more than 1,000 rose stems.

A few days later, after they have been refrigerated and shipped via aircraft, the roses Maria cut will be selling for premium prices in stores from New York to London. Ecuadorean roses are quickly becoming the Rolls-Royce of roses. They have huge heads and unusually vibrant colors, including 10 different reds, from bleeding heart crimson to a rosy lover's blush.

Most of Ecuador's 460 or so rose farms are located in the Cayambe and Cotopaxi regions, 10,000 feet up in the Andes about an hour's drive from the capital, Quito. The rose bushes are planted in huge flat fields at the foot of snowcapped volcanoes that rise to more than 20,000 feet. The bushes are protected by 20-foot-high canopies of plastic sheeting. The combination of intense sunlight, fertile volcanic soil, an equatorial location, and high altitude makes for ideal growing conditions, allowing roses to flower almost year-round.

Ecuador's rose industry started some 20 years ago and has been expanding rapidly since. Ecuador is now the world's fourth largest producer of roses. Roses are the nation's fifth largest export, with customers all over the world. Rose farms generate $240 million in sales and support tens of thousands of jobs. In Cayambe, the population has increased in 10 years from 10,000 to 70,000, primarily as a result of the rose industry. The revenues and taxes from rose growers have helped to pave roads, build schools, and construct sophisticated irrigation systems. In 2003, construction was to begin on an international airport between Quito and Cayambe from which Ecuadorean roses will begin their journey to flower shops all over the world.

Maria works Monday to Saturday, and earns $210 a month, which she says is an average wage in Ecuador and substantially above the country's $120 a month minimum wage. The farm also provides her with health care and a pension. By employing women such as Maria, the industry has fostered a social revolution in which mothers and wives have more control over their family's spending, especially on schooling for their children.

For all of the benefits that roses have bought to Ecuador, where the gross national income per capita is only $1,080 a year, the industry has come under fire from environmentalists. Large growers have been accused of misusing a toxic mixture of pesticides, fungicides, and fumigants to grow and export unblemished pest-free flowers. Reports claim that workers often fumigate roses in street clothes without protective equipment. Some doctors and scientists claim that many of the industry's 50,000 employees have serious health problems as a result of exposure to toxic chemicals. A 1999 study published by the International Labor Organization claimed that women in the industry had more miscarriages than average and that some 60 percent of all workers suffered from headaches, nausea, blurred vision, and fatigue. Still, the critics acknowledge that their studies have been hindered by a lack of access to the farms, and they do not know what the true situation is. The International Labor Organization has also claimed that some rose growers in Ecuador use child labor, a claim that has been strenuously rejected by both the growers and Ecuadorean government agencies.

In Europe, consumer groups have urged the European Union to press for improved environmental safeguards. In response, some Ecuadorean growers have joined a voluntary program aimed at helping customers identify responsible growers. The certification signifies that the grower has distributed protective gear, trained workers in using chemicals, and hired doctors to visit workers at least weekly. Other environmental groups have pushed for stronger sanctions, including trade sanctions, against Ecuadorean rose growers that are not environmentally certified by a reputable agency. On February 14, however, most consumers are oblivious to these issues; they simply want to show their appreciation to their wives and girlfriends with a perfect bunch of roses.

Sources: G. Thompson, "Behind Roses' Beauty, Poor and Ill Workers," *The New York Times*, February 13, 2003, pp. A1, A27; J. Stuart, "You've Come a Long Way Baby," *The Independent*, February 14, 2003, p. 1; V. Marino, "By Any Other Name, It's Usually a Rosa," *The New York Times*, May 11, 2003, p. A9; and A. DePalma, "In Trade Issue, the Pressure Is on Flowers," *The New York Times*, January 24, 2002, p. 1.

The Changing Demographics of the Global Economy

Hand in hand with the trend toward globalization has been a fairly dramatic change in the demographics of the global economy over the past 30 years. As late as the 1960s, four stylized facts described the demographics of the global economy. The first was U.S. dominance in the world economy and world trade picture. The second was U.S. dominance in world foreign direct investment. Related to this, the third fact was the dominance of large, multinational U.S. firms on the international business scene. The fourth was that roughly half the globe—the centrally planned economies of the Communist world—were off-limits to Western international businesses. As will be explained below, all four of these qualities either have changed or are now changing rapidly.

THE CHANGING WORLD OUTPUT AND WORLD TRADE PICTURE

In the early 1960s, the United States was still by far the world's dominant industrial power. In 1963 the United States accounted for 40.3 percent of world output. By 2004, the United States accounted for nearly 21 percent of world output, still by far the world's largest industrial power but down significantly in relative size since the 1960s (see Table 1.2). Nor was the United States the only developed nation to see its relative standing slip. The same occurred to Germany, France, and the United Kingdom, all nations that were among the first to industrialize. This decline in the U.S. position was not an absolute decline, since the U.S. economy grew at a robust average annual rate of more than 3 percent from 1963 to 2004 (the economies of Germany, France, and the United Kingdom also grew during this time). Rather, it was a relative decline, reflecting the faster economic growth of several other economies, particularly in Asia. For example, as can be seen from Table 1.2, from 1963 to 2004, China's share of world output increased from a trivial amount to 13.2 percent. Other countries that markedly increased their share of world output included Japan, Thailand, Malaysia, Taiwan, and South Korea.

By the end of the 1980s, the U.S. position as the world's leading exporter was threatened. Over the past 30 years, U.S. dominance in export markets has waned as Japan, Germany, and a number of newly industrialized countries such as South Korea and China have taken a larger share of world exports. During the 1960s, the United States routinely accounted for 20 percent of world exports of manufactured goods. But as Table 1.2 shows, the U.S. share of world exports of goods and services had slipped to 10.4 percent by 2004. Despite the fall, the United States still remained the world's largest exporter, ahead of Germany, Japan, France, and the fast-rising economic power, China.

In 1997 and 1998, the dynamic economies of the Asian Pacific region were hit by a serious financial crisis that threatened to slow their economic growth rates for several years. Despite this, their powerful growth may continue over the long run, as will that of several other important emerging economies in Latin America (e.g., Brazil) and Eastern Europe (e.g., Poland). Thus, a further relative decline in the share of world output and world exports accounted for by the United States and other long-established developed nations seems likely. By itself, this is not bad. The relative decline of the United States reflects the growing economic development and industrialization of the world economy, as opposed to any absolute decline in the health of the U.S. economy, which entered the new millennium stronger than ever.

If we look 20 years into the future, most forecasts now predict a rapid rise in the share of world output accounted for by developing nations such as China, India, Indonesia, Thailand, South Korea, Mexico, and Brazil, and a commensurate decline in the share enjoyed by rich industrialized countries such as Great Britain, Germany, Japan, and the United States. The World Bank, for example, has estimated that if current trends continue, by 2020 the Chinese economy could be larger than that of the United States, while

Country	Share of World Output 1963	Share of World Output 2004	Share of World Exports 2004
United States	40.3%	20.9%	10.4%
Germany	9.7	4.3	9.5
France	6.3	3.1	4.8
United Kingdom	6.5	3.1	4.7
Japan	5.5	6.9	5.7
Italy	3.4	2.9	3.8
Canada	3.0	3.5	3.4
China	NA	13.2	5.9

TABLE 1.2

The Changing Pattern of World Output and Trade

Sources: IMF, *World Economic Outlook*, April 2005, and data for 1963 from N. Hood and J. Young, *The Economics of the Multinational Enterprise* (New York: Longman, 1973).

the economy of India will approach that of Germany. The World Bank also estimates that today's developing nations may account for more than 60 percent of world economic activity by 2020, while today's rich nations, which currently account for over 55 percent of world economic activity, may account for only about 38 percent.[39] Forecasts are not always correct, but these suggest that a shift in the economic geography of the world is now under way, although the magnitude of that shift is not totally evident. For international businesses, the implications of this changing economic geography are clear: Many of tomorrow's economic opportunities may be found in the developing nations of the world, and many of tomorrow's most capable competitors will probably also emerge from these regions.

THE CHANGING FOREIGN DIRECT INVESTMENT PICTURE

Reflecting the dominance of the United States in the global economy, U.S. firms accounted for 66.3 percent of worldwide foreign direct investment flows in the 1960s. British firms were second, accounting for 10.5 percent, while Japanese firms were a distant eighth, with only 2 percent. The dominance of U.S. firms was so great that books were written about the economic threat posed to Europe by U.S. corporations.[40] Several European governments, most notably France, talked of limiting inward investment by U.S. firms.

However, as the barriers to the free flow of goods, services, and capital fell, and as other countries increased their shares of world output, non-U.S. firms increasingly began to invest across national borders. The motivation for much of this foreign direct investment by non-U.S. firms was the desire to disperse production activities to optimal locations and to build a direct presence in major foreign markets. Thus, beginning in the 1970s, European and Japanese firms began to shift labor-intensive manufacturing operations from their home markets to developing nations where labor costs were lower. In addition, many Japanese firms invested in North America and Europe—often as a hedge against unfavorable currency movements and the possible imposition of trade barriers. For example, Toyota, the Japanese automobile company, rapidly increased its investment in automobile production facilities in the United States and Europe during the late 1980s and early 1990s. Toyota executives believed that an increasingly strong Japanese yen would price Japanese automobile exports out of foreign markets; therefore, production in the most important foreign markets, as opposed

FIGURE 1.4

Percentage Share of Total FDI Stock, 1980 and 2003

Source: Calculated by author from data in United Nations, *World Investment Report, 2004* (New York and Geneva: United Nations, 2004).

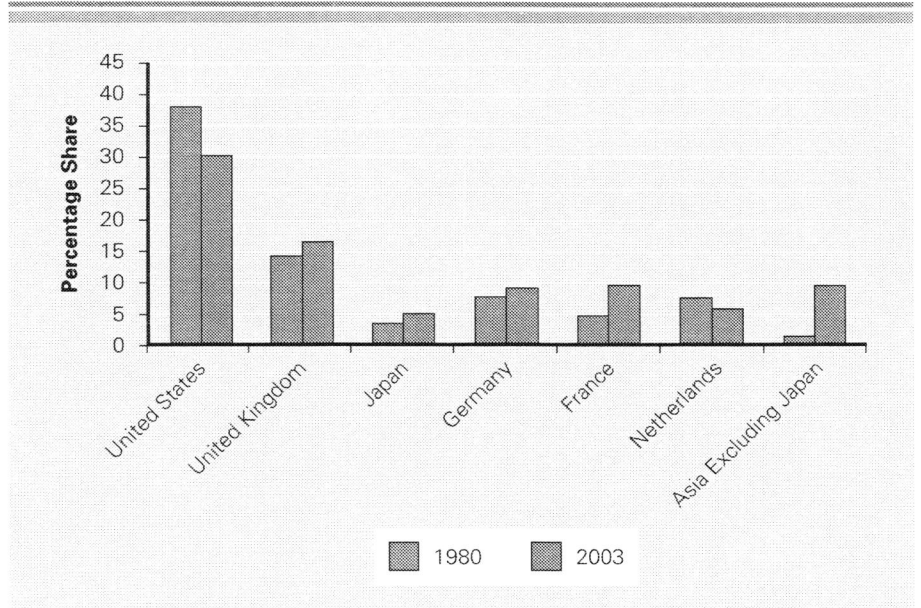

to exports from Japan, made sense. Toyota also undertook these investments to head off growing political pressures in the United States and Europe to restrict Japanese automobile exports into those markets.

One consequence of these developments is illustrated in Figure 1.4, which shows how the stock of foreign direct investment by the world's six most important national sources—the United States, the United Kingdom, Germany, the Netherlands, France, and Japan—changed between 1980 and 2003. (The **stock of foreign direct investment** refers to the total cumulative value of foreign investments.) Figure 1.4 also shows the stock accounted for by firms from Asia, excluding Japan. The share of the total stock accounted for by U.S. firms declined from about 38 percent in 1980 to 30 percent in 2003. Meanwhile, the shares accounted for by France, Japan, and other Asian nations, and the world's developing nations increased markedly. The rise in the share for Asia excluding Japan reflects a growing trend for firms from these countries to invest outside their borders. In 2003, firms based in Asian nations excluding Japan accounted for 9.2 percent of the stock of foreign direct investment, up from only 1.1 percent in 1980. Firms based in Hong Kong, South Korea, Singapore, Taiwan, and mainland China accounted for most of this investment.

Figure 1.5 illustrates two other important trends—the sustained growth in cross-border flows of foreign direct investment that occurred during the 1990s and the emerging importance of developing nations as the destination of foreign direct investment. Throughout the 1990s, the amount of investment directed at both developed and developing nations increased dramatically, a trend that reflects the increasing internationalization of business corporations. A surge in foreign direct investment into developed nations from 1998 to 2000 was followed by a slump from 2001 to 2004 associated with a slowdown in global economic activity after the collapse of the financial bubble of the late 1990s and 2000. Investment directed at developing nations, however, held up relatively well, averaging about $200 billion annually between 1998 and 2004, with China taking the most important share of this. As we shall see later in this book, the sustained flow of foreign investment into developing nations is a very important stimulus for economic growth in those countries, and bodes well for the future of countries such as China, Mexico, and Brazil, all leading beneficiaries of this trend.

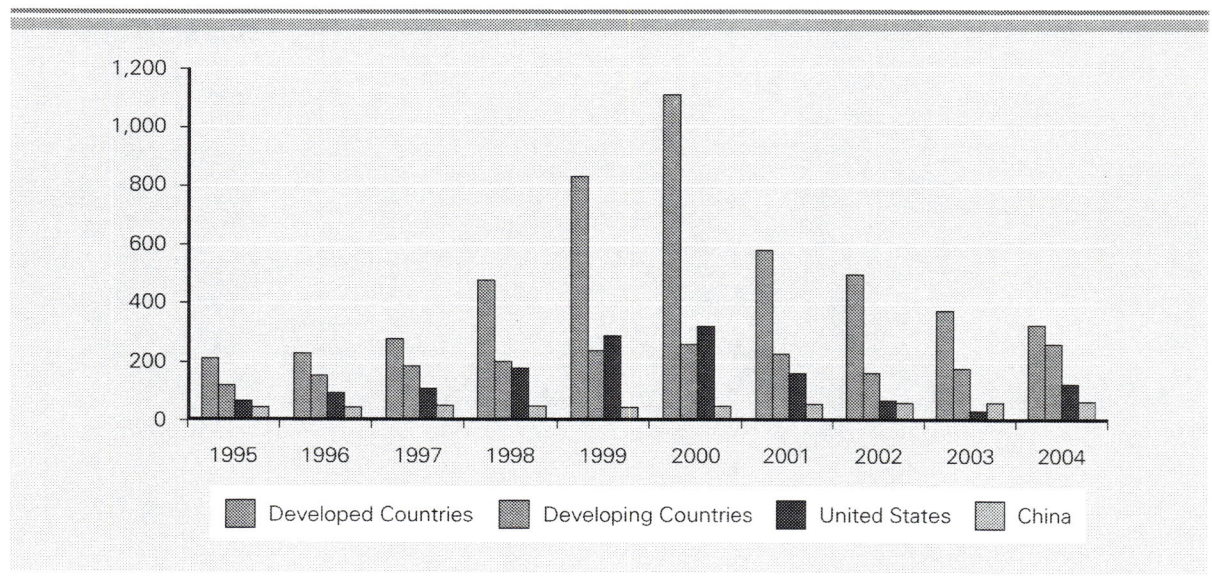

FIGURE 1.5

FDI Inflows, 1995–2004 (in $ billions)

Sources: Calculated by author from data in United Nations, *World Investment Report, 2004* (New York and Geneva: United Nations, 2004), and United Nations Conference on Trade and Development, "World FDI Flows Grew and Estimated 6% in 2004," UNCTAD press release, January 11, 2005.

THE CHANGING NATURE OF THE MULTINATIONAL ENTERPRISE

A **multinational enterprise (MNE)** is any business that has productive activities in two or more countries. Since the 1960s, two notable trends in the demographics of the multinational enterprise have been: (1) the rise of non-U.S. multinationals and (2) the growth of mini-multinationals.

Non-U.S. Multinationals

In the 1960s, global business activity was dominated by large U.S. multinational corporations. With U.S. firms accounting for about two-thirds of foreign direct investment during the 1960s, one would expect most multinationals to be U.S. enterprises. According to the data summarized in Figure 1.6, in 1973, 48.5 percent of the world's 260 largest multinationals were U.S. firms. The second largest source country was the United Kingdom, with 18.8 percent of the largest multinationals. Japan accounted for 3.5 percent of the world's largest multinationals at the time. The large number of U.S. multinationals reflected U.S. economic dominance in the three decades after World War II, while the large number of British multinationals reflected that country's industrial dominance in the early decades of the 20th century.

By 2002 things had shifted significantly. U.S. firms accounted for 28 percent of the world's 100 largest multinationals, followed by France with 14 percent, Germany with 13 percent, and Britain with 12 percent.[41] Although the 1973 data are not strictly comparable with the later data, they illustrate the trend (the 1973 figures are based on the largest 260 firms, whereas the later figures are based on the largest 100 multinationals). The globalization of the world economy has resulted in a relative decline in the dominance of U.S. firms in the global marketplace.

According to UN data, the ranks of the world's largest 100 multinationals are still dominated by firms from developed economies.[42] However, three firms from developing

22　　Part 1　Introduction and Overview

FIGURE 1.6

National Origin of Largest Multinational Corporations, 1973, 1991, 2002

Source: Calculated by author from data in United Nations, *World Investment Report, 2004* (New York and Geneva: United Nations, 2004).

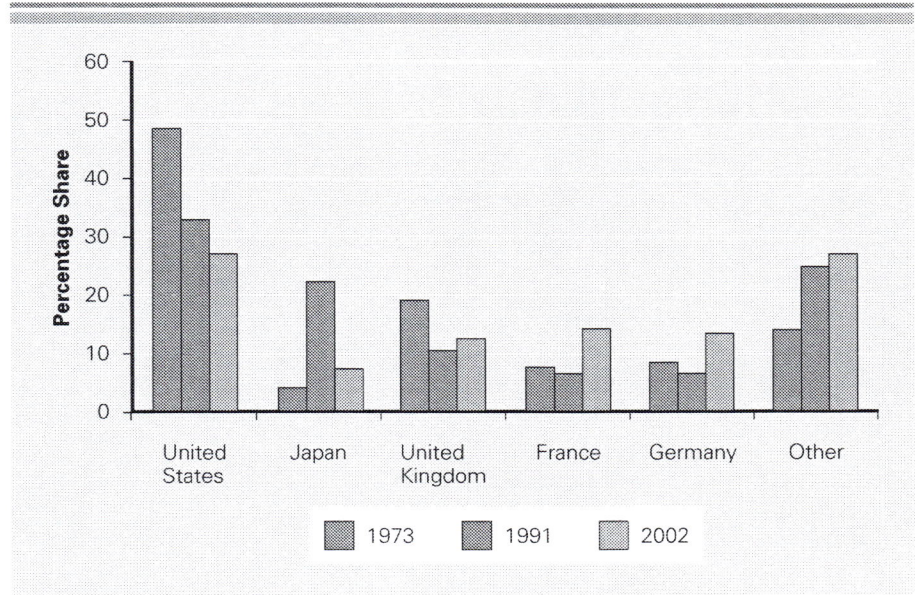

economies entered the UN's list of the 100 largest multinationals. They were Hutchison Whampoa of Hong Kong, China, which ranked 16 in terms of foreign assets; Singtel of Singapore, which was ranked 70; and Cemex of Mexico, which came in at 87.[43] The growth in the number of multinationals from developing economies is evident when we look at smaller firms. In the early 2000s, the largest 50 multinationals from developing economies had foreign sales of $103 billion out of total sales of $453 billion and employed 483,129 people outside of their home countries. Some 22 percent of these companies came from Hong Kong, 16.7 percent from Korea, 8.8 percent from China, and 7.6 percent from Brazil. We can reasonably expect more growth of new multinational enterprises from the world's developing nations. Firms from developing nations can be expected to emerge as important competitors in global markets, further shifting the axis of the world economy away from North America and Western Europe and threatening the long dominance of Western companies. One such rising competitor, Lenovo of China, is profiled in the accompanying Management Focus.

The Rise of Mini-Multinationals

Another trend in international business has been the growth of medium-size and small multinationals (mini-multinationals).[44] When people think of international businesses, they tend to think of firms such as Exxon, General Motors, Ford, Fuji, Kodak, Matsushita, Procter & Gamble, Sony, and Unilever—large, complex multinational corporations with operations that span the globe. Although most international trade and investment is still conducted by large firms, many medium-size and small businesses are becoming increasingly involved in international trade and investment. We have already discussed examples in this chapter—Bridgewater Pottery, and Cardiac Science—and we have noted how the rise of the Internet is lowering the barriers that small firms face in building international sales.

For another example, consider Lubricating Systems, Inc., of Kent, Washington. Lubricating Systems, which manufactures lubricating fluids for machine tools, employs 25 people and generates sales of $6.5 million. It's hardly a large, complex multinational, yet more than $2 million of the company's sales are generated by exports to a score of countries, including Japan, Israel, and the United Arab Emirates. Lubricating Systems also has set up a joint venture with a German company to serve the European market.[45] Consider also Lixi, Inc., a small U.S. manufacturer of industrial X-ray equipment; 70 percent of

China's Lenovo Acquires IBM's PC Operations

MANAGEMENT FOCUS

In late 2004, the Chinese personal computer manufacturer Lenovo stunned the business world when it announced that it would acquire IBM's personal computer operations for $1.25 billion. Lenovo, formerly known as Legend, was founded in 1984 by a group of young Chinese scientists with government financing. The company started as a distributor of computers and printers, selling IBM, ACT, and Hewlett-Packard brands. In the late 1980s, however, the company moved into manufacturing and began to design, make, and sell its own personal computers. Taking advantage of China's low labor costs, Lenovo quickly emerged as a low-cost provider.

By 2004, the company led the PC market in China, where it had a 26 percent share. But for Lenovo's founders, this was not enough. They were worried about the entry of efficient foreign competitors, such as Dell, into the Chinese market. Lenovo might have low labor costs, but its 2.3 percent share of global PC sales left it trailing far behind Dell and Hewlett-Packard, which held 18.3 percent and 15.7 percent of the global market, respectively. Dell and HP could realize substantial economies of scale from their global volume. As a result, increasingly they were able to match Lenovo on costs. At the same time, Lenovo's managers wondered whether it was time to expand internationally and turn Lenovo into a global brand. To deal with Dell at home, and expand into the global marketplace, Lenovo's managers realized that they needed to do two things: (1) attain greater scale economies to further lower costs, which meant more sales volume, and (2) match Western companies on product innovation, differentiation, and brand.

Their solution was to acquire IBM's PC business, which held 6 percent of the global market in 2004. The IBM purchase not only gave Lenovo potential scale economies and global reach, but also brought Lenovo IBM's renowned engineering skills, exemplified by the company's best-selling line of ThinkPad laptop computers, and IBM's extensive sales force and long-established customers. Top executives at Lenovo were smart enough to realize that the acquisition would have little value if IBM's managers and engineers left the company, so they made another surprising decision—they moved Lenovo's global headquarters to New York! Moreover, the former head of IBM's PC division, Stephen Ward, was appointed CEO of Lenovo, while Yang Yuanqing, the former CEO of Lenovo, will become chairman, and Lenovo's Mary Ma will be CFO. The 30-member top management team is split down the middle—half Chinese, half American—and boasts more women than men. English has been declared the company's new business language. The goal, according to Yang, is to transform Lenovo into a truly global corporation capable of going head-to-head with Dell in the battle for dominance in the global PC business.

Sources: D. Barboza, "An Unknown Giant Flexes Its Muscles," *The New York Times*, December 4, 2004, pp. B1, B3; D. Roberts and L. Lee, "East Meets West," *BusinessWeek*, May 9, 2005, pp. 1–4; and C. Forelle, "How IBM's Ward Will Lead China's Largest PC Company," *The Wall Street Journal*, April 21, 2005, p. B1.

www.mhhe.com/hill

Lixi's $4.5 million in revenues comes from exports to Japan.[46] Or take G. W. Barth, a manufacturer of cocoa-bean roasting machinery based in Ludwigsburg, Germany. Employing just 65 people, this small company has captured 70 percent of the global market for cocoa-bean roasting machines.[47] International business is conducted not just by large firms but also by medium-size and small enterprises.

THE CHANGING WORLD ORDER

Between 1989 and 1991 a series of remarkable democratic revolutions swept the Communist world. For reasons that are explored in more detail in Chapter 2, in country after country throughout Eastern Europe and eventually in the Soviet Union itself, Communist Party governments collapsed like the shells of rotten eggs. The Soviet Union is now receding into history, having been replaced by 15 independent republics. Czechoslovakia has divided itself into two states, while Yugoslavia dissolved into a bloody civil war, now thankfully over, among its five successor states.

Many of the former Communist nations of Europe and Asia seem to share a commitment to democratic politics and free market economics. If this continues, the opportunities for international businesses may be enormous. For half a century, these countries were essentially closed to Western international businesses. Now they present a host of export and investment opportunities. Just how this will play out over the next 10 to 20 years is difficult to say. The economies of many of the former Communist states are still relatively undeveloped, and their continued commitment to democracy and free market economics cannot be taken for granted. Disturbing signs of growing unrest and totalitarian tendencies continue to be seen in several Eastern European and Central Asian states. Thus, the risks involved in doing business in such countries are high, but so may be the returns.

In addition to these changes, more quiet revolutions have been occurring in China and Latin America. Their implications for international businesses may be just as profound as the collapse of communism in Eastern Europe. China suppressed its own prodemocracy movement in the bloody Tiananmen Square massacre of 1989. Despite this, China continues to move progressively toward greater free market reforms. If what is occurring in China continues for two more decades, China may move from Third World to industrial superpower status even more rapidly than Japan did. If China's gross domestic product (GDP) per capita grows by an average of 6 percent to 7 percent, which is slower than the 8 percent growth rate achieved during the last decade, then by 2020 this nation of 1.273 billion people could boast an average income per capita of about $13,000, roughly equivalent to that of Spain's today.

The potential consequences for international business are enormous. On the one hand, with nearly 1.3 billion people, China represents a huge and largely untapped market. Reflecting this, between 1983 and 2004, annual foreign direct investment in China increased from less than $2 billion to $64 billion. On the other hand, China's new firms are proving to be very capable competitors, and they could take global market share away from Western and Japanese enterprises (for example, see the Management Focus about Lenovo). Thus, the changes in China are creating both opportunities and threats for established international businesses.

As for Latin America, both democracy and free market reforms also seem to have taken hold. For decades, most Latin American countries were ruled by dictators, many of whom seemed to view Western international businesses as instruments of imperialist domination. Accordingly, they restricted direct investment by foreign firms. In addition, the poorly managed economies of Latin America were characterized by low growth, high debt, and hyperinflation—all of which discouraged investment by international businesses. Now much of this seems to be changing. Throughout most of Latin America, debt and inflation are down, governments are selling state-owned enterprises to private investors, foreign investment is welcomed, and the region's economies have expanded. These changes have increased the attractiveness of Latin America, both as a market for exports and as a site for foreign direct investment. At the same time, given the long history of economic mismanagement in Latin America, there is no guarantee that these favorable trends will continue. As in the case of Eastern Europe, substantial opportunities are accompanied by substantial risks.

THE GLOBAL ECONOMY OF THE 21ST CENTURY

As discussed, the past quarter century has seen rapid changes in the global economy. Barriers to the free flow of goods, services, and capital have been coming down. The volume of cross-border trade and investment has been growing more rapidly than global output, indicating that national economies are becoming more closely integrated into a single, interdependent, global economic system. As their economies advance, more nations are joining the ranks of the developed world. A generation ago, South Korea and Taiwan were viewed as second-tier developing nations. Now they boast large economies, and their firms are major players in many global industries from shipbuilding and steel to electronics and chemicals. The move toward a global economy has been further strengthened

by the widespread adoption of liberal economic policies by countries that had firmly opposed them for two generations or more. Thus, in keeping with the normative prescriptions of liberal economic ideology, in country after country we are seeing state-owned businesses privatized, widespread deregulation adopted, markets opened to more competition, and commitment increased to removing barriers to cross-border trade and investment. This suggests that over the next few decades, countries such as the Czech Republic, Poland, Brazil, China, India, and South Africa may build powerful market-oriented economies. In short, current trends indicate that the world is moving rapidly toward an economic system that is more favorable for international business.

But it is always hazardous to use established trends to predict the future. The world may be moving toward a more global economic system, but globalization is not inevitable. Countries may pull back from the recent commitment to liberal economic ideology if their experiences do not match their expectations. Periodic signs, for example, indicate a retreat from liberal economic ideology in Russia. Russia has experienced considerable economic pain as it tries to shift from a centrally planned economy to a market economy. If Russia's hesitation were to become more permanent and widespread, the liberal vision of a more prosperous global economy based on free market principles might not occur as quickly as many hope. Clearly, this would be a tougher world for international businesses.

Also, greater globalization brings with it risks of its own. This was starkly demonstrated in 1997 and 1998 when a financial crisis in Thailand spread first to other East Asian nations and then in 1998 to Russia and Brazil. Ultimately the crisis threatened to plunge the economies of the developed world, including the United States, into a recession. We explore the causes and consequences of this and other similar global financial crises in Chapter 11. Even from a purely economic perspective, globalization is not all good. The opportunities for doing business in a global economy may be significantly enhanced, but as we saw in 1997–98, the risks associated with global financial contagion are also greater. Still, as explained later in this book, firms can exploit the opportunities associated with globalization, while at the same time reducing the risks through appropriate hedging strategies.

The Globalization Debate

Is the shift toward a more integrated and interdependent global economy a good thing? Many influential economists, politicians, and business leaders seem to think so.[48] They argue that falling barriers to international trade and investment are the twin engines driving the global economy toward greater prosperity. They say increased international trade and cross-border investment will result in lower prices for goods and services. They believe that globalization stimulates economic growth, raises the incomes of consumers, and helps to create jobs in all countries that participate in the global trading system. The arguments of those who support globalization are covered in detail in Chapters 5, 6, and 7. As we shall see, there are good theoretical reasons for believing that declining barriers to international trade and investment do stimulate economic growth, create jobs, and raise income levels. As described in Chapters 6 and 7, empirical evidence lends support to the predictions of this theory. However, despite the existence of a compelling body of theory and evidence, globalization has its critics.[49] Some of these critics have become increasingly vocal and active, taking to the streets to demonstrate their opposition to globalization. Here we look at the rising tide of protests against globalization and briefly review the main themes of the debate concerning the merits of globalization. In later chapters we elaborate on many of the points mentioned below.

ANTIGLOBALIZATION PROTESTS

Street demonstrations against globalization date to December 1999, when more than 40,000 protesters blocked the streets of Seattle in an attempt to shut down a World Trade Organization meeting being held in the city. The demonstrators were protesting against

Demonstrators at the WTO meeting in Seattle in December 1999 began looting and rioting in the city's downtown area.

a wide range of issues, including job losses in industries under attack from foreign competitors, downward pressure on the wage rates of unskilled workers, environmental degradation, and the cultural imperialism of global media and multinational enterprises, which was seen as being dominated by what some protesters called the "culturally impoverished" interests and values of the United States. All of these ills, the demonstrators claimed, could be laid at the feet of globalization. The World Trade Organization was meeting to try to launch a new round of talks to cut barriers to cross-border trade and investment. As such, it was seen as a promoter of globalization and a legitimate target for the antiglobalization protesters. The protests turned violent, transforming the normally placid streets of Seattle into a running battle between "anarchists" and Seattle's bemused and poorly prepared police department. Pictures of brick-throwing protesters and armored police wielding their batons were duly recorded by the global media, which then circulated the images around the world. Meanwhile, the World Trade Organization meeting failed to reach agreement, and although the protests outside the meeting halls had little to do with that failure, the impression took hold that the demonstrators had succeeded in derailing the meetings.

Emboldened by the experience in Seattle, antiglobalization protesters have turned up at almost every major meeting of a global institution. In February 2000, they demonstrated at the World Economic Forum meetings in Davos, Switzerland, and vented their frustrations against global capitalism by trashing that hated symbol of U.S. imperialism, a McDonald's restaurant. In April 2000, demonstrators disrupted talks being held at the World Bank and International Monetary Fund, and in September 2000, 12,000 demonstrated at the annual meeting of the World Bank and IMF in Prague. In April 2001, demonstrations and police firing tear gas and water cannons overshadowed the Summit of the Americas meeting in Quebec City, Canada. In June 2001, 40,000 protesters marched against globalization at the European Union summit in Göteborg, Sweden. The march was peaceful until a core of masked anarchists wielding cobblestones created bloody mayhem. In July 2001, antiglobalization protests in Genoa, Italy, where the heads of the eight largest economies were meeting (the so-called G8 meetings), turned violent, and in the now familiar ritual of running battles between protesters and police, a protester was killed, giving the antiglobalization movement its first martyr. Smaller scale protests have occurred in several countries, such as France, where antiglobalization protesters destroyed a McDonald's restaurant in August 1999 to protest the impoverishment of French culture by American imperialism (see the Country Focus, "Protesting Globalization in France," for details).

While violent protests may give the antiglobalization effort a bad name, it is clear from the scale of the demonstrations that support for the cause goes beyond a core of anarchists. Large segments of the population in many countries believe that globalization has detrimental effects on living standards and the environment, and the media have often fed on this fear. In 2004 and 2005, for example, CNN news anchor Lou Dobbs ran a series that was highly critical of the trend by American companies to take advantage of globalization and "export jobs" overseas. Both theory and evidence suggest that many of these fears are exaggerated, but this may not have been communicated clearly and both politicians and businesspeople need to do more to counter these fears. Many protests against globalization are tapping into a general sense of loss at the passing of a world in which barriers of time and distance, and vast differences in economic institutions, political institutions, and the level of development of different nations, produced a world rich in the diversity of human cultures. This world is now passing into history. However, while the rich citizens of the developed world may have the luxury of mourning the fact that they can now see McDonald's restaurants and Starbucks coffeehouses on their vacations to exotic locations such as Thailand, fewer complaints are heard from the citizens of those countries, who welcome the higher living standards that progress brings.

GLOBALIZATION, JOBS, AND INCOME

One concern frequently voiced by globalization opponents is that falling barriers to international trade destroy manufacturing jobs in wealthy advanced economies such as the United States and the United Kingdom. The critics argue that falling trade barriers allow firms to move manufacturing activities to countries where wage rates are much lower.[50] D. L. Bartlett and J. B. Steele, two journalists for the *Philadelphia Inquirer* who gained notoriety for their attacks on free trade, cite the case of Harwood Industries, a U.S. clothing manufacturer that closed its U.S. operations, where it paid workers $9 per hour, and shifted manufacturing to Honduras, where textile workers receive 48 cents per hour.[51] Because of moves such as this, argue Bartlett and Steele, the wage rates of poorer Americans have fallen significantly over the past quarter of a century.

In the last few years, the same fears have been applied to services, which have increasingly been outsourced to nations with lower labor costs (see the opening case). The popular feeling is that when corporations such as Dell, IBM, or Citigroup outsource service activities to lower cost foreign suppliers—as all three have done—they are "exporting jobs" to low-wage nations and contributing to higher unemployment and lower living standards in their home nations (in this case the United States). Some lawmakers in the United States have responded by calling for legal barriers to job outsourcing.

Supporters of globalization reply that critics of these trends miss the essential point about free trade—the benefits outweigh the costs.[52] They argue that free trade will result in countries specializing in the production of those goods and services that they can produce most efficiently, while importing goods and services that they cannot produce as efficiently. When a country embraces free trade, there is always some dislocation—lost textile jobs at Harwood Industries, or lost call center jobs at Dell—but the whole economy is better off as a result. According to this view, it makes little sense for the United States to produce textiles at home when they can be produced at a lower cost in Honduras or China (which, unlike Honduras, is a major source of U.S. textile imports). Importing textiles from China leads to lower prices for clothes in the United States, which enables consumers to spend more of their money on other items. At the same time, the increased income generated in China from textile exports increases income levels in that country, which helps the Chinese to purchase more products produced in the United States, such as pharmaceuticals from Amgen, Boeing jets, Intel-based computers, Microsoft software, and Cisco routers.

The same argument can be made to support the outsourcing of services to low-wage countries. By outsourcing its customer service call centers to India, Dell can reduce its cost structure, and thereby its prices for PCs. U.S. consumers benefit from this development. As prices for PCs fall, Americans can spend more of their money on other goods and services. Moreover, the increase in income levels in India allows Indians to purchase more U.S. goods and services, which helps to create jobs in the United States. In this manner, supporters of globalization argue that free trade benefits *all* countries that adhere to a free trade regime.

Nevertheless, some supporters of globalization concede that the wage rate enjoyed by unskilled workers in many advanced economies may have declined in recent years.[53] However, the evidence on this is decidedly mixed.[54] A United States Federal Reserve study found that in the seven years preceding 1996, the earnings of the best-paid 10 percent of U.S. workers rose in real terms by 0.6 percent annually while the earnings of the 10 percent at the bottom of the heap fell by 8 percent. In some areas, the fall was much greater.[55] Another study of long-term trends in income distribution concluded,

> Nationwide, from the late 1970s to the late 1990s, the average income of the lowest-income families fell by over 6 percent after adjustment for inflation, and the average real income of the middle fifth of families grew by about 5 percent. By contrast, the average real income of the highest-income fifth of families increased by over 30 percent.[56]

While globalization critics argue that the decline in unskilled wage rates is due to the migration of low-wage manufacturing jobs offshore and a corresponding reduction in demand for unskilled workers, supporters of globalization see a more complex picture. They maintain that the apparent decline in real wage rates of unskilled workers owes far more to a technology-induced shift within advanced economies away from jobs where the only qualification was a willingness to turn up for work every day and toward jobs that require significant education and skills. They point out that many advanced economies report a shortage of highly skilled workers and an excess supply of unskilled workers. Thus, growing income inequality is a result of the wages for skilled workers being bid up by the labor market and the wages for unskilled workers being discounted. If one agrees with this logic, a solution to the problem of declining incomes is to be found not in limiting free trade and globalization, but in increasing society's investment in education to reduce the supply of unskilled workers.[57]

Some research also suggests that the evidence of growing income inequality may be suspect. Robert Lerman of the Urban Institute believes that the finding of inequality is based on inappropriate calculations of wage rates. Reviewing the data using a different methodology, Lerman has found that far from income inequality increasing, an index of wage rate inequality for all workers actually fell by 5.5 percent between 1987 and 1994.[58] A 2002 study by the Organization for Economic Cooperation and Development, whose members include the 20 richest economies in the world, also suggests a more complex picture. The study noted that while the gap between the poorest and richest segments of society in some OECD countries had widened, this trend was by no means universal.[59] In the United States, for example, the OECD study found that while income inequality increased from the mid-1970s to the mid-1980s, it did not widen further in the next decade. The report also notes that in almost all countries, real income levels rose over the 20-year period looked at in the study, including the incomes of the poorest segment of most OECD societies. To add to the mixed research results, a 2002 U.S. study that included data from 1990 to 2000 concluded that during those years, falling unemployment rates brought gains to low-wage workers and fairly broad-based wage growth, especially in the latter half of the 1990s. The income of the worst-paid 10 percent of the population actually rose twice as fast as that of the average worker during 1998–2000.[60] If such trends continued into the 2000s—and they may not have—the argument that globalization leads to growing income inequality may lose some of its punch.

60

Hill: International
Business: Competing in the
Global Marketplace, Sixth
Edition

I. Introduction and
Overview

1. Globalization

© The McGraw–Hill
Companies, 2007

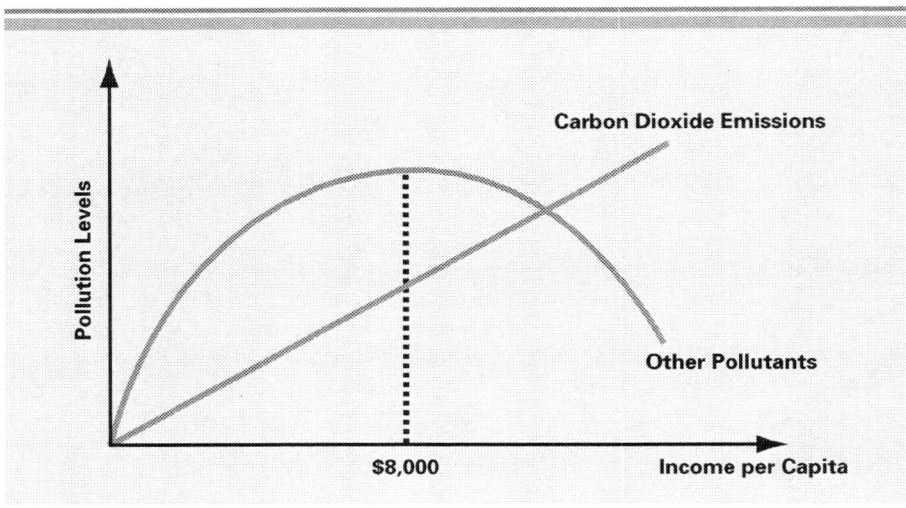

FIGURE 1.7

Income Levels and
Environmental Pollution

GLOBALIZATION, LABOR POLICIES, AND THE ENVIRONMENT

A second source of concern is that free trade encourages firms from advanced nations to move manufacturing facilities to less developed countries that lack adequate regulations to protect labor and the environment from abuse by the unscrupulous.[61] Globalization critics often argue that adhering to labor and environmental regulations significantly increases the costs of manufacturing enterprises and puts them at a competitive disadvantage in the global marketplace vis-à-vis firms based in developing nations that do not have to comply with such regulations. Firms deal with this cost disadvantage, the theory goes, by moving their production facilities to nations that do not have such burdensome regulations or that fail to enforce the regulations they have.

If this is the case, one might expect free trade to lead to an increase in pollution and result in firms from advanced nations exploiting the labor of less developed nations.[62] This argument was used repeatedly by those who opposed the 1994 formation of the North American Free Trade Agreement (NAFTA) between Canada, Mexico, and the United States. They painted a picture of U.S. manufacturing firms moving to Mexico in droves so that they would be free to pollute the environment, employ child labor, and ignore workplace safety and health issues, all in the name of higher profits.[63]

Supporters of free trade and greater globalization express doubts about this scenario. They argue that tougher environmental regulations and stricter labor standards go hand in hand with economic progress.[64] In general, as countries get richer, they enact tougher environmental and labor regulations.[65] Because free trade enables developing countries to increase their economic growth rates and become richer, this should lead to tougher environmental and labor laws. In this view, the critics of free trade have got it backward—free trade does not lead to more pollution and labor exploitation, it leads to less. By creating wealth and incentives for enterprises to produce technological innovations, the free market system and free trade could make it easier for the world to cope with pollution and population growth. Indeed, while pollution levels are rising in the world's poorer countries, they have been falling in developed nations. In the United States, for example, the concentration of carbon monoxide and sulphur dioxide pollutants in the atmosphere decreased by 60 percent between 1978 and 1997, while lead concentrations decreased by 98 percent—and these reductions have occurred against a background of sustained economic expansion.[66]

A number of econometric studies have found consistent evidence of a hump-shaped relationship between income levels and pollution levels (see Figure 1.7).[67] As an economy grows and income levels rise, initially pollution levels also rise. However, past some point, rising income levels lead to demands for greater environmental protection, and pollution levels then fall. A seminal study by Grossman and Krueger found that the turning point generally occurred before per capita income levels reached $8,000.[68]

While the hump-shaped relationship depicted in Figure 1.7 seems to hold across a wide range of pollutants—from sulphur dioxide to lead concentrations and water quality—carbon dioxide emissions are an important exception, rising steadily with higher income levels. Given that increased atmospheric carbon dioxide concentrations are implicated in global warming, this should be a concern. The solution to the problem, however, is probably not to roll back the trade liberalization efforts that have fostered economic growth and globalization, but to get the nations of the world to agree to tougher standards on limiting carbon emissions. Although United Nations—sponsored talks have had this as a central aim since the 1992 Earth Summit in Rio de Janeiro, there has been little success in moving toward the ambitious goals for reducing carbon emissions laid down in the Earth Summit and subsequent talks in Kyoto, Japan, in part because the largest emitter of carbon dioxide, the United States, has refused to sign global agreements that it claims would unreasonably retard economic growth.

Supporters of free trade also point out that it is possible to tie free trade agreements to the implementation of tougher environmental and labor laws in less developed countries. NAFTA, for example, was passed only after side agreements had been negotiated that committed Mexico to tougher enforcement of environmental protection regulations. Thus, supporters of free trade argue that factories based in Mexico are now cleaner than they would have been without the passage of NAFTA.[69]

They also argue that business firms are not the amoral organizations that critics suggest. While there may be some rotten apples, most business enterprises are staffed by managers who are committed to behave in an ethical manner and would be unlikely to move production offshore just so they could pump more pollution into the atmosphere or exploit labor. Furthermore, the relationship between pollution, labor exploitation, and production costs may not be that suggested by critics. In general, a well-treated labor force is productive, and it is productivity rather than base wage rates that often has the greatest influence on costs. The vision of greedy managers who shift production to low-wage countries to exploit their labor force may be misplaced.

GLOBALIZATION AND NATIONAL SOVEREIGNTY

Another concern voiced by critics of globalization is that today's increasingly interdependent global economy shifts economic power away from national governments and toward supranational organizations such as the World Trade Organization, the European Union, and the United Nations. As perceived by critics, unelected bureaucrats now impose policies on the democratically elected governments of nation-states, thereby undermining the sovereignty of those states and limiting the nation's ability to control its own destiny.[70]

The World Trade Organization (WTO) is a favorite target of those who attack the headlong rush toward a global economy. As noted earlier, the WTO was founded in 1994 to police the world trading system established by the General Agreement on Tariffs and Trade. The WTO arbitrates trade disputes between the 148 states that are signatories to the GATT. The arbitration panel can issue a ruling instructing a member state to change trade policies that violate GATT regulations. If the violator refuses to comply with the ruling, the WTO allows other states to impose appropriate trade sanctions on the transgressor. As a result, according to one prominent critic, U.S. environmentalist, consumer rights advocate, and presidential candidate Ralph Nader:

> Under the new system, many decisions that affect billions of people are no longer made by local or national governments but instead, if challenged by any WTO member nation, would be deferred to a group of unelected bureaucrats sitting behind closed doors in Geneva (which is where the headquarters of the WTO are located). The bureaucrats can decide whether or not people in California can prevent the destruction of the last virgin forests or determine if carcinogenic pesticides can be banned from their foods; or whether European countries have the right to ban dangerous biotech hormones in meat. . . . At risk is the very basis of democracy and accountable decision making.[71]

Protesting Globalization in France

COUNTRY FOCUS One night in August 1999, 10 men under the leadership of local sheep farmer and rural activist Jose Bove crept into the town of Millau in central France and vandalized a McDonald's restaurant under construction, causing an estimated $150,000 damage. These were no ordinary vandals, however, at least according to their supporters, for the "symbolic dismantling" of the McDonald's outlet had noble aims, or so it was claimed. The attack was initially presented as a protest against unfair American trade policies. The European Union had banned imports of hormone-treated beef from the United States, primarily because of fears that hormone-treated beef might lead to health problems (although EU scientists had concluded there was no evidence of this). After a careful review, the World Trade Organization stated the EU ban was not allowed under trading rules that the EU and United States were party to, and that the EU would have to lift it or face retaliation. The EU refused to comply, so the U.S. government imposed a 100 percent tariff on imports of certain EU products, including French staples such as foie gras, mustard, and Roquefort cheese. On farms near Millau, Bove and others raised sheep whose milk was used to make Roquefort. They felt incensed by the American tariff and decided to vent their frustrations on McDonald's.

Bove and his compatriots were arrested and charged. They quickly became a focus of the antiglobalization movement in France that was protesting everything from a loss of national sovereignty and "unfair" trade policies that were trying to force hormone-treated beef on French consumers, to the invasion of French culture by alien American values, so aptly symbolized by McDonald's. Lionel Jospin, France's prime minister, called the cause of Jose Bove "just." Allowed to remain free pending his trial, Bove traveled to Seattle in December to protest against the World Trade Organization, where he was feted as a hero of the antiglobalization movement. In France, Bove's July 2000 trial drew some 40,000 supporters to the small town of Millau, where they camped outside the courthouse and waited for the verdict. Bove was found guilty and sentenced to three months in jail, far less than the maximum possible sentence of five years. His supporters wore T-shirts claiming, "The world is not merchandise, and neither am I."

About the same time in the Languedoc region of France, California winemaker Robert Mondavi had reached agreement with the mayor and council of the village of Aniane and regional authorities to turn 125 acres of wooded hillside belonging to the village into a vineyard. Mondavi planned to invest $7 million in the project and hoped to produce top-quality wine that would sell in Europe and the United States for $60 a bottle. However, local environmentalists objected to the plan, which they claimed would destroy the area's unique ecological heritage. Jose Bove, basking in sudden fame, offered his support to the opponents, and the protests started. In May 2001, the Socialist mayor who had approved the project was defeated in local elections in which the Mondavi project had become the major issue. He was replaced by a Communist, Manuel Diaz, who denounced the project as a capitalist plot designed to enrich wealthy U.S. shareholders at the cost of his villagers and the environment. Following Diaz's victory, Mondavi announced he would pull out of the project. A spokesman noted, "It's a huge waste, but there are clearly personal and political interests at play here that go way beyond us."

So are the French opposed to foreign investment? The experience of McDonald's and Mondavi seems to suggest so, as does the associated news coverage, but look closer and a different reality seems to emerge. McDonald's has more than 800 restaurants in France and continues to do very well there. In fact, France is one of the most profitable markets for McDonald's. The level of foreign investment in France reached record levels in the late 1990s and early 2000. Between 1998 and 2003 France received $270 billion in inward investment, far more than other large EU nations. In 2000, France recorded 563 major inward investment deals, a record, and American companies accounted for the largest number, some 178. French enterprises are also investing across borders at record levels. Given all of the talk about American cultural imperialism, it is striking that a French company, Vivendi, acquired two of the propagators of American cultural values: Universal Pictures and publisher Houghton Mifflin. And French politicians seem set on removing domestic barriers that make it difficult for French companies to compete effectively in the global economy.

Sources: "Behind the Bluster," *The Economist*, May 26, 2001; "The French Farmers' Anti-global Hero," *The Economist*, July 8, 2000; C. Trueheart, "France's Golden Arch Enemy?" *Toronto Star*, July 1, 2000; J. Henley, "Grapes of Wrath Scare Off U.S. Firm," *The Economist*, May 18, 2001, p. 11; and United Nations, *World Investment Report, 2004* (New York and Geneva: United Nations, 2004).

In contrast to Nader's rhetoric, many economists and politicians maintain that the power of supranational organizations such as the WTO is limited to what nation-states collectively agree to grant. They argue that bodies such as the United Nations and the WTO exist to serve the collective interests of member states, not to subvert those interests. Supporters of supranational organizations point out that the power of these bodies rests largely on their ability to persuade member states to follow a certain action. If these bodies fail to serve the collective interests of member states, those states will withdraw their support and the supranational organization will quickly collapse. In this view, real power still resides with individual nation-states, not supranational organizations.

GLOBALIZATION AND THE WORLD'S POOR

Critics of globalization argue that despite the supposed benefits associated with free trade and investment, over the past hundred years or so the gap between the rich and poor nations of the world has gotten wider. In 1870 the average income per capita in the world's 17 richest nations was 2.4 times that of all other countries. In 1990 the same group was 4.5 times as rich as the rest.[72] While recent history has shown that some of the world's poorer nations are capable of rapid periods of economic growth—witness the transformation that has occurred in some Southeast Asian nations such as South Korea, Thailand, and Malaysia—there appear to be strong forces for stagnation among the world's poorest nations. A quarter of the countries with a GDP per capita of less than $1,000 in 1960 had growth rates of less than zero from 1960 to 1995, and a third had growth rates of less than 0.05 percent.[73] Critics argue that if globalization is such a positive development, this divergence between the rich and poor should not have occurred.

Although the reasons for economic stagnation vary, several factors stand out, none of which have anything to do with free trade or globalization.[74] Many of the world's poorest countries have suffered from totalitarian governments, economic policies that destroyed wealth rather than facilitated its creation, endemic corruption, scant protection for property rights, and war. Such factors help explain why countries such as Afghanistan, Cambodia, Cuba, Haiti, Iraq, Libya, Nigeria, Sudan, Vietnam, and Zaire have failed to improve the economic lot of their citizens during recent decades. A complicating factor is the rapidly expanding populations in many of these countries. Without a major change in government, population growth may exacerbate their problems. Promoters of free trade argue that the best way for these countries to improve their lot is to lower their barriers to free trade and investment and to implement economic policies based on free market economics.[75]

Many of the world's poorer nations are being held back by large debt burdens. Of particular concern are the 40 or so "highly indebted poorer countries" (HIPCs), which are home to some 700 million people. Among these countries, the average government debt burden is equivalent to 85 percent of the value of the economy, as measured by gross domestic product, and the annual costs of serving government debt consumes 15 percent of the country's export earnings.[76] Servicing such a heavy debt load leaves the governments of these countries with little left to invest in important public infrastructure projects, such as education, health care, roads, and power. The result is the HIPCs are trapped in a cycle of poverty and debt that inhibits economic development. Free trade alone, some argue, is a necessary but not sufficient prerequisite to help these countries bootstrap themselves out of poverty. Instead, large-scale debt relief is needed for the world's poorest nations to give them the opportunity to restructure their economies and start the long climb toward prosperity. Supporters of debt relief also argue that new democratic governments in poor nations should not be forced to honor debts that were incurred and mismanaged long ago by their corrupt and dictatorial predecessors.

In the late 1990s, a debt relief movement began to gain ground among the political establishment in the world's richer nations.[77] Fueled by high-profile endorsements from Irish rock star Bono (who has been a tireless and increasingly effective advocate for debt relief), Pope John Paul II, the Dalai Lama, and influential Harvard economist Jeffrey Sachs, the debt relief movement was instrumental in persuading the United States to enact legislation in 2000 that provided $435 million in debt relief for HIPCs. More importantly perhaps, the United States also backed an IMF plan to sell some of its gold reserves and use the proceeds to help with debt relief. The IMF and World Bank have now picked up the banner and have embarked on a systematic debt relief program.

For such a program to have a lasting effect, however, debt relief must be matched by wise investment in public projects that boost economic growth (such as education), and by the adoption of economic policies that facilitate investment and trade. The rich nations of the world also can help by reducing barriers to the importation of products from the world's poorer nations, particularly tariffs on imports of agricultural products and textiles. High tariff barriers and other impediments to trade make it difficult for poor countries to export more of their agricultural production. The World Trade Organization has estimated that if the developed nations of the world eradicated subsidies to their agricultural producers and removed tariff barriers to trade in agriculture this would raise global economic welfare by $128 billion, with $30 billion of that going to developing nations, many of whom are highly indebted. The faster growth associated with expanded trade in agriculture could reduce the number of people living in poverty by as much as 13 percent by 2015, according to the WTO.[78]

U2's Bono has actively lobbied to have the unpayable debt of poor countries written off.

Debt relief is not new; it has been tried before.[79] Too often in the past, however, the short-term benefits were squandered by corrupt governments who used their newfound financial freedom to make unproductive investments in military infrastructure or grandiose projects that did little to foster long-run economic development. Developed nations contributed to past failures by refusing to open their markets to the products of poor nations. If such a scenario can be avoided this time, the entire world will benefit.

Managing in the Global Marketplace

Much of this book is concerned with the challenges of managing in an international business. An **international business** is any firm that engages in international trade or investment. A firm does not have to become a multinational enterprise, investing directly in operations in other countries, to engage in international business, although multinational enterprises are international businesses. All a firm has to do is export or import products from other countries. As the world shifts toward a truly integrated global economy, more firms, both large and small, are becoming international businesses. What does this shift toward a global economy mean for managers within an international business?

As their organizations increasingly engage in cross-border trade and investment, managers need to recognize that the task of managing an international business differs from that of managing a purely domestic business in many ways. At the most fundamental level, the differences arise from the simple fact that countries are different. Countries differ in their cultures, political systems, economic systems, legal systems, and levels of economic development. Despite all the talk about the emerging global village, and despite the trend toward globalization of markets and production, as we shall see in this book, many of these differences are very profound and enduring.

Hill: International
Business: Competing in the
Global Marketplace, Sixth
Edition

I. Introduction and
Overview

1. Globalization

© The McGraw–Hill
Companies, 2007

65

Differences between countries require that an international business vary its practices country by country. Marketing a product in Brazil may require a different approach from marketing the product in Germany; managing U.S. workers might require different skills than managing Japanese workers; maintaining close relations with a particular level of government may be very important in Mexico and irrelevant in Great Britain; the business strategy pursued in Canada might not work in South Korea; and so on. Managers in an international business must not only be sensitive to these differences, but they must also adopt the appropriate policies and strategies for coping with them. Much of this book is devoted to explaining the sources of these differences and the methods for successfully coping with them.

A further way in which international business differs from domestic business is the greater complexity of managing an international business. In addition to the problems that arise from the differences between countries, a manager in an international business is confronted with a range of other issues that the manager in a domestic business never confronts. The managers of an international business must decide where in the world to site production activities to minimize costs and to maximize value added. They must decide whether it is ethical to adhere to the lower labor and environmental standards found in many less developed nations. Then they must decide how best to coordinate and control globally dispersed production activities (which, as we shall see later in the book, is not a trivial problem). The managers in an international business also must decide which foreign markets to enter and which to avoid. They must choose the appropriate mode for entering a particular foreign country. Is it best to export its product to the foreign country? Should the firm allow a local company to produce its product under license in that country? Should the firm enter into a joint venture with a local firm to produce its product in that country? Or should the firm set up a wholly owned subsidiary to serve the market in that country? As we shall see, the choice of entry mode is critical because it has major implications for the long-term health of the firm.

Conducting business transactions across national borders requires understanding the rules governing the international trading and investment system. Managers in an international business must also deal with government restrictions on international trade and investment. They must find ways to work within the limits imposed by specific governmental interventions. As this book explains, even though many governments are nominally committed to free trade, they often intervene to regulate cross-border trade and investment. Managers within international businesses must develop strategies and policies for dealing with such interventions.

Cross-border transactions also require that money be converted from the firm's home currency into a foreign currency and vice versa. Because currency exchange rates vary in response to changing economic conditions, managers in an international business must develop policies for dealing with exchange rate movements. A firm that adopts a wrong policy can lose large amounts of money, while a firm that adopts the right policy can increase the profitability of its international transactions.

In sum, managing an international business is different from managing a purely domestic business for at least four reasons: (1) countries are different, (2) the range of problems confronted by a manager in an international business is wider and the problems themselves more complex than those confronted by a manager in a domestic business, (3) an international business must find ways to work within the limits imposed by government intervention in the international trade and investment system, and (4) international transactions involve converting money into different currencies.

In this book we examine all these issues in depth, paying close attention to the different strategies and policies that managers pursue to deal with the various challenges created when a firm becomes an international business. Chapters 2 and 3 explore how countries differ from each other with regard to their political, economic, legal, and cultural institutions. Chapter 4 takes a detailed look at the ethical issues that arise in international business. Chapters 5 to 9 look at the international trade and investment environment within which international businesses must operate. Chapters 10 and 11 re-

Hill: International
Business: Competing in the
Global Marketplace, Sixth
Edition

I. Introduction and
Overview

1. Globalization

© The McGraw–Hill
Companies, 2007

view the international monetary system. These chapters focus on the nature of the foreign exchange market and the emerging global monetary system. Chapters 12 to 14 explore the strategy and structure of international businesses. Chapters 15 to 20 look at the management of various functional operations within an international business, including production, marketing, human relations, accounting, and finance. By the time you complete this book, you should have a good grasp of the issues that managers working within international business have to grapple with on a daily basis, and you should be familiar with the range of strategies and operating policies available to compete more effectively in today's rapidly emerging global economy.

Chapter Summary

This chapter sets the scene for the rest of the book. It shows how the world economy is becoming more global and reviews the main drivers of globalization, arguing that they seem to be thrusting nation-states toward a more tightly integrated global economy. We looked at how the nature of international business is changing in response to the changing global economy; we discussed some concerns raised by rapid globalization; and we reviewed implications of rapid globalization for individual managers. The chapter made the following points:

1. Over the past two decades, we have witnessed the globalization of markets and production.

2. The globalization of markets implies that national markets are merging into one huge marketplace. However, it is important not to push this view too far.

3. The globalization of production implies that firms are basing individual productive activities at the optimal world locations for the particular activities. As a consequence, it is increasingly irrelevant to talk about American products, Japanese products, or German products, since these are being replaced by "global" products.

4. Two factors seem to underlie the trend toward globalization: declining trade barriers and changes in communication, information, and transportation technologies.

5. Since the end of World War II, barriers to the free flow of goods, services, and capital have been lowered significantly. More than anything else, this has facilitated the trend toward the globalization of production and has enabled firms to view the world as a single market.

6. As a consequence of the globalization of production and markets, in the last decade world trade has grown faster than world output, foreign direct investment has surged, imports have penetrated more deeply into the world's industrial nations, and competitive pressures have increased in industry after industry.

7. The development of the microprocessor and related developments in communication and information processing technology have helped firms link their worldwide operations into sophisticated information networks. Jet air travel, by shrinking travel time, has also helped to link the worldwide operations of international businesses. These changes have enabled firms to achieve tight coordination of their worldwide operations and to view the world as a single market.

8. In the 1960s, the U.S. economy was dominant in the world, U.S. firms accounted for most of the foreign direct investment in the world economy, U.S. firms dominated the list of large multinationals, and roughly half the world—the centrally planned economies of the Communist world—was closed to Western businesses.

9. By the mid-1990s, the U.S. share of world output had been cut in half, with major shares now being accounted for by Western European and Southeast Asian economies. The U.S. share of worldwide foreign direct investment had also fallen, by about two-thirds. U.S. multinationals were now facing competition from a large number of Japanese and European multinationals. In addition, the emergence of mini-multinationals was noted.

36   **Part 1** Introduction and Overview

10. One of the most dramatic developments of the past 20 years has been the collapse of communism in Eastern Europe, which has created enormous long-run opportunities for international businesses. In addition, the move toward free market economies in China and Latin America is creating opportunities (and threats) for Western international businesses.

11. The benefits and costs of the emerging global economy are being hotly debated among businesspeople, economists, and politicians. The debate focuses on the impact of globalization on jobs, wages, the environment, working conditions, and national sovereignty.

12. Managing an international business is different from managing a domestic business for at least four reasons: (*i*) countries are different, (*ii*) the range of problems confronted by a manager in an international business is wider and the problems themselves more complex than those confronted by a manager in a domestic business, (*iii*) managers in an international business must find ways to work within the limits imposed by governments' intervention in the international trade and investment system, and (*iv*) international transactions involve converting money into different currencies.

Critical Thinking and Discussion Questions

1. Describe the shifts in the world economy over the past 30 years. What are the implications of these shifts for international businesses based in Great Britain? North America? Hong Kong?

2. "The study of international business is fine if you are going to work in a large multinational enterprise, but it has no relevance for individuals who are going to work in small firms." Evaluate this statement.

3. How have changes in technology contributed to the globalization of markets and production? Would the globalization of production and markets have been possible without these technological changes?

4. "Ultimately, the study of international business is no different from the study of domestic business. Thus, there is no point in having a separate course on international business." Evaluate this statement.

5. How might the Internet and the associated World Wide Web affect international business activity and the globalization of the world economy?

6. If current trends continue, China may be the world's largest economy by 2050. Discuss the possible implications of such a development for
   a. The world trading system.
   b. The world monetary system.

c. The business strategy of today's European and U.S.-based global corporations.
   d. Global commodity prices.

7. Read the Country Focus in this chapter on the Ecuadorean rose industry, then answer the following questions:
   a. How has participation in the international rose trade helped Ecuador's economy and its people? How has the rise of Ecuador as a center for rose growing benefited consumers in developed nations who purchase the roses? What do the answers to these questions tell you about the benefits of international trade?
   b. Why do you think that Ecuador's rose industry only began to take off 20 years ago? Why do you think it has grown so rapidly?
   c. To what extent can the alleged health problems among workers in Ecuador's rose industry be laid at the feet of consumers in the developed world and their desire for perfect Valentine's Day roses?
   d. Do you think governments in the developed world should place trade sanctions on Ecuador roses if reports of health issues among Ecuadorean rose workers are verified? What else might they do to improve the situation in Ecuador?

Research Task  globalEDGE.msu.edu

Use the globalEDGE™ site to complete the following exercises:

1. Your company has developed a new product that is expected to achieve high penetration

rates in all the countries where it is introduced, regardless of the average income status of the local populace. Considering the costs of the product launch, the management team has de-

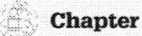
cided to initially introduce the product only in countries that have a sizable population base. You are required to prepare a preliminary report with the top ten countries of the world in terms of population size. Since growth opportunities are another major concern, the average population growth rates should be also listed for management's consideration.

2. You are working for a company that is considering investing in a foreign country. Management has requested a report regarding the attractiveness of alternative countries based on the potential return of FDI. Accordingly, the ranking of the top 25 countries in terms of FDI attractiveness is a crucial ingredient for your report. A colleague mentioned a potentially useful tool called the "FDI Confidence Index" which is updated periodically. Find this index, and provide additional information regarding how the index is constructed.

Wipro Ltd.—The New Face of Global Competition

CLOSING CASE Fifteen years ago, Wipro Ltd. of India was a jumbled conglomerate selling everything from cooking oil and personal care products to knockoffs of Dell microcomputers and lightbulbs. Now it is a fast-growing information technology company at the forefront of India's rapidly expanding technology sector. In the year ending March 2005, Wipro generated more than $1.87 billion in sales, the majority from export contracts in information technology services. Its sales have grown by more than 25 percent a year since 1997, and that growth shows no sign of slowing. The company is very profitable, earning $363 million in net income in the year ending March 2005.

Wipro's move into technology began in 1989 when General Electric entered into a joint venture with Wipro, Wipro GE Medical Systems, to make and sell GE ultrasound scanners under license in India. At the time, Wipro's technology revenues were tiny, just $15 million. While sales of GE scanners in India did not take off as quickly as expected, GE quickly realized it had found a cheap source of talented engineers and programmers. India has a solid base of technology-focused universities and colleges that turn out many engineers every year. The vast majority speak English. While software programmers in the United States with two to four years of experience make $64,000 a year, similarly skilled individuals in India can be had for as little as $2 an hour, and programmers at Wipro on average earn $10,000 a year. That might not sound like a lot, but in India, where the annual per capita income is still less than $500, it can translate into a very good living.

GE quickly set aside $5 million a year to hire Wipro software programmers to write code for GE's ultrasound machines and its CT scanners. By the mid-1990s, senior GE managers began to encourage other units to follow the medical division's lead and outsource information technology work to Indian companies. As a result, at one point during the mid-1990s Wipro was getting as much as 50 percent of its revenues from General Electric. However, along the way GE taught Wipro a hard lesson. GE was soon contracting out work to other Indian information technology companies, playing them off against each other in its drive for ever lower costs. To hold onto its GE business, Wipro found that it had to improve its own operating efficiency, so Wipro looked at what GE was doing, and copied it. Wipro's joint venture with GE helped in this regard, since it gave Wipro a window into GE's relentless push for operating efficiencies. Thus, following GE's lead, Wipro was one of the first Indian companies to adopt the Six Sigma process for improving operating efficiency made famous by GE. Today, Wipro executives credit much of their success in the international market to the hard lessons it learned about efficiency as a GE vendor.

By the late 1990s, GE began to turn its attention from simply buying software from India, to using the country as a base for data entry, processing credit card applications, and other clerical tasks that could be performed over the Internet. About this time, other Western companies such as American Express and British Airways began doing the same thing. GE estimates that it cut operating costs $300 million a year by shifting such work to India. Wipro was a major beneficiary.

Today Wipro's 39,000 technology employees write software, integrate back-office solutions, design semiconductors, debug applications, take orders, and field help calls for some of the biggest companies in the world. Its customers still include General Electric along with Hewlett-Packard, Home Depot, Nokia, Sony, and Weyerhaeuser. By using the Internet, Wipro can maintain and manage software applications for companies all over the world in real time. Typical is Wipro's relationship with Weyerhaeuser, one of the world's largest timber companies. Wipro's involvement with Weyerhaeuser began in 1999 when two employees conducted a modest on-site analysis at Weyerhaeuser's U.S. headquarters just south of Seattle. By 2003, Wipro was supporting a broad array of Weyerhaeuser's information systems including logistics, sales, and human resource applications from Bangalore, India. Overall, Wipro estimates it can save clients as much as 40 percent of the cost of maintaining such systems. In a highly competitive global economy, the imperative for companies such as Weyerhaeuser to outsource is compelling.

Wipro, however, is not content to remain in the low-margin end of the software business. The company increasingly is moving upstream into high value-added applications. For example, in 2002, Wipro signed a deal to design and engineer tape storage devices for Storage Technology. In 2004, Wipro took over responsibility for all development work on this product line from 200 employees in Minneapolis. Wipro is also moving rapidly into high value-added software services, such as establishing global supply chain or billing systems for large corporations, a business that is currently dominated by Western consulting outfits such as IBM, EDS, and Accenture.

As Wipro expands its business, it is also taking steps to become a more global company. Around the world, Wipro has been hiring local nationals to lead its sales push. The company now has a direct sales presence in 35 countries, most of which are staffed by local nationals. By 2005, the company hopes that three-quarters of the employees that customers see will be local nationals—in Europe the figure is already 90 percent. According to a Wipro spokesman, using locals "provides the cultural and linguistic ties that make clients smile, and help us build stronger relationships." Wipro is also buying local companies to give it instant industry presence. In November 2002, Wipro paid $26 million for American Management Systems, buying not just credibility but also 90 consultants and 50 existing client relationships in the energy business. While these consultants will manage contact with U.S. customers, much of the software development work will be moved to Bangalore.

In something of a departure from its historic strategy, since 2000 Wipro has also been moving some product development work out of India to developed nations. It now has nine development centers in Europe and the United States. These centers focus on product development work where more communication between Wipro engineers and the client is required than with the typical outsourcing contract, and where language is an issue. In Germany, for example, Wipro has found that it can win more business if not only its salespeople are German, but also some development work is done locally by German engineers.

Sources: K. H. Hammonds, "The New Face of Global Competition," *Fast Company*, February 2003, pp. 90–97; M. Kripalani and P. Engardio, "The Live Wire of Indian High Tech," *BusinessWeek*, January 20, 2003, pp. 70–71; F. Hayes, "Outsourcing Angst," *Computer World*, March 17, 2003, p. 11; J. Solomon and E. Cherney, "Outsourcing to India Sees a Twist," *The Wall Street Journal*, April 1, 2004, p. A2; J. Solomon and K. Kranhold, "Western Exposure: In India's Outsourcing Boom, GE Played a Starring Role," *The Wall Street Journal*, March 23, 2005, p. A1; and A. Campoy, "Think Locally: Indian Outsourcing Companies Have Finally Begun to Crack the European Market," *The Wall Street Journal*, September 27, 2004, p. R8.

Case Discussion Question

1. How did outsourcing work to Wipro improve General Electric's ability to compete in the global economy? Does such outsourcing harm or benefit the American economy?

2. Did General Electric help to create Wipro? How?

3. If India's information technology companies continue to prosper, over time what do you think will happen to the income differential between software programmers in the United States and India? What are the implications for the American economy?

4. Since 2000, Wipro has moved abroad, establishing sales offices in 35 nations and design centers in nine. Why is Wipro doing this? What would happen to the company if it did not follow this strategy?

5. What does the rise of Wipro teach you about the nature of the global economy in the first decade of the 21st century?

Notes

1. World Trade Organization, trade statistics database accessed May 2005 at http://stat.wto.org/Home/WSDBHome.aspx.

2. Thomas L. Friedman, *The World Is Flat* (New York: Farrar, Straus and Giroux, 2005).

3. Ibid.

4. T. Levitt, "The Globalization of Markets," *Harvard Business Review*, May–June 1983, pp. 92–102.

5. U.S. Department of Commerce, "A Profile of U.S. Exporting Companies, 2000–2001," February 2003. Report available at www.census.gov/foreign-trade/aip/index.html#profile.

6. Ibid.

7. C. M. Draffen, "Going Global: Export Market Proves Profitable for Region's Small Businesses," *Newsday*, March 19, 2001, p. C18.

8. W. J. Holstein, "Why Johann Can Export, but Johnny Can't," *BusinessWeek*, November 4, 1991, pp. 64–65.

9. See F. T. Knickerbocker, *Oligopolistic Reaction and Multinational Enterprise* (Boston: Harvard Business School Press, 1973), and R. E. Caves, "Japanese Investment in the U.S.: Lessons for the Economic Analysis of Foreign Investment," *The World Economy* 16 (1993), pp. 279–300.

10. I. Metthee, "Playing a Large Part," *Seattle Post-Intelligencer*, April 9, 1994, p. 13.

11. D. Pritchard, "Are Federal Tax Laws and State Subsidies for Boeing 7E7 Selling America Short?" *Aviation Week*, April 12, 2004, pp. 74–75.

12. D. Barboza, "An Unknown Giant Flexes Its Muscles," *The New York Times*, December 4, 2004, p. B1, B3.

13. W. M. Bulkeley, "IBM to Export Highly Paid Jobs to India," *The Wall Street Journal*, December 15, 2003, pp. B1, B3.

14. R. B. Reich, *The Work of Nations* (New York: A. A. Knopf, 1991).

15. United Nations, "The UN in Brief," www.un.org/Overview/brief.html.

16. J. A. Frankel, "Globalization of the Economy," National Bureau of Economic Research, Working Paper No. 7858, 2000.

17. J. Bhagwati, *Protectionism* (Cambridge, MA: MIT Press, 1989).

18. F. Williams, "Trade Round Like This May Never Be Seen Again," *Financial Times*, April 15, 1994, p. 8.

19. W. Vieth, "Major Concessions Lead to Success for WTO Talks," *Los Angeles Times*, November 14, 2001, p. A1, and "Seeds Sown for Future Growth," *The Economist*, November 17, 2001, pp. 65–66.

20. United Nations, *World Investment Report, 2004* (New York and Geneva: United Nations, 2004).

21. Ibid.

22. World Trade Organization, *International Trade Trends and Statistics, 2003* (Geneva: WTO, 2003), and WTO press release, "World Trade for 2003: Prospects for 2004," April 4, 2004, available at www.wto.org.

23. United Nations, *World Investment Report, 2004,* and United Nations Conference on Trade and Development, "World FDI Flows Grew an Estimated 6% in 2004," UNCTAD press release, January 11, 2005.

24. World Trade Organization, *International Trade Statistics, 2004* (Geneva: WTO, 2004); United Nations, *World Investment Report, 2004;* and United Nations Conference on Trade and Development, "World FDI Flows Grew an Estimated 6% in 2004."

25. United Nations, *World Investment Report, 2004.*

26. Moore's Law is named after Intel founder Gordon Moore.

27. Frankel, "Globalization of the Economy."

28. J. G. Fernald and V. Greenfield, "The Fall and Rise of the Global Economy," *Chicago Fed Letters*, April 2001, pp. 1–4.

29. Data compiled from various sources and listed by CyberAtlas at http://cyberatlas.internet.com/big_picture/.

30. Data on the number of host computers can be found at www.isc.org/index.pl?/ops/ds/.

31. www.forrester.com/ER/Press/ForrFind/0,1768,0,00.html.

32. For a counterpoint, see "Geography and the Net: Putting It in Its Place," *The Economist*, August 11, 2001, pp. 18–20.

33. M. Dickerson, "All Those Inflated Expectations Aside, Many Firms Are Finding the Internet Invaluable in Pursuing International Trade," *Los Angeles Times*, October 14, 1998, p. 10. The company's Web site is www.cardiacscience.com.

34. A. Stewart, "Easier Access to World Markets," *Financial Times*, December 3, 1997, p. 8.

35. Frankel, "Globalization of the Economy."

36. Data from Bureau of Transportation Statistics, 2001.

37. Fernald and Greenfield, "The Fall and Rise of the Global Economy."

38. Data located at www.bts.gov/publications/us_international_trade_and_freight_transportation_trends/2003/index.html.

39. "War of the Worlds," *The Economist: A Survey of the Global Economy*, October 1, 1994, pp. 3–4.

40. Ibid.

41. United Nations, *World Investment Report, 2004.*

42. Ibid.

43. Ibid.

44. S. Chetty, "Explosive International Growth and Problems of Success among Small and Medium Sized Firms," *International Small Business Journal*, February 2003, pp. 5–28.

45. R. A. Mosbacher, "Opening Up Export Doors for Smaller Firms," *Seattle Times*, July 24, 1991, p. A7.

46. "Small Companies Learn How to Sell to the Japanese," *Seattle Times*, March 19, 1992.

47. Holstein, "Why Johann Can Export, but Johnny Can't."

48. J. E. Stiglitz, *Globalization and Its Discontents* (New York: W. W. Norton, 2003); J. Bhagwati, *In Defense of Globalization* (New York: Oxford University Press, 2004); and Friedman, *The World Is Flat.*

49. See, for example, Ravi Batra, *The Myth of Free Trade* (New York: Touchstone Books, 1993); William Greider, *One World, Ready or Not: The Manic Logic of Global Capitalism* (New York: Simon and Schuster, 1997); and D. Radrik, *Has Globalization Gone Too Far?* (Washington, DC: Institution for International Economics, 1997).

50. James Goldsmith, "The Winners and the Losers," in *The Case against the Global Economy*, ed. J. Mander and E. Goldsmith (San Francisco: The Sierra Book Club, 1996). Lou Dobbs, *Exporting America* (New York: Time Warner Books, 2004).

51. D. L. Bartlett and J. B. Steele, "America: Who Stole the Dream," *Philadelphia Inquirer*, September 9, 1996.

52. For example, see Paul Krugman, *Pop Internationalism* (Cambridge, MA: MIT Press, 1996).

53. Peter Gottschalk and Timothy M. Smeeding, "Cross-National Comparisons of Earnings and Income Inequality," *Journal of Economic Literature* 35 (June 1997), pp. 633–87, and Susan M. Collins, *Exports, Imports, and the American Worker* (Washington, DC: Brookings Institution, 1998).

54. B. Milanovic and L. Squire, "Does Tariff Liberalization Increase Wage Inequality?" *National Bureau of Economic Research*, Working Paper No. 11046, January 2005.

55. "A Survey of Pay. Winners and Losers," *The Economist*, May 8, 1999, pp. 5–8.

56. Jared Bernstein, Elizabeth C. McNichol, Lawrence Mishel, and Robert Zahradnik, "Pulling Apart: A State by State Analysis of Income Trends," *Economic Policy Institute*, January 2000.

57. See Krugman, *Pop Internationalism*, and D. Belman and T. M. Lee, "International Trade and the Performance of US Labor Markets," in *U.S. Trade Policy and Global Growth*, ed. R. A. Blecker (New York: Economic Policy Institute, 1996).

58. See Robert Lerman, "Is Earnings Inequality Really Increasing? Economic Restructuring and the Job Market," Brief No. 1 (Washington, DC: Urban Institute, March 1997).

59. M. Forster and M. Pearson, "Income Distribution and Poverty in the OECD Area," *OECD Economic Studies* 34 (2002).

60. Bernstein, McNichol, Mishel, and Zahradnik, "Pulling Apart: A State by State Analysis of Income Trends."

61. E. Goldsmith, "Global Trade and the Environment," in J. Mander and E. Goldsmith, *The Case against the Global Economy* (San Francisco: Sierra Club, 1996).

62. P. Choate, *Jobs at Risk: Vulnerable U.S. Industries and Jobs under NAFTA* (Washington, DC: Manufacturing Policy Project, 1993).

63. Ibid.

64. B. Lomborg, *The Skeptical Environmentalist* (Cambridge: Cambridge University Press, 2001).

65. H. Nordstrom and S. Vaughan, *Trade and the Environment*, World Trade Organization Special Studies No. 4 (Geneva: WTO, 1999).

66. Figures are from "Freedom's Journey: A Survey of the 20th Century. Our Durable Planet," *The Economist*, September 11, 1999, p. 30.

67. For an exhaustive review of the empirical literature, see B. R. Copeland and M. Scott Taylor, "Trade, Growth and the Environment," *Journal of Economic Literature*, March 2004, pp. 7–77.

68. G. M. Grossman and A. B. Krueger, "Economic Growth and the Environment," *Quarterly Journal of Economics* 110 (1995), pp. 353–78.

69. Krugman, *Pop Internationalism*.

70. R. Kuttner, "Managed Trade and Economic Sovereignty," in *U.S. Trade Policy and Global Growth*, ed. R. A. Blecker (New York: Economic Policy Institute, 1996).

71. Ralph Nader and Lori Wallach, "GATT, NAFTA, and the Subversion of the Democratic Process," in *US Trade Policy and Global Growth*,

ed. R. A. Blecker (New York: Economic Policy Institute, 1996), pp. 93–94.

72. Lant Pritchett, "Divergence, Big Time," *Journal of Economic Perspectives* 11, no. 3 (Summer 1997), pp. 3–18.

73. Ibid.

74. W. Easterly, "How Did Heavily Indebted Poor Countries Become Heavily Indebted?" *World Development*, October 2002, pp. 1677–96.

75. See D. Ben-David, H. Nordstrom, and L. A. Winters, *Trade, Income Disparity and Poverty. World Trade Organization Special Studies No. 5* (Geneva: WTO, 1999).

76. William Easterly, "Debt Relief," *Foreign Policy*, November–December 2001, pp. 20–26.

77. Jeffrey Sachs, "Sachs on Development: Helping the World's Poorest," *The Economist*, August 14, 1999, pp. 17–20.

78. World Trade Organization, *Annual Report 2003* (Geneva: WTO, 2004).

79. Easterly, "Debt Relief."

chapter two 2

The Managerial Process of Crafting and Executing Strategy

(©Dale O'Dell/CORBIS)

Unless we change our direction we are likely to end up where we are headed.

—Ancient Chinese proverb

If we can know where we are and something about how we got there, we might see where we are trending—and if the outcomes which lie naturally in our course are unacceptable, to make timely change.

—Abraham Lincoln

If you don't know where you are going, any road will take you there.

—The Koran

Management's job is not to see the company as it is . . . but as it can become.

—John W. Teets
Former CEO

Crafting and executing strategy are the heart and soul of managing a business enterprise. But exactly what is involved in developing a strategy and executing it proficiently? And who besides top management has strategy-making, strategy-executing responsibility? In this chapter we present an overview of the managerial ins and outs of crafting and executing company strategies. Special attention will be given to management's direction-setting responsibilities—charting a strategic course, setting performance targets, and choosing a strategy capable of producing the desired outcomes. We will also examine which kinds of strategic decisions are made at which levels of management and the roles and responsibilities of the company's board of directors in the strategy-making, strategy-executing process.

WHAT DOES THE PROCESS OF CRAFTING AND EXECUTING STRATEGY ENTAIL?

Crafting and executing a company's strategy is a five-phase managerial process:

1. Developing a strategic vision of where the company needs to head and what its future product-customer-market-technology focus should be.
2. Setting objectives and using them as yardsticks for measuring the company's performance and progress.
3. Crafting a strategy to achieve the desired outcomes and move the company along the strategic course that management has charted.
4. Implementing and executing the chosen strategy efficiently and effectively.
5. Monitoring developments and initiating corrective adjustments in the company's long-term direction, objectives, strategy, or execution in light of the company's actual performance, changing conditions, new ideas, and new opportunities.

Figure 2.1 displays this process. Let's examine this five-phase strategy-making, strategy-executing framework in enough detail to set the stage for the forthcoming chapters and to give you a bird's-eye view of what the rest of this book is about.

DEVELOPING A STRATEGIC VISION: PHASE 1 OF THE STRATEGY-MAKING, STRATEGY-EXECUTING PROCESS

Very early in the strategy-making process, a company's senior managers must wrestle with the issue of what directional path the company should take and what changes in the company's product-market-customer-technology focus would improve its current market position and future prospects. Deciding to commit the company to one path

figure 2.1   **The Strategy-Making, Strategy-Executing Process**

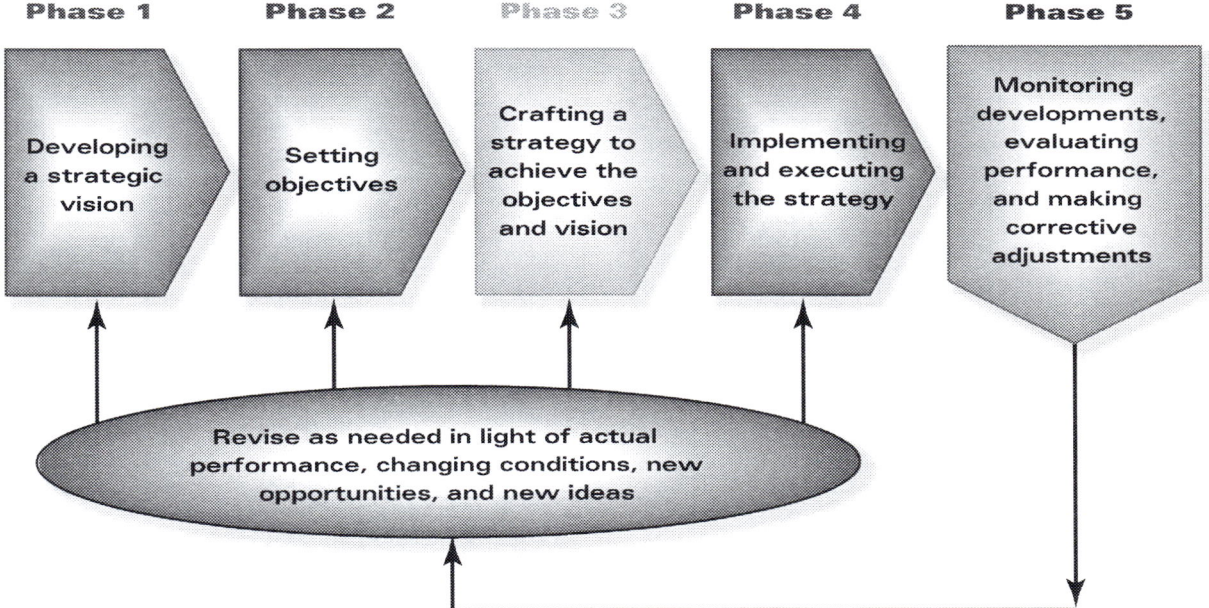

versus another pushes managers to draw some carefully reasoned conclusions about how to try to modify the company's business makeup and the market position it should stake out. A number of direction-shaping factors need to be considered in deciding where to head and why such a direction makes good business sense—see Table 2.1.

Top management's views and conclusions about the company's direction and the product-customer-market-technology focus constitute a **strategic vision** for the company. A strategic vision delineates management's aspirations for the business, providing a panoramic view of "where we are going" and a convincing rationale for why this makes good business sense for the company. A strategic vision thus points an organization in a particular direction, charts a strategic path for it to follow in preparing for the future, and molds organizational identity. A clearly articulated strategic vision communicates management's aspirations to stakeholders and helps steer the energies of company personnel in a common direction. For instance, Henry Ford's vision of a car in every garage had power because it captured the imagination of others, aided internal efforts to mobilize the Ford Motor Company's resources, and served as a reference point for gauging the merits of the company's strategic actions.

Well-conceived visions are distinctive and specific to a particular organization; they avoid generic, feel-good statements like "We will become a global leader and the first choice of customers in every market we choose to serve"—which could apply to any of hundreds of organizations.[1] And they are not the product of a committee charged with coming up with an innocuous but well-meaning one sentence vision that wins consensus approval from various stakeholders. Nicely worded vision statements with no specifics about the company's product-market-customer-technology focus are suspect. A strategic vision proclaiming management's quest "to be the market leader" or "to be the first choice of customers" or "to be the most innovative" or "to be recog-

core concept
A *strategic vision* is a road map showing the route a company intends to take in developing and strengthening its business. It paints a picture of a company's destination and provides a rationale for going there.

table 2.1   **Factors to Consider in Deciding to Commit the Company to One Directional Path versus Another**

External Considerations	Internal Considerations
• Is the outlook for the company promising if it simply maintains its present product/market/customer/technology focus? Does sticking with the company's present strategic course present attractive growth opportunities?	• What are our ambitions for the company? What industry standing does management want the company to have?
• Are changes under way in the market and competitive landscape enhancing or weakening the outlook for the company's present business?	• Will the company's present business generate sufficient growth and profitability in the years ahead to please shareholders?
• What, if any, new customer groups and/or geographic markets should the company get in position to serve?	• What organizational strengths ought the company be trying to leverage in terms of adding new products or services and/or getting into new businesses?
• Which emerging market opportunities should the company pursue and which ones should it avoid?	• Is the company stretching its resources too thin by trying to compete in too many markets or segments? Are some pieces of the company's business unprofitable?
• Should the company plan to abandon any of the markets, market segments, or customer groups we are currently serving?	• Is the company's technological focus too broad or too narrow? Are any changes needed?

nized as the best company in the industry" offer scant guidance about a company's directions and what management intends to do to get there.

For a strategic vision to function as a valuable managerial tool, it must provide understanding of what management wants its business to look like and provide managers with a reference point in making strategic decisions and preparing the company for the future. It must say something definitive about how the company's leaders intend to position the company beyond where it is today. A good vision always needs to be a bit beyond a company's reach, but progress toward the vision is what unifies the efforts of company personnel. Table 2.2 lists some characteristics of an effective vision statement.

A sampling of vision statements currently in use shows a range from strong and clear to bland and ill-conceived. A surprising number of the vision statements found on company Web sites and in annual reports are dull, blurry, and uninspiring—they come across as having been written by a committee to attract consensus from a variety of organizational stakeholders and having been developed only because it is fashionable for companies to have an official vision statement.[2] Few corporate executives want to risk the embarrassment of being without a vision statement. The one- or two-sentence vision statement a company makes available to the public, of course, provides only a glimpse of what company executives are really thinking and where the company is headed and why. Having a vision is not a panacea but rather a useful management tool for giving an organization a sense of direction. Like any tool, it can be used properly or improperly, either strongly conveying a company's strategic course or not. Table 2.3 provides a list of the most common shortcomings in company vision statements.

Illustration Capsule 2.1 contains the strategic vision for Exelon, one of the leading and best-managed electric and gas utility companies in the United States. Illustration Capsule 2.2 provides examples of strategic visions of several prominent companies and nonprofit organizations. See if you can tell which ones are mostly meaningless or nice-sounding and which ones are managerially useful in communicating "where we are headed and the kind of company we are trying to become".

20   Part 1 | Concepts and Techniques for Crafting and Executing Strategy

table 2.2   **Characteristics of an Effectively Worded Vision Statement**

Graphic	A well-stated vision paints a picture of the kind of company that management is trying to create and the market position the company is striving to stake out.
Directional	A well-stated vision says something about the company's journey or destination and signals the kinds of business and strategic changes that will be forthcoming.
Focused	A well-stated vision is specific enough to provide managers with guidance in making decisions and allocating resources.
Flexible	A well-stated vision is not a once-and-for-all-time pronouncement—visions about a company's future path may need to change as events unfold and circumstances change.
Feasible	A well-stated vision is within the realm of what the company can reasonably expect to achieve in due time.
Desirable	A well-stated vision appeals to the long-term interests of stakeholders—particularly shareowners, employees, and customers.
Easy to communicate	A well-stated vision is explainable in less than 10 minutes and ideally can be reduced to a simple, memorable slogan (like Henry Ford's famous vision of "a car in every garage").

Source: Reprinted by permission of Harvard Business School Press. From *Leading Change* by John P. Kotter. Boston, MA, p. 72. Copyright © 1996 by the Harvard Business School Publishing Corporation; all rights reserved.

A Strategic Vision Is Different from a Mission Statement   Whereas the chief concern of a strategic vision is with "where we are going and why," a company mission statement usually deals with a company's *present* business scope and purpose—"who we are, what we do, and why we are here." *A company's mission is defined by the buyer needs it seeks to satisfy, the customer groups and market segments it is endeavoring to serve, and the resources and technologies that it is deploying in trying to please its customers.* (Many companies prefer the term business purpose to mission statement, but the two phrases are essentially conceptually identical and are used interchangeably.) A typical example is the mission statement of Trader Joe's (a unique grocery chain):

> The mission of Trader Joe's is to give our customers the best food and beverage values that they can find anywhere and to provide them with the information required for informed buying decisions. We provide these with a dedication to the highest quality of customer satisfaction delivered with a sense of warmth, friendliness, fun, individual pride, and company spirit.

> The distinction between a strategic vision and a mission statement is fairly clear-cut: A strategic vision portrays a company's future business scope ("where we are going") whereas a company's mission typically describes its present business scope and purpose ("who we are, what we do, and why we are here").

The mission statements that one finds in company annual reports or posted on company Web sites typically provide a brief overview of the company's present business purpose and raison d'être and sometimes its geographic coverage or standing as a market leader. They may or may not single out the company's present products/services, the buyer needs it is seeking to satisfy, the customer groups it serves, or its technological and business capabilities. But company mission statements almost never say anything about where the company is headed, the anticipated changes in its business, or its aspirations.

Occasionally, companies couch their mission in terms of making a profit. The notion that a company's mission or business purpose is to make a profit is misguided—profit is more correctly an *objective* and a *result* of what a company does. Making a profit is the obvious intent of every com-

table 2.3 **Common Shortcomings in Company Vision Statements**

1. Incomplete—short on specifics about where the company is headed or what kind of company management is trying to create.
2. Vague—doesn't provide much indication of whether or how management intends to alter the company's current product/market/customer/technology focus.
3. Bland—lacking in motivational power.
4. Not distinctive—could apply to most any company (or at least several others in the same industry).
5. Too reliant on such superlatives as *best, most successful, recognized leader, global or worldwide leader,* or *first choice of customers.*
6. Too generic—fails to identify the business or industry to which it is supposed to apply. The statement could apply to companies in any of several industries.
7. So broad that it really doesn't rule out most any opportunity that management might opt to pursue.

mercial enterprise. It is management's answer to "make a profit doing what and for whom?" that reveals the substance of a company's mission and gives it an identity apart from any other profit-seeking company. Such companies as Charles Schwab, Caterpillar, Toyota, Wal-Mart, and Nokia are each striving to earn a profit for shareholders; but plainly the fundamentals of their business are substantially different when it comes to "who we are and what we do." If a company's mission statement is to have any managerial value or reveal anything useful about its business, it must direct attention to the particular market arena in which it operates—the buyer needs it seeks to satisfy, the customer groups and market segments it is endeavoring to serve, and the types of resources and technologies that it is deploying in trying to please its customers.

Linking the Vision with Company Values

In the course of deciding "who we are and where we are going," many companies also come up with a statement of values to guide the company's pursuit of its vision. By **values,** we means the beliefs, business principles, and practices that are incorporated into the way the company operates and the behavior of company personnel. Values relate to such things as treatment of employees and customers, integrity, ethics, innovativeness, emphasis on quality or service, social responsibility, and community citizenship. Company values statements tend to contain between four and eight values, which, ideally, are tightly connected to and reinforce the company's vision, strategy, and operating practices. Home Depot has embraced eight values (entrepreneurial spirit, excellent customer service, giving back to the community, respect for all people, doing the right thing, taking care of people, building strong relationships, and creating shareholder value) in its quest to become the world's largest home improvement retailer by operating warehouse stores filled with a wide assortment of products at the lowest prices with trained associates giving absolutely the best customer service in the industry. Intel's corporate values of discipline, risk taking, quality, customer orientation, a results-oriented atmosphere, and being a great place to work guide the company's business behavior and pursuit of its "core mission" of "being the building block supplier to the Internet economy." At Intel, all employee badges are emblazoned with the company's values and employees are trained in over 40 behaviors exemplifying those values. DuPont, which calls itself "a science company" and makes a wide array of

> **core concept**
> A company's ***values*** are the beliefs, business principles, and practices that guide the conduct of its business, the pursuit of its strategic vision, and the behavior of company personnel.

22   Part 1 | Concepts and Techniques for Crafting and Executing Strategy

illustration capsule 2.1
Exelon's Strategic Vision

Exelon, an electric and gas utility company recently created by the merger of Philadelphia Electric Company and Commonwealth Edison, has the following vision statement:

EXELON—ONE COMPANY, ONE VISION

Exelon strives to build exceptional value—by becoming the best and most consistently profitable electricity and gas company in the United States. To succeed, we must . . .

Live up to our commitments	● Keep the lights on. ● Perform safely—especially nuclear operations. ● Constantly improve our environmental performance. ● Act honorably and treat everyone with respect, decency, and integrity. ● Continue building a high performance culture that reflects the diversity of our communities. ● Report our results, opportunities, and problems honestly and reliably.
Perform at world-class levels	● Relentlessly pursue greater productivity, quality, and innovation. ● Understand the relationships among our businesses and optimize the whole. ● Promote and implement policies that build effective markets. ● Adapt rapidly to changing markets, politics, economics and technology to meet our customers' needs. ● Maximize the earnings and cash flow from our assets and businesses and sell those that do not meet our goals.
Invest in our consolidating industry	● Develop strategies based on learning from past successes and failures. ● Implement systems and best practices that can be applied to future acquisitions. ● Prioritize acquisition opportunities based on synergies from scale, scope, generation and delivery integration, and our ability to profitably satisfy . . . regulatory obligations. ● Make acquisitions that will best employ our limited investment resources to produce the most consistent cash flow and earnings accretion. ● Return earnings to shareholders when higher returns are not available from acquisition opportunities.

COMMENTARY ON EXELON'S VISION

While the one-sentence vision is definitely overly general and void of direction, what rescues it (and makes the overall vision statement managerially useful) are the specifics that follow. The three things that management says the company must do to succeed and the accompanying bullet points convey a reasonably clear sense of where management intends to take the company and what the company is endeavoring to do in order to deliver exceptional value to stakeholders. But Exelon's vision statement is still somewhat vague on where management is trying to take the company in terms of its future product/market/customer/technology focus.

Source: Company documents.

products, stresses four values—safety, ethics, respect for people, and environmental stewardship; the first three have been in place since the company was founded over 200 years ago by E. I. du Pont. Loblaw, a major grocery chain in Canada, focuses on just two main values in operating its stores—competence and honesty; it expects employees to display both, and top management strives to promote only those employees who are smart and honest.

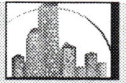

illustration capsule 2.2
Examples of Strategic Visions—How Well Do They Measure Up?

Using the information in Tables 2.2 and 2.3, critique the adequacy and merit of the following eight vision statements, ranking them from 1 (best) to 8 (in need of substantial improvement).

RED HAT LINUX

To extend our position as the most trusted Linux and open source provider to the enterprise. We intend to grow the market for Linux through a complete range of enterprise Red Hat Linux software, a powerful Internet management platform, and associated support and services.

WELLS FARGO

We want to satisfy all of our customers' financial needs, help them succeed financially, be the premier provider of financial services in every one of our markets, and be known as one of America's great companies.

WYETH

Our vision is to lead the way to a healthier world. By carrying out this vision at every level of our organization, we will be recognized by our employees, customers, and shareholders as the best pharmaceutical company in the world, resulting in value for all. We will achieve this by:

- Leading the world in innovation by linking pharmaceutical, biotech, and vaccines technologies
- Making quality, integrity, and excellence hallmarks of the way we do business
- Attracting, developing, and motivating the best people
- Continually growing and improving our business

GENERAL ELECTRIC

We will become number one or number two in every market we serve, and revolutionize this company to have the speed and agility of a small enterprise.

THE DENTAL PRODUCTS DIVISION OF 3M CORPORATION

Become THE supplier of choice to the global dental professional markets, providing world-class quality and innovative products. [All employees of the division wear badges bearing these words, and whenever a new product or business procedure is being considered, management asks "Is this representative of THE leading dental company?"]

NIKE

To bring innovation and inspiration to every athlete in the world.

HEINZ

Our vision, quite simply, is to be the world's premier food company, offering nutritious, superior tasting foods to people everywhere. Being the premier food company does not mean being the biggest but it does mean being the best in terms of consumer value, customer service, employee talent, and consistent and predictable growth.

INTEL

Our vision: Getting to a billion connected computers worldwide, millions of servers, and trillions of dollars of e-commerce. Intel's core mission is being the building block supplier to the Internet economy and spurring efforts to make the Internet more useful. Being connected is now at the center of people's computing experience. We are helping to expand the capabilities of the PC platform and the Internet . . . We have seen only the early stages of deployment of digital technologies.

Sources: Company documents and Web sites.

Company managers connect values to the strategic vision in one of two ways. In companies with long-standing and deeply entrenched values, managers go to great lengths to explain how the vision is compatible with the company's value set, occasionally reinterpreting the meaning of existing values to indicate their relevance in pursuing the strategic vision. In new companies or companies with weak or incomplete sets of values, top management considers what values, beliefs, and operating principles will help drive the vision forward. Then new values that fit the vision are drafted and circulated among managers and employees for discussion and possible modification.

A final values statement that connects to the vision and that reflects the beliefs and principles the company wants to uphold is then officially adopted. A number of companies combine their vision and values into a single statement or document that is provided to all company personnel and often posted on the company's Web site.

Of course, sometimes there is a wide gap between a company's stated values and its actual conduct. Enron, for example, touted four corporate values—respect, integrity, communication, and excellence—but flagrant disregard for these values by some top officials in their management of the company's financial and accounting practices and energy-trading activities triggered the company's implosion. Once one of the world's Big Five public accounting firms, Arthur Andersen was renowned for its commitment to the highest standards of audit integrity, but its high-profile audit failures and partner approval of shady accounting at Enron, WorldCom, and other companies led to Andersen's demise.

Communicating the Strategic Vision

Developing a well-conceived vision is necessary but not sufficient. Effectively communicating the strategic vision down the line to lower-level managers and employees is as important as the strategic soundness of the journey and destination for which top management has opted. If company personnel don't know what management's vision is and don't buy into the rationale for the direction management wants the company to head, they are unlikely to wholeheartedly commit themselves to making the vision a reality. Furthermore, company personnel need to believe that top management has a sound basis for where it is trying to take the company, and they need to understand why the strategic course that management has charted is both reasonable and beneficial. Winning the support of organization members for the vision nearly always means putting "where we are going and why" in writing, distributing the statement organizationwide, and having executives personally explain the vision and its rationale to as many people as feasible. Ideally, executives should present their vision for the company in a manner that reaches out and grabs people. An engaging and convincing vision can have enormous motivational value—for the same reason that a stonemason finds building a magnificent cathedral more inspiring than laying stones. When top management articulates a vivid and compelling picture of what the company needs to do and why, organizational members begin to say, "This has a lot of merit. I want to be involved and contribute to making it happen." The more that a vision evokes positive support and excitement, the greater its impact in terms of arousing a committed organizational effort and getting people to move in a common direction.[3]

Most organization members will rise to the challenge of pursuing a path that may significantly enhance the company's competitiveness and market prominence, win big applause from buyers and turn them into loyal customers, or produce important benefits for society as a whole. Presenting the vision as an endeavor that could make the company the world leader or greatly improve the well-being of customers and/or society is far more motivating than stressing the payoff for shareholders—it goes without saying that the company intends to profit shareholders. Unless most managers and employees are also shareholders (because the company incentivizes employees via a stock ownership plan), they are unlikely to be energized by a vision that does little more than enrich shareholders.

core concept
An effectively communicated vision is management's most valuable tool for enlisting the commitment of company personnel to actions that will make the vision a reality.

Executive ability to paint a convincing and inspiring picture of a company's journey and destination is an important element of effective strategic leadership.

Expressing the Essence of the Vision in a Slogan   The task of effectively conveying the vision to company personnel is made easier when management's vision of where to head is captured in a catchy slogan. A number of organizations have summed up their visions in a brief phrase:

- Levi Strauss & Company: "We will clothe the world by marketing the most appealing and widely worn casual clothing in the world."
- Microsoft Corporation: "Empower people through great software—any time, any place, and on any device."
- Mayo Clinic: "The best care to every patient every day."
- Scotland Yard: "To make London the safest major city in the world."
- Greenpeace: "To halt environmental abuse and promote environmental solutions."
- Charles Schwab: "To provide customers with the most useful and ethical financial services in the world."

Creating a short slogan to illuminate an organization's direction and purpose and then using it repeatedly as a reminder of the "where we are headed and why" helps keep organization members on the chosen path. But it is important to bear in mind that developing a strategic vision is not a wordsmithing exercise to come up with a snappy slogan. Rather, it is an exercise in thinking carefully about where a company needs to head to be successful. It involves selecting the market arenas in which to participate, putting the company on a clearly defined strategic course, and making a commitment to follow that course.

Breaking Down Resistance to a New Strategic Vision   It is particularly important for executives to provide a compelling rationale for a dramatically *new* strategic vision and company direction. When company personnel don't understand or accept the need for redirecting organizational efforts, they are prone to resist change. Hence, reiterating the basis for the new direction, addressing employee concerns head-on, calming fears, lifting spirits, and providing updates and progress reports as events unfold all become part of the task in mobilizing support for the vision and winning commitment to needed actions. Just stating the case for a new direction once is not enough. Executives must repeat the reasons for the new direction often and convincingly at company gatherings and in company publications, and they must reinforce their pronouncements with updates about how the latest information confirms the choice of direction and the validity of the vision. Unless and until more and more people are persuaded of the merits of management's new vision and the vision gains wide acceptance, it will be a struggle to move the organization down the newly chosen path.

Recognizing Strategic Inflection Points   Sometimes there's an order-of-magnitude change in a company's environment that dramatically alters its prospects and mandates radical revision of its strategic course. Intel's chairman Andrew Grove calls such occasions *strategic inflection points*—Illustration Capsule 2.3 relates Intel's two encounters with strategic inflection points and the resulting alterations in its strategic vision. As the Intel example forcefully demonstrates, when a company reaches a strategic inflection point, management has some tough decisions to make about the company's course. Often it is a question of what to do to sustain company success, not just how to avoid possible disaster. Responding to unfolding changes in the marketplace in timely fashion lessens a company's chances of becoming trapped in a stagnant or declining business or letting attractive new growth opportunities slip away.

The Payoffs of a Clear Vision Statement   In sum, a well-conceived, forcefully communicated strategic vision pays off in several respects: (1) it crystallizes senior executives' own views about the firm's long-term direction; (2) it reduces the risk

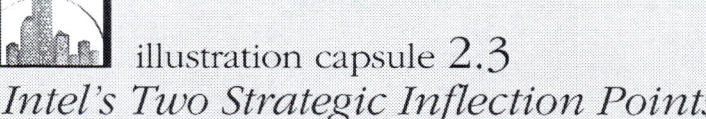

illustration capsule 2.3
Intel's Two Strategic Inflection Points

Intel Corporation has encountered two strategic inflection points within the past 20 years. The first came in the mid-1980s, when memory chips were Intel's principal business and Japanese manufacturers, intent on dominating the memory chip business, began cutting their prices 10 percent below the prices charged by Intel and other U.S. memory chip manufacturers. Each time U.S. companies matched the Japanese price cuts, the Japanese manufacturers responded with another 10 percent price cut. Intel's management explored a number of strategic options to cope with the aggressive pricing of its Japanese rivals—building a giant memory chip factory to overcome the cost advantage of Japanese producers, investing in research and development (R&D) to come up with a more advanced memory chip, and retreating to niche markets for memory chips that were not of interest to the Japanese.

At the time, Gordon Moore, Intel's chairman and cofounder, and Andrew Grove, Intel's chief executive officer (CEO), jointly concluded that none of these options offered much promise and that the best long-term solution was to abandon the memory chip business even though it accounted for 70 percent of Intel's revenue. Grove, with the concurrence of both Moore and the board of directors, then proceeded to commit Intel's full energies to the business of developing ever more powerful microprocessors for personal computers. (Intel had invented microprocessors in the early 1970s but had recently been concentrating on memory chips because of strong competition and excess capacity in the market for microprocessors.)

Grove's bold decision to withdraw from memory chips, absorb a $173 million write-off in 1986, and go all out in microprocessors produced a new strategic vision for Intel—becoming the preeminent supplier of microprocessors to the personal computing industry, making the personal computer (PC) the central appliance in the workplace and the home, and being the undisputed leader in driving PC technology forward. Grove's new vision for Intel and the strategic course he charted in 1985 produced spectacular results. Since 1996, over 80 percent of the world's PCs have been made with Intel microprocessors and Intel has become the world's most profitable chip maker.

The company encountered a second inflection point in 1998, opting to refocus on becoming the preeminent building block supplier to the Internet economy (see Illustration Capsule 2.2) and spurring efforts to make the Internet more useful. Starting in early 1998 and responding to the mushrooming importance of the Internet, Intel's senior management launched major new initiatives to direct attention and resources to expanding the capabilities of both the PC platform and the Internet. It was this strategic inflection point that led to Intel's latest strategic vision of playing a major role in getting a billion computers connected to the Internet worldwide, installing millions of servers, and building an Internet infrastructure that would support trillions of dollars of e-commerce and serve as a worldwide communication medium.

Source: Andrew S. Grove, *Only the Paranoid Survive,* (New York: Doubleday-Currency, 1996) and information posted at www.intel.com.

of rudderless decision making; (3) it is a tool for winning the support of organizational members for internal changes that will help make the vision a reality; (4) it provides a beacon for lower-level managers in forming departmental missions, setting departmental objectives, and crafting functional and departmental strategies that are in sync with the company's overall strategy; and (5) it helps an organization prepare for the future. When management is able to demonstrate significant progress in achieving these five benefits, the first step in organizational direction setting has been successfully completed.

SETTING OBJECTIVES: PHASE 2 OF THE STRATEGY-MAKING, STRATEGY-EXECUTING PROCESS

The managerial purpose of setting **objectives** is to convert the strategic vision into specific performance targets—results and outcomes the company's management wants to achieve—and then use these objectives as yardsticks for tracking the company's progress and performance. Well-stated objectives are *quantifiable, or measurable,* and contain a *deadline for achievement.* As Bill Hewlett, co-founder of Hewlett-Packard, shrewdly observed, "You cannot manage what you cannot measure . . . And what gets measured gets done."[4] The experiences of countless companies and managers teach that precisely spelling out *how much* of *what kind* of performance *by when* and then pressing forward with actions and incentives calculated to help achieve the targeted outcomes will boost a company's actual performance. It definitely beats setting vague targets like "increase profits," "reduce costs," "become more efficient," or "boost sales," which specify neither how much nor by when, and then living with whatever results company personnel deliver.

> **core concept**
> **Objectives** are an organization's performance targets—the results and outcomes it wants to achieve. They function as yardsticks for tracking an organization's performance and progress.

Ideally, managers ought to use the objective-setting exercise as a tool for truly *stretching an organization to reach its full potential.* Challenging company personnel to go all out and deliver big gains in performance pushes an enterprise to be more inventive, to exhibit some urgency in improving both its financial performance and its business position, and to be more intentional and focused in its actions. *Stretch objectives* help build a firewall against contentment with slow, incremental improvements in organizational performance. As Mitchell Leibovitz, CEO of the auto parts and service retailer Pep Boys, once said, "If you want to have ho-hum results, have ho-hum objectives."

What Kinds of Objectives to Set: The Need for a Balanced Scorecard

Two very distinct types of performance yardsticks are required: those relating to *financial performance* and those relating to *strategic performance*—outcomes that indicate a company is strengthening its marketing standing, competitive vitality, and future business prospects. The following are examples of commonly used financial and strategic objectives:

Financial Objectives	Strategic Objectives
• An *x* percent increase in annual revenues	• Winning an *x* percent market share
• Annual increases in after-tax profits of *x* percent	• Achieving lower overall costs than rivals
• Annual increases in earnings per share of *x* percent	• Overtaking key competitors on product performance or quality or customer service
• Annual dividend increases of *x* percent	• Deriving *x* percent of revenues from the sale of new products introduced within the past five years
• Profit margins of *x* percent	
• An *x* percent return on capital employed (ROCE) or shareholders' equity (ROE)	• Achieving technological leadership
	• Having better product selection than rivals
• Increased shareholder value—in the form of an upward-trending stock price and annual dividend increases	• Strengthening the company's brand-name appeal
• Strong bond and credit ratings	• Having stronger national or global sales and distribution capabilities than rivals
• Sufficient internal cash flows to fund new capital investment	• Consistently getting new or improved products to market ahead of rivals
• Stable earnings during periods of recession	

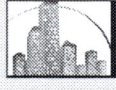 illustration capsule 2.4
Examples of Company Objectives

UNILEVER
(Strategic and Financial Objectives)

Grow annual revenues by 5%–6% annually; increase operating profit margins from 11%–16% percent within 5 years; trim the company's 1200 food, household, and personal care products down to 400 core brands; focus sales and marketing efforts on those brands with potential to become respected, market-leading global brands; and streamline the company's supply chain.

THE KROGER COMPANY
(Strategic and Financial Objectives)

Reduce our operating and administrative cost by $500 million by year-end 2003; leverage our $51 billion size to achieve greater economies of scale; reinvest in our core business to increase sales and market share; and grow earnings per share by 10%–12% in 2002–2003 and by 13%–15% annually starting in 2004.

DUPONT
(Financial and Strategic Objectives)

To achieve annual revenue growth of 5%–6% and annual earnings-per-share growth averaging 10%. Grow per-share profits faster than revenues by (a) increasing productivity, (b) selling enough new products each year that average prices and average margins rise, and (c) using surplus cash to buy back shares. Sell the company's low-margin textiles and interiors division (with sales of $6.6 billion and operating profits of only $114 million); this division makes Lycra and other synthetic fibers for carpets and clothes.

HEINZ
(Financial and Strategic Objectives)

Achieve earnings per share in the range of $2.15–$2.25 in 2004; increase operating cash flow by 45% to $750 million; reduce net debt by $1.3 billion in 2003 and further strengthen the company's balance sheet in 2004; continue to introduce new and improved food products; remove the clutter in company product offerings by reducing the number of SKUs (stock keeping units); increase spending on trade promotion and advertising by $200 million to strengthen the recognition and market shares of the company's core brands; and divest non-core underperforming product lines.

SEAGATE TECHNOLOGY
(Strategic Objectives)

Solidify the company's No. 1 position in the overall market for hard-disk drives; get more Seagate drives into popular consumer electronics products (i.e. video recorders); take share away from Western Digital in providing disk drives for Microsoft's Xbox; and capture a 10% share of the market for 2.5-inch hard drives for notebook computers by 2004.

3M CORPORATION
(Financial and Strategic Objectives)

To achieve annual growth in earnings per share of 10% or better, on average; a return on stockholders' equity of 20%–25%; a return on capital employed of 27% or better; and have at least 30% of sales come from products introduced in the past four years.

Sources: Company documents; *Business Week* (July 28, 2003), p. 106; *Business Week* (September 8, 2003), p. 108.

Achieving acceptable financial results is a must. Without adequate profitability and financial strength, a company's pursuit of its strategic vision, as well as its long-term health and ultimate survival, is jeopardized. Further subpar earnings and a weak balance sheet alarm shareholders and creditors and put the jobs of senior executives at risk. But good financial performance, by itself, is not enough. Of equal or greater importance is a company's strategic performance—outcomes that indicate whether a company's market position and competitiveness are deteriorating, holding steady, or improving. Illustration Capsule 2.4 shows selected objectives of several prominent companies.

Improved Strategic Performance Fosters Better Financial Performance   A company's financial performance measures are really *lagging indicators*

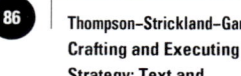
that reflect the results of past decisions and organizational activities. But a company's past or current financial performance is not a reliable indicator of its future prospects—poor financial performers often turn things around and do better, while good financial performers can fall on hard times. The best and most reliable *leading indicators* of a company's future financial performance and business prospects are strategic outcomes that indicate whether the company's competitiveness and market position are stronger or weaker. For instance, if a company has set aggressive strategic objectives and is achieving them—such that its competitive strength and market position are on the rise—then there's reason to expect that its future financial performance will be better than its current or past performance. If a company is losing ground to competitors and its market position is slipping—outcomes that reflect weak strategic performance (and, very likely, failure to achieve its strategic objectives)—then its ability to maintain its present profitability is highly suspect. Hence, the degree to which a company's managers set, pursue, and achieve stretch strategic objectives tends to be a reliable leading indicator of its ability to generate higher profits from business operations.

The Balanced Scorecard Approach: A Combination of Strategic and Financial Objectives The balanced scorecard approach for measuring company performance requires setting both financial and strategic objectives and tracking their achievement. Unless a company is in deep financial difficulty, such that its very survival is threatened, company managers are well advised to put more emphasis on achieving strategic objectives than on achieving financial objectives whenever a trade-off has to be made. *The surest path to sustained future profitability quarter after quarter and year after year is to relentlessly pursue strategic outcomes that strengthen a company's business position and, ideally, give it a growing competitive advantage over rivals.* What ultimately enables a company to deliver better financial results from operations is the achievement of strategic objectives that improve its competitiveness and market strength.

Illustration Capsule 2.5 describes why a growing number of companies are utilizing both financial and strategic objectives to create a "balanced scorecard" approach to measuring company performance.

A Need for Both Short-Term and Long-Term Objectives As a rule, a company's set of financial and strategic objectives ought to include both short-term and long-term performance targets. Having quarterly or annual objectives focuses attention on delivering immediate performance improvements. Targets to be achieved within three to five years prompt considerations of what to do *now* to put the company in position to perform better down the road. A company that has an objective of doubling its sales within five years can't wait until the third or fourth year to begin growing its sales and customer base. By spelling out annual (or perhaps quarterly) performance targets, management indicates the *speed* at which longer-range targets are to be approached.

Short-range objectives can be identical to long-range objectives if an organization is already performing at the targeted long-term level. For instance, if a company has an ongoing objective of 15 percent profit growth every year and is currently achieving this objective, then the company's long-range and short-range objectives for increasing profits coincide. The most important situation in which short-range objectives differ from long-range objectives occurs when managers are trying to elevate organizational performance and cannot reach the long-range target in just one year. Short-range objectives then serve as stairsteps or milestones.

The Concept of Strategic Intent A company's objectives sometimes play another role—that of signaling unmistakable **strategic intent** to make quantum gains in

illustration capsule 2.5
Organizations That Use a Balanced Scorecard Approach to Objective Setting

In recent years organizations like Exxon Mobil, CIGNA, United Parcel Service, Sears, Nova Scotia Power, Duke Children's Hospital, and the City of Charlotte, North Carolina—among numerous others—have used the "Balanced Scorecard" approach to objective setting in all or parts of their operations. This approach, developed and fine-tuned by two Harvard professors, stems from the recognition that exclusive reliance on financial performance measures, which really are lag indicators (i.e., they report the consequences of past actions), induced company managers to take actions that make the company's near-term financial performance look good and to neglect the lead indicators (i.e., the drivers of future financial performance). The solution: measure the performance of a company's strategy and make strategic objectives an integral part of a company's set of performance targets. The balanced scorecard approach to objective setting advocates using a company's strategic vision and strategy as the basis for determining what specific strategic and financial outcomes are appropriate measures of the progress a company is making. The intent is to use the balanced scorecard (containing a carefully chosen combination of strategic and financial performance indicators tailored to the company's particular business) as a tool for managing strategy and measuring its effectiveness.

Four of the initial users of the balanced scorecard approach were money-losing operations that were trailing the industry. Each had new management teams that were implementing strategies that required market repositioning and becoming more customer-driven. All four needed to adopt a new set of cultural values and priorities as well as cost reduction measures. At these four companies, use of a balanced scorecard, consisting of both financial targets (the lag indicators) and strategic targets (the lead indicators of future financial performance), not only served as a vehicle for helping communicate the strategy to organization personnel but also caused the organization to become more strategy-focused.

During the past decade, growing numbers of companies have adopted a balanced scorecard approach, believing that a mix of financial and strategic performance targets is superior to a purely financial set of performance measures and that winning in the marketplace requires paying close attention to whether the company's present strategy is boosting its competitiveness and promoting the development of a sustainable competitive advantage.

core concept
A company exhibits *strategic intent* when it relentlessly pursues an ambitious strategic objective and concentrates its full resources and competitive actions on achieving that objective.

competing against key rivals and establish itself as a clear-cut winner in the marketplace, often against long odds.[5] A company's strategic intent can entail becoming the dominant company in the industry, unseating the existing industry leader, delivering the best customer service of any company in the industry (or the world), or turning a new technology into products capable of changing the way people work and live. Ambitious companies almost invariably begin with strategic intents that are out of proportion to their immediate capabilities and market positions. But they are undeterred by a grandiose objective that may take a sustained effort of 10 years or more to achieve. So intent are they on reaching the target that they set aggressive stretch objectives and pursue them relentlessly, sometimes even obsessively. Capably managed, up-and-coming enterprises with strategic intents exceeding their present reach and resources often prove to be more formidable competitors over time than larger cash-rich rivals with modest market ambitions. Nike's strategic intent during the 1960s was to overtake Adidas, which connected nicely with Nike's core purpose "to experience the emotion of competition, winning, and crushing competitors." Throughout the 1980s, Wal-Mart's strategic intent was to "overtake Sears" as the largest U.S. retailer (a feat accomplished in 1991). For some years, Toyota has been driving to overtake General Motors as the world's largest motor vehicle producer (and it surpassed Ford Motor Company in total vehicles sold in 2003, to rank in second place).

Sometimes a company's strategic intent serves as a rallying cry for managers and employees. When Yamaha overtook Honda in the motorcycle market, Honda responded with "*Yamaha wo tsubusu*" ("We will crush, squash, slaughter Yamaha"). Canon's strategic intent in copying equipment was to "beat Xerox." In the 1960s, Komatsu, Japan's leading earth-moving equipment company, had little market presence outside Japan, depended on its small bulldozers for most of its revenue, and was less than one-third the size of its U.S. rival Caterpillar. But Komatsu's strategic intent was to eventually "encircle Caterpillar" with a broader product line and then compete globally against Caterpillar—its motivating battle cry among managers and employees was "beat Caterpillar." By the late 1980s, Komatsu was the industry's second-ranking company, with a strong sales presence in North America, Europe, and Asia plus a product line that included industrial robots and semiconductors as well as a broad selection of earth-moving equipment.

The Need for Objectives at All Organizational Levels   Objective setting should not stop with top management's establishing of companywide performance targets. Company objectives need to be broken down into performance targets for each separate business, product line, functional department, and individual work unit. Company performance can't reach full potential unless each area of the organization does its part and contributes directly to the desired companywide outcomes and results. This means setting performance targets for each organization unit that support—rather than conflict with or negate—the achievement of companywide strategic and financial objectives.

The ideal situation is a team effort in which each organizational unit strives to produce results in its area of responsibility that contribute to the achievement of the company's performance targets and strategic vision. Such consistency signals that organizational units know their strategic role and are on board in helping the company move down the chosen strategic path and produce the desired results.

The Need for Top-Down Rather Than Bottom-Up Objective Setting
To appreciate why a company's objective-setting process needs to be more top-down than bottom-up, consider the following example: Suppose that the senior executives of a diversified corporation establish a corporate profit objective of $500 million for next year. Suppose further that, after discussion between corporate management and the general managers of the firm's five different businesses, each business is given a stretch profit objective of $100 million by year-end (i.e., if the five business divisions contribute $100 million each in profit, the corporation can reach its $500 million profit objective). A concrete result has thus been agreed on and translated into measurable action commitments at two levels in the managerial hierarchy. Next, suppose that the general manager of business unit A, after some analysis and discussion with functional area managers, concludes that reaching the $100 million profit objective will require selling 1 million units at an average price of $500 and producing them at an average cost of $400 (a $100 profit margin times 1 million units equals $100 million profit). Consequently, the general manager and the manufacturing manager settle on a production objective of 1 million units at a unit cost of $400, and the general manager and the marketing manager agree on a sales objective of 1 million units and a target selling price of $500. In turn, the marketing manager, after consultation with regional sales

32   Part 1 | Concepts and Techniques for Crafting and Executing Strategy

personnel, breaks the sales objective of 1 million units into unit sales targets for each sales territory, each item in the product line, and each salesperson. It is logical for organizationwide objectives and strategy to be established first so that they can guide objective setting and strategy making at lower levels.

A top-down process of setting objectives ensures that the financial and strategic performance targets established for business units, divisions, functional departments, and operating units are directly connected to the achievement of companywide objectives. This integration of objectives has two powerful advantages: (1) it helps produce *cohesion* among the objectives and strategies of different parts of the organization, and (2) it helps *unify internal efforts* to move the company along the chosen strategic path. Bottom-up objective setting, with little or no guidance from above, nearly always signals an absence of strategic leadership on the part of senior executives.

CRAFTING A STRATEGY: PHASE 3 OF THE STRATEGY-MAKING, STRATEGY-EXECUTING PROCESS

A company's senior executives obviously have important strategy-making roles. An enterprise's chief executive officer (CEO), as captain of the ship, carries the mantles of chief direction setter, chief objective setter, chief strategy maker, and chief strategy implementer for the total enterprise. Ultimate responsibility for *leading* the strategy-making, strategy-executing process rests with the CEO. In some enterprises the CEO or owner functions as strategic visionary and chief architect of strategy, personally deciding which of several strategic options to pursue, although senior managers and key employees may well assist with gathering and analyzing background data and advising the CEO on which way to go. Such an approach to strategy development is characteristic of small owner-managed companies and sometimes large corporations that have been founded by the present CEO—Michael Dell at Dell Computer, Bill Gates at Microsoft, and Howard Schultz at Starbucks are prominent examples of corporate CEOs who exert a heavy hand in shaping their company's strategy.

In most companies, however, the heads of business divisions and major product lines; the chief financial officer; and vice presidents (VPs) for production, marketing, human resources, and other functional departments have influential strategy-making roles. Normally, a company's chief financial officer is in charge of devising and implementing an appropriate financial strategy; the production VP takes the lead in developing and executing the company's production strategy; the marketing VP orchestrates sales and marketing strategy; a brand manager is in charge of the strategy for a particular brand in the company's product lineup, and so on.

But it is a mistake to view strategy-making as exclusively a top management function, the province of owner-entrepreneurs, CEOs, and other senior executives. The more wide-ranging a company's operations are, the more that strategy making is a collaborative team effort involving managers (and sometimes key employees) down through the whole organizational hierarchy. Take a company like Toshiba—a $43 billion corporation with 300 subsidiaries, thousands of products, and operations extending across the world. It would be a far-fetched error to assume that a few senior executives in Toshiba headquarters have either the expertise or a sufficiently detailed understanding of all the relevant factors to wisely craft all the strategic initiatives taken in Toshiba's numerous and diverse organizational units. Rather, it takes

core concept

Every company manager has a strategy-making, strategy-executing role—it is flawed thinking to look on the tasks of managing strategy as something only high-level managers do.

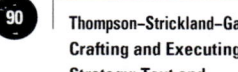
involvement on the part of Toshiba's whole management team to craft and execute the thousands of strategic initiatives that constitute the whole of Toshiba's strategy.

Major organizational units in a company—business divisions, product groups, functional departments, plants, geographic offices, distribution centers—normally have a leading or supporting role in the company's strategic game plan. Because senior executives in the corporate office seldom know enough about the situation in every geographic area and operating unit to direct every strategic move made in the field, it is common practice for top-level managers to delegate strategy-making authority to middle- and lower-echelon managers who head the organizational subunits where specific strategic results must be achieved. The more that a company's operations cut across different products, industries, and geographical areas, the more that headquarters executives are prone to delegate considerable strategy-making authority to on-the-scene personnel who have firsthand knowledge of customer requirements, can better evaluate market opportunities, and are better able to keep the strategy responsive to changing market and competitive conditions. While managers farther down in the managerial hierarchy obviously have a narrower, more specific strategy-making, strategy-executing role than managers closer to the top, the important understanding here is that in most of today's companies *every company manager typically has a strategy-making, strategy-executing role—ranging from minor to major—for the area he or she heads.* Hence, the notion that an organization's strategists are at the top of the management hierarchy and that midlevel and frontline managers and employees merely carry out their directives is misguided.

With decentralized decision making becoming common at companies of all stripes, it is now typical for key pieces of a company's strategy to originate in a company's middle and lower ranks.[6] For example, in a recent year, Electronic Data Systems conducted a yearlong strategy review involving 2,500 of its 55,000 employees and coordinated by a core of 150 managers and staffers from all over the world.[7] J. M. Smucker Company, well known for its jams and jellies, formed a team of 140 employees (7 percent of its 2,000-person workforce) who spent 25 percent of their time over a six-month period looking for ways to rejuvenate the company's growth. Involving teams of people to dissect complex situations and come up with strategic solutions is becoming increasingly necessary in many businesses. Not only are many strategic issues too far-reaching or too involved for a single manager to handle, but they often cut across functional areas and departments, thus requiring the contributions of many disciplinary experts and the collaboration of managers from different parts of the organization. A valuable strength of collaborative strategy making is that the group of people charged with crafting the strategy can easily include the very people who will also be charged with implementing and executing it. Giving people an influential stake in crafting the strategy they must later help implement and execute not only builds motivation and commitment but also allows them to be held accountable for putting the strategy into place and making it work—the oft-used excuse of "It wasn't my idea to do this" won't fly.

In some companies, top management makes a regular practice of encouraging individuals and teams to develop and champion proposals for new product lines and new business ventures. The idea is to unleash the talents and energies of promising "corporate intrapreneurs," letting them try out untested business ideas and giving them the room to pursue new strategic initiatives. Executives serve as judges of which proposals merit support, give company intrapreneurs the needed organizational and budgetary support, and let them run with the ball. Thus, important pieces of company strategy originate with those intrapreneuring individuals and teams who succeed in championing a proposal through the approval stage and then end up being charged with the lead role in launching new products, overseeing the company's entry into new geographic markets, or heading up new business ventures. W. L. Gore and Associates, a privately owned company famous for its Gore-Tex waterproofing film, is an avid and highly successful practitioner of the corporate intrapreneur approach to strategy making. Gore expects all employees to initiate improvements and to display innovativeness. Each employee's intrapreneuring contributions are prime considerations in determining raises, stock option bonuses, and promotions. W. L. Gore's commitment to intrapreneuring has produced a stream of product innovations and new strategic initiatives that has kept the company vibrant and growing for nearly two decades.

The Strategy-Making Pyramid

It thus follows that *a company's overall strategy is really a collection of strategic initiatives and actions* devised by managers and key employees up and down the whole organizational hierarchy. The larger and more diverse the operations of an enterprise, the more points of strategic initiative it has and the more managers and employees at more levels of management that have a relevant strategy-making role. Figure 2.2 shows who is generally responsible for devising what pieces of a company's overall strategy.

In diversified, multibusiness companies where the strategies of several different businesses have to be managed, the strategy-making task involves four distinct types or levels of strategy, each of which involves different facets of the company's overall strategy:

1. *Corporate strategy* consists of the kinds of initiatives the company uses to establish business positions in different industries, the approaches corporate executives pursue to boost the combined performance of the set of businesses the company has diversified into, and the means of capturing cross-business synergies and turning them into competitive advantage. Senior corporate executives normally have lead responsibility for devising corporate strategy and for choosing among whatever recommended actions bubble up from the organization below. Key business-unit heads may also be influential, especially in strategic decisions affecting the businesses they head. Major strategic decisions are usually reviewed and approved by the company's board of directors. We will look deeper into the strategy-making process at diversified companies when we get to Chapter 9.

2. *Business strategy* concerns the actions and the approaches crafted to produce successful performance in one specific line of business. The key focus here is crafting responses to changing market circumstances and initiating actions to strengthen market position, build competitive advantage, and develop strong competitive capabilities. Orchestrating the development of business-level strategy is the responsibility of the manager in charge of the business. The business head has at least two other strategy-related roles: (1) seeing that lower-level strategies are well conceived, consistent with each other, and adequately matched to the overall business strategy, and (2) getting major business-level strategic moves approved by corporate-level officers (and sometimes the board of directors) and keeping them informed of market developments and emerging strategic issues. In diversified companies, business-unit heads may have the additional obligation of making sure business-level objectives and strategy conform to corporate-level objectives and strategy themes.

figure 2.2   **A Company's Strategy-Making Hierarchy**

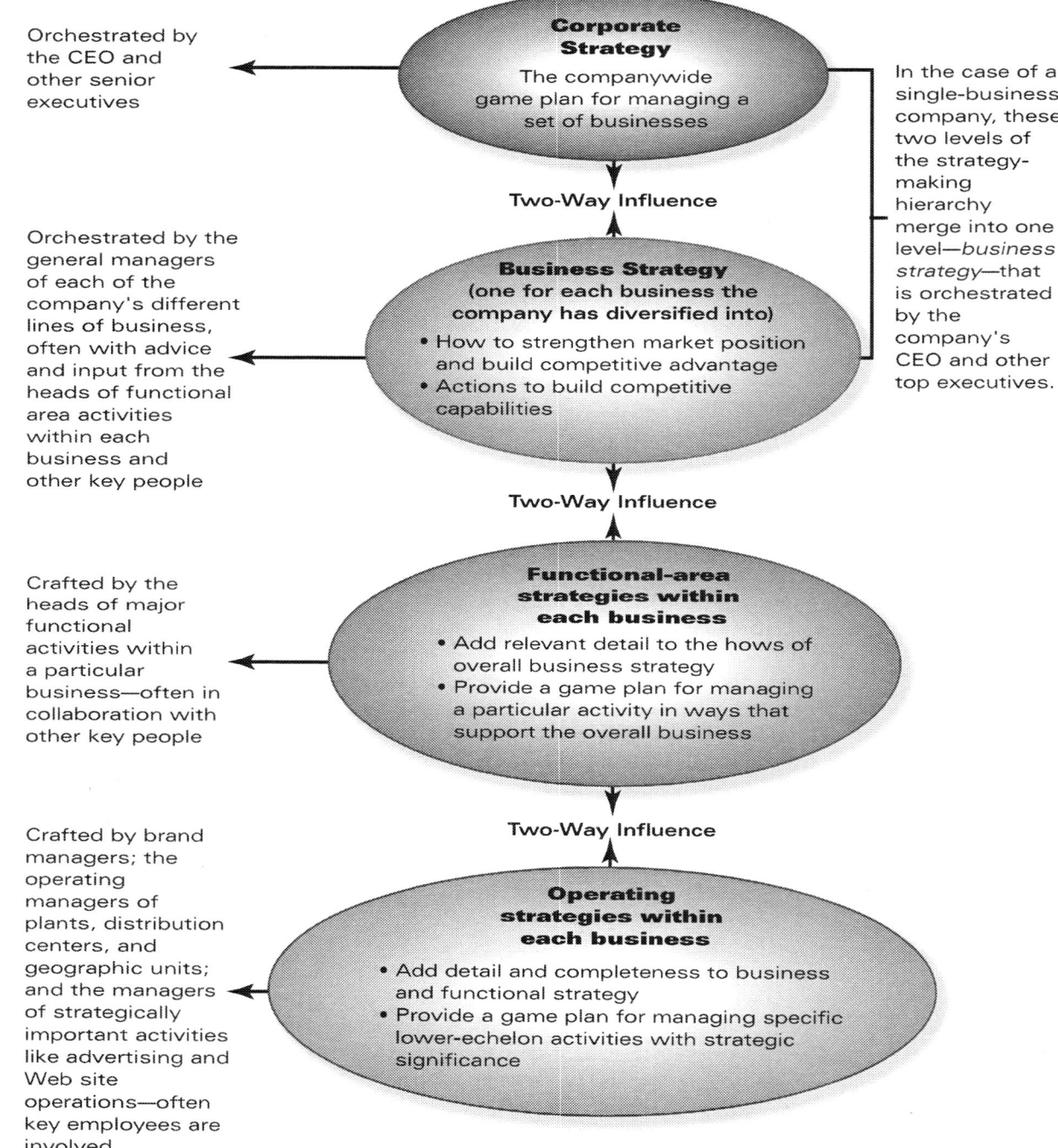

Orchestrated by the CEO and other senior executives

Corporate Strategy
The companywide game plan for managing a set of businesses

In the case of a single-business company, these two levels of the strategy-making hierarchy merge into one level—*business strategy*—that is orchestrated by the company's CEO and other top executives.

Two-Way Influence

Orchestrated by the general managers of each of the company's different lines of business, often with advice and input from the heads of functional area activities within each business and other key people

Business Strategy
(one for each business the company has diversified into)
• How to strengthen market position and build competitive advantage
• Actions to build competitive capabilities

Two-Way Influence

Crafted by the heads of major functional activities within a particular business—often in collaboration with other key people

Functional-area strategies within each business
• Add relevant detail to the hows of overall business strategy
• Provide a game plan for managing a particular activity in ways that support the overall business

Two-Way Influence

Crafted by brand managers; the operating managers of plants, distribution centers, and geographic units; and the managers of strategically important activities like advertising and Web site operations—often key employees are involved

Operating strategies within each business
• Add detail and completeness to business and functional strategy
• Provide a game plan for managing specific lower-echelon activities with strategic significance

3. *Functional-area strategies* concern the actions, approaches, and practices to be employed in managing particular functions or business processes or key activities within a business. A company's marketing strategy, for example, represents the managerial game plan for running the sales and marketing part of the business. A company's new product development strategy represents the managerial game plan for keeping the company's product lineup fresh and in tune with what buyers are looking for. Functional-area strategies add specifics to the hows of business-level strategy. Plus, they aim at establishing or strengthening a business unit's competencies and capabilities in performing strategy-critical activities so as to enhance the business's market position and standing with customers. The primary role of a functional-area strategy is to *support* the company's overall business strategy and competitive approach.

Lead responsibility for functional-area strategies within a business is normally delegated to the heads of the respective functions, with the general manager of the business having final approval and perhaps even exerting a strong influence over the content of particular pieces of functional-area strategies. To some extent, functional managers have to collaborate and coordinate their strategy-making efforts to avoid uncoordinated or conflicting strategies. For the overall business strategy to have maximum impact, a business's marketing strategy, production strategy, finance strategy, customer service strategy, new product development strategy, and human resources strategy should be compatible and mutually reinforcing rather than serving their own narrower purposes. If inconsistent functional-area strategies are sent up the line for final approval, the business head is responsible for spotting the conflicts and getting them resolved.

4. *Operating strategies* concern the relatively narrow strategic initiatives and approaches for managing key operating units (plants, distribution centers, geographic units) and specific operating activities with strategic significance (advertising campaigns, the management of specific brands, supply chain–related activities, and Web site sales and operations). A plant manager needs a strategy for accomplishing the plant's objectives, carrying out the plant's part of the company's overall manufacturing game plan, and dealing with any strategy-related problems that exist at the plant. A company's advertising manager needs a strategy for getting maximum audience exposure and sales impact from the ad budget. Operating strategies, while of limited scope, add further detail and completeness to functional-area strategies and to the overall business strategy. Lead responsibility for operating strategies is usually delegated to frontline managers, subject to review and approval by higher-ranking managers.

Even though operating strategy is at the bottom of the strategy-making hierarchy, its importance should not be downplayed. A major plant that fails in its strategy to achieve production volume, unit cost, and quality targets can undercut the achievement of company sales and profit objectives and wreak havoc with strategic efforts to build a quality image with customers. Frontline managers are thus an important part of an organization's strategy-making team because many operating units have strategy-critical performance targets and need to have strategic action plans in place to achieve them. One cannot reliably judge the strategic importance of a given action simply by the strategy level or location within the managerial hierarchy where it is initiated.

In single-business enterprises, the corporate and business levels of strategy making merge into one level—business strategy—because the strategy for the whole company involves only one distinct line of business. Thus, a single-business enterprise has only three levels of strategy: (1) business strategy for the company as a whole, (2) functional-area strategies for each main area within the business, and (3) operating strategies undertaken by lower-echelon managers to flesh out strategically significant aspects for the company's business and functional area strategies. Proprietorships, partnerships, and owner-managed enterprises may have only one or two strategy-making levels since in small-scale enterprises the whole strategy-making, strategy-executing function can be handled by just a few key people.

Uniting the Strategy-Making Effort

Ideally, the pieces and layers of a company's strategy should fit together like a jigsaw puzzle. To achieve this unity, the strategizing process generally has proceeded from the corporate level to the business level and then from the business level to the functional and operating levels. *Midlevel and frontline managers cannot do good strategy making without understanding the company's long-term direction and higher-level strategies.* The strategic disarray that occurs in an organization when senior managers don't set forth a clearly articulated companywide strategy is akin to what would happen to a football team's offensive performance if the quarterback decided not to call a play for the team but instead let each player pick whatever play he thought would work best at his respective position. In business, as in sports, all the strategy makers in a company are on the same team and the many different pieces of the overall strategy crafted at various organizational levels need to be in sync and united. Anything less than a unified collection of strategies weakens company performance.

> **core concept**
> A company's strategy is at full power only when its many pieces are united.

Achieving unity in strategy making is partly a function of communicating the company's basic strategy themes effectively across the whole organization and establishing clear strategic principles and guidelines for lower-level strategy making. Cohesive strategy making down through the hierarchy becomes easier to achieve when company strategy is distilled into pithy, easy-to-grasp terminology that can be used to drive consistent strategic action throughout the company.[8] The greater the numbers of company personnel who know, understand, and buy in to the company's basic direction and strategy, the smaller the risk that people and organization units will go off in conflicting strategic directions when decision making is pushed down to frontline levels and many people are given a strategy-making role. Good communication of strategic themes and guiding principles thus serves a valuable strategy-unifying purpose.

Merging the Strategic Vision, Objectives, and Strategy into a Strategic Plan

Developing a strategic vision, setting objectives, and crafting a strategy are basic direction-setting tasks. They map out the company's direction, its short-range and long-range performance targets, and the competitive moves and internal action approaches to be used in achieving the targeted business results. Together, they constitute a **strategic plan** for coping with industry and competitive conditions, the expected actions of the industry's key players, and the challenges and issues that stand as obstacles to the company's success.[9]

> **core concept**
> A company's **strategic plan** lays out its future direction, performance targets, and strategy.

In companies committed to regular strategy reviews and the development of explicit strategic plans, the strategic plan may take the form of a written document that is circulated to managers (and perhaps to selected employees). In small privately owned companies, strategic plans exist mostly in the form of oral understandings and commitments among managers and key employees about where to head, what to accomplish, and how to proceed. Short-term performance targets are the part of the strategic plan most often spelled out explicitly and communicated to managers and employees. A number of companies summarize key elements of their strategic plans in the company's annual report to shareholders, in postings on their Web site, in press releases, or in statements provided to the business media. Other companies, perhaps for reasons of competitive sensitivity, make only vague, general statements about their strategic plans that could apply to most any company.

IMPLEMENTING AND EXECUTING THE STRATEGY: PHASE 4 OF THE STRATEGY-MAKING, STRATEGY-EXECUTING PROCESS

Managing strategy implementation and execution is an operations-oriented, make-things-happen activity aimed at shaping the performance of core business activities in a strategy-supportive manner. It is easily the most demanding and time-consuming part of the strategy-management process. To convert strategic plans into actions and results, a manager must be able to direct organizational change, motivate people, build and strengthen company competencies and competitive capabilities, create a strategy-supportive work climate, and meet or beat performance targets.

Management's action agenda for implementing and executing the chosen strategy emerges from assessing what the company, given its particular operating practices and organizational circumstances, will have to do differently or better to execute the strategy proficiently and achieve the targeted performance. Each company manager has to think through the answer to "What has to be done in my area to execute my piece of the strategic plan, and what actions should I take to get the process under way?" How much internal change is needed depends on how much of the strategy is new, how far internal practices and competencies deviate from what the strategy requires, and how well the present work climate/culture supports good strategy execution. Depending on the amount of internal change involved, full implementation and proficient execution of company strategy (or important new pieces thereof) can take several months to several years.

In most situations, managing the strategy-execution process includes the following principal aspects:

- Staffing the organization with the needed skills and expertise, consciously building and strengthening strategy-supportive competencies and competitive capabilities, and organizing the work effort.
- Developing budgets that steer ample resources into those activities critical to strategic success.
- Ensuring that policies and operating procedures facilitate rather than impede effective execution.
- Using the best-known practices to perform core business activities and pushing for continuous improvement. Organizational units have to periodically reassess how things are being done and diligently pursue useful changes and improvements in how the strategy is being executed.
- Installing information and operating systems that enable company personnel to better carry out their strategic roles day in and day out.

- Motivating people to pursue the target objectives energetically and, if need be, modifying their duties and job behavior to better fit the requirements of successful strategy execution.
- Tying rewards and incentives directly to the achievement of performance objectives and good strategy execution.
- Creating a company culture and work climate conducive to successful strategy implementation and execution.
- Exerting the internal leadership needed to drive implementation forward and keep improving strategy execution. When the organization encounters stumbling blocks or weaknesses, management has to see that they are addressed and rectified quickly.

Good strategy execution involves creating strong "fits" between strategy and organizational capabilities, between strategy and the reward structure, between strategy and internal operating systems, and between strategy and the organization's work climate and culture. The stronger these fits—that is, the more that the company's capabilities, reward structure, internal operating systems, and culture facilitate and promote proficient strategy execution—the better the execution and the higher the company's odds of achieving its performance targets. Furthermore, deliberately shaping the performance of core business activities around the strategy helps unite the organization.

INITIATING CORRECTIVE ADJUSTMENTS: PHASE 5 OF THE STRATEGY-MAKING, STRATEGY-EXECUTING PROCESS

The fifth phase of the strategy-management process—evaluating the company's progress, assessing the impact of new external developments, and making corrective adjustments—is the trigger point for deciding whether to continue or change the company's vision, objectives, strategy, and/or strategy-execution methods. So long as the company's direction and strategy seem well matched to industry and competitive conditions and performance targets are being met, company executives may decide to stay the course. Simply fine-tuning the strategic plan and continuing with ongoing efforts to improve strategy execution are sufficient.

But whenever a company encounters disruptive changes in its external environment, questions need to be raised about the appropriateness of its direction and strategy. If a company experiences a downturn in its market position or shortfalls in performance, then company managers are obligated to ferret out whether the causes relate to poor strategy, poor execution, or both and then to take timely corrective action. A company's direction, objectives, and strategy have to be revisited anytime external or internal conditions warrant. It is to be expected that a company will modify its strategic vision, direction, objectives, and strategy over time.

Likewise, it is not unusual for a company to find that one or more aspects of implementing and executing the strategy are not going as well as intended. Proficient strategy execution is always the product of much organizational learning. It is achieved unevenly—coming quickly in some areas and proving nettlesome and problematic in

> **core concept**
> A company's vision, objectives, strategy, and approach to strategy execution are never final; managing strategy is an ongoing process, not an every now and then task.

others. Periodically assessing what aspects of strategy execution are working well and what needs improving is normal and desirable. Successful strategy execution entails vigilantly searching for ways *to continuously improve* and then making corrective adjustments whenever and wherever it is useful to do so.

CORPORATE GOVERNANCE: THE ROLE OF THE BOARD OF DIRECTORS IN THE STRATEGY-MAKING, STRATEGY-EXECUTING PROCESS

Although senior managers have *lead responsibility* for crafting and executing a company's strategy, it is the duty of the board of directors to exercise strong oversight and see that the five tasks of strategic management are done in a manner that benefits shareholders (in the case of investor-owned enterprises) or stakeholders (in the case of not-for-profit organizations). In watching over management's strategy-making, strategy-executing actions and making sure that executive actions are not only proper but also aligned with the interests of stakeholders, a company's board of directors have three obligations to fulfill:

1. *Be inquiring critics and overseers.* Board members must ask probing questions and draw on their business acumen to make independent judgments about whether strategy proposals have been adequately analyzed and whether proposed strategic actions appear to have greater promise than alternatives. If executive management is bringing well-supported and reasoned strategy proposals to the board, there's little reason for board members to aggressively challenge and try to pick apart everything put before them. Asking incisive questions is usually sufficient to test whether the case for management's proposals is compelling and to exercise vigilant oversight. However, when the company's strategy is failing or is plagued with faulty execution, and certainly when there is a precipitous collapse in profitability, board members have a duty to be proactive, expressing their concerns about the validity of the strategy and/or operating methods, initiating debate about the company's strategic path, having one-on-one discussions with key executives and other board members, and perhaps directly intervening as a group to alter the company's executive leadership and, ultimately, its strategy and business approaches.

2. *Evaluate the caliber of senior executives' strategy-making and strategy-executing skills.* The board is always responsible for determining whether the current CEO is doing a good job of strategic leadership (as a basis for awarding salary increases and bonuses and deciding on retention or removal). Boards must also exercise due diligence in evaluating the strategic leadership skills of other senior executives in line to succeed the CEO. When the incumbent CEO steps down or leaves for a position elsewhere, the board must elect a successor, either going with an insider or deciding that an outsider is needed to perhaps radically change the company's strategic course.

3. *Institute a compensation plan for top executives that rewards them for actions and results that serve stakeholder interests, and most especially those of shareholders.* A basic principle of corporate governance is that the owners of a corporation delegate operating authority and managerial control to top management in return for compensation. In their role as an agent of shareholders, top executives have a clear and unequivocal *duty* to make decisions and operate the company in accord with shareholder interests (but this does not mean disregarding the interests of other stakeholders, par-

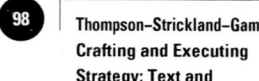
ticularly those of employees, with whom they also have an agency relationship). Most boards of directors have a compensation committee, composed entirely of outside directors, to develop a salary and incentive compensation plan that makes it in the self-interest of executives to operate the business in a manner that benefits the owners; the compensation committee's recommendations are presented to the full board for approval. But in addition to creating compensation plans intended to align executive actions with owner interests, it is incumbent on the board of directors to put a halt to self-serving executive perks and privileges that simply enrich the personal welfare of executives. Numerous media reports have recounted instances in which boards of directors have gone along with opportunistic executive efforts to secure excessive, if not downright obscene, compensation of one kind or another (multimillion-dollar interest-free loans, personal use of corporate aircraft, lucrative severance and retirement packages, outsized stock incentive awards, and so on).

The number of prominent companies that have fallen on hard times because of the actions of scurrilous or out-of-control CEOs, the growing propensity of disgruntled stockholders to file lawsuits alleging director negligence, and the escalating costs of liability insurance for directors all underscore the responsibility that a board of directors has for overseeing a company's strategy-making, strategy-executing process and ensuring that management actions are proper and responsible. Moreover, holders of large blocks of shares (mutual funds and pension funds), regulatory authorities, and the financial press consistently urge that board members, especially outside directors, be active and diligent in their oversight of company strategy and maintain a tight rein on executive actions.

Every corporation should have a strong, independent board of directors that has the courage to curb management actions they believe are inappropriate or unduly risky.[10] Boards of directors that lack the backbone to challenge a strong-willed or "imperial" CEO or that rubber-stamp most anything the CEO recommends without probing inquiry and debate (perhaps because the board is stacked with the CEO's cronies) abdicate their duty to represent shareholder interests. The whole fabric of effective corporate governance is undermined when boards of directors shirk their responsibility to maintain ultimate control over the company's strategic direction, the major elements of its strategy, and the business approaches management is using to implement and execute the strategy. Boards of directors thus have a very important oversight role in the strategy-making, strategy-executing process.

key points

The managerial process of crafting and executing a company's strategy consists of five interrelated and integrated tasks:

1. *Developing a strategic vision of where the company needs to head and what its product-market-customer-technology focus should be.* The vision must provide long-term direction, infuse the organization with a sense of purposeful action, and communicate to stakeholders what management's aspirations for the company are.

2. *Setting objectives.* The role of objectives is to convert the strategic vision into specific performance outcomes for the company to achieve. Objectives need to spell out *how much* of *what kind* of performance *by when*, and they need to require a significant amount of organizational stretch. A balanced scorecard approach to measuring company performance entails setting both *financial objectives* and

strategic objectives. Judging how well a company is doing by its financial performance is not enough—financial outcomes are "lagging indicators" that reflect the impacts of past decisions and organizational activities. But the "lead indicators" of a company's future financial performance are its current achievement of strategic targets that indicate a company is strengthening its marketing standing, competitive vitality, and business prospects.

3. *Crafting a strategy to achieve the desired outcomes and move the company toward where it wants to go.* Crafting strategy is concerned principally with forming responses to changes under way in the external environment, devising competitive moves and market approaches aimed at producing sustainable competitive advantage, building competitively valuable competencies and capabilities, and uniting the strategic actions initiated in various parts of the company. The more wide-ranging a company's operations, the more that strategy making is a team effort. The overall strategy that emerges in such companies is really a collection of strategic actions and business approaches initiated partly by senior company executives, partly by the heads of major business divisions, partly by functional-area managers, and partly by operating managers on the frontlines. The larger and more diverse the operations of an enterprise, the more points of strategic initiative it has and the more managers and employees at more levels of management that have a relevant strategy-making role. A single business enterprise has three levels of strategy—business strategy for the company as a whole, functional-area strategies for each main area within the business, and operating strategies undertaken by lower-echelon managers to flesh out strategically significant aspects for the company's business and functional area strategies. In diversified, multibusiness companies, the strategy-making task involves four distinct types or levels of strategy: corporate strategy for the company as a whole, business strategy (one for each business the company has diversified into), functional-area strategies within each business, and operating strategies. Typically, the strategy-making task is more top-down than bottom-up, with higher-level strategies serving as the guide for developing lower-level strategies.

4. *Implementing and executing the chosen strategy efficiently and effectively.* Managing the implementation and execution of strategy is an operations-oriented, make-things-happen activity aimed at shaping the performance of core business activities in a strategy-supportive manner. Converting a company's strategy into actions and results tests a manager's ability to direct organizational change, motivate people with a reward and incentive compensation system tied to good strategy execution and the achievement of target outcomes, build and strengthen company competencies and competitive capabilities, create a strategy-supportive work climate, and deliver the desired results. The quality of a company's operational excellence in executing the chosen strategy is a major driver of how well the company ultimately performs.

5. *Evaluating performance and initiating corrective adjustments in vision, long-term direction, objectives, strategy, or execution in light of actual experience, changing conditions, new ideas, and new opportunities.* This phase of the strategy management process is the trigger point for deciding whether to continue or change the company's vision, objectives, strategy, and/or strategy execution methods. Sometimes it suffices to simply fine-tune the strategic plan and continue with efforts to improve strategy execution. At other times, major overhauls are required.

Developing a strategic vision and mission, setting objectives, and crafting a strategy are basic direction-setting tasks; together, they constitute a *strategic plan* for coping with industry and competitive conditions, the actions of rivals, and the challenges and issues that stand as obstacles to the company's success.

Boards of directors have a duty to shareholders to play a vigilant supervisory role in a company's strategy-making, strategy-executing process. They are obligated to (1) critically appraise and ultimately approve strategic action plans, (2) evaluate the strategic leadership skills of the CEO and others in line to succeed the incumbent CEO, and (3) institute a compensation plan for top executives that rewards them for actions and results that serve stakeholder interests, and most especially those of shareholders. Boards of directors that are not aggressive and forceful in fulfilling these responsibilities undermine the fabric of effective corporate governance.

exercise

1. Go to the investors section of www.heinz.com and read the letter to the shareholders in the company's fiscal 2003 annual report. Is the vision for Heinz articulated by Chairman and CEO William R. Johnson sufficiently clear and well defined? Why or why not? Are the company's objectives well stated and seemingly appropriate? What about the strategy that Johnson outlines for the company? If you were a shareholder, would you be satisfied with what Johnson has told you about the company's direction, performance targets, and strategy?

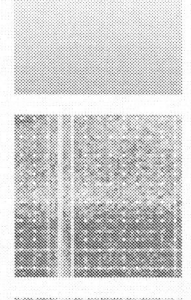
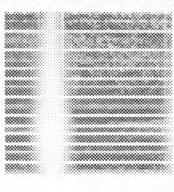
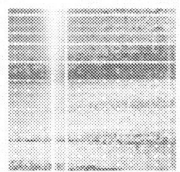

Part 3

Strategy analysis

Part contents

In this part you will find the following chapters:

Introduction

Part 2 set up the economic logic that gives us the tools for analysing and formulating strategy. The key concept introduced here is essentially the logic of competitive advantage supported by specific frameworks such as industry analysis, generic strategies and the value chain. The strength of these concepts lies in the way of thinking about strategy. These are intellectual constructs – they are not cookbooks into which one uncritically feeds data. They apply in different ways to different contexts. By themselves they have limited interest. Their value lies in the way in which they can be applied in different circumstances. Part 3 contains a variety of different contexts for which specific strategies have to be formulated.

Chapter 6 articulates the nature of strategic positioning. We call this the market-based view and others have called it the activity-based view. What strategic positioning is about is what activities have to be pursued in chosen markets so as to gain competitive advantage. Positioning is about the deployment of cost and differentiation-based advantages. It is about the identification of distinctive cost strategies and distinctive differentiation strategies. In practice we see the need for detailed analysis of markets and industries, first, to see what the 'rules' are and how to play them but, second (hopefully) to see how we might innovate with our strategies so as to break the rules and get ahead. In industry terms this means understanding how we can be better than our competitors. In market terms it means understanding what the customer wants. Strategy is about value creation and value analysis is an important element of this chapter.

Chapter 7 steps back into the firm and asks what capabilities are needed for the desired positioning to be achieved. This has become known as the resource-based view often captured in the term 'core competence'. This approach to strategy has become very widespread but suffers from a high degree of subjectivity and lack of agreement about terminology and definitions. This chapter sets out to review some of the main contributions and to indicate a basic language to which we might all subscribe. Core competence, like competitive advantage, is an intellectual construct that is useful because it can be deployed in a wide range of situations. The chapter goes on to examine how competence-based competition can be conducted in practice and suggests some practical ways of relating these ideas to value creation.

Following Chapters 6 and 7 we should now have the ability to develop our own strategic theory of the firm comprising both a view of competitive advantage and core competence *and* the way in which they support and complement each other.

Chapter 8 adds a number of important practical dimensions to the strategic theory that has come from Chapters 6 and 7. Basically it introduces the timeline in the form of life cycle analysis – a notable deficiency of Porter-style work is its static character with only a nodding acknowledgement of the importance of dynamics. In exploring different parts of the time line, going from embryonic stages to decline, the chapter picks out some salient issues. First, we discuss entrepreneurs and start-ups – individualism and idiosyncrasy of both people and events but subject to some overarching strategy context. Second, we examine entry strategies, where we look at the extraordinary difficulty of gaining a foothold in attractive industries in the teeth of organized opposition. Third, we look at turnarounds. These come about typically (but not exclusively) when differentiation advantages have been competed away, the strategy is worn out, and performance is not acceptable. This chapter sets out to put strategic thinking into practical contexts, suggesting as we go along how elements such as personal leadership may be crucial.

Chapter 9 shifts the focus from the single business to the multibusiness portfolio. This is the arena of corporate strategy where the task of the corporate centre is to choose what portfolio it wants and to design and manage the organization structure and its management processes. There are other key tasks: the mission statement and the choice of strategic objectives are discussed in Chapter 1. Managing performance is mentioned in many places but Chapter 18 is devoted to the analysis and measurement of performance. In Chapter 9 the key issue is the way in which the portfolio creates value. This revolves around the economies of scope that we introduced and discussed in Part 2, often called synergy by practitioners and relatedness by analysts and academics. Depending on how synergies arise, there are implications for the fit of strategy and structure and for the styles by which the organization is managed. These are discussed in Chapter 9 and also recur throughout Part 4.

Chapter 10 continues the corporate-level theme with mergers and acquisitions (M&A). These are the biggest and riskiest decisions that most companies make. Mistakes can destroy a company but companies can also grow and prosper very quickly. This chapter lays out the context for M&A decisions and explores in some detail the planning of an acquisition and then its implementation. M&A is a highly controversial area: the risks are very high, the rewards are enticing, but the track record of companies is very varied with perhaps more glaring failures than conspicuous successes. But remember that we said strategy is about risk – a theme we return to in Chapter 14.

Chapter 11 introduces the international domain. This again is controversial and risky (you should be getting used to the idea that these are defining characteristics of strategy) because of the difficulties inherent in moving out of one's home base to international markets and to international suppliers. Globalization is presented in its specialized meaning as global standardization (e.g. the 'world car'). This forms the basis for discussion of the two contrasting strategies of global standardization versus local differentiation. These are a replay of our old friends cost and efficiency on one hand, and differentiation on the other. Not surprisingly, therefore, there is the possibility of combining globalization and localization into a joint approach characterized as 'transnational'. Some think this is just a theoretical possibility but it has led to widespread discussion about the nature of the multinational firm. The chapter concludes with a profile of the 'flagship firm', a concept originated by Alan Rugman in which he portrays how some international firms can sit at the nexus of opposing forces – international versus local forces, global customers versus global suppliers, and different host governments. Overall the theme for the international company is how to blend and balance host-country-specific advantages (CSAs) with firm-specific advantages (FSAs).

Chapter 12 uses the 'new economy' as a rallying cry. This rests on the observation that information technology and knowledge intensity, driven by highly successful R&D programmes over the last forty years, have transformed the cost conditions and demand conditions to which we became accustomed on the old manufacturing-based economy. Cost structures have become predominantly fixed cost in nature with vanishingly small variable costs. Markets have been transformed by the flood of new products that have redefined the elements of consumer leisure time and the patterns of consumer expenditure. Also significant (but quite how much is not yet known) is the emergence of a consumer phenomenon based on standardization and complementarity.[1] Customers increasingly and consciously buy products that conform to known standards and that technically complement their existing products and the products that other people have (one buys a new 'Wintel' computer because your Windows-based software and that of your friends will run on it). This means that we are increasingly buying products because other people have them.[2] It also results in very large, quasi-monopolistic market positions for some companies (e.g. Microsoft), dependency positions for others so that, for example, one is obliged to buy Microsoft's operating systems, and expensive market failures for others (On-Digital versus BSkyB). Business risk has risen markedly in these conditions. Strategies have to be adapted to these specific conditions. Maybe, also, these industries are becoming a bigger proportion of the whole economy. Chapter 12 and some of the case studies at the end of the book discuss the reasons why these new economy characteristics have taken hold and indicates how new economy strategies represent significant adaptations to the strategies common in the traditional manufacturing economy.

The chapters cover the areas depicted below in the strategy resources concepts map and the strategy process concepts map (introduced in Chapters 1 and 2 of this book). The shaded boxes represent the primary focuses of this part of the book. The non-shaded boxes are covered in other parts of this book. The degree of shading in the boxes reflects the degree to which these topics are covered here and also indicates the interconnections explored in each chapter.

The maps show that this section concentrates heavily on resource concepts but only lightly on process concepts. Notably this section says little about 'direction', taking it largely for granted and leaving it mainly to the introduction in Part 1 and to the discussions in Part 5. Throughout this part there are references and allusions to process issues. Sometimes the organization structure issues are covered in some depth. Overall, however, process issues are covered in detail in Part 4 but the allusions herein are important in setting the stage.

---

[1] Strictly speaking it is a re-emergence: it was well known back in the nineteenth century as a characteristic of utilities (e.g. railways and the telegraph) but in a sense was forgotten as manufacturing-style cost conditions became pervasive in the twentieth century.

[2] This is characteristic of fashion products as well, where the benefit is psychological rather than practical.

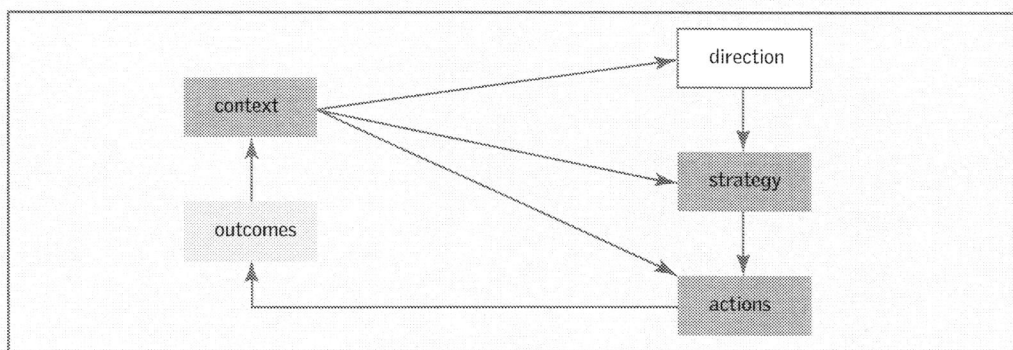

Figure 1.6 Strategy resources concepts map

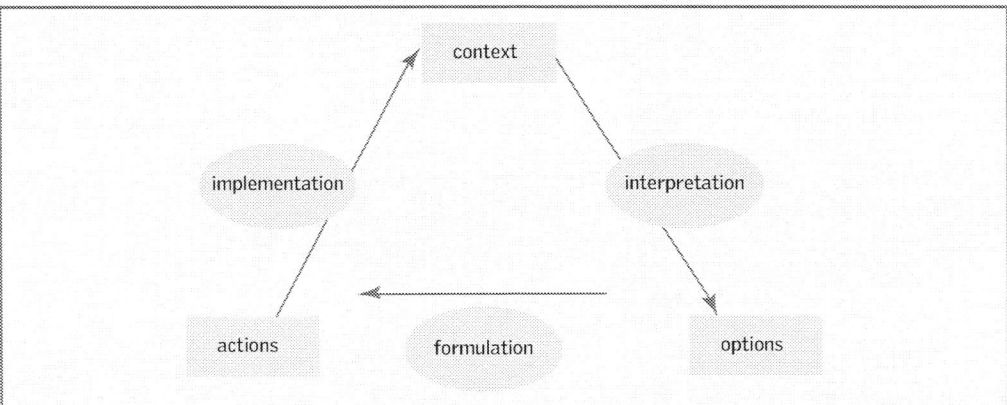

Figure 2.2 Strategy process concepts map

McGee–Thomas–Wilson:
Strategy: Analysis and
Practice, Text and Cases

6. Competitive strategy: the
analysis of strategic
position

Text

© The McGraw–Hill
Companies, 2006

107

Chapter 6

Competitive strategy: the analysis of strategic position

Chapter contents

Introduction

This chapter sets out the essence of strategy as the denial of perfect competition and the search for firm-specific advantages that we call competitive advantage. Chapter 3 developed the economic concepts that underpin the operation of markets. These concepts give us the frameworks and the language for analysing markets and costs. Chapter 4 set out the large-scale macro forces that can shape the fortunes of firms. In Chapter 5 we saw the fundamental importance of the idea of competitive advantage. In this chapter we set out the basic framework of competitive strategy and how it enables us to analyse the market-based view that is, as its name suggests, the positioning of the firm in its markets versus competitors. The central pillar of this is *competitive advantage*. Chapter 8 presents the *resource-based view*.

This focuses on the distinctive nature of the resources and capabilities that are required to produce competitive advantage. The central pillar of this is *core competence*. Chapter 8 concludes by relating the ideas of competitive advantage and core competence to managerial tools such as SWOT analysis, PEST analysis, and critical success factor analysis.

Much of this chapter is built upon Porter's original description (1980) of generic competitive strategies, where strategies are characterized as being cost or differentiation based on the one hand or narrow versus broad focus on the other hand (see Figure 6.1). This derives directly from the economist's view of strategy as explained in Chapter 5, where competition can be seen as cost based at one extreme and pure differentiation based at the other extreme. It also includes fundamental ideas of economies of scope (from Chapter 3) that are reflected in the vertical axis of Figure 6.1. This idea of a generic strategy is a powerful foundation for understanding the nature and variety of competitive strategies. A generic strategy is a simple typology that captures the essential economic forces at work in a market (the demand side) and in an industry (the supply side). Porter suggested that there are three generic strategies to choose from, and each business unit can have its own strategy. According to Porter, a business can strive to supply a product or service more cost-effectively than its competitors (cost leadership), it can strive to add value to the product or service through differentiation and command higher prices (differentiation), or it can narrow its focus to a special product-market segment which it can monopolize (focus). Not following any of these strategies characterizes a firm as being 'stuck in the middle'. The choice of generic strategy should be based on the firm's business unit's strengths and weaknesses, and a comparison of those with the strengths and weaknesses of competitors.

Generic strategy ideas are pervasive in strategy analysis but not for their operational value. They provide a sound conceptual framework from which more operational ideas can be developed. This chapter develops the ideas of cost advantage and differentiation advantage beyond the introduction given in the previous chapter. It then goes on to look at two powerful grouping concepts – markets segments and strategic groups. The former is well developed in marketing and is explored here for its basis for differentiation strategies and for pricing and value capture. Strategic groups is the idea of industries within industries. It is useful in trying to understand complex industry structures. But it is also valuable in looking ahead to ways in which industries might evolve.

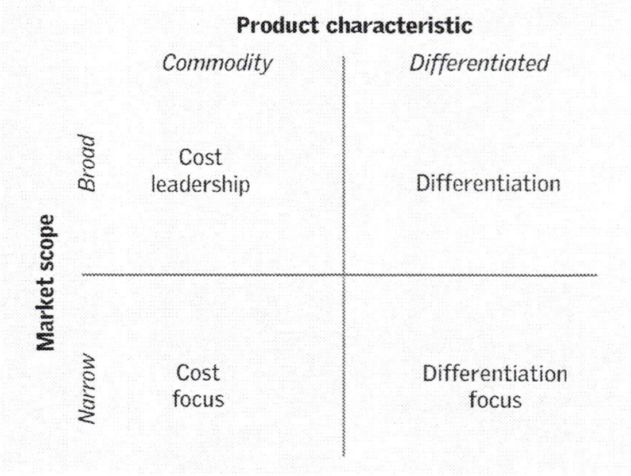

Product characteristic

	Commodity	Differentiated
Broad	Cost leadership	Differentiation
Narrow	Cost focus	Differentiation focus

Market scope (vertical axis label)

Figure 6.1 Porter's generic strategies
Source: Porter, 1980 Chapter 2. Reprinted with the permission of The Free Press, a Division of Simon and Schuster Adult Publishing Group, from *Competitive Strategy* by Micheal E Porter. Copyright © 1980, 1998 by the Free Press. All rights reserved.

Industry transformation looks at bigger, more revolutionary changes in structure. Finally, we look at business models. This phrase has become current in the new world of e-business, being used to show how the internet creates new rules and new ways of making profits – hence the ideas of new business models.

All of the ideas in this chapter contribute to the way in which the firm positions itself in markets to gain competitive advantage. The concepts and frameworks can be deceptively simple, even generic. But the applications require care with data and with interpretation. Above all, application requires a strong grasp of what the competitive strategy concepts are and how to think through their implications. This chapter should be powerful in helping you turn concepts and frameworks into tools for strategic thinking.

6.1 Industry analysis and competitive strategy: the market-based view

In this section we develop the market-based view in some more detail. Building on Chapter 4, we look at cost analysis, especially at the nature of economies of scale and learning effects, as the basis for cost leadership strategies. We consider further the nature of advantage and the different forms in which it can be seen. Finally, we look at some practical advice when formulating competitive strategy.

6.1.1 Cost advantage

The microeconomics of strategy is built initially on an understanding of the nature of costs. Cost for economists is essentially opportunity cost, the sacrifice of the alternatives forgone in producing a product or service. Thus, the cost of a factory building is the set of houses or shops that might have been built instead. The cost of capital is the interest that could have been earned on the capital invested, had it been invested elsewhere. In practice, money prices may not reflect opportunity costs because of uncertainty, imperfect knowledge, natural and contrived barriers to movements of resources, taxes and subsidies, and the existence of externalities (spillover effects of private activities on to other parties; for example, pollution imposes costs on more than just the producer of pollution). Opportunity cost provides the basis for assessing costs of managerial actions, such as in 'make or buy' decisions, and in all those situations where alternative courses of action are being considered.

Costs are also collected and reported routinely both for purposes of stewardship and for control. The behaviour of these costs in relation to the scale of output is of much importance. We see, for example, that break-even analysis is based on the extent to which costs vary in relation to output (in the short term) or are fixed in relation to output. The distinction between fixed and variable costs has implications for the flexibility a firm has in pricing to meet competitive conditions. Thus, one would always wish to price above variable cost per unit in order to maintain positive cash flow. Fixed costs in this example are sunk costs;

they are paid and inescapable, and the only relevant costs are those that are affected by the decision under consideration. It is the behaviour of costs in the long term that has strategic implications for firms and for the structure of industries. The long term is the time horizon under consideration and affects what is considered to be 'fixed'. In the very long term, all economic factors are variable, whereas in the very short term, nearly all economic conditions are fixed and immutable. An economy of scale refers to the extent to which unit costs (costs per unit of output) fall as the scale of the operation (for example, a factory) increases (in other words, as more capital-intensive methods of operation can be employed).

In Figure 6.2 we can see that Plant 1 exhibits increasing returns to scale or, simply, economies of scale. By contrast, Plant 2 shows decreasing returns to scale, diseconomies of scale. The strategic significance of economies of scale depends on the minimum efficient plant size (MES). This is important in relation to market size. The higher the ratio of MES to market size, the larger the share of the market taken by one plant, and the more market power that can be exercised by the firm owning the plant.

Table 6.1 contains estimates of the ratio of MES to market size for various industries in the US and the UK. It is evident, for example, that the refrigerator industry will be much more *concentrated* than the shoe industry (it will have many fewer players) because economies of scale are so much bigger in relation to the market size.

The major sources of economies of scale are usually described as:

* Indivisibilities and the spreading of fixed costs.

* The engineering characteristics of production.

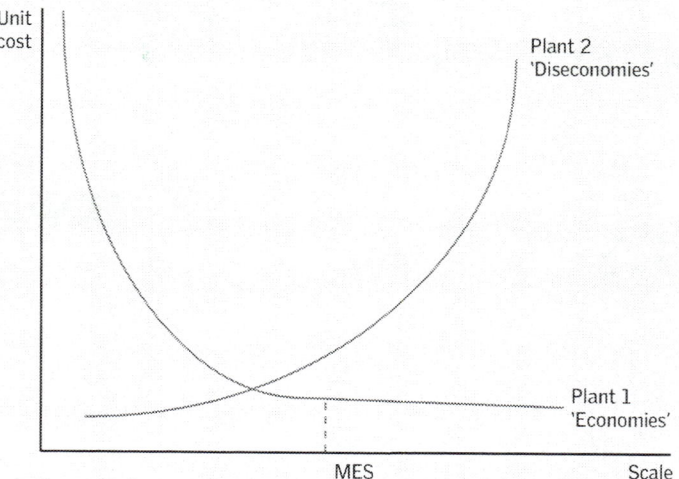

Figure 6.2 Minimum efficient plant size

Indivisibility means that an input cannot be scaled down from a certain minimum size and can only be scaled up in further minimum size units. Thus, costs per unit diminish after the initial investment until a further new block of investment is required. The original examples of 'specialization' (the term coined by Adam Smith) were often engineering in nature. As volumes go up, it is usually cheaper to make work tasks more specialized – as exemplified dramatically in Henry Ford's mass production assembly line operations in the first decade of the last century. Economies of scale also arise because of the physical properties of processing units. This is exemplified by the well-known cube-square rule. Production capacity is usually determined by the volume of the processing unit (the cube of its linear dimensions), whereas cost more often arises from the surface area (the cost of the materials involved). As capacity increases, the average cost decreases, because the ratio of surface area to cube diminishes. (For a full discussion of economies of scale, *see* Besanko, Dranove and Shanley (2000) Chapter 5.)

These general principles apply to functional areas other than production. In marketing, there are important indivisibilities that arise out of branding and the creation of reputation effects. There are important scale effects in advertising, as the costs of campaign preparation can be spread over larger (for example, global) markets. Research and development requires substantial minimum investments – another indivisibility – in advance of production, and the costs of R&D therefore fall as sales volumes increase. Purchasing in bulk exhibits economies of scale, in that the price per unit falls as the number of purchased items goes up. Sometimes this is because of monopolistic buying power (for example, supermarkets in

Table 6.1 Minimum efficient scale for selected industries in the UK and the USA

Industry	% Increase in average costs at ½ MES[1]	MES as % of market	
		UK	USA
Cement	26.0	6.1	1.7
Steel	11.0	15.4	2.6
Glass bottles	11.0	9.0	1.5
Bearings	8.0	4.4	1.4
Fabrics	7.6	1.8	0.2
Refrigerators	6.5	83.3	14.1
Petroleum refining	4.8	11.6	1.9
Paints	4.4	10.2	1.4
Cigarettes	2.2	30.3	6.5
Shoes	1.5	0.6	0.2

[1] This gives a measure of the sensitivity of costs across the range of plant sizes.

Source: Scherer and Ross (1990) *The Economics of Mutiplant Operations*, Tables 3.11 and 3.15.

the UK). But each purchase does have a certain element of fixed costs attached to it (writing contracts, negotiation time, setting up production runs) and these may be significant. The experience curve, sometimes called the learning curve, has similar strategic implications. The experience curve is an empirical estimate of the proportion by which unit costs fall as experience of production increases. An 80 per cent experience curve arises when costs fall to 80 per cent of their previous level after production has doubled (see Figure 6.3). Strategically, this means that a firm which establishes itself first in the market and manages to build a cost advantage by being twice the size of its nearest competitor would have a 20 per cent production cost advantage over this competitor if an 80 per cent experience curve existed. Experience and learning effects arise where there are complex, labour-intensive tasks. The firm can facilitate learning through management and supervisory activities and coaching. It can also use incentives to reward learning.

In general, economies of scale and experience effects provide the basis in terms of cost advantage for those strategies that depend on cost leadership. The objective of cost leadership strategies is to realize a price discount to the customer and/or a margin premium that reflects the size of the cost advantage. Cost advantages are also available through vertical integration and the exercise of buying power.

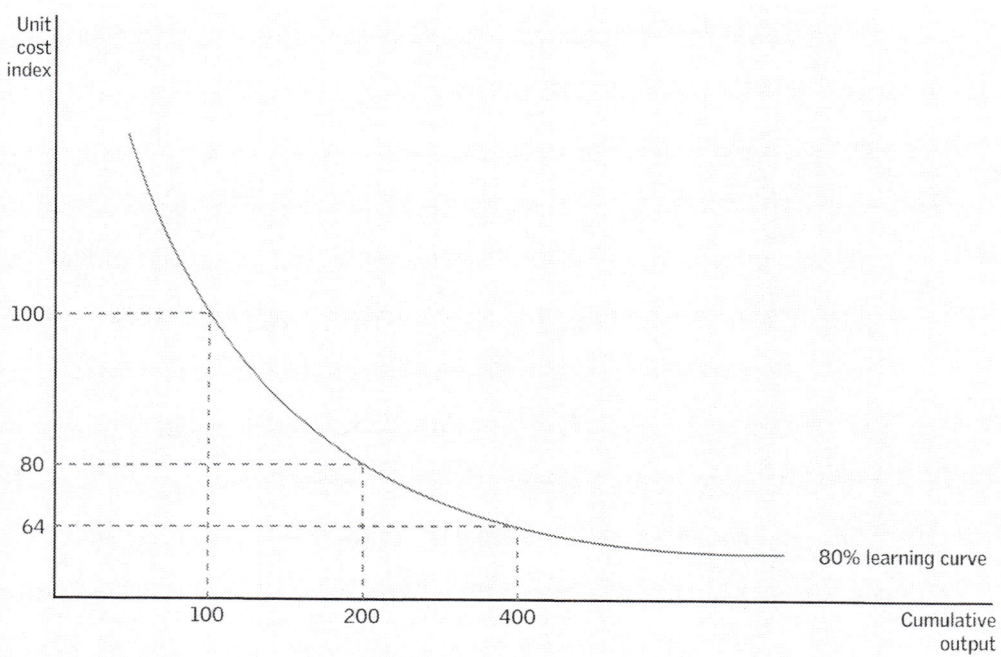

Figure 6.3 The learning curve
Source: Besanko et al., 2000, p. 197. Reprinted with permission of John Wiley and Sons Ltd.

The example in Figure 6.4 is taken from a case study on Du Pont's attempt in the 1970s to dominate the market for titanium dioxide in the USA by virtue of its superior cost position. The cost advantage is based on economies of scale, on experience effects, on vertical integration, and on lower raw material prices. In total, the cost advantage over typical competitors is around 40 per cent. As a result, the competitors were unable to stop Du Pont building scale-efficient new plant to take advantage of market growth – a classic example of a pre-emptive strategy. Similar arguments lay behind the analysis of the rapid growth of Japanese companies in the 1970s. Significant economies of scale gave the opportunity for lower prices, the building of market share, even lower costs, and the gradual dominance of markets. In general, the analysis of first mover advantage relies on the existence of significant scale and experience effects, a price-sensitive market, and the willingness to commit capital ahead of competition.

6.1.2 Differentiation advantage

We first encountered product differentiation in Chapter 3, where we saw that it was a characteristic of imperfect markets where 'non-price' strategies are important. Product differentiation is the act of making products different from one another. This might involve tangible differences such as quality, reliability, performance or design. Alternatively (or in addition) it might be based on intangible elements such as reputation and branding.

	Ilmenite Chloride	Rutile Chloride *1972 cents/lb*	Difference
From exhibit 3	18.80	21.50	−2.70
Less depreciation	−3.00	−2.50	−0.50
Capital charge	6.80	5.60	1.20
	22.60	24.60	−2.00
Learning effect	−4.75	0.00	−4.75
Scale effect	−3.75	0.00	−3.75
Integration effect	−1.30	0.00	−1.30
Capacity effect	1.30	1.00	0.30
Cost per lb	14.10	25.60	−11.50

capital charge = investment requirements per lb multiplied by hurdle rate (say 15%)
learning effect = 79% learning curve and double the experience
scale effect = 85% doubling effect and twice the scale
capacity effect = differences in capacity utilisation

Figure 6.4 Du Pont's calculation of its cost advantage
Source: Du Pont in Titanium Dioxide (A), Harvard Business School case 9-385-40 (1984) exhibits 2 and 3.

Thus, Subaru's cars might be differentiated on the basis of their performance characteristics as attested by their success in motor sport. But Mercedes would rely heavily on accumulated reputation in addition to other tangible differentiators such as build quality.

Differentiation[1] requires the investment of resources – typically time, capital cost and higher variable costs – in a risky bet that the customer will respond to the differentiated product by buying it at a premium price and/or more frequently. The bet is risky because the attempt to differentiate might fail:

1 product quality might fail to improve as a result of the product development activity;

2 a competitor does it better (for example Jaguar is involved in an attempt to catch up with the differentiation power of the German brands BMW and Mercedes);

3 customers fail to respond to the new proposition (see, for example, the failure of laser disks in the consumer electronics market);

4 the costs of differentiation might be in excess of the gains from differentiation – the capital costs and any higher variable costs might not be offset by the new price–volume combination. The classic case of this is IBM's attempts to differentiate its personal computers from the stream of IBM-compatible new entrants in the 1980s. IBM offered a new operating system, OS2, but the benefits of this were not apparent to customers who preferred to stay with the Microsoft DOS system that had become the industry standard.

Successful differentiation makes the market less perfect (see the discussion in Chapter 3) because the firm that has created the differentiation has in fact created a firm-specific imperfection. Product differentiation is therefore the process of creating a competitive advantage by making the product (or service) different from those of rivals to the extent that superior performance results.

In Table 6.2 we can see that there are different bases for cost advantage and differentiation advantage. Cost leadership typically requires large (mass) markets in which minimum efficient plant sizes can be reached. Differentiation, by contrast, prospers in market segments in which different customer needs can be identified and products designed for those needs. The approaches to the market are distinctive. Cost leadership is accompanied by price (low price) strategies, whereas differentiation is based in non-price strategies. Different competences are also indicated. Cost leadership is usually manufacturing and procurement based, whereas differentiation activity is marketing based and R&D intensive. Michael Porter argued, controversially, that firms could not do both and if they tried they would get 'stuck in

---

[1] It is important to distinguish product differentiation from differentiation as applied to organization structure. The building blocks of organization structure are differentiation and integration. In this context differentiation is the way in which a company allocates people and resources to different organization tasks – the greater the number of functions and activities, the higher is the level of differentiation (see p. 56).

	Cost leadership	Differentiation
Cost advantage	Scale and scope	None required
Differentiation advantage	Low (price strategies)	High (non-price strategies)
Market segmentation	Low (mass market)	High (many markets)
Distinctive competences	Manufacturing and buying	Marketing, R&D

Table 6.2 Comparison of cost and differentiation strategies

the middle'. However, his position clearly depends on a particular view of the competences that support cost and differentiation positions. The case box (below) describes the emergence of the scale economy brander in the food processing industry.

Case box: The scale economy brander

The consumer packaged goods industries (including the food processing industry) enjoyed halcyon days in the 1960s when manufacturers were dominant. This was a period when mass markets in processed foods were growing quickly, retail distribution was highly fragmented, economies of scale were available, and processing technologies were proprietary. These substantial economic advantages were buttressed by the creation of mass marketing systems comprising national media advertising, national sales forces and increasingly sophisticated marketing support services. The visible output of this business system was the brand, the repository of guarantees to the customer of product qualities arising from proprietary technology. The creation of the brand was subject to many economies of marketing scale, and fostered scale economies available elsewhere in the system. The brand was the visible symbol of the manufacturer's strength, and was the visible barrier to entry behind which grew a series of oligopolies earning monopoly rents. There were seven entry barriers around these brand positions:

1 National sales force and distribution: 'filling up the backroom and stealing shelf space'.
2 Listing muscle: fragmented retailers felt they had to stock the leading brands on manufacturers' terms.
3 Intensive media advertising bought at preferential rates and defrayed across large volumes.
4 Superior product quality arising from proprietary processing technology and/or from consumer perceptions.
5 Low-cost processing either from superior technology or from scale economies.
6 Sophisticated support services, e.g. market research, product management support structure, advertising skills.
7 Discounts on raw material purchases based on volume.

Branding economics was all about premium prices, consumer pull and economies of scale. The association of market share and profitability was well attested in this regime of the scale economy brander. Behind the brand lay a technology edge and a new management structure and style – the style of the marketing company.

These marketing companies came in two forms. The first was the multinational major branders (e.g. Unilever, BSN, Heinz). These were multinational companies operating multiple, related consumer goods businesses across the world, with strong perceived product differentiation accompanied by strong branding. These companies have been traditionally multi-domestic in character as opposed to global (Porter 1986) or transnational (Bartlett and Ghoshal 1989) (see the discussion in Chapter 11 on the nature of international advantage).

The second was the national major branders (e.g. St Ivel). These were nationally based and focused companies with very high levels of marketing support for a product range which, by the standards of the multinationals, were more limited.

Source: McGee and Segal-Horn, 1992.

Questions for discussion

1 Why was it possible for scale and differentiation effects to be simultaneously present?

2 What effect do you think this could have on the pattern of competition?

Sources of differentiation advantage

Product differentiation opportunities arise from the physical characteristics of the product, from the technological foundations of the product, and from the nature of customers and markets. As a shorthand we can observe that 'quality' reflects the physical characteristics of the product; 'innovation' captures the technological dimension; and 'customer responsiveness' reflects market and customer factors. If we correlate these with the tangibility/intangibility dimension we can see Table 6.3 describing the arena in which product differentiation works.

Table 6.3 is a simple representation of the complexity of differentiation. However, you can see the elements that can make up differentiation. Performance and reliability of products (such as durable goods, computers, cars, washing machines) are obvious characteristics but

Dimensions of differentiation	Tangible	Intangible
Quality	Performance and Reliability	Reputation
Innovation	New functional attributes New usage patterns	Modernity
Customer responsiveness	New distribution system	Brand Relationship management

Table 6.3 Dimensions of differentiation

ones which can be imitated. However, reputation is less easily gained and less easily lost. So a Rolls-Royce reputation for automobile quality may linger for a long time even if the objective data on tangible characteristics might suggest that others have long since caught up.[2] Innovation allows for a reshaping of the way in which the product works and the way in which customers use the product. Thus laptop computers are an innovation sitting alongside the desktop alternatives but operating in different ways and places and requiring different technical solutions. Sometimes innovation captures a style (which we have called modernity) that reflects lifestyle choices. Thus, architectural innovation may have tangible effects on the nature of buildings but much of the benefit may be felt in the feel, style and texture of the space. The (high) fashion industry is one where intangibles are predominant and functionality unimportant. Customer responsiveness captures the extent to which products have value because of the degree and style of interaction between buyer and seller. Dell Computers offer the lesson that product features are not all-important. Michael Dell's innovation was to identify that customers valued close interaction between buyer and seller through the distribution system. Dell's competitive advantage rests on the closeness of links to the customer and the entire business is about creating the logistics that give the customer maximum choice and timeliness of choice.

Dell Computers is a good example of how differentiation advantages can be built in self-reinforcing pyramids. Dell innovated, created a new tangible marketing and distribution process, and has also created an enviable reputation and brand name. The more diverse the bases and dimensions of differentiation, the more powerful will be the differentiation effect. As a result companies that are successful at this (see the scale economy branders above) become infused with the differentiation culture. Witness, or example, how the scale economy branders such as Procter & Gamble, General Foods, Unilever and others are known as marketing companies despite their very considerable talents in manufacturing and other non-marketing functions. The prime source of advantage is differentiation secured through core competences (see Chapter 7) in marketing.

Differentiation covers many approaches to the customer. It might rest on a broad market appeal or it might rely on narrow market niches in which it offers highly specific solutions for customers. Figure 6.5 suggests a methodology by which you can begin an assessment of the market and the potential for differentiation. In looking at the product and customer dimensions in this figure you are trying to work out whether this is a market in which common needs prevail or where there is a diversity of needs. Where you might identify commonality and make your differentiation investments accordingly, you are open to the niche player who might target a niche in your market to which a more specific and valuable customer proposition can be made. In mature markets this process of continuous segmentation

---

[2] This is *not* true of the Rolls-Royce reputation for aero engines which continues to be high on both tangible and intangible dimensions.

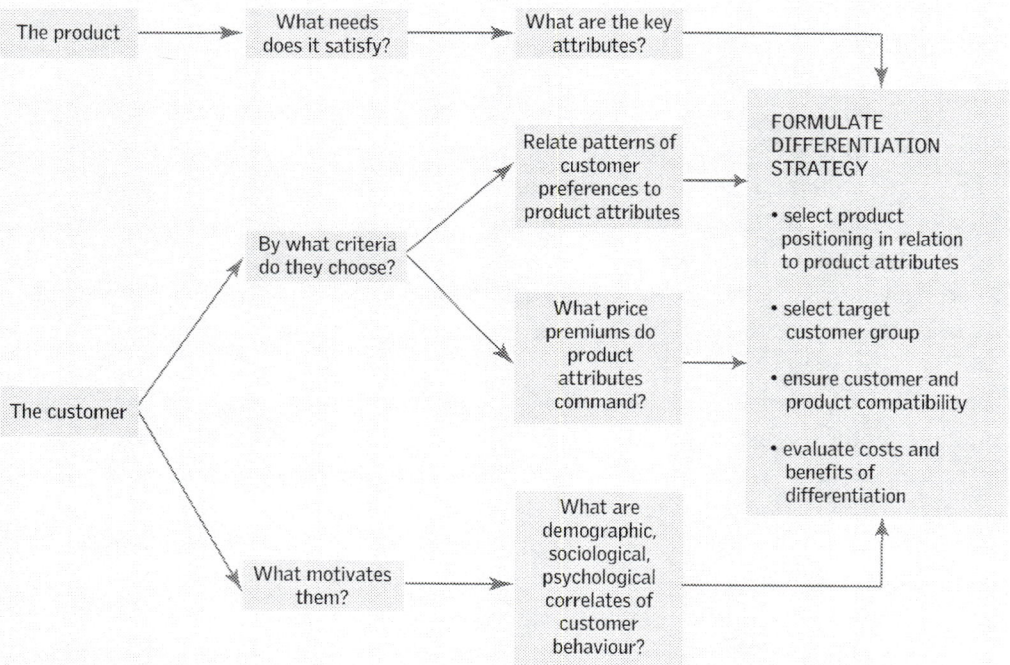

Figure 6.5 Identifying differentiation potential
Source: Adapted from Grant, 2002, p. 287.

allows smaller firms to chip away at the bigger but broader positions of the market leaders. Conversely a niche play is susceptible to innovation by large players such that the niche offer is swept up in a bigger and better offer that covers many segments. The decline of small and medium-size retailers is testament to the ability of large retailers to provide an unmatchable price proposition together with different differentiation propositions.

6.1.3 Competitive advantage

In the case examples on retailing in Chapter 5 we drew the connection between strategy choices and profitability. We argued that strategy choices are resource allocation decisions that enable the firm to create distinctive assets and capabilities (this is the language of core competences, as we shall see below). These enable the firm to create imperfections in markets that are specific to itself and therefore the firm can capture the benefits of this positioning in terms of higher prices or lower costs or both. Figure 6.6 illustrates the point. A successful strategy can earn superior financial returns because it has an unfair advantage, that is, it creates, exploits and defends firm-specific imperfections in the market vis-à-vis competitors. We deliberately use the term unfair advantage as a colloquial simile for competitive advantage in order to underline that such advantages are achieved in the face of organized opposition, both from competitors that wish to emulate your success and from customers that will exercise bargaining power to achieve lower prices.

In theory, competitive advantage is the *delivering of superior value to customers and, in doing so, earning an above average return for the company and its stakeholders.* These twin criteria impose a difficult hurdle for companies because competitive advantage cannot be bought by simply cutting prices or by simply adding quality without reflecting the cost premium in higher price. Competitive advantage requires the firm to be sustainably different from its competitors in such a way that customers are prepared to purchase at a suitably high price. Classic perfect competition works on the basis that all products are so alike as to be commodities and that competition takes place solely on the basis of price. The search for competitive advantage is the search for differences from competitors, and for purchase on the basis of value (that is, the offer of an attractive performance-to-price ratio). Competitive advantage is a statement of positioning in the market and consists of the following elements:

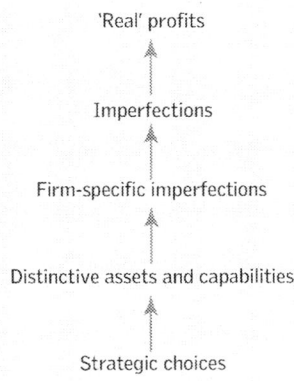

Figure 6.6 Firm-specific imperfections as the source of profits

- A statement of competitive *intent*
- Outward evidence of *advantage* to the customer
- Some combination of:
  - superior delivered cost position
  - a differentiated product
  - protected niches
- Evidence of *direct benefits*, which:
  - are perceived by a sizeable customer group
  - these customers value and are willing to pay for
  - cannot be readily obtained elsewhere, both now and in the foreseeable relevant future

The sustainability of competitive advantage depends on the following:

- *Power* – maintaining the levels of commitments in resource terms relative to competitors
- *Catching-up* – ease of copying and nullifying the advantages
- *Keeping ahead* – productivity of one's own continuous search for enhanced or new advantages
- *The changing game* – rate of change of customer requirements
- *The virtuous circle* – the self-sustainability and mutual reinforcing of existing advantages

Economists argue that competitive advantages are by their nature temporary in character and therefore decay quickly. This is to argue that product markets and the market for underlying resources is reasonably competitive. Indeed, much of the analysis of competitive advantage is concerned with assessing just how defensible, durable and large the advantages can be. The Porter five forces framework (Porter 1980) (*see* Figure 5.1) provides a useful basis for categorizing and understanding the industry economics that lie behind competitive advantage and Figure 5.3 summarizes the competitive forces. Notice that the barriers to entry shown in Figure 5.3 are, in essence, the competitive advantages that are available in the industry. They represent the cost premiums that entrants would have to pay in order to enter the industry and compete on equal terms. In other words, these are the imperfections that the incumbents have created (or are the beneficiaries of). It is important to note that the barriers to entry may be generic, meaning that the incumbents do not have advantages over each other, but have a shared advantage with a shared rent. Or the barriers may be firm-specific, implying that different

Supplier/buyer power	**Barriers to entry**
• Relative concentration	• Scale economies and experience
• Relative importance of product to the provider and the user	• Product differentiation
• Credible threat of vertical integration	• Capital requirements
• Substitution possibilities	• Switching requirements
• Control of information	• Access to distribution
• Switching costs	• Scale-independant cost advantages
	• Level of expected retaliation
Intensity of rivalry *High if...*	**Pressure from substitutes**
• Several equally strong players	• Benefits not product features
• Low/no growth in market	• Sideways competition
• High fixed costs and cyclical demand	• Comparative price/performance
• Few chances for differentiation	• Comparative technology life cycle
• Large-scale capacity increments	• What business are you in?
• Different 'culture' or players	• Backing by rich competitor
• High strategic stakes	
• Major exit barriers	

Figure 6.7 Behind the competitive forces

incumbents are protected by different advantages and are themselves different from one another. Barriers are also entrant-specific in that different potential entrants have different assets and therefore different ways in which they might compete.

Figures 6.8 and 6.9 show a reworking of Porter's generic strategy table (Figure 6.1) to emphasize that the three routes to advantage are potentially reinforcing. Figure 6.9 outlines

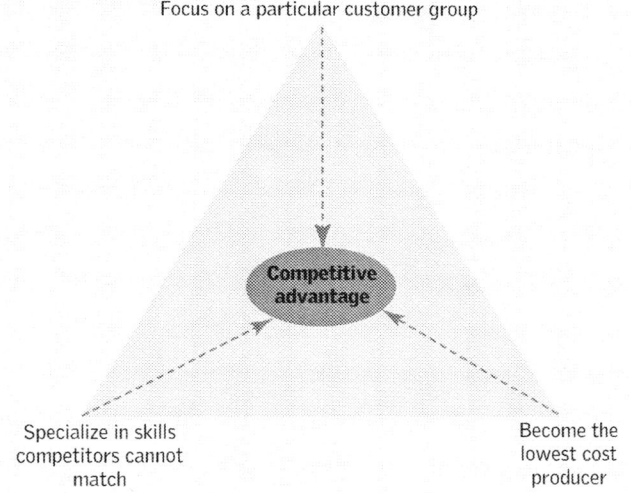

Figure 6.8 Three major routes to competitive advantage

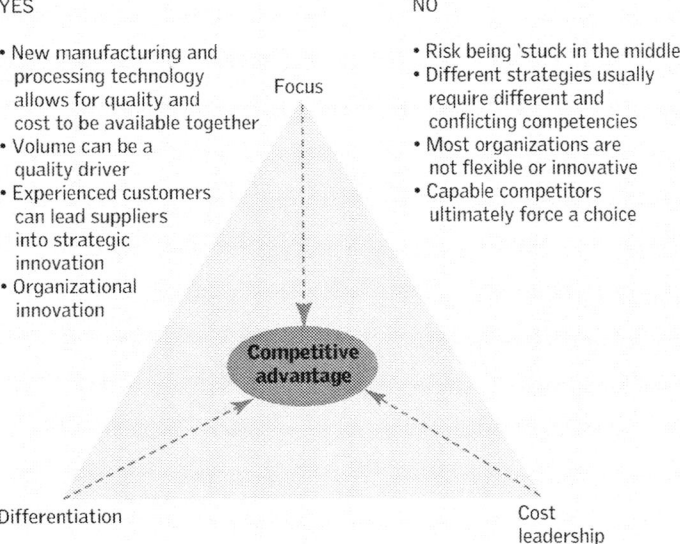

Figure 6.9 Is more than one generic strategy possible?

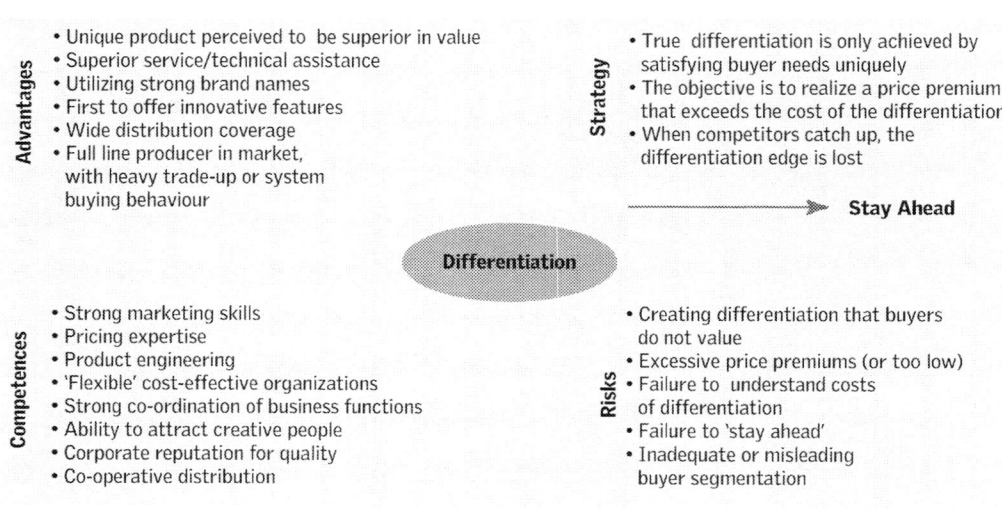

Figure 6.10 The differentiation strategy

the arguments for and against more than one generic strategy. The argument rests on the point that the different strategies require different resources and capabilities and, therefore, different organizational forms and cultures. The alternative argument suggests that new technologies are leading to more similarities in the strategies.

Figures 6.10, 6.11 and 6.12 summarize the generic strategies in terms of the essence of the strategy, the nature of its advantages, the competences required and the risks that it has

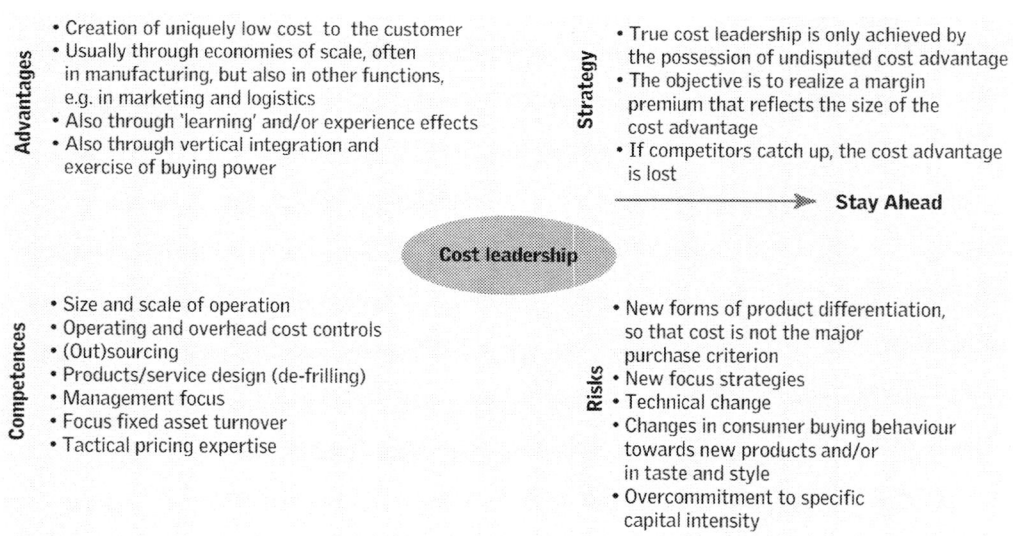

Figure 6.11 The cost leadership strategy

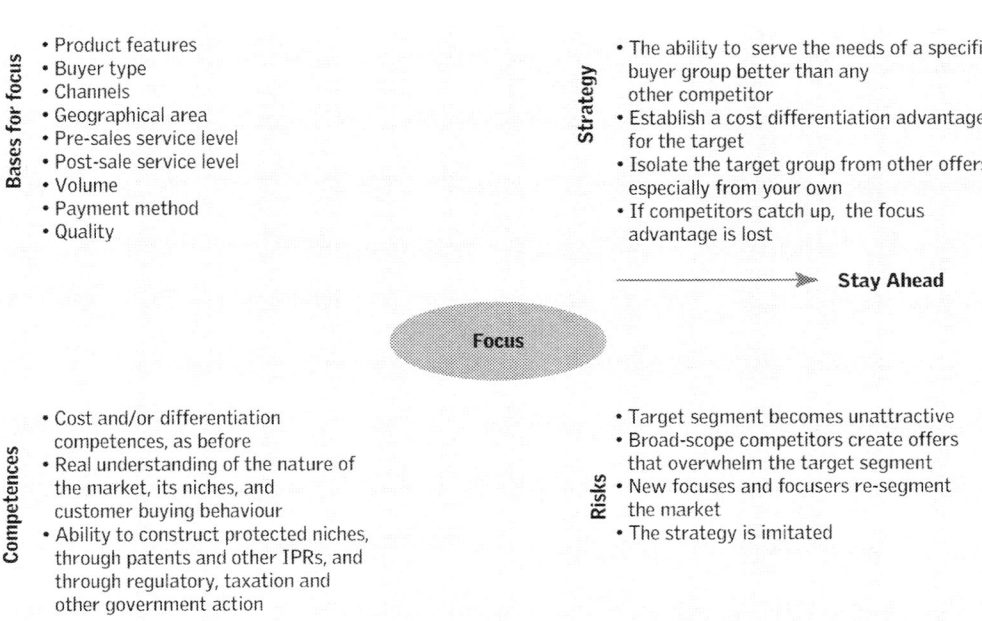

Bases for focus
- Product features
- Buyer type
- Channels
- Geographical area
- Pre-sales service level
- Post-sale service level
- Volume
- Payment method
- Quality

Strategy
- The ability to serve the needs of a specific buyer group better than any other competitor
- Establish a cost differentiation advantage for the target
- Isolate the target group from other offers, especially from your own
- If competitors catch up, the focus advantage is lost

Stay Ahead

Focus

Competences
- Cost and/or differentiation competences, as before
- Real understanding of the nature of the market, its niches, and customer buying behaviour
- Ability to construct protected niches, through patents and other IPRs, and through regulatory, taxation and other government action

Risks
- Target segment becomes unattractive
- Broad-scope competitors create offers that overwhelm the target segment
- New focuses and focusers re-segment the market
- The strategy is imitated

Figure 6.12 The focus strategy

to face. This should reinforce the idea that strategy is about making a commitment and about the deliberate calculation and taking of risk.

Figure 6.13 shows the implications of composite differentiation and cost strategies. The figure arrays cost advantage against a composite differentiation and

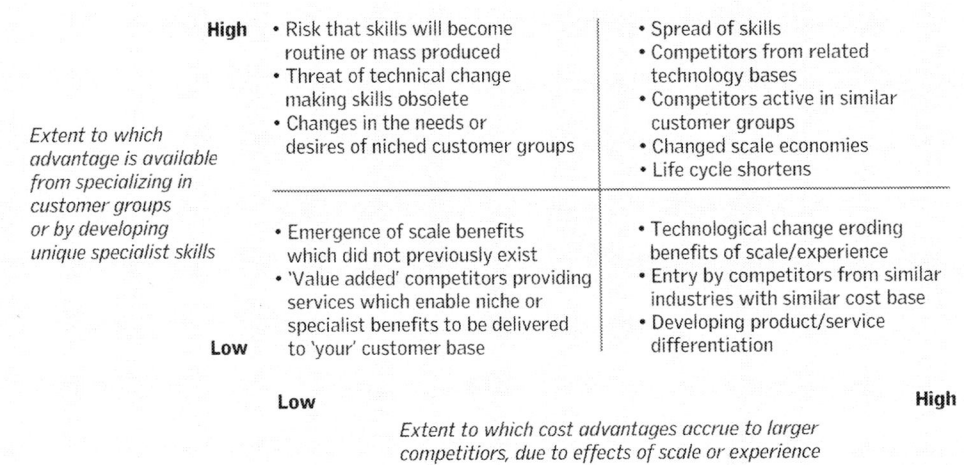

High

Extent to which advantage is available from specializing in customer groups or by developing unique specialist skills

Low

- Risk that skills will become routine or mass produced
- Threat of technical change making skills obsolete
- Changes in the needs or desires of niched customer groups

- Spread of skills
- Competitors from related technology bases
- Competitors active in similar customer groups
- Changed scale economies
- Life cycle shortens

- Emergence of scale benefits which did not previously exist
- 'Value added' competitors providing services which enable niche or specialist benefits to be delivered to 'your' customer base

- Technological change eroding benefits of scale/experience
- Entry by competitors from similar industries with similar cost base
- Developing product/service differentiation

Low   **High**

Extent to which cost advantages accrue to larger competitiors, due to effects of scale or experience

Figure 6.13 How industry dynamics shape competitive threats

focus dimension. For example, where there are high cost advantages and high differentiation advantages, the risk for the company is that the supporting skills might become mass produced or that technological change will outmode the skills. Conversely, where the advantages from both sources are small, then there might be entry from other industries where the skills are similar. The point of the figure is to demonstrate how patterns of advantage (and the supporting patterns of skill and capability) can be eroded by shifts in the competitive environment. Nothing is safe from competitive threat in the long term – the variables of concern to the firm are (i) how large is my advantage, and (ii) for how long can I retain it?

Figure 6.14 takes the same dimensions and draws out the implications for industry structure. The combination of low advantages from both sides leads eventually to a perfectly competitive market. By contrast, the combination of large (high) advantages from both sides yields a kind of specialization, where each large player dominates a large segment. Where there are low-cost advantages but high differentiation/focus advantages, we often see a variety of small or medium-sized speciality firms with protectable niche positions. The position of high-cost advantage and no differentiation effects is typically the profile of a monopoly supplier, such as a water or power utility.

Industries and firms differ markedly in the size and shape of the advantages that are available. In Figure 6.15 we array the number of advantages against the size of the advantages. The point of origin is the perfectly competitive solution, where there are very few

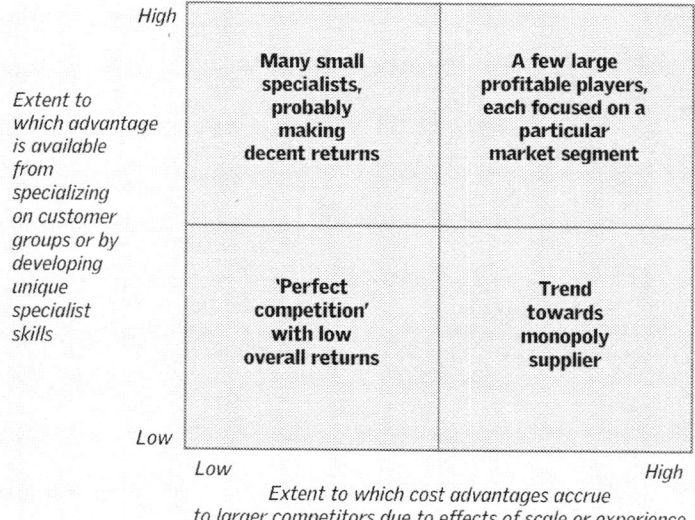

Figure 6.14 Industry dynamics and competitive advantage

advantages and/or the advantages are extremely small. The typical comparison is between the 'blockbusters' and the 'inch by inch' polar alternatives. The blockbuster situation arises where there are very few, usually one or two, sources of advantage, but these are very large in size. The prescription pharmaceuticals industry is like this. Its sources of advantage are research and development (including product registration) and sales force. But products are protected by patent and are typically price insensitive in the markets, so the advantages are huge. Perhaps more typical in most situations is the pattern of multiple sources, but each being of small consequence – the inch by inch situation. This would be typical of much of retailing, where there are a great many ways to compete through choice of product ranges, locations, sourcing policy, staff training and skills, and so on. A more dramatic example is Formula One racing, where the racing teams are very close to each other in terms of performance, but performance does depend on myriad different dimensions. What Formula One does demonstrate is that it is possible for the compounding of many different sources of small advantage to result in predictable and sustainable differences between teams. The source of performance differences here lies in the way in which the resources and capabilities are systematically managed – another resource-based argument.

Read the case box on the video gaming industry and interpret the rules of the game in terms of Porter's five forces analysis. Do this for the original rules of the game and for the new rules that Sony is trying to establish. What benefits is Sony expecting to gain? How would you expect its competitors to react?

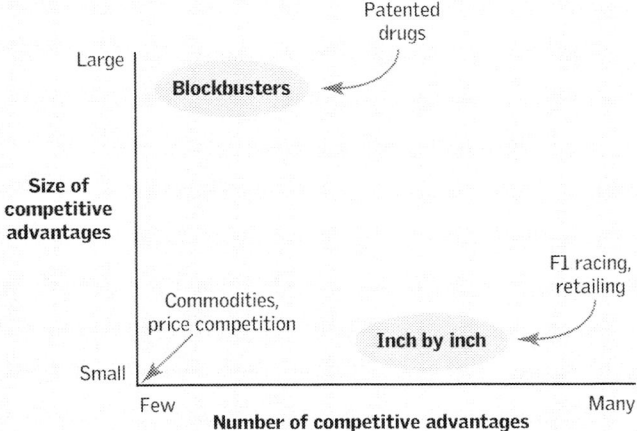

Figure 6.15 Degrees of competitive advantage

Case box: Changing the game in video gaming industry

Something funny is going on in the video gaming business. Sony, the market leader, is changing the technological and business rules that have defined this cut-throat industry for two decades. By doing so, it hopes both to improve its fortunes – earlier this year the company admitted that its revenues and profits had unexpectedly plunged – and to fend off a challenge from Microsoft, which launched its first games console, the Xbox, in 2001. Though motivated by Sony's self-interest, these new rules are also good news for consumers, whether they are seasoned gamers or occasional players, since they impose some stability on a volatile and cyclical industry.

The existing rules are simple: every five years or so, console-makers release new consoles that are far more powerful than the previous generation. The current crop consists of Sony's PlayStation 2, Microsoft's Xbox and Nintendo's GameCube. The PlayStation 2, launched in March 2000, is the most successful by far, with over 60 million units sold, compared with around 15 million units each for the Xbox and GameCube. Just as shaving companies make money on blades rather than razors, the industry works by selling consoles at knock-down prices and making a profit on the games. A game typically costs $50, around $10 of which is passed from publisher to console-maker as a licence fee.

The result is a regular 'console cycle', as one generation succeeds the next. At the end of each cycle, gamers abandon their old consoles and buy new ones, and the whole process starts again. Games written for one console do not work on another, so they also have to buy a completely new set of games. But since each new console cycle offers a great leap forward in computing power, gamers are prepared to play along. Console-makers like the cycle too, since it isolates them from the broader economic climate. The current gaming boom occurred despite a wobbly American economy; the last but one, in 1991–93, came amid a global recession. Console-makers also like it that with each cycle, the playing field is levelled, and the industry in effect starts again from scratch. Microsoft entered the market in the current cycle with its Xbox; its model was Sony, which had launched its first console, the PlayStation, in the previous cycle.

But Sony has changed the rules, by subverting this state of affairs in three ways. First, it made its PlayStation 2 console 'backwards compatible' with the original PlayStation – in other words, games written for the old console also work on the new one. This gave PlayStation owners an incentive to remain loyal to Sony from one cycle to the next. By choosing a PlayStation 2, rather than an Xbox or GameCube, they could protect their existing investment in games. Sony says this policy of backwards compatibility will be maintained when the PlayStation 3 appears in 2005 or 2006: it will be able to run games designed for previous consoles. Since each generation is so much more powerful than the last, this trick is relatively easy to pull off by getting a console to impersonate, or emulate, its less powerful predecessors.

Next, Sony did not kill off the PlayStation when it launched the PlayStation 2, but instead cut its price and aimed it at new, more price-sensitive markets. In 2002, Sony sold 20 million PlayStation 2s and 4 million PlayStations – compared with sales of about 6 million each for the Xbox and GameCube. In other words, successive console cycles are starting to overlap.

Sony's third move is intended to extend this trend still further. It has just launched the PSX, a home-entertainment device that combines a PlayStation 2 with a DVD recorder, a hard-disk based video recorder, satellite and analogue TV tuners, and photo-album and music playback features. As well as cutting down on spaghetti-like wiring behind the TV, this jack-of-all-trades is the first example of Sony's new strategy to combine its games consoles with other consumer-electronics devices. By throwing in PlayStation 2 functionality with other devices at a small premium – made easier by Sony's recent cramming of a PlayStation 2 on to a single chip – it hopes to broaden the market and appeal to people who would not normally dream of buying a stand-alone games console. 'Once they get it down to a single chip, then economies of scale come in, and the potential for integrated devices becomes very real,' says Nick Gibson of Games Investor Consulting.

Playing to win

Together, these three moves have the effect of damping the industry's cyclicality, maintaining loyalty and widening ownership. They also make life more difficult for Microsoft, which is expected to be Sony's chief rival in the next cycle. The Xbox, which was launched more than a year after the PlayStation 2, could never have caught it up in sales. Instead, it was widely seen as Microsoft's trial run for the next round, in which the Xbox 2 will battle the PlayStation 3 on more equal terms. Sony's strategy changes that calculation. As the winner of the previous cycle, it has the most to gain by trying to reduce the industry's cyclicality, in order to maintain its dominance. By overlapping console cycles and spreading the PlayStation 2 into a range of other devices, it hopes to make the coming fight between the Xbox 2 and the PlayStation 3 just one front in a larger battle on a wider landscape. Indeed, says Toby Scott of *Games Analyst*, an industry publication, it now makes sense to consider the PlayStation's collective market share across multiple console cycles. Since Microsoft is now under pressure to make the Xbox 2 backwards compatible too, the next cycle will arguably not start from scratch after all.

That does not mean the console cycle is dead. But it will matter less, which is good news for consumers. In the old days when consoles were killed off and there was no backwards compatibility, says Mr Scott, 'gamers were the playthings of manufacturers'. The changing dynamics of the industry now mean that buying a console, particularly late in the cycle, is much less dangerous than it used to be. If you buy a console this Christmas, in short, you are much less likely to end up getting stuck with a turkey.

Source: 'Changing the Game', *The Economist*, 4 December 2003.

6.2 Strategic market segments

In Chapter 3 we saw that the basis for market segmentation lies in the existence of different responses to price (and other marketing variables) by individuals or groups of individuals. Earlier in this chapter we saw how differentiation activities are intimately related to the existence of market segments. One of the most creative endeavours in strategy making has been the seeking out of new markets or market niches to which customized products can be directed. In general we can see that a market can be divided into strategic segments based on product range and on associated price differentials. Figure 6.16 illustrates the general case.

Customers are faced by an offer curve that summarizes the range of options open to them. This shows what groups of customers exist for each combination of product performance and price. Thus, group A is content with a low product specification and a correspondingly low price. Group B is the larger segment, where both the product specification and price are higher. Group C is higher still on both counts, the premium market. Given this offer curve, firms would be unwilling, in general, to offer a product at point X for two reasons. First, it does not fall into any of the established segments A, B or C. Second it falls above the offer curve, meaning that it is overpriced for that level of product performance. Another way of putting it is to say that at that price the product is underspecified. The shape of the offer curve depends on customer price sensitivities – how much are they prepared to pay for extra product performance? It also depends on the cost characteristics of the product. Thus, the premium product may require different product development routines, and specialized attention in production and marketing. The existence of only a small market for the premium product is likely, due to the high costs

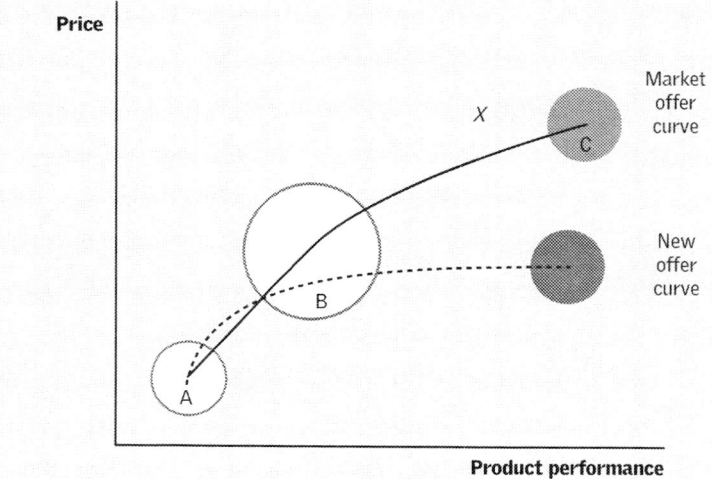

Figure 6.16 The offer curve

involved and the level of the minimum price that has to be charged in order to make a profit. Innovation in the market can transform the offer curve, as shown in Figure 6.16. The innovation, for example, could be due to cost reductions in product development and manufacturing so that lower prices can be charged. A good example is the way the Lexus intruded on the premium car market in Europe and the USA by creating its own version of a premium offer at lower prices than Mercedes. The unfair advantage was the application of the Toyota production system to the Lexus (which is Toyota's premium brand), giving Toyota considerable cost advantage over Mercedes.

Another way of looking at strategic segmentation is to compare price and differentiation patterns across a market. Figure 6.17 suggests a pattern of locations along which the price differentiation trade-off takes place. Starting from point A you can charge relatively higher prices for modest increases in differentiation. This, however, flattens out so that a plateau is achieved around point B, where the price is relatively stable whatever the level of differentiation. This implies a stable price point at which product changes make little difference. Eventually the plateau is broken because differentiation differences are so large as to be able to command higher prices. In this example point C represents a journey through progressively steep trade-offs where customers are prepared to pay disproportionately high prices for modest changes in differentiation. This locus of trade-offs enables us to locate different market positioning strategies. Around point A but below the curve we could see low-cost strategies being deployed. Around point C but above the curve we could see premium-quality strategies. Below the curve and to the right of the mass market located at B we could see a combination of low-cost and high-quality strategies in region D. Although strategies

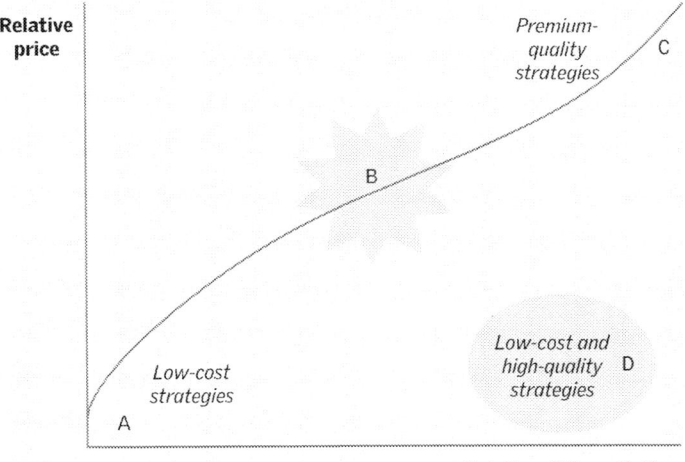

Figure 6.17 Strategic segmentation

around A, B and C are stable and consistent in relation to each other, the offerings in D have the potential to destabilize the market.

6.2.1 Identifying segmentation variables

The bases for segmentation have always been major issue for companies. The conventional approach is to look at the characteristics of buyers and the characteristics of products, as in Figure 6.18. This is a very well known approach and is probably more useful for identifying existing patterns of segmentation than for discovering new and untested segments. Figure 6.18 should remind you of the earlier section on differentiation because the drivers are very much the same in each case. This is to be expected, but what is difficult to do is to develop new bases for segmentation and differentiation. However, the more that all competitors follow the same logic, the more likely they are to end up with the same kinds of strategies. By definition these will cancel out and competitive advantage will be elusive.

The end-of-chapter case study describes the move from 2G standards in mobile telephony to 3G standards. This describes the value proposition of the 3G service, the differentiation required and the segmentation on which it is based. 3G allows for internet connection to mobile telephones, whereas the 2G standard has become almost a commodity-style offer.

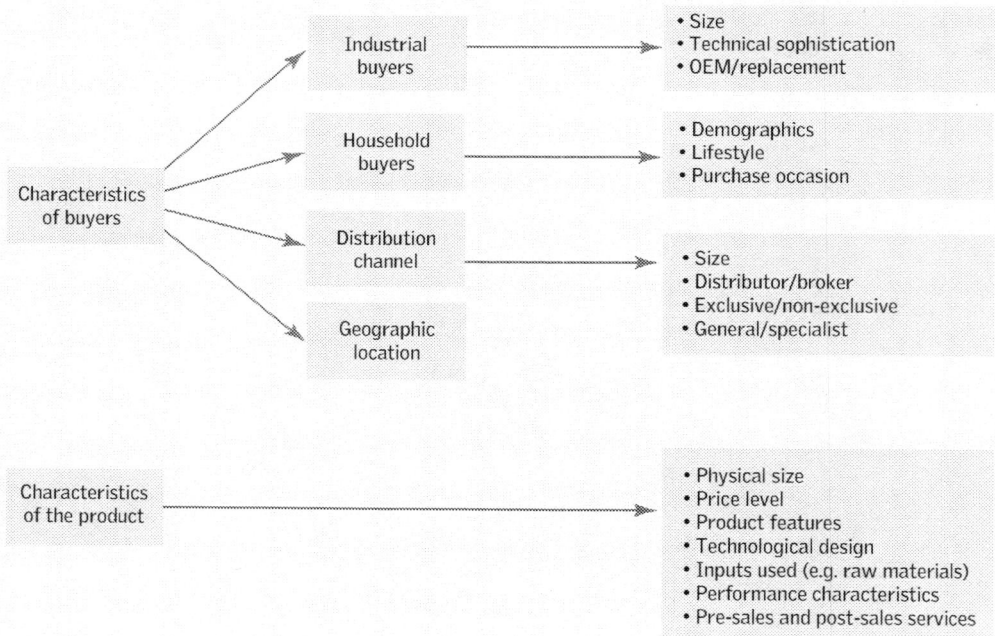

Figure 6.18 Bases for segmentation
Source: Grant, 2002, p. 121.

You should use this example to think about how new technology and development of standards require effective segmentation and differentiation for success.

The analysis of strategic segments leads towards the firm's choice of pricing strategy. In assessing pricing options the firm is essentially concentrating on issues of *value*; that is. how to price in order to gain value to the firm while still delivering value to the customer. The next section addresses this.

6.2.2 Value creation and value analysis

The concept of value is central to economics and to the understanding of competitive advantage. The theory of value in economics deals with the determination of final market prices (as opposed to factor prices, which are determined by the theory of distribution).

Perceived benefit and consumer surplus

If you buy a car for $15 000 but it is worth $20 000 to you in terms of the services it renders, then you are better off by $5000. This is known as the consumer surplus. Given a choice of cars with identical service values, you would (rationally) buy the cheaper car – this would save you money and increase your consumer surplus. The idea of consumer surplus is a profit idea – it is the 'profit' that the consumer makes from a purchase. If the 'consumer' was a firm buying a machine for $15 000 but as a result lowering its costs by $20 000, the value created by the purchase (i.e. the profit) is $5000.

In tabular form:

> *Perceived gross benefit*
> > *less   user costs*
> > *less   transactions costs*
> = *Perceived net benefit*
> > *less   price paid*
> = *Consumer surplus*

Value maps

A firm must deliver consumer surplus to compete successfully. Value maps illustrate the competitive implications of consumer surplus analysis. The vertical axis shows the price of the product and the horizontal axis shows quality or performance characteristics of the product. Each point corresponds to a particular price–quality combination. At any time, the series of price–quality combinations available to consumers is shown by an upward-sloping schedule, an indifference curve. The slope shows the trade-off between price and quality; the steeper the slope, the higher the extra price to be paid for increased quality. This is an 'indifference' curve because at each point on the curve the consumer surplus is the same. Above the curve is lower consumer surplus, because prices are higher. Below the curve is higher consumer surplus because prices are lower. Without any innovations in product or process, any firm wishing to price below the indifference curve to gain volume will do so at the expense of profit. Genuine innovation might enable a competitor to make a different 'offer' in the form of a new indifference curve below the original one. This will offer higher consumer surplus, will divert volume towards the new competitor and take volume and profit away from the non-innovating competitor.

This is illustrated in Figure 6.19 by the luxury car market in the USA (the example is taken from Besanko *et al.* 2000). When the Japanese luxury automobiles Lexus, Infiniti and Acura were introduced in the late 1980s they offered comparable quality to Mercedes but at lower prices. Not surprisingly they gained market share. Eventually the Japanese firms increased prices and Mercedes lowered price, converging on a new and lower indifference curve. Overall the consumer gained – consumer surplus increased. The suppliers would have benefited if their costs had fallen by at least an equivalent amount.

Value creation and pricing

As goods move along the supply chain and into and along the firm's value chain, economic value is created. Firm A in Figure 6.20 illustrates the different value creation packages:

* Consumer surplus is benefit less price paid: B – P

* Firm profit (or producer surplus) is price paid by the consumer less costs: P – C

* Total value created is consumer surplus and firm profit: B – C

* Value added (as measured in the national accounts and used as a measure of output of the economy) is technically firm profit less costs of raw materials: P – RM

The firm's pricing decision can be seen as critical in partitioning total value between consumers and firms. A high price claims more for the firm, giving less to the consumer and running the risk that Firm B, for example, might opt for lower prices and attract volume

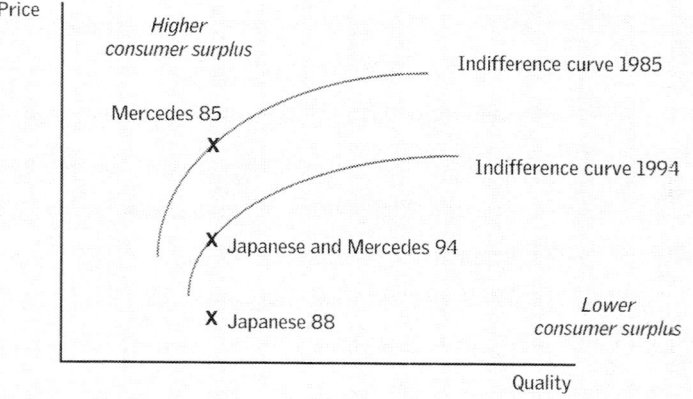

Figure 6.19 Value maps

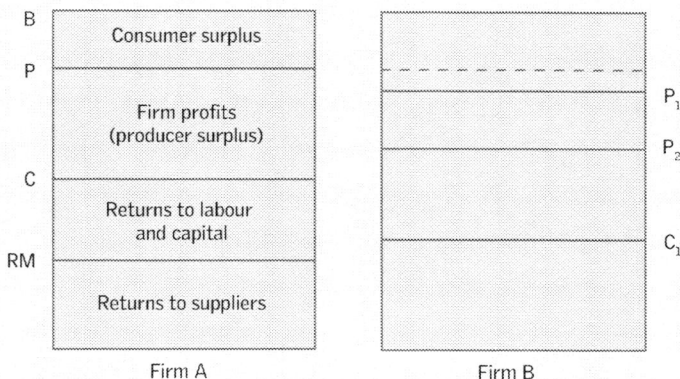

Figure 6.20 Pricing, consumer surplus and profit

away from Firm A. With similar costs competitive forces will move the market towards a common price level P. However, if Firm B is innovative and reduces costs to C_1, then it has the option of various prices below P, such as P_1 or P_2. The choice of price depends on the price elasticity of demand.

Pricing, price elasticity, costs and profits

Table 6.4 illustrates the interactions between price elasticity for the firm (not the market) and type of advantage – differentiation (benefit) or cost. The four boxes tell different stories:

* With a cost advantage and high price elasticity, it pays to underprice competitors to gain share.

* With a differentiation (benefit) advantage and high price elasticity, it pays to maintain price parity and let the differentiation advantage increase volume and thereby pull profits through.

* With cost advantage and low price elasticity the best option is a margin strategy whereby prices are maintained and profits are increased through the margin benefit.

* With a differentiation (benefit) advantage and low price elasticity, a margin strategy is again indicated where prices can be substantially raised because of the low elasticity and high benefits – profits accrue through increased margins with only small volume offsets.

In setting prices the task is to create a competitive advantage by (i) creating unique value to consumers (best possible consumer surplus) and (ii) creating above average profits for the firm. If every firm were like Firm A in Figure 6.20, there would be no competitive advantage. If one firm can innovate and create lower costs (like Firm B) or higher benefits, then a competitive advantage is possible for a range of possible prices depending on the price elasticities

Table 6.4 Pricing, advantage and profits

	Cost advantage	**Differentiation (benefit) advantage**
High price elasticity	SHARE STRATEGY Underprice competitors to gain share	SHARE STRATEGY Maintain price parity and let differentiation gain share
Low price elasticity	MARGIN STRATEGY Maintain price parity and gain profits through high margins	MARGIN STRATEGY Charge price premium relative to competitors

of demand and the type and scale of advantage available to the innovating firm. In this situation Firm B would wish to identify the 'break-even price elasticity', that is the elasticity that would enable it to identify the borderline between a share strategy and a margin strategy.

6.3 Strategic groups

In the same way that there are segments on the demand side, there are groups on the supply side. We call these strategic groups. From Figure 6.14 you can see that we have arrayed differentiation characteristics against cost characteristics to obtain a map of different locations for firms within an industry. In this case we looked in terms of the consequences for profits for firms in different locations. The dimensions of this matrix are strategic choices and thus difficult to change and difficult to imitate. Strategic groups are configurations of this kind. They represent substructures within an industry that enable us to identify groups of firms with similar strategies.

A strategic group is formed when:

> *A firm within a group makes strategic decisions that cannot readily be imitated by firms outside the group without substantial costs, significant elapsed time, or uncertainty about the outcome of those decisions.* (McGee and Thomas, 1986, p. 150)

Strategic groups are based on the notion of mobility barriers, the sources of which are illustrated in Table 6.5:

> *Mobility barriers are a corollary to the existence of strategic groups. They are factors which deter or inhibit the movement of a firm from one strategic position to another and, more generally, the expansion of firms in one group to a position held by another group. Therefore a mobility barrier is essentially a limitation on replicability or imitation. It acts like an entry barrier, but it acts for the group within the industry rather than for the industry as a whole.*
>
> *A group structuring carries no meaning without costs attached to the imitation of strategy by other firms. Mobility barriers thus reflect the decisions of firms and*

Table 6.5 Sources of mobility barriers

Market-related strategies	Supply and cost characteristics	Characteristics of firms

Product line
User technologies
Market segmentation
Distribution channels
Brand names
Geographic coverage
Selling systems
	Economies of scale:
	  production
	  marketing
	  administration
	Manufacturing processes
	R&D capability
	Marketing and distribution systems
		Ownership
		Organisation structure
		Control systems
		Management skills
		Boundaries of firms:
		  diversification
		  vertical integration
		Firm size
		Relationships with influence groups

Source: McGee and Thomas (1986) Strategic Management Journal, p. 151.

are a way of defining the set of key strategies available to a firm. The essential characteristic is relative cost advantage over all other competitors. The remedy for cost disadvantage of this kind probably involves investment expenditure on tangible or intangible assets with significant elapsed time before the investment comes to fruition. Moreover, the investment expenditures are irreversible ... and there will typically be considerable uncertainty attached to the outcome of the investment expenditures. (McGee and Thomas, 1986, p. 153)

6.3.1 The implications of strategic groups

Groups may exist for many different reasons. Investments in distinctive assets and therefore in competitive advantage are risky investments and firms may have quite different risk aversion postures. Thus, strategic positions, which are the outcome of patterns of decisions over time, can be seen in terms of return–risk trade-offs calculated ex ante. Corporate structure may also affect the nature of strategic groupings. Business units can vary considerably in their relationship with their corporate parents and may pursue different goal structures in ways that lead to strategy differences (see Sjostrom 1995). More generally, the historical development of an industry bestows differential advantages on firms depending on their timing of entry (first mover advantages versus follower advantages), geographical location (country-specific advantages), and sheer luck. Whatever the historical genesis of strategic groups, the essential characteristic is similarity along key strategic dimensions. The patterns of similarity and the extent of variety in an industry will have consequences along three dimensions:

1 the structure of the industry and its evolution over time;

2 the nature of competition; and

3 implications for relative performance of firms.

Industry structure analysis is intended to identify the nature and range of profit-earning possibilities for the participants. There are benchmark but simple models of perfect competition and monopoly (see Chapter 3), but the real interest lies in oligopolistic market structures within which different groups of firms may behave in systematically different ways protected (at least for a time) by their mobility barriers. Figure 6.14 illustrates the variety of structural types. Where there are significant opportunities available for both cost and differentiation there will be firms or groups of firms with different strategies and differing expansion paths. This becomes more important as the concept of industry becomes more fluid as entry conditions change, as boundaries become flexible and as 'new' industry groupings are formed (e.g. new media industries, new electronic commerce industries). Industry definition is in itself a form of classification process. Strategic group analysis provides a more fundamental basis for assessing future strategic possibilities and the emergence of new industry boundaries.

Strategic groups affect the nature of competition. Because of their structural similarities, firms in the same group are likely to respond in the same way to disturbances from outside the group and to competitive activities within the group. Here we can see oligopolistic interdependence at work on the basis of ability to imitate the moves of rivals. The interdependence here does not arise from targeting the same customers (although this may be a consequence of similar strategies) but stems solely from the possession of structural similarities.

The ability to explain the relative performance of firms is a central theme in strategic management research. Wide variation in profitability is characteristic of many industries and means that industry structural characteristics are not likely to be a good or stable predictor of profitability. However, mobility barriers (i.e. strategy differences) can explain persistent differences in profit rates between groups in an industry. Porter (1979) argued that the pattern and intensity of inter-group competition and the consequences for profitability in the industry depends on three factors:

1 *The number and size distribution of groups.* Other things held constant, the more numerous and more equal in size are the strategic groups, the higher is the rivalry. On the other hand, if one strategic group constitutes a small portion of an industry while another is a very large portion, then strategic asymmetry is likely to have little impact on rivalry since the power of the small group to influence the large group is probably low.

2 *The strategic distance between groups.* This is the degree to which strategies in different groups differ in terms of the key strategic decision variables. The greater this distance, the more difficult tacit co-ordination becomes and the more vigorous rivalry will be in the industry.

3 *The market interdependence between groups.* Diversity of strategies increases rivalry between groups the most, where market interdependence is high. However, those

strategic groups that possess high mobility barriers are relatively more insulated from rivalry. On the other hand, when strategic groups are targeting very different segments, their effect on each other is much less severe.

Profits may be differentially affected across strategic groups for other reasons:

* There may be differences in bargaining power that some strategic groups may have towards customers and/or suppliers. These differences may be due to differences in scale, threat of vertical integration or product differentiation following from differing strategies.

* There may be differences in the degree of exposure of strategic groups to *substitute products* produced by other industries.

* There may be great differences in the degree to which firms *within* the group compete with each other. While mutual dependence should be fully recognized within groups that contain few firms, it may be difficult to sustain if there are numerous firms in the strategic group or if the risk profiles of the firms differ.

There are also firm-specific factors that influence profitability within a group:

* *Differences in firms' scale within the strategic group.* Although firms within the same strategic groups are likely to be similar in the scales of their operations, differences in scale *may* exist and may work to the disadvantage of smaller firms in the group where there are aspects of the strategy subject to economies of scale.

* *Differences in the cost of mobility into a strategic group.* If there are absolute cost advantages of being early in establishing brand names, locating raw materials, etc., a later entrant in a specific strategic group may face some disadvantages with respect to established firms. Timing is in this case a factor that may impact profit differences. This may also be the case if an established firm also possesses assets from its operations in other industries that could be jointly utilized.

* *Ability of the firm to execute or implement its strategy* in an operational sense. Some firms may be superior in their ability to organize and manage operations, develop creative advertising themes, make technological breakthroughs with given inputs of resources and the like. While these are not structural advantages of the sort created by mobility barriers, they may be relatively stable advantages if the market for managers, scientists and creative personnel is imperfect. Those firms in a group with superior abilities to execute strategies will be more profitable than others firms in the same group.

6.3.2 Strategic mapping

It is convenient and conventional to turn the multidimensional concept of strategic groups into a practical tool by drawing strategic maps. These are two-dimensional replications of the larger group structure within which the important strategic dimensions can be seen and through which key opportunities and threats can be depicted. The key steps in this process are (following Fiegenbaum et al., 1990, and Fiegenbaum and Thomas, 1990):

1 choice of the strategy space (industry);
2 choice of organizational levels to be incorporated (corporate, business or functional);
3 identification of the variables which best capture firms' strategies;
4 identification of stable time periods;
5 clustering of firms into strategic groups.

The main issue concerning choice of strategic space relates to the identification of the boundaries of the 'industry'. The concept of industry is fuzzy but in practice we often over-rely on Standard Industrial Classification (SIC) codes. However, these mirror product variation and are typically bounded by nationality. The term strategic space is used as an alternative to industry to indicate that the relevant criterion for choice is competitive interaction.

When choosing the organizational level at which to analyse firms' strategies one must not simply focus on business level characteristics such as product and geographical scope, and relative emphasis on cost versus differentiation. Corporate parenting can provide a significant element of the eventual competitive advantage and it would be an oversimplification to exclude corporate effects. Similarly, functional strategies such as advertising intensity and sales force characteristics can be critical investments in support of the business strategy.

On the identification of the variables representing firms' strategies it is common to argue that there are a small number of dimensions that capture the essence of strategy differences between firms and between groups. This suggests that it is entirely possible to adopt a pragmatic approach. Typically an in-depth case study can reflect the views of industry participants, can give peer group judgements on competitors' strategies, and can also give the analyst a database for independent judgement. The alternative is to use clustering and other statistical techniques to determine, de facto, what groups exist and then to interpret the groupings using independent data on strategy dimensions. This is typically the route taken by academic researchers.[3]

---

[3] A number of different methods exist for clustering firms into groups. Analysis of empirical research indicates that most researchers use cluster analysis. Once strategic variables have been identified, researchers generally use clustering techniques to form groups so that homogeneity is at its maximum internally and at its minimum externally. There is considerable debate about the nature of cluster analysis; see Ketchen and Shook (1996) for a review of the way it has been used in strategy research. The advantage of cluster analysis is that it indicates the distance that exists between strategic groups and between companies within the same strategic group. The distance between groups can be considered as approximating the height of mobility barriers while the distance between firms can be used as a basis to analyse the differences between them. The main difficulty with cluster analysis is that it identifies clusters regardless of the presence or absence of any underlying structure (Ketchen and Shook, 1996). Then there remains the question of how to describe and empirically validate the dimensions that the analysis reveals.

Much research in strategic management has studied industry change over long periods of time. This contrasts with research in economics where the emphasis has been much more on cross-section, relatively short-period studies. When studying strategic groups longitudinally there is a problem about identifying the nature of change and the way it affects the groupings. The typical approach is to think in terms of 'punctuated equilibria'. Periods of stability are punctuated by periods of change within which strategies are changed, new positions taken up, and rivalry adjusts in response. Firms' strategies and industry structure are seen in equilibrium during each strategic time period. When the equilibrium ends (maybe because of exogenous shocks in the environment or alternatively triggered by autonomous firm actions), some firms change their strategies, new strategic groups are formed and others disappear. Statistical techniques can be used to identify the relatively stable sub-periods within which strategic groups are identifiable (see Bogner, Thomas and McGee 1996) and the transition points or periods from one equilibrium to the next.

6.3.3 Strategic groups in practice

We illustrate these points by looking at a study of the food processing industry in Europe at the time of the enactment of the European Single Market Act 1987–1992 (McGee and Segal-Horn 1990 and 1992). This looked across conventional market (national) boundaries and asked how the industry might evolve given the exogenous legislation shocks to the industry.

The practical question concerned the possible emergence of a pan-European food industry from the existing mosaic of separate nationally focused industries, i.e. transnational companies emerging from multidomestic structures. This possibility was mooted in the context of the Single European Act, conceived in 1987 for implementation by 1992. This was expected to reduce the costs of access to separate European markets and, along with expectations about increasing homogeneity of consumers across Europe, constituted external triggers for structural change.

The approach to this was to develop a model of 'strategic space' on to which the prospective movements of firms could be mapped. A historical overview enabled the identification of periods of stability and the conditions causing breaks between periods. On the basis of this history, key variables were identified as the basis for strategic group identification. These were market scope (territories covered), marketing intensity and brand strength, manufacturing focus, and R&D intensity (the latter two were not statistically validated). These were used to identify the strategic group configuration in 1990, enabling the identification of at least four distinct groupings. However, the real interpretive power of the configuration lay in the specification of the mobility barriers between the groups. The strategic space idea is the converse of the strategic group, i.e. why is there no group present in a particular location on an n-dimensional map. The first possible answer is that some spaces are currently infeasible and the asset structures implied by that space are competitively dominated by other asset structures. The second possible answer is that some spaces have never been entered because the construction of the implied assets was not thought to be competitively viable. This second insight allowed the analysis of certain empty spaces to suggest that certain assets could technically be constructed (e.g. European marketing systems and brands) and that changing market conditions might yield a pay-off for those new asset structures.

Thus the strategic group/space analysis allowed the juxtaposition of a changing market situation in Europe with a lowering of mobility barriers between existing groups and the empty spaces. The conclusion drawn is that certain kinds of new asset structures of firms are very likely to be constructed and that these will fall into two or three key new groups. The processes by which this might happen can be identified, including a wave of mergers and acquisitions. The consequences for competition both in the transition period and for a period of subsequent stability can be analysed, although the time period over which the transition will take place could not be identified. The analysis is distinctive in that it is almost entirely prospective in character, laying out a framework for analysing future change in the industry.

Figures 6.21, 6.22, 6.23 and 6.24 summarize the analysis. Figure 6.21 shows the existing strategic group structure in the late 1980s. Figure 6.22 summarizes the mobility barriers that protect each group. Figure 6.23 contains the strategic space analysis and Figure 6.24 shows the authors' conjectures about the group configuration in 2000. The dimensions of the matrix are key strategic decisions faced by firms in this industry, namely geographical coverage of the EC (representing internationalization strategy) and marketing intensity (representing brand focus). The map distinguishes different kinds of brand players, national versus European in scope, and cost-based own-label suppliers.

The authors conclude:

> *First, two major new strategies are likely to emerge, the pan-European own label supplier and the pan-European brander. Second, the strategic space analysis tells us something about the pathways to achieving these positions. Third, it also tells us something about the nature of competition both en route and in the new structure. This approach does not tell us how long the process of change will take, nor does it say*

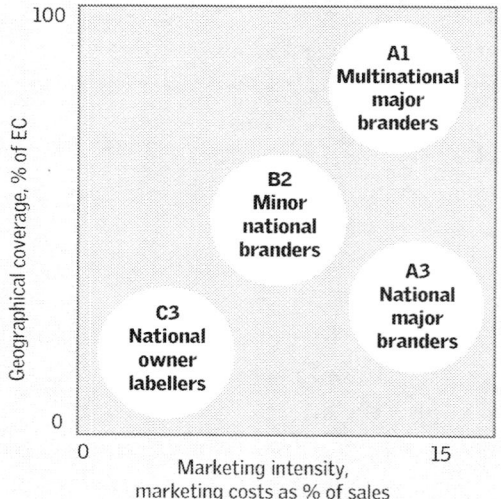

Figure 6.21 European food processing industry strategic groups, late 1980s
Source: McGee and Segal-Horn (1990) *Journal of Marketing Management*. Reproduced with permission of Westburn Publishers Ltd.

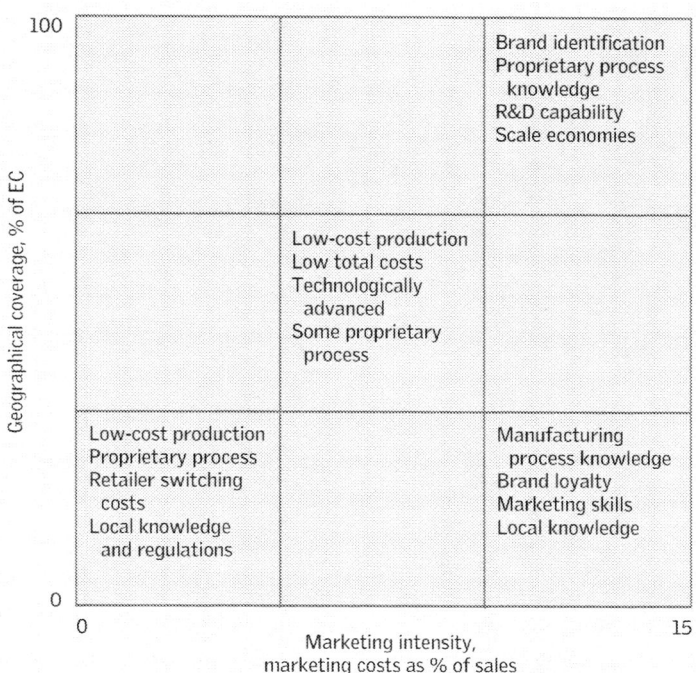

Figure 6.22 European food processing industry mobility barriers, late 1980s
Source: McGee and Segal-Horn (1990) *Journal of Marketing Management*. Reproduced with permission of Westburn Publishers Ltd.

who will be the winners and losers. It does, however, say a great deal about the characteristics of the winners and losers. (McGee and Segal-Horn, 1990, p. 190)

After the passage of time since this paper was written, it is interesting to reflect on the extent to which the pan-European brander space has been occupied. At that time it seemed like an attractive space since it offered economies of scale across a European market that was showing signs of converging consumer tastes, developing its logistics networks and creating fewer larger factories. In the 1990s it becomes clear that Unilever, Nestlé and Mars were beginning to focus on just such a strategy (Johnson and Scholes 1999, p. 129).[4]

Strategic group maps do not have to be historical and therefore 'backward-looking'. History is important in developing an understanding of the nature of mobility barriers and the time and cost involved in investing to overcome them. However, one can assess the present and make forward-looking conjectures. For example, Figure 6.25 is a speculative map constructed in 1996 of retail banking in 2000 in order to assess the implications of new

---

[4] Note that the Pan-European group emerges with lower marketing/sales ratios because transnationals (and trans-regionals) save costs by eliminating duplication of marketing costs across country markets.

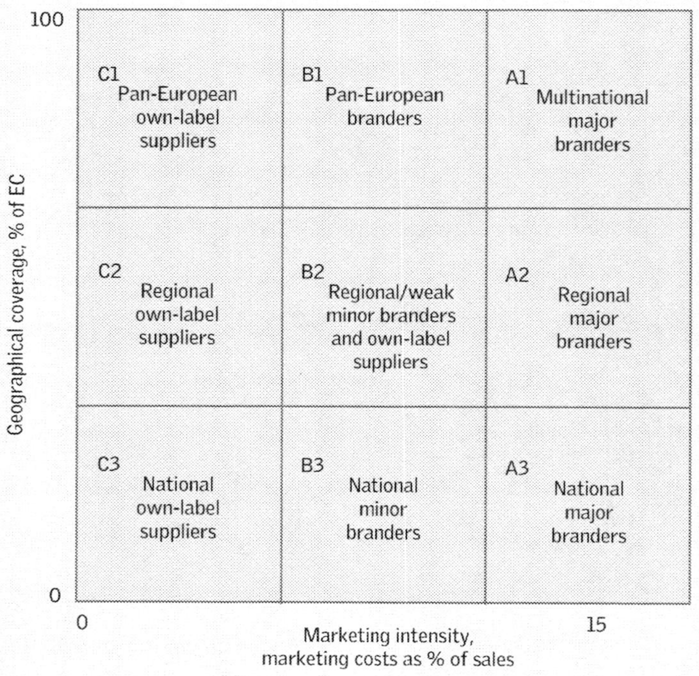

Figure 6.23 European food processing industry strategic space analysis
Source: McGee and Segal-Horn (1990) *Journal of Marketing Management*. Reproduced with permission of Westburn Publishers Ltd.

possibilities such as banking through the internet. The two strategy dimensions are degree of vertical integration and brand novelty. Traditional banks have a 'complete' value chain and do everything in-house whereas the new e-banks focus for the most part on electronic distribution and sub-contract everything else such as cheque processing. The new e-banks have enormous brand novelty indicated by the plethora of 'cute' names such as Egg, Goldfish and Smile. Thus, we have two utterly distinct groups. The first question to ask is, are these groups highly rivalrous, or is the emergence of the new group merely indicative of a new market segment? This poses a degree of threat to traditional banks which need to ask whether they can remain where they are with some strategic adaptation such as opening of new electronic channels of distribution in parallel to their existing channels (viz. the High Street). Or should they seek to develop some brand novelty? Or perhaps deconstruct their integrated value chains into separate upstream and downstream businesses? Or is there a different dimension on which they can play, for instance TV banking? For the new e-banks the question is, to what extent is this strategic group defensible? Should a highly deconstructed value chain be supported by a series of alliances to secure access to best-in-class highly complementary activities?

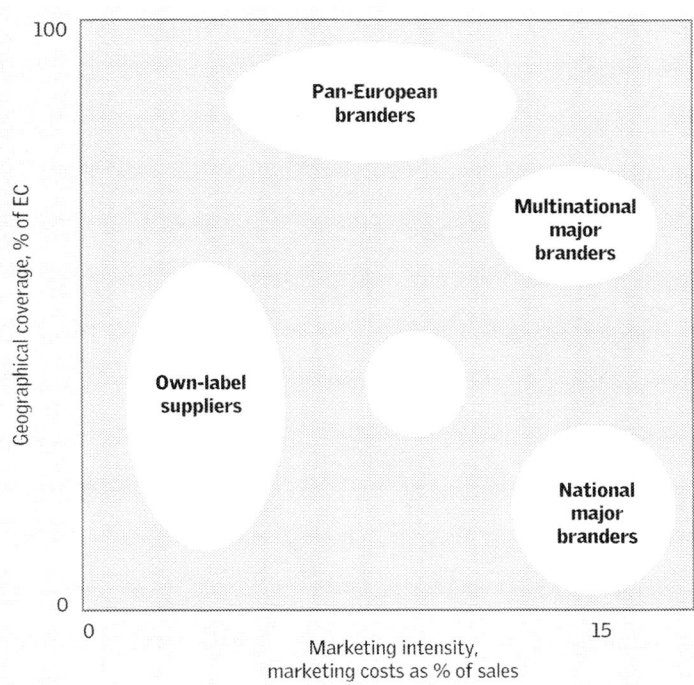

Figure 6.24 European food processing industry strategic groups, 2000
Source: McGee and Segal-Horn (1990) *Journal of Marketing Management*. Reproduced with permission of Westburn Publishers Ltd.

These two examples demonstrate some key themes:

1 Strategic group analysis enriches our discussion of the nature of strategic choice.

2 The formation of groups reflects strategy innovations and risky decisions.

3 The stability of group structures over time tells us, through mobility barriers, about sustainability.

4 The nature of mobility barriers forces us to think about the investments that underpin market position and competitive advantage. It points us towards the nature of resources and the idea of core competences.

Any analysis of group structures leads very quickly from history to predictive ability. The essence of strategic decision is investment in distinctive assets against an uncertain future and therefore strategy innovations and industry evolution are closely linked. Innovation disturbs the industry equilibrium and foreshadows the emergence of new ways of competing and new group structures. Ex ante analysis of possible strategy innovations gives an indication of new strategy dimensions and therefore the nature, pattern and intensity of future rivalry. The pay-offs from this approach can be summarized in terms of interpretation, framework and language, viz.:

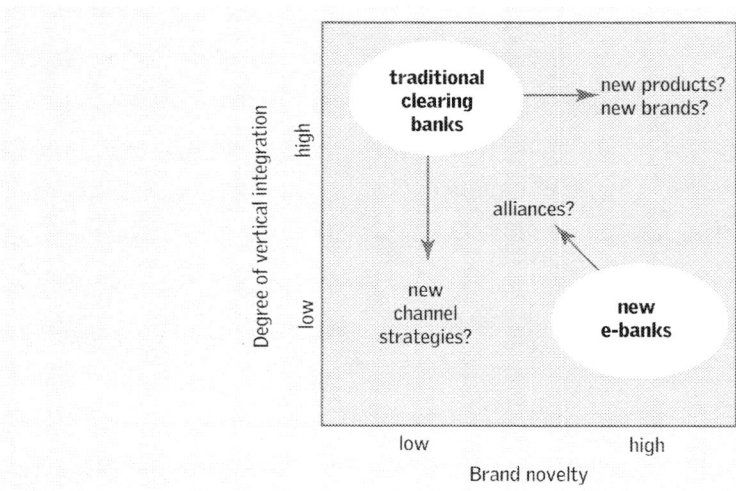

Figure 6.25 UK retail banking, 2000

1 a richer *interpretation* of current industry structures and the interaction of firm asset (tangible and intangible) structures with intra-industry competition;

2 a conceptual *framework* for analysing change over time and across industries;

3 a *language* for interpreting change in terms of asset structures of firms and the ensuing effects on competition in the long run.

6.4 Industry transformation

It is common to observe that change is endemic and many consulting firms have been very successful in promoting programmes of strategic change. However, many also note that strategies by their nature are not things that one changes readily or frequently. Strategies involve investment in lumpy and sticky assets without the comfort of knowing that mistakes can be easily undone. Nevertheless, markets and industries do evolve and grow. Growth very often is continuous and cumulative, especially when research and development follows cumulative trajectories. The experience of the last quarter of a century shows that new knowledge has very often moved sideways into adjacent industries and done an excellent job of unsettling long-held beliefs and strategies. Thus, new materials such as plastics have undermined the steel industry and the coming of the internet has caused major changes in distribution industries. So are there any patterns in the way in which industries are transformed? In what ways does Porter's famous picture of the five forces change systematically? Figure 6.26 suggests the major possibilities.

The principal industry transformation routes, as a result of which the five forces are reconfigured, are:

1 redefining the market

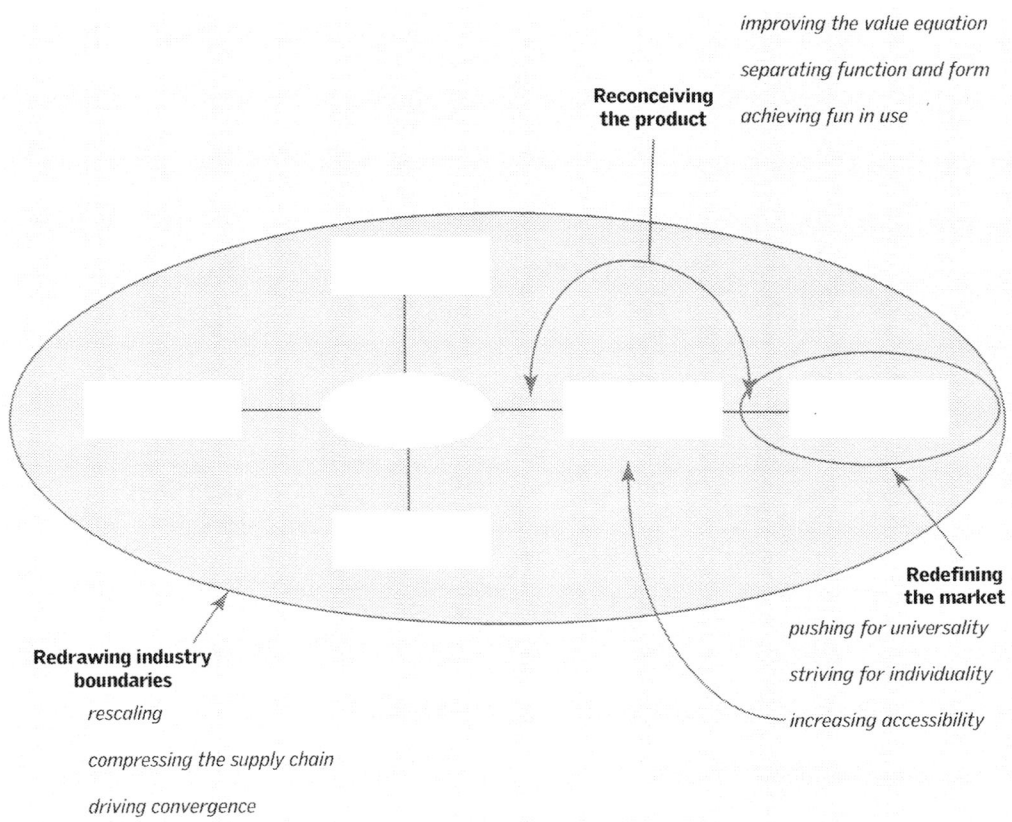

improving the value equation

separating function and form

Reconceiving the product   *achieving fun in use*

Redefining the market

pushing for universality

striving for individuality

increasing accessibility

Redrawing industry boundaries

rescaling

compressing the supply chain

driving convergence

Figure 6.26 Industry transformation routes

2   reconceiving the product

3   redrawing the industry boundaries

Market redefinitions involve changing the relationship with the customer. At one level firms may seek universality, that is, striving to get a wider take-up of their products across hitherto distinct market segments. This is the approach typically taken in internationalization and we could say that Coca-Cola has succeeded in achieving a universal market. The opposite approach is individualization with segments of one person – an approach typical in modern electronic and internet-based industries. Most redefinition strategies have some element of higher accessibility involving major changes in logistics and distribution.

Rethinking the role of the product is also an attempt to capture changes that are taking place in the psychology of consumers. There have been fundamental and controversial changes in the nature of drinks on offer to young people (alco-pops, for example), where the producers have been trying to tap into the rapid changes that are taking place.

146 | McGee-Thomas-Wilson:
Strategy: Analysis and
Practice, Text and Cases | 6. Competitive strategy: the
analysis of strategic
position | Text | © The McGraw-Hill
Companies, 2006

Similarly, sports cars are being redefined as toys for the retired. Product changes typically involve changing the value equation (benefit–cost ratio to the customer).

Redrawing industry boundaries stems from major changes in the underling economics of production and of the supply chain in general. The drivers of change are usually rescaling to obtain economies, and driving convergence and eliminating variety to the same end. A simple way of reducing costs has been to outsource more and more but this in itself is not strategic – it is more a rebalancing of the location of costs along the chain. More significant is the compressing of the supply chain, where new technology raises the possibility of changing the nature of the operations in the chain with the effect of changing the product and its cost characteristics.

In Chapter 5 and in this chapter we have often referred to the 'economic model' that captures the essential economic characteristics and cash flows of the firm. In assessing strategic position we wish to be able to relate the intended strategic position and the nature of the competitive advantage to the performance of the firm. In the next section we introduce the idea of the business model.

6.5 Business model

This is a widely used term intended to provide the link between an intended strategy, its functional and operational requirements, and the performance (typically cash flows and profits) that is expected. It usually applies to single businesses where a specific competitive strategy can be identified but it can also apply to those multi-business portfolios that are linked by strong synergies and therefore have common or similar strategies.

Chesbrough and Rosenbloom (2002) cite their experience in turning up 107,000 references to 'business model' on the World Wide Web while only finding three citations in the academic literature. In the usual practitioner sense, a business model is the method of doing business by which a company can sustain itself – that is, generate revenue. The business model spells out how a company makes money by specifying where it is positioned in the value chain. A more precise definition has been offered by the consultants KM Lab (2000): 'business model is a description of how your company intends to create value in the marketplace. It includes that unique combination of products, services, image and distribution that your company carries forward. It also includes the underlying organization of people and operational infrastructure that they use to accomplish their work.'

Chesbrough and Rosenbloom (2002) describe the functions of a business model as:

* to articulate the value proposition
* to identify a market segment
* to define the structure of the value chain
* to estimate the cost structure and profit potential

* to describe the position of the firm within the supply chain
* to formulate the strategic logic by which the firm will gain and hold advantage

The simple Du Pont accounting identities are a good starting point for identifying a business model. Thus:

$$\pi = (p - c)Q - F$$

and

$$NA = WC + FA$$

where

π is profits
p is price
c is variable costs
Q is quantity sold
F is fixed costs
NA is net assets
WC is working capital
FA is fixed assets

An intended strategy should have specific effects on the variables in these equations. For example, a cost leadership strategy would be expected to reduce variable costs, to increase fixed costs, and to increase fixed assets – according to the economies of scale available. Accordingly, profits and return on investment (π/NA) will be expected to increase because the rise in fixed costs and fixed assets due to the investment will be more than offset by the increase in contribution margin $(p - c)$. A more ambitious business model might also specify a price reduction that will result in a volume increase through the medium of a high price elasticity and no imitation by competitors. The validity of such an assumption about lack of competitor response depends on judgements about competitor cost levels and their willingness to sacrifice margin for volume.

Similarly, a differentiation strategy would be expected to raise both costs and prices. Costs would go up because of the variable costs (such as quality and service levels) and fixed costs (such as advertising and R&D) of differentiation. Prices would be expected to increase disproportionately if the value to customers was sufficiently high to make the product price inelastic. This business model then calls for a higher margin game, offset to some degree by higher fixed costs. A more ambitious model might also aim for a volume increase on the basis of higher product 'value' stimulating demand (a rising demand curve rather than a negatively sloped one).

What the business model does is to articulate the logic of the intended strategy in terms of the specific operations that have to take place. With this detailed plan the consequences for cash flows can be determined and the link between (intended) strategy and (expected) performance can be established. Beyond the obvious benefit of quantifying the strategic logic of the firm, the business model also enables sensitivity testing and risk analysis. In the case of the cost leadership example the intention might be to reduce variable costs by a target percentage. The implications of a shortfall in cost reduction can easily be calculated and expressed in terms of the percentage change in profits in relation to a given percentage shortfall from the target cost reduction. Where the business model calls for price changes, the implications of competitor imitation or non-imitation can also be calculated.

In practice a business model can be articulated in terms of detailed plans and budgets that provide guidance to managers relating to their operational responsibilities. The logic that drives plans and budgets lies within the business model. The business model itself is the mechanism through which a business intends to generate revenue and profits. Figure 6.27 shows a schematic (Yip, 2004) that describes the process from inputs to customers – in many ways this is simply a restyled value chain. This should not be surprising – the value chain is an activity map on to which can be placed assets and costs. Figure 6.28 shows an application to the existing mobile telephony business (*see* end of chapter case study). The merit of this is the explicit nature of the choices made and from this the implications for cash flows will follow. A different example is shown in Figure 6.29. This describes the leasing operations of a London bank. This shows clearly the performance dimensions at the top of the figure. Shareholder value is decomposed into components such as market share, price and costs. The bottom of the figure shows the drivers of the cash flows, starting with characteristics such as flexibility and moving upwards to a higher level of aggregation to customer satisfaction and brand strength from which the cash flows stem directly. This is an unusual picture of a business

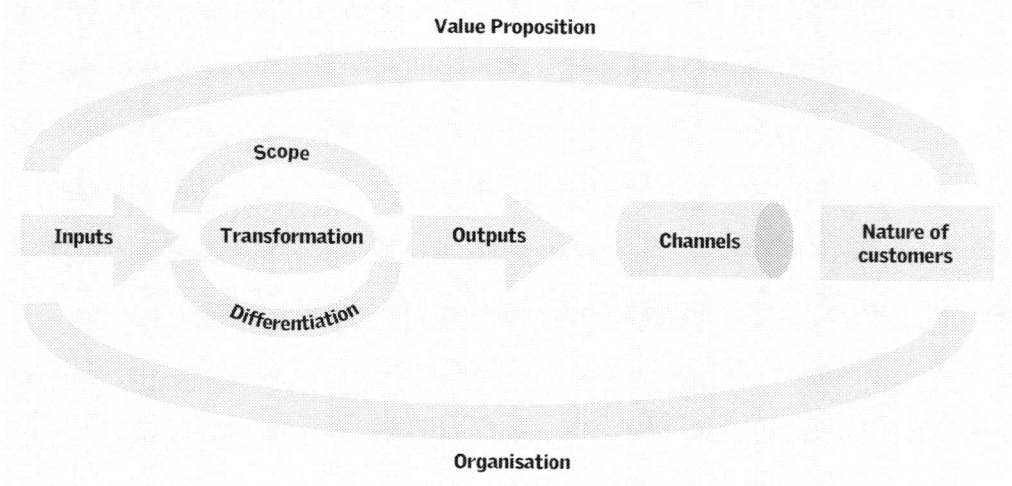

Figure 6.27 Elements of a business model
Source: Yip, 2004.

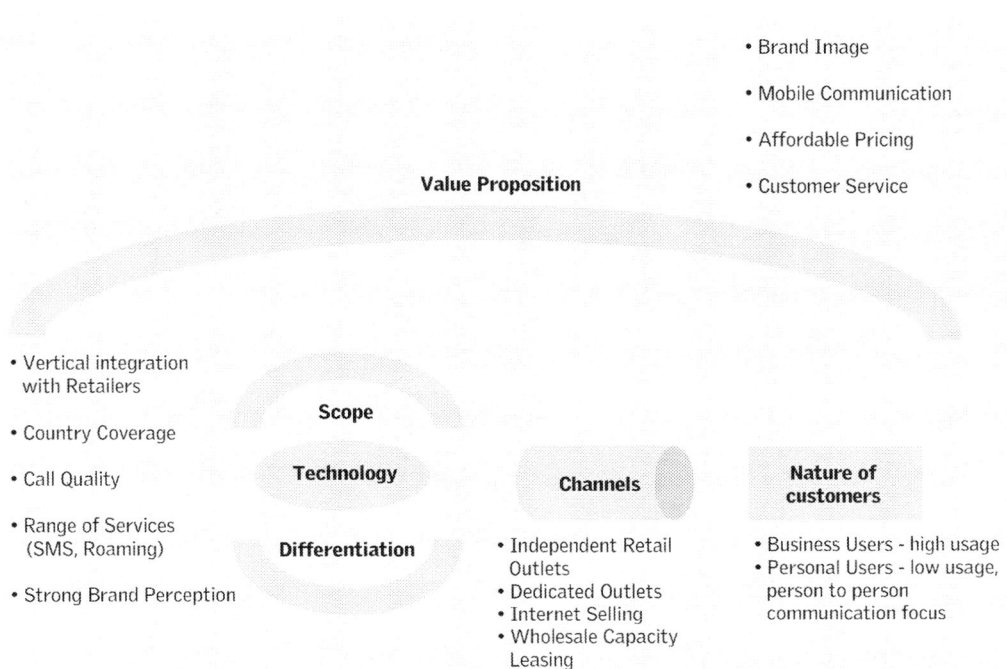

Figure 6.28 The 2G business model
Source: Puri, 2004.

model because it is not faithful to the value chain idea – only selected activities are shown. You should look at this and ask yourself (i) is this likely to be an accurate model if some variables are excluded? (ii) not all the variables are observable and quantifiable – does this matter? and (iii) what extra information would you require (hint: consider sensitivity analysis)?

6.5.1 Commitment and sustainability

The business model has become a standard part of the business lexicon to indicate the way cash flows are underpinned by a strategic logic. For the business model to be genuinely useful it needs to reflect the sustainability and defensibility of its strategic position and the nature of the commitment that is required in the strategic assets of the firm. Recall the strategy cycle (Figure 5.9) and note that the top line requires a balancing of resources and assets with the market position. The resource and asset component of this is discussed in the next chapter. Sustainability of the strategic position is to do with the imitability (or otherwise) of the competitive advantage. The five forces model gives an indication of the overall attractiveness of the industry – attractiveness means the degree to which the profits of the industry players are protected from erosion by the five competitive forces. More specifically, sustainability is to do with the insulation of the net cash flows (and the net present value of

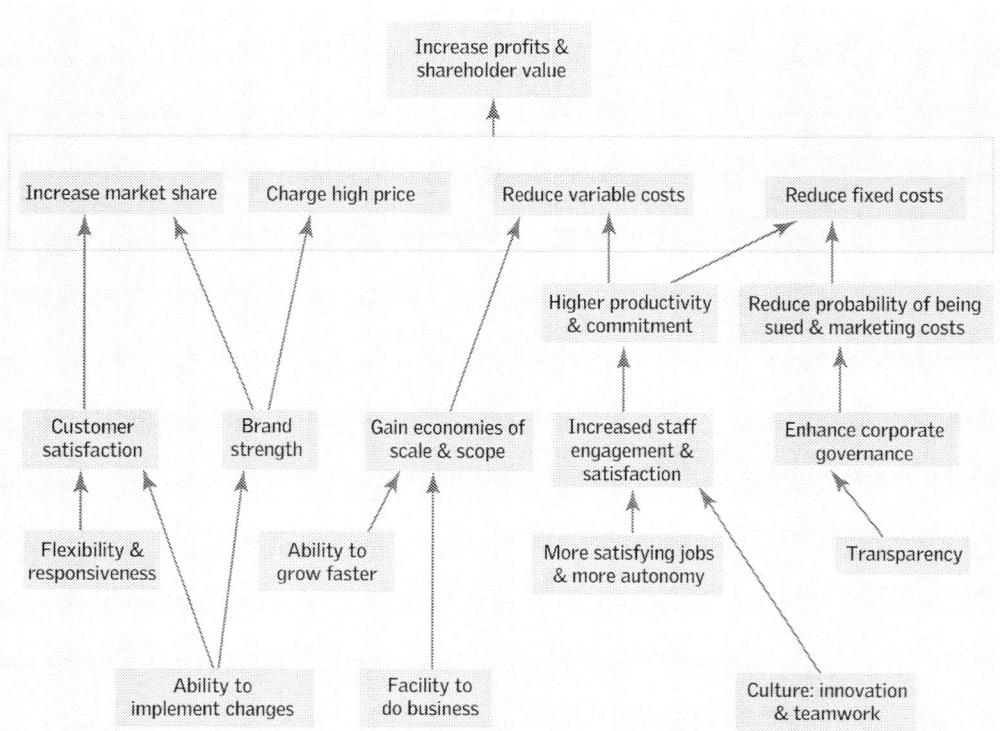

Figure 6.29 London bank: leasing business model
Source: Tello, 2004.

the firm) from attack by any individual competitor. A failing of the generic five forces model is its inability to move beyond the industry on average or in general. Sustainability analysis involves analysing potential responses by competitors and potential entrants and the impact of those actions on the degree of competition and on the cash flows that are generated by the competitive advantage of the incumbent firm. Richard Rumelt invented the term iso-lating mechanisms to refer to the economic forces that limit the extent to which a competitive advantage can be neutralized or duplicated. Isolating mechanisms are to the firm what entry barriers are to an industry – they are the forces that inhibit other firms from competing away profits from incumbent firms. There are different approaches to identifying and classifying isolating mechanisms (*see* Rumelt 1984; Ghemawat 1991, 1994a, 1994b; Yao 1988). Besanko *et al.* (2000) put them in two distinct groups.

Impediments to imitation

These isolating mechanisms prevent firms from imitating and/or surpassing the resources, competences and strategic assets that underpin the incumbent's advantage. Thus, many firms compete in the executive car markets but few, if any, can match the approach of BMW and Mercedes. Note, however, the concerted efforts of Audi, Jaguar and Lexus to do so. In the soft drinks industry Coca-Cola has been unrivalled in fostering its brand name as a symbol of uniqueness. These impediments include legal restrictions, superior access to inputs or to customers, and intangible barriers (resource-based) to imitating the incumbent's core competences.

Early mover advantages

Once a firm establishes a competitive advantage then certain economic forces can protect its position. We saw earlier in this chapter the example of Du Pont in titanium dioxide. Its first move pre-empted the market by establishing a requirement for sufficiently large size to attain competitive costs that there was insufficient room in the market for followers. Similarly, Microsoft's position as the effective standard in the personal computer industry (see Chapter 13 for an analysis of network effects) has meant that no follower has been able to create a value proposition for consumers such that they would be willing to incur the costs of switching to a new (and presumably much improved) standard. These impediments are all related to market size and scale economies, and also to technological change and the creation of legally recognized or de facto standards.

Firms usually analyse isolating mechanisms through a process of competitor analysis (*see* Channon, 1988). This can take a variety of forms but usually contains a number of common headings:

- Identifying which competitors to track
  - existing direct competitors
  - new and potential entrants

- Establishing a competitor database
  - surveying sources of competitor intelligence
  - collecting data regularly and systematically
  - building and using the database

- Analysing competitor strategies
  - functional strategies
    - marketing
    - production/operations
    - R&D
    - financing strategy
  - business unit strategies
  - corporate/group objectives
  - long-term financial capability

Competitor analysis is capable of giving insight into ways in which the incumbent's core competences might be imitated or outflanked. Sometimes this can be done by direct observation of the activities of competitors and making appropriate inferences. A longer-range warning might come from studying the stated and sometimes covert intentions of significant competitors. Thus, Citibank and Chase Manhattan might have credited the possible appearance of HSBC[5] as a global competitor as it began its move out of its Hong Kong base in the early 1980s. It is now bigger than Chase.

These ideas are captured in the case box below, which discusses changes in the business model for large pharmaceutical companies.

Case box: Big trouble for Big Pharma

Why Big Pharma urgently needs a new business model

When GlaxoWellcome and SmithKlineBeecham announced their merger in 2000 to form GlaxoSmithKline (GSK), the world's second-largest drug firm, its new boss, Jean-Pierre Garnier, said that the merged firms would be 'the kings of science.' This week GSK unveiled its crown jewels: a full pipeline of compounds in research and development, the result of a £2.6 billion ($4.5 billion), 16,000-researcher-strong effort. 82 new drugs and 20 vaccines are in development, 44 of them moving into later-stage trials. Yet if Mr Garnier hoped that these numbers would impress his shareholders, he had to think again: GSK's share price actually fell on the news. Like investors in many other big drug firms, GSK's shareholders have little confidence that many of its new compounds will earn them a cent anytime soon. Of the 20 drugs that GSK plans to put into final-phase human testing in the next three years, the chances are, on current industry averages, that less than half of them will make it to market.

Next, consider Merck. On November 20th, news that the firm was stopping development of a diabetes drug after finding tumours in lab mice was met with dismay – and a wave of selling that knocked 11% off the firm's already-battered share price. With another vaunted project – an experimental anti-depressant – also failing last month, Merck's near-term pipeline now looks horribly empty. Even an upbeat profit forecast for next year, on December 3rd, did not cheer investors much.

Merck and GSK are not alone. In 1998–2002, according to Lehman Brothers, Big Pharma firms launched on average 59 drugs per year. In 2002–06, reckons Lehman, they will launch just 50 per year. Moreover, as many patents for the industry's existing products expire in the next five years, competition from generic-drug makers will threaten $30 billion (one-fifth) of annual sales in America alone, says AT Kearney, a consultancy.

When the drugs don't work

Big Pharma now faces two big challenges. First, control costs better. Stuart Walker, head of the Centre for Medicines Research International, reckons that total industry spending on R&D

---

[5] Formerly the Hong Kong and Shanghai Banking Corporation.

will reach $50 billion this year, over 25% up on 1998. Sales and marketing overheads have soared, too. In the past four years, says Dean Hart, head of North American sales at Takeda, a Japanese drug firm, the number of sales representatives employed by drug firms in America has risen by 54%, to 90,000. Each rep costs on average $200,000 a year. Sales, general and administrative expenses account for 17% of a typical big American firm's revenues, says Christopher White of AT Kearney. In the drug industry, such overheads (even excluding the big American sales forces) account for 33% of revenues. Standard management practices such as consolidating procurement, outsourcing personnel and finance functions and automating transaction processing all compare poorly with other industries, says Mr White. Many firms still make pills in-house, a job perhaps better done by a contract manufacturer.

But the tougher challenge is to improve the productivity of R&D. As Mr Walker points out, it is not just the number of new products that has fallen in recent years, but also their originality. Less than 30% of drugs launched last year were first or second in their class. The proportion was far higher in the late 1990s. Roughly 40% of R&D spending by Big Pharma is now on 'line extensions' – improving existing drugs, not creating entirely new ones.

Many big drug firms have begun to license more of their technology and products from outside companies, especially biotechnology start-ups: having slumped in recent years, the value of biotech firms is now rising again. Novartis has set up a big R&D centre in Cambridge, Massachusetts, in part to better position itself to collaborate with outside academics. Eli Lilly's InnoCentive subsidiary runs a website where problems confronting drugmakers, such as how to generate a particular compound in chemical synthesis, are posted to be tackled by more than 25,000 registered problem-solvers as far afield as Russia and China. For a reward of $10,000–100,000, the firm gets a solution that would have cost more time and money to solve itself.

Others hope to improve the way they manage in-house R&D. Wyeth is encouraging its researchers to perform their tasks better by changing how it pays them. Unusually for the industry, its scientists get to share a bonus pool which depends, in part, on how many new drugs they launch each year. There used to be a temptation for Wyeth's early-stage researchers to throw their work 'over the wall' before it was ready to the scientists who run clinical trials, says Robert Ruffolo, the firm's head of research. Because early-stage researchers now share incentives with later-stage scientists, the later-stage researchers have begun to 'pull' the development of the most promising compounds forward. A corresponding 'push' from early-stage workers hastens the process. GSK fundamentally reorganised its R&D in 2001, splitting its more creative arm into smaller 'centres of excellence', and enlarging the arm that enjoys economies of scale. Mr Garnier claims that his 'best of both worlds' strategy is now paying off.

The industry's bloated overheads appear to be driving its decisions on the sort of drugs it seeks to develop. Like a supermodel who will not get out of bed for less than $10,000 a day, Big Pharma has decided that it is simply not worth investing in anything but a blockbuster.

This means that lesser, albeit interesting, compounds fall by the wayside. An oft-quoted figure from the Tufts Centre for the Study of Drug Development puts the average cost of bringing a new drug to market at $897m. But as F.M. Scherer, an economist, points out, this is an average cost for big firms producing drugs for chronic diseases. Other firms can bring drugs for other complaints – infectious diseases or rare conditions, say – to the market for around $100m–200m.

Big Pharma also needs to do something about its poorly trained, generalised sales force, which is simply not equipped to chase smaller, more specialised markets. Most sales calls end, at best, with just a few seconds of a doctor's time, laments Mr Hart of Takeda. Some reps do not even make it past the reception desk before dropping off their free samples. Drug firms lag behind other industries in the way they use information technology to discriminate between profitable and unprofitable customers. Only one in five drug companies invests in any sales force training beyond initial courses offered to recruits. Who, after all, needed to bother with trifles such as training and IT when, without much effort, a drug such as Lipitor, Pfizer's cholesterol-lowering medicine, was making sales of $8.6 billion last year alone?

Can Big Pharma achieve transformation without changes at the top? The bosses of big drugs firms have been horribly slow to grasp the enormity of their problems. Until recently, Merck's boss, Raymond Gilmartin, has been reluctant to license much technology from outside, instead putting his faith in the firm's own scientists. With Merck's in-house R&D now struggling, it will be no surprise if Mr Gilmartin's head is the first to roll.

Source: 'Big Trouble for Big Pharma', *The Economist*, 4 December 2003.
© The Economist Newspaper Limited, London (4 December 2003).

6.6 Summary

This chapter has examined the notion of competitive advantage from the viewpoint of establishing and defending strategic position in the marketplace. This requires a deep understanding of the economic drivers of the firm, its essential cost position, its approach to differentiating itself in the market from its competitors, and its chosen position in the market in terms of ability to exploit natural economies of scale and scope. We have also looked at what competitive advantage means to customers and to firms and the ways firms have of understanding their positions in terms of strategic market segments (on the demand side) and of strategic groups (on the supply side). This leads to an understanding pricing and value and the sustainability of value over time. Any competitive strategy has to be turned into action – the notion of the business model is the way in which the firm's individual theory of its business (its competitive strategy) is turned into cash flows. A proper understanding of the business model leads to an appreciation of how the strategy might be sustained into the future (sustainability).

In the next chapter we turn our attention to the assessment of strategic capability, those core competences that underpin competitive advantage and are the target of the firm's strategic investment programmes.

Key terms

Bargaining power *225*

Break-even price elasticity *222*

Business model *234*

Consumer surplus *219*

Early mover advantages *239*

Economies of scope *196*

Experience curve *200*

First mover advantage *201*

Indivisibilities *199*

Industry transformation *232*

Isolating mechanisms *238*

Learning curve *200*

Market-based view *195*

Mobility barriers *222*

Offer curve *216*

Positioning *195*

Price elasticity *221*

Punctuated equilibria *227*

Strategic groups *222*

Strategic maps *225*

Strategic market segments *216*

Strategic space *227*

Stuck in the middle *202*

Sunk costs *197*

Theory of value *219*

Unfair advantage *206*

Value maps *219*

Recap questions and assignments

1   Read the case box on the video gaming industry and interpret the rules of the game in terms of Porter's five forces analysis. Do this for the original rules of the game and for the new rules that Sony is trying to establish. What benefits does Sony expect to gain? How would you expect its competitors to react?

2   Read the case box that discusses changes in the business model for large pharmaceutical companies. Identify the original business model by which these companies have traditionally earned high profits. Why has this model become unsustainable? Is this because industry forces have gradually eroded the traditional imperfections upon which firms could build their profits? Or, alternatively, have there been significant shifts in the business environment that have outdated their strategies. Define the new business model. What are its risks?

Online LearningCentre

When you have read this chapter, log on to the Online Learning Centre website at www.mcgraw-hill.co.uk/textbooks/mcgee to explore chapter-by-chapter test questions, further reading and more online study tools for strategy.

244   CASE STUDY

Case 1 Mobile telephony and the move from 2G to 3G standards

The 3G business model

The transition from 2G to 3G business model is not a radical step change. With the introduction of WAP and GPRS services, the 2G business model is continually evolving. The proposed 3G business model is the culmination of this evolution. Of course business models are dynamic, like strategy, and will continually alter with rapid technology introduction (Yip 2004).

The 3G business model is muddied by the number of services that an operator can offer. The 3G platform allows enhanced data services and therefore the complexity of the service offering is increased. Obviously, since 3G is essentially offering 2G services, part of the business model stays the same; however, many new business models need to be amalgamated with this existing voice telephony model.

The 3G business model identifies two distinct uses a mobile operator may offer its customer base: a provider of communication and a mobile exchange. The network operator must try to provide the characteristics that will make each of these offerings successful in the marketplace and build a business model that will be sustainable.

3G as communication provider

The role of the communications provider is to allow customers to send and receive communications over the mobile network to which they are connected.

- **The value proposition** – in this case, is similar to that in the 2G case. Mobility and convenience of communication is clearly an advantage to the customer. The value proposition is enhanced by a strong brand image that confers the psychological risk reduction of branding on the customer. The newest entrant to the market, 3 UK, may suffer from this as they have no particular brand image at present. Negative publicity over network problems will further disadvantage the company, which has obviously spent millions in trying to build a brand. Although Vodafone and Orange may hold premium place in the branding stakes, it is important to realize that a branding strategy needs to be aligned with the customers you intend to target. Vodafone's premium position may be a disadvantage if pressure on call charges increases. Customers are looking to pay the least they can for what is now viewed as a commodity market and Vodafone's perceived higher prices may put customers off.

- **Differentiation** – is the step that operators must take if indeed they are to price calls higher than competitors. In the 2G world, Vodafone (and to a certain extent O_2) was able to create the impression that its network was of higher quality and dropped less calls than T-Mobile and Orange. These factors lead business customers and other high-value users to subscribe to the Vodafone connection as being the premium network. In the world of 3G, voice will be the main driver and to protect revenues operators must establish a differentiation between themselves and competitors. Handset range is a potential differentiator. 3 UK has suffered badly from being unable to provide customers with a handset range that meets the standards of the newest 2G phones. 3G phones need significant improvement in aesthetics and battery power if they are to be considered a viable alternative to the current crop of 2G phones. The average customer is looking for a phone that can be considered a fashion accessory and it could take some time before 3G phones reach this stage (Morrison 2003). Another strong avenue of differentiation must be customer service. T-Mobile ploughed millions of pounds into the renovation of the customer service department before and after rebranding from One2One. One2One was always associated with poor levels of customer service and high levels of churn. Rebranding meant that T-Mobile was focusing on new market segments and customer services had to be of industry standard before marketing to these customers could occur.

◈ **The channels of distribution** – are also not greatly changed for this particular 3G offering. Independent retailers offer an excellent way of getting phones to market and do not require the expense of building expensive prime-located stores. Carphone Warehouse dominate this market and more than 27 per cent of customers say that it would be the first place they would go if they wanted to find out more about their phone (ICM Research 2003). Interestingly, dedicated retailers Orange and Vodafone, which have invested large sums in building up the branding of their stores, come second and third in the poll. O_2 and T-Mobile stores lag further behind after a string of independents such as The Link and Phones 4 U. The findings show that the companies that lead the branding stakes are also foremost in the minds of customers when they are thinking about their phones. Vodafone and Orange consistently score higher on brand awareness surveys than other networks and customers automatically think of these brands when they want to make changes to the way they use their phones (Wolff Olins 2004).

Preferred mobile phone retailers

Retailer	Percentage of customers
Carphone Warehouse	27%
Orange shops	18%
Vodafone shops	16%
The Link	16%
Phones 4 U	9%
O_2 shops	5%
T-Mobile shops	5%

Source: ICM Research, 2003.

246   CASE STUDY

- **Segmentation of customers** – is an extremely important stage that requires operators to begin thinking in different ways. Operators must think of the consumer base as different sub-groups, which can be characterized by different needs, some of which will overlap. Remembering that voice is very much the main driver, tariff plans must be altered to accommodate the needs of a majority of these groups. In August 2003, 51 per cent of customers on 3 UK admitted to voice and SMS being the primary reason they purchased a new phone and connection (Deutsche Bank 2003). An analysis of the market shows that there are many types of users, each with different usage patterns of voice and SMS products. By mapping these on to axes we can see which particular services operators will have to target when putting together tariffs to appeal to these different segments. The business community can be seen as a large range of users that primarily use voice services but may be high users of text messages as well. Users in an older demographic can be considered low users of either service, with mobility and convenience being their main concern. The main group of users relates to customers in a middle-age demographic, but even this must be segmented. Traditional users continue to use their handset as a voice-calling instrument and do not use other services heavily. Prepay customers look to receive more calls and send more SMS messages, while the upwardly mobile users are high-worth customers that use their phone for all occasions. Between these groups are students, who look to minimize payments by sending SMS messages, and children under 15, who may have parental limits on the amount they spend. It must be remembered that there are many other variables to be considered when deciding tariff and this analysis is simply a guide.

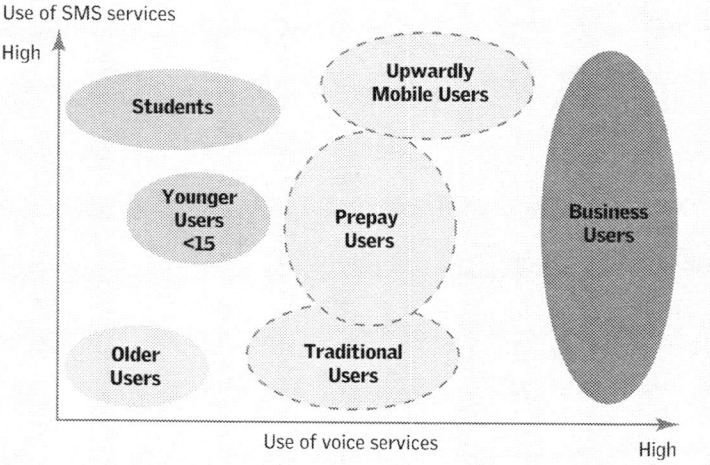

3G voice and SMS services segmentation

Other segmentation factors

Factor	High-end user	Low-end user
Handset style	Upwardly mobile user	Older user
Price sensitivity	Prepay user	Business user
Interconnect allowances	Upwardly mobile user	Older user
International options	Upwardly mobile user; students	Younger users

Source: Puri, 2004.

Case Questions

1 Describe the strategy being followed to move to the 3G standard.

2 What are the bases for differentiation and segmentation? Try to describe these in terms of Table 6.3 and Figures 6.5 and 6.18.

3 Is there anything novel about the approach described here?

4 Can you suggest alternative, new ways for differentiating innovative products?

Further reading and references

Bartlett, C and Ghoshal, S (1989) *Managing Across Borders*, Hutchinson, London.

Besanko, D, Dranove, D and Shanley, M (2000) *The Economics of Strategy*, (2nd edition), John Wiley & Sons, New York.

Bogner, WC, Thomas, H and McGee, J (1996) 'A Longitudinal Study of the Competitive Positions and Entry Paths of European Firms in the US Pharmaceutical Market', *Strategic Managment Journal*, **17**, **2**, pp. 85–107.

Chesbrough, H and Rosenbloom, RS (2002) 'The role of the business model in capturing value from innovation: evidence from Xerox Corporation's technology spin-off companies', *Industrial and Corporate Change*, **11**, **3**, pp. 529–55.

Deutsche Bank (2003) 'European Wireless Review', May, Deutsche Bank Equity Research, London.

Economist, The, 'Big Trouble for Big Pharma', 4 December 2003.

Fiegenbaum, A and Thomas, H (1990) 'Strategic Groups and Performance: The US Insurance Industry 1980–84', *Strategic Management Journal*, **11**, pp. 197–215.

Fiegenbaum, A, Tang, MJ and Thomas, H (1990) 'Strategic Time Periods and Strategic Group Research: Concepts and an Empirical Example', *Journal of Management Studies*, **27**, pp. 133–48.

Ghemawhat, P (1989) 'Du Pont's Titanium Business (A)', Harvard Business School Case Study 9–390–112.

Ghemawat, P (1991) 'Commitment: the Dynamic of Strategy', Free Press, New York.

Ghemawat, P (1994a) 'Du Pont in Titanium Dioxide (A)', Harvard Business School Case Study 9–385–140.

Ghemawat, P (1994b) 'Capacity Expansion in the Titanium Dixoide Industry', *Journal of Industrial Economics*, XXXIII, December, pp. 145–63.

Grant, RM (2002) *Contemporary Strategy Analysis*, 4th edition, Basil Blackwell, Oxford.

HMSO (1978) *A Review of Monopolies and Mergers Policy*, cmnd 7198, London.

ICM Research (2003) 'Do People Want More from their Mobiles?', ICM Research Review, July, pp. 3–4, ICM Research, London.

Johnson, G and Scholes, K (1999) *Exploring Corporate Strategy*, Prentice Hall, Hemel Hempstead.

Ketchen, DJ and Shook, CL (1996) 'The Application of Cluster Analysis in Strategic Management Research: An Analysis and Critique', *Strategic Management Journal* **17**, pp. 441–58.

Kitchen, S (2000) 'Connections in the Wireless World', Warwick Business School, September.

KM Lab (2000) www.Kmlab.com/4Gwarfare.html, 20 June.

MacMillan, I and McGrath, RG (1997) 'Discovering New Points of Differentiation', *Harvard Business Review*, July/August, pp. 3–11.

McGee, J and Thomas, H (1986) 'Strategic Groups: Theory, Research and Taxonomy', *Strategic Management Journal*, **7**, **2**, pp. 141–60.

McGee, J and Segal-Horn, S (1990) 'Strategic Space and Industry Dynamics', *Journal of Marketing Management*, **6**, **3**, pp. 175–93.

McGee, J and Segal-Horn, S (1992) 'Will There Be a European Food Processing Industry?' in S Young and J Hamill (eds) *Europe and the Multinationals: Issues and Responses for the 1990s*, Edward Elgar.

McGee, J and Channon, DF (eds) (2005) *The Encyclopaedic Dictionary of Strategic Management*, 2nd edition, Blackwell Publishing, Oxford.

Miller, D (1992) 'The Generic Strategy Trap', *Journal of Business Strategy*, **13**, **1**, pp. 37–42.

Morrison, D (2003) 'Calling up a New Strategy', *New Media Age*, October, pp. 24–7.

Porter, ME (1979) 'The Structure within Industries and Company Performance', *Review of Economics and Statistics*, **61**, May, pp. 214–27.

Porter, ME (1980) *Competitive Strategy: Techniques for Analysing Industries and Competitors*, Free Press, New York.

Porter, ME (1985) *Competitive Advantage*, Free Press, New York.

Porter, ME (1986) *Competition in Global Industries*, Harvard Business School Press, Boston.

Puri, R (2004) 'Mobile Telephony: The Move from 2G to 3G Standards', Warwick Business School, September.

Rumelt, RP (1984) 'Towards a Strategic Theory of the Firm', in RB Lamb (ed.) *Competitive Strategic Management*, Prentice-Hall, pp. 566–70.

Rumelt, RP (1991) 'How much does industry matter?' *Strategic Management Journal*, **12**, pp. 167–85.

Scherer, FM and Ross, D (1990) *The Economics of Multiplant Operations*, Harvard University Press, Boston.

Sjostrom, C (1995) 'Corporate Effects on Industry Competition: a Strategic Groups Analysis', unpublished doctoral dissertation, University of Oxford.

Tello, M (2004) 'Opportunities in the Leasing Market for London-based Banks', Warwick Business School, September.

Wolff Olins (2004) 'Significance of Mobile Branding', Wolff Olins Orange Case Study, April, Wolff Olins Brand Consultancy, London.

Yao, D (1988) 'Beyond the reach of the invisible hand: impediments to economic activity, market failures, and profitability', *Strategic Management Journal*, Special Issue, **9**, pp. 59–70.

Yip, G. (2004) 'Using Strategy to Change your Business Model', *Business Strategy Review*, **15**, **2** (Summer), pp. 17–24.

Chapter 7

Competitive strategy: the analysis of strategic capability

Introduction

In setting out to understand strategic management we are in effect building our own strategic theory of the firm. The usual starting point of this endeavour is provided in Chapters 5 and 6, which describe the behaviour of firms in markets, the nature of competition, and the search for unique and sustainable market positions. To attain competitive advantage is to open the door to higher profits, other things being equal. This chapter sets out the internal agenda for the firm seeking to create competitive advantage. What resources and capabilities should the firm create and protect that will be the critical underpinning of its desired competitive advantage? In common parlance this is the concern with 'core competences'. In the academic discourse this is the resource-based view (RBV) of the firm in which it is recognized that firms are internally heterogeneous and in effect possess unique clusters of resources. Thus firms in the same industries and markets will very likely have different strategies and different performance levels. Critics of the market-based view (MBV) have argued that it is nonsensical to place the MBV at the centre of strategy making, leaving the inside of the firm to operate as a black box. Some, therefore, use the RBV to place the firm, rather than the industry or the market, at the centre of strategy making. However, the emphasis of this chapter is that the RBV and the MBV provide complementary perspectives on how to compete and jointly provide the basis for a strategic theory of the firm.[1]

7.1 The resource-based view in theory

Economists see the firm as a bundle of productive resources, where resources are defined as inputs into the firm's operations so as to produce goods and services. In this view resources are generic and specific categories are not suggested, but typical examples include patents, capital equipment, and skilled and unskilled human resources. Strategists go further and distinguish capabilities from resources. A capability is the ability to perform a task or activity that involves complex patterns of co-ordination and co-operation between people and other resources. Capabilities would include research and development expertise, customer service and high-quality manufacturing. Skills, by contrast, are more specific, relating to narrowly defined activities such as typing, machine maintenance and book-keeping.

Strategists are interested in those resources and capabilities that can earn rents (a surplus of revenue over cost). These collectively are known as strategic assets or core competences[2] and are a subset of but distinct from those other resources and capabilities that do not distinctively support the competitive advantage. The strategic task for the firm is to sustain these rent streams over time by creating and protecting the competitive advantage and the strategic assets that together underpin them. The inherent value of the strategic assets for the firm depends on the ways in which the firm combines, co-ordinates and deploys these assets in concert with the other firm-specific and more generic resources and capabilities.

The internal economy of the firm can be seen as sets of discrete activities (e.g. a product line), each of which leads to market positions and each of which is supported by assets of resources and capabilities. *Similar* activities (for example the Ford Mondeo and Ford Focus product lines) share some common strategic assets and some common generic assets. This sharing can lead to economies of scale (if different components share the same production line), to economies of scope (where products might go through common distribution

---

[1] However, this is to ignore important contributions such as the theory of the growth of the firm by Edith Penrose (1954) and the evolutionary theory of Nelson and Winter (1982).

[2] But note that there are many other labels, such as distinctive capabilities from Selznick (1957), that are and have been current.

channels), and experience effects. *Complementary* activities require dissimilar sets of strategic assets which would then require degrees of co-ordination (for example marketing activities and production activities). The skills of co-ordination and internal co-operation are in fact high-level capabilities with considerable strategic significance.

In the real world of uncertainty and imperfect information the firm may have (and usually does have) considerable problems in knowing which particular configurations of its strategic assets will maximize profits. Managers do not have perfect knowledge of future states of the world, of alternative actions that could be taken, or of the pay-offs from adopting various alternatives. Moreover, the way a manager chooses to allocate resources will be a function of past personal experience, the firm's experience, values, biases and personality. Accordingly, even if two managers were given identical bundles of resources they would use them in different ways. The result is that a firm's set of resources and capabilities will diverge from those of its competitors over time. Managers in competing firms in the same markets do not face the same sets of choices – rather, they have different menus with different choices. The future, as firms sees it, is to a greater or lesser degree uncertain and unknowable and their capacities for addressing the unknowable are diverse. Further, no amount of information gathering can resolve this fundamental uncertainty of what the future will hold.

Case box: The game of chess

If the theory of chess were really fully known there would be nothing left to play. The theory would show which of the three possibilities (white wins, tie or black wins) actually holds and, accordingly, the play would be decided before it starts … human difficulty necessitates the use of incomplete, heuristic methods of playing, which constitute 'good' chess; and without it there would be no element of 'struggle' and 'surprise' in the game.

Rationality and full information would give us the ability to solve well-specified problems like chess. The initial resources (i.e. whether you start with white or black) would fully determine the outcome. Furthermore, no one would read or write books on how to play chess well, because all the optimal moves would already be known. In practice, people differ widely in their ability to play chess and many find that studying books on chess ('rules' for winning) improves their play. People rely on heuristics, on search, on experience and on training to aid their decisions. Such individuals can learn better heuristics and search patterns from books and can improve their performance.

If we assume in both chess and in strategy that no one knows all the 'rules' then there can exist rules for riches that can benefit many participants. Indeed, half the firms in any industry could improve their status by becoming average. Neither in chess nor in strategy is there a fully fledged theory with optimization procedures in place. Participants have therefore to make progress by adopting heuristics (or intellectual constructs) that help them make sense of the possible varieties of moves and counter-moves. There cannot exist simple nostrums or simple rules for riches that apply universally.

Thus, strategy making is a long way from the simplistic assumptions of the economic model. Strategies tend to be unique and idiosyncratic and simplistic theories for success are usually 'magic theories', i.e. theories which explain everything but predict nothing.[3] Nor are there simple rules for riches, i.e. there are no automatic rules that provide benefits in the long run. The case box above uses the game of chess as an analogy.

This means that strategic management is not captured in the form of a strategic theory of the firm in a way that enables equations to be identified, data collected and analysed and simple rules be inferred. Strategic management is much more eclectic and diverse. Contexts external to the firm and internal to the firm are highly idiosyncratic. This places a premium on the ability to diagnose situations and formulate options. The specific routes to high performance are many and varied and not readily susceptible to simple generalizations. This goes some way to explaining why the RBV is widely seen as lacking specificity and definable concepts, and having no traceable connection to real performance improvements.

7.2 The language of the resource-based view: what is core competence?

In Chapter 5, we introduced the resource-based view with a figure similar to Figure 7.1. The top line of this diagram shows how the firm's investment programmes are directed towards the creation and development of resources and capabilities, and that these underpin the positional advantage from which superior value can be delivered to customers. The bottom line shows the value and financial consequences, in terms of the capacity of the firm to finance its investment programmes. The resource-based view focuses on the resources and capabilities of the firm, asserting that it is the distinctiveness of these that enables sustainable positional

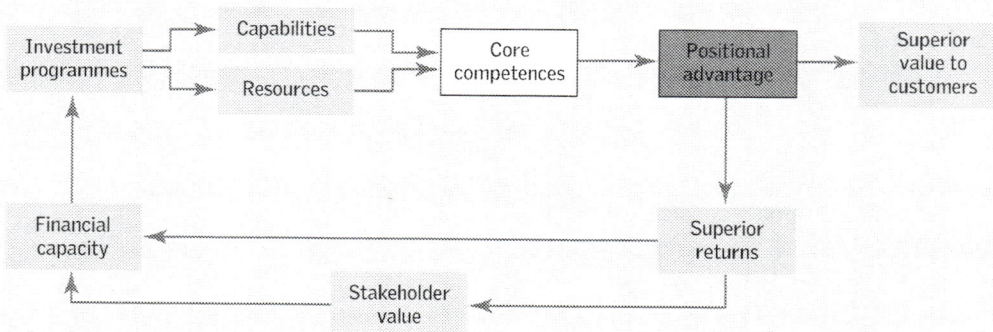

Figure 7.1 Competitive advantage and core competence

---

[3] Lave C and J March (1993) *An Introduction to Models in the Social Sciences*, University Press of America, NY.

7.2 THE LANGUAGE OF THE RESOURCE-BASED VIEW: WHAT IS CORE COMPETENCE?   255

advantages to be constructed. The added element in this diagram is the presence of core competences as representing those resources and capabilities that are distinctive to the firm. As a result, competitive advantage is seen as the joint product of core competences and positional advantage. What many writers observe is that imperfections in the resource and capability markets are more in number and larger in size than those in product markets. This places the burden on firms to pay attention to the underpinnings of competitive advantage in resource and capability terms. What many writers have also observed is that markets are changeable and even volatile, but it is quite difficult to get firms to change their internal cultures and processes quickly enough to keep pace with market changes.

Here we follow Grant's (1991 and 1998) lead in using 'resources' to describe inputs that can in general be purchased on open markets and customized for use by the purchasers. Thus, production capacity might be generally available, but will be configured for specific use by each purchaser. The activities of individual purchasers may lead to imperfections in supply markets. For example, a company may seek to monopolize certain raw materials through acquisition, or maybe through offering long-term supply contracts. But, on their own, few resources are immediately productive. By contrast, the 'capabilities' described here are firm-specific. They are developed internally against the specific needs and ambitions of each company. They often depend on tacit knowledge, are path-dependent in that they emerge and develop over time, and are not in the form of assets that can be traded. These resources and capabilities have individual characteristics, but a large part of their value-in-use to a firm is related to their configuration and their co-ordination. Figure 7.2 compares typical resources and typical capabilities (we introduced their distribution in Figure 5.7 on p. 165). The distinctiveness of the firm's specific set of resources and capabilities is a function of which resources to acquire and what capabilities to develop (the *configuration* issue), the way in which each of these is developed (the *firm-specificity* issue), and the way in which they are internally managed to create positional advantage (the *co-ordination* issue).

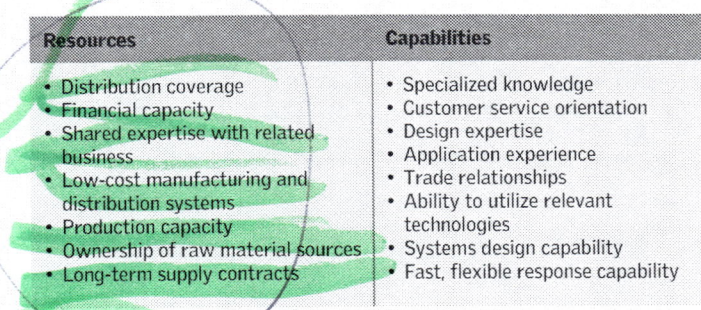

Resources	Capabilities
• Distribution coverage • Financial capacity • Shared expertise with related business • Low-cost manufacturing and distribution systems • Production capacity • Ownership of raw material sources • Long-term supply contracts	• Specialized knowledge • Customer service orientation • Design expertise • Application experience • Trade relationships • Ability to utilize relevant technologies • Systems design capability • Fast, flexible response capability

Figure 7.2 Resources and capabilities

7.2.1 Prahalad and Hamel on core competence

The language of assets, resources and capabilities can be confusing. The Grant (1998) distinction between resources and capabilities is as easy a distinction as any to maintain. However, it is laborious to keep referring to strategic resources and capabilities as those that systematically and uniquely underpin the competitive advantage relative to those other resources and capabilities that do not. Thus it is attractive to refer to these as core competences, the language popularized by Prahalad and Hamel in the *Harvard Business Review* (1990). They provided an unusual metaphor:

> *The diversified corporation is a large tree. The trunk and the major limbs are core products, the smaller branches are business units; the leaves, flowers, and fruit are end products. The root system that provides nourishment, sustenance, and stability is the core competence. You can miss the strength of competitors by looking only at their end products, in the same way you miss the strength of a tree if you look only at its leaves ...*
>
> *Core competences are the collective learning in the organization, especially how to coordinate diverse production skills and integrate multiple streams of technologies.*

7.2.2 BCG and capabilities-based competition

Prahalad and Hamel's approach is to define core competence as the combination of individual technologies and production skills that underlie a company's product lines. Sony's core competence in miniaturization allows it to make everything from the Sony Walkman to video cameras and digital cameras. Honda's core competence in engines and powertrains allows it compete from lawnmowers to racing cars. But this latter example shows a difficulty in their approach in that Honda's dealer network would be invisible – because of the focus on competences that lead directly to products. A development of their idea is contained in a Boston Consulting Group paper in 1992[4] on 'capabilities-based' competition. This contained four basic principles:

1   the building blocks of strategy are not products and markets but business processes;

2   competitive success depends on transforming these key processes into strategic capabilities that consistently provide superior value to the customer;

3   companies create these capabilities by making strategic investments in a support infrastructure that links together and transcends traditional strategic business units;

4   because capabilities necessarily cross functions, the champion of a capabilities-based strategy is the chief executive officer.

---

[4] Stalk, G, P Evans and L Shulman (1992) 'Competing on Capabilities', *Harvard Business Review*, March/April.

McGee–Thomas–Wilson:
Strategy: Analysis and
Practice, Text and Cases

7. Competitive strategy: the
analysis of strategic
capability

Text

© The McGraw–Hill
Companies, 2006

169

This approach has the real merit of focusing on business processes as the integrative glue that binds together the various lower-level ingredients and on the investments that are required to make this effective. Unfortunately, the continued use of capabilities makes for some confusion. The essence of the idea here is that these business processes should connect to real customer needs. Things are only strategic when they begin and end with the customer because that is where value is sensed and created. The box below is an extract from the same paper and summarizes the five dimensions on which a company's strategic resources and capabilities should aim to outperform the competition.

- ◈ **Speed:**   the ability to respond quickly to customer or market demands and to incorporate new ideas and technologies quickly into products

- ◈ **Consistency:**   the ability to produce a product that unfailingly satisfies customers' expectations

- ◈ **Acuity:**   the ability to see the competitive environment clearly and thus to anticipate and respond to customers' evolving needs and wants

- ◈ **Agility:**   the ability to adapt simultaneously to many different business environments

- ◈ **Innovativeness:** the ability to generate new ideas and to combine existing elements to create new sources of value

Source: Stalk, Evans and Shulman, 1992.

Boston Consulting Group present this discussion in the language of strategic capabilities in an attempt to avoid an overuse of competences, which is a feature of the Prahalad and Hamel approach.

7.2.3 Amit and Schoemaker on strategic assets

A similar approach can be seen in another classic paper from the same era. Amit and Schoemaker (1993) build on the resource and capability language to create 'strategic assets'. By resources they mean stocks of available factors of production that are owned and controlled by the firm. Capabilites refer to the firm's capacity to deploy resources, usually in combination, using organizational processes to effect a desired end. They are information-based, tangible and intangible processes that are firm-specific and are developed over time through complex interactions with each other and with the firm's resources. Unlike resources, capabilities are based on developing, sharing and exchanging information through the firm's human capital – as information-based assets they are often called 'invisible assets'. The authors describe 'strategic assets' as:

> *the set of difficult to trade and imitate, scarce, appropriable and specialised resources and capabilities that (underpin) the firm's competitive advantage.*

In practice it is difficult to draw clear distinctions between the core competences of Prahalad and Hamel, the capabilities-based competition of Boston Consulting Group, and the strategic assets of Amit and Schoemaker. They all convey the sense of firm-specific assets that are typically process and information based and intangible in character.

There are other assets and activities in the value chain, notable complementary assets that, when linked to strategic assets (core competences), are necessary for the existence of the competitive advantage. Thus, a research-based pharmaceuticals company such as Merck or SmithKlineGlaxo would identify research expertise as a core competence but would regard management of government regulations as a complementary asset, essential but not unique. Many other assets and activities in the firm can be classified as 'make-or-buy', that is, the firm makes a financial calculation as to make or buy. Figure 7.3 distinguishes 'strategic assets' from 'complementary' assets and 'make-or-buy' assets. Strategic assets are those that are truly distinctive and unique to the firm and provide the underpinning of positional advantage in product markets. Complementary assets are those assets that are jointly required with the strategic assets in order to produce and deliver the product or service. Thus, product development might be a strategic asset, but production capacity is required for product trials and for product adaptations, even though that capacity is not unique to the firm. These assets are sometimes called co-specialized assets, in that they are complementary to the specialized assets and (lightly) customized to interface with them. Make-or-buy assets are those that you choose to include in the assets portfolio solely on the basis of financial calculations. For example, the decision to own or lease company cars might be made solely on financial criteria, because there are no strategic implications. In principle, if there are no strategic implications (which means that there is no need to customize the assets for specific purposes), then there will, in general, be a free outside market. This in turn generally means that the market is able to supply cheaper than is possible internally. You can see from this that the pressure to outsource can be very high and depends critically on the characteristics of supply markets.

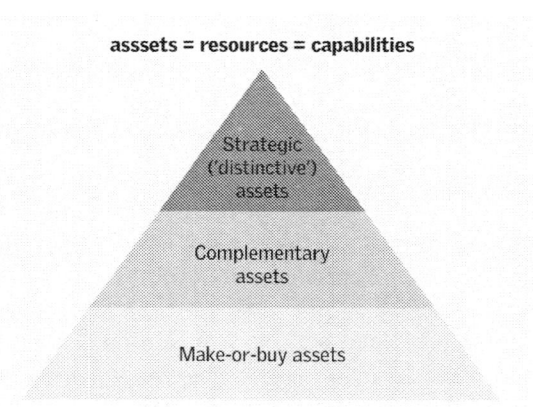

asssets = resources = capabilities

Strategic ('distinctive') assets

Complementary assets

Make-or-buy assets

Figure 7.3 The asset triangle

7.2.4 Core competence = distinctive capability = strategic asset

In this chapter we propose to follow the terminology shown in Figure 7.1. This means that we follow the definition of resources and capabilities as discussed by Grant (1998) and that we use the term 'core competences' to cover the capabilities language of Boston Consulting

Group and the strategic assets approach of Amit and Schoemaker. This language of core competences is nevertheless abstract and hard to put into practice. This reflects the idiosyncratic and unique nature of the strategic problems faced by individual firms. But it also reflects the need to have a clear concept upon which to base strategic thinking. The two building blocks of strategy (identified so far in this book) are competitive advantage and core competence. They are both intellectual constructs. Each relies on situational characteristics for their application in practice. Each provides a way of thinking so that strategists can develop a 'theory in use' that applies to their own situation. Gary Hamel (1994) has attempted to codify the idea of core competence further. He offers the following essential characteristics of a core competence:

1   A competence is a bundle of constituent skills and technologies rather than a discrete skill or technology and a core competence is the integration of a variety of individual skills.

2   A core competence is not an asset in the accounting sense of the word. A factory, a distribution channel or brand cannot be a core competence but an aptitude to manage that factory, that channel or that brand may constitute a core competence.

3   A core competence must make a disproportionate contribution to customer-perceived value. The distinction between core and non-core competence thus rests on a distinction between the relative impacts on customer value.

4   A core competence must also be competitively unique. This means either that (i) a competence is held uniquely by one firm in the competitive set or that (ii) a competence that is ubiquitous across an industry must be held at a superior level in the firm (for example, powertrains are ubiquitous in the automobile industry but one could argue that Honda has unique strength in this area and thus it is a core competence for Honda).

5   From the corporate (multi-business) perspective[5] a core competence should provide an entrée into new markets. A particular competence may be core from the perspective of an individual business, but from a corporate perspective it will not be core if there is no way of imagining an array of new product-markets issuing from it.[6]

The language of core competence has become widespread. Core competence and competitive advantage together have become the central conceptual terms in the analysis of competitive strategy. We define core competence quite simply as:

> *the underlying capability that is the distinguishing characteristic of the organization.*

♦   It is the way we do things.

♦   It is how we organize the way we do things.

---

[5]   See Chapter 9 for an explanation of the way in which competitive advantage should be deployed across multiple businesses within one company.

[6]   For an excellent example, see the case study Canon: Competing on Capabilities, HBS in the text and cases version of this book.

◆ It is how we *communicate* systematically this knowledge and build upon it.

◆ It is understanding the difference, and building bridges, between tangible and intangible assets, tacit and explicit knowledge, and individual and team knowledge and skill.

More formally, we define core competences as:

> *the set of firm-specific skills and cognitive processes directed towards the attainment of competitive advantage.* (McGee and Segal-Horn, 1997)

Core competence is a fundamental concept in our understanding of what strategy making is. It is *only* through core competence that the firm attains competitive advantage and is therefore the mainspring of sustainable distinctiveness. But it is also the lens through which the world is seen and interpreted. Different firms (and people) see different things in their environments and this is a function of their inheritance and their experience. In the same way, firms (and people) differ in the way in which they see themselves and therefore in their understanding of what they might achieve. In this way we can see core competences as the link between managerial cognition and the economics of the firm (*see* Figure 7.4). The key tasks of a strategy analyst are interpreting the external environment, understanding the dynamics of markets and of competition, and understanding the internal dynamics of one's own organization. Core competences provide the links to these economic assessments through a clarity of perception about the shared values and beliefs in the firm (often explicit in the mission statement), through tacit knowledge and understandings (that are possibly unique to the firm), and through flexible routines and recipes that enable non-standard challenges to be comprehended.

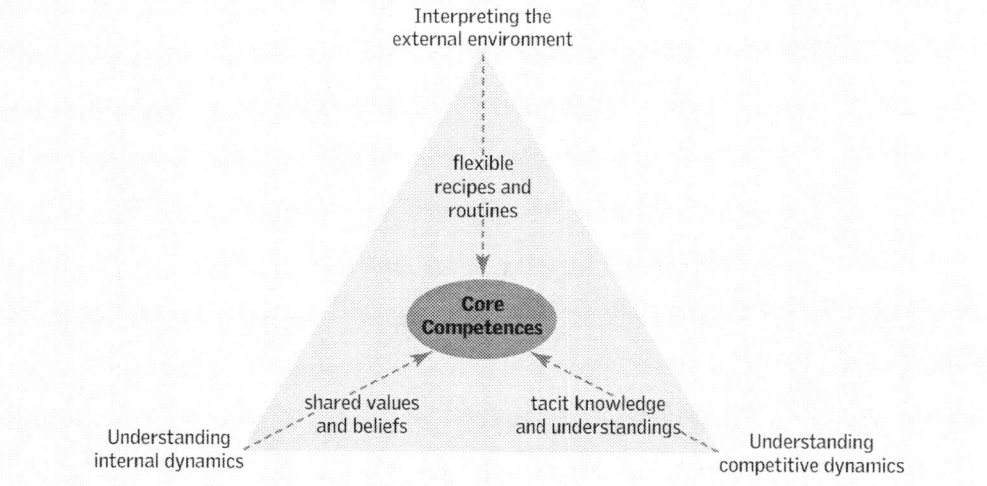

Figure 7.4 Core competences as the link between managerial cognition and the economics of the firm
Source: McGee and Segal-Horn, 1997.

7.3 Related issues and the management of core competences

There are some mistakes that managers make very frequently. The first is to assume that acquiring and leveraging generic resources will be a major source of advantage in a new market. Advantage requires some degree of difference between firms and this requires the construction of assets that are unique to the firm. Another common mistake is to overestimate the transferability of specific assets and capabilities to a new product market. Assets are unique to the firm in relation to the use for which they have been designed. New uses require some degree of further customization or re-adaptation. Even where the firm has constructed unique assets, it is easy to overestimate their capability to compete in highly profitable markets. This is merely to say that strategic choices are highly risky. Even if one can create a distinctive asset base it does not necessarily follow that customers will like the product offering that follows. Through this observation, you can see that competitive advantage is a composite of a resource-based view and a market-based view. Both are necessary: neither is necessary and sufficient on its own.

7.3.1 Resource leverage

Managers often neglect ways of creating advantage from a resource-based perspective. It is common to see firms paying much attention to the detail of product positioning in attempts to create those pieces of unique advantage that can make a difference. However, attention to the resource side can have significant pay-offs. For example, the approach of the Japanese automobile assemblers, especially Toyota,[7] show the benefits from rearranging the supply chain in such a way that essential customer values such as reliability can be fundamentally changed. There are five ways in which management can leverage its resources so as to create the conditions under which a core competence can emerge.[8] The idea of leverage (a much-used word of strategists) is to focus attention and effort an a specific object to the exclusion of rival objects so as to create a desired outcome. The exercise of leverage requires clear strategic intent and the possession of the relevant assets and competences.

Concentrating resources: convergence and focus

Convergence is the idea of focusing resources on few rather than many objectives and focus itself prevents the dilution of resources being applied to a specific target. The basic principle is the concentration of resources and the avoidance of dissipation of effort.

---

[7] See 'Competitive Advantage the Toyota Way' by Gary Fane, Reza Vagheti, Cheryl Van Deusen and Louis Woods, *Business Strategy Review*, 14, 4, 51–60, Winter 2003.

[8] This is taken from Gary Hamel and CK Prahalad (1993) 'Strategy as Stretch and Leverage', *Harvard Business Review*, March/April.

Accumulating resources: extracting and borrowing

Extraction is the ability to surface resources and capabilities that exist within the firm but might be lying concealed or dormant. The capacity to draw from the stockpile of resources is a facet of the ability to learn. Borrowing resources is the ability to tap into the resources of other companies. A simple example is the use of one company's basic research as an input to another company's commercialization. Thus Sony commercialized the transistor that was pioneered by Bell Laboratories. As Hamel and Prahalad (1993) point out:

> *Increasingly, technology is stateless. It crosses borders in the form of scientific papers, foreign sponsorship of university research, international licensing, cross border equity stakes in high-tech start-ups and international academic conferences. Tapping into the market for technology is a potentially important source of resource leverage.*

Complementing resources: blending and balancing

Blending resources is similar to what we called co-specialization (above). How resources fit together in planned and unplanned ways gives the possibility to transform the value of resources while using them. Blending requires integrative skills such as technological integration, functional integration and new product development. The blending of functional skills is a new way of restating the nature of general management. This traditionally has involved the integration of functions such as production, marketing and R&D. Balancing requires the firm's resources and capabilities to be able to support a business model. Unbalanced firms would have gaps such that resources and capabilities would be required from others for a sustainable revenue stream to be achieved. A balanced firm may benefit from tapping into the resources of others but has a defensible position on its own.

Conserving resources: co-opting and shielding

Conserving resources simply means retaining resources so that they are reusable – the basis for economies of scope. The issue is how to retain knowledge in the memory banks so that it is addressable and recyclable to other activities. Co-option has the same theme as recycling but involves collaborative efforts to work collectively towards new standards or new products. Shielding resources is about not wasting non-renewable resources (such as cash) on difficult targets. Attacking competitors directly in their home markets is an example of a difficult target where the probabilities are more of failure than of success. The example of Canon taking on Xerox in plain paper copying is a classic example. Xerox's R&D budgets were very much higher than those of Canon, but Canon chose to compete in areas where the Xerox business model was weak, e.g. small machines, third-party distribution systems and machine reliability.[9]

---

[9] See the case study Canon: Competing on Capabilities, HBS in the text and cases version of this book.

Recovering resources: expediting success

Pace is a significant dimension of performance. The faster the cycle time from investment through to sales, the quicker that resources can be renewed and redeveloped (see Figure 7.1, where the strategy cycle indicates the process). The speed at which Japanese automakers and motorcycle manufacturers operated gave these companies higher cash flows than their Western counterparts but also more up-to-date products and a greater ability to respond to changing markets.

7.3.2 Identifying intangibles

The expression 'intangible' is being applied more and more frequently to resources and to capabilities. For our purposes it refers to the following:

- Intellectual property rights of patents, trademarks, copyright and registered designs
- Trade secrets
- Contracts and licences
- Databases
- Information in the public domain
- Personal and organizational networks
- The know-how of employees, advisers, suppliers and distributors
- The reputation of products and of the company
- The culture of the organization

Richard Hall conducted a study of the relative contribution of intangible resources and capabilities to business success.[10] Some of the results are summarized in Tables 7.1, 7.2 and 7.3. Table 7.1 summarizes the average weightings for each intangible drawn from the above list. Hall found that the results were common and systematic across a wide sample of companies. Four factors stood out as most important namely, company reputation, product reputation, employee know-how and organization culture. By contrast, intellectual property rights and trade secrets were by far the least significant. Table 7.2 unpacks the employee know-how factor seen in Table 7.1. Here CEOs were asked which business function was the most important contributor to employee know-how. Operations scores highly because of the high tacit content of know-how (learning by experience). In contrast, in finance, know-how has a large external knowledge content, which means that skills can be formalized and transferred. The importance attached to sales and marketing by both manufacturers and retailers is to be expected, whereas the contribution of technology is quite modest.

---

[10] Richard Hall (1992) 'The Strategic Analysis of Intangible Resources', *Strategic Management Journal*, 13, 135–44.

Table 7.1 Relative importance of intangible resources in overall business success

Ranking (1 = highest, 2 = lowest)	Average weight (crucial = 10, insignificant = 1)
1 Company reputation	8.6
2 Product reputation	8.4
3 Employee know-how	8.1
4 Organization culture	7.9
5 Networks	7.1
6 Specialist physical resources	6.1
7 Databases	6.0
8 Supplier know-how	5.8
9 Distributor know-how	5.3
10 Public knowledge	5.2
11 Contracts	4.7
12 Intellectual property rights	3.2
13 Trade secrets	2.9

Sample size = 95
Source: Hall, 1992. © Copyright 1992, John Wiley and Sons Ltd. Reproduced with permission.

Table 7.2 Percentage of CEOs quoting the function as the most important area of employee know-how

	Total sample	Manufacturing	Retailing
Operations	43	27	8
Sales and marketing	29	46	46
Technology	17	18	31
Finance	6	0	15
Other	5	9	0
Total	100	100	100

Source: Hall, 1992. © Copyright 1992, John Wiley and Sons Ltd. Reproduced with permission.

Table 7.3 Replacement periods

	Average replacement period (years)
Company reputation	10.8
Product reputation	6.0
Employee know-how	4.6
Networks	3.4
Supplier know-how	3.1
Databases	2.1
Distributor know-how	1.6

Source: Hall, 1992. © Copyright 1992, John Wiley and Sons Ltd. Reproduced with permission.

Table 7.3 looks at the time it takes to replace an intangible asset. The question posed was, How many years would it take to replace the *particular resource* if you had to start from scratch? This gives an indication of protection from new entrants depending on the transferability of existing reputation. Reputational resources dominate this list. Company reputation, in particular, gives strong incumbents a significant advantage. By contrast, much know-how can be replaced or rebuilt over quite a short period (around three years), suggesting that speedy imitation is quite probable in most situations.

The importance of reputation suggests that it should receive constant management attention. The distinction between company and product is interesting, implying, first, that attention to both is probably necessary and, second, that in multi-business companies the corporate name could have a significant halo effect across businesses and product lines. The experience of companies such as Sony, Hewlett-Packard and IBM provide good examples of this. The high scores for employee know-how support the idea of invisible assets that are information and experience rich. This is clearly fertile ground for the development of core competences. In Table 7.1 the term culture has a specific meaning: it refers to ability to manage change, ability to innovate, teamworking ability, participative management style, perception of high quality standards, and perception of high standards of customer service. These are also ingredients that are information and experience rich.

7.3.3 What determines the value of a core competence?

Figure 7.5 summarizes the conditions that determine the value of a core competence (strategic asset). The basic foundations of value are *imitability*, *durability*, *substitutability*

Figure 7.5 Value of a core competence
Source: Peteraf, 1993.

and *appropriability*. The ability of competitors to imitate your assets is in part to do with *physical uniqueness*. More subtle issues around inimitability are:

◆ Path dependency – cumulative learning and experience over time, which is difficult to replicate over short periods.

◆ Causal ambiguity – not really knowing what it is that is the important element in a complex asset.

◆ First-mover advantage – the pre-emption of a market by being the first to create scale efficient assets.

Substitutability is often an unknown, in that new technologies can emerge which very quickly outdate older solutions. For example, the battle between satellite and cable television systems is still raging – substitutability is high, but it is not clear which standard will prevail. Appropriability is an important but subtle issue. A central question about a strategic asset is: Who can capture the value that is created? Is it the firm? Could it be the skilled technicians? Might it be patent owners? Perhaps there are long-term supply contracts?

7.4 Linking core competence to competitive advantage

The resource-based view (RBV) is not a theory in its own right. But coupled with the market-based view (MBV) it enables the strategist to link the firm's internal behavioural

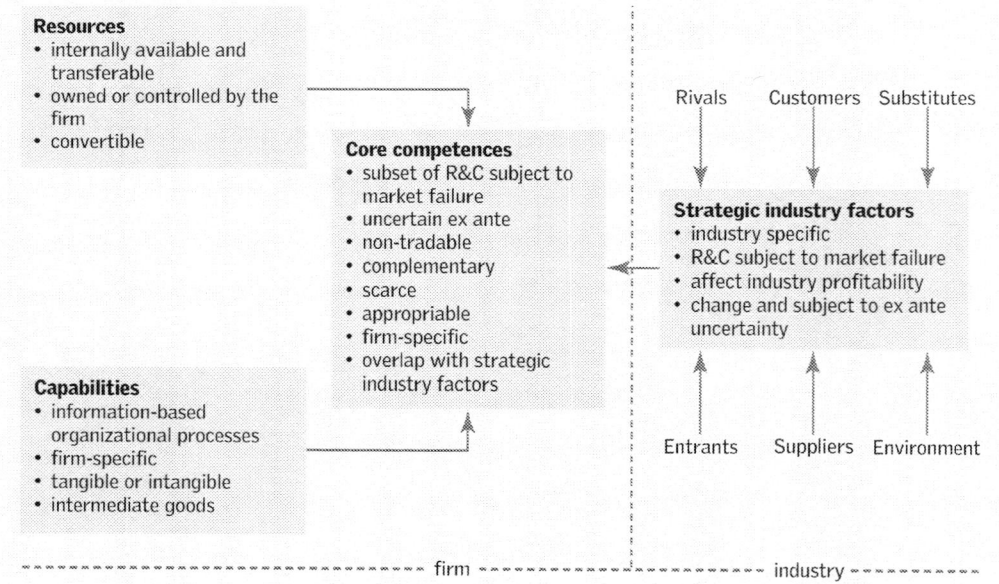

Figure 7.6 Strategic industry factors and core competences
Source: Amit and Schoemaker, 1993.

decisions and organizational choices with the need to secure a defensible positional advantage in the market. RBV and MBV together provide a theory-in-use for the strategist. Figure 7.1 shows the link between RBV and MBV as a juxtaposition of core competence and competitive advantage. Amit and Schoemaker (1993) went a stage further. Their full model is shown in Figure 7.6, adapted only to use the phrase core competence for strategic asset. The extra dimension (compared to Figure 7.1) provided here is contained in the phrase 'strategic industry factors'. These are the sources of market imperfections that firms can capture as elements in their competitive advantage.[11]

From our earlier discussion of industry analysis and Porter's five forces we obtained a general description of the characteristics of an industry. Porter's model provides five generic characteristics and others have suggested more, such as government and deeper environmental variables. Other ad hoc analyses have developed over the years, particularly the idea of key success factors (KSFs). Later in this chapter we suggest a way of using KSFs in practice, but in general KSFs can be seen as those elements in the industry that are deemed as *important* for customers. Strategic industry factors are a way of articulating KSFs as those elements in the industry and in the market that are subject to market failure and therefore where firms can provide them they will have an advantage. Using our language of advantage, these factors are those firm-specific imperfections that represent competitive advantage. Amit and Schoemaker synthesize contributions from many writers in producing this list of characteristics that apply to strategic industry factors.

1 They are determined through a complex interaction among industry rivals, new entrants, customers, regulators, innovators, suppliers and other stakeholders.

2 They are strategic in that they are subject to market failures and may be the basis for competition among rivals.

3 They are known ex post but not ex ante; in particular, not all aspects of their development and interactions with other factors in the market will be known or controllable.

4 Their development takes time, skill and capital: they may be specialized to particular uses.

5 Investments in them are largely irreversible (i.e. sunk costs).

6 Their pace of accumulation is affected by own prior knowledge and experience and that of rivals (i.e. path dependent) and cannot be readily increased (doubling the investment will not usually halve the time).

7 Their value to any particular firm will depend on its control of other factors – the complementarity property.

---

[11] Economists often refer to these imperfections as market failures, that is, inabilities to trade in these factors in perfect markets. Our view of competitive advantage as firm-specific imperfections in the market rests on this notion of market failure.

You will observe that this list is similar to, and is a development of, the discussion in section 5.1, where we discussed the essential ingredients of strategy. In examining Figure 7.6 you will see that the list of core competences has similarities to the list of strategic industry factors. This is not an accident, nor is it an error. The difference is that firms seek to design their core competences in anticipation of their usefulness in creating and sustaining an intended competitive advantage. The strategic industry factors are those imperfections in the market that have succeeded. The core competences are ex ante in nature; they are intentions. The strategic industry factors are ex post, those characteristics that have actually worked in the market to produce competitive advantage.

7.4.1 Competence-based competition in practice

In 1977 Dan Bricklin, an MBA student at the Harvard Business School, developed on his Apple computer a type of 'electronic blackboard' that allowed him to display a grid of numbers linked together by formulae. His professor told him (allegedly) that it had no future as a product. Why? Because software was (and is) easily imitated. There was virtually no entry barrier. There were established firms selling mainframe languages to do pro-forma calculations. Moreover, the Apple was a mere toy! What was wrong with the professor's reasoning?

In 1973 one of the authors wrote a case on the Japanese motorcycle industry. The final discussion question asked, Should Honda enter the emerging global automobile business? It was a 'giveaway' question – anyone who said 'yes' flunked, because markets were saturated, efficient competitors existed in Japan, the USA and in Europe. Honda had little or no experience in automobiles and it had no automobile distribution system or access to one. In 1985 his wife drove a Honda! What was wrong with this answer?

This was a common fault in the strategy analyses of that period. Why was it that Canon could beat Xerox? How did Komatsu manage to beat Caterpillar? The fault lay in the lack of a proper resource-based perspective. There are three parts in an answer to this question: strategic intent, strategic innovation and core competences.

Strategic intent

Strategic intent has a particular meaning in encouraging people to go beyond 'business as usual'. It appeals to the resource language that we reported above, particularly the sense of concentration, convergence and focus, and to the idea of resource leverage.

It has been argued that US firms seeking strategic fit have often found themselves overtaken by firms, especially the Asian conglomerates, driven by long-term visions of the future, which are then relentlessly and ruthlessly pursued with *strategic intent*. Companies such as CNN, Honda, NEC and Sony have succeeded (according to this argument) because of their sustained obsession with achieving global dominance in their industries. This obsession has been labelled strategic intent (Hamel and Prahalad 1989). The significance of this is that the intent of these companies was out of proportion to their existing resources and capabilities.

McGee–Thomas–Wilson:
Strategy: Analysis and
Practice, Text and Cases

7. Competitive strategy: the
analysis of strategic
capability

Text

© The McGraw–Hill
Companies, 2006

181

Table 7.4 The Xerox position in 1980

	Xerox
Technology	Leading edge product technology: 7000 patents
Distribution	Worldwide direct sales: 7000 in USA, 5000 in Europe, 3000 in Japan
Financing	Leasing
R&D investment	$600 million p.a.
Manufacturing	Worldwide network of plants
Scale	Market share = 90%
Image	Photocopy = Xerox

Source: Ackenhusen (1992) 'Canon: Competing on Capabilities', case study.

This gap between ambition and resources is known as strategic stretch. These companies had to expand and adapt their current stock of resources and create new ones. They were more concerned with 'leveraging' resources than with achieving strategic fit between their current resources and their industry environments.

Strategic intent can thus be used as a psychological target which provides a focus that all members of the organization seek to adopt. Becoming the industry leader or dominating a specific segment are frequent missionary goals. The fundamental focus of the firm's strategy commits well beyond its current resource profile. The prophecies can therefore become self-fulfilling provided that employees have faith in their leadership and that, in many cases, the existing industry leaders fail to recognize that the challenge is on. The logic of expansion coupled with economies of scope provides an economic basis for justifying strategic intent. However, there are limits to economies of scope which arise when industries and markets require more variety than the fixed factors that sustain scope effects can support.

Strategic intent implies a stretch beyond current resources, capabilities and means. But for those companies that have adopted this style it became a necessity and was not a luxury.

Table 7.5 How Canon rewrote the rules of the game

	Xerox existing business	Canon's new rules
Customer definition	Medium/large companies	Small companies/individuals
Use pattern	Centralised copying	Decentralised
Product	High copy volume features	Utility, value for money
Distribution	Own sales force	Office products dealers
Service	Own network	By dealers
Financing	Lease	Sale
Technology	Leading edge dry toner	Low cost liquid toner

Source: Ackenhusen (1992) 'Canon: Competing on Capabilities', case study.

Strategic innovation

Strategic investments are bets against an unknowable future. These bets often require technical progress and substantial investment in R&D and in new products. In 1980 Xerox had a stranglehold on the copier industry. IBM were poised to enter, attracted by Xerox's huge profits. Canon also had an interest in fine optics and precision mechanics on the basis of their existing camera business. On whom would you have bet? Table 7.4 shows the Xerox hand.

The barriers to entry were formidable. In IBM's favour was their own large scale that meant it could probably afford to spend as much money as Xerox (but note that Kodak had had the same thoughts earlier without too much success). Canon had no obvious points of superiority given the nature of the market and the strategic industry factors that were present at that time. The idea of strategic innovation is to rewrite the rules of the game. Table 7.5 catches the essence of what Canon did to outflank Xerox and one can do similar analyses to show how Komatsu outflanked Caterpillar by changing the point of competition from quality to cost and reliability, and how Honda managed to enter the global automobile industry by emphasizing quality.

Strategic innovation leads to a new form of competitive advantage, a different conception of the required core competences and a different business model through which the cash could be seen to flow. In the case of the Apple computer and Dan Bricklin's spreadsheet invention, the spreadsheet became the killer application that placed the new Apple personal computer on millions of desks by appealing to a similar sense that Canon identified – the customers' wish to have desktop capability.

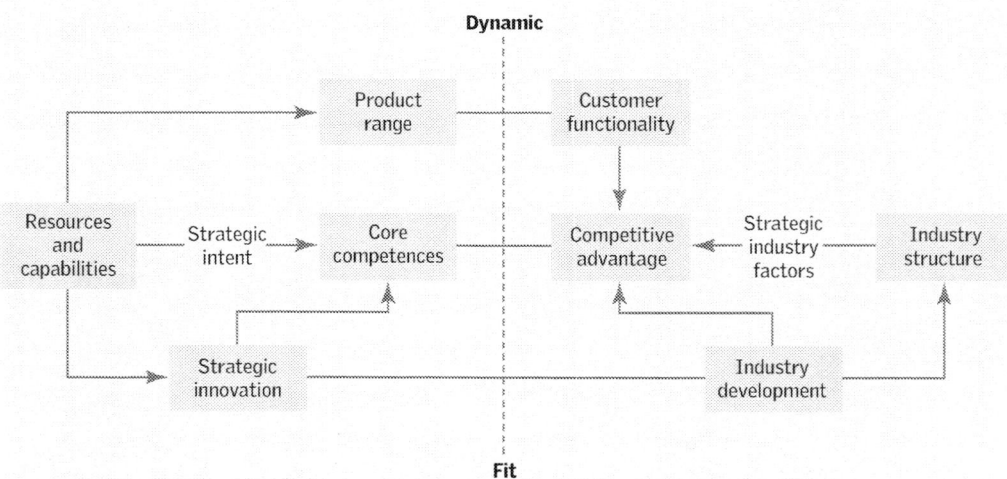

Figure 7.7 Matching resources and markets: linking the inside and the outside

Core competence

The core competences in each of these examples were created by investments in the operational and organizational infrastructure of the strategic innovators. The new capabilities spawned through these investments were linked across business units and the learning and experience of diverse business units was captured and leveraged across the company. Canon's distinctive management processes (compared to Xerox) were high levels of decentralization, strong internal co-ordination processes and external co-operation. Canon exemplified the value of external co-operation through importing knowledge from strategic alliance partners and joint ventures The complex core competences that arose could be described as (i) a high pace of learning and innovation, (ii) a long-term approach to developing capabilities, and (iii) the systematic transfer of competences across businesses and into new businesses.

The risks associated with the Japanese approach – most of the examples have been Japanese companies – is that an overdependence on a resource-based perspective can lock you into your own view of the world, away from changing markets and customer preferences. In an earlier discussion of the strategy cycle in Chapter 5 we commented on how Marks & Spencer became trapped in their own conception of the world just as the textile market became more fashion conscious, new entrants were appearing and product offers were changing rapidly (the strategic industry factors were obviously in a process of change).

How do we balance the inside view with the outside view? Figure 7.7 summarizes inside and outside perspectives and the links between them. The firm is driven by the link of resources and capabilities through strategic intent to core competences. This is the crux of the firm's intended strategy culminating in the match between core competences and competitive advantage. A failed strategy would have empty boxes in the middle of the diagram. The core competences are captured in products which have to match customer functionality. The dynamics of the process are shown by strategic innovation which through 'newgame' strategies match with and/or drive industry development.

The demand side, the outside, is captured by the link between industry structure through strategic industry factors to competitive advantage. Industry structure has multiple industry factors and competitive advantages associated with it. The firm's task is to identify one of the set and match with it – this implies a set of customer functionalities to be satisfied. The dynamics are captured through industry development and other exogenous factors.

The design of the firm's theory-in-use is shown by the strategic fit between core competences and competitive advantage. The practical present-day fit is shown by the fit between product range and customer functionality. The dynamic fit is between strategic innovation and industry development. Lack of fit in the short term can be a result of (i) the requirements of the outside moving too quickly for the inside to keep pace, or (ii) by the strategic drive from the inside missing its targets. There may be a short-term fit that erodes because the dynamic linkages through innovation and industry development do not work properly.

7.4.2 The role of learning

When we compare product markets and resource markets, we can see that fundamentally competition is a contest for the acquisition of skills. Moreover, competition in product markets is a superficial expression of the more fundamental competition over competences. Looked at in this way, the dynamics of markets, of industries and of firms is about 'learning' rather than technical theories of product market evolution; hence, all the current concern with the 'learning organization' and with 'knowledge management'. Core competences arise through the collective learning of the firm, through accumulated experience with the coordination of diverse production skills and the integration of multiple streams of technology. Prahalad and Hamel (1990) take the proposition further. They argue that core competences span across businesses and products within a corporation – they can support several products or businesses. Thus, they argue that the narrow focus of strategic business units is dysfunctional. It is also clear that core competences have temporal dominance over products. They evolve slower than the products that they make possible, or core competences support several generations of essentially the same product classes. Figure 7.8 suggests a framework within which all these strands can be seen. The focus of the diagram is on the way in which the resource-based view is becoming accepted as the genesis of advantage in the firm, but also reflects the modern debate about the contribution of learning and knowledge to our understanding of how firms compete. Chapters 16 and 19 take this discussion further.

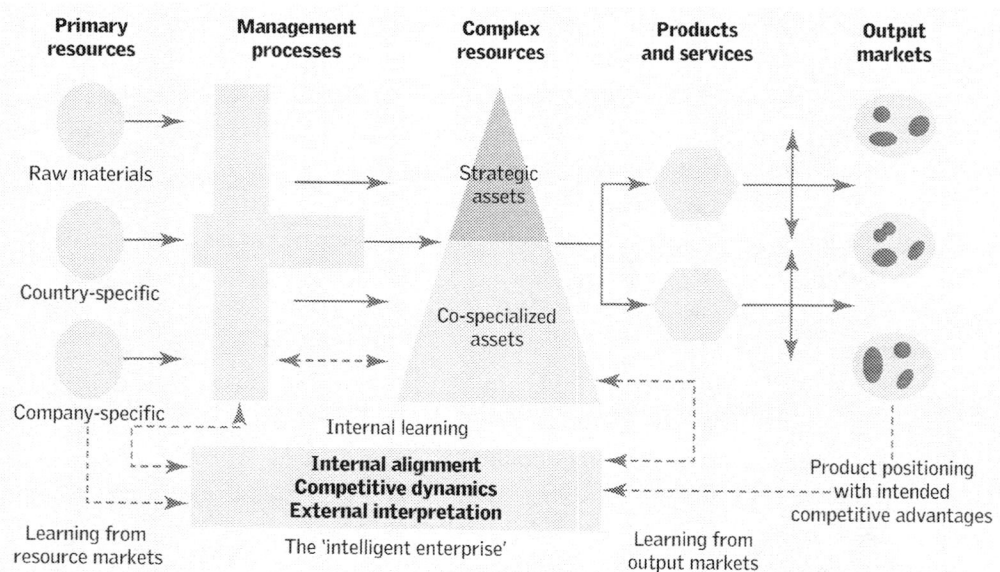

Figure 7.8 A synthesis of positioning, the resource-based view and learning
Source: McGee and Segal-Horn, 1997.

7.5 Competitive strategy in practice

We start from the premise that there can be great differences between the abilities of firms to succeed – there are fundamental inequalities between most competitors. This contrasts with the conventional economics textbook view of perfect competition that holds that firms are essentially similar, if not the same, and that over time their performances will converge on a minimum rate of return on capital. Less efficient firms will be obliged to exit and the more efficient firms will be subject to imitation. But the competitive strategy view of the firm is that understanding and manipulating the factors that cause these inequalities, so as to give the firm a sustainable competitive advantage, largely govern long-term business success. These factors vary widely; so different businesses, even within the same industry, often need to be doing different things. Thus, there are many strategies open to firms. The usual starting point is to recognize that strategy is the outcome of the resolution of several different, conflicting forces. These are summarized in Figure 7.9. Society has expectations of its business organizations. Owners, managers and other implementers of strategy have their own personal values and ambitions. The company has strengths and weaknesses, and the industry context offers opportunities and threats. The traditional top-down view of strategy is encapsulated in the *strategic planning view*. This involves deciding on long-term objectives and strategic direction, eliminating or minimizing weaknesses, avoiding threats, building on and defending strengths, and taking advantage

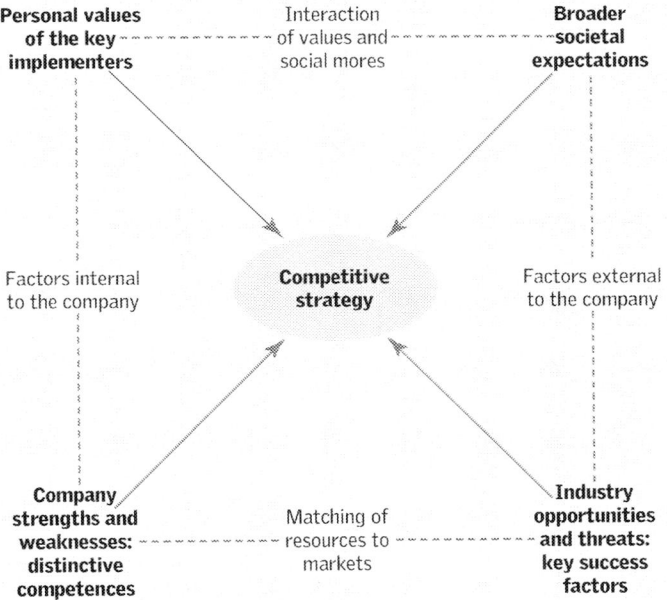

Figure 7.9 An overview of the influences on competitive strategy

of opportunities. But, from reading this chapter, it should be clear that given the strategic direction, the key strategic decision is product market selection. This should be based on the existence of long-term viable business opportunities (not merely the existence of growing markets), together with the prospect of creating the relevant core competences. Viable business opportunities depend on:

◆ The existence of valuable market segments.

◆ The existence of a sustainable positional advantage.

◆ The creation of the appropriate strategic assets.

In conducting the assessment of viable business opportunity, the term *key success factors* is often used. Intuitively, this means 'What do we have to do to succeed?' We can put some analytical flesh on these bones. Figures 7.10 and 7.11 illustrate the process (see Grant 1991). There is a set of key questions to ask:

◆ Is there a market?

◆ Do we have some advantage?

◆ Can we survive the competition?

These lead us into two pieces of analysis: the analysis of customers and demand, and the analysis of competition (summarized in Figure 7.10). Figure 7.11 shows how these can be put together to identify key success factors in three different industries. The key success factors represent the strategic logic(s) (there is usually more than one) available. In the steel industry, the key success factors revolve around low cost, cost efficiencies and scale effectiveness, with some scope for speciality steels. In the fashion industry, key success factors are about differentiation, coupled with an element of low cost. Differentiation has speed of response characteristics, but the industry and the market are so broad that there are

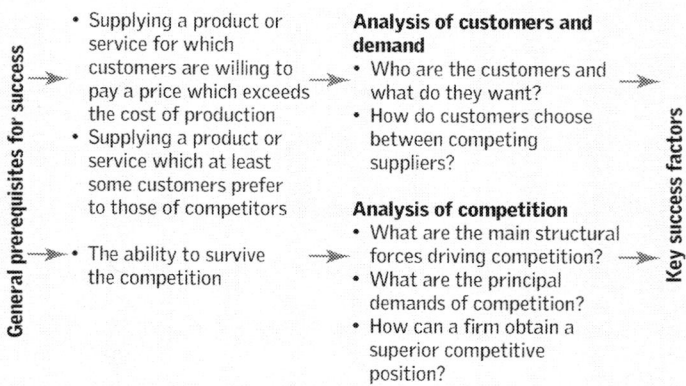

Figure 7.10 Identifying key success factors

Industry	What do customers want? (analysis of demand)	How do firms survive competition? (analysis of competition)	Key success factors
Steel	Customers include automobiles, engineering, and container industries. Customers acutely price sensitive. Also require product consistency and reliability of supply. Specific technical specifications required for special steels.	Competition primarily on price. Competition intense due to declining demand, high fixed costs and low-cost imports. Strong trade union bargaining power. Transport costs high. Scale economies important.	Cost efficiency through scale-efficient plants, low-cost location, rapid adjustment of capacity to output, low labour costs. In special steels, scope for differentiation through quality.
Fashion clothing	Demand fragmented by garment, style, quality, colour. Customers willing to pay price premium for fashion, exclusivity, and quality. Retailers seek reliability and speed of supply.	Low barriers to entry and exit. Low seller concentration. Few scale economies. Strong retail buying power. Price and non-price competition both strong.	Combine effective differentiation with low-cost operation. Key differentiation variables are speed of response to changing fashions, style, reputation with retailers/consumers. Low wages and overheads important.
Grocery supermarkets	Customers want low prices, convenient location and wide range of products.	Markets localized, concentration normally high. But customer price sensitivity encourages vigorous price competition. Exercise of bargaining power a key determinant of purchase price. Scale economies in operations and advertising.	Low-cost operation requires operational efficiency, scale efficient stores, large aggregate purchases to maximize buying power, low wage costs. Differentiation requires large stores to provide wide product and customer convenience facilities.

Figure 7.11 Identifying key success factors in three industries

distinctive segments, some of which are cost driven, while others are differentiation driven. This industry provides a good example of the multiplicity of available strategies.

In formulating competitive strategy, there are some important things to remember:

* *Resources are limited*, opportunities are infinite. The essence of strategy lies in saying 'Yes' to only some of the options and, therefore, 'No' to many others. *Trade-offs* are essential to strategy – they reflect the need for choice and they purposefully limit what a company offers.

* Always factor in *opportunity costs*. A dollar invested 'here' is a dollar not invested 'there', or not given back to shareholders.

* The essence of strategy is choosing to perform activities *differently* than rivals.

* In the long run, what matters is not how fast you are running, but whether you are *running faster than your competitors*.

* A company can only outperform rivals if it can establish a difference that it can sustain. So always test for the *sustainability* of your competitive advantage. Competitors are likely to view relieving you of your competitive advantage as their cardinal duty. Further, not all of them are likely to be stupid.

* The competitive value of individual activities cannot be separated from the whole. So, *fit* locks out imitators by creating a value chain that is stronger than its weakest link.

♦ The long-run test of any strategy lies not in what it contributes to market share or profit margins but in what it contributes to long-term *return on investment*.

♦ Strategic positions should have a *time horizon* of a decade or more, not just of a single planning cycle and/or product cycle.

7.5.1 Managing the business for value

Firms are often poor at devising practical procedures for carrying out the strategy analyses of the kind suggested in this chapter. The ideas are frequently expressed only as concepts. Data is often not collected nor organized as evidence to test out alternative possibilities. This section outlines one way of capturing the analysis of competitive advantage.

Competitive advantage is about creating value both for the customer and for the firm. The first task is to define what this means in practice. Thus, value to the customer can be defined as:

1 firm's ability to position a product better/different than competitors;

2 firm's ability to persuade customers to recognize, purchase and value the difference.

Value to the firm can be defined as

1 firm's ability to create and sustain core competences that underpin the positioning at manageable cost premiums;

2 firm's ability to run (the rest of) the business efficiently and at best practice levels.

These definitions can be operationalized according the schema shown in Figure 7.12. The four elements of value are coded as positioning, customer persuasion, capability and efficiency. Note that efficiency is not enough! Each of these requires strategic indicators by which performance can be measured. The figure suggests some starting points.

Strategic indicators		Company 1	Benchmark
Price: performance segment maps	Positioning		
Repeats; price premium; share	Customer		
Peer ratings; tech benchmarking	Capability		
Engineering studies cost analysis	Efficiency		
Financial indicators	Sales margins asset T/O RoI		

Figure 7.12 Managing the business for value

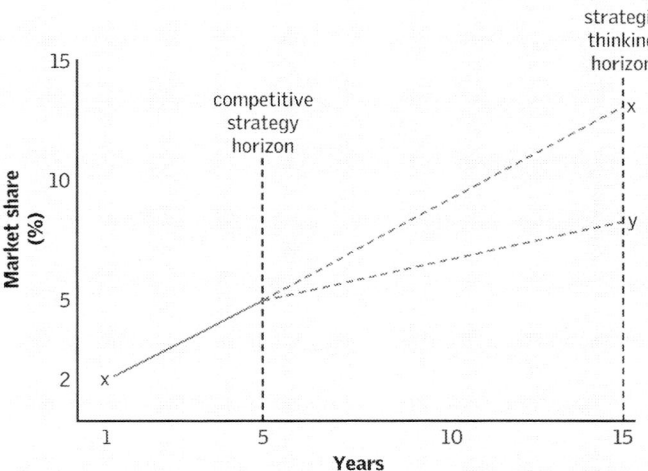

Figure 7.13 Positioning the business for growth

Then data should be collected to identify the firm's own performance on these measures and then some benchmark comparisons. To complement this strategic performance analysis financial indicators can also be shown remembering that these reflect the outcomes of previous strategies whereas the strategic indicators will presage future financial performance.

7.5.2 Positioning the business for growth

Competitive strategy will usually have a limited time scale over which assessments can be made reliably. This is usually related to the tangibility of assets and to the speed with which the product life cycle operates. As a rule of thumb firms can see to the end of the current product life cycle and are actively engaged in the planning and the next cycle. The cycle beyond that is much less clearly seen. Thus, in practice, we can expect firms to see one and a half life cycles ahead (subject to the life expectancy of their capital assets). Thus, if a car manufacturer has a product life cycle of four years, we would expect it to be able to see and forecast about six or seven years ahead. So how do we plan beyond this if the numbers are missing? Figure 7.13 shows the break in our planning horizons.

The shorter period of competitive strategy horizon (shown for example as five years) should not and does not mean that we do not do any strategic thinking beyond that. One way of dealing with this is to compare

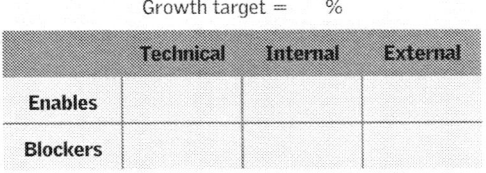

Figure 7.14 Enables and blockers

alternative growth targets (shown in the figure). For each of these, identify the enables and the blockers and assess the nature of these as either technical, internal or external (*see* Figure 7.14). An enabler might, for example, be a creative and productive research team and it would be internal in nature. A blocker might be the growth of low-cost manufacturing capability among competitors and it would be external in character. An example of a technical issue might be the development of new technical standards (such as for DVD rewriting) and this might either be an enabler or a blocker depending on the firm's capabilities.

Longer-term strategic thinking requires both enables and blockers to be managed properly. Thus we would expect a focus on the key enables to develop measures and information sources, to create an intelligence system to track their progress. The need is to assess and keep assessing the prior probability of these enables occurring. The blockers are more difficult. The task is to identify the blockers, sort them into groups according to their common factors, discover the underlying forces and dynamics, and to develop strategies to shift the blocks or to get round them (note how in the reprographics industry in the 1970s Canon developed an R&D strategy to get around Xerox's network of blocking patents). For blockers we need (as for enables) to assess and track over time the prior probability of controlling the blockers and moderating their influence. This analysis should then be repeated for different growth targets. The outcomes will of course be quite qualitative and multidimensional, but Figure 7.15 suggests a way of summarizing the outputs.

The vertical axis is the prior probabilities of facilitating the enables and controlling the blockers (a joint probability of achieving a target would be one way of operationalizing this). The horizontal axis is time. The first part of this is a commitment period during which the foundations are being established (typically the first part of a J-curve), shown here for example as four years. Beyond this period we are looking for a confidence that growth can be managed – *the ring of confidence* in the figure, or not, i.e. *the undesirable region*. More generally you would expect to see a curve showing the prior probabilities rising over time. The key question is whether the probabilities are sufficiently high early enough. The bad position is when the probabilities remain low well beyond the commitment period. Conversely, happiness occurs when they rise quickly.

Approaches such as this one require considerable judgement and they often will defy the objective tests implied by quantification. However, the advantage here is of applying a systematic procedure that is rooted in the economics of the firm, in the nature of customer behaviour and that seeks to balance opportunity against risk.

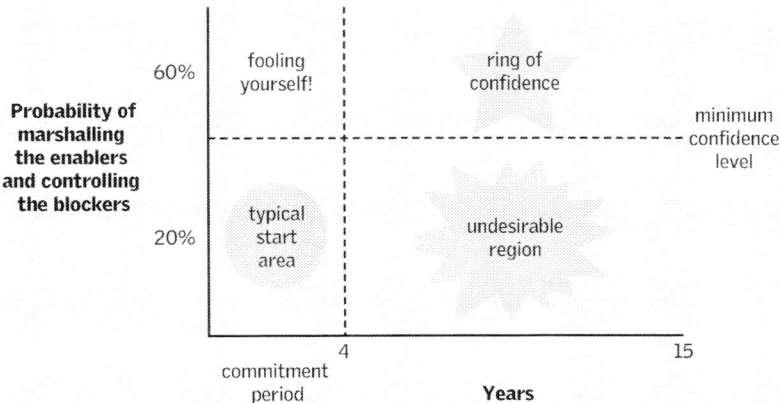

Figure 7.15 Positioning the business for growth: assessing feasibility

7.6 Summary

This chapter asserts that competitive advantage and core competence are two key intellectual constructs that together provide the foundation for understanding strategy. Competitive advantage is the basis for the market-based view, providing us with a way of assessing the positioning of the firm relative to its competitors. Core competence is one of many phrases that capture the resource-based view. The idea of *the underlying capability that is the distinguishing characteristic of the organization* and that underpins competitive advantage.

We have reviewed the various languages of the resource-based view, mentioning resources, capabilities, competences and strategic assets. However, rather than pursue semantic differences between such an array of titles, we have chosen to follow the definition of resources and capabilities as discussed by Grant (1998) and to use the term 'core competences' to cover the capabilities language of Boston Consulting Group and the strategic assets approach of Amit and Schoemaker. Further, we suggest Hamel's clarification as both practical and theoretically sound, namely:

1 A competence is a bundle of constituent skills and technologies rather than a discrete skill or technology and a core competence is the integration of a variety of individual skills.

2 A core competence is not an asset in the accounting sense of the word. A factory, a distribution channel or brand cannot be a core competence but an aptitude to manage that factory, that channel or that brand may constitute a core competence.

3   A core competence must make a disproportionate contribution to customer-perceived value. The distinction between core and non-core competence thus rests on a distinction between the relative impacts on customer value.

4   A core competence must also be competitively unique. This means either that (i) a competence is held uniquely by one firm in the competitive set or that (ii) a competence that is ubiquitous across an industry must be held at a superior level in the firm.

5   From the corporate (multi-business) perspective a core competence should provide an entrée into new markets. A particular competence may be core from the perspective of an individual business, but from a corporate perspective it will not be core if there is no way of imagining an array of new product-markets issuing from it.

The language of the resource-based view can be confusing and it is no surprise that the concept of core competence has been difficult to apply. However, it is an intellectual construct in just the same way that competitive advantage is, and it should be used to clarify thinking. It is not intended as a simple framework or tool (such as SWOT or PEST) that contains within it simple practical guidelines. The second half of the chapter is devoted to practical applications of the core competence concept. Core competence leads directly into issues of resource leverage (for value and profit). We discuss the importance of identifying intangibles. We have discussed the link to competitive advantage using the language of strategic industry factors and fey success factors. We have looked at strategic intent, strategic innovation and the role of learning. What core competence does is to focus attention on the managerial processes, information content and communications that are the intangible heart of the resource-based view. Core competences are hardly ever tangible assets – they reflect intangible, sometimes designed but sometimes informal managerial process. As intangibles it is then not surprising that firms are essentially different from one another (as opposed to the traditional view of economists who hold that firms are essentially similar in the long term). Bringing competitive advantage and core competence together as competitive strategy in practice we see how managing the business for value and managing the business for growth depends on both concepts.

In the following chapters we explore how strategy (i.e. competitive advantage plus core competence) is manifested in a number of different situations. In Chapter 8 we look at competitive strategy in a variety of different situations. Chapter 9 introduces multi-business or corporate strategy and Chapter 10 develops this into mergers and acquisitions. Chapter 11 focuses on international strategy and Chapter 12 asks how these ideas translate into the world of the 'new economy'.

7.6 SUMMARY   281

Key terms

Capabilities *252*

Causal ambiguity *266*

Core competences *252*

Co-specialized assets *258*

First mover advantage *266*

Intangibles *263*

Leverage *261*

Market-based view (MBV) *252*

Path dependency *266*

Resource-based view (RBV) *251*

Rents *252*

Resources *252*

Strategic assets *252*

Strategic fit *269*

Strategic intent *268*

Strategic stretch *269*

Sustainable positional advantage *254*

Recap questions and assignments

Guide answers to these questions are given on the Online Learning Centre website.

1 Undertake a resource audit of an organization with which you are familiar, then identify which resources, if any, are unique in the sense that they are difficult to imitate. Has the organization gained competitive advantage as a result of this uniqueness?

2 Refer to Question 2 (Chapter 5). For these same two companies identify the core competences and show where they are located within their value choices.

3 Refer to Question 3 (Chapter 5). For the same organization show how its core competences are contained within the SWOT analysis. Convert your SWOT analysis into a diagram based on Figure 7.7.

Online LearningCentre

When you have read this chapter, log on to the Online Learning Centre website at www.mcgraw-hill.co.uk/textbooks/mcgee to explore chapter-by-chapter test questions, further reading and more online study tools for strategy.

Case 1 How Dell keeps from stumbling: It's the supply chain, says its boss, Dick Hunter

In the high-tech universe, Dell Computer Corp. is a force of nature. In less than 20 years, company founder Michael S. Dell has amassed a personal fortune of $16 billion and built a $25 billion company, besting the likes of IBM, Hewlett-Packard, and Compaq Computer in the process. Along the way, his build-to-order model has blossomed into a new manufacturing paradigm. Impressively, the Austin (Tex.) company also has weathered the technology meltdown—at least so far. Rival Gateway Inc. just posted its second consecutive quarterly loss, and Hewlett-Packard Co. is planning to eliminate 3,000 management jobs. Outside the PC sector, things are far worse: Cisco Systems Inc. is slashing up to 8,500 jobs after writing off $2.5 billion in unsold inventory.

What insulates Dell from these troubles? Says Dick L. Hunter, the vice-president overseeing supply-chain management, the difference comes from Dell's super-efficient supply chain. 'Michael [Dell] focuses relentlessly on driving low-cost material from the supplier through the supply chain to our customers,' he says. The low-cost producer, he adds, will be the ultimate winner, and that's reflected in Dell's steadily rising market share. According to IDC in Framingham, Mass, Dell nabbed top spot in global PC sales in the first quarter, with a 13.1% share. Hunter brought 25 years of manufacturing experience to Dell. Before joining the company in 1998, he worked in operations and supply-chain management for General Electric, Texas Instruments, and Ericsson. Today, in addition to his supply-chain responsibilities, he manages Dell's largest manufacturing site, a cluster of four factories in Austin that produces most of the systems sold in the Americas. Hunter recently spoke with *Business Week* Industries Editor Adam Aston about the nuts and bolts—and chips and monitors—of Dell's supply-chain operations.

Q: How central to Dell's success is the efficiency of its supply chain?
A: It's absolutely critical. Materials costs account for about 74% of our revenues. We spent around $21 billion on materials last year. Shaving 0.1% off [that] can have a bigger impact than, say, improving manufacturing productivity by 10%.

Q: Dell is famously lean. How does that affect your performance?
A: We carry about five days' worth of inventory. Our competitors carry 30, 45, or even 90 days' worth. This is critical because in our industry, materials costs fall by about 1% per week. So if a competitor has four weeks' worth of inventory and we have one week's, right there we have 3% worth of materials cost advantage. That can mean a 2% or 3% advantage on the bottom line.

Q: Dell has been growing at double-digit rates for its entire life span. Does software play a big role in that?
A: A couple of years ago, realizing we couldn't grow to $75 billion with the tools we had in

place, we selected i2 Technologies' software. Now, 10 months later, all our global manufacturing sites are operating on the same i2 resource-planning and execution systems.

Q: And the result?

A: We now schedule every line in every factory around the world every two hours—we only bring into the factory two hours' worth of materials. With i2, we typically run a factory with about five or six hours' worth of inventory on hand, including work in progress. This increased the cycle time at our factories and reduced warehouse space. We replaced this space with more manufacturing lines.

Q: It takes a tightly knit supplier base to deliver on a schedule like that. How many suppliers do you rely on?

A: Our top 30 suppliers represent about 75% of our total costs. Throw in the next 20, and that comes to about 95%. We deal with all of those top 50 daily, many of them many times a day.

Q: How do the new systems help you manage supply crises?

A: The software tells us where we are. We monitor practically every part, every day. If we're running out of a part, it might be because demand is outstripping supply. We'd try to solve the supply problem first. We'd call the supplier to see if he can increase the next shipment. If it's a generic part—like a hard drive—we might check alternate suppliers. Once we've exhausted our supply options, we go to the sales and marketing guys to help shift the demand to something else. This happens within a few hours.

Q: But isn't demand beyond your control?

A: One of coolest things about Dell is that we talk to 10,000-plus customers every day. That gives us 10,000 opportunities to balance supply and demand. If I'm running out of a part, then I know ahead of time. I'd communicate with our sales department and we'd move demand to material that we have. For example, we can alter lead times. We might extend the lead time on a high-demand item from the standard 4 to 5 days to 10. In this case, we know statistically how much demand will move. Or we may do a promotion. If we're short on Sony 17-inch monitors, we could offer a 19-inch model at a lower price, or even at the 17-inch price. We know if we do this an awful lot of demand will move. We can alter pricing and product mixes in real time via Dell.com. Our competitors that are building to sell through retail channels can't do that.

Q: What effect does this have on excess inventory?

A: Perpetual balance of supply and demand is my main goal in life. If I'm in perpetual balance, I can always meet my customers' delivery expectations. It also helps to minimize excess and obsolete inventory. Dell writes off between 0.05% and 0.1% of total material costs in excess and obsolete inventory—that's about $21 million across our global business in a year. In other industries that figure is probably 4% to 5%. Our competitors probably

284   CASE STUDY

have to write off 2% to 3% worth of excess and obsolete inventory. There's no way we'd end up with months of inventory someplace. If we see two or three days of softening demand for a particular product, alarm bells go off. On an end-of-life product, we'll name a number—say 50,000 more of this computer model will be built. Then that's it — we will not build a 50,001st.

Q: At this volume of transactions, and at this speed, how do you coordinate your suppliers?
A: All of the data goes back and forth on the Internet. From the long-term planning data—volume expectations over the next 4 to 12 weeks—to the two-hourly execution systems, which are making automatic requests for replenishment, every supplier can view our order information via the Web.

Q: How far has automation gone—are even your smallest suppliers wired up?
A: The issue isn't how to get the last 5% online—that's easy, everyone can see our information via the Web. The real question is: How do I get true machine-to-machine connection between me and my supplier, because today there is still manual intervention by the supplier to get the data off the Web. We're fairly automated internally at Dell. Now we want to get the suppliers connected machine-to-machine.

Q: Are you advising the suppliers on particular technologies?
A: Yes. We have a lot of leverage with our suppliers. And all of them understand our model and supply-chain management systems. We constantly ask them, 'How can you become more like Dell?' We're very loyal to these guys. I'd say just two or three of our top suppliers have changed in the past three years.

Q: So what's the next step?
A: Folks ask if five days of inventory is the best Dell can do. Heck no, we can get to two.

Q: How have Dell's operations been affected by the PC downturn?
A: We had 1,700 layoffs a couple of months ago. And our use of contract workers fluctuates depending on the cycle. As we have a downturn, we will have a smaller percentage of contract workers. As we increase production, we have a higher percent. But this recession could be a very good thing for Dell. We're able to pass on lower costs to our customers more quickly, which allows us to gain market share and put a hurt on our competitors.

Q: Some big names, such as Cisco, have been burned by excess inventory. Your thoughts?
A: Our goal is to replace inventory with information. The more information we get to our suppliers quickly, the faster we build product, the faster we receive materials from suppliers, the faster [we] alleviate a problem like Cisco is having. Cisco might have communication problems in the supply chain about what's real demand and what's real supply. It could be that they had bad high forecasting, and the suppliers never knew better.

Reprinted from *Business Week Online*, March 14, 2002 by special permission.
© 2002 by the McGraw-Hill Companies, Inc.

Case Questions

1   What resources and capabilities does Hunter identify in his answer?

2   Which of these do you think are core competences? Why?

3   How does Dell keep the inside (the firm) and the outside (the industry and the market) in balance?

198

McGee–Thomas–Wilson:
Strategy: Analysis and
Practice, Text and Cases

7. Competitive strategy: the
analysis of strategic
capability

Text

© The McGraw–Hill
Companies, 2006

286   CASE STUDY

Case 2   Brand extension, with jacuzzi

Should luxury-goods firms go into the hotel business?

Giorgio Armani is already one of the most diversified brands in fashion. As well as haute couture and everyday clothes, Mr Armani and his eponymous firm create scent, cosmetics, spectacles, watches and accessories. Dedicated followers of Mr Armani's minimalist aesthetics can buy furniture at Casa Armani, chocolate, other sweets, jam and even marmalade at Armani dolce and flowers at Armani fiore. There are Armani cafes and restaurants in Paris, New York, London and other cities. An Armani nightclub recently opened in Milan. Now the great Giorgio is branching out further still. On 22 February his firm announced a $1 billion hotel venture with Dubai's Emaar Properties, the Middle East's largest property developer. Mr Armani will be in charge of the design for ten new luxury hotels and four resorts, to be built in the next six-to-eight years.

Armani's is the boldest move so far by a luxury-goods company into the hotel business. But it is by no means the first. In September 2000, a hotel designed by Donatella Versace opened on Australia's Gold Coast. In February 2001, Bulgari, an Italian jeweller, announced a joint-venture with Ritz-Carlton, the luxury-hotel division of Marriott, to build six or seven hotels and one or two resorts. Bulgari and Marriott are each investing some $70m. The first Bulgari hotel, located immediately behind Milan's La Scala opera house, will (belatedly) open in May. Salvatore Ferragamo, an Italian shoemaker, has designed four hotels in Florence, his hometown. The latest Ferragamo hotel, the Continentale, opened in January last year.

Does it make sense for designers of luxury goods to go into a tricky service business? Hotels are not even a good hedge against the fickleness of the fashion world. Travel and luxury follow the same economic cycle. In the first half of last year both industries were in bad shape because of the war in Iraq, SARS and the rise of the euro. (Many luxury-goods firms are from euro-zone countries, but their revenues are mostly in dollars or yen.) In the second half of the year the two industries both started to recover, albeit timidly. Armani and Bulgari say that their hotels are managed by outside professional managers, and that they are only in charge of making the hotels beautiful. Mr Armani considers hotels a logical extension of his aim of promoting his brand in all walks of life (can Armani toilet paper be far behind?). Rita Clifton, chairman of Interbrand, a consultancy, says that this strategy can work. A strong product, strong images and a strong experience, such as staying at a fashion designer's hotel, can combine to make a super-strong brand, claims Ms Clifton.

To fit the firm's luxurious image, Bulgari says that its hotels must be as upmarket as it is possible to be. Because small is considered more exclusive, Armani and Bulgari plan to launch mostly smallish five-star hotels. Armani's Dubai hotel, due to open in 2007, will be an exception, however, with 250 rooms. Bulgari's Milan hotel will have no more than 60 rooms.

Losing control of their brand is the biggest risk for luxury firms expanding abroad or venturing into a new line of business. Over the years, Pierre Cardin, Yves St Laurent and Christian Dior have each lost their good names by doling out licences all over the world to firms that did not deliver the appropriate quality. Calvin Klein's current troubles are related to the company's loss of control of the distribution of its wares in many countries. Designers' hotels can create good publicity, as they have done for Ferragamo with its easily controllable properties in Florence. Even if Bulgari's hotels turn out not to make any money, the venture could be considered an expensive, yet effective, advertising campaign, says Antoine Colonna of Merrill Lynch in Paris. Mr Armani's hotel plans are altogether more ambitious, and the danger of brand dilution much greater. Armani says that the management company for its hotel venture will be headquartered in Milan rather than Dubai, and that Mr Armani will be fully in charge of design. So far Mr Armani has managed to control his brand tightly despite dabbling in many different businesses. Hotels, however, are a bigger challenge than flowers and marmalade.

Source: 'Brand extension, with jacuzzi', *The Economist*, 26 February 2004.
© The Economist Newspaper Limited, London (26 February 2004).

Case Questions

1 What are the core competences of the typical luxury-goods business and Armani in particular?

2 Explain why these core competences are to be transferred to other businesses such as hotels.

3 What would be the limits to this?

4 To what extent is the core competence of Armani dependent on Giorgio Armani himself? How might his family plan for life after Giorgio?

Further reading and references

Ackenhusen, M (1992) 'Canon: competing on capabilities', INSEAD case study, reprinted in B de Wit and R Meyer (1998) *Strategy: Process, Context, and Content*, 2nd edition, International Thomson Business Press, London.

Amit, R and Schoemaker, PJ (1993) 'Strategic assets and organisational rent', *The Strategy Management Journal*, **14**, pp. 33–46, reprinted in Segal-Horn, S (ed) (1998) *The Strategy Reader*, Blackwell Business.

Barnet, JB (1991) 'Firm Resources and Sustained Competitive Advantage', *Journal of Management*, **17**, pp. 99–120.

Besanko, D, Dranove, D and Shandley, M (2000) *The Economics of Strategy*, 2nd edition, John Wiley & Sons, New York.

Collis, D and Montgomery, C (1995) 'Competing on Capabilities', *Harvard Business Review*, **73**, **4**, pp. 118–28.

Fane, G, Vagheti, R, Van Deusen, C and Woods, L (2003) 'Competitive Advantage the Toyota Way', *Business Strategy Review*, **14**, **4**, Winter, pp. 51–60.

Grant, RM (1991) 'The Resource-Based Theory of Competitive Advantage: Implications for Strategy Formulation', *California Management Review*, Spring, pp. 114–35.

Grant, RM (1998) *Contemporary Strategy Analysis*, 3rd edition, Basil Blackwell, Oxford.

Hall, Richard (1992) 'The Strategic Analysis of Intangible Resources', *Strategic Management Journal*, **13**, pp. 135–44.

Hamel, G (1994) 'The Concept of Core Competence', Chapter 1 in G Hamel and A Heene (eds) *Competence Based Competition*, in the Strategic Management Series, John Wiley & Sons.

Hamel, G and Heene, A (eds) (1994) *Competence Based Competition*, the Strategic Management Series, John Wiley & Sons, Chichester.

Hamel, G and Prahalad, CK (1989) 'Strategic Intent', *Harvard Business Review*, **67**, **3**, pp. 63–76.

Hamel, G and Prahalad, CK (1993) 'Strategy as Stretch and Leverage', *Harvard Business Review*, **71**, **2**, pp. 75–84.

Lave, C and March, J (1993) *An Introduction to Models in the Social Sciences*, University Press of America, NY.

McGee, J and Segal-Horn, S (1997) 'Global Competences in Service Multinationals', in Thomas, H and O'Neal, D (eds) *Strategic Discovery: Competing in New Arenas*, the Strategic Management Series, J Wiley & Sons, Chichester, pp. 49–77.

Nelson, RR and Winter, SG (1982) *An Evolutionary Theory of Economic Change*, Harvard University Press, Boston.

Penrose, E (1995) *The Theory of the Growth of the Firm*, 3rd edition (original edition 1954), Oxford University Press.

Peteraf, MA (1993) 'The Cornerstones of Competitive Advantage; a Resource-based View', *Strategic Management Journal*, **14, 2**, pp. 179–91.

Porter, ME (1980) *Competitive Strategy: Techniques for Analysing Industries and Competitors*, Free Press, New York.

Porter, ME (1985) *Competitive Advantage*, Free Press, New York.

Prahalad, CK and Hamel, G (1990) 'The Core Competence of the Corporation', *Harvard Business Review*, May/June, pp. 79–91, reprinted in S Segal-Horn (1998) (ed.) *The Strategy Reader*, Blackwell Business.

Schoemaker, P (1992) 'How to Link Strategic Vision to Core Capabilities', *Sloan Management Review*, Fall, pp. 67–81.

Segal-Horn, S (ed.) (1998) *The Strategy Reader*, Blackwell Business, Oxford.

Selznick, P (1957) *Leadership and Administration*, University of California Press.

Stalk, G, Evans, P and Shulman, LE (1992) 'Competing on Capabilities: the new Rules of Corporate Strategy', *Harvard Business Review*, **70, 2**, pp. 57–69.

Corporate-Level Strategy:

Creating Value through Diversification

>chapter objectives

After reading this chapter, you should have a good understanding of:

- How managers can create value through diversification initiatives.

- The reasons for the failure of many diversification efforts.

- How corporations can use related diversification to achieve synergistic benefits through economies of scope and market power.

- How corporations can use unrelated diversification to attain synergistic benefits through corporate restructuring, parenting, and portfolio analysis.

- The various means of engaging in diversification—mergers and acquisitions, joint ventures/strategic alliances, and internal development.

- The benefits and potential drawbacks of real options analysis (ROA) in making resource allocation decisions under conditions of high uncertainty.

- Managerial behaviors that can erode the creation of value.

orporate-level strategy addresses two related issues: (1) what businesses should a corporation compete in, and (2) how can these businesses be managed so they create "synergy"—that is, more value by working together than if they were freestanding units? As we will see, these questions present a key challenge for today's managers. Many diversification efforts fail or, in many cases, provide only marginal returns to shareholders. Thus, determining how to create value through entering new markets, introducing new products, or developing new technologies is a vital issue in strategic management.

We begin by discussing why diversification initiatives, in general, have not yielded the anticipated benefits. Then, in the next three sections of the chapter, we explore the two key alternative approaches: related and unrelated diversification. With related diversification, corporations strive to enter product-markets that share some resources and capabilities with their existing business units or increase their market power. Here we suggest four means of creating value: leveraging core competencies, sharing activities, pooled negotiating power, and vertical integration. With unrelated diversification, there are few similarities in the resources and capabilities among the firm's business units, but value can be created in multiple ways. These include restructuring, corporate parenting, and portfolio analysis approaches. Whereas the synergies to be realized with related diversification come from *horizontal relationships* among the business units, the synergies from unrelated diversification are derived from *hierarchical relationships* between the corporate office and the business units.

The last three sections address (1) the various means that corporations can use to achieve diversification, (2) real options analysis, and (3) managerial behaviors (e.g., self-interest) that serve to erode shareholder value. We address merger and acquisitions (M&A), joint ventures/strategic alliances, and internal development. Each of these involves the evaluation of important trade-offs. We also discuss the benefits and potential drawbacks of real options analysis (ROA)—an increasingly popular technique for making resource allocation decisions. Detrimental managerial behaviors, often guided by a manager's self-interest, are "growth for growth's sake," egotism, and antitakeover tactics. Some of these behaviors raise ethical issues because managers, in some cases, are not acting in the best interests of a firm's shareholders.

The pioneering discount broker Charles Schwab and Company became the industry leader through its focus on the customer and the innovative use of information technology. Faced with intense competition from deep-discount Internet brokerages in the late 1990s, Schwab tried to greatly expand its services to wealthy clientele by acquiring U.S. Trust. Below, we discuss why things didn't work out as planned.

"Clicks and mortar" broker Charles Schwab Corp. bought U.S. Trust Corp. in mid-2000 for $3.2 billion, joining a 147-year-old private-client wealth management firm with a leading provider of discount investor services.[1] Schwab paid a premium of 63.5 percent to U.S. Trust shareholders. The steep premium for U.S. Trust reflects the broker's deep pockets as well as its interest in becoming a full-service investment firm. At the time of the acquisition, Schwab was the nation's number one Internet and discount broker and number four financial services company overall.

Several synergies were expected from this acquisition. According to Schwab, the move expanded on its already developed offerings for wealthy clientele, including Schwab's Advisor Source and Signature Services. Schwab saw great potential for growth in the market represented by high-net-worth individuals and hoped its combination of Internet savvy and U.S. Trust's high-touch business lines would be tailor-made for that segment. In all, Schwab expected to leverage on its core competency in investor services to build greater market power.

But the news out of Charles Schwab and Co. has not been good. The bear market took a big bite out of Schwab's trading volume, revenues, and profits. With investment returns eroding, customers were much more sensitive to brokerage and commission fees. The management shake-up at U.S. Trust Corp. in October 2002 also raised serious questions. In its eagerness to tap upscale markets and become more than the people's broker, did the normally savvy Schwab miss serious warning signs at U.S. Trust? What went wrong?

The apparent synergies have not worked out, and deeper incompatibilities surfaced. Former U.S. Trust employees claimed that Schwab was overly enamored by the glossy brand and pedigreed clients of U.S. Trust. The company was too optimistic about Schwab's ability to direct their high-end clients to U.S. Trust, but very few Schwab customers have $2 million in assets, the minimum for U.S. Trust's pricey hand holding. Even those referred were often turned down by the subsidiary. Therefore, the main hope for the acquisition—stopping Schwab's richest customers from defecting to full-service brokerages such as Merrill Lynch—has not panned out. Also, many key managers left when their retention agreements expired in May 2002, taking their clients with them.

By mid-2004, more than 300 wealth advisers had departed. Wealth advisers are the core of U.S. Trust's businesses because they have the direct relationships with the wealthy families that make up its core clientele. When advisers leave, clients often follow them. U.S. Trust has been forced to offer hefty pay packages and bonuses to retain some of its top talent.

Perhaps, the core problem has been a clash between the two cultures. The low-cost discount-broker culture of Schwab discouraged big pay packages and provided only limited services to clients. U.S. Trust, with its plush dining rooms and lavish pay packages, prides itself on its highly personal service to wealthy families. Schwab executives complained about U.S. Trust's arrogance and refusal to adapt to fast-changing financial markets and customer demands. U.S. Trust executives, in contrast, frowned on Schwab's lack of sophistication and obsessive focus on cutting costs. According to one U.S. Trust executive, "It's like the battle between old wealth versus new wealth. U.S. Trust represented the established wealth and complicated needs of wealthy families. Schwab was the upstart that saw the market in more simple terms."

Another major problem has been technology. Despite reports of federal regulators' hinting at system-related problems, Schwab thought it was manageable and was content with its inspection of U.S. Trust's system. However, it eventually discovered the magnitude of the problem when the computer systems failed to detect suspicious patterns of cash transactions. The bank had to pay $10 million in July 2001 to settle charges by the New York State Banking Department and Federal Reserve that it was not complying with anti–money laundering rules. (The bank did not admit or deny fault.) The severity of the technology problem is illustrated by the fact that U.S. Trust did not even use the standard Windows operating system until the late 1990s. Furthermore, its 30 branches are not on a single computer system, hindering back-office operations such as order processing.

Compounding the problems after the compliance fiasco, U.S. Trust started screening clients so closely that it alienated them. This consumed time and money that could otherwise have been spent generating new business. Cost cutting has been another area of concern. U.S. Trust's executives dragged their feet on consolidating their numerous bank charters and cutting costs at offices outside New York, adding to the disappointing performance. Several weak branches will likely be closed.

With problems mounting, Schwab replaced U.S. Trust CEO Jeffrey S. Maurer and the president, Amribeth S. Rahe. They named Alan J. Weber, former head of Citibank's international operations, to be CEO and president. Weber faces the Herculean task of making things work. "The wild card is whether Schwab can transform a high-net-worth business from (one of) steady earnings growth to more dynamic earnings growth," says a Wall Street analyst. It seems that marrying up has not been the ticket to wealth it was supposed to be.

Schwab is not alone in having a disappointing experience with an acquisition. Many large multinational firms and recent big acquirers have failed to effectively integrate their acquisitions, paid too high a premium for the target's common stock, or were unable to understand how the acquired firm's assets would fit with their own lines of business. And, at times, top executives may not have acted in the best interests of shareholders. That is, the motive for the acquisition may have been to enhance the executives' power and prestige rather than improve shareholder returns. At times, the only other people who may have benefited were the shareholders of the *acquired* firms.

Exhibit 6.1 summarizes some of the bottom line results of several studies that were conducted over a variety of time periods. Here are a few examples of the enormous amount of shareholder wealth that has been lost within a few years after some of the more recent well-chronicled acquisitions and mergers.[2]

- Glaxo/SmithKline (2000) $40 billion lost
- Chase/J. P. Morgan (2000) $26 billion lost
- SBC/Ameritech (1999) $68 billion lost
- WorldCom/MCI (1998) $94 billion lost
- Daimler/Chrysler (1998) $36 billion lost

Many acquisitions ultimately result in divestiture—an admission that things didn't work out as planned. In fact, some years ago, a writer for *Fortune* magazine lamented, "Studies show that 33 percent to 50 percent of acquisitions are later divested, giving corporate marriages a divorce rate roughly comparable to that of men and women."[3]

Admittedly, we have been rather pessimistic so far. Clearly, many diversification efforts have worked out very well—whether through mergers and acquisitions, strategic alliances and joint ventures, or internal development. We will discuss many success stories throughout this chapter. Next, we will discuss the primary rationales for diversification.

>>Making Diversification Work: An Overview

Not all diversification moves, including those involving mergers and acquisitions, erode performance. For example, acquisitions in the oil industry, such as British Petroleum PLC's purchases of Amoco and Arco, are performing well, as is the merger of Exxon and Mobil. Similarly, many leading high-tech firms, such as Microsoft and Intel, have

Exhibit 6.1

Diversification and Corporate Performance: A Disappointing History

The summaries of the studies below consistently support the notion that attaining the intended payoffs from diversification efforts is very elusive.

- Michael Porter of Harvard University studied the diversification records of 33 large, prestigious U.S. companies from 1950 to 1986 and found that most of them had divested many more acquisitions than they had kept. The corporate strategies of most companies had dissipated rather than enhanced shareholder value. By taking over companies and breaking them up, corporate raiders had thrived on failed strategies.

- Another study evaluated the stock market reaction to 600 acquisitions over the period between 1975 and 1991. The results indicated that the acquiring firms suffered an average 4 percent drop in market value (after adjusting for market movements) in the three months following the acquisitions announcement.

- A study conducted jointly by *BusinessWeek* and Mercer Management Consulting, Inc., analyzed 150 acquisitions worth more than $500 million that took place between July 1990 and July 1995. Based on total stock returns from three months before the announcement and up to three years after the announcement:
  - 30 percent substantially eroded shareholder returns.
  - 20 percent eroded some returns.
  - 33 percent created only marginal returns.
  - 17 percent created substantial returns.

- In a study by Salomon Smith Barney of U.S. companies acquired since 1997 in deals for $15 billion or more, the stocks of the acquiring firms have, on average, underperformed the S&P stock index by 14 percentage points and underperformed their peer group by 4 percentage points after the deals were announced.

- A study of 12,023 acquisitions from 1980 to 2001 found that acquiring-firm shareholders lost 12 cents per dollar spent on acquisition, for a total loss of $240 billion from 1998 through 2001, whereas they lost only $7 billion in all of the 1980s, or 1.6 cents per dollar spent. The 1998 to 2001 aggregate dollar loss of acquiring-firm shareholders is so large because of a small number of acquisitions with negative synergy gains by firms with extremely high valuations. Without these acquisitions, the wealth of acquiring-firm shareholders would have increased.

Sources: Moeller, S. B., Schlingemann, F. P., & Stulz, R. M. 2005. Wealth destruction on a massive scale? A study of acquiring-firm returns in the recent merger wave. *Journal of Finance* (forthcoming); Lipin, S., & Deogun, N. 2000. Big mergers of the 90s prove disappointing to shareholders. *The Wall Street Journal*, October 30: C1; Dr. G. William Schwert, University of Rochester study cited in Pare, T. P. 1994. The new merger boom. *Fortune*, November 28: 96; and, Porter, M. E. 1987. From competitive advantage to corporate strategy. *Harvard Business Review*, 65(3): 43.

dramatically increased their revenues, profits, and market values through a wide variety of diversification moves, including mergers and acquisitions, strategic alliances and joint ventures, and internal development.

So the question becomes: Why do some diversification efforts pay off and others produce disappointing results? In this chapter we will address this question. Whereas Chapter 5 focused on business-level strategy—that is, how to achieve sustainable advantages in a given business or product market—this chapter addresses two related issues: (1) What businesses should a corporation compete in? and (2) How should these businesses be managed to jointly create more value than if they were freestanding units?

Diversification initiatives—whether through mergers and acquisitions, strategic alliances and joint ventures, or internal development—must be justified by the creation of value for shareholders. But this is not always the case. For example, as noted earlier, acquiring firms typically pay high premiums when they acquire a target firm. However, you and I, as private investors, can diversify our portfolio of stocks very cheaply. With the advent of the intensely competitive online brokerage industry, we can acquire hundreds (or thousands) of shares for a transaction fee of as little as $10.00 or less—a far cry from the 30 to 40 percent (or higher) premiums that corporations typically must pay to acquire companies.

Given the seemingly high inherent downside risks and uncertainties, it might be reasonable to ask why companies should even bother with diversification initiatives. The answer, in a word, is *synergy,* derived from the Greek word *synergos,* which means "working together." This can have two different, but not mutually exclusive, meanings. First, a firm may diversify into *related* businesses. Here, the primary potential benefits to be derived come from *horizontal relationships;* that is, businesses sharing intangible resources (e.g., core competences) and tangible resources (e.g., production facilities, distribution channels). Additionally, firms can enhance their market power through pooled negotiating power and vertical integration. As we will see in this chapter, Procter & Gamble enjoys many synergies from having businesses that share distribution resources.

Second, a corporation may diversify into *unrelated* businesses. In these instances, the primary potential benefits are derived largely from *hierarchical relationships;* that is, value creation derived from the corporate office. Examples of the latter would include leveraging some of the support activities in the value chain that we discussed in Chapter 3, such as information systems or human resource practices. Cooper Industries, another firm we will discuss, has followed a successful strategy of unrelated diversification. There are few similarities in the products it makes or the industries in which it competes. However, the corporate office adds value through such activities as superb human resource practices as well as planning and budgeting systems.

It is important to note that the aforementioned horizontal (derived from related diversification) and hierarchical (derived from related and unrelated diversification) relationships are not mutually exclusive. Many firms that diversify into related areas benefit from information technology expertise in the corporate office, and firms diversifying into unrelated areas often benefit from the "best practices" of sister businesses even though their products, markets, and technologies may differ dramatically.

Exhibit 6.2 provides an overview of how we will address the various means by which firms create value through both related and unrelated diversification and also include a summary of some examples that we will address in this chapter.[4]

>>Related Diversification: Economies of Scope and Revenue Enhancement

As discussed earlier, related diversification enables a firm to benefit from horizontal relationships across different businesses in the diversified corporation by leveraging core competencies and sharing activities (e.g., production facilities and distribution facilities). This enables a corporation to benefit from economies of scope. *Economies of scope* refers to cost savings from leveraging core competencies or sharing related activities among businesses in the corporation. A firm can also enjoy greater revenues if two businesses attain higher levels of sales growth combined than either company could attain independently.

For example, a sporting goods store with one or several locations may acquire other stores. This enables it to leverage, or reuse, many of its key resources—favorable reputation, expert staff and management skills, efficient purchasing operations—the basis

Exhibit 6.2

Creating Value through Related and Unrelated Diversification

Related Diversification: Economies of Scope

Leveraging core competences
- 3M leverages its competencies in adhesives technologies to many industries, including automotive, construction, and telecommunications.

Sharing activities
- McKesson, a large distribution company, sells many product lines, such as pharmaceuticals and liquor, through its superwarehouses.

Related Diversification: Market Power

Pooled negotiating power
- The Times Mirror Company increases its power over customers by providing "one-stop shopping" for advertisers to reach customers through multiple media—television and newspapers—in several huge markets such as New York and Chicago.

Vertical integration
- Shaw Industries, a giant carpet manufacturer, increases its control over raw materials by producing much of its own polypropylene fiber, a key input to its manufacturing process.

Unrelated Diversification: Parenting, Restructuring, and Financial Synergies

Corporate restructuring and parenting
- The corporate office of Cooper Industries adds value to its acquired businesses by performing such activities as auditing their manufacturing operations, improving their accounting activities, and centralizing union negotiations.

Portfolio management
- Novartis, formerly Ciba-Geigy, uses portfolio management to improve many key activities, including resource allocation and reward and evaluation systems.

of its competitive advantage(s), over a larger number of stores.[5] Let's next address how to create value by leveraging core competencies.

Leveraging Core Competencies

The concept of core competencies can be illustrated by the imagery of the diversified corporation as a tree.[6] The trunk and major limbs represent core products; the smaller branches are business units; and the leaves, flowers, and fruit are end products. The core competencies are represented by the root system, which provides nourishment, sustenance, and stability. Managers often misread the strength of competitors by looking only at their end products, just as we can fail to appreciate the strength of a tree by looking only at its leaves. Core competencies may also be viewed as the "glue" that binds existing businesses together or as the engine that fuels new business growth.

Core competencies reflect the collective learning in organizations—how to coordinate diverse production skills, integrate multiple streams of technologies, and market and merchandise diverse products and services. The theoretical knowledge necessary to put a radio on a chip does not in itself assure a company of the skill needed to produce a miniature radio approximately the size of a business card. To accomplish this, Casio, a giant electronic products producer, must synthesize know-how in miniaturization, microprocessor design, material science, and ultrathin precision castings. These are the same skills that it applies in its miniature card calculators, pocket TVs, and digital watches.

For a core competence to create value and provide a viable basis for synergy among the businesses in a corporation, it must meet three criteria.[7]

- ***The core competence must enhance competitive advantage(s) by creating superior customer value.*** It must enable the business to develop strengths relative to the competition. Every value-chain activity has the potential to provide a viable basis for building on a core competence.[8] At Gillette, for example, scientists developed the Mach 3 and Sensor Excel after the introduction of the tremendously successful Sensor System because of a thorough understanding of several phenomena that underlie shaving. These include the physiology of facial hair and skin, the metallurgy of blade strength and sharpness, the dynamics of a cartridge moving across skin, and the physics of a razor blade severing hair. Such innovations are possible only with an understanding of such phenomena and the ability to combine such technologies into innovative products. Customers have consistently been willing to pay more for such technologically differentiated products.

- ***Different businesses in the corporation must be similar in at least one important way related to the core competence.*** It is not essential that the products or services themselves be similar. Rather, at least one element in the value chain must require similar skills in creating competitive advantage if the corporation is to capitalize on its core competence. At first glance you might think that motorcycles, clothes, and restaurants have little in common. But at Harley-Davidson, they do.[9] Harley-Davidson has capitalized on its exceptionally strong brand image as well as merchandising and licensing skills to sell accessories, clothing, and toys and has licensed the Harley-Davidson Café in New York City—further evidence of the strength of its brand name and products.

- ***The core competencies must be difficult for competitors to imitate or find substitutes for.*** As we discussed in Chapter 5, competitive advantages will not be sustainable if the competition can easily imitate or substitute them. Similarly, if the skills associated with a firm's core competencies are easily imitated or replicated, they are not a sound basis for sustainable advantages. Consider Sharp Corporation, a $17 billion consumer electronics giant.[10] It has a set of specialized core competencies in optoelectronics technologies that are difficult to replicate and contribute to its competitive advantages in its core businesses. Its most successful technology has been liquid crystal displays (LCDs) that are critical components in nearly all of Sharp's products. Its expertise in this technology enabled Sharp to succeed in videocassette recorders (VCRs) with its innovative LCD viewfinder and led to the creation of its Wizard, a personal electronic organizer.

Strategy Spotlight 6.1 discusses how UPS leverages its core competence in logistics. It ships broken Toshiba laptops to its facility in Louisville, Kentucky, to diagnose and repair them.

Sharing Activities

As we saw above, leveraging core competencies involves transferring accumulated skills and expertise across business units in a corporation. When carried out effectively, this leads to advantages that can become quite sustainable over time. Corporations also can achieve synergy by sharing tangible activities across their business units. These include

STRATEGY SPOTLIGHT   6.1

UPS: Leveraging Its Core Competence in Logistics

Toshiba has recently handed over its entire laptop repair operation to United Parcel Service (UPS) Supply Chain Solutions, the shipper's $2.4 billion logistics outsourcing division. UPS will ship broken Toshiba laptops to its facility in Louisville, Kentucky, where UPS will diagnose and repair defects. The facility consists of a campus that occupies 2 million square feet devoted to more than 70 companies. Consumers will enjoy an immediate benefit. In the past, repairs could take weeks, depending on whether Toshiba needed components from Japan. However, since the UPS repair site is adjacent to its air hub, customers should get their machines back, as good as new, in a matter of days.

Why would Toshiba let a shipping company repair its laptops? Simply put, the challenge of computer repair is more logistical than technical. "Moving a unit around and getting replacement parts consumes most of the time," says Mark Simons, general manager of Toshiba's digital products division. "The actual service only takes about an hour." Plus, UPS already has experience in this area. The company has repaired Lexmark and Hewlett-Packard printers since 1996 and has performed initial inspections on laptops being returned by Toshiba since 1999.

The expanded relationship with Toshiba is another step in UPS's strategy to broaden its business beyond package delivery into commerce services. Its new marketing mission in 2004 was to market a set of capabilities that go along with its new slogan, "Synchronizing the world of commerce." According to Larry Bloomenkranz, Vice President, Global Brand Management and Advertising, "It's not just the same old UPS. We are a one-brand supplier up and down the supply chain." UPS currently works with clients to manage inventory, ordering, and customs processes, and it has just introduced a service to dispose of unwanted electronics.

If Toshiba's customers are satisfied with the new UPS repair services, other electronics manufacturers will likely also consider UPS as an outsourcing partner. As pointed out by Roger Kay, Vice President for Client Computing at research firm IDC, "A logistics partner who can also do repair is a rare and wonderful thing." Clearly, UPS is able to leverage its core competencies in logistics (e.g., shipping, spare parts supply management) into the seemingly unrelated area of laptop repair to enhance its revenues and profitability.

Sources: James, G. 2004. The next delivery? Computer repairs by UPS. *Business 2.0*, July: 30; Blanchard, D. 2004. It takes a supply chain village. *www.logisticstoday.com*, November: 9; and, Podmolik, M. 2004. UPS promotes commerce, supply-chain capabilities. *B to B*, 89(12): 18.

value-creating activities such as common manufacturing facilities, distribution channels, and sales forces. As we will see, sharing activities can potentially provide two primary payoffs: cost savings and revenue enhancements.

Deriving Cost Savings through Sharing Activities   Typically, this is the most common type of synergy and the easiest to estimate. Peter Shaw, head of mergers and acquisitions at the British chemical and pharmaceutical company ICI refers to cost savings as "hard synergies" and contends that the level of certainty of their achievement is quite high. Cost savings come from many sources, including elimination of jobs, facilities, and related expenses that are no longer needed when functions are consolidated, or from economies of scale in purchasing. Cost savings are generally highest when one company acquires another from the same industry in the same country. Shaw Industries, recently acquired by Berkshire Hathaway, is the nation's largest carpet producer. Over the years, it has dominated the competition through a strategy of acquisition which has enabled Shaw, among other things, to consolidate its manufacturing operations in a few, highly efficient plants and to lower costs through higher capacity utilization.

It is important to note that sharing activities inevitably involve costs that the benefits must outweigh. One often overlooked cost is the greater coordination required to manage a shared activity. Even more important is the need to compromise the design or performance of an activity so that it can be shared. For example, a salesperson handling the products of two business units must operate in a way that is usually not what either unit would choose if it were independent. If the compromise erodes the unit's effectiveness, then sharing may reduce rather than enhance competitive advantage.

Enhancing Revenue and Differentiation through Sharing Activities
Often an acquiring firm and its target may achieve a higher level of sales growth together than either company could on its own. Shortly after Gillette acquired Duracell, it confirmed its expectation that selling Duracell batteries through Gillette's existing channels for personal care products would increase sales, particularly internationally. Gillette sold Duracell products in 25 new markets in the first year after the acquisition and substantially increased sales in established international markets. In a similar vein, a target company's distribution channel can be used to escalate the sales of the acquiring company's product. Such was the case when Gillette acquired Parker Pen. Gillette estimated that it could gain an additional $25 million in sales of its own Waterman pens by taking advantage of Parker's distribution channels.

Firms also can enhance the effectiveness of their differentiation strategies by means of sharing activities among business units. A shared order-processing system, for example, may permit new features and services that a buyer will value. Also, sharing can reduce the cost of differentiation. For instance, a shared service network may make more advanced, remote service technology economically feasible. To illustrate the potential for enhanced differentiation though sharing, consider $5.1 billion VF Corporation—producer of such well-known brands as Lee, Wrangler, Vanity Fair, and Jantzen.

> VF's acquisition of Nutmeg Industries and H. H. Cutler provided it with several large customers that it didn't have before, increasing its plant utilization and productivity. But more importantly, Nutmeg designs and makes licensed apparel for sports teams and organizations, while Cutler manufactures licensed brand-name children's apparel, including Walt Disney kids' wear. Such brand labeling enhances the differentiation of VF's apparel products. According to VF President Mackey McDonald, "What we're doing is looking at value-added knitwear, taking our basic fleece from Basset-Walker [one of its divisions], embellishing it through Cutler and Nutmeg, and selling it as a value-added product." Additionally, Cutler's advanced high-speed printing technologies will enable VF to be more proactive in anticipating trends in the fashion-driven fleece market. Claims McDonald, "Rather than printing first and then trying to guess what the customer wants, we can see what's happening in the marketplace and then print it up."[11]

As a cautionary note, managers must keep in mind that sharing activities among businesses in a corporation can have a negative effect on a given business's differentiation. For example, with the merger of Chrysler and Daimler-Benz, many consumers may lower their perceptions of Mercedes's quality and prestige if they feel that common production components and processes are being used across the two divisions. And the Jaguar division of Ford Motor Company may be adversely affected as consumers come to understand that it shares many components with its sister divisions at Ford, including Lincoln.

Strategy Spotlight 6.2 discusses how Freemantle Media leverages its hit television show *American Idol* through its core competences and shared activities to create multiple revenue streams.

>>Related Diversification: Market Power

In the previous section, we explained how leveraging core competencies and sharing activities help firms create economies of scale and scope through related diversification. In this section, we discuss how companies achieve related diversification through market power. We also address the two principal means by which firms achieve synergy through market power: *pooled negotiating power* and *vertical integration*. It is important to recognize that managers have limits on their ability to use market power for diversification,

STRATEGY SPOTLIGHT   6.2

American Idol: Far More than Just a Television Show

American Idol is one of several of FremantleMedia's (FM) hit television shows. FM is a division of German media giant Bertlesmann, which has approximately $20 billion in revenues. Some of FM's other well-known television shows are *The Apprentice, The Swan,* and at a ripe old age of 48—*The Price Is Right.*

First shown in the United States in June 2002, *American Idol* became a tremendous overnight success. Although the show may be crass and occasionally cruel, it is undeniably brilliant. It's become the ultimate testament to a singular business achievement: FM has become extremely successful at creating truly global programming. In part, that is due to the creative minds at Fremantle; it has some of the best professionals in the business who have a talent for developing shows that appeal to huge populations with different backgrounds and circumstances.

Amazingly, FM, which created *Pop Idol* in Britain in 2001, is now rolling out the show in its 30th country. There's *Belgium Idool, Portugal Idolos, Deutschland Sucht den SuperStar* (Germany), *SuperStar KZ* (Kazakhstan), and of course, the largest and best-known show, *American Idol,* in the United States. *American Idol* is the primary reason that Fremantle's revenue is up 9 percent to more than $1 billion since the show was launched. According to Fremantle's CEO Tony Cohen, "*Idol* has become a national institution in lots of countries." To illustrate, fans cast more than 65 million votes for the *American Idol* finale in May, 2004—that is two-thirds as many people as voted in the 2004 U.S. presidential election.

The real key to Fremantle's success is not just adapting its television hits to other countries, but systematically leveraging its core product—television shows—to create multiple revenue streams. In essence, the "Fremantle Way" holds lessons not just for show business but for all business. It enables a company to use its core competence of making products of mass appeal and then to customize them for places with widely varying languages, cultures, and mores. It then milks the hits for every penny through tie-ins, spinoffs, innovative uses of technology, and marketing masterstrokes.

The *Idol* franchise has created a wide variety of new revenue streams for Fremantle's German parent, Bertelsmann. Here's how much *American Idol* has generated in its first two years since its June 2002 launch:

- *Products ($50 million).* Brand extensions range from videogames and fragrances to a planned microphone-shaped soap-on-a-rope. Fremantle receives a licensing fee from manufacturers.

- *TV Licensing ($75 million).* For its rights fee, Fox gets to broadcast the show and, in turn, sell ads and lucrative sponsorships.

- *Compact Discs (CDs) ($130 million).* The most successful performers on the *Idols* shows have sold millions of CDs; more than one-third of the revenue goes to BMG, which, like Fremantle, is an affiliate of Bertelsmann.

- *Concerts ($35 million).* Although artists and their management get the bulk of the take, concerts sell records and merchandise and promote the next *Idol* show.

In addition, Fremantle Licensing Worldwide signed Warner Brothers Publications to produce and distribute *Idol* audition books with CDs for the United States, Canada, United Kingdom, and Australia. The new books/CDs—*Pop Idol* (UK), *Australian Idol,* and *Canadian Idol*—join the *American Idol* book/CD.

Sources: Sloan, P. 2004. The reality factory. *Business 2.0,* August: 74–82; Cooney, J. 2004. In the news. *License!,* March: 48; and, Anonymous. 2005. Fox on top in Feb; NBC languishing at the bottom. www.indiantelevision.com, March 2.

because government regulations can sometimes restrict the ability of a business to gain very large shares of a particular market.

When General Electric (GE) announced a $41 billion bid for Honeywell, the European Union stepped in. GE's market clout would have expanded significantly as a result of the deal, with GE supplying over one-half the parts needed to build several aircraft engines. The commission's concern, causing them to reject the acquisition, was that GE could use its increased market power to dominate the aircraft engine parts market and crowd out competitors.[12] Thus, while managers need to be aware of the strategic advantages of market power, they must at the same time be aware of regulations and legislation.

Pooled Negotiating Power

Similar businesses working together or the affiliation of a business with a strong parent can strengthen an organization's bargaining position in relation to suppliers and customers and enhance its position vis-à-vis competitors. Compare, for example, the position of an independent food manufacturer with the same business within Nestlé. Being part of Nestlé Corporation provides the business with significant clout—greater bargaining power with suppliers and customers—since it is part of a firm that makes large purchases from suppliers and provides a wide variety of products to its customers. Access to the parent's deep pockets increases the business's strength relative to rivals. Further, the Nestlé unit enjoys greater protection from substitutes and new entrants. Not only would rivals perceive the unit as a more formidable opponent, but the unit's association with Nestlé would also provide greater visibility and improved image.

Consolidating an industry can also increase a firm's market power. This is clearly an emerging trend in the multimedia industry.[13] All of these mergers and acquisitions have a common goal: to control and leverage as many news and entertainment channels as possible. In total, more than $261 billion in mergers and acquisitions in the media industry were announced in 2000—up 12 percent from 1999. For example, consider the Tribune Company's $8 billion purchase of the Times Mirror Company.

> The merger doubled the size of the Tribune and secured its position among the top tier of major media companies. The enhanced scale and scope helped it to compete more effectively and grow more rapidly in two consolidating industries—newspaper and television broadcasting. The combined company would increase its power over customers by providing a "one-stop shop" for advertisers desiring to reach consumers through multiple media in enormous markets such as Chicago, Los Angeles, and New York. The company has estimated its incremental revenue from national and cross-media advertising will grow from $40 to $50 million in 2001 to $200 million by 2005. The combined company should also increase its power relative to its suppliers. The company's enhanced size is expected to lead to increased efficiencies when purchasing newsprint and other commodities.[14]

When acquiring related businesses, a firm's potential for pooled negotiating power vis-à-vis its customers and suppliers can be very enticing. However, managers must carefully evaluate how the combined businesses may affect relationships with actual and potential customers, suppliers, and competitors. For example, when PepsiCo diversified into the fast-food industry with its acquisitions of Kentucky Fried Chicken, Taco Bell, and Pizza Hut (since spun off as Tricon, Inc.), it clearly benefited from its position over these units that served as a captive market for its soft-drink products. However, many competitors such as McDonald's have refused to consider PepsiCo as a supplier of its own soft-drink needs because of competition with Pepsi's divisions in the fast-food industry. Simply put, McDonald's did not want to subsidize the enemy! Thus, although acquiring related businesses can enhance a corporation's bargaining power, it must be aware of the potential for retaliation.

Vertical Integration

Vertical integration represents an expansion or extension of the firm by integrating preceding or successive productive processes.[15] That is, the firm incorporates more processes toward the original source of raw materials (backward integration) or toward the ultimate consumer (forward integration). For example, an automobile manufacturer might supply its own parts or make its own engines to secure sources of supply. Or it might control its own system of dealerships to ensure retail outlets for its products. Similarly, an oil refinery might secure land leases and develop its own drilling capacity to

216

Dess–Lumpkin–Eisner:
Strategic Management:
Text and Cases, Third

II. Strategic Formulation

6. Corporate–Level
Strategy: Creating Value
through Diversification

© The McGraw–Hill
Companies, 2007

STRATEGY SPOTLIGHT

6.3

Vertical Integration at Shaw Industries

Shaw Industries (now part of Berkshire Hathaway) is an example of a firm that has followed a very successful strategy of vertical integration. By relentlessly pursuing both backward and forward integration, Shaw has become the dominant manufacturer of carpeting products in the United States. According to CEO Robert Shaw, "We want to be involved with as much of the process of making and selling carpets as practical. That way, we're

in charge of costs." For example, Shaw acquired Amoco's polypropylene fiber manufacturing facilities in Alabama and Georgia. These new plants provide carpet fibers for internal use and for sale to other manufacturers. With this backward integration, fully one-quarter of Shaw's carpet fiber needs are now met in-house. In early 1996 Shaw began to integrate forward, acquiring seven floor-covering retailers in a move that suggested a strategy to consolidate the fragmented industry and increase its influence over retail pricing. Exhibit 6.3 provides a simplified depiction of the stages of vertical integration for Shaw Industries.

Sources: White, J. 2003. Shaw to home in on more with Georgia Tufters deal. *HFN: The Weekly Newspaper for the Home Furnishing Network,* May 5: 32; Shaw Industries. 1993, 2000. Annual reports; and Server, A. 1994. How to escape a price war. *Fortune,* June 13: 88.

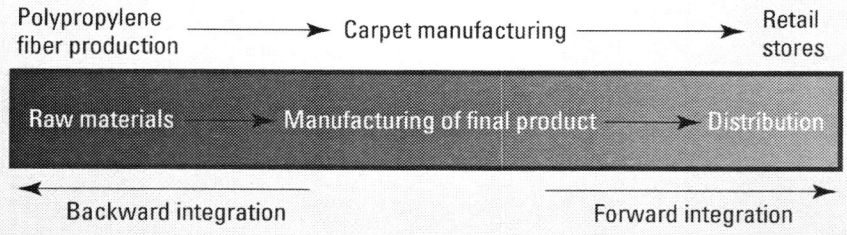

Exhibit 6.3 *Simplified Stages of Vertical Integration: Shaw Industries*

ensure a constant supply of crude oil. Or it could expand into retail operations by owning or licensing gasoline stations to guarantee customers for its petroleum products.

Clearly, vertical integration can be a viable strategy for many firms. Strategy Spotlight 6.3 discusses Shaw Industries, a carpet manufacturer that has attained a dominant position in the industry via a strategy of vertical integration. Shaw has successfully implemented strategies of both forward and backward integration.

Benefits and Risks of Vertical Integration   Although vertical integration is a means for an organization to reduce its dependence on suppliers or its channels of distribution to end users, it represents a major decision that an organization must carefully consider. The benefits associated with vertical integration—backward or forward—must be carefully weighed against the risks.[16]

The *benefits* of vertical integration include (1) a secure supply of raw materials or distribution channels that cannot be "held hostage" to external markets where costs can fluctuate over time, (2) protection and control over assets and services required to produce and deliver valuable products and services, (3) access to new business opportunities and new forms of technologies, and (4) simplified procurement and administrative procedures since key activities are brought inside the firm, eliminating the need to deal with a wide variety of suppliers and distributors.

Winnebago, the leader in the market for drivable recreational vehicles with a 19.3 percent market share, illustrates some of vertical integration's benefits.[17] The word Winnebago means "big RV" to most Americans. And the firm has a sterling reputation for great quality. The firm's huge northern Iowa factories do everything from extruding aluminum for body parts to molding plastics for water and holding tanks and dashboards. Such vertical integration at the factory may appear to be outdated and expensive, but it guarantees excellent quality. The Recreational Vehicle Dealer Association started giving a quality award in 1996, and Winnebago has won it every year.

The *risks* of vertical integration include (1) the costs and expenses associated with increased overhead and capital expenditures to provide facilities, raw material inputs, and distribution channels inside the organization; (2) a loss of flexibility resulting from the inability to respond quickly to changes in the external environment because of the huge investments in vertical integration activities that generally cannot be easily deployed elsewhere; (3) problems associated with unbalanced capacities or unfilled demand along the value chain; and (4) additional administrative costs associated with managing a more complex set of activities. Exhibit 6.4 summarizes the benefits and risks of vertical integration.

In making decisions associated with vertical integration, four issues should be considered.[18]

1. *Is the company satisfied with the quality of the value that its present suppliers and distributors are providing?* If the performance of organizations in the vertical chain—both suppliers and distributors—is satisfactory, it may not, in general, be appropriate for a company to perform these activities themselves. Firms in the athletic footwear industry such as Nike and Reebok have traditionally outsourced the manufacture of their shoes to countries such as China and Indonesia where labor costs are low. Since the strengths of these companies are typically in design and marketing, it would be advisable to continue to outsource production operations and continue to focus on where they can add the most value.

2. *Are there activities in the industry value chain presently being outsourced or performed independently by others that are a viable source of future profits?* Even if a firm is outsourcing value-chain activities to companies that are doing a credible job, it may be missing out on substantial profit opportunities. To illustrate, consider the automobile industry's profit pool. As you may recall from Chapter 5, there is much more potential profit in many downstream activities (e.g., leasing, warranty, insurance, and service) than in the manufacture of automobiles. Not surprising, carmakers such as Ford and General Motors are undertaking forward integration strategies to become bigger players in these high-profit activities.

Exhibit 6.4
Benefits and Risks of Vertical Integration

Benefits

-   A secure source of raw materials or distribution channels.
-   Protection of and control over valuable assets.
-   Access to new business opportunities.
-   Simplified procurement and administrative procedures.

Risks

-   Costs and expenses associated with increased overhead and capital expenditures.
-   Loss of flexibility resulting from large investments.
-   Problems associated with unbalanced capacities along the value chain.
-   Additional administrative costs associated with managing a more complex set of activities.

3. *Is there a high level of stability in the demand for the organization's products?* High demand or sales volatility would not be conducive to a vertical integration strategy. With the high level of fixed costs in plant and equipment as well as operating costs that accompany endeavors toward vertical integration, widely fluctuating sales demand can either strain resources (in times of high demand) or result in unused capacity (in times of low demand). The cycles of "boom and bust" in the automobile industry are a key reason why the manufacturers have increased the amount of outsourced inputs in recent years.

4. *How high is the proportion of additional production capacity actually absorbed by existing products or by the prospects of new and similar products?* The smaller the proportion of production capacity to be absorbed by existing or future products, the lower is the potential for achieving scale economies associated with the increased capacity—either in terms of backward integration (toward the supply of raw materials) or forward integration (toward the end user). Alternatively, if there is excess capacity in the near term, the strategy of vertical integration may be viable if there is the anticipation of future expansion of products.

Analyzing Vertical Integration: The Transaction Cost Perspective

Another approach that has proved very useful in understanding vertical integration is the *transaction cost perspective.*[19] According to this perspective, every market transaction involves some *transaction costs.* First, a decision to purchase an input from an outside source leads to *search* costs (i.e., the cost to find where it is available, the level of quality, etc.). Second, there are costs associated with *negotiating.* Third, a *contract* needs to be written spelling out future possible contingencies. Fourth, parties in a contract have to *monitor* each other. Finally, if a party does not comply with the terms of the contract, there are *enforcement* costs. Transaction costs are thus the sum of search costs, negotiation costs, contracting costs, monitoring costs, and enforcement costs. These transaction costs can be avoided by internalizing the activity, in other words, by producing the input in-house.

A related problem with purchasing a specialized input from outside is the issue of *transaction-specific investments.* For example, when an automobile company needs an input specifically designed for a particular car model, the supplier may be unwilling to make the investments in plant and machinery necessary to produce that component for two reasons. First, the investment may take many years to recover but there is no guarantee the automobile company will continue to buy from them after the contract expires, typically in one year. Second, once the investment is made, the supplier has no bargaining power. That is, the buyer knows that the supplier has no option but to supply at ever-lower prices because the investments were so specific that they cannot be used to produce alternative products. In such circumstances, again, vertical integration may be the only option.

Vertical integration, however, gives rise to a different set of costs. These costs are referred to as *administrative costs.* Coordinating different stages of the value chain now internalized within the firm causes administrative costs to go up. Decisions about vertical integration are, therefore, based on a comparison of transaction costs and administrative costs. If transaction costs are lower than administrative costs, it is best to resort to market transactions and avoid vertical integration. For example, McDonald's may be the world's biggest buyer of beef, but they do not raise cattle. The market for beef has low transaction costs and requires no transaction-specific investments. On the other hand, if transaction costs are higher than administrative costs, vertical integration becomes an attractive strategy. Most automobile manufacturers produce their own engines because the market for engines involves high transaction costs and transaction-specific investments.

Vertical Integration: Further Considerations   As many companies would attest, successfully executing strategies of vertical integration can be very difficult. For example, Unocal, a major petroleum refiner, which once owned retail gas stations, was slow to capture the potential grocery and merchandise side business that might have resulted from customer traffic to its service stations. Unocal lacked the competencies to develop a separate retail organization and culture. The company eventually sold the assets and brand to Tosco (now part of Phillips Petroleum Co.). Eli Lilly, the pharmaceutical firm, tried to achieve forward integration by acquiring a pharmaceutical mail-order business in 1994, but it was unsuccessful in increasing market share because it failed to integrate its operations. Two years later, Lilly wrote off the venture.

Last, as with our earlier discussion of pooled negotiating power, managers must carefully consider the impact that vertical integration may have on existing and future customers, suppliers, and competitors. After Lockheed Martin, a dominant defense contractor, acquired Loral Corporation, an electronics supplier, for $9.1 billion, it had an unpleasant and unanticipated surprise. Loral, as a captive supplier of Lockheed, is now perceived and treated as a competitor by many of its previous customers. McDonnell Douglas (MD), for example, announced that it would switch its business from Loral to other suppliers of electronic systems such as Litton Industries or Raytheon. Thus, before Lockheed Martin can realize any net synergies from this acquisition, it must make up for the substantial lost business resulting from MD's (now part of Boeing) decision to switch suppliers.

In these two sections we have addressed four means by which firms can achieve synergies through related diversification: leveraging core competences, sharing activities, pooled negotiating power, and vertical integration. In Strategy Spotlight 6.4, we address how Procter & Gamble strengthened its competitive position by combining all four means. We next turn our attention to unrelated diversification.

>>Unrelated Diversification: Financial Synergies and Parenting

With unrelated diversification, unlike related diversification, few benefits are derived from *horizontal relationships*—that is, the leveraging of core competencies or the sharing of activities across business units within a corporation. Instead, potential benefits can be gained from *vertical (or hierarchical) relationships*—the creation of synergies from the interaction of the corporate office with the individual business units. There are two main sources of such synergies. First, the corporate office can contribute to "parenting" and restructuring of (often acquired) businesses. Second, the corporate office can add value by viewing the entire corporation as a family or "portfolio" of businesses and allocating resources to optimize corporate goals of profitability, cash flow, and growth. Additionally, the corporate office enhances value by establishing appropriate human resource practices and financial controls for each of its business units.

Corporate Parenting and Restructuring

So far, we have discussed how corporations can add value through related diversification by exploring sources of synergy *across* business units. In this section, we will discuss how value can be created *within* business units as a result of the expertise and support provided by the corporate office. Thus, we look at these as *hierarchical* sources of synergy.

The positive contributions of the corporate office have been referred to as the "parenting advantage."[20] Many firms have successfully diversified their holdings without

220

Dess–Lumpkin–Eisner:
Strategic Management:
Text and Cases, Third

II. Strategic Formulation

6. Corporate–Level
Strategy: Creating Value
through Diversification

© The McGraw–Hill
Companies, 2007

STRATEGY SPOTLIGHT

6.4

Procter & Gamble: Using Multiple Means to Achieve Synergies

To accomplish successful related diversification, a company must combine multiple facets of its business to create synergies across the organization. Procter & Gamble (P&G) is a prime example of such a firm. Using related diversification, it creates synergies by leveraging core competencies, sharing activities, pooling negotiating power, and vertically integrating certain product lines as part of its corporate-level strategy. The following excerpt from a speech by Clayt Daley, Procter & Gamble's chief financial officer, illustrates how the company has done this.

Remarks to Financial Analysts

Today, we already sell 10 brands with sales of one billion dollars or more. Seven of these 10 brands surpassed the billion-dollar sales mark during the '90s. And, in total, these 10 brands accounted for more than half of our sales growth during the decade. Beyond these 10, there are several brands with the potential to achieve a billion dollars in sales by 2005. Olay could surpass a billion dollars in sales in 2001, Iams by 2002.

P&G's unmatched lineup of billion-dollar leadership brands generates consistently strong returns. In virtually every case, P&G's leading brands achieve higher margins and deliver consistently strong shareholder returns. Having a stable of such strong global brands creates significant advantages for P&G—and our total company scale multiplies those advantages.

We can obviously take advantage of our purchasing power for things as varied as raw materials and advertising media. We can leverage the scale of our manufacturing and logistics operations. But we can do far more.

We have the scale of our intellectual property—the knowledge and deep insight that exists throughout our organization. We have scale in our technologies—the enormous breadth of expertise we have across our product categories. There is scale in our go-to-market capabilities and our global customer relationships.

Let me give you three quick examples. First, scale of consumer knowledge. We are able to learn, reapply, and multiply knowledge across many brands with a similar target audience. For example, teens. The teen market is global. Teens in New York, Tokyo, and Caracas wear the same clothes, listen to the same music, and have many of the same attitudes. We have categories they buy and use: cosmetics, hair care, skin care, personal cleansing and body products, feminine protection, snacks and beverages, oral care, and others. Our scale enables us to develop unique insights on teens—like how to identify teen chat leaders—and then reapply that across all our teen-focused businesses.

Another way we can leverage scale is through the transfer of product technologies across categories. We can connect seemingly unrelated technologies to create surprising new products. Our new Crest White Strips are a great example of the innovation that can result. This new product provides a major new tooth-whitening benefit that can be achieved in the home. We have combined our knowledge in oral hygiene, and our knowledge of bleaching agents, with a special film technology to provide a safe and effective product that can whiten teeth within 14 days.

Another important source of scale is our go-to-market capability. No other consumer products company works with retailers the way we do. Our Customer Business Development approach is a fundamentally different way of working with our trade partners. We seek to build businesses across common goals.

We bring a philosophy that encourages a simple, transparent shopping experience—with simple, transparent pricing, efficient assortment, efficient in-store promotion, and efficient replenishment. This approach has helped us build extremely strong relationships with our customers. For example, in the annual Cannondale "Power-Ranking Survey," U.S. retailers consistently ranked P&G at the top on brands, consumer information, supply-chain management, category management, and more.

Source: Daley, C. 2000. Remarks to Financial Analysts. Speech excerpt. Procter & Gamble Company, September 28.

strong evidence of the more traditional sources of synergy (i.e., horizontally across business units). Diversified public corporations such as BTR, Emerson Electric, and Hanson and leveraged buyout firms such as Kohlberg, Kravis, Roberts & Company, and Clayton, Dublilier & Rice are a few examples.[21] These parent companies create value through management expertise. How? They improve plans and budgets and provide especially competent central functions such as legal, financial, human resource management, procurement, and the like. Additionally, they help subsidiaries make wise choices in their own acquisitions, divestitures, and new internal development decisions. Such contributions often help business units to substantially increase their revenues and profits. Consider Texas-based Cooper Industries' acquisition of Champion International, the spark plug company, as an example of corporate parenting.[22]

Cooper applies a distinctive parenting approach designed to help its businesses improve their manufacturing performance. New acquisitions are "Cooperized"—Cooper audits their manufacturing operations; improves their cost accounting systems; makes their planning, budgeting, and human resource systems conform with its systems; and centralizes union negotiations. Excess cash is squeezed out through tighter controls and reinvested in productivity enhancements, which improve overall operating efficiency. As one manager observed, "When you get acquired by Cooper, one of the first things that happens is a truckload of policy manuals arrives at your door." Such active parenting has been effective in enhancing the competitive advantages of many kinds of manufacturing businesses.

Restructuring is another means by which the corporate office can add substantial value to a business.[23] The central idea can be captured in the real estate phrase "buy low and sell high." Here, the corporate office tries to find either poorly performing firms with unrealized potential or firms in industries on the threshold of significant, positive change. The parent intervenes, often selling off parts of the business; changing the management; reducing payroll and unnecessary sources of expenses; changing strategies; and infusing the company with new technologies, processes, reward systems, and so forth. When the restructuring is complete, the firm can either "sell high" and capture the added value or keep the business in the corporate family and enjoy the financial and competitive benefits of the enhanced performance.[24]

For the restructuring strategy to work, the corporate management must have both the insight to detect undervalued companies (otherwise the cost of acquisition would be too high) or businesses competing in industries with a high potential for transformation.[25] Additionally, of course, they must have the requisite skills and resources to turn the businesses around, even if they may be in new and unfamiliar industries.

Restructuring can involve changes in assets, capital structure, or management. *Asset restructuring* involves the sale of unproductive assets, or even whole lines of businesses, that are peripheral. In some cases, it may even involve acquisitions that strengthen the core business. *Capital restructuring* involves changing the debt-equity mix, or the mix between different classes of debt or equity. Although the substitution of equity with debt is more common in buyout situations, occasionally the parent may provide additional equity capital. *Management restructuring* typically involves changes in the composition of the top management team, organizational structure, and reporting relationships. Tight financial control, rewards based strictly on meeting short- to medium-term performance goals, and reduction in the number of middle-level managers are common steps in management restructuring. In some cases, parental intervention may even result in changes in strategy as well as infusion of new technologies and processes.

Hanson, plc, a British conglomerate, made numerous such acquisitions in the United States in the 1980s, often selling these firms at significant profits after a few years of successful restructuring efforts. Hanson's acquisition and subsequent restructuring of the SCM group is a classic example of the restructuring strategy. Hanson acquired SCM, a diversified manufacturer of industrial and consumer products (including Smith-Corona typewriters, Glidden paints, and Durkee Famous Foods), for $930 million in 1986 after a bitter takeover battle. In the next few months, Hanson sold SCM's paper and pulp operations for $160 million, the chemical division for $30 million, Glidden paints for $580 million, and Durkee Famous Foods for $120 million, virtually recovering the entire original investment. In addition, Hanson also sold the SCM headquarters in New York for $36 million and reduced the headquarters staff by 250. They still retained several profitable divisions, including the titanium dioxide operations and managed them with tight financial controls that led to increased returns.[26]

Portfolio Management

During the 1970s and early 1980s, several leading consulting firms developed the concept of portfolio matrices to achieve a better understanding of the competitive position of an overall portfolio (or family) of businesses, to suggest strategic alternatives for each of the businesses, and to identify priorities for the allocation of resources. Several studies have reported widespread use of these techniques among American firms.[27]

The key purpose of portfolio models was to assist a firm in achieving a balanced portfolio of businesses.[28] This consisted of businesses whose profitability, growth, and cash flow characteristics would complement each other and add up to a satisfactory overall corporate performance. Imbalance, for example, could be caused either by excessive cash generation with too few growth opportunities or by insufficient cash generation to fund the growth requirements in the portfolio. Monsanto, for example, used portfolio planning to restructure its portfolio, divesting low-growth commodity chemicals businesses and acquiring businesses in higher-growth industries such as biotechnology.

The Boston Consulting Group's (BCG) growth/share matrix is among the best known of these approaches.[29] In the BCG approach, each of the firm's strategic business units (SBUs) is plotted on a two-dimensional grid in which the axes are relative market share and industry growth rate. The grid is broken into four quadrants. Exhibit 6.5 depicts the BCG matrix. Following are a few clarifications:

1. Each circle represents one of the corporation's business units. The size of the circle represents the relative size of the business unit in terms of revenues.
2. Relative market share, measured by the ratio of the business unit's size to that of its largest competitor, is plotted along the horizontal axis.
3. Market share is central to the BCG matrix. This is because high relative market share leads to unit cost reduction due to experience and learning curve effects and, consequently, superior competitive position.

Each of the four quadrants of the grid has different implications for the SBUs that fall into the category:

- *Stars* are SBUs competing in high-growth industries with relatively high market shares. These firms have long-term growth potential and should continue to receive substantial investment funding.

- *Question marks* are SBUs competing in high-growth industries but having relatively weak market shares. Resources should be invested in them to enhance their competitive positions.

- *Cash cows* are SBUs with high market shares in low-growth industries. These units have limited long-run potential but represent a source of current cash flows to fund investments in "stars" and "question marks."

- *Dogs* are SBUs with weak market shares in low-growth industries. Because they have weak positions and limited potential, most analysts recommend that they be divested.

In using portfolio strategy approaches, a corporation tries to create synergies and shareholder value in a number of ways.[30] Since the businesses are unrelated, synergies

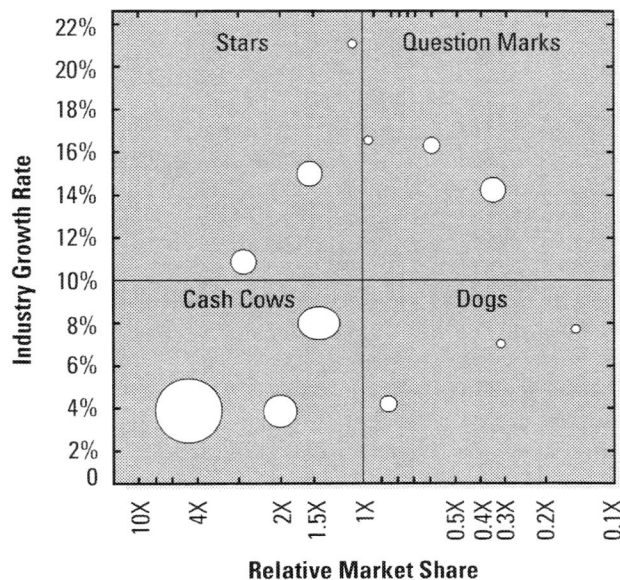

Industry Growth Rate (y-axis): 22%, 20%, 18%, 16%, 14%, 12%, 10%, 8%, 6%, 4%, 2%, 0

Stars   Question Marks
Cash Cows   Dogs

Relative Market Share (x-axis): 10X, 4X, 2X, 1.5X, 1X, 0.5X, 0.4X, 0.3X, 0.2X, 0.1X

Exhibit 6.5   The Boston Consulting Group (BCG) Portfolio Matrix

that develop are those that result from the actions of the corporate office with the individual units (i.e., hierarchical relationships) instead of among business units (i.e., horizontal relationships). First, portfolio analysis provides a snapshot of the businesses in a corporation's portfolio; therefore, the corporation is in a better position to allocate resources among the business units according to prescribed criteria (e.g., use cash flows from the "cash cows" to fund promising "stars"). Second, the expertise and analytical resources in the corporate office provide guidance in determining what firms may be attractive (or unattractive) acquisitions. Third, the corporate office is able to provide financial resources to the business units on favorable terms that reflect the corporation's overall ability to raise funds. Fourth, the corporate office can provide high-quality review and coaching for the individual businesses. Fifth, portfolio analysis provides a basis for developing strategic goals and reward/evaluation systems for business managers. For example, managers of cash cows would have lower targets for revenue growth than managers of stars, but the former would have higher threshold levels of profit targets on proposed projects than the managers of star businesses. Compensation systems would also reflect such realities. Cash cows understandably would be rewarded more on the basis of cash that their businesses generate than would managers of star businesses. Similarly, managers of star businesses would be held to higher standards for revenue growth than managers of cash cow businesses.

To see how companies can benefit from portfolio approaches, consider Ciba-Geigy.

In 1994 Ciba-Geigy adopted portfolio planning approaches to help it manage its business units, which competed in a wide variety of industries, including chemicals, dyes, pharmaceuticals, crop protection, and animal health.[31] It placed each business unit in a category corresponding to the BCG matrix. The business unit's goals, compensation programs, personnel selection, and resource allocation were strongly associated with the category within which the business was placed. For example, business units classified as "cash cows" had much higher hurdles for obtaining financial resources (from the corporate office) for expansion than "question marks" since the latter were businesses for which Ciba-Geigy had high hopes for accelerated future growth and profitability. Additionally, the compensation of a business unit manager in a cash cow would be strongly associated with its success in generating cash to fund other businesses, whereas a manager of a question mark business would be rewarded on his or her ability to increase revenue growth and market share. The portfolio planning approaches appear to be working. In 2004, Ciba-Geigy's (now Novartis) revenues and net income stood at $22 billion and $5.0 billion, respectively. This represents a rather modest 40 percent increase in revenues but a most impressive 150 percent growth in net income over a seven-year period.

Despite the potential benefits of portfolio models, there are also some notable downsides. First, they compare SBUs on only two dimensions, making the implicit but erroneous assumption that (1) those are the only factors that really matter and (2) every unit can be accurately compared on that basis. Second, the approach views each SBU as a stand-alone entity, ignoring common core business practices and value-creating activities that may hold promise for synergies across business units. Third, unless care is exercised, the process becomes largely mechanical, substituting an oversimplified graphical model for the important contributions of the CEO's (and other corporate managers's) experience and judgment. Fourth, the reliance on "strict rules" regarding resource allocation across SBUs can be detrimental to a firm's long-term viability. For example, according to one study, over one-half of all the businesses that should have been cash users (based on the BCG matrix) were instead cash providers.[32] Finally, while colorful and easy to comprehend, the imagery of the BCG matrix can lead to some troublesome and overly simplistic prescriptions. According to one author:

> The dairying analogy is appropriate (for some cash cows), so long as we resist the urge to oversimplify it. On the farm, even the best-producing cows eventually begin to dry up. The farmer's solution to this is euphemistically called "freshening" the cow: The farmer arranges a date for the cow with a bull, she has a calf, the milk begins flowing again. Cloistering the cow—isolating her from everything but the feed trough and the milking machines—assures that she will go dry.[33]

To see what can go wrong, consider Cabot Corporation.

> Cabot Corporation supplies carbon black for the rubber, electronics, and plastics industries. Following the BCG matrix, Cabot moved away from its cash cow, carbon black, and diversified into stars such as ceramics and semiconductors in a seemingly overaggressive effort to create more revenue growth for the corporation. Predictably, Cabot's return on assets declined as the firm shifted away from its core competence to unrelated areas. The portfolio model failed by pointing the company in the wrong direction in an effort to spur growth—away from their core business. Recognizing its mistake, Cabot Corporation returned to its mainstay carbon black manufacturing and divested unrelated businesses. Today the company is a leader in its field with $1.8 billion in 2003 revenues.[34]

Caveat: Is Risk Reduction a Viable Goal of Diversification?

Analysts and academics have suggested that one of the purposes of diversification is to reduce the risk that is inherent in a firm's variability in revenues and profits over time. In essence, the argument is that if a firm enters new products or markets that are affected differently by seasonal or economic cycles, its performance over time will be more stable. For example, a firm manufacturing lawn mowers may diversify into snow blowers to even out its annual sales. Or a firm manufacturing a luxury line of household furniture may introduce a lower-priced line since affluent and lower-income customers are affected differently by economic cycles.

At first glance the above reasoning may make sense, but there are some problems with it. First, a firm's stockholders can diversify their portfolios at a much lower cost than a corporation. As we have noted in this chapter, individuals can purchase their shares with almost no premium (e.g., only a small commission is paid to a discount broker), and they don't have to worry about integrating the acquisition into their portfolio. Second, economic cycles as well as their impact on a given industry (or firm) are difficult to predict with any degree of accuracy.

Notwithstanding the above, some firms have benefited from diversification by lowering the variability (or risk) in their performance over time. Consider Emerson Electronic.

> Emerson Electronic is a $16 billion manufacturer that has enjoyed an incredible run—43 consecutive years of earnings growth![35] It produces a wide variety of products, including measurement devices for heavy industry, temperature controls for heating and ventilation systems, and power tools sold at Home Depot. Recently, many analysts questioned Emerson's purchase of companies that sell power systems to the volatile telecommunications industry. Why? This industry is expected to experience, at best, minimal growth. However, CEO David Farr maintained that such assets could be acquired inexpensively because of the aggregate decline in demand in this industry. Additionally, he argued that the other business units, such as the sales of valves and regulators to the now-booming oil and natural gas companies, were able to pick up the slack. Therefore, while net profits in the electrical equipment sector (Emerson's core business) sharply decreased, Emerson's overall corporate profits increased 1.7 percent.

In summary, risk reduction in and of itself is rarely viable as a means to create shareholder value. It must be undertaken with a view of a firm's overall diversification strategy.

>>The Means to Achieve Diversification

In the prior three sections, we have addressed the types of diversification (e.g., related and unrelated) that a firm may undertake to achieve synergies and create value for its shareholders. In this section, we address the means by which a firm can go about achieving these desired benefits.

We will address three basic means. First, through acquisitions or mergers, corporations can directly acquire the assets and competencies of other firms. Second, corporations may agree to pool the resources of other companies with their resource base. This approach is commonly known as a joint venture or strategic alliance. Although these two forms of partnerships are similar in many ways, there is an important difference. Joint ventures involve the formation of a third-party legal entity where the two (or more) firms each contribute equity, whereas strategic alliances do not. Third, corporations may diversify into new products, markets, and technologies through internal development. This approach, sometimes called corporate entrepreneurship, involves the leveraging and combining of a firm's own resources and competencies to create synergies and enhance shareholder value.

Mergers and Acquisitions

The rate of mergers and acquisitions (M&A) had dropped off beginning in 2001. This trend was largely a result of a recession, corporate scandals, and a declining stock market. However, the situation has changed dramatically. Recently, several large mergers and acquisitions were announced. These include:[36]

- Sprint's merger with Nextel for $39 billion.
- Johnson & Johnson's $25 billion acquisition of medical device maker Guidant.
- Exelon's acquisition of Public Service Enterprise Group for $12 billion.
- SBC's purchase of AT&T for $16 billion.
- Procter & Gamble's purchase of Gillette for $54 billion.
- Kmart Holding Corp.'s acquisition of Sears, Roebuck & Co. for $11 billion.

218   Part 2   Strategic Formulation

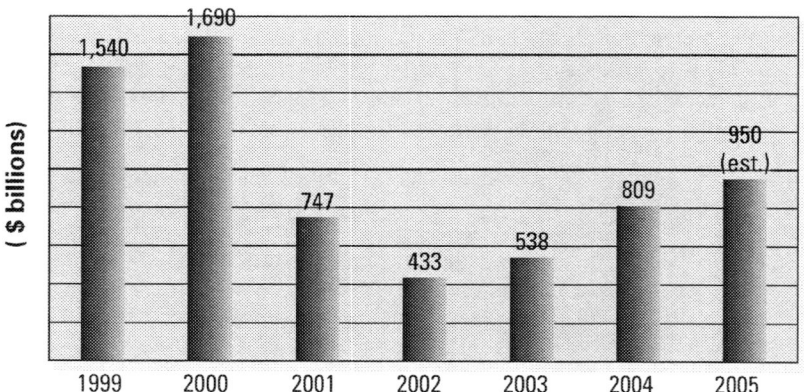

Let's make some deals
The value of U.S. mergers and acquisitions has been steadily increasing since 2002.

Exhibit 6.6   U.S. Mergers and Acquisitions

Sources: Thomson Financial; and, Coy, P., Thornton, E., Arndt, M. Grow, B. 2005. Shake rattle, and merge. *Business Week*, January 10:34.

Exhibit 6.6 illustrates the dramatic increase in merger and acquisition activity in the United States in the past few years. While the volume is not expected soon to reach the peak level of 1999 and 2000, when the dollar amount totaled over $3 trillion, several factors help to explain the recent rise. First, there is the robust economy and the increasing corporate profits that have boosted stock prices and cash. For example, the Standard & Poor's 500 stock index companies, including financial companies, have a record $2 trillion in cash and other short-term assets, according to S&P Compustat.

Second, the weak U.S. dollar makes U.S. assets more attractive to other countries. That is, from the perspective of a foreign acquirer, compared to any other period in recent memory, U.S. companies are "cheap" today. For example, a Euro which was worth only 80 cents in 1999 was worth $1.25 by early 2005. This makes U.S. companies a relative bargain for a European acquirer. And third, stricter governance standards are requiring poorly performing CEOs and boards of directors to consider unsolicited offers. In essence, top executives and board members are less likely to be protected by anti-takeover mechanisms such as greenmail, poison pills and golden parachutes (which we will discuss at the end of the chapter).

Next, we will address some of the motives and potential benefits of mergers and acquisitions as well as their potential limitations.

Motives and Benefits   Growth through mergers and acquisitions has played a critical role in the success of many corporations in a wide variety of high-technology and knowledge-intensive industries. Here, market and technology changes can occur very quickly and unpredictably.[37] Speed—speed to market, speed to positioning, and speed to becoming a viable company—is critical in such industries. For example, Alex Mandl, then AT&T's president, was responsible for the acquisition of McCaw Cellular. Although many industry experts felt the price was too steep, he believed that cellular technology was a critical asset for the telecommunications business and that it would have been extremely difficult to build that business from the ground up. Mandl claimed, "The plain fact is that acquiring is much faster than building."[38]

As we discussed earlier in the chapter, mergers and acquisitions also can be a means of *obtaining valuable resources that can help an organization expand its product offerings and services.* For example, Cisco Systems, a dominant player in networking equipment, acquired more than 70 companies from 1993 to early 2000.[39] This provides Cisco with access to the latest in networking equipment. Then it uses its excellent sales force to market the new technology to its corporate customers and telephone companies. Cisco also provides strong incentives to the staff of acquired companies to stay on. In order to realize the greatest value from its acquisitions, Cisco also has learned to integrate acquired companies efficiently and effectively.[40]

Mergers and acquisitions also can *provide the opportunity for firms to attain the three bases of synergy that were addressed earlier in the chapter—leveraging core competencies, sharing activities, and building market power.* Consider Procter & Gamble's $54 billion proposed acquisition of Gillette.[41] First, it should help Procter & Gamble to leverage its core competencies in marketing and product positioning in the area of grooming and personal care brands. For example, P&G has experience in repositioning brands such as Old Spice in this market (which recently passed Gillette's Right Guard brand to become No. 1 in the deodorant market). Gillette has very strong brands in razors and blades. Thus, P&G's marketing expertise should help it to enhance its market position. Second, there are opportunities to share value-creating activities. Gillette will benefit from P&G's stronger distribution network in developing countries where the potential growth rate for the industry's products remains higher than in the United States, Europe, or Japan. Consider the insight of A. F. Lafley, P&G's CEO:

> When I was in Asia in the 90s, we had already gone beyond the top 500 cities in China. Today, we're way down into the rural areas. So we add three, four, five Gillette brands, and we don't even have to add a salesperson.

Finally, the addition of Gillette will enhance P&G's market power. In recent years, the growth of powerful global retailers such as Wal-Mart, Carrefour, and Costco has eroded much of the consumer goods industry's pricing power. A central part of P&G's recent strategy has been to focus its resources on enhancing its core brands. Today, 16 of its brands (each with revenues of over $1 billion) account for $30 billion of the firm's $51.4 billion in total revenues. Gillette, with $10.5 billion in total revenues, adds five brands which also have revenues of over $1 billion. P&G anticipates that its growing stable of "superbrands" will help it to weather the industry's tough pricing environment and enhance its power relative to large, powerful retailers.

Merger and acquisition activity also can *lead to consolidation within an industry and can force other players to merge.*[42] In the pharmaceutical industry, the patents for many top-selling drugs are expiring and M&A activity is expected to heat up.[43] For example, SG Cowen Securities predicts that between 2000 and 2005, U.S. patents will expire on pharmaceutical products with annual domestic sales of approximately $34.6 billion. Clearly, this is an example of how the political-legal segment of the general environment (discussed in Chapter 2) can affect a corporation's strategy and performance. Although health care providers and patients are happy about the lower-cost generics that will arrive, drug firms are being pressed to make up for lost revenues. Combining top firms such as Pfizer Inc. and Warner-Lambert Co. as well as Glaxo Wellcome and SmithKline Beecham has many potential long-term benefits. They not only promise significant postmerger cost savings, but also the increased size of the combined companies brings greater research and development possibilities.

Two other industries where consolidation is the primary rationale are telecommunications and software.[44] In 2004, Cingular Wireless became number one in the industry by acquiring AT&T Wireless Communications. Subsequently, Sprint agreed to buy Nextel to form a stronger number three. SBC Communications Inc. desires to have full ownership of Cingular, but BellSouth does not want to sell its 40 percent ownership. Will SBC simply buy all of BellSouth? Says SBC chief operating officer (COO) Randall Stephenson, "I don't want to speculate, but who knows? This industry is going to continue to consolidate." In software, the primary motive for merger is to offer customers a fuller portfolio of products. Many niche players are selling out to serial buyers like Oracle Corp., which recently acquired PeopleSoft Inc. after a long and heated struggle. Symantec Corp. agreed to acquire Veritas Software Corporation for $13.5 billion. Such consolidation raises questions about whether smaller players such as McAfee, BEA Systems, and Siebel Systems are big enough to remain independent. According to Joseph M. Tucci, president and CEO of data-storage giant EMC, "This is going to be a big boys' game. They're going to move very aggressively and quickly."

Strategy Spotlight 6.5 discusses how Ken Hendricks was able to successfully consolidate the highly fragmented, and low-margin industry of roofing supplies. The example shows that industry consolidation can take place in lesser known, and more mundane, industries.

Corporations can also *enter new market segments by way of acquisitions.* Although Charles Schwab & Co. is best known for providing discount trading services for middle America, it clearly is interested in other target markets.[45] In late 2000 Schwab surprised its rivals by paying $2.7 billion to acquire U.S. Trust Corporation, a 147-year-old-financial services institution that is a top estate planner for the wealthy, as noted in the chapter's opening case. However, Schwab is in no way ignoring its core market. The firm also purchased Cybercorp Inc., a Texas brokerage company, for $488 million. That firm offers active online traders sophisticated quotes and stock-screening tools.

Potential Limitations   As noted in the previous section, mergers and acquisitions provide a firm with many potential benefits. However, at the same time, there are many potential drawbacks or limitations to such corporate activity.[46]

First, *the takeover premium that is paid for an acquisition is very high.* Two times out of three, the stock price of the acquiring company falls once the deal is made public. Since the acquiring firm often pays a 30 percent to 40 percent premium for the target company, the acquirer must create synergies and scale economies that result in sales and market gains exceeding the premium price. Firms paying higher premiums set the performance hurdle even higher. For example, Household International paid an 82 percent premium to buy Beneficial, and Conseco paid an 83 percent premium to acquire Green Tree Financial. Historically, paying a high premium over the stock price has been a largely unprofitable strategy.

Second, *competing firms often can imitate any advantages realized or copy synergies that result from the M&A.* Thus, a firm can often see its advantages quickly evaporate if it plans to achieve competitive advantage through M&A activity. Unless the advantages are sustainable and difficult to copy, investors will not be willing to pay a high premium for the stock. Similarly, the time value of money must be factored into the stock price. M&A costs are paid up front. Conversely, firms pay for research and development, ongoing marketing, and capacity expansion over time. This stretches out the payments needed to gain new competencies. The M&A argument is that a large initial investment is worthwhile because it creates long-term advantages. However, stock analysts want to see immediate results from such a large cash outlay. If the acquired firm does not produce results quickly, investors often sell the stock, driving the price down.

Third, *managers' credibility and ego can sometimes get in the way of sound business decisions.* If the M&A does not perform as planned, managers who pushed for the deal find that their reputation may be at stake. Sometimes, this can lead these managers

6.5 STRATEGY SPOTLIGHT

How Ken Hendricks Consolidated the Roofing Industry

As a child growing up in Janesville, Wisconsin, Ken Hendricks sensed the contempt "the country club set" had for his blue-collar family because of his father's humble job as a roofer. "They looked down their noses at him," Hendricks says. "He went to work every single day of his life. That wasn't good enough? Some kid got to go to a fancy school and that made him different than me? That just sets in your gut."

Whatever has driven Mr. Hendricks, he has become a remarkable success. Last year, his Beloit, Wisconsin–based American Builders & Contractors Supply (ABC) was the largest wholesaler of roofing supplies in the United States and among the largest supplies of vinyl sidings and windows. In 2004, the firm netted $67 million in profits on revenues of $1.8 billion. And as the sole owner of the privately held company, Hendricks joined the Forbes 400 with an estimated net worth of $850 million.

In his early years, Ken worked as an independent roofer, picking up jobs where he could, and subcontracting out some of the work. He had his big break when a major hailstorm hit a small town near where he lived. He met with the insurance company's claims adjuster and he offered to charge his normal pricing in exchange for a contract that combined all of the damaged roofs. (Most of his rivals typically inflated their prices in order to exploit the situation.) Eventually word spread, and before he was 30 years old, he had about 500 roofers working for him around the country.

Several years later—after selling off his business and settling into a leisurely life pursuing a sideline of renovating real estate—he began thinking about the need for a national distribution chain. He recalled that as a contractor he was constantly frustrated by dealing with dozens of suppliers, none of which could sell everything he needed.

Sources: Armstrong, D. 2004. Up on the roof. *Forbes*, November 29: 184–188; and Welles, E. O. 2001. Roll your own. *Inc.*, February: 68–72.

And he sensed that there was a tremendous amount of complacency, waste, and room for improvement.

In 1982, Hendricks bought his first three distributors and intensified his acquisition activities over the next 15 years. By 1997, Hendricks had 157 outlets, $789 million in revenues, and a profit of $10 million. In total, he has made over 60 acquisitions, and ABC now has 280 locations in the United States.

He made it work by negotiating volume discounts with manufacturers and exercising very tight cost control. He used to deliver shingles to job sites with used trucks instead of buying new ones. He recycles pallets and sells them back to the manufacturer. ABC's point-of-sales system was built with a $20,000 software package, and it is still the heart of the company's computer system today.

Although Hendricks does not have the latest customer-relationship software, he does have an understanding of customer needs. "I've been up on the roof. I know what those guys are going through. My whole life has been about making that profession respectable."

But how will the competition from the big hardware and home-improvement chains affect ABC? Replies Hendricks, "We've got 256 different shingles by brand, weight, and color. Home Depot's not going to waste the shelf space. It's a low-margin business."

A testimony from a satisfied customer exemplifies ABC's commitment to excellent customer service. Robert Shannon, a contractor in Mineola, New York, has 50 roofers working for him. That makes him a very desirable customer for ABC as well as Home Depot. Some bad customer-service experiences soured him on Home Depot, and he is now loyal to ABC. Says Shannon, "They've delivered shingles overnight from Boston, stuff I needed the next day. No other supplier does that. They understand if you have nine crew members standing around with nothing to do, that costs money."

to protect their credibility by funneling more money, or escalating their commitment, into an inevitably doomed operation. Further, when a merger fails and a firm tries to unload the acquisition, managers often find that they must sell at a huge discount. These problems further compound the costs and weaken the stock price.

Fourth, *there can be many cultural issues that may doom the intended benefits from M&A endeavors.* Consider, for example, the insights of Joanne Lawrence, who played an important role as vice president and director of communications and investor relations at SmithKline Beecham, in the merger between SmithKline and the Beecham Group, a diversified consumer-oriented group headquartered in the United Kingdom.[47]

The key to a strategic merger is to create a new culture. This was a mammoth challenge during the SmithKline Beecham merger. We were working at so many different cultural levels, it was dizzying. We had two national cultures to blend—American and British—that compounded the challenge of selling the merger in two different markets with two different shareholder bases. There were also two different business cultures: One was very strong, scientific, and academic; the other was much more commercially oriented. And then we had to consider within both companies the individual businesses, each of which has its own little culture.[48]

Strategic Alliances and Joint Ventures

Strategic alliances and joint ventures are assuming an increasingly prominent role in the strategy of leading firms, both large and small.[49] Such cooperative relationships have many potential advantages. Among these are entering new markets, reducing manufacturing (or other) costs in the value chain, and developing and diffusing new technologies.[50]

Entering New Markets   Often a company that has a successful product or service wants to introduce it into a new market. However, it may not have the requisite marketing expertise because it does not understand customer needs, know how to promote the product, or have access to the proper distribution channels.

The partnerships formed between Time-Warner, Inc., and three African American–owned cable companies in New York City are examples of joint ventures created to serve a domestic market. Time-Warner built a 185,000-home cable system in the city and asked the three cable companies to operate it. Time-Warner supplied the product, and the cable companies supplied the knowledge of the community and the know-how to market the cable system. Joining with the local companies enabled Time-Warner to win the acceptance of the cable customers and to benefit from an improved image in the black community.

Reducing Manufacturing (or Other) Costs in the Value Chain   Strategic alliances (or joint ventures) often enable firms to pool capital, value-creating activities, or facilities in order to reduce costs. For example, Molson Companies and Carling O'Keefe Breweries in Canada formed a joint venture to merge their brewing operations. Although Molson had a modern and efficient brewery in Montreal, Carling's was outdated. However, Carling had the better facilities in Toronto. In addition, Molson's Toronto brewery was located on the waterfront and had substantial real estate value. Overall, the synergies gained by using their combined facilities more efficiently added $150 million of pretax earnings during the initial year of the venture. Economies of scale were realized and facilities were better utilized.

Developing and Diffusing New Technologies   Strategic alliances also may be used to build jointly on the technological expertise of two or more companies in order to develop products technologically beyond the capability of the companies acting independently. STMicroelectronics (ST) is a high-tech company based in Geneva, Switzerland, that has thrived—largely due to the success of its strategic alliances.[51] The firm develops and manufactures computer chips for a variety of applications such as mobile phones, set-top boxes, smart cards, and flash memories. In 1995 it teamed up with Hewlett-Packard to develop powerful new processors for various digital applications that are now nearing completion. Another example was its strategic alliance with Nokia to develop a chip that would give Nokia's phones a longer battery life. Here, ST produced a chip that tripled standby time to 60 hours—a breakthough that gave Nokia a huge advantage in the marketplace.

The firm's CEO, Pasquale Pistorio, was among the first in the industry to form R&D alliances with other companies. Now ST's top 12 customers, including HP, Nokia, and Nortel, account for 45 percent of revenues. According to Pistorio, "Alliances are in our DNA." Such relationships help ST keep better-than-average growth rates, even in difficult times. That's because close partners are less likely to defect to other suppliers. ST's financial results are most impressive. During 2000 its revenues grew 55 percent—nearly double the industry average.

Despite their promise, many alliances and joint ventures fail to meet expectations for a variety of reasons. First, without the proper partner, a firm should never consider undertaking an alliance, even for the best of reasons. Each partner should bring the desired complementary strengths to the partnership. Ideally, the strengths contributed by the partners are unique; thus synergies created can be more easily sustained and defended over the longer term. The goal must be to develop synergies between the contributions of the partners, resulting in a win–win situation for both. Moreover, the partners must be compatible and willing to trust each other. Unfortunately, often little attention is given to nurturing the close working relationships and interpersonal connections that bring together the partnering organizations. The human or people factors are not carefully considered or, at worst, they are dismissed as an unimportant consideration.

Internal Development

Firms can also diversify by means of corporate entrepreneurship and new venture development. In today's economy, internal development is such an important means by which companies expand their businesses that we have devoted a whole chapter to it (see Chapter 12). Sony and the Minnesota Mining & Manufacturing Co. (3M), for example, are known for their dedication to innovation, R&D, and cutting-edge technologies. For example, 3M has developed its entire corporate culture to support its ongoing policy of generating at least 25 percent of total sales from products created within the most recent four-year period. During the 1990s, 3M exceeded this goal by achieving about 30 percent of sales per year from new internally developed products.

Many companies use some form of internal development to extend their product lines or add to their service offerings. This approach to internal development is used by many large publicly held corporations as well as small firms. An example of the latter is Rosa Verde, a small but growing business serving the health care needs of San Antonio, Texas.

> This small company began with one person who moved from Mexico to San Antonio, Texas, to serve the health care needs of inner-city residents.[52] Beginning as a sole proprietor, Dr. Lourdes Pizana started Rosa Verde Family Health Care Group in 1995 with only $10,000 obtained from credit card debt. She has used a strategy of internal development to propel the company to where it is today—six clinics, 30 doctors, and a team of other health care professionals.
>
> How was Dr. Pizana able to accomplish this in such a short time? She emphasizes the company's role in the community, forging links with community leaders. In addition, she hires nearly all her professional staff as independent contractors to control costs. These professionals are paid based on the volume of work they do rather than a set salary; Pizana splits her revenue with them, thus motivating them to work efficiently. Her strategy is to grow the company from the inside out through high levels of service, commitment to the community she serves, and savvy leadership. By committing to a solid plan, Pizana has proven that internal growth and development can be a successful strategy.

The luxury hotel chain Ritz-Carlton has long been recognized for its exemplary service. In fact, it is the only service company ever to win two Malcolm Baldrige National Quality Awards. It has built on this capability by developing a highly successful internal venture to offer leadership development programs—both to its employees as well as to outside companies. We address this internal venture in Strategy Spotlight 6.6.

Compared to mergers and acquisitions, firms that engage in internal development are able to capture the value created by their own innovative activities without having to "share the wealth" with alliance partners or face the difficulties associated with combining activities across the value chains of several companies or merging corporate cultures. Another advantage is that firms can often develop new products or services at a relatively lower

STRATEGY SPOTLIGHT

The Ritz-Carlton Leadership Center: A Successful Internal Venture

Companies worldwide often strive to be the "Ritz-Carlton" of their industries. Ritz-Carlton, the large luxury hotel chain, is the only service company to have won the prestigious Malcolm Baldrige National Quality Award twice—in 1992 and 1999 (one year after being acquired by Marriott). It also has placed first in guest satisfaction among luxury hotels in the most recent J.D. Power & Associates hotel survey.

Until a few years ago, being "Ritz-Carlton-like" was just a motivational simile. However, in 2000, the company launched the Ritz-Carlton Leadership Center, where it offers 12 leadership development programs for its employees and seven benchmarking seminars and workshops to outside companies. It also conducts 35 off-site presentations on such topics as "Creating a Dynamic Employee Orientation," and "The Key to Retaining and Selecting Talented Employees." (Incidentally, Ritz-Carlton's annual turnover rate among nonmanagement employees is 25 percent—roughly half the average rate for U.S. luxury hotels.)

Within its first four years of operation, 800 different companies from such industries as health care, banking and finance, hospitality, and the automotive industries have participated in the Leadership Center's programs. And to date it has generated over $2 million in revenues. Ken Yancey, CEO of the nonprofit small-business consultancy, Score, says the concepts he learned, like "the three steps of service," apply directly to his business. "Hotels are about service to a client," he says. "And we are too."

To give a few specifics on one of the Leadership Center's programs, consider its "Legendary Service I" course. The topics that are covered include empowerment, using customer recognition to boost loyalty, and Ritz-Carlton's approach to quality. The course lasts two days and costs $2,000 per attendee. Well-known companies that have participated include Microsoft, Morgan Stanley, and Starbucks.

Sources: McDonald, D. 2004. Roll out the blue carpet. *Business 2.0.* May: 53; and Johnson, G. 2003. Nine tactics to take your corporate university from good to GREAT. *Training.* July/August: 38–41.

cost and thus rely on their own resources rather than turning to external funding. There are also potential disadvantages. Internal development may be time consuming; thus, firms may forfeit the benefits of speed that growth through mergers or acquisitions can provide. This may be especially important among high-tech or knowledge-based organizations in fast-paced environments where being an early mover is critical. Thus, firms that choose to diversify through internal development must develop capabilities that allow them to move quickly from initial opportunity recognition to market introduction.

>>Real Options Analysis: A Useful Tool

Real options analysis (ROA) is an investment analysis tool from the field of finance. It has been slowly, but increasingly, adopted by consultants and executives to support strategic decision making in firms. What does real options analysis consist of and how can it be appropriately applied to the investments required to initiate strategic decisions? To understand *real* options it is first necessary to have a basic understanding of what *options* are.

Options exist when the owner of the option has the right but not the obligation to engage in certain types of transactions. The most common are stock options. A stock option grants the holder the right to buy (call option) or sell (put option) shares of the stock at a fixed price (strike price) at some time in the future.[53] Another aspect of stock options important to note is that the investment to be made immediately is small, whereas the investment to be made in the future is generally larger. For example, an option to buy a rapidly rising stock currently priced at $50 might cost as little as $.50.[54] An important point to note is that owners of such a stock option have limited their losses to $.50 per share, while the upside potential is unlimited. This aspect of options is attractive because options offer the prospect of high gains with relatively small up-front investments that represent limited losses.

Dess–Lumpkin–Eisner:
Strategic Management:
Text and Cases, Third
Edition

II. Strategic Formulation

6. Corporate–Level
Strategy: Creating Value
through Diversification

© The McGraw–Hill
Companies, 2007

233

The phrase "real options" applies to situations where options theory and valuation techniques are applied to real assets or physical things as opposed to financial assets. Some of the most common applications of real options are with property and insurance. A real estate option grants the holder the right to buy or sell a piece of property at an established price some time in the future. The actual market price of the property may rise above the established (or strike) price—or the market value may sink below the strike price. If the price of the property goes up, the owner of the option is likely to buy it. If the market value of the property drops below the strike price, the option holder is unlikely to execute the purchase. In the latter circumstance, the option holder has limited his or her loss to the cost of the option, but during the life of the option retains the right to participate in whatever the upside potential might be. Casualty insurance is another variation of real options. With casualty insurance, the owner of the property has limited the loss to the cost of the insurance, while the upside potential is the actual loss, ranging, of course, up to the limit of the insurance.[55]

Applications of Real Options Analysis to Strategic Decisions

The concept of options can also be applied to strategic decisions where management has flexibility; that is, the situation will permit management to decide whether to invest additional funds to grow or accelerate the activity, perhaps delay in order to learn more, shrink the scale of the activity, or even abandon it. Decisions to invest in business activities such as R&D, motion pictures, exploration and production of oil wells, and the opening and closing of copper mines often have this flexibility.[56] Important issues to note are the following:

- Real options analysis is appropriate to use when investments can be staged; in other words, a smaller investment up front can be followed by subsequent investments. In short, real options can be applied to an investment decision that gives the company the right, but not the obligation, to make follow-on investments.

- The strategic decision makers have "tollgates" or key points at which they can decide whether to continue, delay, or abandon the project. In short, the executives have the flexibility. There are opportunities to make other go or no–go decisions associated with each phase.

- It is expected that there will be increased knowledge about outcomes at the time of the next investment and that additional knowledge will help inform the decision makers about whether to make additional investments (i.e., whether the option is in the money or out of the money).

Many strategic decisions have the characteristic of containing a series of options. The phenomenon is called "embedded options," a series of investments in which at each stage of the investment there is a go/no–go decision. For example, pharmaceutical companies have successfully used real options analysis in evaluating decisions about investments in pharmaceutical R&D projects since the early 1990s.[57] Pharmaceuticals have at least four stages of investments: basic research yielding compounds and the three FDA-mandated phases of clinical trials. Generally, each phase is more expensive to undertake than the previous phase. However, as each phase unfolds, management knows more about the underlying drug and the many sources of uncertainty, including the technical difficulties with the drugs themselves as well as external market conditions, such as the results of competitors' research.[58] Management can make the decision to invest more with the intent of speeding up the process, delay the start of the next phase, reduce investment, or even abandon the R&D.[59]

As noted above, the use of real options analysis can provide the firm with many opportunities for learning. In many cases, such learning can extend beyond the specific investment or project at hand. For example, consider Eli Lilly's 1984 investment in a start-up biotechnology firm, Hybritech:[60]

> Within two years of making its investment in Hybritech, Eli Lilly acquired the firm outright, acquiring full access to drugs that Hybritech was pursuing. The first and primary benefit for Eli Lilly was access to a drug before it had been approved by the FDA, allowing them to acquire it at a much lower cost than if they had waited for FDA approval. They also acquired access to Hybritech's management and existing knowledge—another benefit. The benefit easiest to overlook, however, was learning how to partner with a biotechnology start-up with different expertise (i.e., Eli Lilly was engaged in chemical-based science; Hybritech was genetically based). This enabled them to learn how to better work with their biotechnology partners and how to transmit that information inside Eli Lilly more efficiently. They wrote an option to acquire Hybritech and also wrote an option to learn how to partner with other biotechnology firms. Long term, the latter appears to have been the more valuable real option. Lilly has brought more drugs to market from its collaboration with its partners than has nearly anyone else. Lilly's recent FDA-approved drug, Cialis, resulted from a partnership with another biotechnology firm, Icos.

Strategy Spotlight 6.7 provides two examples of companies using ROA to guide their decision-making process.

Potential Pitfalls of Real Options Analysis

Despite the many benefits that can be gained from using real options analysis, managers must be aware of its potential limitations or pitfalls. Below we will address three major issues.[61]

Agency Theory and the Back-Solver Dilemma   Let's assume that companies adopting a real-options perspective invest heavily in training and that their people understand how to effectively estimate variance—that is, the amount of dispersion or range that is estimated for potential outcomes. Such training can help them use ROA. However, it does not solve another inherent problem: managers may have an incentive and the know-how to "game the system." Most electronic spreadsheets permit users to simply back-solve any formula; that is, you can type in the answer you want and ask what values are needed in a formula to get that answer. If managers know that a certain option value must be met in order for the proposal to get approved, they can back-solve the model to find a variance estimate needed to arrive at the answer that upper management desires. What would be the manager's motive to do this?

Agency problems are typically inherent in investment decisions. They may occur when the managers of a firm are separated from its owners—that is, when managers act as "agents" rather than "principals" (owners). Such problems could occur because a manager may have something to gain by not acting in the owner's best interests, or the interests of managers and owners are not co-aligned. Agency theory suggests that as managerial and owner interests diverge, managers will follow the path of their own self-interests. Sometimes this is to secure better compensation. At other times, those interests involve exerting less effort. In terms of securing better compensation, agency problems arise because managers who propose projects may believe that if their projects are approved, they stand a much better chance of getting promoted. So while managers have an incentive to propose projects that *should* be successful, they also have an incentive to propose projects that *might* be successful. And because of the subjectivity involved in formally modeling a real option, managers may have an incentive to choose variance values that increase the likelihood of approval.

Managerial Conceit: Overconfidence and the Illusion of Control   Often, poor decisions are the result of such traps as biases, blind spots, and other human frailties. Much of this literature falls under the concept of *managerial conceit.*[62]

6.7 STRATEGY SPOTLIGHT

Applications of Real Options Analysis

The following two examples illustrate how real options analysis (ROA) is enjoying increasing popularity among strategists facing the task of allocating resources in an era of great uncertainty. In the first example, a privately held biotechnology firm is using ROA to analyze an internal development decision. In the second example pharmaceutical giant Merck uses this tool to decide whether to enter into a strategic alliance. In each of these cases, ROA led to a different decision outcome than that of more traditional net present value (NPV) analysis. NPV is the sum of costs and revenues for the life of the project, discounted typically by current interest rates to reflect the time value of money.

- A privately held biotechnology firm had developed a unique technology for introducing the coat protein of a particular virus into animal feedstock. Ingesting the coat protein generated an immune response, thus protecting the animal from the virus. The firm was at the beginning of the preclinical trials stage, the first of a series of tests required by FDA regulation and conducted through the FDA subagency called the Center for Veterinary Medicine. The company expected the stage to take 18 months and cost $2 million. Long-standing experience indicated that 95 percent of new drug investigations are abandoned during this phase. Subsequent stages would decrease somewhat in terms of the possibility of rejection, but costs would rise, with a total outflow from 2002 through anticipated launch in 2007 of at least $18.5 million. The company's best estimate of the market from 2007 through 2017 was about $85 million per year, with the possibility of taking as much as a 50 percent market share. In short, there was huge potential, but in the interim there was tremendous chance of failure (i.e., high risk), significant early outflows, and delayed inflows. Analysis using a traditional NPV analysis yielded a negative $2 million with an 11 percent risk-adjusted discount rate. Viewing the investment as a multistage option, however, and incorporating management's flexibility to change its decision at a minimum of four points between 2002 and 2007, changes the valuation markedly. A real options analysis approach to the analysis demonstrated a present value of about $22 million. The question was not whether to risk $18.5 million, but whether to invest $2 million today for the opportunity to earn $22 million.

- Merck has applied real options analysis to a number of its strategic decisions. One was the agreement it signed with Biogen, which in the late 1990s had developed an asthma drug. Instead of purchasing Biogen outright, Merck created a real options arrangement. Merck paid Biogen $15 million up front and retained the right to invest up to an additional $130 million at various points as the biotechnology company reached specified milestones. In essence, Merck purchased a stream of options: the right to scale up and scale down, or even abandon, the option. Merck's potential in the deal was unlimited, while its downside risk was limited to the extent of the milestone payments. Analysis suggested that the present value of the deal was about $275 million, considerably more than the present value of the up-front and milestone payments. Using traditional NPV methods would have killed this deal. However, real options analysis encouraged Merck to undertake the arrangement, in part, because Merck was in the process of learning about the underlying technology. Biogen, on the other hand, gained the advantage of committed cash flow to continue development—provided that developments from the various phases continued to be favorable.

Sources: Stockley, R. L., Jr., Curtis, S., Jafari, J., and Tibbs, K. 2003. The option value of an early-stage biotechnology investment. *Journal of Applied Finance*, 15(2): 44–55; and Mauboussin, M. H. 1999. Get real: Using real options in security analysis. *Equity Research Series by Credit Suite/First Boston*, 10, June 23: 18.

Understanding how these traps affect decision makers can help to improve decision making.

First, managerial conceit occurs when managers who have made successful choices in the past may come to believe that they possess superior expertise for managing uncertainty. They believe that their abilities can, therefore, reduce the risks inherent in decision making to a much greater extent than they actually can. Such managers are more likely to shift away from analysis to trusting their own judgment. In the case of real options, they can simply declare that any given decision is a real option and proceed as before. If asked to formally model their decision, they are more likely to employ variance estimates that support their viewpoint.

Second, employing the real-options perspective can encourage decision makers toward a bias for action. Such a bias may lead to carelessness. Managerial conceit is as much a problem (if not more so) for small decisions as for big ones. Why? The cost to write the first stage of an option is much smaller than the cost of full commitment, and managers pay less attention to small decisions than to large ones. Because real options are designed to minimize potential losses while preserving potential gains, any problems that arise are likely to be smaller at first, causing less concern for the manager. Managerial conceit could suggest that managers will assume that those problems are the easiest to solve and control—a concern referred to as the illusion of control. Managers may fail to respond appropriately because they overlook the problem or believe that since it is small, they can easily resolve it. Thus, managers may approach each real-option decision with less care and diligence than if they had made a full commitment to a larger investment.

Managerial Conceit: Irrational Escalation of Commitment A strength of a real options perspective is also one of its Achilles heels. Both real options and decisions involving escalation of commitment require specific environments with sequential decisions.[63] As the escalation-of-commitment literature indicates, simply separating a decision into multiple parts does not guarantee that decisions made will turn out well. This condition is potentially present whenever the exercise decision retains some uncertainty, which most still do. The decision to abandon also has strong psychological factors associated with it that affect the ability of managers to make correct exercise decisions.[64]

An option to exit requires reversing an initial decision made by someone in the organization. Organizations typically encourage managers to "own their decisions" in order to motivate them. One result is that as managers invest themselves in their decision, it proves harder for them to lose face by reversing course. In effect, for managers making the decision, it feels as if they made the wrong decision in the first place, even if it was initially a good decision. The more specific the manager's human capital becomes, the harder it is to transfer it to other organizations. Hence, there is a greater likelihood that managers will stick around and try to make an existing decision work. They are more likely to continue an existing project even if it should perhaps be ended.[65]

>>How Managerial Motives Can Erode Value Creation

Thus far in the chapter we have implicitly assumed that CEOs and top executives are "rational beings"; that is, they act in the best interests of shareholders to maximize long-term shareholder value. In the real world, however, this is not the case. Frequently, they may act in their own self-interest. Next we address some managerial motives that can serve to erode, rather than enhance, value creation. These include "growth for growth's sake," excessive egotism, and the creation of a wide variety of antitakeover tactics.

Growth for Growth's Sake

There are huge incentives for executives to increase the size of their firm, and many of these are hardly consistent with increasing shareholder wealth. Top managers, including the CEO, of larger firms typically enjoy more prestige, higher rankings for their companies on the Fortune 500 list (which is based on revenues, not profits), greater incomes, more job security, and so on. There is also the excitement and associated recognition of making a major acquisition. As noted by Harvard's Michael Porter, "There's a tremendous allure to mergers and acquisitions. It's the big play, the dramatic gesture. With one stroke of the pen you can add billions to size, get a front-page story, and create excitement in markets."[66]

In recent years many high-tech firms have suffered from the negative impact of their uncontrolled growth. Consider, for example, Priceline.com's ill-fated venture into an online service to offer groceries and gasoline.[67] A myriad of problems—perhaps most importantly, a lack of participation by manufacturers—caused the firm to lose more than $5 million a *week* prior to abandoning these ventures. Similarly, many have questioned the profit potential of Amazon.com's recent ventures into a variety of products such as tools and hardware, cell phones, and service. Such initiatives are often little more than desperate moves by top managers to satisfy investor demands for accelerating revenues. Unfortunately, the increased revenues often fail to materialize into a corresponding hike in earnings.

At times, executives' overemphasis on growth can result in a plethora of ethical lapses, which can have disastrous outcomes for their companies. A good example (of bad practice) is Joseph Bernardino's leadership at Andersen Worldwide. Bernardino had a chance early on to take a hard line on ethics and quality in the wake of earlier scandals at clients such as Waste Management and Sunbeam. Instead, according to former executives, he put too much emphasis on revenue growth. Consequently, the firm's reputation quickly eroded when it audited and signed off on the highly flawed financial statements of such infamous firms as Enron, Global Crossing, and WorldCom. WorldCom, in fact, is recognized as the biggest financial fraud of all time. Bernardino ultimately resigned in disgrace in March 2002, and his firm was dissolved later that year.[68]

Egotism

Most would agree that there is nothing wrong with ego, per se. After all, a healthy ego helps make a leader confident, clearheaded, and able to cope with change. CEOs, by their very nature, are typically fiercely competitive people in the office as well as on the tennis court or golf course. However, sometimes when pride is at stake, individuals will go to great lengths to win—or at least not to back down. Consider the following anecdote:

> When Warner Bros. CEO Robert Daly walked into the first postmerger gathering of senior Time Warner management in the Bahamas, he felt a hand on his shoulder. It was a Time Inc. executive whom he had never met. The magazine man asked the studio executive if he ever considered that General Motors purchased $30 million worth of advertising in Time Inc. publications before Daly acquired *Roger and Me*, a scathing cinematic indictment of the carmaker.
>
> Daly replied, "No. Did you consider that Warner Bros. spent over $50 million on *Batman* before *Time* ran its lousy review of the movie?" The Time executive smiled, patted his new colleague's shoulder and suggested that they continue their jobs in their own way!

Egos can get in the way of a "synergistic" corporate marriage. Few executives (or lower-level managers) are exempt from the potential downside of excessive egos. Consider, for example, the reflections of General Electric's former CEO Jack Welch, considered by many to be the world's most admired executive. He admitted to his regrettable decision for GE to acquire Kidder Peabody.[69] According to Welch, "My hubris got in the way in the Kidder Peabody deal. [He was referring to GE's buyout of the soon-to-be-troubled Wall Street firm.] I got wise advice from Walter Wriston and other directors who said, 'Jack, don't do this.' But I was bully enough and on a run to do it. And I got whacked right in the head." In addition to poor financial results, Kidder Peabody was wracked by a widely publicized trading scandal that tarnished the reputations of both GE and Kidder Peabody. Welch ended up selling Kidder in 1994.

The business press has included many stories of how egotism and greed have infiltrated organizations. Some incidents are considered rather astonishing, such as Tyco's former (and now convicted) CEO Dennis Kozlowski's well-chronicled purchase of a $6,000 shower curtain and vodka-spewing, full-size replica of Michaelangelo's David.[70] Other well-known examples of power grabs and extraordinary consumption of compensation and perks include

STRATEGY SPOTLIGHT 6.8

Poison Pills: How Antitakeover Strategies Can Raise Ethical Issues

Poison pills are almost always good for managers but not always so good for shareholders. They present managers with an ethical dilemma: How can they balance their own interests with their fiduciary responsibility to shareholders?

Here's how poison pills work. In the event of a takeover bid, existing shareholders have the option to buy additional shares of stock at a discount to the current market price. This action is typically triggered when a new shareholder rapidly accumulates more than a set percentage of ownership (usually 20 percent) through stock purchases. When this happens, managers fear that the voting rights and increased proportional ownership of the new shareholder might be a ploy to make a takeover play.

To protect existing shareholders, stock is offered at a discount, but only to existing shareholders. As the existing owners buy the discounted stock, the stock is diluted (i.e., there are now more shares, each with a lower value). If there has been a takeover offer at a set price per share, the overall price for the company immediately goes up since there are now more shares. This assures stockholders of receiving a fair price for the company.

Sounds good, but here's the problem. Executives on the company's board of directors retain the right to allow the stock discount. The discounted stock price for existing shareholders may or may not be activated when a takeover is imminent. This brings in the issue of motive: Why did the board enact the poison pill provision in the first place? At times, it may have been simply to protect the existing shareholders. At other times, it may have been to protect the interests of those on the board of directors. In other words, the board may have enacted the rule not to protect shareholders, but to protect their own jobs.

When the board receives a takeover offer, the offering company will be aware of the poison pill provision. This gives negotiating power to board members of the takeover target. They may include as part of the negotiation that the new company keep them as members of the board. In exchange, the board members would not enact the discounted share price; existing stockholders would lose, but the jobs of the board members would be protected.

When a company offers poison pill provisions to shareholders, the shareholders should keep in mind that things are not always as they seem. The motives may reflect concern for shareholders. But on the other hand...

Sources: Vicente, J. P. 2001. Toxic treatment: Poison pills proliferate as Internet firms worry they've become easy marks. *Red Herring*, May 1 and 15: 195; Chakraborty, A., & Baum, C. F. 1998. Poison pills, optimal contracting and the market for corporate control: Evidence from Fortune 500 firms. *International Journal of Finance*, 10(3): 1120–1138; Sundaramurthy, C. 1996. Corporate governance within the context of antitakeover provisions. *Strategic Management Journal*, 17: 377–394.

executives at Enron, the Rigas family who were convicted of defrauding Adelphia of roughly $1 billion, former CEO Bernie Ebbers's $408 million loan from WorldCom, and so on. However, executives in the United States clearly don't have a monopoly on such deeds. Consider, for example, Jean-Marie Messier, former CEO of Vivendi Universal.[71]

> In striving to convert a French utility into a global media conglomerate, Messier seldom passed up a chance for self-promotion. Although most French executives have a preference for discreet personal lives, Messier hung out with rock stars and moved his family into a $17.5 million Park Avenue spread paid for by Vivendi. He pushed the company to the brink of collapse by running up $19 billion in debt from an acquisition spree and confusing investors with inconsistent financial transactions which are now under investigation by authorities in both the United States and France. Not one to accept full responsibility, less than five months after his forced resignation, he published a book, *My True Diary*, that blames a group of French business leaders for plotting against him. And his ego is clearly intact: At a recent Paris press conference, he described his firing as a setback for French capitalism.

Antitakeover Tactics

Unfriendly or hostile takeovers can occur when a company's stock becomes undervalued. A competing organization can buy the outstanding stock of a takeover candidate in sufficient quantity to become a large shareholder. Then it makes a tender offer to gain full control of the company. If the shareholders accept the offer, the hostile firm buys the target company and either fires the target firm's management team or strips them of their power. For this reason, antitakeover tactics are common. Three of these are greenmail, golden parachutes, and poison pills.[72]

The first, *greenmail*, is an effort by the target firm to prevent an impending takeover. When a hostile firm buys a large block of outstanding target company stock and the target firm's management feels that a tender offer is impending, they offer to buy the stock back from the hostile company at a higher price than the unfriendly company paid for it. The positive side is that this often prevents a hostile takeover. On the downside, the same price is not offered to preexisting shareholders. However, it protects the jobs of the target firm's management.

The second strategy is a *golden parachute*. A golden parachute is a prearranged contract with managers specifying that, in the event of a hostile takeover, the target firm's managers will be paid a significant severance package. Although top managers lose their jobs, the golden parachute provisions protect their income.

Strategy Spotlight 6.8 illustrates how poison pills are used to prevent takeovers. *Poison pills* are means by which a company can give shareholders certain rights in the event of a takeover by another firm. In addition to "poison pills," they are also known as shareholder rights plans.

As you can see, antitakeover tactics can often raise some interesting ethical issues.

Summary

A key challenge for today's managers is to create "synergy" when engaging in diversification activities. As we discussed in this chapter, corporate managers do not, in general, have a very good track record in creating value in such endeavors when it comes to mergers and acquisitions. Among the factors that serve to erode shareholder values are paying an excessive premium for the target firm, failing to integrate the activities of the newly acquired businesses into the corporate family, and undertaking diversification initiatives that are too easily imitated by the competition.

We addressed two major types of corporate-level strategy: related and unrelated diversification. With *related diversification* the corporation strives to enter into areas in which key resources and capabilities of the corporation can be shared or leveraged. Synergies come from horizontal relationships between business units. Cost savings and enhanced revenues can be derived from two major sources. First, economies of scope can be achieved from the leveraging of core competencies and the sharing of activities. Second, market power can be attained from greater, or pooled, negotiating power and from vertical integration.

When firms undergo *unrelated diversification* they enter product markets that are dissimilar to their present businesses. Thus, there is generally little opportunity to either leverage core competencies or share activities across business units. Here, synergies are created from vertical relationships between the corporate office and the individual business units. With unrelated diversification, the primary ways to create value are corporate restructuring and parenting, as well as the use of portfolio analysis techniques.

Corporations have three primary means of diversifying their product markets—mergers and acquisitions, joint ventures/strategic alliances, and internal development. There are key trade-offs associated with each of these. For example, mergers and acquisitions are typically the quickest means to enter new markets and provide the corporation with a high level of control over the acquired business. However, with the expensive premiums that often need to be paid to the shareholders of the target firm and the challenges associated with integrating acquisitions, they can also be quite expensive. Strategic alliances between two or more firms, on the other hand, may be a means of reducing risk since they involve the sharing and combining of resources. But such joint initiatives also provide a firm with less control (than it would have with an acquisition) since governance is shared between two independent entities. Also, there is a limit to the potential upside for each partner because returns must be shared as well. Finally, with internal development, a firm is able to capture all of the value from its initiatives (as opposed to sharing it with a merger or alliance partner). However, diversification by means of internal development can be very time-consuming—a disadvantage that becomes even more important in fast-paced competitive environments.

Traditional tools such as net present value (NPV) analysis are not always very helpful in making resource allocation decisions under uncertainty. Real options analysis (ROA) is increasingly used to make better quality decisions in such situations. We also addressed the potential limitations of ROA.

Finally, some managerial behaviors may serve to erode shareholder returns. Among these are "growth for growth's sake," egotism, and antitakeover tactics. As we discussed, some of these issues—particularly antitakeover tactics—raise ethical considerations because the managers of the firm are not acting in the best interests of the shareholders.

Summary Review Questions

1. Discuss how managers can create value for their firm through diversification efforts.
2. What are some of the reasons that many diversification efforts fail to achieve desired outcomes?
3. How can companies benefit from related diversification? Unrelated diversification? What are some of the key concepts that can explain such success?
4. What are some of the important ways in which a firm can restructure a business?
5. Discuss some of the various means that firms can use to diversify. What are the pros and cons associated with each of these?
6. Discuss some of the actions that managers may engage in to erode shareholder value.

Experiential Exercise

Time Warner (formerly AOL Time Warner) is a firm that follows a strategy of related diversification. Evaluate its success (or lack thereof) with regard to how well it has: (1) built on core competencies, (2) shared infrastructures, and (3) increased market power.

Rationale for Related Diversification	Successful/Unsuccessful?	Why?
1. Build on core competencies		
2. Share infrastructures		
3. Increase market power		

1. What were some of the largest mergers and acquisitions over the last two years? What was the rationale for these actions? Do you think they will be successful? Explain.

2. Discuss some examples from business practice in which an executive's actions appear to be in his or her self-interest rather than the corporation's well-being.

3. Discuss some of the challenges that managers must overcome in making strategic alliances successful. What are some strategic alliances with which you are familiar? Were they successful or not? Explain.

4. Use the Internet and select a company that has recently undertaken diversification into new product markets. What do you feel were some of the reasons for this diversification (e.g., leveraging core competencies, sharing infrastructures)?

Application Questions Exercises

1. In recent years there has been a rash of corporate downsizing and layoffs. Do you feel that such actions raise ethical considerations? Why or why not?

2. What are some of the ethical issues that arise when managers act in a manner that is counter to their firm's best interests? What are the long-term implications for both the firms and the managers themselves?

Ethics Questions

References

1. Craig, S., & Brown, K. 2004. Schwab ousts Pottruck as CEO; Founder returns to take the helm. *Wall Street Journal*, July 21: A1; Tabb, L. 2004. Wealth management: Can a leopard change its spots? www.wallstreetand_tech.com, November; Frank, R. 2004. U.S. Trust feels effects of switch; Schwab unit was perceived as ousted CEO's deal; shake-up is likely in offing. *Wall Street Journal*, July 21: A8; Lee, L. 2002, Closed eyes, open wallet. *BusinessWeek*, November 4: 116–117; Shilling, A. G. 2003. Wall Street's fat. *Forbes*, April 14: 242; and Schwab acquires U.S. Trust. 2000. *CNN Money* (online), January 13.

2. Hammonds, K. H. 2002. The numbers don't lie. *Fast Company*, September: 80.

3. Pare, T. P. 1994. The new merger boom. *Fortune*, November 28: 96.

4. Our framework draws upon a variety of sources, including Goold, M., & Campbell, A. 1998. Desperately seeking synergy. *Harvard Business Review*, 76(5): 131–143; Porter, M. E. 1987. From advantage to corporate strategy. *Harvard Business Review*, 65(3): 43–59; and Hitt, M. A., Ireland, R. D., & Hoskisson, R. E. 2001. *Strategic management: competitiveness and globalization* (4th ed.). Cincinnati, OH: South-Western.

5. Collis, D. J., & Montgomery, C. A. 1987. *Corporate strategy: Resources and the scope of the firm*. New York: McGraw-Hill.

6. This imagery of the corporation as a tree and related discussion draws on Prahalad, C. K., & Hamel, G. 1990. The core competence of the corporation. *Harvard Business Review*, 68(3): 79–91. Parts of this section also draw on Picken, J. C., & Dess, G. G. 1997. *Mission critical*: chap. 5. Burr Ridge, IL: Irwin Professional Publishing.

7. This section draws on Prahalad & Hamel, op. cit.; and Porter, op. cit.

8. A recent study that investigates the relationship between a firm's technology resources, diversification, and performance can be found in Miller, D. J. 2004. Firms' technological resources and the performance effects of diversification. A longitudinal study. *Strategic Management Journal*, 25: 1097–1119.

9. Harley-Davidson. 1993. Annual report.

10. Collis & Montgomery, op. cit.

11. Henricks, M. 1994. VF seeks global brand dominance. *Apparel Industry Magazine*, August: 21–40; VF Corporation. 1993. First quarter corporate summary report. *1993 VF Annual Report*.

12. Hill, A., & Hargreaves, D. 2001. Turbulent times for GE-Honeywell deal. *Financial Times*, February 28: 26.

13. Lowry, T. 2001. Media. *BusinessWeek*, January 8: 100–101.

14. The Tribune Company. 1999. *Annual report*.

15. This section draws on Hrebiniak, L. G., & Joyce, W. F. 1984. *Implementing strategy*. New York: MacMillan; and Oster, S. M. 1994. *Modern competitive analysis*. New York: Oxford University Press.

16. The discussion of the benefits and costs of vertical integration draws on Hax, A. C., & Majluf, N. S. 1991. *The strategy concept and process: A pragmatic approach*: 139. Englewood Cliffs, NJ: Prentice Hall.

17. Fahey, J. 2005. Gray winds. *Forbes*. January 10: 143.

18. This discussion draws on Oster, op. cit.; and Harrigan, K. 1986. Matching vertical integration strategies to competitive conditions. *Strategic Management Journal*, 7(6): 535–556.

19. For a scholarly explanation on how transaction costs determine the boundaries of a firm, see Oliver E. Williamson's pioneering books *Markets and Hierarchies: Analysis and Antitrust Implications* (New York: Free Press, 1975) and

The Economic Institutions of Capitalism (New York: Free Press, 1985).

20. Campbell, A., Goold, M., & Alexander, M. 1995. Corporate strategy: The quest for parenting advantage. *Harvard Business Review,* 73(2): 120–132; and Picken & Dess, op. cit.

21. Anslinger, P. A., & Copeland, T. E. 1996. Growth through acquisition: A fresh look. *Harvard Business Review,* 74(1): 126–135.

22. Campbell et al., op. cit.

23. This section draws on Porter, op. cit.; and Hambrick, D. C. 1985. Turnaround strategies. In Guth, W. D. (Ed.). *Handbook of business strategy:* 10-1–10-32. Boston: Warren, Gorham & Lamont.

24. There is an important delineation between companies that are operated for a long-term profit and those that are bought and sold for short-term gains. The latter are sometimes referred to as "holding companies" and are generally more concerned about financial issues than strategic issues.

25. Casico. W. F. 2002. Strategies for responsible restructuring. *Academy of Management Executive,* 16(3): 80–91; and Singh, H. 1993. Challenges in researching corporate restructuring. *Journal of Management Studies,* 30(1): 147–172.

26. Cusack, M. 1987. *Hanson Trust: A review of the company and its prospects.* London: Hoare Govett.

27. Hax & Majluf, op. cit. By 1979, 45 percent of Fortune 500 companies employed some form of portfolio analysis, according to Haspelagh, P. 1982. Portfolio planning: Uses and limits. *Harvard Busines Review,* 60: 58–73. A later study conducted in 1993 found that over 40 percent of the respondents used portfolio analysis techniques, but the level of usage was expected to increase to more than 60 percent in the near future: Rigby, D. K. 1994. Managing the management tools. *Planning Review,* September–October: 20–24.

28. Goold, M., & Luchs, K. 1993. Why diversify? Four decades of management thinking. *Academy of Management Executive,* 7(3): 7–25.

29. Other approaches include the industry attractiveness–business strength matrix developed jointly by General Electric and McKinsey and Company, the life-cycle matrix developed by Arthur D. Little, and the profitability matrix proposed by Marakon. For an extensive review, refer to Hax & Majluf, op. cit.: 182–194.

30. Porter, op. cit.: 49–52.

31. Collis, D. J. 1995. Portfolio planning at Ciba-Geigy and the Newport investment proposal. Harvard Business School Case No. 9-795-040. Novartis AG was created in 1996 by the merger of Ciba-Geigy and Sandoz.

32. Buzzell, R. D., & Gale, B. T. 1987. *The PIMS Principles: Linking Strategy to Performance.* New York: Free Press; and Miller, A., & Dess, G. G. 1996. *Strategic Management,* (2nd ed.). New York: McGraw-Hill.

33. Seeger, J. 1984. Reversing the images of BCG's growth share matrix. *Strategic Management Journal,* 5(1): 93–97.

34. Picken & Dess, op. cit.; Cabot Corporation. 2001. 10-Q filing, Securities and Exchange Commission, May 14.

35. Koudsi, S. 2001. Remedies for an economic hangover. *Fortune,* June 25: 130–139.

36. Coy, P., Thornton, E., Arndt, M., & Grow, B. 2005. Shake, rattle, and merge. *BusinessWeek,* January 10: 32–35; and Anonymous. 2005. Love is in the air. *Economist,* February 5: 9.

37. For an interesting study of the relationship between mergers and a firm's product-market strategies, refer to Krisnan, R. A., Joshi, S., & Krishnan, H. 2004. The influence of mergers on firms' product-mix strategies. *Strategic Management Journal,* 25: 587–611.

38. Carey, D., moderator. 2000. A CEO roundtable on making mergers succeed. *Harvard Business Review,* 78(3): 146.

39. Shinal, J. 2001. Can Mike Volpi make Cisco sizzle again? *BusinessWeek,* February 26: 102–104; Kambil, A. Eselius, E. D., & Monteiro, K. A. 2000. Fast venturing: The quick way to start Web businesses. *Sloan Management Review,* 41(4): 55–67; and Elstrom, P. 2001. Sorry, Cisco: The old answers won't work. *BusinessWeek,* April 30: 39.

40. Like many high-tech firms during the economic slump that began in mid-2000, Cisco Systems has experienced declining performance. On April 16, 2001, it announced that its revenues for the quarter closing April 30 would drop 5 percent from a year earlier—and a stunning 30 percent from the previous three months—to about $4.7 billion. Furthermore, Cisco announced that it would lay off 8,500 employees and take an enormous $2.5 billion charge to write down inventory. By late October 2002, its stock was trading at around $10, down significantly from its 52-week high of $70. Elstrom, op. cit.: 39.

41. Coy, P., Thornton, E., Arndt, M. & Grow, B. 2005, Shake, rattle, and merge. *BusinessWeek,* January 10: 32–35; and, Anonymous. 2005. The rise of the superbrands. *Economist,* February 5: 63–65; and, Sellers, P. 2005. It was a no-brainer. *Fortune,* February 21: 96–102.

42. For a discussion of the trend toward consolidation of the steel industry and how Lakshmi Mittal is becoming a dominant player, read Reed, S., & Arndt, M. 2004. The Raja of steel. *BusinessWeek,* December 20: 50–52.

43. Barrett, A. 2001. Drugs. *BusinessWeek,* January 8: 112–113.

44. Coy, P., et al. 2005, op. cit.

45. Whalen, C. J., Pascual, A. M., Lowery, T., & Muller, J. 2001. The top 25 managers. *BusinessWeek,* January 8: 63.

46. This discussion draws upon Rappaport, A., & Sirower, M. L. 1999. Stock or cash? The trade-offs for buyers and sellers in mergers and acquisitions. *Harvard Business Review,* 77(6): 147–158; and Lipin, S., & Deogun, N. 2000. Big mergers of 90s prove disappointing to shareholders. *Wall Street Journal,* October 30: C1.

47. Mouio, A. (Ed.). 1998. Unit of one. *Fast Company,* September: 82.

48. Ibid.

49. For scholarly perspectives on the role of learning in creating value in strategic alliances, refer to Anard, B. N., & Khanna, T. 2000. Do firms learn to create value? *Strategic*

Management Journal, 12(3): 295–317; and Vermeulen, F., & Barkema, H. P. 2001. Learning through acquisitions. *Academy of Management Journal,* 44(3): 457–476.

50. This section draws on Hutt, M. D., Stafford, E. R., Walker, B. A., & Reingen, P. H. 2000. Case study: Defining the strategic alliance. *Sloan Management Review,* 41(2): 51–62; and Walters, B. A., Peters, S., & Dess, G. G. 1994. Strategic alliances and joint ventures: Making them work. *Business Horizons,* 4: 5–10.

51. Edmondson, G., & Reinhardt, A. 2001. From niche player to Goliath. *BusinessWeek,* March 12: 94–96.

52. Clayton, V. 2000. Lourdes Pizana's passions: Confessions and lessons of an accidental business owner. *E-Merging Business,* Fall–Winter: 73–75.

53. Hoskin, R. E. 1994. *Financial Accounting.* New York: Wiley.

54. We know stock options as derivative assets—that is, "an asset whose value depends on or is derived from the value of another, the underlying asset": Amram, M., & Kulatilaka, N. 1999. *Real options: Managing strategic investment in an uncertain world:* 34. Boston: Harvard Business School Press.

55. Neufville, R. de. 2001. Real options: Dealing with uncertainty in systems planning and design, paper presented to the Fifth International Conference on Technology Policy and Innovation at the Technical University of Delft, Delft, Netherlands, June 29.

56. For an interesting discussion on why it is difficult to "kill options," refer to Royer, I. 2003. Why bad projects are so hard to kill. *Harvard Business Review,* 81(2): 48–57.

57. Triantis, A., et al. 2003. University of Maryland roundtable on real options and corporate practice. *Journal of Applied Corporate Finance,* 15(2): 8–23.

58. Interesting insights on how CEOs use their financial preferences in making decisions is found in Prince, E. T. 2005. The fiscal behavior of CEOs. *MIT Sloan Management Review,* 46(3): 23–26.

59. For a more in-depth discussion of ROA, refer to Copeland, T. E., & Keenan, P. T. 1998. Making real options real. *McKinsey Quarterly,* 3; and Luehrman, T. A. 1998. Strategy as a portfolio of real options. *Harvard Business Review,* September–October.

60. Janney, J. J., & Dess, G. G. 2004. Can real-options analysis improve decision making? Promises and pitfalls. *Academy of Management Executive,* 18(4): 60–75.

61. This section draws on Janney, J. J., & Dess, G. G. 2004. Can real options analysis improve decision-making? Promises and pitfalls. *Academy of Management Executive,* 18(4): 60–75. For additional insights on pitfalls of real options, consider McGrath, R. G. 1997. A real options logic for initiating technology positioning investment. *Academy of Management Review,* 22(4): 974–994; Coff, R. W., & Laverty, K. J. 2001. Real options on knowledge assets: Panacea or Pandora's box. *Business Horizons,* 73: 79, McGrath, R. G. 1999. Falling forward: Real options reasoning and entrepreneurial failure. *Academy of Management Review,* 24(1): 13–30; and, Zardkoohi, A. 2004.

62. For an understanding of the differences between how managers say they approach decisions and how they actually do, March and Shapira's discussion is perhaps the best. March, J. G., & Shapira, Z. 1987. Managerial perspectives on risk and risk-taking. *Management Science,* 33(11): 1404–1418.

63. A discussion of some factors that may lead to escalation in decision making is included in Choo, C. W. 2005. Information failures and organizational disasters. *MIT Sloan Management Review,* 46(3): 8–10.

64. For an interesting discussion of the use of real options analysis in the application of wireless communications, which helped to lower the potential for escalation, refer to McGrath, R. G., Ferrier, W. J., & Mendelow, A. L. 2004. Real options as engines of choice and heterogeneity. *Academy of Management Review,* 29(1): 86–101.

65. One very useful solution for reducing the effects of managerial conceit is to incorporate an "exit champion" into the decision process. Exit champions provide arguments for killing off the firm's commitment to a decision. For a very insightful discussion on exit champions, refer to Royer, I. 2003. Why bad projects are so hard to kill. *Harvard Business Review,* 81(2): 49–56.

66. Porter, op. cit.: 43–59.

67. Angwin, J. S., & Wingfield, N. 2000. How Jay Walker built WebHouse on a theory that he couldn't prove. *Wall Street Journal,* October 16: A1, A8.

68. *BusinessWeek.* 2003. The fallen. January 13: 80–82.

69. The Jack Welch example draws upon Sellers, P. 2001. Get over yourself. *Fortune,* April 30: 76–88.

70. Polek, D. 2002. The rise and fall of Dennis Kozlowski. *BusinessWeek,* December 23: 64–77.

71. *BusinessWeek.* 2003. op. cit.: 80.

72. This section draws on Weston, J. F., Besley, S., & Brigham, E. F. 1996. *Essentials of Managerial Finance* (11th ed.): 18–20. Fort Worth, TX: Dryden Press, Harcourt Brace.

chapter six

Beyond Competitive Strategy

Other Important Strategy Choices

(© Royalty-Free / CORBIS)

Strategies for taking the hill won't necessarily hold it.

—**Amar Bhide**

The sure path to oblivion is to stay where you are.

—**Bernard Fauber**

Successful business strategy is about actively shaping the game you play, not just playing the game you find.

—**Adam M. Brandenburger and Barry J. Nalebuff**

Don't form an alliance to correct a weakness and don't ally with a partner that is trying to correct a weakness of its own. The only result from a marriage of weaknesses is the creation of even more weaknesses.

—**Michel Robert**

Once a company has settled on which of the five generic strategies to employ, attention turns to what other *strategic actions* it can take to complement its choice of a basic competitive strategy. Several decisions have to be made:

- What use to make of strategic alliances and collaborative partnerships.

- Whether to bolster the company's market position via merger or acquisitions.

- Whether to integrate backward or forward into more stages of the industry value chain.

- Whether to outsource certain value chain activities or perform them in-house.

- Whether and when to employ offensive and defensive moves.

- Which of several ways to use the Internet as a distribution channel in positioning the company in the marketplace.

This chapter contains sections discussing the pros and cons of each of the above complementary strategic options. The next-to-last section in the chapter discusses the competitive importance of timing strategic moves—when it is advantageous to be a first-mover and when it is better to be a fast-follower or late-mover. The chapter concludes with a brief look at the need for strategic choices in each functional area of a company's business (R&D, production, sales and marketing, finance, and so on) to support its basic competitive approach and complementary strategic moves.

Figure 6.1 shows the menu of strategic options a company has in crafting a strategy and the order in which the choices should generally be made. The portion of Figure 6.1 below the competitive strategy options illustrates the structure of this chapter and the topics that will be covered.

STRATEGIC ALLIANCES AND COLLABORATIVE PARTNERSHIPS

During the past decade, companies in all types of industries and in all parts of the world have elected to form strategic alliances and partnerships to complement their own strategic initiatives and strengthen their competitiveness in domestic and international markets. This is an about-face from times past, when the vast majority of companies were content to go it alone, confident that they already had or could independently

246

Thompson–Strickland–Gamble:
Crafting and Executing
Strategy: Text and
Readings, 14th Edition

I. Concepts and
Techniques for Crafting
and Executing Strategy

6. Beyond Competitive
Strategy: Other Important
Strategy Choices

© The McGraw–Hill
Companies, 2004

142   Part 1 | Concepts and Techniques for Crafting and Executing Strategy

figure 6.1   **A Company's Menu of Strategy Options**

Basic Competitive Strategy Options
(A company's first strategic choice)

Overall Low-Cost
Provider?

Broad
Differentiation?

Best-Cost
Provider?

Focused
Differentiation?

Focused
Low-Cost Provider?

Complementary Strategic Options
(A company's second set of
strategic choices)

Employ strategic alliances and
collaborative partnerships?

Outsource selected
value chain activities?

Merge with or acquire other
companies?

Initiate offensive
strategic moves?

Integrate backward or forward?

Employ defensive strategic moves?

Use the Internet as a distribution
channel and, if so, to what extent?

Functional-Area Strategies to Support the Above Strategic Choices

| R&D Engineering | Production | Marketing & Sales | Human Resources | Finance |

(A company's third set of strategic choices)

Timing a Company's Strategic Moves in the Marketplace

First-Mover?   Fast-Follower?   Late-Mover?

(A company's fourth set of strategic choices)

develop whatever resources and know-how were needed to be successful in their markets. But globalization of the world economy, revolutionary advances in technology across a broad front, and untapped opportunities in national markets in Asia, Latin America, and Europe that are opening up, deregulating, and/or undergoing privatization have made partnerships of one kind or another integral to competing on a broad geographic scale.

Many companies now find themselves thrust into two very demanding competitive races: (1) *the global race to build a presence in many different national markets* and join the ranks of companies recognized as global market leaders, and (2) *the race to seize opportunities on the frontiers of advancing technology* and build the resource strengths and business capabilities to compete successfully in the industries and product markets of the future.[1] Even the largest and most financially sound companies have concluded that simultaneously running the races for global market leadership and for a stake in the industries of the future requires more diverse and expansive skills, resources, technological expertise, and competitive capabilities than they can assemble and manage alone. Such companies, along with others that are missing the resources and competitive capabilities needed to pursue promising opportunities, have determined that the fastest way to fill the gap is often to form alliances with enterprises having the desired strengths. Consequently, these companies form **strategic alliances** or collaborative partnerships in which two or more companies join forces to achieve mutually beneficial strategic outcomes. Strategic alliances go beyond normal company-to-company dealings but fall short of merger or full joint venture partnership with formal ownership ties. (Some strategic alliances, however, do involve arrangements whereby one or more allies have minority ownership in certain of the other alliance members.)

> **core concept**
> *Strategic alliances* are collaborative partnerships where two or more companies join forces to achieve mutually beneficial strategic outcomes.

The Pervasive Use of Alliances

Strategic alliances and collaborative partnerships have thus emerged as an attractive means of breaching technology and resource gaps. More and more enterprises, especially in fast-changing industries, are making strategic alliances a core part of their overall strategy. Alliances are so central to Corning's strategy that the company describes itself as a "network of organizations." Toyota has forged long-term strategic partnerships with many of its suppliers of automotive parts and components. Microsoft collaborates very closely with independent software developers that create new programs to run on the next-generation versions of Windows. Oracle is said to have over 15,000 alliances. Time Warner, IBM, and Microsoft each have over 200 partnerships with e-business enterprises. Genentech, a leader in biotechnology and human genetics, has a partnering strategy to increase its access to novel biotherapeutics products and technologies and has formed alliances with over 30 companies to strengthen its research and development (R&D) pipeline. Since 1998, Samsung, a South Korean corporation with $34 billion in sales, has entered into 34 major strategic alliances involving such companies as Sony, Yahoo, Hewlett-Packard, Intel, Microsoft, Dell, Mitsubishi, and Rockwell Automation. Studies indicate that large corporations are commonly involved in 30 to 50 alliances and that a number have hundreds of alliances. One recent study estimated that about 35 percent of corporate revenues in 2003 came from activities involving strategic alliances, up from 15 percent in 1995.[2]

> Alliances have become so essential to the competitiveness of companies in many industries that they are a core element of today's business strategies.

In the personal computer (PC) industry, alliances are pervasive because the different components of PCs and the software to run them are supplied by so many different companies—one set of companies provides the microprocessors, another group makes the motherboards, another the monitors, another the disk drives, another the memory chips, and so on. Moreover, their facilities are scattered across the United States, Japan, Taiwan, Singapore, Malaysia, and parts of Europe. Close collaboration is required on product development, logistics, production, and the timing of new product releases. To bring all these diverse enterprises together in a common effort to advance PC technology and PC capabilities, Intel has formed collaborative partnerships with numerous makers of PC components and software developers. Intel's strategic objective has been to foster collaboration on bringing next-generation PC-related products to market in parallel so that PC users can get the maximum benefits from new PCs running on Intel's next-generation microprocessors. Without extensive cooperation among Intel, the makers of other key PC components, PC makers, and software developers in both new technology and new product development, there would be all kinds of delays and incompatibility problems in introducing better-performing PC hardware and software products—obstacles that would dampen the benefits that PC users could get from utilizing Intel's latest generations of chips and lower Intel's chip sales.

> While a few companies have the resources and capabilities to pursue their strategies alone, it is becoming increasingly common for companies to pursue their strategies in collaboration with suppliers, distributors, makers of complementary products, and sometimes even select competitors.

Why and How Strategic Alliances Are Advantageous

The value of a strategic alliance stems not from the agreement or deal itself but rather from the capacity of the partners to defuse organizational frictions, collaborate effectively over time, and work their way through the maze of changes that lie in front of them—technological and competitive surprises, new market developments (which may come at a rapid-fire pace), and changes in their own priorities and competitive circumstances. Collaborative partnerships nearly always entail an *evolving* relationship whose benefits and competitive value ultimately depend on mutual learning, cooperation, and adaptation to changing industry conditions. *The best alliances are highly selective, focusing on particular value chain activities and on obtaining a particular competitive benefit.* Competitive advantage can emerge if the combined resources and capabilities of a company and its allies give it an edge over rivals.

The most common reasons why companies enter into strategic alliances are to collaborate on technology or the development of promising new products, to overcome deficits in their technical and manufacturing expertise, to acquire altogether new competencies, to improve supply chain efficiency, to gain economies of scale in production and/or marketing, and to acquire or improve market access through joint marketing agreements.[3] A company that is racing for global market leadership can enhance its chances for success by using alliances to:

- *Get into critical country markets quickly* and accelerate the process of building a potent global market presence.
- *Gain inside knowledge about unfamiliar markets and cultures* through alliances with local partners. For example, U.S., European, and Japanese companies wanting to build market footholds in the fast-growing Chinese market have pursued partnership arrangements with Chinese companies to help in dealing with government regulations, to supply knowledge of local markets, to provide guidance on adapting their products to better match the buying preferences of Chinese consumers, to set up local manufacturing capabilities, and to assist in distribution, marketing, and promotional activities.

- *Access valuable skills and competencies* that are concentrated in particular geographic locations, such as software design competencies in the United States, fashion design skills in Italy, and efficient manufacturing skills in Japan.

A company that is racing to stake out a strong position in a technology or industry of the future can enhance its market standing by using alliances to:

- *Establish a stronger beachhead* for participating in the target technology or industry.
- *Master new technologies and build new expertise and competencies faster* than would be possible through internal efforts.
- *Open up broader opportunities* in the target industry by melding the firm's own capabilities with the expertise and resources of partners.

Allies can learn much from one another in performing joint research, sharing technological know-how, and collaborating on complementary new technologies and products—sometimes enough to enable them to pursue other new opportunities on their own. Manufacturers typically pursue alliances with parts and components suppliers to gain the efficiencies of better supply chain management and to speed new products to market. By joining forces in components production and/or final assembly, companies may be able to realize cost savings not achievable with their own small volumes—Volvo, Renault, and Peugeot formed an alliance to join forces in making engines for their large car models because none of the three needed enough such engines to operate its own engine plant economically. Manufacturing allies can also learn much about how to improve their quality control and production procedures by studying one another's manufacturing methods. IBM and Dell Computer formed an alliance whereby Dell agreed to purchase $16 billion in parts and components from IBM for use in Dell's PCs, servers, and workstations over a three-year period; Dell determined that IBM's growing expertise and capabilities in PC components justified using IBM as a major supplier even though Dell and IBM competed in supplying laptop computers and servers to corporate customers. Johnson & Johnson and Merck entered into an alliance to market Pepcid AC; Merck developed the stomach distress remedy and Johnson & Johnson functioned as marketer—the alliance made Pepcid products the best-selling remedies for acid indigestion and heartburn. United Airlines, American Airlines, Continental, Delta, and Northwest created an alliance to form Orbitz, an Internet travel site designed to compete with Expedia and Travelocity to provide consumers with low-cost airfares, rental cars, lodging, cruises, and vacation packages.

> The competitive attraction of alliances is in allowing companies to bundle competencies and resources that are more valuable in a joint effort than when kept within a single company.

Strategic cooperation is a much-favored, indeed necessary, approach in industries where new technological developments are occurring at a furious pace along many different paths and where advances in one technology spill over to affect others (often blurring industry boundaries). Whenever industries are experiencing high-velocity technological change in many areas simultaneously, firms find it virtually essential to have cooperative relationships with other enterprises to stay on the leading edge of technology and product performance even in their own area of specialization.

Alliances and Partnerships with Foreign Companies

Cooperative strategies and alliances to penetrate international markets are also common between domestic and foreign firms. Such partnerships are useful in putting together the capabilities to do business over a wider number of country markets. For example, the policy of the Chinese government has long been one of giving privileged market access to only a few select outsiders and requiring the favored outsiders to partner in one way or another with local enterprises. This policy has made alliances with local Chinese companies a strategic necessity for outsiders desirous of gaining a foothold in the vast and fast-growing Chinese market.

Why Many Alliances Are Unstable or Break Apart

The stability of an alliance depends on how well the partners work together, their success in adapting to changing internal and external conditions, and their willingness to renegotiate the bargain if circumstances so warrant. A successful alliance requires real in-the-trenches collaboration, not merely an arm's-length exchange of ideas. Unless partners place a high value on the skills, resources, and contributions each brings to the alliance and the cooperative arrangement results in valuable win–win outcomes, it is doomed. A surprisingly large number of alliances never live up to expectations. A 1999 study by Accenture, a global business consulting organization, revealed that 61 percent of alliances either were outright failures or were "limping along." Many alliances are dissolved after a few years. The high "divorce rate" among strategic allies has several causes—diverging objectives and priorities, an inability to work well together, changing conditions that render the purpose of the alliance obsolete, the emergence of more attractive technological paths, and marketplace rivalry between one or more allies.[4] Experience indicates that alliances stand a reasonable chance of helping a company reduce competitive disadvantage but very rarely have they proved a durable device for achieving a competitive edge.

> Many alliances break apart without reaching their potential because of frictions and conflicts among the allies.

The Strategic Dangers of Relying Heavily on Alliances and Collaborative Partnerships

The Achilles heel of alliances and cooperative strategies is the danger of becoming dependent on other companies for *essential* expertise and capabilities over the long term. To be a market leader (and perhaps even a serious market contender), a company must ultimately develop its own capabilities in areas where internal strategic control is pivotal to protecting its competitiveness and building competitive advantage. Moreover, some alliances hold only limited potential because the partner guards its most valuable skills and expertise; in such instances, acquiring or merging with a company possessing the desired resources is a better solution.

MERGER AND ACQUISITION STRATEGIES

> No company can afford to ignore the strategic and competitive benefits of acquiring or merging with another company to strengthen its market position and open up avenues of new opportunity.

Mergers and acquisitions are much-used strategic options. They are especially suited for situations in which alliances and partnerships do not go far enough in providing a company with access to the needed resources and capabilities. Ownership ties are more permanent than partnership ties, allowing the operations of the merger/acquisition participants to be tightly integrated and creating more in-house control and autonomy. A **merger** is a pooling of equals, with the newly created company often taking on a new name. An **acquisition** is a combination in which one company, the acquirer, purchases and absorbs the operations of another, the acquired. The difference between a merger and an acquisition relates more to the details of ownership, management control, and financial arrangements than to strategy and competitive advantage. The resources, competencies, and competitive capabilities of the newly created enterprise end up much the same whether the combination is the result of acquisition or merger.

Many mergers and acquisitions are driven by strategies to achieve one of five strategic objectives:[5]

> **core concept**
> A *merger* is a pooling of two or more companies as equals, with the newly created company often taking on a new name. An *acquisition* is a combination in which one company purchases and absorbs the operations of another.

1. *To pave the way for the acquiring company to gain more market share and, further, create a more efficient operation out of the combined companies by closing high-cost plants and eliminating surplus capacity industrywide*—The merger that formed DaimlerChrysler was motivated in large part by the fact that the motor vehicle industry had far more production capacity worldwide than was needed; management at both Daimler Benz and Chrysler believed that the efficiency of the two companies could be significantly improved by shutting some plants and laying off workers, realigning which models were produced at which plants, and squeezing out efficiencies by combining supply chain activities, product design, and administration. Quite a number of acquisitions are undertaken with the objective of transforming two or more otherwise high-cost companies into one lean competitor with average or below-average costs.

2. *To expand a company's geographic coverage*—Many industries exist for a long time in a fragmented state, with local companies dominating local markets and no company having a significantly visible regional or national presence. Eventually, though, expansion-minded companies will launch strategies to acquire local companies in adjacent territories. Over time, companies with successful growth via acquisition strategies emerge as regional market leaders and later perhaps as a company with national coverage. Often the acquiring company follows up on its acquisitions with efforts to lower the operating costs and improve the customer service capabilities of the local businesses it acquires.

3. *To extend the company's business into new product categories or international markets*—PepsiCo acquired Quaker Oats chiefly to bring Gatorade into the Pepsi family of beverages, and PepsiCo's Frito-Lay division has made a series of acquisitions of foreign-based snack foods companies to begin to establish a stronger presence in international markets. Companies like Nestlé, Kraft, Unilever, and Procter & Gamble—all racing for global market leadership—have made acquisitions an integral part of their strategies to widen their geographic reach and broaden the number of product categories in which they compete.

4. *To gain quick access to new technologies and avoid the need for a time-consuming R&D effort*—This type of acquisition strategy is a favorite of companies racing to establish attractive positions in emerging markets. Such companies need to fill in technological gaps, extend their technological capabilities along some promising new paths, and position themselves to launch next-wave products and services. Cisco Systems purchased over 75 technology companies to give it more technological reach and product breadth, thereby buttressing its standing as the world's biggest supplier of systems for building the infrastructure of the Internet. Intel has made over 300 acquisitions since 1997 to broaden its technological base, put it in a stronger position to be a major supplier of Internet technology, and make it less dependent on supplying microprocessors for PCs. Between 1996 and 2001, Lucent Technologies acquired 38 companies in the course of its strategic drive to be the technology leader in telecommunications networking. Gaining access to desirable

technologies via acquisition enables a company to build a market position in attractive technologies quickly and serves as a substitute for extensive in-house R&D programs.

5. *To try to invent a new industry and lead the convergence of industries whose boundaries are being blurred by changing technologies and new market opportunities*—In such acquisitions, the company's management is betting that a new industry is on the verge of being born and wants to establish an early position in this industry by bringing together the resources and products of several different companies. Examples include the merger of AOL and media giant Time Warner and Viacom's purchase of Paramount Pictures, CBS, and Blockbuster—both of which reflected bold strategic moves predicated on beliefs that all entertainment content will ultimately converge into a single industry and be distributed over the Internet. (Neither of these mergers and strategic bets, however, have proved successful.)

In addition to the above objectives, there are instances in which acquisitions are motivated by a company's desire to fill resource gaps, thus allowing the new company to do things it could not do before. Illustration Capsule 6.1 describes how Clear Channel Worldwide has used mergers and acquisitions to build a leading global position in outdoor advertising and radio and TV broadcasting.

All too frequently, mergers and acquisitions do not produce the hoped-for outcomes. Combining the operations of two companies, especially large and complex ones, often entails formidable resistance from rank-and-file organization members, hard-to-resolve conflicts in management styles and corporate cultures, and tough problems of integration. Cost savings, expertise sharing, and enhanced competitive capabilities may take substantially longer than expected or, worse, may never materialize at all. Integrating the operations of two fairly large or culturally diverse companies is hard to pull off—only a few companies that use merger and acquisition strategies have proved they can consistently make good decisions about what to leave alone and what to meld into their own operations and systems. In the case of mergers between companies of roughly equal size, the management groups of the two companies frequently battle over which one is going to end up in control.

A number of previously applauded mergers/acquisitions have yet to live up to expectations—the merger of AOL and Time Warner, the merger of Daimler Benz and Chrysler, Hewlett-Packard's acquisition of Compaq Computer, and Ford's acquisition of Jaguar. The AOL Time Warner merger has proved to be mostly a disaster, partly because AOL's rapid growth has evaporated, partly because of a huge clash of corporate cultures, and partly because most of the expected benefits have yet to materialize. Ford paid a handsome price to acquire Jaguar but has yet to make the Jaguar brand a major factor in the luxury-car segment in competition against Mercedes, BMW, and Lexus. Novell acquired WordPerfect for $1.7 billion in stock in 1994, but the combination never generated enough punch to compete against Microsoft Word and Microsoft Office—Novell sold WordPerfect to Corel for $124 million in cash and stock less than two years later. In 2001 electronics retailer Best Buy paid $685 million to acquire Musicland, a struggling 1300-store music retailer that included stores operating under the Musicland, Sam Goody, Suncoast, Media Play, and On Cue names. But Musicland's sales, already declining, dropped even further. In June 2003 Best Buy "sold" Musicland to a Florida investment firm. No cash changed hands and the "buyer" received shares of stock in Best Buy in return for assuming Musicland's liabilities.

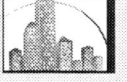 illustration capsule 6.1

How Clear Channel Has Used Mergers and Acquisitions to Become a Global Market Leader

In 2003, Clear Channel Worldwide was the fourth largest media company in the world behind Disney, Time Warner, and Viacom/CBS. The company, founded in 1972 by Lowry Mays and Billy Joe McCombs, got its start by acquiring an unprofitable country-music radio station in San Antonio, Texas. Over the next 10 years, Mays learned the radio business and slowly bought other radio stations in a variety of states. Going public in 1984 helped the company raise the equity capital needed to fuel its strategy of expanding by acquiring radio stations in additional geographic markets.

In the late 1980s, following the decision of the Federal Communications Commission to loosen the rules regarding the ability of one company to own both radio and TV stations, Clear Channel broadened its strategy and began acquiring small, struggling TV stations. Soon thereafter, Clear Channel became affiliated with the Fox network, which was starting to build a national presence and challenge ABC, CBS, and NBC. Meanwhile, the company began selling programming services to other stations, and in some markets where it already had stations it took on the function of selling advertising for crosstown stations it did not own.

By 1998, Clear Channel had used acquisitions to build a leading position in radio and television stations. Domestically, it owned, programmed, or sold airtime for 69 AM radio stations, 135 FM stations, and 18 TV stations in 48 local markets in 24 states. The TV stations included affiliates of FOX, UPN, ABC, NBC, and CBS. Clear Channel was also beginning to expand internationally. It purchased an ownership interest in a domestic Spanish-language radio broadcaster; owned two radio stations and a cable audio channel in Denmark; and acquired ownership interests in radio stations in Australia, Mexico, New Zealand, and the Czech Republic.

In 1997, Clear Channel acquired Phoenix-based Eller Media Company, an outdoor advertising company with over 100,000 billboard facings. This was quickly followed by additional acquisitions of outdoor advertising companies, the most important of which were ABC Outdoor in Milwaukee, Wisconsin; Paxton Communications (with operations in Tampa and Orlando, Florida); Universal Outdoor; and the More Group, with outdoor operations and 90,000 displays in 24 countries.

Then in October 1999, Clear Channel merged with AM-FM, Inc. After divesting some 125 properties needed to gain regulatory approval, Clear Channel Communications (the name adopted by the merged companies) operated in 32 countries and included 830 radio stations, 19 TV stations, and more than 425,000 outdoor displays. Several additional acquisitions were completed during the 2000–2002 period.

Clear Channel's strategy was to buy radio, TV, and outdoor advertising properties with operations in many of the same local markets; share facilities and staffs to cut costs; improve programming; and sell advertising to customers in packages for all three media simultaneously. Packaging ads for two or three media not only helped Clear Channel's advertising clients distribute their messages more effectively but also allowed the company to combine its sales activities and have a common sales force for all three media, achieving significant cost savings and boosting profit margins.

In 2003, Clear Channel Worldwide (the company's latest name) owned radio and television stations, outdoor displays, and entertainment venues in 66 countries around the world. Clear Channel operated 1,184 radio and 34 television stations in the United States and had equity interests in over 240 radio stations internationally. It also operated a national radio network in the United States with about 180 million weekly listeners. In addition, the company operated over 700,000 outdoor advertising displays, including billboards, street furniture, and transit panels around the world. The company's Clear Channel Entertainment division was a leading promoter, producer, and marketer of about 30,000 live entertainment events annually and also owned leading athlete management and marketing companies.

Sources: www.clearchannel.com, September 2003, and *Business Week,* October 19, 1999, p. 56

VERTICAL INTEGRATION STRATEGIES: OPERATING ACROSS MORE STAGES OF THE INDUSTRY VALUE CHAIN

Vertical integration extends a firm's competitive and operating scope within the same basic industry. It involves expanding the firm's range of activities backward into sources of supply and/or forward toward end users. Thus, if a manufacturer invests in facilities to produce certain component parts that it formerly purchased from outside suppliers, it remains in essentially the same industry as before. The only change is that it has operations in two stages of the industry value chain. Similarly, if a paint manufacturer, Sherwin-Williams for example, elects to integrate forward by opening a national chain of retail stores to market its paint products directly to consumers, it remains in the paint business even though its competitive scope extends from manufacturing to retailing.

Vertical integration strategies can aim at *full integration* (participating in all stages of the industry value chain) or *partial integration* (building positions in selected stages of the industry's total value chain). A firm can pursue vertical integration by starting its own operations in other stages in the industry's activity chain or by acquiring a company already performing the activities it wants to bring in-house.

The Strategic Advantages of Vertical Integration

> **core concept**
> A vertical integration strategy has appeal *only* if it significantly strengthens a firm's competitive position.

The only good reason for investing company resources in vertical integration is to strengthen the firm's competitive position.[6] Vertical integration has no real payoff profitwise or strategywise unless it produces sufficient cost savings to justify the extra investment, adds materially to a company's technological and competitive strengths, or truly helps differentiate the company's product offering.

Integrating Backward to Achieve Greater Competitiveness   Integrating backward generates cost savings only when the volume needed is big enough to capture the same scale economies suppliers have and when suppliers' production efficiency can be matched or exceeded with no drop-off in quality and new product development capability. Backward integration is most likely to reduce costs when suppliers have sizable profit margins, the item being supplied is a major cost component, and the needed technological skills and product development capability are easily mastered or can be gained by acquiring a supplier with the desired expertise. Integrating backward can sometimes significantly enhance a company's technological capabilities and give it expertise needed to stake out positions in the industries and products of the future. Intel, Cisco, and many other Silicon Valley companies have been active in acquiring companies that will help them speed the advance of Internet technology and pave the way for next-generation families of products and services.

Backward vertical integration can produce a differentiation-based competitive advantage when a company, by performing activities in-house that were previously outsourced, ends up with a better-quality offering, improves the caliber of its customer service, or in other ways enhances the performance of its final product. On occasion, integrating into more stages along the industry value chain can add to a company's differentiation capabilities by allowing it to build or strengthen its core competencies, better master key skills or strategy-critical technologies, or add features that deliver greater customer value. Smithfield Foods, the largest pork processing company in the United States, has integrated backward into hog production because by having direct control over genetics, feed, and other aspects of the hog-raising process, it can introduce branded products—such as Smithfield Lean Generation Pork—that stand out from other pork products on the market.

Other potential advantages of backward integration include decreasing the company's dependence on suppliers of crucial components and lessening the company's vulnerability to powerful suppliers inclined to raise prices at every opportunity. Stockpiling, contracting for fixed prices, multiple sourcing, forming long-term cooperative partnerships, and using substitute inputs are not always attractive ways for dealing with uncertain supply conditions or with economically powerful suppliers. Companies that are low on a key supplier's customer priority list can find themselves waiting on shipments every time supplies get tight. If this occurs often and wreaks havoc in a company's own production and customer relations activities, backward integration can be an advantageous strategic solution.

Integrating Forward to Enhance Competitiveness The strategic impetus for forward integration is to gain better access to end users and better market visibility. In many industries, independent sales agents, wholesalers, and retailers handle competing brands of the same product; having no allegiance to any one company's brand, they tend to push whatever sells and earns them the biggest profits. Halfhearted commitments by distributors and retailers can frustrate a company's attempt to boost sales and market share, give rise to costly inventory pileups and frequent underutilization of capacity, and disrupt the economies of steady near-capacity production. In such cases, it can be advantageous for a manufacturer to integrate forward into wholesaling or retailing via company-owned distributorships or a chain of retail stores. But often a company's product line is not broad enough to justify stand-alone distributorships or retail outlets. This leaves the option of integrating forward into the activity of selling directly to end users—perhaps via the Internet. Bypassing regular wholesale/retail channels in favor of direct sales and Internet retailing may lower distribution costs, produce a relative cost advantage over certain rivals, and result in lower selling prices to end users.

The Strategic Disadvantages of Vertical Integration

Vertical integration has some substantial drawbacks, however. It boosts a firm's capital investment in the industry, increasing business risk (what if industry growth and profitability go sour?) and perhaps denying financial resources to more worthwhile pursuits. A vertically integrated firm has vested interests in protecting its technology and production facilities. Because of the high costs of abandoning such investments before they are worn out, fully integrated firms tend to adopt new technologies slower than partially integrated or nonintegrated firms. Second, integrating forward or backward locks a firm into relying on its own in-house activities and sources of supply (which later may prove more costly than outsourcing) and potentially results in less flexibility in accommodating buyer demand for greater product variety. In today's world of close working relationships with suppliers and efficient supply chain management systems, very few businesses can make a case for integrating backward into the business of suppliers just for the purposes of ensuring a reliable supply of materials and components or to reduce production costs.

Third, vertical integration poses all kinds of capacity-matching problems. In motor vehicle manufacturing, for example, the most efficient scale of operation for making axles is different from the most economic volume for radiators, and different yet again for both engines and transmissions. Building the capacity to produce just the right number of axles, radiators, engines, and transmissions in-house—and doing so at the lowest unit costs for each—is much easier said than done. If internal capacity for making transmissions is deficient, the difference has to be bought externally. Where internal capacity for radiators proves excessive, customers need to be found for the surplus. And if by-products are generated—as occurs in the processing of many chemical products—they require arrangements for disposal.

Fourth, integration forward or backward often calls for radically different skills and business capabilities. Parts and components manufacturing, assembly operations, wholesale distribution and retailing, and direct sales via the Internet are different businesses with different key success factors. A manufacturer that integrates backward into components production may find that its expertise in advancing the technology of such components is deficient compared to the capabilities of companies that specialize in the manufacture of particular components. Most automakers, for example, have learned that they lack the capabilities to develop next-generation parts and components for their vehicles compared to what can be achieved by partnering with components specialists who have greater depth of knowledge and expertise. Managers of a manufacturing company should consider carefully whether it makes good business sense to invest time and money in developing the expertise and merchandising skills to integrate forward into wholesaling and retailing. Many manufacturers learn the hard way that company-owned wholesale/retail networks present many headaches, fit poorly with what they do best, and don't always add the kind of value to their core business they thought they would. Selling to customers via the Internet poses still another set of problems—it is usually easier to use the Internet to sell to business customers than to consumers.

Integrating backward into parts and components manufacture isn't as simple or profitable as it sounds, either. Producing some or all of the parts and components needed for final assembly can reduce a company's flexibility to make desirable changes in using certain parts and components—it is one thing to design out a component made by a supplier and another to design out a component being made in-house. Companies that alter designs and models frequently in response to shifting buyer preferences often find outsourcing the needed parts and components cheaper and less complicated than in-house manufacturing. Most of the world's automakers, despite their expertise in automotive technology and manufacturing, have concluded that purchasing many of their key parts and components from manufacturing specialists results in higher quality, lower costs, and greater design flexibility than does the vertical integration option.

Weighing the Pros and Cons of Vertical Integration   All in all, a strategy of vertical integration can have both important strengths and weaknesses. Which way the scales tip depends on (1) whether vertical integration can enhance the performance of strategy-critical activities in ways that lower cost, build expertise, or increase differentiation; (2) the impact of vertical integration on investment costs, flexibility and response times, and the administrative costs of coordinating operations across more value chain activities; and (3) whether vertical integration substantially enhances a company's competitiveness. Vertical integration strategies have merit according to which capabilities and value chain activities truly need to be performed in-house and which can be performed better or cheaper by outsiders. Absent solid benefits, integrating forward or backward is not likely to be an attractive competitive strategy option. In a growing number of instances, companies are proving that focusing on a narrower portion of the industry value chain and relying on outsiders to perform the remaining value chain activities is a more flexible and economical strategy.

OUTSOURCING STRATEGIES: NARROWING THE BOUNDARIES OF THE BUSINESS

Over the past decade, outsourcing the performance of some value chain activities traditionally performed in-house has become increasingly popular. Some companies have found vertical integration to be so competitively burdensome that they have deintegrated and withdrawn from some stages of the industry value chain. Moreover, a number of single-business enterprises have begun outsourcing a variety of value chain activities formerly performed in-house to enable them to better concentrate their energies on a narrower, more strategy-critical portion of the overall value chain. Outsourcing strategies thus involve a conscious decision to abandon or forgo attempts to perform certain value chain activities internally and instead to farm them out to outside specialists and business partners. The two driving themes behind outsourcing are that (1) outsiders can often perform certain activities better or cheaper and (2) outsourcing allows a firm to focus its entire energies on its core business—those activities at the center of its expertise (its core competencies) and that are the most critical to its competitive and financial success.

Advantages of Outsourcing

Outsourcing pieces of the value chain to narrow the boundaries of a firm's business makes strategic sense whenever:

- *An activity can be performed more cheaply by outside specialists.* Many PC makers, for example, have shifted from assembling units in-house to using contract assemblers because of the sizable scale economies associated with purchasing PC components in large volumes and assembling PCs. Cisco outsources most all production and assembly of its routers and switching equipment to contract manufacturers that together operate 37 factories, all linked to Cisco facilities via the Internet.

- *An activity can be performed better by outside specialists.* An automaker can obtain higher-caliber navigation systems and audio systems for its cars by sourcing them from companies with specialized know-how and manufacturing expertise than it can from trying to make them in-house.

- *The activity is not crucial to the firm's ability to achieve sustainable competitive advantage and won't hollow out its core competencies, capabilities, or technical know-how.* Outsourcing of maintenance services, data processing, customer billing, employee benefits administration, Web site operations, and other administrative support activities to specialists has become commonplace. American Express, for instance, recently entered into a seven-year, $4 billion deal whereby IBM's Services division will host American Express's Web site, network servers, data storage, and help-desk support; American Express indicated that it would save several hundred million dollars by paying only for the services it needed when it needed them (as opposed to funding its own full-time staff).

- *It reduces the company's risk exposure to changing technology and/or changing buyer preferences.* Outsourcing, for example, puts the burden on outside suppliers of components to keep pace with advancing technology as it affects their component business; should a components supplier fall behind on developing next-generation components or should its component lose out to a different type of component incorporating another type of technology, then the outsourcing company can simply shift suppliers. Likewise, a PC maker that decides to outsource rather than make monitors for its PCs can readily shift its purchases to liquid crystal display (LCD) or flat-panel monitors as more and more buyers of its PCs shift away from ordering conventional cathode ray tube (CRT) monitors. Had a PC maker opted years ago to produce CRT monitors in-house, then it would have less flexibility in accommodating growing buyer preferences for LCD monitors and its investment in facilities to produce CRT monitors would be at risk.

- *It streamlines company operations in ways that cut the time it takes to get newly developed products into the marketplace, lower internal coordination costs, or improve organizational flexibility.* Hewlett-Packard can speed the introduction of next-generation printers by collaborating with outside suppliers of printer components on both new printer design and new model release dates and then holding suppliers accountable for meeting the established specifications and deadlines. Were Hewlett-Packard to make all its printer components in-house, its lead times for getting newly designed models to market would be longer and more cumbersome in terms of bureaucratic hassle, internal resistance, and coordination costs. Major advances in the methods of supply chain management are allowing companies to employ very efficient and effective outsourcing strategies; moreover, outside suppliers tend to be more responsive to requests from their major customers than internal company groups are to requests from another internal group.

- *It allows a company to concentrate on strengthening and leveraging its core competencies.* Ideally, outsourcing allows a company to focus on a distinctive competence in some competitively important activity that results in sustainable competitive advantage over rivals.

core concept

A company should generally *not* perform any value chain activity internally that can be performed more efficiently or effectively by its outside business partners—the chief exception is when an activity is strategically crucial and internal control over that activity is deemed essential.

Often, many of the advantages of performing value chain activities in-house can be captured and many of the disadvantages avoided by forging close, long-term cooperative partnerships with key suppliers and tapping into the important competitive capabilities that able suppliers have painstakingly developed. In years past, many companies maintained arm's-length relationships with suppliers, insisting on items being made to precise specifications and negotiating long and hard over price.[7] Although a company might place orders with the same supplier repeatedly, there was no firm expectation that the orders would continue; price usually determined which supplier was awarded an order, and companies maneuvered for leverage over suppliers to get the lowest possible prices. The threat of switching suppliers was the company's primary weapon. To make this threat credible, sourcing from several suppliers was preferred to dealing with only a single supplier.

Today, most companies are abandoning such approaches in favor of alliances and strategic partnerships with a small number of highly capable suppliers. Cooperative relationships are replacing contractual, purely price-oriented relationships. Relying on outside specialists to perform certain value chain activities offers a number of strategic advantages:[8]

- Obtaining higher quality and/or cheaper components or services than internal sources can provide.

- Improving the company's ability to innovate by allying with "best-in-world" suppliers who have considerable intellectual capital and innovative capabilities of their own.

- Enhancing the firm's strategic flexibility should customer needs and market conditions suddenly shift—seeking out new suppliers with the needed capabilities already in place is frequently quicker, easier, less risky, and cheaper than hurriedly retooling internal operations to disband obsolete capabilities and put new ones in place.

- Increasing the firm's ability to assemble diverse kinds of expertise speedily and efficiently.

- Allowing the firm to concentrate its resources on performing those activities internally that it can perform better than outsiders and/or that it needs to have under its direct control.

Dell Computer's partnerships with the suppliers of PC components have allowed it to operate with fewer than four days of inventory, to realize substantial savings in inventory costs, and to get PCs equipped with next-generation components into the marketplace in less than a week after the newly upgraded components start shipping. Cisco's contract suppliers work so closely with Cisco that they can ship Cisco products to Cisco customers without a Cisco employee ever touching the gear; Cisco management claims its system of alliances saves $500 million to $800 million annually.[9] Hewlett-Packard, IBM, Silicon Graphics (now SGI), and others have sold plants to suppliers and then contracted to purchase the output. Starbucks finds purchasing coffee beans from independent growers to be far more advantageous than trying to integrate backward into the coffee-growing business.

The Pitfalls of Outsourcing

The biggest danger of outsourcing is that a company will farm out too many or the wrong types of activities and thereby hollow out its own capabilities. In such cases, a company loses touch with the very activities and expertise that over the long run determine its success. Cisco guards against loss of control and protects its manufacturing expertise by designing the production methods that its contract manufacturers must use. Cisco keeps the source code for its designs proprietary so it can remain the source of all improvements and innovations. Further, Cisco utilizes online technology to monitor the factory operations of contract manufacturers around the clock, enabling it to know immediately when problems arise and whether to get involved.

USING OFFENSIVE STRATEGIES TO SECURE COMPETITIVE ADVANTAGE

Competitive advantage is nearly always achieved by successful *offensive* strategic moves—initiatives calculated to yield a cost advantage, a differentiation advantage, or a resource advantage. In contrast, *defensive* strategies, discussed later in this chapter, can protect competitive advantage but rarely are the basis for creating the advantage. How long it takes for a successful offensive to create an edge varies with the competitive circumstances.[10] It can be short if the requisite resources and capabilities are already in place awaiting deployment or if buyers respond immediately (as can occur with a dramatic price cut, an imaginative ad campaign, or an especially appealing new product). Securing a competitive edge can take much longer if winning consumer acceptance of an innovative product will take some time or if the firm may need several years to debug a new technology or put new network systems or production capacity in place. Ideally, an offensive move builds competitive advantage quickly; the longer it takes, the more likely it is that rivals will spot the move, see its potential, and begin a counterresponse. The size of the advantage can be large (as in pharmaceuticals, where patents on an important new drug produce a substantial advantage) or small (as in apparel, where popular new designs can be imitated quickly).

However, competent, resourceful competitors can be counted on to counterattack with initiatives to overcome any market disadvantage they face—few companies will allow themselves to be outcompeted without a fight.[11] Thus, to sustain an initially won competitive advantage, a firm must come up with follow-on offensive and defensive moves. Unless the firm initiates one series of offensive and defensive moves after another to protect its market position and retain customer favor, its market advantage will erode.

> **core concept**
> Competent, resourceful rivals will exert strong efforts to overcome any competitive disadvantage they face—they won't be outcompeted without a fight.

Basic Types of Offensive Strategies

Most every company must at times go on the offensive to improve its market position. While offensive attacks may or may not be aimed at particular rivals, they usually are motivated by a desire to win sales and market share at the expense of other companies in the industry. There are six basic types of strategic offensives:[12]

1. Initiatives to match or exceed competitor strengths.
2. Initiatives to capitalize on competitor weaknesses.
3. Simultaneous initiatives on many fronts.
4. End-run offensives.
5. Guerrilla offensives.
6. Preemptive strikes.

Initiatives to Match or Exceed Competitor Strengths   There are two instances in which it makes sense to mount offensives aimed at neutralizing or overcoming the strengths and capabilities of rival companies. The first is when a company has no choice but to try to whittle away at a strong rival's competitive advantage. The second is when it is possible to gain profitable market share at the expense of rivals despite whatever resource strengths and capabilities they have. Attacking a powerful rival's strengths may be necessary when the rival has either a *superior product offering* or *superior organizational resources and capabilities*. Advanced Micro Devices (AMD), wanting to grow its sales of microprocessors for PCs, has on several occasions elected to attack Intel head-on, offering a faster alternative to Intel's Pentium chips at a lower price. Believing that the company's survival depends on eliminating the performance gap between AMD chips and Intel chips, AMD management has been willing to risk that a head-on offensive might prompt Intel to counter with lower prices of its own and accelerated development of faster Pentium chips.

The classic avenue for attacking a strong rival is to offer an equally good product at a lower price.[13] This can produce market share gains if the targeted competitor has sound reasons for not resorting to price cuts of its own and if the challenger convinces buyers that its product is just as good. However, such a strategy increases total profits only if the gains in additional unit sales are enough to offset the impact of lower prices and thinner margins per unit sold. A more potent and sustainable basis for mounting a price-aggressive challenge is to *first achieve a cost advantage* and then hit competitors with a lower price.[14]

Other strategic options for attacking a competitor's strengths include leapfrogging into next-generation technologies to make the rival's products obsolete, adding new features that appeal to the rival's customers, running comparison ads, constructing major new plant capacity in the rival's backyard, expanding the product line to match the rival model for model, and developing customer service capabilities that the targeted rival doesn't have.

As a rule, challenging a rival on competitive grounds where it is strong is an uphill struggle. Success can be long in coming and usually hinges on developing some kind of important edge over the target rival, whether it be lower cost, better service, a product with attractive differentiating features, or unique competitive capabilities (fast design-to-market times, greater technical know-how, or agility in responding to shifting customer requirements). Absent good prospects for added profitability and a more solid competitive position, offensives aimed at attacking a stronger rival head-on are ill-advised. General Motors, for instance, repeatedly attacked rival carmakers with aggressive rebates and 0 percent financing (at a cost of about $3,100 per vehicle sold) in 2001–2002, but it failed to gain more than 1 percent additional market share.[15]

Initiatives to Capitalize on Competitor Weaknesses Initiatives that exploit competitor weaknesses stand a better chance of succeeding than do those that challenge competitor strengths, especially if the weaknesses represent important vulnerabilities and the rival is caught by surprise with no ready defense.[16] Options for attacking the competitive weaknesses of rivals include:

- Going after the customers of those rivals whose products lag on quality, features, or product performance.
- Making special sales pitches to the customers of those rivals who provide subpar customer service.
- Trying to win customers away from rivals with weak brand recognition (an attractive option if the aggressor has strong marketing skills and a recognized brand name).
- Emphasizing sales to buyers in geographic regions where a rival has a weak market share or is exerting less competitive effort.
- Paying special attention to buyer segments that a rival is neglecting or is weakly equipped to serve.

There are times when a defender facing a direct attack from a strong rival will be motivated to look for opportunities elsewhere rather than counterattack with strong moves of its own.[17]

Simultaneous Initiatives on Many Fronts On occasion a company may see merit in launching a grand offensive involving multiple initiatives (price cuts, increased advertising, additional performance features, new models and styles, customer service improvements, and such promotions as free samples, coupons, rebates, and in-store displays) launched more or less concurrently across a wide geographic front. Such all-out campaigns can force a rival into many defensive actions to protect different pieces of its customer base simultaneously and thus divide its attention. Multifaceted offensives have their best chance of success when a challenger not only comes up with an especially attractive product or service but also has the brand awareness and distribution clout to get buyers' attention. A high-profile market blitz, buttressed with advertising and special deals, may well entice large numbers of buyers to switch their brand allegiance.

End-Run Offensives   The idea of an end-run offensive is to maneuver *around* competitors, capture unoccupied or less contested market territory, and change the rules of the competitive game in the aggressor's favor.[18] Examples include:

- *Introducing new products that redefine the market and the terms of competition*— Digital cameras have changed the rules of competition for members of the film-based camera and photo-processing industries. Wireless communications firms are employing end-run offensives to wreak havoc with the landline businesses of AT&T and the regional Bells.

- *Launching initiatives to build strong positions in geographic areas where close rivals have little or no market presence*—The race for global market leadership in PCs, servers, and Internet infrastructure products is prompting some contenders to launch early end-run offensives to build positions in less contested markets in Latin America and Asia (China and India have one-third of the world's population).

- *Trying to create new segments by introducing products with different attributes and performance features to better meet the needs of selected buyers*—Witness the success that Lexus, Acura, Infinity, and BMW have had with carlike sport-utility vehicles. This initiative works well when new product versions satisfy certain buyer needs that heretofore have been ignored or neglected.

- *Leapfrogging into next-generation technologies to supplant existing technologies, products and/or services*—The makers of thin, trim flat-panel monitors and LCD TVs are moving aggressively to improve the cost-effectiveness of their technology and production processes to leapfrog the technology of heavier, more bulky CRT monitors and TVs.

Guerrilla Offensives   Guerrilla offensives are particularly well suited to small challengers who have neither the resources nor the market visibility to mount a full-fledged attack on industry leaders.[19] Guerrilla offensives use the hit-and-run principle—an underdog tries to grab sales and market share wherever and whenever it catches rivals napping or spots an opening through which to lure customers away. Guerrilla offensives can involve making scattered, random raids on the leaders' customers with such tactics as occasional lowballing on price (to win a big order or steal a key account); surprising key rivals with sporadic but intense bursts of promotional activity (offering a 20 percent discount for one week to draw customers away from rival brands); or undertaking special campaigns to attract buyers away from rivals plagued with a strike or problems in meeting delivery schedules.[20] Guerrillas can promote the quality of their products when rivals have quality control problems or announce guaranteed delivery times when competitors' deliveries are running behind or significantly boost their commitment to prompt technical support when buyers are frustrated by the caliber of the support offered by industry leaders.

Preemptive Strikes   Preemptive strategies involve moving first to secure an advantageous position that rivals are prevented or discouraged from duplicating. What makes a move preemptive is its one-of-a-kind nature—whoever strikes first stands to acquire competitive assets that rivals can't readily match. There are several ways a firm can bolster its competitive capabilities with preemptive moves: (1) securing exclusive or dominant access to the best distributors in a particular geographic region or country; (2) moving to obtain the most favorable site along a heavily traveled thoroughfare, at a new interchange or intersection, in a new shopping mall, in a natural beauty spot, close to cheap transportation or raw material supplies or market outlets, and so on; and (3) tying up the most reliable, high-quality suppliers via exclusive partnership, long-term contracts, or acquisition.[21] To be successful, a preemptive move doesn't have to totally block rivals from following or copying; it merely needs to give a firm a prime position that is not easily circumvented.

Choosing Which Rivals to Attack

Offensive-minded firms need to analyze which of their rivals to challenge as well as how to mount that challenge. The following are the best targets for offensive attacks:[22]

- *Market leaders that are vulnerable*—Offensive attacks make good sense when a company that leads in terms of size and market share is not a true leader in terms of serving the market well. Signs of leader vulnerability include unhappy buyers, an inferior product line, a weak competitive strategy with regard to low-cost leadership or differentiation, strong emotional commitment to an aging technology the leader has pioneered, outdated plants and equipment, a preoccupation with diversification into other industries, and mediocre or declining profitability. Offensives to erode the positions of market leaders have real promise when the challenger is able to revamp its value chain or innovate to gain a fresh cost-based or differentiation-based competitive advantage.[23] To be judged successful, attacks on leaders don't have to result in making the aggressor the new leader; a challenger may "win" by simply becoming a stronger runner-up. Caution is well advised in challenging strong market leaders—there's a significant risk of squandering valuable resources in a futile effort or precipitating a fierce and profitless industrywide battle for market share.

- *Runner-up firms with weaknesses where the challenger is strong*—Runner-up firms are an especially attractive target when a challenger's resource strengths and competitive capabilities are well suited to exploiting their weaknesses.

- *Struggling enterprises that are on the verge of going under*—Challenging a hard-pressed rival in ways that further sap its financial strength and competitive position can weaken its resolve and hasten its exit from the market.

- *Small local and regional firms with limited capabilities*—Because small firms typically have limited expertise and resources, a challenger with broader capabilities is well positioned to raid their biggest and best customers—particularly those who are growing rapidly, have increasingly sophisticated requirements, and may already be thinking about switching to a supplier with more full-service capability.

Choosing the Basis for Attack

A firm's strategic offensive should, at a minimum, be tied to what it does best—its core competencies, resource strengths, and competitive capabilities. Otherwise the prospects for success are indeed dim. The centerpiece of the offensive can be an important core competence, a unique competitive capability, much-improved performance features, an innovative new product, technological superiority, a cost advantage in manufacturing or distribution, or some kind of differentiation advantage. If the challenger's resources and competitive strengths amount to a competitive advantage over the targeted rivals, so much the better.

USING DEFENSIVE STRATEGIES TO PROTECT THE COMPANY'S POSITION

> It is just as important to discern when to fortify a company's present market position with defensive actions as it is to seize the initiative and launch strategic offensives.

In a competitive market, all firms are subject to offensive challenges from rivals. The purposes of defensive strategies are to lower the risk of being attacked, weaken the impact of any attack that occurs, and influence challengers to aim their efforts at other rivals. While defensive strategies usually don't enhance a firm's competitive advantage, they can definitely help fortify its competitive position, protect its most valuable resources and capabilities from imitation, and defend whatever competitive advantage it might have. Defensive strategies can take either of two forms: blocking challengers and signaling the likelihood of strong retaliation.

Blocking the Avenues Open to Challengers

> There are many ways to throw obstacles in the path of challengers.

The most frequently employed approach to defending a company's present position involves actions that restrict a challenger's options for initiating competitive attack. There are any number of obstacles that can be put in the path of would-be challengers.[24] A defender can participate in alternative technologies to reduce the threat that rivals will attack with a better technology. A defender can introduce new features, add new models, or broaden its product line to close off gaps and vacant niches to would-be challengers. It can thwart the efforts of rivals to attack with a lower price by maintaining economy-priced options of its own. It can try to discourage buyers from trying competitors' brands via such actions as lengthening warranty coverages, offering free training and support services, developing the capability to deliver spare parts to users faster than rivals can, providing coupons and sample giveaways to buyers most prone to experiment, and making early announcements about impending new products or price changes to induce potential buyers to postpone switching. It can challenge the quality or safety of rivals' products in regulatory proceedings—a favorite tactic of the pharmaceutical firms in trying to delay the introduction of competing prescription drugs. Finally, a defender can grant dealers and distributors volume discounts or better financing terms to discourage them from experimenting with other suppliers, or it can convince them to handle its product line *exclusively* and force competitors to use other distribution outlets.

Signaling Challengers That Retaliation Is Likely

The goal of signaling challengers that strong retaliation is likely in the event of an attack is either to dissuade challengers from attacking at all or to divert them to less threatening options. Either goal can be achieved by letting challengers know the battle will cost more than it is worth. Would-be challengers can be signaled by:[25]

- Publicly announcing management's commitment to maintain the firm's present market share.
- Publicly committing the company to match competitors' terms or prices.
- Maintaining a war chest of cash and marketable securities.
- Making an occasional strong counterresponse to the moves of weak competitors to enhance the firm's image as a tough defender.

Thompson–Strickland–Gamble:
Crafting and Executing
Strategy: Text and
Readings, 14th Edition

I. Concepts and
Techniques for Crafting
and Executing Strategy

6. Beyond Competitive
Strategy: Other Important
Strategy Choices

© The McGraw–Hill
Companies, 2004

265

STRATEGIES FOR USING THE INTERNET AS A DISTRIBUTION CHANNEL

As the Internet continues to weave its way into the fabric of everyday business and personal life, and as the second wave of Internet entrepreneurship takes root, companies of all types are addressing how best to make the Internet a fundamental part of their business and their competitive strategies. Few if any businesses can escape making some effort to use Internet applications to improve their value chain activities. This much is a given—anything less risks competitive disadvantage. Companies across the world are deep into the process of implementing a variety of Internet technology applications; the chief question companies face at this point is what additional Internet technology applications to incorporate into day-to-day operations. But the larger and much tougher *strategic* issue is how to make the Internet a fundamental part of a company's competitive strategy—in particular, how much emphasis to place on the Internet as a distribution channel for accessing buyers. *Managers must decide how to use the Internet in positioning the company in the marketplace*—whether to use the company's Web site as *simply a means of disseminating product information* (with traditional distribution channel partners making all sales to end users), as a *secondary* or *minor* channel for making sales, as *one of several important distribution channels for generating sales to end users,* as *the primary distribution channel,* or as *the exclusive channel for accessing customers.*[26] Let's look at each of these strategic options in turn.

> Companies today must wrestle with the issue of how to use the Internet in positioning themselves in the marketplace—whether to use their Web site as a way to disseminate product information, as a minor distribution channel, as one of several important distribution channels, as the primary distribution channel, or as the company's only distribution channel.

Using the Internet Just to Disseminate Product Information

Operating a Web site that only disseminates product information—but that relies on click-throughs to the Web sites of distribution channel partners for sales transactions (or that informs site users where nearby retail stores are located)—is an attractive market positioning option for manufacturers and wholesalers that already have retail dealer networks and face nettlesome channel conflict issues if they try to sell online in direct competition with their dealers. A manufacturer or wholesaler that aggressively pursues online sales to end users is signaling both a weak strategic commitment to its dealers and a willingness to cannibalize dealers' sales and growth potential. To the extent that strong partnerships with wholesale and/or retail dealers are critical to accessing end users, selling direct to end users via the company's Web site is a very tricky road to negotiate. A manufacturer's efforts to use its Web site to sell around its dealers is certain to anger its wholesale distributors and retail dealers may respond by putting more effort into marketing the brands of rival manufacturers who don't sell online. In sum, the manufacturer may stand to lose more sales through its dealers than it gains from its own online sales effort. Moreover, dealers may be in better position to employ a brick-and-click strategy than a manufacturer because dealers have a local presence to complement their online sales approach (which consumers may find appealing). Consequently, in industries where the strong support and goodwill of dealer networks is essential, manufacturers may conclude that their Web site should be designed to partner with dealers rather than compete with them—just as the auto manufacturers are doing with their franchised dealers.

Using the Internet as a Minor Distribution Channel

A second strategic option is to use online sales as a relatively minor distribution channel for achieving incremental sales, gaining online sales experience, and doing marketing research. If channel conflict poses a big obstacle to online sales, or if only a small fraction of buyers can be attracted to make online purchases, then companies are well advised to pursue online sales with the strategic intent of gaining experience, learning more about buyer tastes and preferences, testing reaction to new products, creating added market buzz about their products, and boosting overall sales volume a few percentage points. Nike, for example, has begun selling some of its footwear online, giving buyers the option of specifying certain colors and features. Such a strategy is unlikely to provoke much resistance from dealers and could even prove beneficial to dealers if footwear buyers become enamored with custom-made shoes that can be ordered through and/or picked up at Nike retailers. A manufacturer may be able to glean valuable marketing research data from tracking the browsing patterns of Web site visitors and incorporating what generates the most interest into its mainstream product offerings. The behavior and actions of Web surfers are a veritable gold mine of information for companies seeking to respond more precisely to buyer preferences.

Brick-and-Click Strategies: An Appealing Middle Ground

Employing a brick-and-click strategy to sell directly to consumers while at the same time using traditional wholesale and retail channels can be an attractive market positioning option in the right circumstances. With a brick-and-click strategy, sales at a company's Web site can serve as either one of several important distribution channels through which the company accesses end users or as its primary distribution channel. Software developers, for example, have come to rely on the Internet as a highly effective distribution channel to complement sales through brick-and-mortar wholesalers and retailers. Selling online directly to end users has the advantage of cutting out the costs and margins of software wholesalers and retailers (often 35 to 50 percent of the retail price). In addition, allowing customers to download their software purchases immediately eliminates the costs of producing and packaging CDs. However, software developers are still strongly motivated to continue to distribute their products through wholesalers and retailers (to maintain broad access to existing and potential users who, for whatever reason, may be reluctant to buy online).

Despite the channel conflict that exists when a manufacturer sells directly to end users at its Web site in head-to-head competition with its distribution channel allies, there are three major reasons why manufacturers might want to aggressively pursue online sales and establish the Internet as an important distribution channel alongside traditional channels:

1. The manufacturer's profit margin from online sales is bigger than that from sales through wholesale/retail channels.

2. Encouraging buyers to visit the company's Web site helps educate them to the ease and convenience of purchasing online, thus encouraging more and more buyers to migrate to buying online (where company profit margins are greater).

3. Selling directly to end users allows a manufacturer to make greater use of build-to-order manufacturing and assembly as a basis for bypassing traditional distribution channels entirely. Dell Computer, for instance, has used online sales to make

build-to-order options a cost-effective reality. Similarly, several motor vehicle companies have initiated actions to streamline build-to-order manufacturing capabilities and reduce delivery times for custom orders from 30–60 days to as few as 5–10 days; most vehicle manufacturers already have software on their Web sites that permits motor vehicle shoppers to select the models, colors, and optional equipment they would like to have. In industries where build-to-order options can result in substantial cost savings along the industry value chain and permit sizable price reductions to end users, companies have to consider making build-to-order and sell-direct an integral part of their market positioning strategy. Over time, such a strategy could increase the rate at which sales migrate from distribution allies to the company's Web site.

A combination brick-and-click market positioning strategy is highly suitable when online sales have a good chance of *evolving* into a manufacturer's primary distribution channel. In such instances, incurring channel conflict in the short term and competing against traditional distribution allies makes good strategic sense.

Many brick-and-mortar companies can enter online retailing at relatively low cost—all they need is a Web store and systems for filling and delivering individual customer orders. Brick-and-click strategies have two big strategic appeals for wholesale and retail enterprises: They are an economic means of expanding a company's geographic reach, and they give both existing and potential customers another choice of how to communicate with the company, shop for product information, make purchases, or resolve customer service problems. Brick-and-mortar distributors and retailers (as well as manufacturers with company-owned retail stores) can shift to brick-and-click strategies by using their current distribution centers and/or retail stores for picking orders from on-hand inventories and making deliveries. Walgreen's, a leading drugstore chain, allows customers to order a prescription online and then pick it up at a local store (using the drive-through window, in some cases). In banking, a brick-and-click strategy allows customers to use local branches and ATMs for depositing checks and getting cash while using online systems to pay bills, check account balances, and transfer funds. Many industrial distributors are finding it efficient for customers to place their orders over the Web rather than phoning them in or waiting for salespeople to call in person. Illustration Capsule 6.2 describes how Office Depot has successfully migrated from a traditional brick-and-mortar distribution strategy to a combination brick-and-click distribution strategy.

Strategies for Online Enterprises

A company that elects to use the Internet as its exclusive channel for accessing buyers is essentially an online business from the perspective of the customer. The company's Web site becomes its online store for making sales and delivering customer services. Except for advertising, the company's Web site functions as the sole point of all buyer–seller contact. Many so-called pure dot-com enterprises have chosen this strategic approach—prominent examples include eBay, Amazon.com, Yahoo, Buy.com, and Priceline.com. For a company to succeed in using the Internet as its exclusive distribution channel, its product or service must be one for which buying online holds strong appeal. Furthermore, judging from the evidence thus far, an online company's strategy must incorporate the following features:

- *The capability to deliver unique value to buyers*—Winning strategies succeed in drawing buyers because of the value being delivered. This means that online

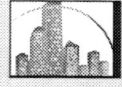

illustration capsule 6.2
Office Depot's Brick-and-Click Strategy

Office Depot was in the first wave of retailers to adopt a combination brick-and-click strategy. In 1996, it began allowing business customers to use the Internet to place orders. Businesses could thus avoid having to make a call, generate a purchase order, and pay an invoice—while still getting same-day or next-day delivery from one of Office Depot's local stores.

Office Depot built its Internet business around its existing network of 1,059 retail stores in 12 countries plus its 22 delivery centers and warehouses, 1,900 delivery trucks, 1,400 account managers, 60 sales offices, and 13 regional call centers that handled large business customers. It already had a solid brand name and enough purchasing power with its suppliers to counter discount-minded online rivals trying to attract buyers of office supplies on the basis of superlow prices. Office Depot's incremental investment to enter the e-commerce arena was minimal since all it needed to add was a Web site where customers could see pictures and descriptions of the 14,000 items it carried, their prices, and in-stock availability. Office Depot's marketing costs to make customers aware of its Web store option ran less than $10 million.

In setting up customized Web pages for 37,000 corporate and educational customers, Office Depot designed sites that allowed the customer's employees varying degrees of freedom to buy supplies. A clerk might be able to order only copying paper, toner cartridges, computer disks, and paper clips up to a preset dollar limit per order, while a vice president might have carte blanche to order any item Office Depot sold. Office Depot's online prices were the same as its store prices; the company's strategy was to promote Web sales on the basis of service, convenience, and lower customer costs for order processing and inventories.

In 2003, over 50 percent of Office Depot's major customers were ordering most of their supplies online because of the convenience and the savings in transactions costs. Bank of America, for example, was ordering 85 percent of its office supplies online from Office Depot.

Customers reported that using the Web site cut their transaction costs by up to 80 percent; plus, Office Depot's same-day or next-day delivery capability allowed them to reduce the amount of office supplies they kept in inventory.

Web site sales cost Office Depot less than $1 per $100 of goods ordered, compared with about $2 for phone and fax orders. And since Web sales eliminate the need to key in transactions, order-entry errors have been virtually eliminated and product returns cut by 50 percent. Billing is handled electronically.

Office Depot's online unit accounted for $2.1 billion in sales in 2002, up sharply from $982 million in 2000, making Office Depot the second-largest online retailer behind Amazon.com. Online sales were about 20 percent of the Office Depot's overall sales. Its online operations have been profitable from the start. Industry experts believe that Office Depot's success is based on the company's philosophy of maintaining a strong link between the Internet and its stores. "Office Depot gets it," noted one industry analyst. "It used the Net to build deeper relationships with customers."

Sources: www.officedepot.com, September 2003, and "Office Depot's e-Diva," *Business Week Online* (www.businessweek.com), August 6, 2001; Laura Lorek, "Office Depot Site Picks Up Speed." *Interactive Week* (www.zdnet.com/intweek), June 25, 2001; "Why Office Depot Loves the Net," *Business Week,* September 27, 1999, pp. EB 66, EB 68; and *Fortune,* November 8, 1999, p. 17.

businesses must usually attract buyers on the basis of something more than just low price—indeed, many dot-coms are already working to tilt the basis for competing away from low price and toward build-to-order systems, convenience, superior product information, attentive online service, and other ways to attract customers to buying online.

- *Deliberate efforts to engineer a value chain that enables differentiation, lower costs, or better value for the money*—For a company to win in the marketplace with an online-only distribution strategy, its value chain approach must hold potential for low-cost leadership, competitively valuable differentiating attributes, or a best-cost provider advantage. If a firm's strategy is to attract customers by selling at cut-rate prices, then it must possess cost advantages in those activities it performs, and it must outsource the remaining activities to low-cost specialists. If an online seller is going to differentiate itself on the basis of a superior buying experience and top-notch customer service, then it needs to concentrate on having an easy-to-navigate Web site, an array of functions and conveniences for customers, "Web reps" who can answer questions online, and logistical capabilities to deliver products quickly and accommodate returned merchandise. If it is going to deliver more value for the money, then it must manage value chain activities so as to deliver upscale products and services at lower costs than rivals. Absent a value chain that puts the company in an attractive position to compete head-to-head against other online and brick-and-mortar rivals, such a distribution strategy is unlikely to produce attractive profitability.

- *An innovative, fresh, and entertaining Web site*—Just as successful brick-and-mortar retailers employ merchandising strategies to keep their stores fresh and interesting to shoppers, Web merchandisers must exert ongoing efforts to add innovative site features and capabilities, enhance the look and feel of their sites, heighten viewer interest with audio and video, and have fresh product offerings and special promotions. Web pages need to be easy to read and interesting, with lots of eye appeal. Web site features that are distinctive, engaging, and entertaining add value to the experience of spending time at the site and are thus strong competitive assets.

- *A clear focus on a limited number of competencies and a relatively specialized number of value chain activities in which proprietary Internet applications and capabilities can be developed*—Low-value-added activities can be delegated to outside specialists. A strong market position is far more likely to emerge from efforts to develop proprietary Internet applications than from using third-party developers' software packages, which are also readily available to imitative rivals. Outsourcing value chain activities for which there is little potential for proprietary advantage allows an enterprise to concentrate on the ones for which it has the most expertise and through which it can gain competitive advantage.

- *Innovative marketing techniques that are efficient in reaching the targeted audience and effective in stimulating purchases (or boosting ancillary revenue sources like advertising)*—Web sites have to be cleverly marketed. Unless Web surfers hear about the site, like what they see on their first visit, and are intrigued enough to return again and again, the site will not generate enough revenue to allow the company to survive. Marketing campaigns that result only in heavy site traffic and lots of page views are seldom sufficient; the best test of effective marketing is the ratio at which page views are converted into revenues (the "look-to-buy" ratio). For example, in 2001 Yahoo's site traffic averaged 1.2 *billion* page views daily but generated only about $2 million in daily revenues; in contrast, the traffic at brokerage firm Charles Schwab's Web site averaged only 40 *million* page views per day but resulted in an average of $5 million daily in online commission revenues.

- *Minimal reliance on ancillary revenues*—Online businesses have to charge fully for the value delivered to customers rather than subsidizing artificially low prices with revenues collected from advertising and other ancillary sources. Companies should view site-advertising revenues and other revenue extras as a way to boost the profitability of an already profitable core businesses, *not* as a means of covering core business losses.

The Issue of Broad versus Narrow Product Offerings   Given that shelf space on the Internet is unlimited, online sellers have to make shrewd decisions about how to position themselves on the spectrum of broad versus narrow product offerings.

A one-stop shopping strategy like that employed by Amazon.com has the appealing economics of helping spread fixed operating costs over a wide number of items and a large customer base. Amazon has diversified its product offerings beyond books to include electronics, computers, housewares, music, DVDs, videos, cameras, toys, baby items and baby registry, software, computer and video games, cell phones and service, tools and hardware, travel services, magazine subscriptions, and outdoor-living items; it has also allowed small specialty-item e-tailers to market their products on the Amazon Web site. The company's tag line "Earth's Biggest Selection" seems accurate: In 2002, Amazon offered some 34 million items at its Web sites in the United States, Britain, France, Germany, Denmark, and Japan. Other e-tailers, such as Expedia and Hotel.com, have adopted classic focus strategies—building a Web site aimed at a sharply defined target audience shopping for a particular product or product category. "Focusers" seek to build customer loyalty based on attractively low prices, better value, wide selection of models and styles within the targeted category, convenient service, nifty options, or some other differentiating attribute. They pay special attention to the details that will please their narrow target audience.

The Order Fulfillment Issue   Another big strategic issue for dot-com retailers is whether to perform order fulfillment activities internally or to outsource them. Building central warehouses, stocking them with adequate inventories, and developing systems to pick, pack, and ship individual orders all require substantial start-up capital but may result in lower overall unit costs than would paying the fees of order fulfillment specialists who make a business of providing warehouse space, stocking inventories, and shipping orders for e-tailers. Outsourcing is likely to be economical unless an e-tailer has high unit volume and the capital to invest in its own order fulfillment capabilities. Buy.com, an online superstore consisting of some 30,000 items, obtains products from name-brand manufacturers and uses outsiders to stock and ship those products; thus, its focus is not on manufacturing or order fulfillment but rather on selling.

CHOOSING APPROPRIATE FUNCTIONAL-AREA STRATEGIES

A company's strategy is not complete until company managers have made strategic choices about how the various functional parts of the business—R&D, production, human resources, sales and marketing, finance, and so on—will be managed in support of its basic competitive strategy approach and the other important competitive moves being taken. Normally, functional-area strategy choices rank third on the menu of choosing among the various strategy options, as shown in Figure 6.1 (see p. 142). But whether commitments to particular functional strategies are made before or after the choices of complementary strategic options shown in Figure 6.1 is beside the point— what's really important is what the functional strategies are and how they mesh to enhance the success of the company's higher-level strategic thrusts.

In many respects, the nature of functional strategies is dictated by the choice of competitive strategy. For example, a manufacturer employing a low-cost provider strategy needs an R&D and product design strategy that emphasizes cheap-to-incorporate features and facilitates economical assembly and a production strategy that stresses capture of scale economies and actions to achieve low-cost manufacture (such as high labor productivity, efficient supply chain management, and automated production processes), and a low-budget marketing strategy. A business pursuing a high-end differentiation strategy needs a production strategy geared to top-notch quality and a marketing strategy aimed at touting differentiating features and using advertising and a trusted brand name to "pull" sales through the chosen distribution channels. A company using a focused differentiation strategy (like Krispy Kreme) needs a marketing strategy that stresses growing the niche (getting more people hooked on Krispy Kreme doughnuts), keeping buyer interest at a high level, and protecting the niche against invasion by outsiders.

Beyond very general prescriptions, it is difficult to say just what the content of the different functional-area strategies should be without first knowing what higher-level strategic choices a company has made, the industry environment in which it operates, the resource strengths that can be leveraged, and so on. Suffice it to say here that company personnel—both managers and employees charged with strategy-making responsibility down through the organizational hierarchy—must be clear about which higher-level strategies top management has chosen and then must tailor the company's functional-area strategies accordingly.

FIRST-MOVER ADVANTAGES AND DISADVANTAGES

When to make a strategic move is often as crucial as *what* move to make. Timing is especially important when *first-mover advantages* or *disadvantages* exist.[27] Being first to initiate a strategic move can have a high payoff in terms of strengthening a company's market position and competitiveness when (1) pioneering helps build a firm's image and reputation with buyers; (2) early commitments to new technologies, new-style components, distribution channels, and so on can produce an absolute cost advantage over rivals; (3) first-time customers remain strongly loyal to pioneering firms in making repeat purchases; and (4) moving first constitutes a preemptive strike, making imitation extra hard or unlikely. The bigger the first-mover advantages, the more attractive making the first move becomes.[28] In the Internet gold-rush era, several companies that were first with a new technology, network solution, or business model enjoyed lasting first-mover advantages in gaining the visibility and reputation needed to emerge as the dominant market leader—America Online, Amazon.com, Yahoo, eBay, and Priceline.com are cases in point. But a first-mover also needs to be a fast learner (so as to sustain any advantage of being a pioneer), and it helps immensely if the first-mover has deep financial pockets, important competencies and competitive capabilities, and high-quality management. Just being a first-mover by itself is seldom enough to yield competitive advantage. The proper target in timing a strategic move is not that of being the first company to do something but rather that of being the first competitor to put together the precise combination of features, customer value, and sound revenue-cost-profit economics that gives it an edge over rivals in the battle for market leadership.[29]

> **core concept**
> Because there are often important advantages to being a first-mover, competitive advantage can spring from *when* a move is made as well as from *what* move is made.

However, being a fast-follower or even a wait-and-see late-mover doesn't always carry a significant or lasting competitive penalty. There are times when a first-mover's skills, know-how, and actions are easily copied or even surpassed, allowing late-movers to catch or overtake the first-mover in a relatively short period. And there are times when there are actually *advantages* to being an adept follower rather than a first-mover. Late-mover advantages (or first-mover disadvantages) arise when (1) pioneering leadership is more costly than imitating followership and only negligible experience or learning-curve benefits accrue to the leader—a condition that allows a follower to end up with lower costs than the first-mover; (2) the products of an innovator are somewhat

Thompson–Strickland–Gamble:
Crafting and Executing
Strategy: Text and
Readings, 14th Edition

I. Concepts and
Techniques for Crafting
and Executing Strategy

6. Beyond Competitive
Strategy: Other Important
Strategy Choices

© The McGraw–Hill
Companies, 2004

168   Part 1 | Concepts and Techniques for Crafting and Executing Strategy

primitive and do not live up to buyer expectations, thus allowing a clever follower to win disenchanted buyers away from the leader with better-performing next-generation products; and (3) technology is advancing rapidly, giving fast-followers the opening to leapfrog a first-mover's products with more attractive and full-featured second- and third-generation products.

In weighing the pros and cons of being a first-mover versus a fast-follower, it is important to discern when the race to market leadership in a particular industry is a marathon rather than a sprint. In marathons, a slow-mover is not unduly penalized—first-mover advantages can be fleeting, and there's ample time for followers to play catch-up.[30] For instance, it took seven years for videocassette recorders to find their way into 1 million U.S. homes but only a year and a half for 10 million users to sign up for Hotmail. The lesson here is that there is a market-penetration curve for every emerging opportunity; typically, the curve has an inflection point at which all the pieces of the business model fall into place, buyer demand explodes, and the market takes off. The inflection point can come early on a fast-rising curve or farther on up a slow-rising curve. Any company that seeks competitive advantage by being a first-mover should thus first pose some hard questions: Does market takeoff depend on the development of complementary products or services that currently are not available? Is new infrastructure required before buyer demand can surge? Will buyers need to learn new skills or adopt new behaviors? Will buyers encounter high switching costs? Are there influential competitors in a position to derail the efforts of a first-mover? When the answers to any of these questions are yes, then a company must be careful not to pour too many resources into getting ahead of the market opportunity—the race is likely going to be more of a 10-year marathon than a 2-year sprint. But being first out of the starting block is competitively important if it produces clear and substantial benefits to buyers and competitors will be compelled to follow.

While being an adept fast-follower has the advantages of being less risky and skirting the costs of pioneering, rarely does a company have much to gain from being a slow-follower and concentrating on avoiding the "mistakes" of first-movers. Habitual late-movers, while often able to survive, are usually fighting to retain their customers and scrambling to keep pace with more progressive and innovative rivals. For a habitual late-mover to catch up, it must count on first-movers to be slow learners—plus it has to hope that buyers will be slow to gravitate to the products of first-movers, again giving it time to catch up. And it has to have competencies and capabilities that are sufficiently strong to allow it to close the gap fairly quickly once it makes its move. Counting on all first-movers to stumble or otherwise be easily overtaken is usually a bad bet that puts a late-mover's competitive position at risk.

Illustration Capsule 6.3 describes the challenges that late-moving telephone companies have in winning the battle to supply high-speed Internet access and overcoming the first-mover advantages of cable companies.

key points

Once a company has selected which of the five basic competitive strategies to employ in its quest for competitive advantage, it must then decide whether to supplement its choice of a basic competitive strategy approach with strategic actions relating to forming alliances and collaborative partnerships, pursuing mergers and acquisitions, integrating forward or backward, outsourcing certain value chain activities, making offensive and defensive moves, and what use to make of the Internet in selling directly to end users, as shown in Figure 6.1.

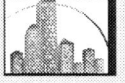 illustration capsule 6.3
The Battle in Consumer Broadband: First-Movers versus Late-Movers

In 1988 an engineer at the Bell companies' research labs figured out how to rush signals along ordinary copper wire at high speed using digital technology, thus creating the digital subscriber line (DSL). But the regional Bells, which dominated the local telephone market, showed little interest over the next 10 years, believing it was more lucrative to rent T-1 lines to businesses that needed fast data transmission capability and rent second phone lines to households wanting an Internet connection that didn't disrupt their regular telephone service. Furthermore, telephone executives were skeptical about DSL technology—there were a host of technical snarls to overcome, and early users encountered annoying glitches. Many executives doubted that it made good sense to invest billions of dollars in the infrastructure needed to roll out DSL to residential and small business customers, given the success they were having with T-1 and second-line rentals. As a consequence, the Bells didn't seriously begin to market DSL until the late 1990s, two years after the cable TV companies began their push to market cable broadband.

Cable companies were more than happy to be the first-movers in marketing broadband service via their copper cable wires, chiefly because their business was threatened by satellite TV technology and they saw broadband as an innovative service they could provide that the satellite companies could not. (Delivering broadband service via satellite has yet to become a factor in the marketplace, winning only a 1 percent share in 2003.) Cable companies were able to deploy broadband on their copper wire economically because during the 1980s and early 1990s most cable operators had spent about $60 billion to upgrade their systems with fiber-optic technology in order to handle two-way traffic rather than just one-way TV signals and thereby make good on their promises to local governments to develop "interactive" cable systems if they were awarded franchises. Although the early interactive services were duds, technicians discovered in the mid-1990s that the two-way systems enabled high-speed Internet hookups.

With Internet excitement surging in the late 1990s, cable executives saw high-speed Internet service as a no-brainer and began rolling it out to customers in 1998, securing about 362,000 customers by year-end versus only about 41,000 for DSL. Part of the early success of cable broadband was due to a cost advantage in modems—cable

executives, seeing the potential of cable broadband several years earlier, had asked CableLabs to standardize the technology for cable modems, a move that lowered costs and made cable modems marketable in consumer electronics stores. DSL modems were substantially more complicated, and it took longer to drive the costs down from several hundred dollars each to under $100—today, both cable and phone companies pay about $50 for modems, but cable modems got there much sooner.

As cable broadband began to attract more and more attention, the regional Bells continued to move slowly on DSL. The technical problems lingered, and early users were disgruntled by a host of annoying and sometimes horrendous installation difficulties and service glitches. Not only did providing users with convenient and reliable service prove to be a formidable challenge, but some regulatory issues stood in the way as well. And it continues to be hard to justify multibillion-dollar investments to install the necessary equipment and support systems to offer, market, manage, and maintain DSL service on the vast scale of a regional Bell company. SBC Communications figured it would cost at least $6 billion to roll out DSL to its customers. Verizon estimated that it would take 3.5 to 4 million customers to make DSL economics work, a number it would probably not reach until the end of 2005.

In 2003, high-speed consumer access to the Internet was a surging business with a bright outlook and cable broadband was the preferred choice—70 percent of the market was opting for cable modems supplied by cable TV companies instead of DSL service offered by the local phone companies. While only about 13 million of the 115 million U.S. households had cable Internet access and only 7.3 million had DSL in June 2003, the number of Internet users upgrading to high-speed service was growing by several hundred thousand monthly. Moreover, over half of the households subscribing to cable broadband and DSL were disconnecting their second phone lines, once used to connect to the Internet. While an additional 25 to 30 million households and small businesses were expected to upgrade to broadband in the next several years, it was questionable whether DSL broadband would be able to catch cable broadband in the marketplace. Phone company executives were hopeful that DSL could close the gap, despite its late start.

Source: Shawn Young and Peter Grant, "How Phone Firms Lost to Cable in Consumer Broadband Market," *The Wall Street Journal,* March 13, 2003, pp. A1, A6.

Many companies are using strategic alliances and collaborative partnerships to help them in the race to build a global market presence and in the technology race. Even large and financially strong companies have concluded that simultaneously running both races requires more diverse and expansive skills and competitive capabilities than they can assemble and manage alone. Strategic alliances are an attractive, flexible, and often cost-effective means by which companies can gain access to missing technology, expertise, and business capabilities. The competitive attraction of alliances is to bundle competencies and resources that are more valuable in a joint effort than when kept separate. Competitive advantage emerges when a company acquires valuable resources and capabilities through alliances that it could not readily obtain on its own and that give it an edge over rivals.

Mergers and acquisitions are another attractive strategic option for strengthening a firm's competitiveness. Companies racing for global market leadership frequently make acquisitions to build a market presence in countries where they currently do not compete. Similarly, companies racing to establish attractive positions in the industries of the future merge or make acquisitions to close gaps in resources or technology, build important technological capabilities, and move into position to launch next-wave products and services. When the operations of two companies are combined via merger or acquisition, the new company's competitiveness can be enhanced in any of several ways—lower costs; stronger technological skills; more or better competitive capabilities; a more attractive lineup of products and services; wider geographic coverage; and/or greater financial resources with which to invest in R&D, add capacity, or expand into new areas.

Vertically integrating forward or backward makes strategic sense only if it strengthens a company's position via either cost reduction or creation of a differentiation-based advantage. Otherwise, the drawbacks of vertical integration (increased investment, greater business risk, increased vulnerability to technological changes, and less flexibility in making product changes) outweigh the advantages (better coordination of production flows and technological know-how from stage to stage, more specialized use of technology, greater internal control over operations, greater scale economies, and matching production with sales and marketing). Collaborative partnerships with suppliers and/or distribution allies often permit a company to achieve the advantages of vertical integration without encountering the drawbacks.

Outsourcing pieces of the value chain formerly performed in-house can enhance a company's competitiveness whenever (1) an activity can be performed better or more cheaply by outside specialists; (2) the activity is not crucial to the firm's ability to achieve sustainable competitive advantage and won't hollow out its core competencies, capabilities, or technical know-how; (3) outsourcing reduces the company's risk exposure to changing technology and/or changing buyer preferences; (4) outsourcing streamlines company operations in ways that improve organizational flexibility, cut cycle time, speed decision making, and reduce coordination costs; and/or (5) outsourcing allows a company to concentrate on its core business and do what it does best. In many situations outsourcing is a superior strategic alternative to vertical integration.

A variety of offensive strategic moves can be used to secure a competitive advantage. Strategic offensives can be aimed either at competitors' strengths or at their weaknesses; they can involve end runs or grand offensives on many fronts; they can be designed as guerrilla actions or as preemptive strikes; and the target of the offensive can be a market leader, a runner-up firm, or the smallest and/or weakest firms in the industry.

Defensive strategies to protect a company's position usually take the form of making moves that put obstacles in the path of would-be challengers and fortify the company's present position while undertaking actions to dissuade rivals from even trying to attack (by signaling that the resulting battle will be more costly to the challenger than it is worth).

One of the most pertinent strategic issues that companies face is how to use the Internet in positioning the company in the marketplace—as *only a means of disseminating product information* (with traditional distribution channel partners making all sales to end users), as a *secondary channel,* as *one of several important distribution channels,* as the company's *primary distribution channel,* or as the company's *exclusive channel for accessing customers.*

The timing of strategic moves also has relevance in the quest for competitive advantage. Because of the competitive importance that is sometimes associated with when a strategic move is made, company managers are obligated to carefully consider the advantages or disadvantages that attach to being a first-mover versus a fast-follower versus a wait-and-see late-mover. At the end of the day, though, the proper objective of a first-mover is that of being the first competitor to put together the precise combination of features, customer value, and sound revenue/cost/profit economics that puts it ahead of the pack in capturing an attractive market opportunity. Sometimes the company that first unlocks a profitable market opportunity is the first-mover and sometimes it is not—but the company that comes up with the key is surely the smart mover.

exercises

1. Go to www.google.com and do a search on "strategic alliances." Identify at least two companies in different industries that are making a significant use of strategic alliances as a core part of their strategies. In addition, identify who their alliances are with and describe the purpose of the alliances.

2. Go to www.google.com and do a search on "acquisition strategy." Identify at least two companies in different industries that are using acquisitions to strengthen their market positions. Identify some of the companies that have been acquired, and describe the purpose behind the acquisitions.

chapter eight

Tailoring Strategy to Fit Specific Industry and Company Situations

(©Images.com/CORBIS)

The best strategy for a given firm is ultimately a unique construction reflecting its particular circumstances.

—**Michael E. Porter**

Competing in the marketplace is like war. You have injuries and casualties, and the best strategy wins.

—**John Collins**

It is much better to make your own products obsolete than allow a competitor to do it.

—**Michael A. Cusamano and Richard W. Selby**

In a turbulent age, the only dependable advantage is reinventing your business model before circumstances force you to.

—**Gary Hamel and Liisa Välikangas**

Prior chapters have emphasized the analysis and options that go into matching a company's choice of strategy to (1) industry and competitive conditions and (2) its own resource strengths and weaknesses, competitive capabilities, opportunities and threats, and market position. But there's more to be revealed about the hows of matching the choices of strategy to a company's circumstances. This chapter looks at the strategy-making task in nine other commonly encountered situations:

1. Companies competing in emerging industries.

2. Companies competing in turbulent, high-velocity markets.

3. Companies competing in mature, slow-growth industries.

4. Companies competing in stagnant or declining industries.

5. Companies competing in fragmented industries.

6. Companies pursuing rapid growth.

7. Companies in industry leadership positions.

8. Companies in runner-up positions.

9. Companies in competitively weak positions or plagued by crisis conditions.

We selected these situations to shed still more light on the factors that managers need to consider in tailoring a company's strategy. When you finish this chapter, you will have a stronger grasp of the factors that managers have to weigh in choosing a strategy and what the pros and cons are for some of the heretofore unexplored strategic options that are open to a company.

STRATEGIES FOR COMPETING IN EMERGING INDUSTRIES

An *emerging industry* is one in the formative stage. Examples include wireless Internet communications, high-definition TV and liquid crystal display (LCD) TV screens, assisted living for the elderly, online education, organic food products, e-book publishing, and electronic banking. Many companies striving to establish a strong foothold in an emerging industry are in a start-up mode; they are busily perfecting technology, adding people, acquiring or constructing facilities, gearing up operations, and trying to broaden distribution and gain buyer acceptance. The business models and strategies of companies in an emerging industry are unproved—what appears to be a promising business concept and strategy may never generate attractive bottom-line profitability. Often, there are important product design problems and technological problems that remain to be worked out.

Challenges When Competing in Emerging Industries

Competing in emerging industries presents managers with some unique strategy-making challenges:[1]

- Because the market is new and unproved, there may be much speculation about how it will function, how fast it will grow, and how big it will get. The little historical information available is virtually useless in making sales and profit projections. There's lots of guesswork about how rapidly buyers will be attracted and how much they will be willing to pay. For example, there is still uncertainty about how quickly the demand for high-definition TV sets will grow following the 2003 law requiring all U.S. TV stations to broadcast digital programs.

- In many cases, much of the technological know-how underlying the products of emerging industries is proprietary and closely guarded, having been developed in-house by pioneering firms; patents and unique technical expertise are key factors in securing competitive advantage. In other cases, the technology is multifaceted, entailing parallel or collaborative efforts on the part of several enterprises and perhaps competing technological approaches.

- Often, there is no consensus regarding which of several competing technologies will win out or which product attributes will prove decisive in winning buyer favor—as is the case in high-speed Internet access where cable modems, digital subscriber line (DSL), and wireless technologies are competing vigorously. Until market forces sort these things out, wide differences in product quality and performance are typical. Rivalry therefore centers on each firm's efforts to get the market to ratify its own strategic approach to technology, product design, marketing, and distribution.

- Entry barriers tend to be relatively low, even for entrepreneurial start-up companies. Large, well-known, opportunity-seeking companies with ample resources and competitive capabilities are likely to enter if the industry has promise for explosive growth or if its emergence threatens their present business. For instance, many traditional local telephone companies, seeing the potent threat of wireless communications technology, have opted to enter the mobile communications business in one way or another.

- Strong learning and experience curve effects may be present, allowing significant price reductions as volume builds and costs fall.

- Since in an emerging industry all buyers are first-time users, the marketing task is to induce initial purchase and to overcome customer concerns about product features, performance reliability, and conflicting claims of rival firms.

- Many potential buyers expect first-generation products to be rapidly improved, so they delay purchase until technology and product design mature and second- or third-generation products appear on the market.

- Sometimes, firms have trouble securing ample supplies of raw materials and components (until suppliers gear up to meet the industry's needs).

- Undercapitalized companies, finding themselves short of funds to support needed R&D and get through several lean years until the product catches on, end up merging with competitors or being acquired by financially strong outsiders looking to invest in a growth market.

The two critical strategic issues confronting firms in an emerging industry are (1) how to finance initial operations until sales and revenues take off, and (2) what market segments and competitive advantages to go after in trying to secure a front-runner position.[2] Competitive strategies keyed either to low cost or differentiation are usually viable. Focusing makes good sense when resources and capabilities are limited and the industry has too many technological frontiers or too many buyer segments to pursue at once. The lack of established "rules of the game" gives industry participants considerable freedom to experiment with a variety of different strategic approaches. Nonetheless, a firm with solid resource capabilities, an appealing business model, and a good strategy has a golden opportunity to shape the rules and establish itself as the recognized industry front-runner.

Strategic Avenues for Competing in an Emerging Industry

Dealing with all the risks and opportunities of an emerging industry is one of the most challenging business strategy problems. To be successful in an emerging industry, companies usually have to pursue one or more of the following strategic avenues:[3]

1. Try to win the early race for industry leadership with risk-taking entrepreneurship and a bold creative strategy. Broad or focused differentiation strategies keyed to technological or product superiority typically offer the best chance for early competitive advantage.

2. Push to perfect the technology, improve product quality, and develop additional attractive performance features.

3. As technological uncertainty clears and a dominant technology emerges, adopt it quickly. (However, while there's merit in trying to be the industry standard-bearer on technology and to pioneer the dominant product design, firms have to beware of betting too heavily on their own preferred technological approach or product design—especially when there are many competing technologies, R&D is costly, and technological developments can quickly move in surprising new directions.)

4. Form strategic alliances with key suppliers to gain access to specialized skills, technological capabilities, and critical materials or components.

5. Acquire or form alliances with companies that have related or complementary technological expertise as a means of helping outcompete rivals on the basis of technological superiority.

6. Try to capture any first-mover advantages associated with early commitments to promising technologies.

7. Pursue new customer groups, new user applications, and entry into new geographical areas (perhaps using strategic partnerships or joint ventures if financial resources are constrained).

> Strategic success in an emerging industry calls for bold entrepreneurship, a willingness to pioneer and take risks, an intuitive feel for what buyers will like, quick response to new developments, and opportunistic strategy making.

8. Make it easy and cheap for first-time buyers to try the industry's first-generation product. Then, as the product becomes familiar to a wide portion of the market, begin to shift the advertising emphasis from creating product awareness to increasing frequency of use and building brand loyalty.

9. Use price cuts to attract the next layer of price-sensitive buyers into the market.

> The early leaders in an emerging industry cannot rest on their laurels; they must drive hard to strengthen their resource capabilities and build a position strong enough to ward off newcomers and compete successfully for the long haul.

The short-term value of winning the early race for growth and market share leadership has to be balanced against the longer-range need to build a durable competitive edge and a defendable market position.[4] Well-financed outsiders are certain to move in with aggressive strategies as industry sales start to take off and the perceived risk of investing in the industry lessens. A rush of new entrants, attracted by the growth and profit potential, may crowd the market and force industry consolidation to a smaller number of players. Resource-rich latecomers, aspiring to industry leadership, may be able to become major players by acquiring and merging the operations of weaker competitors and then launching strategic offensives to build market share and gain quick brand-name recognition. Strategies must be aimed at competing for the long haul; often, this means sacrificing some degree of short-term profitability in order to invest in the resources, capabilities, and market recognition needed to sustain early successes.

Young companies in fast-growing markets face three strategic hurdles: (1) managing their own rapid expansion, (2) defending against competitors trying to horn in on their success, and (3) building a competitive position extending beyond their initial product or market. Up-and-coming companies can help their cause by selecting knowledgeable members for their boards of directors, by hiring entrepreneurial managers with experience in guiding young businesses through the start-up and takeoff stages, by concentrating on out-innovating the competition, and perhaps by merging with or acquiring another firm to gain added expertise and a stronger resource base.

STRATEGIES FOR COMPETING IN TURBULENT, HIGH-VELOCITY MARKETS

More and more companies are finding themselves in industry situations characterized by rapid technological change, short product life cycles because of entry of important new rivals into the marketplace, frequent launches of new competitive moves by rivals, and fast-evolving customer requirements and expectations—all occurring at once. Since news of this or that important competitive development arrives daily, it is an imposing task just to monitor and assess developing events. High-velocity change is plainly the prevailing condition in personal computer hardware and software, video games, networking, wireless telecommunications, medical equipment, biotechnology, prescription drugs, and virtually all Internet industries.

Strategic Postures for Coping with Rapid Change

The central strategy-making challenge in a turbulent market environment is managing change.[5] As illustrated in Figure 8.1, a company can assume any of three strategic postures in dealing with high-velocity change:[6]

- *It can react to change.* The company can respond to a rival's new product with a better product. It can counter an unexpected shift in buyer tastes and buyer demand

figure 8.1 **Meeting the Challenge of High-Velocity Change**

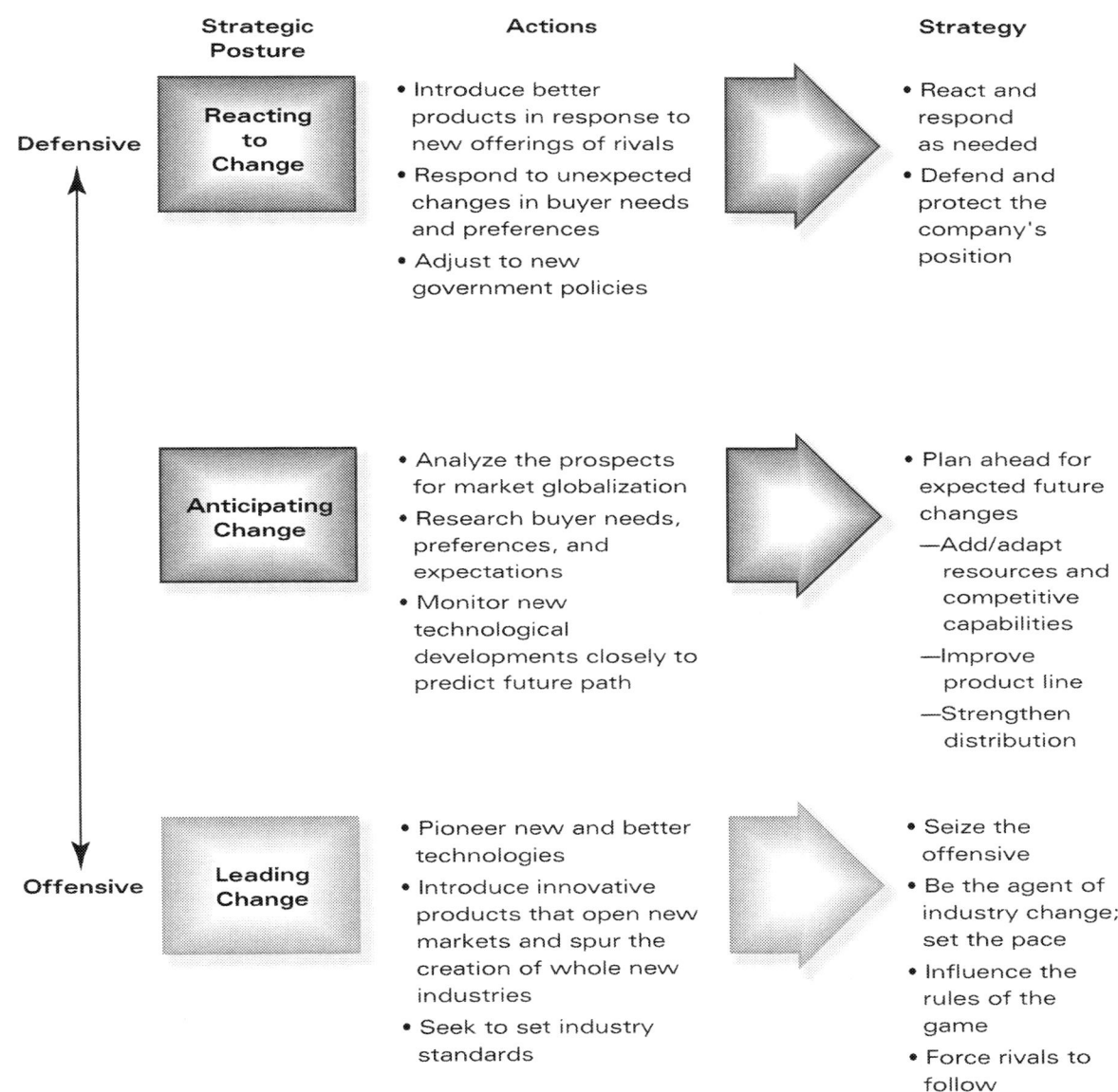

Source: Reprinted by permission of Harvard Business School Press. From *Competing on the Edge: Strategy as Structured Chaos* by Shona L. Brown and Kathleen M. Eisenhardt, Boston, MA 1998, p. 5. Copyright ©1998 by the Harvard Business School Publishing Corporation; all rights reserved.

by redesigning or repackaging its product, or shifting its advertising emphasis to different product attributes. Reacting is a defensive strategy and is therefore unlikely to create fresh opportunity, but it is nonetheless a necessary component in a company's arsenal of options.

- *It can anticipate change, make plans for dealing with the expected changes, and follow its plans as changes occur (fine-tuning them as may be needed).* Anticipation entails looking ahead to analyze what is likely to occur and then preparing and positioning for that future. It entails studying buyer behavior, buyer needs, and buyer expectations to get insight into how the market will evolve, then lining up the necessary production and distribution capabilities ahead of time. Like reacting to change, anticipating change is still fundamentally defensive in that forces outside the enterprise are in the driver's seat. Anticipation, however, can open up new opportunities and thus is a better way to manage change than just pure reaction.

> Reacting to change and anticipating change are basically defensive postures; leading change is an offensive posture.

- *It can lead change.* Leading change entails initiating the market and competitive forces that others must respond to—*it is an offensive strategy aimed at putting a company in the driver's seat.* Leading change means being first to market with an important new product or service. It means being the technological leader, rushing next-generation products to market ahead of rivals, and having products whose features and attributes shape customer preferences and expectations. It means proactively seeking to shape the rules of the game.

> Industry leaders are proactive agents of change, not reactive followers and analyzers. Moreover, they improvise, experiment, develop options, and adapt rapidly.

As a practical matter, a company's approach to managing change should, ideally, incorporate all three postures (though not in the same proportion). The best-performing companies in high-velocity markets consistently seek to lead change with proactive strategies that often entail the flexibility to pursue any of several strategic options, depending on how the market actually evolves. Even so, an environment of relentless change makes it incumbent on any company to anticipate and prepare for the future and to react quickly to unpredictable or uncontrollable new developments.

Strategic Moves for Fast-Changing Markets

Competitive success in fast-changing markets tends to hinge on a company's ability to improvise, experiment, adapt, reinvent, and regenerate as market and competitive conditions shift rapidly and sometimes unpredictably.[7] It has to constantly reshape its strategy and its basis for competitive advantage. While the process of altering offensive and defensive moves every few months or weeks to keep the overall strategy closely matched to changing conditions is inefficient, the alternative—a fast-obsolescing strategy—is worse. The following five strategic moves seem to offer the best payoffs:

1. *Invest aggressively in R&D to stay on the leading edge of technological know-how.* Translating technological advances into innovative new products (and remaining close on the heels of whatever advances and features are pioneered by rivals) is a necessity in industries where technology is the primary driver of change. But it is often desirable to focus the R&D effort on a few critical areas, not only to avoid stretching the company's resources too thin but also to deepen the firm's expertise, master the technology, fully capture learning-curve effects, and become the dominant leader in a particular technology or product category.[8] When a fast-evolving market environment entails many technological areas and product categories, competitors have little choice but to employ some type of focus strategy and concentrate on being the leader in a particular product/technology category.

2. *Develop quick-response capability.* Because no company can predict all of the changes that will occur, it is crucial to have the organizational capability to be able to react quickly, improvising if necessary. This means shifting resources internally, adapting existing competencies and capabilities, creating new competencies and capabilities, and not falling far behind rivals. Companies that are habitual late-movers are destined to be industry also-rans.

3. *Rely on strategic partnerships with outside suppliers and with companies making tie-in products.* In many high-velocity industries, technology is branching off to create so many new technological paths and product categories that no company has the resources and competencies to pursue them all. Specialization (to promote the necessary technical depth) and focus (to preserve organizational agility and leverage the firm's expertise) are desirable strategies. Companies build their competitive position not just by strengthening their own internal resource base but also by partnering with those suppliers making state-of-the-art parts and components and by collaborating closely with both the developers of related technologies and the makers of tie-in products. For example, personal computer companies like Gateway, Dell, Compaq, and Acer rely heavily on the developers and manufacturers of chips, monitors, hard drives, DVD players, and software for innovative advances in PCs. None of the PC makers have done much in the way of integrating backward into parts and components because they have learned that the most effective way to provide PC users with a state-of-the-art product is to outsource the latest, most advanced components from technologically sophisticated suppliers who make it their business to stay on the cutting edge of their specialization and who can achieve economies of scale by mass-producing components for many PC assemblers. An outsourcing strategy also allows a company the flexibility to replace suppliers that fall behind on technology or product features or that cease to be competitive on price. The managerial challenge here is to strike a good balance between building a rich internal resource base that, on the one hand, keeps the firm from being at the mercy of its suppliers and allies and, on the other hand, maintains organizational agility by relying on the resources and expertise of capable (and perhaps "best-in-world") outsiders.

4. *Initiate fresh actions every few months, not just when a competitive response is needed.* In some sense, change is partly triggered by the passage of time rather than solely by the occurrence of events. A company can be proactive by making *time-paced moves*—introducing a new or improved product every four months, rather than when the market tapers off or a rival introduces a next-generation model.[9] Similarly, a company can expand into a new geographic market every six months rather than waiting for a new market opportunity to present itself; it can also refresh existing brands every two years rather than waiting until their popularity wanes. The keys to successfully using time pacing as a strategic weapon are choosing intervals that make sense internally and externally, establishing an internal organizational rhythm for change, and choreographing the transitions. 3M Corporation has long pursued an objective of having 25 percent of its revenues come from products less than four years old, a force that established the rhythm of change and created a relentless push for new products. Recently, the firm's CEO upped the tempo of change at 3M by increasing the percentage from 25 percent to 30 percent.

5. *Keep the company's products and services fresh and exciting enough to stand out in the midst of all the change that is taking place.* One of the risks of rapid change is that products and even companies can get lost in the shuffle. The marketing challenge here is to keep the firm's products and services in the limelight and, further, to keep them innovative and well matched to the changes that are occurring in the marketplace.

Cutting-edge know-how and first-to-market capabilities are very valuable competitive assets in fast-evolving markets. Moreover, action-packed competition demands that a company have quick reaction times and flexible, adaptable resources—organizational

> In fast-paced markets, in-depth expertise, speed, agility, innovativeness, opportunism, and resource flexibility are critical organizational capabilities.

agility is a huge competitive asset. Even so, companies will make mistakes and some things a company does are going to work better than others. When a company's strategy doesn't seem to be working well, it has to quickly regroup—probing, experimenting, improvising, and trying again and again until it finds something that strikes the right chord with buyers and that puts it in sync with market and competitive realities.

STRATEGIES FOR COMPETING IN MATURING INDUSTRIES

A maturing industry is one that is moving from rapid growth to significantly slower growth. An industry is said to be mature when nearly all potential buyers are already users of the industry's products. In a mature market, demand consists mainly of replacement sales to existing users, with growth hinging on the industry's abilities to attract the few remaining new buyers and to convince existing buyers to up their usage. Consumer goods industries that are mature typically have a growth rate under 5 percent—roughly equal to the growth of the customer base or economy as a whole.

Industry Changes Resulting from Market Maturity

An industry's transition to maturity does not begin on an easily predicted schedule. Industry maturity can be forestalled by the emergence of new technological advances, product innovations, or other driving forces that keep rejuvenating market demand. Nonetheless, when growth rates do slacken, the onset of market maturity usually produces fundamental changes in the industry's competitive environment:[10]

1. *Slowing growth in buyer demand generates more head-to-head competition for market share.* Firms that want to continue on a rapid-growth track start looking for ways to take customers away from competitors. Outbreaks of price cutting, increased advertising, and other aggressive tactics to gain market share are common.

2. *Buyers become more sophisticated, often driving a harder bargain on repeat purchases.* Since buyers have experience with the product and are familiar with competing brands, they are better able to evaluate different brands and can use their knowledge to negotiate a better deal with sellers.

3. *Competition often produces a greater emphasis on cost and service.* As sellers all begin to offer the product attributes buyers prefer, buyer choices increasingly depend on which seller offers the best combination of price and service.

4. *Firms have a "topping-out" problem in adding new facilities.* Reduced rates of industry growth mean slowdowns in capacity expansion for manufacturers and slowdowns in new store growth for retail chains. With slower industry growth, adding too much capacity too soon can create oversupply conditions that adversely affect company profits well into the future.

5. *Product innovation and new end-use applications are harder to come by.* Producers find it increasingly difficult to create new product features, find further uses for the product, and sustain buyer excitement.

6. *International competition increases.* Growth-minded domestic firms start to seek out sales opportunities in foreign markets. Some companies, looking for ways to cut costs, relocate plants to countries with lower wage rates. Greater product

standardization and diffusion of technological know-how reduce entry barriers and make it possible for enterprising foreign companies to become serious market contenders in more countries. Industry leadership passes to companies that succeed in building strong competitive positions in most of the world's major geographic markets and in winning the biggest global market shares.

7. *Industry profitability falls temporarily or permanently.* Slower growth, increased competition, more sophisticated buyers, and occasional periods of overcapacity put pressure on industry profit margins. Weaker, less-efficient firms are usually the hardest hit.

8. *Stiffening competition induces a number of mergers and acquisitions among former competitors, drives the weakest firms out of the industry, and produces industry consolidation in general.* Inefficient firms and firms with weak competitive strategies can achieve respectable results in a fast-growing industry with booming sales. But the intensifying competition that accompanies industry maturity exposes competitive weakness and throws second- and third-tier competitors into a survival-of-the-fittest contest.

Strategic Moves in Maturing Industries

As the new competitive character of industry maturity begins to hit full force, any of several strategic moves can strengthen a firm's competitive position: pruning the product line, improving value chain efficiency, trimming costs, increasing sales to present customers, acquiring rival firms, expanding internationally, and strengthening capabilities.[11]

Pruning Marginal Products and Models A wide selection of models, features, and product options sometimes has competitive value during the growth stage, when buyers' needs are still evolving. But such variety can become too costly as price competition stiffens and profit margins are squeezed. Maintaining many product versions works against achieving design, parts inventory, and production economies at the manufacturing levels and can increase inventory stocking costs for distributors and retailers. In addition, the prices of slow-selling versions may not cover their true costs. Pruning marginal products from the line opens the door for cost savings and permits more concentration on items whose margins are highest and/or where a firm has a competitive advantage.

More Emphasis on Value Chain Innovation Efforts to reinvent the industry value chain can have a fourfold payoff: lower costs, better product or service quality, greater capability to turn out multiple or customized product versions, and shorter design-to-market cycles. Manufacturers can mechanize high-cost activities, redesign production lines to improve labor efficiency, build flexibility into the assembly process so that customized product versions can be easily produced, and increase use of advanced technology (robotics, computerized controls, and automatic guided vehicles). Suppliers of parts and components, manufacturers, and distributors can collaborate on the use of Internet technology and e-commerce techniques to streamline various value chain activities and implement cost-saving innovations.

Trimming Costs Stiffening price competition gives firms extra incentive to drive down unit costs. Company cost-reduction initiatives can cover a broad front. Some of the most frequently pursued options are pushing suppliers for better prices, implementing tighter supply chain management practices, cutting low-value activities out of the value chain, developing more economical product designs, reengineering internal processes using e-commerce technology, and shifting to more economical distribution arrangements.

Increasing Sales to Present Customers   In a mature market, growing by taking customers away from rivals may not be as appealing as expanding sales to existing customers. Strategies to increase purchases by existing customers can involve adding more sales promotions, providing complementary items and ancillary services, and finding more ways for customers to use the product. Convenience stores, for example, have boosted average sales per customer by adding video rentals, automated teller machines, gasoline pumps, and deli counters.

Acquiring Rival Firms at Bargain Prices   Sometimes a firm can acquire the facilities and assets of struggling rivals quite cheaply. Bargain-priced acquisitions can help create a low-cost position if they also present opportunities for greater operating efficiency. In addition, an acquired firm's customer base can provide expanded market coverage and opportunities for greater scale economies. The most desirable acquisitions are those that will significantly enhance the acquiring firm's competitive strength.

Expanding Internationally   As its domestic market matures, a firm may seek to enter foreign markets where attractive growth potential still exists and competitive pressures are not so strong. Many multinational companies are expanding into such emerging markets as China, India, Brazil, Argentina, and the Philippines, where the long-term growth prospects are quite attractive. Strategies to expand internationally also make sense when a domestic firm's skills, reputation, and product are readily transferable to foreign markets. For example, even though the U.S. market for soft drinks is mature, Coca-Cola has remained a growth company by upping its efforts to penetrate emerging markets where soft-drink sales are expanding rapidly.

Building New or More Flexible Capabilities   The stiffening pressures of competition in a maturing or already mature market can often be combated by strengthening the company's resource base and competitive capabilities. This can mean adding new competencies or capabilities, deepening existing competencies to make them harder to imitate, or striving to make core competencies more adaptable to changing customer requirements and expectations. Microsoft has responded to competitors' challenges by expanding its already large cadre of talented programmers. Chevron has developed a best-practices discovery team and a best-practices resource map to enhance the speed and effectiveness with which it is able to transfer efficiency improvements from one oil refinery to another.

Strategic Pitfalls in Maturing Industries

> One of the greatest strategic mistakes a firm can make in a maturing industry is pursuing a compromise strategy that leaves it stuck in the middle.

Perhaps the biggest strategic mistake a company can make as an industry matures is steering a middle course between low cost, differentiation, and focusing—blending efforts to achieve low cost with efforts to incorporate differentiating features and efforts to focus on a limited target market. Such strategic compromises typically leave the firm stuck in the middle with a fuzzy strategy, too little commitment to winning a competitive advantage, an average image with buyers, and little chance of springing into the ranks of the industry leaders.

Other strategic pitfalls include being slow to mount a defense against stiffening competitive pressures, concentrating more on protecting short-term profitability than on building or maintaining long-term competitive position, waiting too long to respond to price cutting by rivals, overexpanding in the face of slowing growth, overspending on advertising and sales promotion efforts in a losing effort to combat the growth slowdown, and failing to pursue cost reduction soon enough or aggressively enough.

STRATEGIES FOR FIRMS IN STAGNANT OR DECLINING INDUSTRIES

Many firms operate in industries where demand is growing more slowly than the economy-wide average or is even declining. Although harvesting the business to obtain the greatest cash flow, selling out, or preparing for closedown are obvious end-game strategies for uncommitted competitors with dim long-term prospects, strong competitors may be able to achieve good performance even in a stagnant market environment.[12] Stagnant demand by itself is not enough to make an industry unattractive. Selling out may or may not be practical, and closing operations is always a last resort.

Businesses competing in stagnant or declining industries must resign themselves to performance targets consistent with available market opportunities. Cash flow and return-on-investment criteria are more appropriate than growth-oriented performance measures, but sales and market-share growth are by no means ruled out. Strong competitors may be able to take sales from weaker rivals, and the acquisition or exit of weaker firms creates opportunities for the remaining companies to capture greater market share.

In general, companies that succeed in stagnant industries employ one or more of three strategic themes:[13]

1. *Pursue a focused strategy aimed at the fastest-growing market segments within the industry.* Stagnant or declining markets, like other markets, are composed of numerous segments or niches. Frequently, one or more of these segments is growing rapidly, despite stagnation in the industry as a whole. An astute competitor who zeroes in on fast-growing segments and does a first-rate job of meeting the needs of buyers comprising these segments can often escape stagnating sales and profits and even gain decided competitive advantage. For instance, both Ben & Jerry's and Häagen-Dazs have achieved success by focusing on the growing luxury or superpremium segment of the otherwise stagnant market for ice cream; revenue growth and profit margins are substantially higher for high-end ice creams sold in supermarkets and in scoop shops than is the case in other segments of the ice cream market.

> Achieving competitive advantage in stagnant or declining industries usually requires pursuing one of three competitive approaches: focusing on growing market segments within the industry, differentiating on the basis of better quality and frequent product innovation, or becoming a lower-cost producer.

2. *Stress differentiation based on quality improvement and product innovation.* Either enhanced quality or innovation can rejuvenate demand by creating important new growth segments or inducing buyers to trade up. Successful product innovation opens up an avenue for competing that bypasses meeting or beating rivals' prices. Differentiation based on successful innovation has the additional advantage of being difficult and expensive for rival firms to imitate. Sony has built a solid business selling high-quality multifeatured TVs, an industry where market demand has been relatively flat in the world's industrialized nations for some years. New Covent Garden Soup has met with success by introducing packaged fresh soups for sale in major supermarkets, where the typical soup offerings are canned or dry mixes.

Part 1 | Concepts and Techniques for Crafting and Executing Strategy

3. *Strive to drive costs down and become the industry's low-cost leader.* Companies in stagnant industries can improve profit margins and return on investment by pursuing innovative cost reduction year after year. Potential cost-saving actions include (*a*) cutting marginally beneficial activities out of the value chain; (*b*) outsourcing functions and activities that can be performed more cheaply by outsiders; (*c*) redesigning internal business processes to exploit cost-reducing e-commerce technologies; (*d*) consolidating underutilized production facilities; (*e*) adding more distribution channels to ensure the unit volume needed for low-cost production; (*f*) closing low-volume, high-cost retail outlets; and (*g*) pruning marginal products from the firm's offerings. Japan-based Asahi Glass (a low-cost producer of flat glass), PotashCorp and IMC Global (two low-cost leaders in potash production), Alcan Aluminum, Nucor Steel, and Safety Components International (a low-cost producer of air bags for motor vehicles) have all been successful in driving costs down in competitively tough and largely stagnant industry environments.

These three strategic themes are not mutually exclusive.[14] Introducing innovative versions of a product can *create* a fast-growing market segment. Similarly, relentless pursuit of greater operating efficiencies permits price reductions that create price-conscious growth segments. Note that all three themes are spinoffs of the generic competitive strategies, adjusted to fit the circumstances of a tough industry environment. The most attractive declining industries are those in which sales are eroding only slowly, there is large built-in demand, and some profitable niches remain.

The most common strategic mistakes companies make in stagnating or declining markets are (1) getting trapped in a profitless war of attrition, (2) diverting too much cash out of the business too quickly (thus further eroding performance), and (3) being overly optimistic about the industry's future and spending too much on improvements in anticipation that things will get better.

Illustration Capsule 8.1 describes the creative approach taken by Yamaha to combat the declining demand in the piano market.

STRATEGIES FOR COMPETING IN FRAGMENTED INDUSTRIES

A number of industries are populated by hundreds, even thousands, of small and medium-sized companies, many privately held and none with a substantial share of total industry sales.[15] The standout competitive feature of a fragmented industry is the absence of market leaders with king-sized market shares or widespread buyer recognition. Examples of fragmented industries include book publishing, landscaping and plant nurseries, real estate development, convenience stores, banking, health and medical care, mail order catalog sales, computer software development, custom printing, kitchen cabinets, trucking, auto repair, restaurants and fast food, public accounting, apparel manufacture and apparel retailing, paperboard boxes, hotels and motels, and furniture.

Reasons for Supply-Side Fragmentation

Any of several reasons can account for why the supply side of an industry is fragmented:

- Market demand is so extensive and so diverse that very large numbers of firms can easily coexist trying to accommodate the range and variety of buyer preferences

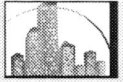

illustration capsule 8.1
Yamaha's Strategy in the Stagnant Piano Industry

For some years now, worldwide demand for pianos has been declining—in the mid-1980s the decline was 10 percent annually. Modern-day parents have not put the same stress on music lessons for their children as prior generations of parents did. In an effort to see if it could revitalize its piano business, Yamaha conducted a market research survey to learn what use was being made of pianos in households that owned one. The survey revealed that the overwhelming majority of the 40 million pianos in American, European, and Japanese households were seldom used. In most cases, the reasons the piano had been purchased no longer applied. Children had either stopped taking piano lessons or were grown and had left the household; adult household members played their pianos sparingly, if at all—only a small percentage were accomplished piano players. Most pianos were serving as a piece of fine furniture and were in good condition despite not being tuned regularly. The survey also confirmed that the income levels of piano owners were well above average.

Beginning in the late 1980s, Yamaha's piano strategists saw the idle pianos in these upscale households as a poten-

tial market opportunity. The strategy that emerged entailed marketing an attachment that would convert the piano into an old-fashioned automatic player piano capable of playing a wide number of selections recorded on disks. Concurrently, Yamaha introduced Disklavier, an upright acoustic player piano model that could record and play back performances up to 90 minutes long, making it simple to monitor student progress.

Over the past 15 years, Yamaha has introduced a host of Disklavier pianos—grand pianos, minigrand, upright, and console designs in a variety of styles and finishes. It has partnered with recording artists and music studios to make thousands of digital disks available for Yamaha piano owners, allowing them to enjoy concert-caliber performances in their home. And it has created a global music education program for both teachers and students—in 2003 Yamaha had about 750,000 students enrolled in its music education programs at some 7,500 locations across the world. Together, these efforts have helped rejuvenate and sustain Yamaha's piano business.

Source: www.yamaha.com.

and requirements and to cover all the needed geographic locations. This is true in the hotel and restaurant industry in New York City, London, or Tokyo, and the market for apparel. Likewise, there is ample room in the marketplace for numerous auto repair outlets, gasoline and convenience store retailers, and real estate firms.

- Low entry barriers allow small firms to enter quickly and cheaply.

- An absence of scale economies permits small companies to compete on an equal cost footing with larger firms.

- Buyers require relatively small quantities of customized products (as in business forms, interior design, kitchen cabinets, and advertising). Because demand for any particular product version is small, sales volumes are not adequate to support producing, distributing, or marketing on a scale that yields advantages to a large firm.

- The market for the industry's product or service is becoming more global, putting companies in more and more countries in the same competitive market arena (as in apparel manufacture).

- The technologies embodied in the industry's value chain are exploding into so many new areas and along so many different paths that specialization is essential just to keep abreast in any one area of expertise.

- The industry is young and crowded with aspiring contenders, with no firm having yet developed the resource base, competitive capabilities, and market recognition to command a significant market share (as in business-to-consumer retailing via the Internet).

Some fragmented industries consolidate over time as growth slows and the market matures. The stiffer competition that accompanies slower growth produces a shake-out of weak, inefficient firms and a greater concentration of larger, more visible sellers. Others remain atomistic because it is inherent in the nature of their businesses. And still others remain stuck in a fragmented state because existing firms lack the resources or ingenuity to employ a strategy powerful enough to drive industry consolidation.

Competitive rivalry in fragmented industries can vary from moderately strong to fierce. Low barriers tend to make entry of new competitors an ongoing threat. Competition from substitutes may or may not be a major factor. The relatively small size of companies in fragmented industries puts them in a relatively weak position to bargain with powerful suppliers and buyers, although sometimes they can become members of a cooperative formed for the purpose of using their combined leverage to negotiate better sales and purchase terms. In such an environment, the best a firm can expect is to cultivate a loyal customer base and grow a bit faster than the industry average. Competitive strategies based on either low cost or product differentiation are viable unless the industry's product is highly standardized or a commodity (like sand, concrete blocks, or paperboard boxes). Focusing on a well-defined market niche or buyer segment usually offers more competitive advantage potential than striving for broad market appeal.

> In fragmented industries competitors usually have wide enough strategic latitude (1) to either compete broadly or focus and (2) to pursue a low-cost, differentiation-based, or best-cost competitive advantage.

Strategy Options for a Fragmented Industry

Suitable competitive strategy options in a fragmented industry include:

- *Constructing and operating "formula" facilities*—This strategic approach is frequently employed in restaurant and retailing businesses operating at multiple locations. It involves constructing standardized outlets in favorable locations at minimum cost and then operating them cost-effectively. Yum! Brands (the parent of Pizza Hut, Taco Bell, KFC, Long John Silver's, and A&W restaurants), Home Depot, Staples, and 7-Eleven pursue this strategy.

- *Becoming a low-cost operator*—When price competition is intense and profit margins are under constant pressure, companies can stress no-frills operations featuring low overhead, high-productivity/low-cost labor, lean capital budgets, and dedicated pursuit of total operating efficiency. Successful low-cost producers in a fragmented industry can play the price-discounting game and still earn profits above the industry average. Many e-tailers compete on the basis of bargain prices; so do local tire retailers and supermarkets and off-brand gasoline stations.

- *Specializing by product type*—When a fragmented industry's products include a range of styles or services, a strategy to focus on one product or service category can be effective. Some firms in the furniture industry specialize in only one furniture type such as brass beds, rattan and wicker, lawn and garden, or early American. In auto repair, companies specialize in transmission repair, body work, or speedy oil changes.

- *Specializing by customer type*—A firm can stake out a market niche in a fragmented industry by catering to those customers who are interested in low prices, unique product attributes, customized features, carefree service, or other extras. A number of restaurants cater to take-out customers; others specialize in fine dining, and still others cater to the sports bar crowd.

- *Focusing on a limited geographic area*—Even though a firm in a fragmented industry can't win a big share of total industrywide sales, it can still try to dominate a local or regional geographic area. Concentrating company efforts on a limited territory can produce greater operating efficiency, speed delivery and customer services, promote strong brand awareness, and permit saturation advertising, while avoiding the diseconomies of stretching operations out over a much wider area. Supermarkets, banks, convenience stores, and sporting goods retailers successfully operate multiple locations within a limited geographic area.

In fragmented industries, firms generally have the strategic freedom to pursue broad or narrow market targets and low-cost or differentiation-based competitive advantages. Many different strategic approaches can exist side by side.

STRATEGIES FOR SUSTAINING RAPID COMPANY GROWTH

Companies that are focused on growing their revenues and earnings at a rapid or above-average pace year after year generally have to craft a portfolio of strategic initiatives covering three horizons:[16]

- *Horizon 1: "Short-jump" strategic initiatives to fortify and extend the company's position in existing businesses*—Short-jump initiatives typically include adding new items to the company's present product line, expanding into new geographic areas where the company does not yet have a market presence, and launching offensives to take market share away from rivals. The objective is to capitalize fully on whatever growth potential exists in the company's present business arenas.

- *Horizon 2: "Medium-jump" strategic initiatives to leverage existing resources and capabilities by entering new businesses with promising growth potential*—Growth companies have to be alert for opportunities to jump into new businesses where there is promise of rapid growth and where their experience, intellectual capital, and technological know-how will prove valuable in gaining rapid market penetration. While Horizon 2 initiatives may take a back seat to Horizon 1 initiatives as long as there is plenty of untapped growth in the company's present businesses, they move to the front as the onset of market maturity dims the company's growth prospects in its present business(es).

- *Horizon 3: "Long-jump" strategic initiatives to plant the seeds for ventures in businesses that do not yet exist*—Long-jump initiatives can entail pumping funds into long-range R&D projects, setting up an internal venture capital fund to invest in promising start-up companies attempting to create the industries of the future, or acquiring a number of small start-up companies experimenting with technologies and product ideas that complement the company's present businesses. Intel, for example, set up a multibillion-dollar venture fund to invest in over 100 different projects and start-up companies, the intent being to plant seeds for Intel's future, broadening its base as a global leader in supplying building blocks for PCs and the worldwide Internet economy. Royal Dutch/Shell, with over $140 billion in revenues and over 100,000 employees, spent over $20 million on rule-breaking, game-changing ideas put forth by free-thinking employees; the objective was to inject a new spirit of entrepreneurship into the company and sow the seeds of faster growth.[17]

| 292 | Thompson–Strickland–Gamble: Crafting and Executing Strategy: Text and Readings, 14th Edition | I. Concepts and Techniques for Crafting and Executing Strategy | 8. Tailoring Strategy to Fit Specific Industry and Company Situations | | © The McGraw–Hill Companies, 2004 |

218   Part 1 | Concepts and Techniques for Crafting and Executing Strategy

figure 8.2 **The Three Strategy Horizons for Sustaining Rapid Growth**

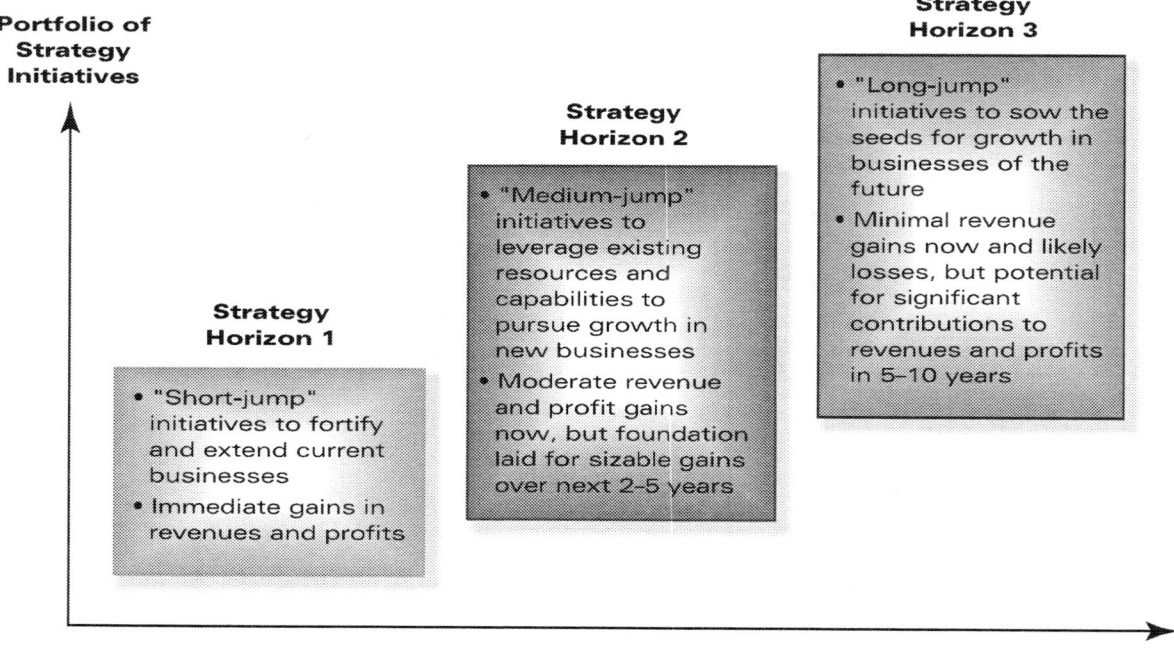

Source: Adapted from Eric D. Beinhocker, "Robust Adaptive Strategies," *Sloan Management Review* 40, No. 3 (Spring 1999), p. 101.

The three strategy horizons are illustrated in Figure 8.2. Managing such a portfolio of strategic initiatives to sustain rapid growth is not easy, however. The tendency of most companies is to focus on Horizon 1 strategies and devote only sporadic and uneven attention to Horizon 2 and 3 strategies. But a recent McKinsey & Company study of 30 of the world's leading growth companies revealed a relatively balanced portfolio of strategic initiatives covering all three horizons. The lesson of successful growth companies is that keeping a company's record of rapid growth intact over the long term entails crafting a diverse population of strategies, ranging from short-jump incremental strategies to grow present businesses to long-jump initiatives with a 5- to 10-year growth payoff horizon.[18] Having a mixture of short-jump, medium-jump, and long-jump initiatives not only increases the odds of hitting a few home runs but also provides some protection against unexpected adversity in present or newly entered businesses.

The Risks of Pursuing Multiple Strategy Horizons

There are, of course, risks to pursuing a diverse strategy portfolio aimed at sustained growth. A company cannot, of course, place bets on every opportunity that appears on its radar screen, lest it stretch its resources too thin. And medium-jump and long-jump initiatives can cause a company to stray far from its core competencies and end up trying to compete in businesses for which it is ill-suited. Moreover, it can be difficult to achieve competitive advantage in medium- and long-jump product families and businesses that prove not to mesh well with a company's present businesses and resource strengths. The payoffs of long-jump initiatives often prove elusive; not all of the seeds a company sows will bear fruit, and only a few may evolve into truly significant contributors to the company's revenue and profit growth. The losses from those long-jump ventures that do not take root may significantly erode the gains from those that do, resulting in disappointingly modest gains in overall profits.

STRATEGIES FOR INDUSTRY LEADERS

The competitive positions of industry leaders normally range from "stronger than average" to "powerful." Leaders typically are well known, and strongly entrenched leaders have proven strategies (keyed either to low-cost leadership or to differentiation). Some of the best-known industry leaders are Anheuser-Busch (beer), Starbucks (coffee drinks), Microsoft (computer software), Callaway (golf clubs), McDonald's (fast food), Gillette (razor blades), Campbell's Soup (canned soups), Gerber (baby food), Hewlett-Packard (printers), Nokia (cell phones), AT&T (long-distance telephone service), Eastman Kodak (camera film), Wal-Mart (discount retailing), Amazon.com (online shopping), eBay (online auctions), and Levi Strauss (jeans).

The main strategic concern for a leader revolves around how to defend and strengthen its leadership position, perhaps becoming the *dominant* leader as opposed to just *a* leader. However, the pursuit of industry leadership and large market share is primarily important because of the competitive advantage and profitability that accrue to being the industry's biggest company. Three contrasting strategic postures are open to industry leaders:[19]

1. Stay-on-the-offensive strategy—The central goal of a stay-on-the-offensive strategy is to be a first-mover and a proactive market leader.[20] It rests on the principle that staying a step ahead and forcing rivals into a catch-up mode is the surest path to industry prominence and potential market dominance—as the saying goes, the best defense is a good offense. Being the industry standard setter entails relentless pursuit of continuous improvement and innovation—being out front with technological improvements, new or better products, more attractive performance features, quality enhancements, improved customer service, ways to cut operating costs, and ways to make it easier and less costly for potential customers to switch their purchases from runner-up firms to its own products. A low-cost leader must set the pace for cost reduction, and a differentiator must constantly initiate new ways to keep its product set apart from the brands of imitative rivals in order to be the standard against which rivals' products are judged. The array of options for a potent stay-on-the-offensive strategy can also include initiatives to expand overall industry demand—spurring the creation of new families of products, making the product more suitable for consumers in emerging-country markets, discovering new uses for the product, attracting new users of the product, and promoting more frequent use.

> The two best tests of success of a stay-on-the-offensive strategy are (1) the extent to which it keeps rivals in a reactive mode, scrambling to keep up, and (2) whether the leader is growing faster than the industry as a whole and wresting market share from rivals.

Furthermore, unless a leader's market share is already so dominant that it presents a threat of antitrust action (a market share under 60 percent is usually safe), a potent stay-on-the-offensive strategy entails actions aimed at growing faster than the industry as a whole and wresting market share from rivals. A leader whose growth does not equal or outpace the industry average is losing ground to competitors.

2.   *Fortify-and-defend strategy*—The essence of "fortify and defend" is to make it harder for challengers to gain ground and for new firms to enter. The goals of a strong defense are to hold on to the present market share, strengthen current market position, and protect whatever competitive advantage the firm has. Specific defensive actions can include:

- Attempting to raise the competitive ante for challengers and new entrants via increased spending for advertising, higher levels of customer service, and bigger R&D outlays.

- Introducing more product versions or brands to match the product attributes that challenger brands have or to fill vacant niches that competitors could slip into.

- Adding personalized services and other extras that boost customer loyalty and make it harder or more costly for customers to switch to rival products.

- Keeping prices reasonable and quality attractive.

- Building new capacity ahead of market demand to discourage smaller competitors from adding capacity of their own.

- Investing enough to remain cost-competitive and technologically progressive.

- Patenting the feasible alternative technologies.

- Signing exclusive contracts with the best suppliers and dealer distributors.

> Industry leaders can strengthen their long-term competitive positions with strategies keyed to aggressive offense, aggressive defense, or muscling smaller rivals and customers into behaviors that bolster its own market standing.

A fortify-and-defend strategy best suits firms that have already achieved industry dominance and don't wish to risk antitrust action. It is also well suited to situations where a firm wishes to milk its present position for profits and cash flow because the industry's prospects for growth are low or because further gains in market share do not appear profitable enough to go after. But a fortify-and-defend strategy always entails trying to grow as fast as the market as a whole (to stave off market-share slippage) and requires reinvesting enough capital in the business to protect the leader's ability to compete.

3.   *Muscle-flexing strategy*—Here a dominant leader plays competitive hardball (presumably in an ethical and competitively legal manner) when smaller rivals rock the boat with price cuts or mount new market offensives that directly threaten its position. Specific responses can include quickly matching and perhaps exceeding challengers' price cuts, using large promotional campaigns to counter challengers' moves to gain market share, and offering better deals to their major customers. Dominant leaders may also court distributors assiduously to dissuade them from carrying rivals' products, provide salespersons with documented information about the weaknesses of competing products, or try to fill any vacant positions in their own firms by making attractive offers to the better executives of rivals that get out of line.

The leader may also use various arm-twisting tactics to pressure present customers not to use the products of rivals. This can range from simply forcefully communicating its displeasure should customers opt to use the products of rivals to pushing them to agree to exclusive arrangements in return for better prices to charging them a higher price if they use any competitors' products. As a final resort, a leader may grant certain customers special discounts or preferred treatment if they do not use any products of rivals.

The obvious risks of a muscle-flexing strategy are running afoul of the antitrust laws (as Microsoft did—see Illustration Capsule 8.2), alienating customers with bullying tactics, and arousing adverse public opinion. A company that tries to throw its weight around to protect and enhance its market dominance has got to be judicious, lest it cross the line from allowable tactics to unethical or illegal competitive practices.

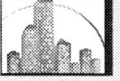 illustration capsule 8.2
How Microsoft Uses Its Muscle to Maintain Its Market Leadership

U.S. district judge Thomas Penfield Jackson concluded in 1999 in *U.S.* v. *Microsoft* that Microsoft repeatedly had used heavy-handed tactics to routinely pressure customers, crush competitors, and throttle competition. Judge Jackson painted Microsoft as a domineering company that rewarded its friends and punished its enemies, pointing to the following examples:

- Gateway and IBM, both of which resisted Microsoft's efforts to dissuade them from using or promoting competitors' products on their PCs, were forced to pay higher prices for installing Microsoft's Windows operating system on their PCs than several other PC makers had to pay.

- Microsoft tried to persuade Netscape to halt its development of platform-level technologies for Windows 95, arguing that Netscape's Navigator browser should be designed to run on Windows 95 only rather than be designed in a way that could serve as an alternative operating system platform and substitute for use of Windows. Microsoft wanted Netscape to agree to a special alliance with Microsoft that would allow Microsoft to incorporate Navigator's functionality into Windows. When Netscape refused, Microsoft withheld information about its Windows 95 code until after it released the new operating system and its own new version of Internet Explorer. Microsoft also refused to give Netscape a license to one of its scripting tools, thereby preventing Netscape from doing business with certain Internet service providers for a time. Simultaneously, Microsoft pressured PC makers to install Internet Explorer as the preferred alternative to Netscape Navigator. When Compaq removed the Internet Explorer icon from the opening screen of its computers and preinstalled the Navigator icon, Microsoft threatened to revoke Compaq's license to install Windows 95.

- Microsoft tried to convince Intel not to ship its newly developed Native Signal Processing (NSP) software (intended to help spark demand for Intel's most advanced microprocessors) because Microsoft felt that NSP represented an incursion into Microsoft's operating system platform territory. It also asked Intel to reduce the number of people working on software at Intel. Microsoft assured Intel that if it would stop promoting NSP, Microsoft would accelerate its own work to incorporate the functions of NSP into Windows. At the same time, Microsoft pressured PC makers not to install Intel's NSP software on their PCs.

- When Compaq Computer entered into an agreement with America Online (AOL) to promote AOL above all other online services and began to ship its computers with the Microsoft Network (MSN) icon removed and the AOL icon installed, Microsoft wrote Compaq a letter stating its intention to terminate Compaq's license for Windows 95 if it did not restore the MSN icon to its original position on the opening screen.

Despite the 1999 decision, Microsoft has continued to flex its muscles. In 2001, the company reduced its support for the language Java in its release of the new Windows XP operating system—Java is favored by Microsoft's longtime rival Sun Microsystems. Microsoft also pressured PC makers to display three of its own icons—for MSN online, Windows Media player, and Internet Explorer—on the Windows XP desktop. And it has consistently used harassing tactics against RealNetworks, a maker of media software that competes directly with Microsoft's Windows Media Player.

Sources: Don Clark, "Microsoft Raises Requirements on Icon Use by Computer Makers," *The Wall Street Journal* (www.wsj.com), August 9, 2001; D. Ian Hopper, "Microsoft Appeals to Supreme Court," Associated Press, August 8, 2001; John R. Wilke and Don Clark, "Senate Judiciary Committee Plans Microsoft Hearings," *The Wall Street Journal* (http://public.wsj.com), July 24, 2001; John R. Wilke and Don Clark, "Microsoft Pulls Back Support for Java," *The Wall Street Journal* (www.wsj.com), July 19, 2001; and transcript of Judge Jackson's findings of fact in *U.S.* v. *Microsoft,* November 5, 1999.

STRATEGIES FOR RUNNER-UP FIRMS

Runner-up or "second-tier" firms have smaller market shares than "first-tier" industry leaders. Some runner-up firms are up-and-coming *market challengers,* employing offensive strategies to gain market share and build a stronger market position. Other runner-up competitors are *focusers*, seeking to improve their lot by concentrating their attention on serving a limited portion of the market. There are, of course, always a number of firms in any industry that are destined to be *perennial runners-up*, lacking the resources and competitive strengths to do more than continue in trailing positions and/or content to follow the trendsetting moves of the market leaders.

Obstacles for Firms with Small Market Shares

In industries where big size is definitely a key success factor, firms with small market shares have some obstacles to overcome: (1) less access to economies of scale in manufacturing, distribution, or marketing and sales promotion; (2) difficulty in gaining customer recognition; (3) weaker ability to use mass media advertising; and (4) difficulty in funding capital requirements.[21] When significant scale economies give large-volume competitors a *dominating* cost advantage, small-share firms have only two viable strategic options: initiate offensive moves to gain sales and market share (so as to build the volume of business needed to approach the scale economies enjoyed by larger rivals) or withdraw from the business (gradually or quickly).

The competitive strategies most underdogs use to build market share and achieve critical scale economies are based on (1) using lower prices to win customers from weak higher-cost rivals; (2) merging with or acquiring rival firms to achieve the size needed to capture greater scale economies; (3) investing in new cost-saving facilities and equipment, perhaps relocating operations to countries where costs are significantly lower; and (4) pursuing technological innovations or radical value chain revamping to achieve dramatic cost savings.

But *it is erroneous to view runner-up firms as inherently less profitable or unable to hold their own against the biggest firms.* Many small and medium-sized firms earn healthy profits and enjoy good reputations with customers.

Strategic Approaches for Runner-Up Companies

Assuming that scale economies or learning-curve effects are relatively small and result in no important cost advantage for big-share firms, runner-up companies have considerable strategic flexibility and can consider any of the following seven approaches.

Offensive Strategies to Build Market Share   A challenger firm needs a strategy aimed at building a competitive advantage of its own. Rarely can a runner-up improve its competitive position by imitating the strategies of leading firms. A cardinal rule in offensive strategy is to avoid attacking a leader head-on with an imitative strategy, regardless of the resources and staying power an underdog may have.[22] Moreover, if a challenger has a 5 percent market share and needs a 20 percent share to earn attractive returns, it needs a more creative approach to competing than just "Try harder."

> Rarely can a runner-up firm successfully challenge an industry leader with a copycat strategy.

Ambitious runner-up companies have to make some waves in the marketplace if they want to make big market share gains. The best "mover-and-shaker" offensives usually involve one of the following approaches:

- Pioneering a leapfrog technological breakthrough.
- Getting new or better products into the market consistently ahead of rivals and building a reputation for product leadership.

- Being more agile and innovative in adapting to evolving market conditions and customer expectations than slower-to-change market leaders.

- Forging attractive strategic alliances with key distributors, dealers, or marketers of complementary products.

- Finding innovative ways to dramatically drive down costs and then using the attraction of lower prices to win customers from higher-cost, higher-priced rivals. A challenger firm can pursue aggressive cost reduction by eliminating marginal activities from its value chain, streamlining supply chain relationships, improving internal operating efficiency, using various e-commerce techniques, and merging with or acquiring rival firms to achieve the size needed to capture greater scale economies.

- Crafting an attractive differentiation strategy based on premium quality, technological superiority, outstanding customer service, rapid product innovation, or convenient online shopping options.

Without a potent offensive strategy to capture added market share, runner-up companies have to patiently nibble away at the lead of market leaders and build sales at a moderate pace over time.

Growth-via-Acquisition Strategy   One of the most frequently used strategies employed by ambitious runner-up companies is merging with or acquiring rivals to form an enterprise that has greater competitive strength and a larger share of the overall market. For an enterprise to succeed with this strategic approach, senior management must have the skills to assimilate the operations of the acquired companies, eliminating duplication and overlap, generating efficiencies and cost savings, and structuring the combined resources in ways that create substantially stronger competitive capabilities. Many banks owe their growth during the past decade to acquisition of smaller regional and local banks. Likewise, a number of book publishers have grown by acquiring small publishers. Cisco Systems has used acquisitions to become a leader in Internet networking products.

Vacant-Niche Strategy   This version of a focused strategy involves concentrating on specific customer groups or end-use applications that market leaders have bypassed or neglected. An ideal vacant niche is of sufficient size and scope to be profitable, has some growth potential, is well suited to a firm's own capabilities, and for one reason or another is hard for leading firms to serve. Two examples where vacant-niche strategies have worked successfully are (1) regional commuter airlines serving cities with too few passengers to fill the large jets flown by major airlines and (2) health-food producers (like Health Valley, Hain, and Tree of Life) that cater to local health-food stores—a market segment traditionally given little attention by Kraft, General Mills, Nestlé, Unilever, Campbell Soup, and other leading food products firms.

Specialist Strategy   A specialist firm trains its competitive effort on one technology, product or product family, end use, or market segment (often one in which buyers have special needs). The aim is to train the company's resource strengths and capabilities on building competitive advantage through leadership in a specific area. Smaller companies that successfully use this focused strategy include Formby's (a specialist in stains and finishes for wood furniture, especially refinishing); Blue Diamond (a California-based grower and marketer of almonds); Canada Dry (known for its ginger ale, tonic water, and carbonated soda water); and American Tobacco (a leader in chewing tobacco and snuff). Many companies in high-tech industries concentrate their energies on being the clear leader in a particular technological niche; their competitive advantage is superior technological depth, technical expertise that is highly valued by customers, and the capability to consistently beat out rivals in pioneering technological advances.

Superior Product Strategy   The approach here is to use a differentiation-based focused strategy keyed to superior product quality or unique attributes. Sales and marketing efforts are aimed directly at quality-conscious and performance-oriented buyers. Fine craftsmanship, prestige quality, frequent product innovations, and/or close contact with customers to solicit their input in developing a better product usually undergird the superior product approach. Some examples include Samuel Adams in beer, Tiffany in diamonds and jewelry, Chicago Cutlery in premium-quality kitchen knives, Baccarat in fine crystal, Cannondale in mountain bikes, Bally in shoes, and Patagonia in apparel for outdoor recreation enthusiasts.

Distinctive-Image Strategy   Some runner-up companies build their strategies around ways to make themselves stand out from competitors. A variety of distinctive-image strategies can be used: creating a reputation for charging the lowest prices, providing prestige quality at a good price, going all-out to give superior customer service, designing unique product attributes, being a leader in new product introduction, or devising unusually creative advertising. Examples include Dr Pepper's strategy in calling attention to its distinctive taste, Apple Computer's making it easier and more interesting for people to use its Macintosh PCs, and Mary Kay Cosmetics' distinctive use of the color pink.

Content Follower Strategy   Content followers deliberately refrain from initiating trendsetting strategic moves and from aggressive attempts to steal customers away from the leaders. Followers prefer approaches that will not provoke competitive retaliation, often opting for focus and differentiation strategies that keep them out of the leaders' paths. They react and respond rather than initiate and challenge. They prefer defense to offense. And they rarely get out of line with the leaders on price. They are content to simply maintain their market position, albeit sometimes struggling to do so. Followers have no urgent strategic questions to confront beyond "What strategic changes are the leaders initiating and what do we need to do to follow along and maintain our present position?" The marketers of private-label products tend to be followers, imitating many of the features of name-brand products and content to sell to price-conscious buyers at prices modestly below those of well-known brands.

STRATEGIES FOR WEAK AND CRISIS-RIDDEN BUSINESSES

A firm in an also-ran or declining competitive position has four basic strategic options. If it can come up with the financial resources, it can launch an *offensive turnaround strategy* keyed either to low-cost or "new" differentiation themes, pouring enough money and talent into the effort to move up a notch or two in the industry rankings and become a respectable market contender within five years or so. It can employ a *fortify-and-defend strategy,* using variations of its present strategy and fighting hard to keep sales, market share, profitability, and competitive position at current levels. It can opt for a *fast-exit strategy* and get out of the business, either by selling out to another firm or by closing down operations if a buyer cannot be found. Or it can employ an *end-game or slow-exit strategy*, keeping reinvestment to a bare-bones minimum and taking actions to maximize short-term cash flows in preparation for an orderly market exit.

> The strategic options for a competitively weak company include waging a modest offensive to improve its position, defending its present position, being acquired by another company, or employing an end-game strategy.

Turnaround Strategies for Businesses in Crisis

Turnaround strategies are needed when a business worth rescuing goes into crisis; the objective is to arrest and reverse the sources of competitive and financial weakness as quickly as possible. Management's first task in formulating a suitable turnaround strategy is to diagnose what lies at the root of poor performance. Is it an unexpected downturn in sales brought on by a weak economy? An ill-chosen competitive strategy? Poor execution of an otherwise workable strategy? High operating costs? Important resource deficiencies? An overload of debt? The next task is to decide whether the business can be saved or whether the situation is hopeless. Understanding what is wrong with the business and how serious its strategic problems are is essential because different diagnoses lead to different turnaround strategies.

Some of the most common causes of business trouble are taking on too much debt, overestimating the potential for sales growth, ignoring the profit-depressing effects of an overly aggressive effort to "buy" market share with deep price cuts, being burdened with heavy fixed costs because of an inability to use plant capacity, betting on R&D efforts but failing to come up with effective innovations, betting on technological long shots, being too optimistic about the ability to penetrate new markets, making frequent changes in strategy (because the previous strategy didn't work out), and being overpowered by more successful rivals. Curing these kinds of problems and achieving a successful business turnaround can involve any of the following actions:

- Selling off assets to raise cash to save the remaining part of the business.
- Revising the existing strategy.
- Launching efforts to boost revenues.
- Pursuing cost reduction.
- Using a combination of these efforts.

Selling Off Assets   Asset-reduction strategies are essential when cash flow is a critical consideration and when the most practical ways to generate cash are (1) through sale of some of the firm's assets (plant and equipment, land, patents, inventories, or profitable subsidiaries) and (2) through retrenchment (pruning of marginal products from the product line, closing or selling older plants, reducing the workforce, withdrawing from outlying markets, cutting back customer service). Sometimes crisis-ridden companies sell off assets not so much to unload losing operations as to raise funds to save and strengthen the remaining business activities. In such cases, the choice is usually to dispose of noncore business assets to support strategy renewal in the firm's core businesses.

Strategy Revision   When weak performance is caused by bad strategy, the task of strategy overhaul can proceed along any of several paths: (1) shifting to a new competitive approach to rebuild the firm's market position; (2) overhauling internal operations and functional-area strategies to better support the same overall business strategy; (3) merging with another firm in the industry and forging a new strategy keyed to the newly merged firm's strengths; and (4) retrenching into a reduced core of products and customers more closely matched to the firm's strengths. The most appealing path depends on prevailing industry conditions, the firm's particular strengths and weaknesses, its competitive capabilities vis-à-vis rival firms, and the severity of the crisis. A situation analysis of the industry, the major competitors, and the firm's own competitive position is a prerequisite for action. As a rule, successful strategy revision must be tied to the ailing firm's strengths and near-term competitive capabilities and directed at its best market opportunities.

Boosting Revenues   Revenue-increasing turnaround efforts aim at generating increased sales volume. There are a number of revenue-building options: price cuts, increased promotion, a bigger sales force, added customer services, and quickly achieved product improvements. Attempts to increase revenues and sales volumes are necessary (1) when there is little or no room in the operating budget to cut expenses and still break even, and (2) when the key to restoring profitability is increased use of existing capacity. If buyers are not especially price-sensitive because of differentiating features, the quickest way to boost short-term revenues may be to raise prices rather than opt for volume-building price cuts.

Cutting Costs   Cost-reducing turnaround strategies work best when an ailing firm's value chain and cost structure are flexible enough to permit radical surgery, when operating inefficiencies are identifiable and readily correctable, when the firm's costs are obviously bloated, and when the firm is relatively close to its break-even point. Accompanying a general belt-tightening can be an increased emphasis on paring administrative overheads, elimination of nonessential and low-value-added activities in the firm's value chain, modernization of existing plant and equipment to gain greater productivity, delay of nonessential capital expenditures, and debt restructuring to reduce interest costs and stretch out repayments.

Combination Efforts   Combination turnaround strategies are usually essential in grim situations that require fast action on a broad front. Likewise, combination actions frequently come into play when new managers are brought in and given a free hand to make whatever changes they see fit. The tougher the problems, the more likely it is that the solutions will involve multiple strategic initiatives—see the story of turnaround efforts at Lucent Technologies in Illustration Capsule 8.3.

Turnaround efforts tend to be high-risk undertakings, and they often fail. A landmark study of 64 companies found no successful turnarounds among the most troubled companies in eight basic industries.[23] Many of the troubled businesses waited too long to begin a turnaround. Others found themselves short of both the cash and entrepreneurial talent needed to compete in a slow-growth industry characterized by a fierce battle for market share. Better-positioned rivals simply proved too strong to defeat in a long, head-to-head contest. Even when successful, turnaround may involve numerous attempts and management changes before long-term competitive viability and profitability are finally restored. A recent study found that troubled companies that did nothing and elected to wait out hard times had only a 10 percent chance of recovery.[24] This same study also found that, of the companies studied, the chances of recovery

illustration capsule 8.3
Lucent Technologies' Turnaround Strategy: Slow to Produce Results

In the fall of 2001, the situation was becoming desperate at Lucent Technologies, an AT&T spinoff that had been heralded as a superstar of the telecommunications equipment industry. The combination of lost sales to competitors and a steep downturn in capital spending for telecommunications equipment had thrown the company into a nosedive, driving its stock price from over $80 a share down to under $10. Revenues had dropped from $38 billion in the fiscal year ending September 1999 to just $21 billion in fiscal year ending September 2001; profits had declined even more precipitously, falling from a positive $3.5 billion to a stunning $14.2 billion loss. Some observers predicted the company could not survive, and most everyone agreed that Lucent's recovery would be slow at best because of a capacity glut in fiber-optic telecommunications systems.

To bolster its sagging outlook, top executives engineered a turnaround strategy that featured:

- Eliminating 15,000 to 20,000 jobs worldwide immediately and eventually cutting the workforce by more than half, from 150,000 to 60,000.

- Consolidating production at a fewer plants and closing the unneeded plants.

- Selling the company's fiber-optic business (for about $4 billion).

- Raising additional cash by selling $1.8 billion in convertible preferred stock.

- Reaching an agreement with its group of banks to realign the terms of $4 billion in loans.

- Dropping certain product lines.

- Spinning off its microelectronics business, Agere Systems, as a separate company.

- Pursuing a number of cost-cutting initiatives aimed at making Lucent a leaner, more efficient maker of telecommunications equipment.

Top executives were confident in predicting that these moves would return Lucent to profitability in 2002, even without a recovery in telecommunications spending. But Lucent's turnaround proved considerably more problematic than expected. In fiscal 2002 (ending September 2002), revenues fell further, to $12.3 billion, and losses amounted to $12 billion. Lucent's struggles to get its business back on track included restoring lost confidence in top management by brining in a new president and CEO, Pat Russo. Russo continued with the restructuring efforts previously announced but also spurred company efforts to grow the company's revenues and reduce the company's break-even sales volumes via additional streamlining of operations.

In the fall of 2003, the company was continuing to lose money and was also experiencing further revenue declines. In the third quarter of fiscal 2003, Lucent reported revenues of $1.96 billion and a loss of $254 million. The company's stock was trading in the $2.00–$2.50 range. Russo forecast that the company would not return to profitability until sometime in 2004. The bright spot in Lucent's outlook was its strong position in third-generation (3G) wireless technology. Lucent management expected that the company would get a major boost from sales of 3G technology products as wireless communications companies began to more aggressively upgrade their networks.

Sources: www.lucent.com, accessed September 22, 2003; Yuki Noguchi, "Lucent Closes Herndon's Chromatis," *Washington Post* (www.washingtonpost.com), August 29, 2001; Simon Romero, "Lucent Maps Out Route to Profit by the End of Next Year," *New York Times* (www.nytimes.com), August 24, 2001; Peter J. Howe, "Lucent Fires 290 More at Massachusetts Sites," *Boston Globe* (www.boston.com), August 24, 2001; and Sara Silver, "Lucent Cuts 2,200 Jobs," Associated Press, August 23, 2001.

were boosted 190 percent if the turnaround strategy involved buying assets that strengthened the company's business in its core markets; companies that both bought assets or companies in their core markets and sold off noncore assets increased their chances of recovery by 250 percent.

Liquidation—the Strategy of Last Resort

Sometimes a business in crisis is too far gone to be salvaged. The problem, of course, is determining when a turnaround is achievable and when it isn't. It is easy for owners or managers to let their emotions and pride overcome sound judgment when a business gets in such deep trouble that a successful turnaround is remote. Closing down a crisis-ridden business and liquidating its assets, however, is sometimes the best and wisest strategy. Of all the strategic alternatives, liquidation is the most unpleasant and painful because of the hardships of job eliminations and the effects of business closings on local communities. Nonetheless, in hopeless situations, an early liquidation effort usually serves owner-stockholder interests better than an inevitable bankruptcy. Prolonging the pursuit of a lost cause merely exhausts an organization's resources further and leaves less to salvage, not to mention the added stress and potential career impairment for all the people involved.

End-Game Strategies

An *end-game, slow-exit,* or *harvesting strategy* steers a middle course between preserving the status quo and exiting as soon as possible. This type of strategy involves a gradual phasing down of the business and even sacrificing market position in return for bigger near-term cash flows or current profitability. The overriding financial objective of a slow-exit or harvest strategy is to reap the greatest possible harvest of cash to deploy to other business endeavors. The operating budget is chopped to a rock-bottom level; reinvestment in the business is held to a bare minimum. Capital expenditures for new equipment are put on hold or given low financial priority (unless replacement needs are unusually urgent); instead, efforts are made to stretch the life of existing equipment and make do with present facilities as long as possible. Promotional expenses may be cut gradually, quality reduced in not-so-visible ways, nonessential customer services curtailed, and the like. Although such actions may result in shrinking sales and market share, if cash expenses can be cut even faster, then after-tax profits and cash flows are bigger (at least temporarily). The business gradually declines, but not before sizable amounts of cash have been harvested.

An end-game, slow-exit, or harvest strategy is a reasonable strategic option for a weak business in the following circumstances:[25]

1. *When the industry's long-term prospects are unattractive*—as seems to be the case for the cigarette industry, for the manufacture and sale of VCRs and videocassettes (which are now being replaced by DVD players and both CDs and DVDs), and for the 3.5-inch floppy disk business.

2. *When rejuvenating the business would be too costly or at best marginally profitable*—as could be the case at Iomega, which is struggling to maintain sales of its Zip drives in the face of rapidly expanding hard disk drives on PCs, or at Polaroid, which has experienced stagnant sales for its instant cameras and film.

3. *When the firm's market share is becoming increasingly costly to maintain or defend*—as could be the case with the makers of film for traditional cameras.

4. *When reduced levels of competitive effort will not trigger an immediate or rapid falloff in sales*—the makers of printers will not likely experience much of a decline in sales of either dot-matrix printers or ribbons if they spend all of their ad budgets on promoting their lines of laser printers.

5. *When the enterprise can redeploy the freed resources in higher-opportunity areas*—the makers of CD players and CDs are better off devoting their resources to the production and sale of DVD players/recorders and DVDs.

6. *When the business is not a crucial or core component of a diversified company's overall lineup of businesses*—gradually letting a sideline business decay is strategically preferable to deliberately letting a mainline or core business decline.

7. *When the business does not contribute other desired features to a company's overall business portfolio*—such features include sales stability, prestige, and a well-rounded product line.

The more of these seven conditions that are present, the more ideal the business is for harvesting and a slow-exit or end-game strategy.

End-game strategies make the most sense for diversified companies that have sideline or noncore business units in weak competitive positions or in unattractive industries. Such companies can withdraw the cash flows from unattractive, noncore business units and reallocate them to business units with greater profit potential or spend them on the acquisition of new businesses.

10 COMMANDMENTS FOR CRAFTING SUCCESSFUL BUSINESS STRATEGIES

Company experiences over the years prove again and again that disastrous strategies can be avoided by adhering to good strategy-making principles. We've distilled the lessons learned from the strategic mistakes companies most often make into 10 commandments that serve as useful guides for developing sound strategies:

1. *Place top priority on crafting and executing strategic moves that enhance the company's competitive position for the long term.* The glory of meeting one quarter's or one year's financial performance targets quickly fades, but an ever-stronger competitive position pays off year after year. Shareholders are never well served by managers who let short-term financial performance considerations rule out strategic initiatives that will meaningfully bolster the company's longer-term competitive position and competitive strength. The best way to ensure a company's long-term profitability is with a strategy that strengthens the company's long-term competitiveness and market position.

2. *Be prompt in adapting to changing market conditions, unmet customer needs, buyer wishes for something better, emerging technological alternatives, and new initiatives of competitors.* Responding late or with too little often puts a company in the precarious position of having to play catch-up. While pursuit of a consistent strategy has its virtues, adapting strategy to changing circumstances is normal and necessary. Moreover, long-term strategic commitments to achieve top quality or lowest cost should be interpreted relative to competitors' products as well as customers' needs and expectations; the company should avoid singlemindedly striving to make the absolute highest-quality or lowest-cost product no matter what.

3. *Invest in creating a sustainable competitive advantage.* Having a competitive edge over rivals is the single most dependable contributor to above-average profitability.

As a general rule, a company must play aggressive offense to build competitive advantage and aggressive defense to protect it.

4. *Avoid strategies capable of succeeding only in the most optimistic circumstances.* Expect competitors to employ countermeasures and expect times of unfavorable market conditions. A good strategy works reasonably well and produces tolerable results even in the worst of times.

5. *Don't underestimate the reactions and the commitment of rival firms.* Rivals are most dangerous when they are pushed into a corner and their well-being is threatened.

6. *Consider that attacking competitive weakness is usually more profitable and less risky than attacking competitive strength.* Attacking capable, resourceful rivals is likely to fail unless the attacker has deep financial pockets and a solid basis for competitive advantage over stronger rivals.

7. *Be judicious in cutting prices without an established cost advantage.* Only a low-cost producer can win at price cutting over the long term.

8. *Strive to open up very meaningful gaps in quality or service or performance features when pursuing a differentiation strategy.* Tiny differences between rivals' product offerings may not be visible or important to buyers.

9. *Avoid stuck-in-the-middle strategies that represent compromises between lower costs and greater differentiation and between broad and narrow market appeal.* Compromise strategies rarely produce sustainable competitive advantage or a distinctive competitive position—a well-executed best-cost producer strategy is the only exception where a compromise between low cost and differentiation succeeds. Usually, companies with compromise strategies end up with average costs, average differentiation, an average image and reputation, a middle-of-the-pack industry ranking, and little prospect of industry leadership.

10. *Be aware that aggressive moves to wrest market share away from rivals often provoke retaliation in the form of a price war—to the detriment of everyone's profits.* Aggressive moves to capture a bigger market share invite cutthroat competition, particularly when the market is plagued with high inventories and excess production capacity.

MATCHING STRATEGY TO ANY INDUSTRY AND COMPANY SITUATION

It is not enough to understand a company's basic competitive strategy options—overall low-cost leadership, broad differentiation, best-cost, focused low-cost, and focused differentiation—and that there are a variety of offensive, defensive, first-mover, and late-mover initiatives and actions to choose from. The lessons of this chapter are (1) that some strategic options are better suited to certain specific industry and competitive environments than others and (2) that some strategic options are better suited to certain specific company situations than others. This chapter portrays the multifaceted task of matching strategy to a firm's external and internal circumstances in nine types of situations.

Rather than try to summarize the main points we made about choosing strategies for these nine sets of circumstances (the relevant principles are not readily capsuled in three or four sentences each), we think it more useful to conclude this chapter by outlining a broader framework for matching strategy to *any* industry and company situation. Aligning a company's strategy with its overall situation starts with a quick diagnosis of the industry environment and the firm's competitive standing in the industry:

1. What basic type of industry environment (emerging, rapid-growth, high-velocity, mature, global, commodity-product) does the company operate in? What strategic options and strategic postures are usually best suited to this generic type of environment?

2. What position does the firm have in the industry (leader, runner-up, or also-ran; strong, weak, or crisis-ridden)? How does the firm's market standing influence its strategic options given the industry and competitive environment—in particular, which courses of action have to be ruled out?

Next, strategists need to factor in the primary external and internal situational considerations (as discussed in Chapters 3 and 4) and decide how all the factors add up. Nearly always, weighing the various considerations makes it clear that some strategic options can be ruled out. Listing the pros and cons of the remaining options can help managers choose the best overall strategy.

The final step is to custom-tailor the chosen generic competitive strategy approach (low-cost, broad differentiation, best-cost, focused low-cost, focused differentiation) to fit *both* the industry environment and the firm's standing vis-à-vis competitors. Here, it is important to be sure that (1) the customized aspects of the proposed strategy are well matched to the firm's competencies and competitive capabilities, and (2) the strategy addresses all issues and problems the firm confronts.

In weeding out less-attractive strategic alternatives and weighing the pros and cons of the most attractive ones, the answers to the following questions often help point to the best course of action:

- What kind of competitive edge can the company *realistically* achieve? Can the company execute the strategic moves necessary to secure this edge?

- Does the company have the organizational capabilities and financial resources to succeed in these moves and approaches? If not, can they be acquired?

- Once built, how can the competitive advantage be protected? Is the company in a position to lead industry change and set the rules by which rivals must compete? What defensive strategies need to be employed? Will rivals counterattack? What will it take to blunt their efforts?

- Are any rivals particularly vulnerable? Should the firm mount an offensive to capitalize on these vulnerabilities? What offensive moves need to be employed?

- What additional strategic moves are needed to deal with driving forces in the industry, specific threats and weaknesses, and any other issues/problems unique to the firm?

table 8.1   **Sample Format for a Strategic Action Plan**

1. Strategic Vision and Mission	5. Supporting Functional Strategies
2. Strategic Objectives	• Production
• Short-term	• Marketing/sales
• Long-term	• Finance
3. Financial Objectives	• Personnel/human resources
• Short-term	• Other
• Long-term	6. Recommended Actions to Improve Company Performance
4. Overall Business Strategy	• Immediate
	• Longer-range

In crafting the overall strategy, there are several pitfalls to avoid:

- Designing an overly ambitious strategic plan—one that overtaxes the company's resources and capabilities.

- Selecting a strategy that represents a radical departure from or abandonment of the cornerstones of the company's prior success—a radical strategy change need not be rejected automatically, but it should be pursued only after careful risk assessment.

- Choosing a strategy that goes against the grain of the organization's culture or conflicts with the values and philosophies of the most senior executives.

- Being unwilling to *commit wholeheartedly* to one of the five competitive strategies—picking and choosing features of the different strategies usually produces so many compromises between low cost, best cost, differentiation, and focusing that the company fails to achieve any kind of advantage and ends up stuck in the middle.

Table 8.1 provides a generic format for outlining a strategic action plan for a single-business enterprise. It contains all of the pieces of a comprehensive strategic action plan that we discussed at various places in these first eight chapters.

| exercises

1. Listed below are eight industries. Classify each one as (a) emerging, (b) turbulent or high-velocity, (c) mature/slow-growth, (d) stagnant/declining, or (e) fragmented. Do research on the Internet, if needed, to locate information on industry conditions and reach a conclusion on what classification to assign each of the following:

    (1) DVD player industry

    (2) Dry cleaning industry

    (3) Poultry industry

    (4) Camera film and film-developing industry

    (5) Wine, beer, and liquor retailing

    (6) Personal computer industry

    (7) Cell phone industry

    (8) Recorded music industry (DVDs, CDs, tapes)

2. Toyota overtook Ford Motor Company in 2003 to become the second largest maker of motor vehicles, behind General Motors. Toyota is widely regarded as having aspirations to overtake General Motors as the global leader in motor vehicles within the next 10 years. Do research on the Internet or in the library to determine what strategy General Motors is pursuing to maintain its status as the industry leader. Then research Toyota's strategy to overtake General Motors.

Chapter 17

Strategy and corporate governance[1]

Introduction

In recent years the importance of governance has become of prime concern in the strategic management of organizations of all kinds. Effective, honest, accountable and transparent modes of governance are now sought of organizations by stakeholders of all varieties.

There is no single model of good governance. However the OECD (2004) has identified corporate governance as one of the key elements in improving economics efficiency and growth as well as enhancing investor confidence. The OECD (2004) describes corporate governance as:

> ... involving a set of relationships between a company's management, its board, its

Chapter contents

---

[1] Contributions to this chapter were made by Derek Condon, Warwick Business School.

shareholders and other stakeholders. Corporate governance also provides the structure through which the objectives of the company are set, and the means of attaining those objectives and monitoring performance are determined. Good corporate governance should provide proper incentives for the board and management to pursue objectives that are in the interests of the company and its shareholders and should facilitate effective monitoring.

The OECD's *Principles of Corporate Governance* go on to say that:

Corporate governance is only part of the larger economic context in which firms operate that includes, for example, macroeconomic policies and the degree of competition in product and factor markets. The corporate governance framework also depends on the legal, regulatory and institutional environment. In addition, factors such as business ethics and corporate awareness of the environment and societal interests of the communities in which a company operates can also have an impact on its reputation and its long-term success.

There have been a number of recent scandals and exposés of alleged poor governance ranging from Enron, through Parmalat to Shell. These failures expose some of the key principles and the importance of governance structures, processes and accountabilities. We outline the case of Enron below.

Case box: The Enron collapse

On 2 December 2001, Enron filed for bankruptcy. On the same day, Irwin Steltzer writing in the Business News of the *Sunday Times* praised Kenneth Lay (Enron's Chairman) for 'converting this American Industry into a lean, mean and internationally competitive machine'. Houston-based Enron went bankrupt amid revelations of hidden debt, inflated profits, questionable accounting and governance. Thousands of workers lost their jobs and millions of investors who hadn't already bolted watched their shares become worthless. Dozens of people, including Enron founder and former Chairman Kenneth Lay, former Chief Executive Jeffrey Skilling and former finance chief Andrew Fastow, have been charged with crimes in the Justice Department's continuing investigation of what caused the collapse. Mr Fastow is among 10 former executives who have pleaded guilty, while Messrs Lay and Skilling are among the 20 who have pleaded innocent and are facing trial. The ventures that once defined Enron as a leader in energy and other markets, such as trading and broadband, are long gone. Unsecured debts in the UK alone reached over £600 million involving Barclays, the Royal Bank of Scotland and Abbey.

Since the collapse of Enron, a key focus has been on how organizations are governed and how boards of directors in particular can let such events happen – and how they might prevent them happening again. The Enron story reveals a board which effectively turned a blind eye to events which should have sounded alarm bells. In brief, the story goes: Enron forged a close relationship with the then Secretary of State for Energy (John Wakeham) in 1990. Wakeham gave Enron permission to build a large gas-fired power station on Teesside. John Wakeham was an accountant by training and was trusted and largely left alone by his two Prime Ministers (Margaret Thatcher and John Major) to secure the deal. In 1994, John Wakeham left the government and joined the main board of Enron. The Tories' policy of energy privatization was vigorously opposed by Labour (especially by its spokesman on industrial affairs, Tony Blair). Once appointed Prime Minister in 1997, Blair began to change policy and secured close relationships with private energy companies and with John Wakeham (now Lord Wakeham, a Tory peer). Enron made small donations to both US political parties, including $10,000 to support the Florida recount in the Presidential elections. Kenneth Lay subsequently secured a seat on a key advisory committee on energy policy (a post previously unavailable to anyone outside government). Enron also lobbied New Labour in the UK.

In 1998, Peter Mandelson (then Trade and Industry Secretary) gave permission for Enron to purchase Wessex Water without referring this decision to anywhere else in the Government. Wessex Water became the core of Enron's new water unit, Azurix. In 1999, Azurix went public and Enron began commercial operation of its nationwide fibre network for high bandwidth uses. Also in 1999, Helen Liddell (Industry Minister) gave Enron permission to build a gas-fired power station on the Isle of Grain, Kent, also without referring the decision elsewhere. By 1999 the Labour government had reversed their energy policies and were strongly backing gas-fired power stations. Labour ministers insisted that the regulation of privatized industries would ensure fair play and healthy business practices.

The response of the Enron board was to recruit the regulators. In October 2000, Claire Spottiswoode, the Gas regulator joined the board of Asturix (the new title of Wessex Water) and in August 2001, Stephen Littlechild, the electricity regulator, was appointed to the board of Teeside Water (a subsidiary of Enron). Following this, the Enron board turned a blind eye to several deals carried out by executives and sanctioned their actions.

These deals put large dents in Enron's funds but were not recorded on the balance sheets. Billions of pounds were used to support these initiatives. In February 2001, a group of Andersen partners met to discuss Enron's accounting and disclosures, but decided to retain the company as a client. Kenneth Lay discussed energy policy with Dick Cheney, US Vice-President, and Cheney's energy task force included some recommendations favourable to Enron. During a public appearance in June 2001, Skilling was hit by a cream pie thrown in protest for Enron allegedly profiteering from California's energy crisis which had begun in May 2000. In August 2001, Skilling resigned as President and CO and Kenneth Lay returned to the position of CEO. In October 2001, the *Wall Street Journal* revealed that Fastow made at least $7 million from running LJM partnerships in order to hedge investment in an internet company. In October 2001, Andersen began shredding Enron-related documents despite knowing of an SEC inquiry.

Enron replaced Fastow as CEO with Jeffrey McMahon from the industrial markets division and the SEC elevated its inquiry into Enron's financial dealings to a formal status. Enron restated its earnings for 1997 to 2001, reducing net income over that time by $586 million and boosting debts by $2.6 billion. By November 2001, major credit rating agencies had downgraded Enron's bonds to junk status at 61 cents per share. The bankruptcy file (for Chapter 11 protection) in December was the biggest in the US at the time ($62 billion in assets).

In 2002 Enron's trading operations were sold to UBS Warburg. Enron received no money but did secure the promise of one-third profits. Enron's board fired Andersen as auditors. Andersen claimed the relationship ended when Enron went into bankruptcy. On 23 January 2002, Kenneth Lay resigned as Chairman and CEO, replaced by Stephen Cooper as acting CEO. The Powers Report, commissioned to investigate blame, spreads the reason for Enron's collapse among Lay, Skilling, Fastow and Andersen, among many others.

Stephen Cooper revealed reorganization plans in May 2002 and one month later a jury found Andersen guilty of obstruction of justice in the investigation of Enron, sealing the demise of the accounting firm in the process. Between October 1998 and November 2001, Lay sold shares with gross proceeds of $184 million; Skilling $71 million; Fastow $34 million and Rebecca Mark $83 million.

By July 2004, the US Government had launched 31 Enron-related prosecutions including the criminal case which brought down Andersen in 2002. It has also set up criminal investigations into around 20 former Enron employees including Lay, Skilling and Fastow. So far, 11 have resulted in convictions or guilty pleas.

Source: authors' own data.

In New York in July 2004, US bankruptcy judge Arthur Gonzalez signed off Enron's plan to exit Chapter 11 bankruptcy protection with no notable adjustments. The reorganization plan aims to pay most of the more than 20,000 creditors about $12 billion of the approximate $63 billion they are owed in cash and stock in one of three new companies created from Enron's remains. Sales are pending for two of those companies – CrossCountry Energy Corp., which comprises Enron's whole or part interest in three domestic natural-gas pipelines, and Portland General Electric, its Pacific Northwest utility. The third is Prisma Energy International Inc., a smattering of pipeline and power assets in 14 countries, mostly in Latin America.

If the sales of CrossCountry and Portland General close later this year as expected, the $11 billion will be distributed to creditors with 92 per cent in cash and 8 per cent in Prisma stock. If one or both of the sales crumble, creditors will receive less cash and more stock in the multiple companies. The Enron name will disappear.

CrossCountry has so far attracted two buyers. In May the first bidder, Texas billionaire and Coastal Corp. founder Oscar Wyatt Jr, offered $2.2 billion. Then, a joint venture of Southern

Union Co. and GE Commercial Finance a unit of General Electric, offered $2.3 billion. Both offers include $430 million in assumed debt. Judge Gonzalez is to consider those and any other bids at a 1 September auction, and he is to approve the winning bid by 9 September.

CrossCountry's holdings include the 2600-mile Transwestern pipeline, which transports natural gas from west Texas, Oklahoma, eastern New Mexico, the San Juan Basin in north-western New Mexico and southern Colorado to California, Arizona and Texas markets; half-ownership with El Paso Corp. of Citrus Corp., a holding company that owns the 5000-mile Florida Gas Transmission pipeline from southeast Texas to Florida; and a less than 2 per cent interest in Northern Border Partners, which transports natural gas from Canada to the Midwest.

Last year Enron announced plans to sell Portland General to an investment group backed by Texas Pacific Group for $1.25 billion in cash and $1.1 billion in assumed debt.

Stephen F. Cooper, Enron's acting CEO and chief restructuring officer, said in a news release:

> Undoubtedly, this was an extremely complex bankruptcy. Today's court approval acknowledges not only the tremendous amount of work that has been accomplished during the last two and a half years, but also the overwhelming support of our economic constituents.

The Enron debacle was seen as a serious failure of strategists at board level. It heralded a new era of reviews and prescriptions for board behaviours and regulation, which will be discussed later in this chapter. A new era, since the first code of good governance originated in the USA in 1978. There were, of course, other high-profile failures in the US WorldCom, Global Crossing and Tyco. In Asia the economic crisis of 1997 was laid firmly at the door of poor governance by the Asian Development Bank. And, in Europe, Parmalat and Shell Oil have also been blamed for poor governance. Clearly not just a problem in US companies; nevertheless, the US Business Roundtable issued a report concerning the roles and composition of boards of directors of large publicly owned companies. Monks and Minnow (1992) argued that the origin of this code was in response to increasingly criminal corporate behaviour and included guidelines to quell the occurrence of hostile takeovers. This focus on board behaviours and processes was essentially about the structure, composition and conduct of boards. The main points identified the chairman's main duties as:

* Overseeing board members' selection and succession.

* Reviewing the organization's performance and allocating its funds.

* Overseeing corporate social responsibility.

* Adherence to the law.

It was not until 1989 that the next code of governance was issued, this time in Hong Kong by the Hong Kong Stock Exchange and this was rapidly followed in 1991 by a best practice set of guidelines issued by the Irish Association of Investment Managers (Aguilera and Cuervo-Cazurra 2004). After this date, the Cadbury Committee Report in the UK (1992) heralded the authorship of many codes of good conduct with Aguilera and Cuervo-Cazurra (2004: 419) concluding that there were 72 codes of good governance by the end of 1999 spread across 24 industrialized and developing countries. Table 17.1 summarizes the position.

The codes produced under different legal systems have often been customized to particular national settings and this has reinforced the governance differences identified by Charkham (1999). However, institutions such as the World Bank and OECD are calling for

Table 17.1 Numbers of codes of governance worldwide (to end 1999)

Country	Total number of codes	
English-origin legal system:		
Australia	4	
Canada	4	
Hong Kong	4	
India	2	
Ireland	2	
Malaysia	1	
Singapore	1	
South Africa	1	
Thailand	1	
UK	11	
USA	17	
French-origin legal system:		
Belgium	4	
Brazil	1	
France	4	
Greece	1	
Italy	2	
Mexico	1	
Netherlands	2	
Portugal	1	
Spain	2	
German-origin legal system:		
Germany	1	
Japan	2	
Korea	1	
Scandinavian-origin legal system:		
Sweden	2	
Total countries	24	**Total codes** 72

Source: adapted from Aguilera and Cuervo-Cazurra, 2004, p. 423.

common principles and common governance structures and processes, at least to a minimum level. *Exogenous* forces are influencing the adoption of reasonably common codes. As organizations become more a part of the global economy for example, the transmission of common practices becomes easier and, some would say, necessary. Government liberalization and the increasing influence of foreign institutional investors also force the pace for common codes and standards. In this way, exogenous pressures force countries to show that their codes of corporate governance are 'legitimate' in the global economy.

17.1 The context of corporate governance

As early as the 1930s, Berle and Means (1932) drew attention to the growing separation of power between the executive management of major public companies and their increasingly diverse and remote shareholders. This view focused on the problem of control. The central question was to what extent could boards control executive management and thereby maintain the rights and influence of the shareholders as owners of the organization? This question has been addressed in terms of agency theory, in particular in economics. In this theory, the *agents* are corporate management, and the *principals* are the shareholders. In agency theory, the board is viewed as an alternative monitoring device which helps to control the agents to further the interests of the principals. It is assumed in agency theory that effective boards will identify with shareholder interests and use their experience in decision making and control to exert leverage over any self-interested tendencies of corporate management – the agents. For boards to exercise their vigilant role over the chief executive officer (CEO), the board needs power (Keasey, Thompson and Wright 1997). For the CEO to engage in self-interested activities there must presumably be a power imbalance between the CEO and the board.

Cadbury (2000) and Cassidy (2000) offer accounts of the rise and rise of corporate governance as an issue in the USA and Europe since the 1980s. Central to their argument about why this issue has risen so far up the policy agenda have been:

- a succession of corporate scandals;
- performance weaknesses of many firms which could be attributed at least in part to poor governance and leadership;
- disjunctures between the compensation of CEOs and executive directors and the financial performance of the companies they are managing (Conyon and Murphy 2000).

Despite these varying accounts, it is clear that there are a common set of *endogenous* pressures and questions which revolve around the purposes, responsibilities, control, leadership and power of boards. These questions include:

- How is oversight to be exercised over those delegated to the executive management of the firm?

636   CHAPTER 17 STRATEGY AND CORPORATE GOVERNANCE

◆ How are owners' interests to be protected?

◆ How are the interests of the other stakeholders such as consumers, employees and local communities to be protected?

◆ Who sets the purpose and direction of the organization and ensures its accountability?

◆ How is power over the organization legitimized and to whom is an organization accountable and responsible?

17.2 Corporate governance in the UK

Modern UK corporate governance regulations began with the Cadbury Report (1992), which reviewed the financial aspects of corporate governance and led to the publication of the Code of Best Practice. This was followed by the Greenbury Committee (1995), which reviewed directors' remuneration, while the Hampel Committee on corporate governance (established in 1995 and reporting in 1998) had a broader remit that built on Cadbury and Greenbury, essentially picking up new issues that had arisen from both reports. Following the report of the Hampel Committee, the first edition of the Combined Code was published by the London Stock Exchange (LSE) Committee on Corporate Governance and was added as an appendix to the LSE Listing Rules. The code superseded all previous codes for UK-listed companies and was derived from Cadbury, Greenbury, Hampel and the LSE's Listing Rules. The principles behind the code were those of market and self-regulation. The code was not legally enforceable, but a company was required to explain how the principles of the code had been followed and to disclose when and why they did not follow the code. If these reasons were not deemed acceptable by the stock market, it would be reflected in the company's stock price.

Since the publication of the first edition of the Combined Code, three other important reports have been published to date. These are the Turnbull Report, which provides guidelines for directors on how to meet the code's provisions on internal control; the Smith Report, which relates to the provisions on audit committees and auditors; and the Higgs Report, which was a review of the role and effectiveness of non-executive directors. The findings of these reports have been incorporated into the latest edition of the Combined Code (Higgs 2003). It represents something of a 'capstone' on the previous reports and it has had a significant impact on the structures and processes of boards in the UK. Like all previous codes, the Combined Code seeks to influence board structure and conduct by means of codes of practice and not through legislation. Boards are expected to *comply or explain* why they have not complied in their reporting mechanisms. The key requirements of the Combined Code are summarized in Table 17.2.

The reasons for not choosing a legal requirement for disclosure and relying on codes of practice lie, on the one hand, in the less than adequate provision of the legal structure in the

Table 17.2 Key elements of the Combined Code

> ### The main disclosures required are:
>
> * A statement of how the board operates and which types of decision are taken by the board and which are delegated to management.
> * Number of meetings of the board and its committees including a list of annual attendance by directors.
> * A description of how performance evaluation of the board, its committees and its directors is conducted.
> * What steps have been taken to ensure that members of the board, especially non-executive directors, understand the views of major shareholders about their organization.
> * A description of how the nomination committee works and why open advertising or an external search agency have not been used in either the appointments of a chairman or a non-executive director.
> * A description of the processes and activities of the remuneration and audit committees.
>
> ### The main principles of the code are:
>
> * Every company should be headed by an effective board which is collectively responsible for the success of the organization.
> * A clear division of responsibilities. The roles of chairman and chief executive should not be exercised by the same individual and no one individual should have unfettered powers of decision. It is worth noting here that almost 10 per cent of UK-listed companies have a joint chairman/chief executive (Hemscott 2003).
> * The board should include a balance of executive and independent non-executive directors.
> * Transparency of all procedures.
> * The board should undertake a formal and rigorous evaluation of its own performance and that of its committees and individual directors.
> * All directors should be submitted for re-election at regular intervals subject to continued satisfactory performance. Refreshing the board with new members should be planned and implemented.
> * Levels of remuneration should be sufficient to attract, retain and motivate directors but this should not include paying more than is necessary for this purpose. There should be a transparent policy on remuneration.
> * Financial reporting should be understandable and transparent and subject to strict internal controls.

UK to ensure good practice and, on the other, to encourage the spirit of self-regulation. For example, UK law rests on the principle that the owners (shareholders) appoint agents (directors) to run the business, and the directors report annually on their stewardship. In practice, in public limited companies (of which there are around 2,000 in the UK), there is a two-link chain of accountability. Management is accountable to directors, and directors are accountable to shareholders. PLCs registered after 1 November 1929 are legally required to have at least two directors. There is no distinction between classes of directors; for instance, between executive (inside or full-time) directors and non-executive (outside and part-time) directors. The law refers only obscurely to chairmen and barely mentions boards. This legal minimalism leads Charkham (1999) to conclude that

> *the superstructure as we know it: boards, board committees, chairmen, non-executive directors are pragmatic adaptations. In law none is essential; to this day ICI could legally be run by two directors, like the consulate of the Roman Republic.*

Many UK boards divide the chairman and chief executive officer (CEO) roles, and the position of chairman is often part time. Chairmen have major responsibilities in determining the size, balance, composition and agenda of the board. They can also play a significant part in handling external relationships with key stakeholders such as government, institutional investors, regulators and banks. Chairmen are normally appointed by non-executive directors. Non-executive directors play an increasingly important role in influencing board processes, heading up important committees of the board such as the audit or remuneration committees. Audit and remuneration committees comprise only non-executive directors and nomination committees are headed by a non-executive director or the chairman, who must meet the independence criteria laid out in the Combined Code.

17.2.1 Compliance with codes of governance in the UK

Conyon (1995) reveals a clear pattern of company adherence to the Cadbury recommendations. There is no statutory requirement for a company to reveal its board committee structure, so the failure of a company to reveal the existence of a committee does not necessarily mean it does not exist. (Since Cadbury, however, it is in companies' interests to be as transparent as possible in reporting non-controversial matters about board structures.) Tables 17.3, 17.4 and 17.5 summarize the main patterns in the data from the Conyon study and is reported in Pettigrew (2004).

Table 17.3 Board composition and size in the UK

	Average size of board	Average number of non-executive directors	Average number of executive directors
FT-SE top 100 Companies	12.30	6.15	6.16
FT-SE mid 250 Companies	8.89	4.57	4.32
FT-SE top 350 companies	9.87	5.02	4.85

Source: Conyon, 1995.

By 2003, these data had hardly changed. On average, a UK-listed board has around 7 directors. FTSE 100 boards are still larger, with an average of 11.5 directors (Hemscott 2003).

Table 17.4   Remuneration committee structures in UK companies, 1994

	Number of companies with remuneration committee	Average size of remuneration committee	Average number of non-executive directors on remuneration committee	Number of non-executive-only remuneration committees
FT-SE top 100 companies	100	4.61	4.28	73
FT-SE mid 250 companies	233	4.07	3.63	161
FT-SE top 350 companies	333	4.23	3.82	234

Source: Conyon, 1995.

Table 17.5   Audit committee structures in UK companies, 1994

	Number of companies with audit committee	Average size of audit committee	Average number of non-executive directors on audit committee	Number of non-executive-only audit committees
FT-SE top 100 companies	100	4.24	4.05	92
FT-SE mid 250 companies	246	3.94	3.59	208
FT-SE top 350 companies	346	4.03	3.73	300

Source: Conyon, 1995.

Again, the Hemscott (2003) survey of boards reveals very few changes in the above data from the Conyon study.

Key points from the Conyon study are:

♦ The overall average board size for the FTSE 350 companies is 9.87. The ratio of non-executive directors to executive directors for large UK companies is approximately equal. The average of 5.02 non-executive directors per company considerably exceeds the Cadbury minimum recommendation of three.

In a 1993 postal survey of 400 of the *Times* 1000 top UK companies between 1988 and 1993, Conyon (1994) found the average proportion of non-executives on the main board in 1993 to be 44 per cent, up from 38 per cent in 1988. There is possibly a rising trend in the use of non-executive directors in large UK plcs.

♦ Table 17.4 indicates close adherence to the Cadbury and institutional shareholders'

640   CHAPTER 17 STRATEGY AND CORPORATE GOVERNANCE

committee recommendations on the creation and composition of remuneration committees. Almost all the FTSE 350 companies have remuneration committees that set top pay. Table 17.4 also shows the minimal presence of executive directors on such committees. Even so, among the 1994 FTSE 100 companies, there were still 33 executive directors who sat on their company's remuneration committee. According to Conyon's 1993 study, in contrast, only 54 per cent of companies sampled had had remuneration committees in 1988.

◆ The Cadbury Report states that 'all listed companies should establish an audit committee' (1992, 4.35, p. 28) in order to help safeguard shareholder interests. Table 17.5 shows that by 1994, 98.9 per cent of the FTSE 350 companies had audit committees and that non-executive directors were a dominant feature of the audit committee. This high disclosure of the existence of audit committees again shows considerable change from the disclosure rate in 1988, when a Bank of England (1988) company survey found that only 56 per cent of the *Times* 1000 top 250 companies reported the existence of audit committees.

The picture that emerges from the Conyon studies (1994 and 1995) is one of substantial change in the prevalence of remuneration and audit committees between 1988 and 1994. Bostock (1995), however, has shown a lesser rate of adoption of board-nominating committees. Nominating committees, when available, may be able to bring a more objective approach to the selection of executive and non-executive board members. Using publicly available data disclosed in company annual reports, Bostock (1995) showed that 53 per cent of the top 100 UK companies by market capitalization did not have a nominating committee. The incidence of nominating committees trebled between 1998 and 1993, yet Conyon (1994) found that only approximately 40 per cent of UK quoted companies had them in 1993, despite the Cadbury code of practice.

The Cadbury code of practice does not recommend companies to split the roles of chairman and chief executive. It does, however, recommend that where the roles are not

Table 17.6 Number of companies with women on the board for 1995

	Number with at least one woman non-executive director	Number with at least one woman executive director	Number with at least one woman board member (exec or non-exec)
FT-SE top 100 companies	34	7	40
FT-SE mid 250 companies	29	7	33
FT-SE top 350 companies	63	14	73

Source: Conyon and Mallin, 1997.

Table 17.7 Percentage of females on the board in 1995

	Percentage of female non-executive directors on main board	Percentage of female executive directors on main board	Percentage of all female directors on main board
FT-SE top 100 companies	3.08	0.56	3.65
FT-SE mid 250 companies	1.44	0.40	1.84
FT-SE top 350 companies	2.02	0.46	2.49

Source: Conyon and Mallin, 1997.

split, there should be a strong independent element, with a recognized senior member, on the board. The Cadbury Committee's own research on compliance (CADS, 1995) shows that by 1994 the roles of chairman and chief executive were split in 82 per cent of UK firms in the top 500 by market capitalization. Conyon's (1994) postal survey of 400 firms in the *Times* 1000 found that, in 1993, 77 per cent of quoted companies had split the two roles, compared with 57 per cent in 1988.

In a slightly later study, Conyon and Mallin (1997) report on women's participation rates in the UK boardrooms. Tables 17.6 and 17.7 report respectively on the number of companies with women on the board, and the percentage of females on the board of UK plcs in 1995.

These data reveal the very limited participation of women in the main boardrooms of the UKs top plcs. IN 1995, there were just 73 companies with at least one female director on the main board and very few of those were executive directors. In 1995 there was only one company in the FTSE 100 with a female CEO. In 2000, this figure had doubled to two. Only 2.49 per cent of the directors were female and females are more likely to be non-executive than executive directors. By 2003, just over one in ten FTSE non-executive posts were held by females and one in forty FTSE executive posts were held by women (Hemscott 2003). Things do not seem to be changing in terms of the gender imbalances in the boardroom. Most strategists are male.

Although the above data show the extent which UK organizations comply with the various codes, the data should not be taken to imply anything about the effectiveness of these boards. Ticking the boxes of compliance and working effectively are two very different processes. In the next sections, we look at board effectiveness generally (i.e. in companies worldwide) and in the UK, referring to a recent empirical study of UK boards by McNulty and Pettigrew (1999).

17.3 Board effectiveness

Conger *et al.* (2001), Ward (2000) and the OECD (2004) all offer principles against which board effectiveness might be judged. In particular, these authors emphasize that the board should be able to exercise judgement in decision making and corporate affairs generally, independently of other influences, particularly the voices of management. Since boards should appoint non-executive directors to exercise independent judgements over key areas such as financial reporting, nomination and remuneration, the board ought to be able to exercise independent and informed judgements away from the day-to-day managerial concerns of the organization. In addition, these authors emphasize the importance of boards being able to access and be supplied with accurate, timely and relevant information in order to carry out their strategic decision making roles effectively. Finally, the role of accountability is emphasized, not only compliance with the law and acting on good faith, but also in the interests of all shareholders and the social responsibilities of the organization. These issues are summarized in the next sections.

17.3.1 The board as a team

Surprisingly, the board as an organizational team has been relatively neglected in empirical study. While there are plenty of studies on teams (and top teams) in organizations (see Katzenbach and Smith 1992; Hambrick *et al.* 1998), there are very few studies of boards using the key variables identified from these team studies. Applying the empirical knowledge of team processes and performance to boards would emphasize a number of key aspects.

First, boards should ensure they focus on the correct issues during their meetings and avoid much of the side-tracking which can take place in groups. For example, this would mean being able to focus on and distinguish between long- and short-term factors with full discussions at board meetings before any strategic decisions are taken. As with all organizational groups, size is important. Extrapolating from the team-based literatures, boards should restrict their size as far as possible to around six or eight members for a small organization to ten or twelve members for a larger organization. All members should feel that they can contribute freely and effectively to meetings and be well prepared in advance of the meeting. Regular meetings with high levels of attendance would also be beneficial in terms of effective decision making.

Second, the board needs to build in maintenance and learning functions to its operations and processes. The board's role as the key strategic decision making body calls for a high level of commitment of all members as well as the ability of those members to learn from experience and apply that learning to decisions and judgements they are required to take. Training and development (e.g. perhaps an induction programme for newly appointed directors) should also be beneficial as should specific training in the key areas of decision making (see Chapter 13) such as strategy, risk and evaluating performance. Like all groups in organizations, some assessment of their own performance as a team and as individuals in that team should ensure greater effectiveness.

17.4 The board and strategic decision making

As the key group in strategic decision making processes, the board needs both to understand how decisions are made (on what basis and with what stated objectives for example) and how they go about decision making as a team. This is another aspect of the interface between organization and strategy (see Chapter 2). In making strategic decisions, the board stamps its mark on the organization and, in turn, the organization becomes a distinctive entity with

Table 17.8 Levels of non-executive board member involvement in strategy

	Taking strategic decisions	Shaping strategic decisions	Shaping the content, context and conduct of strategy
Definition	Influence is exerted inside the boardroom at the end of the capital investment decision process	Influence occurs early in the decision process as part-time board members shape the preparation of capital investment proposals by executives	Influence is continuous and not confined to decision episodes
Board behaviour	Inside the boardroom, boards take decisions to accept, reject or refer capital investment proposals	Consultation with part-time board members by the executive, either formally or informally, while a capital investment proposal is being prepared enables board members to test ideas, raise issues, question assumptions, advise caution, and offer encouragement. *Executives 'sieve' capital investment proposals in anticipation of the need for board approval*	The board develops the context for strategic debate, establishes a methodology for strategy development, monitors strategy content and alters the conduct of the executive in relation to strategy
Board involvement	All boards take strategic decisions	Some boards shape strategic decisions	A minority of boards shape the context, content and conduct of strategy

Source: adapted from McNulty and Pettigrew, 1999.

its own structure, culture and philosophy. A resource-based view of the organization would imply that a key role of the board is to ensure precisely what is the core business or purpose of the organization and to ensure that organizational competences and resources are in place to support that core purpose. This is akin to creating and preserving that 'cherished core ideology' that Collins and Porras (2000) argue is the vital constant of successful organiz-ations when all else around them is subject to change. In essence, the board represents and needs to preserve the glue which holds the organization together and which symbolizes the guiding principles by which key decisions are made.

The board also has the responsibility of overseeing not only its own internal processes in this respect, but also of ensuring that this 'strategy with values' is disseminated effectively throughout the organization and that processes, rewards and organizational structures are aligned with the strategy. Opinions differ about the level of involvement that is both poss-ible and desirable for boards in the strategy process. Some argue that boards should have a proactive or initiating role of shaping strategy. Others contend the board should challenge, question and eventually approve strategic ideas and decisions formulated below the board in the executive team. McNulty and Pettigrew (1999) have examined the contribution to strategy by chairmen and non-executive directors of large UK companies. The collective label of part-time board member was used to refer to individuals performing these two roles (although a limited number of chairmen in the UK have executive and virtually full-time positions). Table 17.8 summarizes the forms of strategic involvement of boards in strategic decision making.

Most non-executives claimed they were much more influential in stopping initiatives than in starting them (McNulty and Pettigrew 1999). The executives interviewed claimed that around 80 per cent of the strategic decisions they took to the boardroom were approved or confirmed by the whole board.

Shaping strategic decisions entails a higher degree of non-executive board member influ-ence. Here the non-executives are consulted and involved earlier in the strategy process and thereby can shape the assumptions, alternatives and actual choices in the process. Shaping also occurs when executives restrict the range of their own proposals (knowing that certain alternatives will not be accepted at board level).

The ultimate way for a board to shape strategy is to fire the CEO and other executive direc-tors. This is happening with increasing frequency in UK boardrooms. The new generation of CEOs entering UK boardrooms are likely to be younger, to have had experience in more than one company and industry, and to have a shorter tenure in post than their predecessors of the 1980s and early 1990s.

17.4.1 The board and performance

Like any process, it is vital that boards have some way of agreeing what the key drivers of performance are. These can include a variety of measures such as financial results, corporate reputation or customer satisfaction, or can be a holistic grouping of such measures. An example of such a broad-based performance measurement system is Kaplan and Norton's (1992) balanced scorecard approach to using multiple measures for assessing performance. These include financial and non-financial measures of performance with a view to assessing future potential as well as assessing current performance.

A broad-based performance measure means boards must be clear about:

* How do our customers see us.

* What we must excel at.

* How we can continue to improve and create value.

* How good our financial performance is.

Each of these measures can be sub-divided into two component parts. These are outcomes, which *measure* the results of actions in the past, and performance drivers (*goals*), which predict future success. This allows future strategies to be reflected in today's goals and targets. Figure 17.1 shows the multi-dimensional nature of the balanced scorecard.

Measures can be metrics such as return on capital employed or return on net assets. They can also include factors such as employee attitudes, extent of customer satisfaction or core competences. *Goals* are future desired states which predict future success.

Of course, such a broad-based performance tool requires boards to be effective at both *prioritizing* strategic decisions (see Chapter 13) and assessing *risk*. The task of the board is to manage risk effectively rather than try to eliminate risk altogether. Bernstein (1996) reminds us that risk is a choice rather than a fate. The degree of risk taken by boards is really an expression of the amount of action (in an uncertain world) they dare to take. In this sense, risk is also an integral part of strategic decision making alongside prioritization. It is also

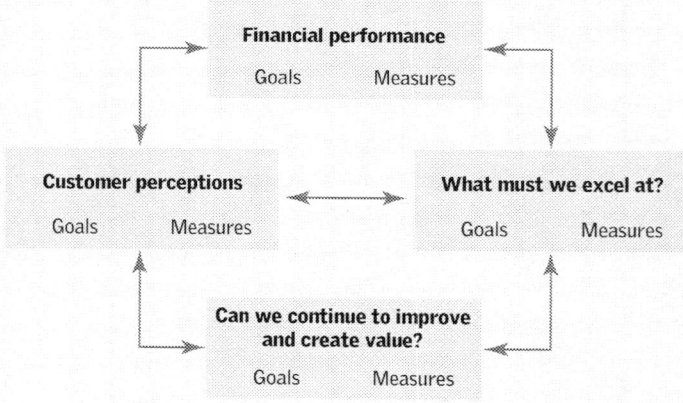

Figure 17.1 The balanced scorecard
Source: adapted from Kaplan and Norton, 1992.

management's responsibility (as well as that of the board) to monitor and assess risk as well as to keep the board informed of future risk-related projects or developments.

Handling risks (and setting the appetite for risk in an organization) are the responsibility both of the board and management. Effective risk management means there must also be good patterns of communication and understanding between the board and the management of an organization. Risks can arise from virtually all organizational activities. Some boards establish risk committees to look explicitly at some of the risk factors outlined in Table 17.9.

The main challenge to boards is to incorporate risk assessments into their own processes and to be able to prioritize significant or key risks (which may range from ethical issues to health and safety). Many practitioners advise that the board should make a detailed risk analysis every time they make (or ratify) a strategic decision. The Turnbull Report recommended a risk-based approach to designing, operating and maintaining a sound system of internal governance. Kirkbride and Letza (2003) note that Turnbull is the first official UK corporate governance document where the role of risk in corporate governance practice has been explicitly included and articulated.

Table 17.9 Some risks facing boards

Source of risk	Examples
Corporate strategy	◆ Strategy and organizational capabilities not aligned ◆ Unsuccessful acquisition ◆ Major change programme goes wrong
Financial	◆ Major accounting irregularities ◆ Fraud ◆ Cash flow problems
Legal	◆ Health and safety risks ◆ Breach of regulatory laws ◆ Failure to protect intellectual property
Supply chain and alliances	◆ Strategic alliances and joint ventures do not work ◆ Supply chain problems (e.g. suppliers) ◆ Overdependence on outsourced services
The operating environment	◆ Not responding to market trends ◆ Failure to innovate ◆ Overdependence on a few customers/suppliers
Human resources	◆ Loss of key people ◆ Poor motivation and communication among staff ◆ Leadership unable to take the organization forward (unable to formulate/implement strategies)
Social responsibility	◆ Stakeholder concerns about ethics of organization ◆ Dealing with unethical suppliers or contractors ◆ Human rights violations

The board is responsible for the company's system of internal control and it is the role of management to implement board policies on risk and control. Reports to the board should provide a balanced assessment of the significant risks and the effectiveness of the internal control mechanisms to handle those risks.

Other risks identified in the Turnbull Report include the following.

Strategic risk

* Changing conditions in the regional, national or world economy having an effect on the company's business
* Becoming a takeover target
* The risk of obsolescent technology
* Being in an industry in decline

Financial risk

* Shortage of cash (liquidity risk)
* Trying to expand the business too quickly
* Having unrecorded liabilities (e.g. guarantees about which senior management is unaware)
* Taking decisions with incomplete or inaccurate financial information.

Compliance risk

* Breaching financial regulations
* Litigation risks
* Breaching the requirements of the Companies Act (or its legal equivalent)
* Incurring tax penalties

Operational risk

* Vulnerability of IT systems to unauthorized access (e.g. hackers)
* Loss of key people
* Succession problems
* Reputation damage or loss

17.5 Boards and corporate social responsibility

A question of increasing importance to all organizations is to what extent the board has ensured that strategic decisions incorporate ethical, socially responsible and sustainable factors. It is the duty of a diligent board to assess and to take into consideration issues of a sustainable environment. In many respects, corporate social responsibility (CSR) is not a separate issue but is one which permeates all board activities (in particular decision making and risk assessment).

An organization which operates in a manner contrary to CSR faces the risk of poor market ratings and adverse publicity. Those which face large ethical concerns also face the results of poor and adverse publicity. A well-known example of this is the case of BP-Amoco which suffered greatly as a result of its exploration activities in Colombia. Eventually accused of working for a corrupt government, BP Amoco suffered bad publicity, a drop in market value and a drastic drop in reputation. Few boards would want to ignore CSR. They would do so at their peril.

Two aspects of formalizing CSR have now become the remit of boards worldwide. The first is known as the 'triple bottom line'. This means that, alongside financial and other hard measures of performance, a measure of CSR (the third measure) should be included as an equal arbiter of performance. The second is known as the 'global compact', resulting from a meeting of the World Economic Forum in 1999. The then UN Secretary General, Kofi Annan, set out nine principles on human rights, labour and the environment that organizations need to address (and be judged against). Table 17.10 summarizes the nine core principles of the global compact.

A study by Contardo and Wilson (2001) revealed a patchy take up of these nine principles by the boards of twenty organizations. These twenty organizations were drawn from ten different nations in order to see if country of origin had any significant impact on the implementation of the nine principles. The results revealed that country of origin had no

Table 17.10 The nine principles of the global compact

Human rights	Businesses should: ◆ Support and respect the protection of international human rights within their sphere of influence ◆ Ensure their own corporations are not involved in human rights abuses (implicitly or explicitly)
Labour	◆ Recognize the right of labour to collective bargaining and freedom of association ◆ Eliminate forced and compulsory labour ◆ Abolish child labour ◆ Eliminate discrimination in terms of employment and occupation
Environment	◆ Take a precautionary approach to environmental challenges ◆ Promote greater environmental responsibility ◆ Encourage the development and diffusion of environmentally friendly technologies

impact at all. The data from this study revealed that boards were experiencing some difficulties in implementing the nine principles, especially in older organizations. Boards in older organizations experienced difficulties in assessing the relative priority of these principles in relation to other externally determined standards (such as International Standards or Health and Safety). In general, the boards of older organizations were making progress in networking with stakeholders in order to try to establish partnerships and had often set up new functions in the organization to deal with CSR issues. For example, Unilever had created a special department addressing CSR issues and had engaged with many stakeholders (including strong critics of the organization) in order to weave environmental consciousness throughout their business. Shell Brazil has introduced a clause in its contracts with distillers forbidding the use of child labour. Shell Brazil was awarded the title 'Child Friendly Company' for its work in discouraging the use of child labour in the production of sugar cane alcohol, which it is legally obliged to sell on its forecourts and include in its gasoline. BASF has established a sustainability council at board level to try to make sustainability a part of everyday processes in the company. Overall, however, the data from Contardo and Wilson (2001) point to a very patchy worldwide take up of the nine principles by a wide range of organizations, with boards in particular finding it difficult to add these responsibilities to their existing portfolio of activities.

17.6 What is an effective board?

There are many autobiographical accounts by practitioners of board effectiveness but few independently conducted analyses of board conduct and performance. Recently a study conducted by Pettigrew and McNulty has generated first-hand data on board conduct, power relationships and strategy processes (Pettigrew and McNulty 1995 and 1998; McNulty and Pettigrew 1999). This study used a multi-method approach combining a survey of the chairmen, CEOs and non-executive directors of the top 500 plcs, with personal interviews with 65 part-time and 43 full-time board members and the analysis of publicly available documentary material.

Most of the board members we interviewed acknowledged that it was somewhat easier to identify the characteristics of an ineffective board than to catalogue the features of an effective one. Indicators of ineffectiveness included:

- Poor chairing of the board
- Over-dominance by the chair
- Marginalization of the non-executives
- Cliques and politicking between and inside board meetings
- Failure to reveal critical information to board members
- Failure to encourage open discussions and allow issue spotting

❖ A board focused on a narrow set of issues and fixated by historical reporting and operational matters

❖ A closed process of recruitment to the board

Looking more broadly at board effectiveness, there are some important conceptual distinctions. These include considering effectiveness both against a set of agreed board purposes and against a trinity of design choices (inputs, processes and outputs); recognizing that effectiveness has to be customized to local circumstances; and being clear that performance in the boardroom is a dynamic issue and may require continuous performance assessment, learning and change. McNulty and Pettigrew (1999) characterized effective boards as 'maximalist' and less effective boards as 'minimalist'. Table 17.11 summarizes their characteristics.

The maximalist board does not have the extreme power asymmetrics to be found in the minimalist board. With greater sharing of power and information, and more clearly defined purposes and roles, better relationships and communication flows are apparent in the maximalist board. In time, with greater trust and better shared understandings between the chair and CEO, the board culture changes. With greater trust, more challenge and dissent becomes

Table 17.11 Characteristics of maximalist (successful) and minimalist (less successful) boards

Characteristics of minimalist boards	Characteristics of maximalist boards
Run by individuals and small factions	Trigger for change often a performance crisis
Big power asymmetries between chair or chair/CEO and rest of board and executive	Top-level change: new personalities and purpose and processes
Non-execs have low legitimacy; selected to maintain power asymmetries; starved of information; confined to the boardroom; isolated from the strategic process	Attempts to distinguish roles more clearly
	Recruitment of new non-executive directors: given greater legitimacy
Board agenda is stylized and predictable in its historical reporting	Board agenda and process opened up
	Space for issue spotting and resolutions
No space to spot issues, even less for dealing with them	Non-execs allowed into strategic process
	Non-execs allowed to roam outside boardroom
Little or no conflict, challenge or dissent	Roaming enhances perspective, judgement, confidence and trust
	Greater trust and openness allows greater challenge and dissent and more informal working and better relationships
	Often tensions about power. Non-execs are prepared to use it, and executives have felt it
	Checks and balances and fluidity of information and relationships allow control and leadership purposes to be realized

possible and more fundamental strategic issues are opened up for discussion and possible resolution. Although there is a more comfortable dynamic balance of power on maximalist boards, there may still be an appropriate tension about power. This tension may be a left-over from the company performance crisis, when the non-executives were prepared to use power and when the executives felt the use of power. Without this tension about power there would be no checks and balances, and without these the apparently contradictory board purposes of control and strategic leadership would be less likely to be realized.

17.7 Summary

This chapter has examined some key aspects of boards and their role in strategic decision making. Board have a strategic and public responsibility to provide direct returns for shareholders and employees, suppliers and have a responsibility towards the communities in which they operate. In the wake of recent corporate scandals and collapses, governments worldwide have been reviewing the role and the processes of governance.

Because the board is in place to lead and control the organization, it should have a clearly defined set of responsibilities and codes of operation. This chapter has outlined the main features of those responsibilities and it has outlined some of the major features of the emerging guidelines.

Although board structures differ from country to country, most countries have a common set of principles of governance, namely that no individual director has unrestrained power to control and direct the organization and that there should be a countervailing influence (on insiders on the board) from outside directors who act as the guardians of board conduct and decision making processes

Key terms

Agency theory 635

Board effectiveness 641

Code of governance 633

Combined Code 636

Corporate social responsibility 633

Governance 629

Legal systems 634

Non-executive directors 636

Online LearningCentre

When you have read this chapter, log on to the Online Learning Centre website at www.mcgraw-hill.co.uk/textbooks/mcgee to explore chapter-by-chapter test questions, further reading and more online study tools for strategy.

Recap questions and assignments

1 Why are governance processes and structures important to our understanding of strategy?

2 With regard to an organization you know well (or is in the pubic domain) what would you assess as its good and less good features in terms of governance structures and processes?

3 What do you see as the key changes and challenges for the future for corporate governance

Case 1 Walt Disney Company: 'The case against Michael Eisner'

Timeline

1984 Following a long period of relative decline, reflected in both its stock price and profits, corporate raider Saul Steinberg launches a takeover bid for Disney. Although unsuccessful it leads to a power struggle that is eventually won by a group of shareholders led by directors Roy E. Disney (nephew of Walt Disney and son of Roy O. Disney the co-founders of Walt Disney Productions) and Stanley Gold (Disney's close friend, attorney and financial advisor). The existing management – Raymond Watson (Chairman) and Ron Miller (CEO), Walt Disney's son-in-law – is replaced by Michael Eisner (Chairman and CEO), the President of Paramount Pictures (a division of Gulf & Western), and Frank Wells (President), a former CEO of Warner Bros (a division of Warner Communications). Both were equals in the sense that they reported directly to the board, with Eisner seen as the 'creative talent' and Wells the 'businessman', an arrangement similar to that found in the original Walt Disney Productions where Walt Disney (creative) was Chairman and CEO and Roy O. Disney (businessman) was President.

Roy E. Disney (who had previously resigned his executive position at the company while remaining on the board of directors) returns as Head of Animation.

Jeffery Katzenberg joins as Head of the Film Division.

1984–94 Over the next 10 years as the stock price rises 6000%, the company opens EuroDisney, makes numerous successful films and TV shows targeting all types of audiences, expands Disney World, buys TV stations and the Anaheim Mighty Ducks ice hockey team. Eisner is lauded as one of the great CEOs of the 1980s and 1990s.

1994 (April) Frank Wells is killed in a helicopter crash.

1994 (July) Katzenberg (seen by many commentator's as Eisner's eventual successor) leaves after a clash with Eisner. Only one month after *The Lion King*, overseen by Katzenberg, becomes the most successful animated film ever.

1994 (July) Eisner undergoes quadruple bypass surgery.

1994 Prince Alwaleed invests in the failing EuroDisney preventing the collapse of the project which is renamed Disneyland Paris.

1995 (Oct)   'Super-agent' Michael Ovitz, frequently described as the 'most powerful man in Hollywood', leaves Creative Artists Agency (CAA) to become Disney President. He is seen as a potential successor to Eisner by many industry insiders and institutional investors.

1995   George Mitchell joins the board.

1996 (Feb)   Disney purchases Capital Cities/ABC for $19 billion. It is the largest media takeover to date and the second largest acquisition of a US firm.

1996   Disney purchases the Anaheim Angels baseball franchise.

1997 (Jan)   Ovitz leaves the company after a public clash with Eisner with a $140 million severance package.

1997   *Business Week* names the Disney board the worst board in America (for the first time).

1999   Disney's lawsuit with Katzenberg, regarding future profit participation, is settled when he accepts a $275 million payout.

2000   Roy E. Disney and Stanley Gold begin their campaign to force the board to develop a programme to identify Eisner's eventual successor and become more independent. The board of directors includes Eisner's friends such as actor Sidney Poitier, architect Robert A.M. Stern, who has designed many Disney properties, and former Sen. George Mitchell, who consults for Disney. The board's judgement is particularly questionable with regard to the compensation packages awarded to Eisner. In the spring of 2001, *Forbes* concluded that in the previous five years, Eisner made $737 million. This was in a period when the company's profits fell and in which the company's stock performed poorly.

2001 (Oct)   Disney acquires the Fox Family Channel for $5.3 billion, a price that is seen by many as far too high.

2002 (Aug)   During the previous five years, Disney performed worse than all but three of the 30 Dow stocks. Eisner's failures are becoming increasingly common-place, they include the poor performance of the ABC network, the leading network, possessing an envied news organization and cutting-edge original programming such as *NYPD Blue* when it was purchased seven years earlier; a botched plan to build an American history theme park; the loss of millions of dollars on an expensive new California Adventure attraction at Disneyland, which failed to draw significant crowds; and a loss of more than $1 billion in an attempt to replicate Yahoo!'s portal with the go.com network.

2003	The Securities and Exchange Commission began investigating whether Disney failed adequately to disclose payments made by the company to directors and their family members in 2001.
2003 (April)	Disney sells Anaheim Angels baseball franchise.
2003 (May)	Disney announces plans to sell its badly performing Disney Stores.
2003 (Nov)	Roy E. Disney learns he will not be entered on the slate of directors for the next election (March 2004).
2003 (Nov)	Roy E. Disney resigns from the board and publishes his letter of resignation in which he claims that some of his associates have been required to report his conversations and activities back to Eisner, the company has lost its creative direction, Eisner is guilty of micro-management and has refused to establish a clear succession plan. He concludes by saying '… it is my sincere belief that it is you who should be leaving not me. Accordingly, I once again call for your resignation or retirement.'
2003 (Dec)	Stanley Gold resigns from the board and publishes his letter of resignation in which he criticizes the board for 'not actively engaging in serious discussions regarding the Company's flawed plans and management's unmet projections and unfilled promises'. He also questions the board's adoption of its Corporate Governance Guidelines which he describes as 'another example of this Board's commitment to image over substance'.
2004 (Jan)	Pixar, the company behind blockbusters such as *Finding Nemo* and *Monsters Inc*, ends its distribution deal with Disney following the failure of the two parties to negotiate a new distribution deal. The five movies created by Pixar for Disney have grossed more than $2.5 billion at the box office.
2004 (Feb)	Comcast announces a hostile bid for Disney ($54 billion in stock). The bid is rejected.
2004 (Feb)	Institutional Shareholder Services (Proxy Advisor) recommends shareholders to withhold their vote on the re-election of Michael Eisner.
2004 (Feb)	Glass Lewis & Co. (Proxy Advisor) recommends shareholders to withhold their vote on the re-election of Michael Eisner and George Mitchell.
2004 (March)	A five and half hour annual shareholder meeting sees 43% of shareholders withhold their vote for Eisner and 24% for Mitchell (final results including proxy voting show 45.37% and 25.69% respectively). Later in the day it is announced that Eisner will be replaced as Chairman of the Board by Mitchell.

656 CASE STUDY

2004 (April)   *Forbes* magazine names Eisner as one of the five worst CEOs in America (based on annualized total return of minus 5% and average compensation over the six year period of $121 170 940).

2004 (April)   Comcast drops bid for Disney (now worth $48 billion).

2004 (Sept)   Eisner announces that he will retire when his contract expires in September 2006. The two-year period of transition to a new CEO is heavily criticized for being too long, increasing uncertainty, handicapping the development of corporate strategy and creating a 'lame duck' CEO. The search for Eisner's successor will be led by Chairman George Mitchell, who will also be leaving the board in September 2006, who announced the company's intention to name the new CEO in June 2005, leading to uncertainty as to whether Eisner would leave the company earlier than planned. Mitchell also announced Robert Iger (a long-time executive at Capital Cities/ABC before its sale to Disney, who became Disney's President in 2000). This was Eisner's personal choice as his successor and the only internal candidate for the post.

Following initial suggestions that he would not rule out continuing to serve on the board and reclaiming the Chairmanship if asked to by the board after his 'retirement', Eisner said in a *Fortune* magazine interview that his assumption is that he would not continue on the board or as Chairman. Mitchell added that 'as far as the Board is concerned that is the end of it.'

The California Public Employees' Retirement System (one of the US's largest investors and a leading advocate for improved corporate governance) called for Eisner's resignation, saying in a press release that Eisner's 'continued presence on the board would prevent the company from the clean break that is needed to restore investor confidence.'

Upcoming   A lawsuit filed by shareholders against Disney is expected to be tried in Delaware's Court of Chancery in October 2004. The suit is challenging Ovitz's $140 million severance package. Eisner, and the directors of the company will defend against allegations that their mishandling of Mr Ovitz's hiring and termination cost shareholders millions.

The defendants will have to face claims they breached their duty to Disney in 1995 when Mr Ovitz negotiated the terms of his employment deal, and in 1996, when he was allowed to leave the company under a 'no-fault' clause.

Attorneys for shareholders argue that Mr Ovitz's performance was so poor in the president's slot that the company should have fired him for cause, a move that would have meant a much smaller severance package. Mr Ovitz's attorneys say the evidence will prove otherwise.

In a pre-trial hearing, the judge ruled that instead of resigning or being fired, Disney's president may have colluded with Mr Eisner to engineer a no-fault departure. In court papers, Mr Ovitz's attorneys have said the $140 million no-fault payment was justified and a bargain, compared with the $320 million in damages that Ovitz could have won had Disney fired him unfairly for cause. If shareholder allegations that Mr Ovitz lied and alienated Disney executives prove to be true, the judge may find that the no-fault termination was unjustified and that Disney's board is to blame for not firing him.

The Disney directors are already in a difficult position as the board never met to approve Ovitz's departure or the payment of his severance package and it is unclear whether the payment ever was properly authorized.

Upcoming Disney and Gold have promised to run an alternate slate of potential Disney directors if the board does not remove Eisner by the March 2005 annual meeting.

The above case covers many of the key issues in the present debate on corporate governance:

1 CEO rewards
2 Chairman/CEO split
3 Succession planning
4 Board independence
5 Effectiveness of the board
6 Communication among and to board members
7 Responsibilities of directors
8 Payments to directors' companies and family members
9 Ceremonial adoption of corporate governance guidelines
10 The role of financial institutions

The letter from Stanley Gold is below:

[Letterhead of Stanley P. Gold]

December 1, 2003

To the Board of Directors of the Walt Disney Company:

It is with regret that I resign effective immediately from the Board of Directors of the Walt Disney Company and second Roy Disney's call for the removal of Michael Eisner as Chairman and C.E.O. I am proud of my more than 15 years of service and my role in reshaping the Company in 1984 by bringing Frank Wells and Michael Eisner to the Company. I do, however, lament that my efforts over the past three years to implement needed changes has only succeeded in creating an insular Board of Directors serving as a bulwark to shield management from criticism and accountability. At this time, I believe there is little that I can achieve by working from within to refocus the Company. I hope that my resignation will serve as a catalyst for change at Disney.

The most recent evidence of the drive for insularity is reflected in the Governance Committee's determination that Roy Disney should no longer serve on the Board, ostensibly because Roy had surpassed the expected retirement age established by the Board's Corporate Governance Guidelines. In fact, these very rules regarding age, by their terms, only apply to non-management directors, not to Roy, who, as the Committee knows, has been deemed a management director. The Committee's decision and George Mitchell's defense of it yesterday are clearly disingenuous. The real reason for the Committee's action is that Roy has become more pointed and vocal in his criticism of Michael Eisner and this Board. This is yet another attempt by this Board to squelch dissent by hiding behind the veil of 'good governance.' What a curious result.

Roy has devoted a lifetime to Disney as both an employee and Director. He has served with renewed vigor during these times of malaise, disappointment and instability at the Company, trying to maintain the morale of employees, focusing on the magic that makes Disney special and attacking bonuses to the CEO and increased compensation for Board members while the Company falters and shareholder value erodes. He and his family have a very large financial stake in the Company. Unlike Messrs. Watson and Murphy who have asked to be replaced, Roy has sought even more involvement only to be told that his input in animation will continue to be minimized and that his role as a Director is no longer welcome. This Board has become an enabler to entrenched management and, in so doing, is not effectively discharging its duties to the shareholders. This conduct has resulted in yet another valuable human asset of the Company slipping away. Within the last year this Board will have managed to cull from its ranks Andrea Van de Kamp and now Roy, two of the staunchest critics of Michael Eisner and the Company's poor performance. I cannot sit idly by as this Board continues to ignore and disenfranchise those who raise questions about the performance of management.

As this Board knows, during my tenure I have tried to be an active, engaged Director. I believe a board should not merely rubber stamp decisions of senior management. I decided in August of 2002 that it was not enough just to express my views in the limited time set aside for our infrequent Board meetings. I therefore began a series of written communications to the Board regarding the Company, its management and the Board. I wrote to express my disagreement and growing concern with management, its policies and the effectiveness of the Board. I focused on the failed initiatives of the Company over the past five or six years and admonished the Board for not actively engaging in serious discussions regarding the Company's flawed plans and management's unmet projections and unfulfilled promises. In particular, I have urged the Board to concentrate on the Company's 'poor performance, lack of credibility and accountability and poor capital allocation.' In an effort to get Directors to seriously assess management's 5-year strategic plan (a plan that is only discussed with this Board, but not submitted for Board approval), I wrote to the Board to detail the Company's unsatisfactory financial performance for the past several years and to suggest a process, a so-called Diagnostic Review, designed to give the non-management directors the tools necessary to evaluate performance and establish a comprehensive framework and baseline from which the Board could be active partners in developing plans to maximize the value of Disney's existing assets and businesses. That approach was opposed by management and then, not surprisingly, rejected by the Board. The Board and its Chairman even criticized me for putting on paper these serious questions about fundamental matters.

I believe the Board's adoption of its Corporate Governance Guidelines was yet another example of this Board's commitment to image over substance. Among other things, those Guidelines were carefully crafted to stifle dissent while allowing those supportive of senior management to continue business as usual. This was apparent when the Board applied its Guidelines to conclude that I was not 'independent' despite the fact that I frequently challenged management at Board meetings and criticized both the Board's and the Company's performance. That decision was initially based on my daughter's employment in a non-executive position at Disney and, then, after that reason became insufficient under the new NYSE Governance Guidelines, because of my association with Roy. This resulted in my further isolation as I was no longer permitted to serve on the Governance and Nominating Committee or the Compensation Committee. On the other hand, John Bryson was deemed 'independent' and appointed Chairman of the Nominating and Governance Committee despite the fact that his wife is an executive officer at Lifetime Entertainment Television, a 50% owned subsidiary of Disney, where she earned in excess of $1 million in total compensation in fiscal 2001. In addition, Senator Mitchell was appointed Presiding Director, despite having been recently employed as a Company consultant and notwithstanding that the law firm of which he was chairman received in excess of $1 million for legal services on behalf of the Company in fiscal 2001.

At the time the Company's new Corporate Governance Guidelines were being considered, I also urged the Board to separate the positions of Chairman of the Board and CEO. This separation would empower the Board and help establish its independence and oversight role. Not only did the Board reject that initiative, the Board failed to give the newly established Presiding Director any real substantive powers.

Continuing through March of this year I wrote to express my concerns regarding the financial performance of the Company and the repeated failures of management to achieve its forecasts. I urged this Board to feel a sense of urgency in dealing with the issues of leadership, performance, operations and accountability. Those efforts failed. Instead, Mr. Eisner was awarded a bonus of $5 million in Disney shares by the Compensation Committee despite objections by Roy and me. I believe that bonuses for senior management must be tied to performance; by that measure, no bonus was warranted.

In a similar vein, I recently wrote to express my objection to the Compensation and Governance Committee's joint recommendations that fees paid to Disney Directors be increased dramatically, that stock grants to Directors be substituted for options (and thereby render meaningless the requirement that Directors own $100,000 in Disney shares) and that greater compensation be paid to the Presiding Director. Raises for the Disney Directors at this time are inappropriate based on my assessment of the Company's performance. I objected to the increase for the Presiding Director on the grounds that it did not reflect a reasonable payment for the only slightly increased duties. Finally, I could not make sense of a share ownership requirement for Directors that would be satisfied by a direct issuance from the Company at the same time Directors' cash compensation was being increased.

It is clear to me that this Board is unwilling to tackle the difficult issues I believe this Company continues to face – management failures and accountability for those failures, operational deficiencies, imprudent capital allocations, the cannibalization of certain Company icons for short-term gain, the enormous loss of creative talent over the last years, the absence of succession planning and the lack of strategic focus. Instead, the Board seems determined to devote its time and energies to adopting policies that focus not on substance, but on process and, in reality, only serve to muzzle and isolate those Directors who recognize that their role is to be active participants in shaping the Company and planning for executive succession. Further, this Board isolates those Directors who believe that Michael Eisner (when measured by the dismal results over the last 7 years) is not up to the challenge. Perhaps acting independently, from outside the Boardroom, not hamstrung by a recently enacted Board policy barring Board members from communicating with shareholders and the media, I can have greater success in shaping the policies, practices and operations of Disney than I had as a member of the Board.

In accordance with Item 6 of Form 8-K and Item 7 of Schedule 14A, I request that you disclose this letter and that you file a copy of this letter as an exhibit to a Company Form 8-K.

Very truly yours,

(Signed) Stanley P. Gold

The letter from Roy Edward Disney is as follows:

Letterhead of Roy Edward Disney

November 30, 2003

Dear Michael,

It is with deep sadness and regret that I send you this letter of resignation from the Walt Disney Company, both as Chairman of the Feature Animation Division and as Vice Chairman of the Board of Directors.

You well know that you and I have had serious differences of opinion about the direction and style of management in the Company in recent years, for whatever reason, you have driven a wedge between me and those I work with even to the extent of requiring some of your associates to report my conversations and activities back to you. I find this intolerable.

Finally, you discussed with the Nominating Committee of the Board of Directors its decision to leave my name off the slate of directors to be elected in the coming years, effectively muzzling my voice on the Board – much as you did with Andrea Van de Kamp last year.

Michael, I believe your conduct has resulted from my clear and unambiguous statements to you and to the Board of Directors that after 19 years at the helm you are no longer the best person to run the Walt Disney Company. You have a very successful first 10 plus years at the Company in partnership with Frank Wells, for which I salute you. But, since Frank's untimely death in 1994, the Company has lost its focus, its creative energy, and its heritage.

As I have said, and as Stanley Gold has documented in letters to you and other members of the Board, this Company, under your leadership, has failed during the last seven years in many ways:

1   The failure to bring back ABC Prime Time from the ratings abyss it has been in for years and your inability to program successfully the ABC Family Channel. Both of these failures have had, and I believe will continue to have, significant adverse impact on shareholder value.

2   Your considered micro-management of everyone around you with the resulting loss of morale throughout this Company.

3   The timidity of your investments in our theme park business. At Disney's California Adventure, Paris, and now in Hong Kong, you have tried to build parks 'on the cheap' and they show it and the attendance figures reflect it.

4   The perception by all our stakeholders – consumers, investors, employees, distributors and suppliers – that the Company is rapacious, soul-less, and always looking for the 'quick buck' rather than long-term value which is leading to a loss of public trust.

5   The creative brain drain of the last several years, which is real and continuing, and damages our Company with the loss of every talented employee.

6   Your failure to establish and build constructive relationships with creative partners, especially Pixar, Miramax, and cable companies distributing our products.

7   Your consistent refusal to establish a clear succession plan.

In conclusion, Michael, it is my sincere belief that it is you who should be leaving and not me. Accordingly, I once again call for your resignation or retirement. The Walt Disney Company deserve fresh, energetic leadership at this challenging time in its history just as it did in 1984 when I headed a restructuring that resulted in your recruitment to the company.

I have and will always have an enormous allegiance and respect for this Company, founded by my uncle Walt, and father, Roy, and to our faithful employees and loyal stockholders.

I don't know if you and other directors can comprehend how painful it is for me and the extended Disney family to arrive at this decision.

In accordance with Item 6 of Form 8-K and Item 7 of Schedule 14A, I request that you disclose this letter and that you file a copy of this letter as an exhibit to a Company Form 8-K.

With sincere regret,

(Signed) Roy Edward Disney

cc. Board of Directors

Case Questions

1 What went wrong on the Disney Board? Suggest ways you might avoid or alleviate these factors.

2 To what extent do you think any of the regulatory and advisory codes of conduct for Boards would have been useful in addressing Disney's problems of governance? Why would they have been useful (or why not)?

3 Examine the letters from Stanley Gold and Roy Disney. What do they reveal about board structures, processes and ethos?

4 What are the implications of poor governance (such as in the Disney case) for strategic thinking and acting in organizations?

Further reading and references

Aguilera, RV and Cuervo-Cazurra, A (2004) Codes of good governance worldwide: what is the trigger? *Organization Studies*, **25**, **3**, pp. 415–43.

Bank of England (1998) 'Composition of Company Boards', *Bank of England Quarterly Bulletin*, May, pp. 242–5.

Berle, AA and Means, GC (1932) *The Modern Corporation and Private Property*, Macmillan, New York.

Bernstein, PL (1996) *Against the Gods: The Remarkable Story of Risk*, Wiley, New York.

Bostock, R (1995) 'Company Responses to Cadbury', *Corporate Governance: An International Review*, **3**, **2**, April, pp. 72–7.

Cadbury Report (1992) *Committee on the Financial Aspects of Corporate Governance*, Moorgate, London.

Cadbury, A (2000) 'The Corporate Governance Agenda', *Corporate Governance: An International Review*, **8**, **1**, pp. 7–15.

CADS (1995) *The Financial Aspects of Corporate Governance: Compliance with the Code of Best Practice*, May, Stock Exchange, London.

Cassidy, DP (2000) 'Wither Corporate Governance in the 21st Century', *Corporate Governance: An International Review*, **8**, **4**, pp. 297–302.

Charkham, JP (1999) *Keeping Good Company: A Study of Corporate Governance in Five Countries* (2nd edition), Oxford University Press, Oxford.

Collins, JC and Porras, JI (2000) *Built to Last: Successful Habits of Visionary Companies*, Random House, New York.

Condon, D (2003) 'The Role of the Turnbull Guidelines and the Management and Identification of Risk in UK Multi-National Companies', PhD in progress Warwick Business School, UK.

Conger, JA, Lawler, EE and Finegold, DL (2001) *Corporate Boards: Strategy for Adding Value at the Top*, Jossey-Bass Pfeiffer, San Francisco and Wiley, Chichester.

Contardo, I and Wilson, DC (2001) 'The United Nations' Global Compact: A Report on Case Study Evidence', Research Paper, Warwick Business School, UK.

Conyon, MJ (1994) 'Corporate Governance Changes in UK Companies between 1988 and 1993', *Corporate Governance: An International Review*, **2**, **2**, pp. 97–109.

Conyon, MJ (1995) *Cadbury in the Boardroom*, in Arthur Anderson Corporate Register, Hemmington Scott, London.

Conyon, MJ and Mallin, C (1997) 'Women in the Boardroom: Evidence from Large UK Companies', *Corporate Governance: An International Review*, 5, 3, pp. 112–17.

Conyon, MJ and Murphy, KJ (2000) 'The Prince and the Pauper? CEO Pay in the US and UK', *The Economic Journal*, 110, F640–F671.

Greenbury, R (1995) *Directors' Remuneration: Report of a Study Group Chaired by Sir Richard Greenbury*, Gee Publishing, London.

Hambrick, DC, Nadler, DA and Tushman, ML (1998) (eds) *Navigating Change: How CEOs, Top Teams and Boards Steer Transformation*, Harvard University Press, Boston, MA.

Hampel, R (1998) *Committee on Corporate Governance: Final Report*, Gee Publishing, London.

Hemscott (2003) 'The current population of non-executive directors', Hemscott Group Limited, London

Higgs, D (2003) Review of the Role and Effectiveness of Non-Executive Directors, Department of Trade and Industry, London. Printed in the United Kingdom by The Stationery Office 19585 809438 01/03.

Hutton, W (1996) *The State We're In*, Vintage Press, London.

Institute of Chartered Accountants (1999) 'Internal Control: Guidance for Directors on the Combined Code', ICA, London.

Institute of Chartered Accountants (1999) 'Implementing Turnbull: A Boardroom Brief', ICA Centre for Business Performance, London.

Kaplan, RS and Norton, DP (1992) The Balanced Scorcard: Measures that Drive Performance, *Harvard Business Review*, Jan/Feb.

Katzenbach, JR and Smith, DK (1992) *The Wisdom of Teams: Creating the High Performance Organization*, Harvard Business School Press, Boston, MA.

Keasey, K, Thompson, S and Wright, M (eds) (1997) *Corporate Governance: Economic Management and Financial Issues*, Oxford University Press, Oxford.

Kirkbride, J and Letza, S (2003) 'Establishing the boundaries of regulation in coporate governance: Is the UK moving toward a process of collibration?', *Business and Society Review*, 108, 4, pp. 463–85.

McNulty, T and Pettigrew, AM (1999) 'Strategists on the Board', *Organization Studies*, 20, 1, pp. 47–74.

Monks, RAG and Minnow, N (1992) *Power and Accountability: Restoring Balance of Power Between Corporations, Owners and Societies*, Harper Business, New York.

OECD (2004) *Principles of Corporate Governance* (available at www.OECD.org).

Pettigrew, AM (2004) 'Corporate Governance', *Distance Learning MBA Notes for Strategy and Practice*, Warwick Business School.

Pettigrew, AM and McNulty, T (1995) 'Power and Influence in and Around the Boardroom', *Human Relations*, **48**, **8**, pp. 845–73.

Pettigrew, AM and McNulty, T (1998) 'Sources and Uses of Power in the Boardroom', *European Journal of Work and Organizational Psychology*, **7**, **2**, pp. 197–214.

Ward, RD (2000) *The Boardroom Insider Guidebook*, New York, Wiley.

Strategic Leadership:

Creating a Learning Organization and an Ethical Organization

>chapter objectives

After reading this chapter, you should have a good understanding of:

- The three key activities in which all successful leaders must be continually engaged.

- The importance of recognizing the interdependence of the three key leadership activities and the salience of power in overcoming resistance to change.

- The crucial role of emotional intelligence (EI) in successful leadership as well as its potential drawbacks.

- The value of creating and maintaining a "learning organization" in today's global marketplace.

- The five central elements of a "learning organization."

- The leader's role in establishing an ethical organization.

- The benefits of developing an ethical organization.

- The high financial and nonfinancial costs associated with ethical crises.

*t*o compete in the global marketplace, organizations need to have strong and effective leadership. This involves the active process of both creating and implementing proper strategies. In this chapter we address key activities in which leaders throughout the organization must be involved to be successful in creating competitive advantages.

In the first section we provide a brief overview of the three key leadership activities. These are (1) setting a direction, (2) designing the organization, and (3) nurturing a culture committed to excellence and ethical behavior. Each of these activities is "necessary but not sufficient"; that is, to be effective, leaders must give proper attention to each of them. We also address the importance of a leader's effective use of power to overcome resistance to change.

The second section discusses the vital role of emotional intelligence (EI) in effective strategic leadership. EI refers to an individual's capacity for recognizing his or her emotions and those of others. It consists of five components: self-awareness, self-regulation, motivation, empathy, and social skills. We also address potential downsides or drawbacks that may result from the ineffective use of EI.

Next we address the important role of a leader in creating a "learning organization." Here leaders must strive to harness the individual and collective talents of individuals throughout the entire organization. Creating a learning organization becomes particularly important in today's competitive environment, which is increasingly unpredictable, dynamic, and interdependent. Clearly, everyone must be involved in learning. It can't be only a few people at the top of the organization. The key elements of a learning organization are inspiring and motivating people with a mission or purpose, empowering employees at all levels, accumulating and sharing internal and external information, and challenging the status quo to enable creativity.

The final section discusses a leader's challenge in creating and maintaining an ethical organization. There are many benefits of having an ethical organization. In addition to financial benefits, it can enhance human capital and help to ensure positive relationships with suppliers, customers, society at large, and governmental agencies. On the other hand, the costs of ethical crises can be very expensive for many reasons. We address four key elements of an ethical organization: role models, corporate credos and codes of conduct, reward and evaluation systems, and policies and procedures.

348

Dess–Lumpkin–Eisner:
Strategic Management:
Text and Cases, Third
Edition

III. Strategic
Implementation

11. Strategic Leadership:
Creating a Learning
Organization and an
Ethical Organization

© The McGraw–Hill
Companies, 2007

Scott A. Livengood was fired as Chief Executive Officer (CEO) of Krispy Kreme on January 19, 2005.[1] He hasn't received very much good news lately. The firm's stock went up 10 percent the day of that announcement. And he received the rather dubious honor of being recognized as one of *Business Week*'s seven "Worst Managers" of 2004.

What brought about the demise of Livengood, a 28-year veteran of the doughnut maker who had been CEO since 1998? Let's look at two of the central issues.

First, under his direction Krispy Kreme expanded far too rapidly. After its initial public offering in 2001, it continued to open stores at breakneck speed. Hoping to cash in on the nation's sweet tooth, the chain created media events in places like New York, San Francisco, and Boston. At times, cars would line up for blocks just to bring a box of the tasty confections to work. Unfortunately, while the craze faded, the costs of operating the franchises did not. By 2003, same-store sales had declined 16 percent, while the company's overhead continued to rise. In short, the brand quickly lost its novelty. Soon Krispy Kreme realized that many of its franchises would fail.

Recent financial results reflect the poor strategy. The once high-flying company posted a $3 million third-quarter loss in November 2004—its second losing quarter of the year. And in February 2005, the firm stated that it would restate earnings for the previous year, lowering previously reported income by as much as 8.6 percent.

Second, there are what *Fortune* has called "shady deals" surrounding how the firm conducted buybacks of some franchises owned by corporate insiders. For example, Krispy Kreme didn't disclose that a California franchise it repurchased in 2004 was partly owned by Livengood's ex-wife, whose stake was valued at $1.5 million. While executives aren't required to disclose transactions with former spouses, Livengood could be in trouble if the deal was made as part of a settlement or in lieu of alimony.

An even more troubling transaction is the 2003 deal in which the chain repurchased six stores in Dallas and Shreveport, Louisiana, that were partly owned by Krispy Kreme's former chairman and current director, Joseph McAleer. McAleer got a pretty good deal—$67 million (or $11 million per store). This comes to more than three times what the firm paid for many other shops! According to David Gourevitch, a former Securities and Exchange Commission (SEC) enforcement attorney, "At some point a transaction is not remotely reasonable, and it approximates a gift or payoff." Worst case scenario: The SEC could impose fines and require some officials to step down.

The SEC continues to investigate the firm and it upgraded its informal inquiry to a formal probe. Although customers may continue to enjoy Krispy Kreme's products, the investors have hardly had a pleasant experience. Krispy Kreme's stock price has continued to sink. By late 2005 it was at $7—less than one-sixth of the $45 peak that it reached in July 2003. This fall reflects a loss of market capitalization of over $2 billion.

Clearly, many of the decisions and actions of Scott A. Livengood were not in the best interests of the firm and its shareholders. In contrast, effective leaders play an important and often pivotal role in the development and implementation of strategies.

This chapter provides insights into how organizations can more effectively manage, change, and cope with increased environmental complexity and uncertainty. Below we will define leadership and introduce what are considered to be the three most important leadership activities as well as the important role of power. The second section focuses on a key trait—emotional intelligence—that has become increasingly recognized as critical to successful leadership. Then, the third major section, "Developing a Learning Organization," provides a useful framework for how leaders can help their firms learn and proactively adapt in the face of accelerating change. Central to this contemporary idea is the concept of empowerment, wherein employees and managers throughout the organization truly come to have a sense of self-determination, meaning, competence, and impact. The fourth section addresses the leader's role in building an ethical organization. Here, we address both the value of an ethical culture for a firm as well as the key elements that it encompasses.

>>Leadership: Three Interdependent Activities

In today's chaotic world, few would argue against the need for leadership, but how do we go about encouraging it? Let's focus on business organizations. Is it enough to merely keep the organization afloat, or is it essential to make steady progress toward some well-defined objective? We believe custodial management is not leadership. Rather, leadership is proactive, goal-oriented, and focused on the creation and implementation of a creative vision. *Leadership is the process of transforming organizations from what they are to what the leader would have them become.* This definition implies a lot: *dissatisfaction* with the status quo, a *vision* of what should be, and a *process* for bringing about change. An insurance company executive recently shared the following insight on leadership, "I lead by the Noah Principle: It's all right to know when it's going to rain, but, by God, you had better build the ark."

Doing the right thing is becoming increasingly important in today's competitive environment. After all, many industries are declining; the global village is becoming increasingly complex, interconnected, and unpredictable; and product and market life cycles are becoming increasingly compressed. Recently, when asked to describe the life cycle of his company's products, the CEO of a supplier of computer components replied, "Seven months from cradle to grave—and that includes three months to design the product and get it into production!" Richard D'Aveni, author of *Hypercompetition,* went even further. He argued that in a world where all dimensions of competition appear to be compressed in time and heightened in complexity, *sustainable* competitive advantages are no longer possible.

Despite the importance of doing the "right thing," leaders must also be concerned about doing "things right." Charan and Colvin argued strongly that implementation (or execution) is also essential to success.

> Any way that you look at it, mastering execution turns out to be the odds-on best way for a CEO to keep his job. So what's the right way to think about that sexier obsession, strategy? It's vitally important—obviously. The problem is that our age's fascination feeds the mistaken belief that developing exactly the right strategy will enable a company to rocket past competitors. In reality, that's less than half the battle.[2]

Thus, leaders are change agents whose success is measured by how effectively they implement a strategic vision and mission.

Accordingly, many authors contend that successful leaders must recognize three interdependent activities that must be continually reassessed for organizations to succeed. As shown in Exhibit 11.1, these are: (1) determining a direction, (2) designing the organization, and (3) nurturing a culture dedicated to excellence and ethical behavior.[3]

The interdependent nature of these three activities is self-evident. Consider an organization with a great mission and a superb organizational structure and design, but a culture that implicitly encourages shirking and unethical behavior. Or a strong culture and organizational design but little direction and vision—in caricature, a highly ethical and efficient buggy whip manufacturer. Or one with a sound direction and strong culture, but counterproductive teams and a "zero-sum" reward system that leads to the dysfunctional situation in which one party's gain is viewed as another party's loss, and collaboration and sharing are severely hampered. Obviously, the examples could go on and on. We contend that much of the failure of today's organizations can be attributed to a lack of equal consideration of these three activities. The imagery of a three-legged stool is instructive: It will collapse if one leg is missing or broken. Let's briefly look at each of these activities. We'll also address the important role of a leader's power in overcoming resistance to change.

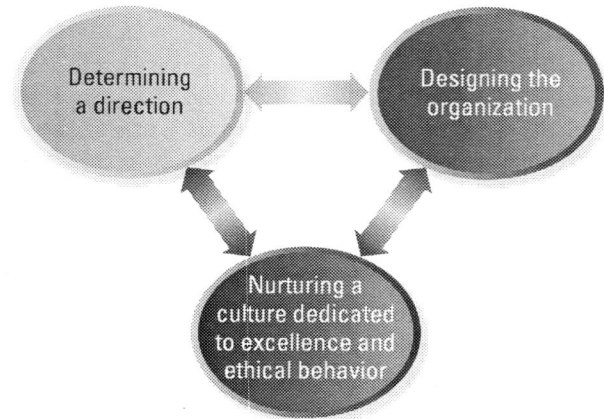

Exhibit 11.1   Three Interdependent Activities of Leadership

Setting a Direction

Leaders need a holistic understanding of an organization's stakeholders. This requires an ability to scan the environment to develop a knowledge of all of the company's stakeholders (e.g., customers, suppliers, shareholders) and other salient environmental trends and events and integrate this knowledge into a vision of what the organization could become. It necessitates the capacity to solve increasingly complex problems, become proactive in approach, and develop viable strategic options. Developing a strategic vision provides many benefits: a clear future direction; a framework for the organization's mission and goals; and enhanced employee communication, participation, and commitment. Strategy Spotlight 11.1 discusses how Chairman Howard Schultz's vision of Starbucks as a "third place" has spurred the firm's remarkable growth.

At times the creative process involves what the CEO of Yokogawa, GE's Japanese partner in the Medical Systems business, called "bullet train" thinking.[4] That is, if you want to increase the speed by 10 miles per hour, you look for incremental advances. However, if you want to double the speed, you've got to think "out of the box" (e.g., widen the track, change the overall suspension system). In today's challenging times, leaders typically need more than just keeping the same train with a few minor tweaks. Instead, they must come up with more revolutionary visions.

Consider how Robert Tillman, CEO of Lowe's, dramatically revitalized his firm by setting a clear and compelling direction. He made it into a formidable competitor to Home Depot, Inc., the Goliath of the home-improvement and hardware retailing industry.[5] In his six years as CEO, Tillman has transformed the $36.5 billion chain, based in Wilkesboro, North Carolina. Its shares have more than doubled over the past four years, while Home Depot's have fallen about 20 percent.

Tillman has redirected Lowe's strategy by responding effectively to research showing that women initiate 80 percent of home projects. While Home Depot has focused on the professionals and male customers, Tillman has redesigned Lowe's stores to give them a brighter appearance, stocked them with more appliances, and focused on higher-margin goods (including everything from Laura Ashley paints to high-end bathroom fixtures). And, like Wal-Mart, Lowe's has one of the best inventory systems in retailing. As a result, Lowe's profits are expected to continue to rise faster than Home Depot's.

11.1   STRATEGY SPOTLIGHT

Howard Schultz's Vision of Starbucks as a "Third Place"

Most people think of Starbucks as an expensive place to get a cup of coffee. However, Chairman Howard Schultz sees the 8,000-store chain as a "third place" for people to hang out besides home and work. That is why the seemingly unrelated service of offering wireless Net access in its stores that started in 2002 turned out to be so successful. Although Starbucks Corp. will not quantify the revenue impact, people using the service typically stay nine times longer than the usual five minutes—almost certainly enough time to consume more lattes. Further, 90 percent of customers who log on are doing so after peak morning hours, which helps to fill the stores during previously slow periods. According to Anne Saunders, Starbucks' senior vice-president of marketing, "If we'd only thought of ourselves as a coffee company, we wouldn't have done this."

The wireless network also inspired a new initiative that could again remake the Seattle-based company. Its recently introduced Hear Music Coffeehouses features dozens of listening stations where people can make custom CDs, at about a dollar a tune, from hundreds of thousands of songs. Eventually, Starbucks plans to have a Hear Music media bar in about half of its stores. In addition to offering this new service, Schultz has said he thinks Starbucks could transform the music business. Although that might be debatable, he's transforming Starbucks once again. And who would have ever thought that Apple and Starbucks might become competitors?

Source: Burrows, P., Hamm, S., Brady, D. & Rowley, I. 2004. Managing for innovation. *BusinessWeek*, October 11: 192–200; and Gray, S. 2005. Starbucks brews broader menu; coffee chain's cup runneth over with breakfast, lunch, music. *Wall Street Journal*, February 9: B9.

Let's now turn to another key leadership activity: the design of the organization's structure, processes, and evaluation and control systems.

Designing the Organization

At times, almost all leaders have difficulty implementing their vision and strategies. Such problems—many of which we discussed in Chapter 10—may stem from a variety of sources, including:

- Lack of understanding of responsibility and accountability among managers.
- Reward systems that do not motivate individuals (or collectives such as groups and divisions) toward desired organizational goals.
- Inadequate or inappropriate budgeting and control systems.
- Insufficient mechanisms to coordinate and integrate activities across the organization.

Successful leaders are actively involved in building structures, teams, systems, and organizational processes that facilitate the implementation of their vision and strategies. For example, we discussed the necessity for consistency between business-level and corporate-level strategies and organizational control in Chapter 9. Clearly, a firm would generally be unable to attain an overall low-cost advantage without closely monitoring its costs through detailed and formalized cost and financial control procedures. In a similar vein, achieving a differentiation advantage would necessitate encouraging innovation, creativity, and sensitivity to market conditions. Such efforts would be typically impeded by the use of a huge set of cumbersome rules and regulations, as well as highly centralized decision making. With regard to corporate-level strategy, in Chapter 9 we addressed how a related diversification strategy would necessitate reward systems that emphasize behavioral measures to promote sharing across divisions within a firm, whereas an unrelated strategy should rely more on financial (or objective) indicators of

STRATEGY SPOTLIGHT 11.2

Marshall Industries: Problems with Incentives

Marshall Industries is a large Los Angeles distributor of 170,000 different electronic components. The company has 30,000 customers and receives supplies from more than 150 suppliers. CEO Rod Rodin became concerned about some irregularities in the company. He saw that an average of 20 percent of monthly sales were being shipped in the last three days of the month. He discovered that divisions within the company were hiding customer returns and opening bad credit accounts to beef up monthly numbers. Employees in divisions with scarce supplies were hiding the supplies from other divisions. Sales representatives, working on commission, were constantly fighting with one another over how commissions should be split on joint sales efforts.

Rodin came to the conclusion that his employees were doing exactly what they were being paid to do. The commission structure encouraged employees to hide re-

turns, put in nonexistent orders the last few days of a month to make their monthly sales goals, and hide resources from one another. The key objective, of course, was sales, but the compensation structure failed to motivate employees in that direction. "Creative accounting" could easily make sure representatives made their sales goals each month whether or not the sales actually occurred. Until Rodin noticed the irregularities, there were few control mechanisms in place to integrate sales activities between divisions.

Rodin's solution? Scrap the commission system. From now on, all salespeople would receive a salary plus a bonus based on company profitability. *Electronic Buyers News* published an editorial criticizing the decision. Most people thought it was a crazy idea. But sometimes crazy ideas work pretty well. Four years after the change, sales had grown from $582 million to $1.2 billion, and the stock price of Marshall Industries had nearly quadrupled. Aligning the goals of employees with the objectives of the company seemed to be just the thing needed to bring control, integration, and coordination out of chaos.

Sources: Dess, G. G., & Picken, J. C. 1999. *Beyond productivity.* New York: AMACOM: Muoio, A. 1998. The truth is, the truth hurts. *Fast Company,* April–May: 93–102; Wilson, T. 1998. Marshall Industries: Wholesale shift to the Web. *InternetWeek,* July 20: 14–15.

performance, such as revenue gains and profitability, since there is less need for collaboration across business units because they would have little in common.

Strategy Spotlight 11.2 focuses on how the reward and evaluation system at Marshall Industries had unintended consequences, making budgeting and control very difficult. However, Rod Rodin, Marshall's CEO, recognized the problem and took decisive and bold action. This example shows how leaders must, at times, make decisions that appear to be counter to "conventional wisdom."

Nurturing a Culture Dedicated to Excellence and Ethical Behavior

In Chapter 9 we discussed how organizational culture can be an effective and positive means of organizational control. Leaders play a key role in developing and sustaining—as well as changing, when necessary—an organization's culture. Strategy Spotlight 11.3 discusses how the leadership at the Container Store has created such an exemplary culture.

Leaders actions can, of course, also have a very detrimental effect on a firm's culture and ethics. Consider Kenneth Lay, the infamous former CEO of Enron. He, along with other top executives, led Enron into a megascandal that resulted in bankruptcy and an investor loss of $67 billion. He will stand trial in Houston, Texas, in early 2006 on criminal conspiracy charges.[6] Sherron Watkins, a former vice president at Enron, provides an interesting example of and perspective on how Lay's actions served to erode Enron's culture and ethical standards:[7]

Ken Lay, although well known for his charitable giving and his verbal commitment to Enron's four core values (Respect, Integrity, Communication, and Excellence), was not quite walking

11.3 STRATEGY SPOTLIGHT

The Container Store: The Best Place to Work in America

The Container Store, a Dallas-based chain of 20 specialty retail stores that sell everything you need to organize your home, office, car, or even your life, has been consistently ranked as one of the "Best Companies to Work For" by *Fortune* magazine. In the five years from 2000 to 2004, they were always ranked in the top three, and they were number one in 2000 and 2001. This is truly surprising considering that the retail industry typically has a very high employee turnover, poorly trained workers on minimum wages, and low skill levels. The Container Store is also one of the 14 companies that Dr. Leonard Berry identified as providing exemplary service through values-driven marketing. What makes the Container Store so special?

First of all, they pay very well. The average salary for salespersons is $36,000—one of the highest salaries in the industry. The benefits are substantial too. But the financial benefits are only a small part of the story. The employees consider the Container Store a happy place to work. It is a community that they belong to. Nearly 40 percent of the company's new hires are referrals from existing employees. The company invests heavily in employee training. Stores welcome new employees with Foundation Week, a week-long orientation to the company, its products, and philosophy along with a welcome box that contains $150 worth of company products as gifts. During the first year, an employee receives 235 hours of training! At the headquarters, the Fun Committee builds a sense of community among employees through lunch-time activities such as silent auctions. At birthday celebrations, teams gather for lunch and cake. It is the birthday person's responsibility to bring cake for the next birthday honoree. The company offers employees yoga classes, chair massages, and an online exercise and nutrition diary personalized to every employee! More importantly, the company's books are open to every employee every day. This helps them make better business decisions.

The company has no thick policy manuals. Instead, they are guided by six Foundational Principles that are easy to remember:

1. "Fill the other guy's basket to the brim." Each employee is trained to work with the customer in creative and imaginative ways to help them choose the best products for organizing.

2. "Man-in-the-desert." A thirsty man reaching an oasis needs more than just water. Similarly, each employee is expected to "astonish" the customer by exceeding his expectations.

3. "1 average person = 3 lousy people. 1 good person = 3 average people. 1 great person = 3 good people." The Container Store seeks only great people. Others may be happy with 9 lousy people!

4. "Intuition does not come to the unprepared mind." The heavy emphasis on training helps to prepare the employees to create unique solutions for customers.

5. "The best selection of products anywhere + the best service anywhere + the best pricing in our markets."

6. "Air of excitement." Three steps into the door and customers realize that they are in a different place.

Kip Tindal, CEO of the Container Store, explains:

TCS's Foundational Principles empower employees to serve the customer in the true sense of the word. Employees are trusted to make whatever decision necessary to help a customer. TCS is said to provide exemplary service through values-driven marketing practices. Its employees delight in helping customers solve problems—and they possess the freedom and confidence to do so. The quest for excellence pays off in human terms, as well as financial terms.

Sources: Gavin, J. H., & Mason, R. O. 2004. The virtuous organization: The value of happiness in the workplace. *Organizational Dynamics*, 33(4): 379–392; and Berry, L. 1999. *Discovering the soul of service: Nine drivers of sustainable business success*. New York: Free Press.

the walk. For example, he always had Enron employees use his sister's travel agency. And not just us; the local Andersen office and Enron's outside attorneys, Vinson and Elkins, were pressured into using her agency as well. Trouble was that it provided neither low cost nor good service. Domestically, you could manage, but when it came to international travel—that agency sucked. I was stuck in Third World countries, where I didn't speak the language, without a hotel room or with an insufficient airline ticket home, despite paperwork that indicated otherwise. The incompetence was hard to understand. I would try using a different agency, but after one or two expense reports, I'd get a finger-wagging voice mail or e-mail reminding me that I needed to use Enron's preferred agency, Travel Agency in the Park. We called it Travel Agency in the Dark.

In some perverse way, Andy Fastow (Enron's Chief Financial Officer) might have justified his behavior by saying to himself, "Well, my LJM partnership is helping Enron meet its financial statement goals. Why can't I just take a little for myself, just like Lay has been taking a little Enron money and transferring it to his sister for all these years?"[8]

Clearly, a leader's ethical behavior can make a strong impact on an organization—for good or for bad. Given the importance of this topic, we address it in detail in the last major section of this chapter.

Managers and top executives must also accept personal responsibility for developing and strengthening ethical behavior throughout the organization. They must consistently demonstrate that such behavior is central to the vision and mission of the organization. Several elements must be present and reinforced for a firm to become a highly ethical organization: role models, corporate credos and codes of conduct, reward and evaluation systems, and policies and procedures.

Overcoming Barriers to Change and the Effective Use of Power

Now that we have discussed the three interdependent activities that leaders perform, we must address a key question: What are the barriers to change that leaders often encounter, and how can they use power to bring about meaningful change in their organizations? After all, people generally have some level of choice about how strongly they support or resist a leader's change initiatives. Why is there often so much resistance? There are many reasons why organizations and managers at all levels are prone to inertia and are slow to learn, adapt, and change.

1. Many people have *vested interests in the status quo.* There is a broad stream of organizational literature on the subject of "escalation," wherein certain individuals (in both controlled laboratory settings and actual management practice) continue to throw "good money at bad decisions" despite negative performance feedback.[9]

2. There are *systemic barriers.* Here, the design of the organization's structure, information processing, reporting relationships, and so forth impede the proper flow and evaluation of information. A bureaucratic structure with multiple layers, onerous requirements for documentation, and rigid rules and procedures will often "inoculate" the organization against change.

3. *Behavioral barriers* are associated with the tendency of managers to look at issues from a biased or limited perspective. This can be attributed to their education, training, work experiences, and so forth. For example, consider an incident shared by David Lieberman, marketing director at GVO, an innovation consulting firm based in Palo Alto, California.

   A company's creative type had come up with a great idea for a new product. Nearly everybody loved it. However, it was shot down by a high-ranking manufacturing representative who exploded: "A new color? Do you have any idea of the spare-parts problem that it will create?" This was not a dimwit exasperated at having to build a few storage racks at the warehouse. He'd been hearing for years about cost cutting, lean inventories, and "focus." Lieberman's comment: "Good concepts, but not always good for innovation."

4. *Political barriers* refer to conflicts arising from power relationships. This can be the outcome of a myriad of symptoms such as vested interests (e.g., the aforementioned escalation problems), refusal to share information, conflicts over resources, conflicts between departments and divisions, and petty interpersonal differences.

5. *Personal time constraints* bring to mind the old saying about "not having enough time to drain the swamp when you are up to your neck in alligators." In effect, Gresham's law of planning states that operational decisions will drive out the time necessary for strategic thinking and reflection. This tendency is accentuated in organizations experiencing severe price competition or retrenchment wherein managers and employees are spread rather thin.

Successful leadership requires effective use of power in overcoming barriers to change.[10] Power refers to a leader's ability to get things done in a way he or she wants them to be done. It is the ability to influence other people's behavior, to persuade them to do things that they otherwise would not do, and to overcome resistance and opposition to changing direction. Effective exercise of power is essential for successful leadership.[11]

A leader derives his or her power from several sources or bases. Numerous classifications of such sources or bases abound in the literature on power. However, the simplest way to understand the bases of power is by classifying them as organizational and personal, as shown in Exhibit 11.2.

Organizational bases of power refer to the power that a person wields because of holding a formal management position. These include legitimate power, reward power, coercive power, and information power. *Legitimate power* is derived from organizationally conferred decision-making authority and is exercised by virtue of a manager's position in the organization. *Reward power* depends on the ability of the leader or manager to confer rewards for positive behaviors or outcomes. *Coercive power* is the power a manager exercises over employees using fear of punishment for errors of omission or commission. *Information power* arises from a manager's access, control, and distribution of information that is not freely available to everyone in an organization.

Apart from the organizationally derived power, a leader might be able to influence subordinates because of his or her personality characteristics and behavior. These would be considered the "personal" bases of power. The personal bases of power are referent power and expert power. The source of *referent power* is a subordinate's identification with the leader. A leader's personal attributes or charisma might influence subordinates and make them devoted to that leader. On the other hand, the source of *expert power* is the leader's

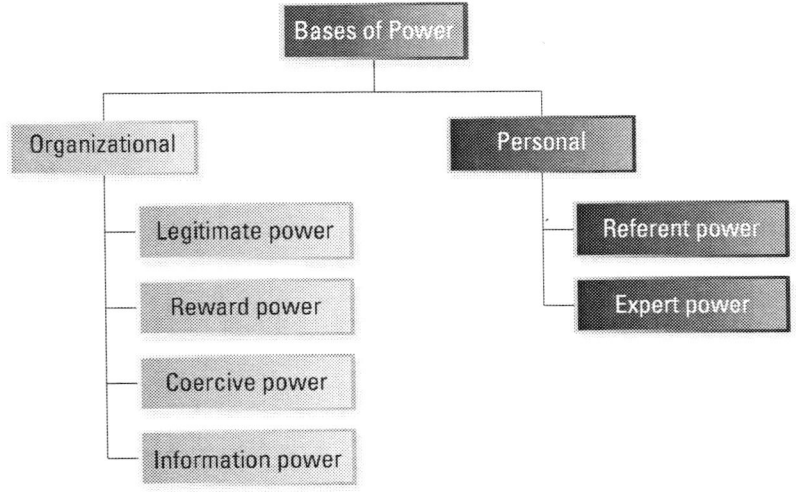

Exhibit 11.2   **A Leader's Bases of Power**

STRATEGY SPOTLIGHT

11.4

William Bratton: Using Multiple Bases of Power

William Bratton, Chief of the Los Angeles Police Department has an enviable track record in turning around police departments in crime-ridden cities. First, while running the police division of Massachusetts Bay Transit Authority (MBTA) in Boston, then as police commissioner of New York in the mid-1990s, and now in Los Angeles since 2002, Chief Bratton is credited with reducing crime and improving police morale in record time. An analysis of his success at each of these organizations reveals very similar patterns both in terms of the problems he faced and the many ways in which he used the different bases of power to engineer a rapid turnaround.

In Boston, New York, and Los Angeles, Chief Bratton faced similar hurdles: organizations wedded to the status quo, limited resources, demotivated staffs, and opposition from powerful vested interests. But he does not give up in the face of these seemingly insurmountable problems. He is persuasive in calls for change, capable of mobilizing the commitment of key players, silencing vocal naysayers, and building rapport with superiors and subordinates while building bridges with external constituencies.

Chief Bratton's persuasion tactics are unconventional, yet effective. When he was running the MBTA police, the Transit Authority decided to buy small squad cars, which are cheaper to buy and to run, but very inadequate for the police officer's task. Instead of arguing, Bratton invited the general manager for a tour of the city. He rode with the general manager in exactly the same type of car that was ordered for ordinary officers, and drove over every pothole on the road. He

moved the seats forward so that the general manager could feel how little leg room was there. And he put on his belt, cuffs, and gun so that the general manager could understand how limited the space was. After two hours in the cramped car, the general manager was ready to change the order and get more suitable cars for the officers!

Another tactic Bratton used effectively was insisting on community meetings between police officers and citizens. This went against the long-standing practice of detachment between police and community to decrease the chances of corruption. The result was that his department had a better understanding of public concerns and rearranged their priorities, which in turn led to better community relations. For internal communications, he relied mainly on professionally produced videos instead of long, boring memos.

Chief Bratton also shows a remarkable talent for building political bridges and silencing naysayers. As he was introducing his zero-tolerance policing approach that aggressively targets "quality of life" crimes such as panhandling, drunkenness, and prostitution, opposition came from the city's courts which feared being inundated by a large number of small-crimes cases. Bratton enlisted the support of Rudolph Giuliani, the mayor of New York, who had considerable influence over the district attorneys, the courts, and the city jail. He also took the case to the *New York Times,* and managed to get the issue of zero-tolerance on the front pages of the newspaper. The courts were left with no alternative but to cooperate.

To a great extent, Bratton's success can be attributed to his understanding of the subtleties of power, including persuasion, motivation, coalition building, empathy for subordinates, and a focus on goals.

Sources: Chan Kim, W., & Renee Mauborgne, R. 2003. Tipping point leadership. *Harvard Business Review,* 81(4): 60–69; and McCarthy, T. 2004. The gang buster. *Time,* January 19: 56–58.

expertise and knowledge in a particular field. The leader is the expert on whom subordinates depend for information that they need to do their jobs successfully.

Successful leaders use the different bases of power, and often a combination of them, as appropriate to meet the demands of a situation, such as the nature of the task, the personality characteristics of the subordinates, the urgency of the issue, and other factors. Leaders must recognize that persuasion and developing consensus are often essential, but so is pressing for action. Clearly, at some point stragglers must be prodded into line.[12] Peter Georgescu, who recently retired as CEO of Young & Rubicam (an advertising and media giant acquired by the UK-based WPP Group in 2000), summarized a leader's dilemma brilliantly (and humorously), "I have knee pads and a .45. I get down and beg a lot, but I shoot people too."[13]

Strategy Spotlight 11.4 addresses some of the subtleties of power. It focuses on William Bratton, Chief of the Los Angeles Police Department, who has enjoyed a very successful career in law enforcement.

>>Emotional Intelligence: A Key Leadership Trait

In the previous section, we discussed three of the salient activities of strategic leadership. In a sense, the focus was on "what leaders *do*." In this section, the issue becomes "who leaders *are*," that is, what are the most important traits (or capabilities) of leaders. Clearly, these two issues are related, because successful leaders possess the valuable traits that enable them to perform effectively in order to create value for their organization.

There has been, as we would expect, a vast amount of literature on the successful traits of leaders, including business leaders at the highest level.[14] These traits include integrity, maturity, energy, judgment, motivation, intelligence, expertise, and so on. However, for simplicity, these traits may be grouped into three broad sets of capabilities:

- Purely technical skills (like accounting or operations research).
- Cognitive abilities (like analytical reasoning or quantitative analysis).
- Emotional intelligence (such as the ability to work with others and a passion for work).

One attribute of successful leaders that has become popular in both the literature and management practice in recent years is "emotional intelligence."[15] Some evidence of this popularity is that *Harvard Business Review* articles published in 1998 and 2000 by psychologist/journalist Daniel Goleman, who is most closely associated with the concept, have become this widely read management journal's most highly requested reprint articles. And two of Goleman's recent books, *Emotional Intelligence* and *Working with Emotional Intelligence*, were both on the *New York Times*'s best-seller lists. Goleman defines emotional intelligence (EI) as the capacity for recognizing one's own emotions and those of others.[16]

Recent studies of successful managers have found that effective leaders consistently have a high level of emotional intelligence.[17] Findings indicate, for example, that EI is a better predictor of life success (economic well-being, satisfaction with life, friendship, family life), including occupational attainments, than IQ. Such evidence has been extrapolated to the catchy phrase: "IQ gets you hired, but EQ (Emotional Quotient) gets you promoted." And surveys show that human resource managers believe this statement to be true, and perhaps even for highly technical jobs such as those of scientists and engineers.

This is not to say that IQ and technical skills are irrelevant. Obviously, they do matter, but they should be viewed as "threshold capabilities." That is, they are the necessary requirements for attaining higher-level managerial positions. EI, on the other hand, is essential for leadership success. Without it, Goleman has argued, a manager can have excellent training, an incisive analytical mind, and many smart ideas but will still not be a great leader.

There are five components of EI: self-awareness, self-regulation, motivation, empathy, and social skill. They are included in Exhibit 11.3. Next, we will briefly discuss each of them.

Self-Awareness

Self-awareness is the first component of EI and brings to mind that Delphic oracle who gave the advice "know thyself" thousands of years ago. Self-awareness involves a person having a deep understanding of his or her emotions, strengths, weaknesses, and drives. People with strong self-awareness are neither overly critical nor unrealistically optimistic. Instead, they are honest with themselves and others.

	Definition	**Hallmarks**
Self-management skills:		
Self-awareness	• The ability to recognize and understand your moods, emotions, and drives, as well as their effect on others.	• Self-confidence • Realistic self-assessment • Self-deprecating sense of humor
Self-regulation	• The ability to control or redirect disruptive impulses and moods. • The propensity to suspend judgment—to think before acting.	• Trustworthiness and integrity • Comfort with ambiguity • Openness to change
Motivation	• A passion to work for reasons that go beyond money or status. • A propensity to pursue goals with energy and persistence.	• Strong drive to achieve • Optimism, even in the face of failure • Organizational commitment
Managing relationships:		
Empathy	• The ability to understand the emotional makeup of other people. • Skill in treating people according to their emotional reactions.	• Expertise in building and retaining talent • Cross-cultural sensitivity • Service to clients and customers
Social skill	• Proficiency in managing relationships and building networks. • An ability to find common ground and build rapport.	• Effectiveness in leading change • Persuasiveness • Expertise in building and leading teams

Source: Adapted and reprinted by permission of *Harvard Business Review.* Exhibit from "What Makes a Leader," by D. Goleman, January 2004. Copyright © 2004 by the Harvard Business School Publishing Corporation; all rights reserved.

Exhibit 11.3

The Five Components of Emotional Intelligence at Work

People generally admire and respect candor. Further, leaders are constantly required to make judgment calls that require a candid assessment of capabilities—their own and those of others. People who assess themselves honestly (i.e., self-aware people) are well suited to do the same for the organizations they run.

Self-Regulation

Biological impulses drive our emotions. Although we cannot do away with them, we can strive to manage them. Self-regulation, which is akin to an ongoing inner conversation, frees us from being prisoners of our feelings. People engaged in such conversation feel bad moods and emotional impulses just as everyone else does. However, they find ways to control them and even channel them in useful ways.

People who are in control of their feelings and impulses are able to create an environment of trust and fairness. In such an environment, political behavior and infighting are sharply reduced and productivity tends to be high. Further, people who have mastered their emotions are better able to bring about and implement change in an organization. When a new initiative is announced, they are less likely to panic; rather, they are able to suspend judgment, seek out information, and listen to executives explain the new program.

Motivation

Successful executives are driven to achieve beyond expectations—their own and everyone else's. They are driven to achieve. Although many people are driven by external factors, such as money and prestige, those with leadership potential are driven by a deeply embedded desire to achieve for the sake of achievement.

How can a person tell if he or she is motivated by a drive for achievement instead of external rewards? Look for a sign of passion for the work itself, such as seeking out creative challenges, a love of learning, and taking pride in a job well done. Also, motivated people have a high level of energy to do things better as well as a restlessness with the status quo. They are eager to explore new approaches to their work.

Empathy

Empathy is probably the most easily recognized component of EI. In a business setting, empathy means thoughtfully considering an employee's feelings, along with other factors, in the process of making intelligent decisions. Empathy is particularly important in today's business environment for at least three reasons: the increasing use of teams, the rapid pace of globalization, and the growing need to retain talent.[18]

When leading a team, a manager is often charged with arriving at a consensus—often in the face of a high level of emotions. Empathy enables a manager to sense and understand the viewpoints of everyone around the table.

Globalization typically involves cross-cultural dialogue that can easily lead to miscues. Empathetic people are attuned to the subtleties of body language; they can hear the message beneath the words being spoken. In a more general sense, they have a deep understanding of the existence and importance of cultural and ethnic differences.

Empathy also plays a key role in retaining talent. As we discussed in Chapter 4, human capital is particularly important to a firm in the knowledge economy when it comes to creating advantages that are sustainable. Leaders need empathy to develop and keep top talent. Today, that's even more important, because when high performers leave, they take their tacit knowledge with them.

Social Skill

While the first three components of emotional intelligence are all self-management skills, the last two—empathy and social skill—concern a person's ability to manage relationships with others. Social skill may be viewed as friendliness with a purpose: moving people in the direction you desire, whether that's agreement on a new marketing strategy or enthusiasm about a new product.

Socially skilled people tend to have a wide circle of acquaintances as well as a knack for finding common ground and building rapport. They recognize that nothing gets done alone, and they have a network in place when the time for action comes.

Social skill can be viewed as the culmination of the other dimensions of EI. People will be effective at managing relationships when they can understand and control their own emotions and can empathize with the feelings of others. Motivation also contributes to social skill. People who are driven to achieve tend to be optimistic, even when confronted with setbacks or failure. And when people are upbeat, their "glow" is cast upon conversations and other social encounters. They are popular, and for good reason.

STRATEGY SPOTLIGHT

11.5

Emotional Intelligence: Pat Croce

Every businessperson knows the story of a highly qualified, well-trained executive who was promoted to a leadership position, only to fail at the job. This is not because the executive didn't have a high IQ or sound technical fundamentals. It is about the presence or lack of *emotional intelligence*. When Pat Croce took over as the new president of the Philadelphia 76ers in May 1996, people were skeptical of his cornball style and unabashed attitude. At his national debut as the president of the 76ers, he erupted with glee as the team wound up with the number one pick at the nationally televised broadcast of the NBA's draft lottery. He leaped to his feet, pumped his fists and slapped the palms of the other team representatives. But that was not all. He then hugged David Stern, the gray-haired, tight-laced NBA commissioner, kissing him on the cheek and patting him on the sleeve of his suit jacket.

People who meet Croce on the street or at work salute him with either a high-five or a "Hey dude." Those

who know him say his high energy and red-bloodedness are infectious and his vivacious style is how he exhibits the virtues of a can-do attitude and never-say-die perseverance. A self-made man, Croce founded a fitness center called the Sports Physical Therapists (SPT), successfully turned it into an 11-state chain, and eventually sold it off for $40 million in 1993.

His record as the basketball baron is no less impressive. His team was the Cinderella story of the NBA. Before he took over, the team's dismal business management and apathetic player attitudes had led to a very unimpressive record. Croce is widely credited with reinvigorating the business with his hurricane-force personality and leading the born-again team to its first chance to compete in the NBA finals in more than a decade. And for all this, Croce has but his emotional intelligence to thank. His self-awareness, motivation, and social skills make him detail-oriented and competitive—the stereotypical qualities of a successful entrepreneur.

Sources: Rosenbloom, J. 2002. Why it's Pat Croce's world. *Inc.*, April: 77–83; www.patcroce.com/NonMember/pages/index.html; and Brokaw, L. 2002. Pat Croce's bottom line. *Fast Company*, January 1: 45–47.

Strategy Spotlight 11.5 discusses Pat Croce's approach to leadership and illustrates some of the components of emotional intelligence. Croce is president of the National Basketball Association's Philadelphia 76ers.

Consider some comments from Dan Goleman, who has made many important contributions to our understanding of EI.

> It would be foolish to assert that good old-fashioned IQ and technical ability are not important ingredients to strong leadership. But the recipe would not be complete without emotional intelligence. It was once thought that the components of emotional intelligence were "nice to have" in business leaders. But now we know that, for the sake of performance, these are ingredients that leaders "need to have."
>
> It is fortunate, then, that emotional intelligence can be learned. The process is not easy. It takes time and, most of all, commitment. But the benefits that come from having a well-developed emotional intelligence, both for the individual and for the organization, make it worth the effort.[19]

Emotional Intelligence: Some Potential Drawbacks and Cautionary Notes

Many great leaders have been found to have great reserves of empathy, interpersonal astuteness, awareness of their own feelings, and an awareness of their impact on others.[20] And, more importantly, they apply these capabilities judiciously as best benefits the situation. In essence, the key to this is self-regulation; having some minimum level of these emotional intelligences will help a person be effective as a leader as long as they are channeled appropriately. However, if a person has a high level of these capabilities it may become "too much of a good thing" if they are allowed to drive inappropriate behaviors. Let's consider two insights from experts that appeared in a 2004 *Harvard Business Review* article:[21]

> . . . there is always a danger in being preoccupied with, or overusing, one aspect of EI. For example, if you overemphasize the emotional intelligence competencies of initiative or achievement, you'll always be changing things at your company. Nobody would know what you are going to do next, which would be quite destabilizing for the organization. If you over-use empathy, you might never fire anybody. If you overuse teamwork, you might never build diversity or listen to a lone voice. Balance is essential.
>
> If you're extremely self-aware but short on empathy, you might come off as self-obsessed. If you're excessively empathetic, you risk being too hard to read. If you're great at self-management but not very transparent, you might seem inauthentic. Finally, at times, leaders have to deliberately avoid getting too close to the troops in order to ensure that they're seeing the bigger picture. Emotionally intelligent leaders know when to rein it in.

Some additional potential drawbacks of EI can be gleaned from the flip side of the benefits from some of its essential components.

Effective Leaders Have Empathy for Others   However, they also must be able to make the "tough decisions." Leaders must be able to appeal to logic and reason and acknowledge others' feelings so that people feel the decisions are correct. However, it is easy to overidentify with others or confuse empathy with sympathy. This will make it more difficult to make the tough decisions.

Effective Leaders Are Astute Judges of People   A danger is that leaders may become judgmental and overly critical about the shortcomings they perceive in others. They are likely to dismiss other people's insights, making them feel disrespected and undervalued.

Effective Leaders Are Passionate about What They Do, and They Show It   This doesn't necessarily mean that they are always cheerleaders. Rather, they may express their passion as persistence in pursuing an objective or a relentless focus on a valued principle. However, there is a fine line between being excited about something and letting your passion close your mind to other possibilities or cause you to ignore realities that others see.

Effective Leaders Create Personal Connections with Their People   Most effective leaders take time to engage employees individually and in groups, listening to their ideas, suggestions and concerns, and responding in ways that make people feel that their ideas are respected and appreciated. However, the downside of such visibility is that if the leader makes too many unannounced visits, it may create a culture of fear and micromanagement. Clearly, striking a correct balance is essential.

Finally, from a moral standpoint, emotional leadership is neither good nor bad. Emotional leaders can be altruistic, focused on the general welfare of the company and its employees, and highly principled. On the other hand, they can be manipulative, selfish, and dishonest. For example, if a person is using leadership solely to gain formal or informal power, that is not leadership at all.[22] Rather, they are using their EI to grasp what people want and pander to those desires in order to gain authority and influence. After all, easy answers sell.

Many people with high emotional intelligence and charisma aren't interested in asking the deeper questions, because they get so much emotional gain from the adoring crowd.[23] For them, that is the end in itself. They are satisfying their own hungers and vulnerabilities—their need to be liked, their need for power and control, or their need to be needed and to feel important—which renders them vulnerable to grandiosity. But that's not leadership. It's hunger for authority.[24]

In the next section, we will discuss some guidelines for developing a "learning organization." In today's competitive environment, the old saying about "a chain is only as strong as the weakest link" applies more than ever before. People throughout organizations must become involved in leadership processes and play greater roles in the formulation and implementation of an organization's strategies and tactics. Put another way, to learn and adapt proactively, firms need "eyes, ears, and brains" throughout all parts of the organization. One person, or a small group of individuals, can no longer think and learn for the entire entity.

>>Developing a Learning Organization

Charles Handy, author of *The Age of Unreason* and *The Age of Paradox* and one of today's most respected business visionaries, shared an amusing story:

> The other day, a courier could not find my family's remote cottage. He called his base on his radio, and the base called us to ask directions. He was just around the corner, but his base managed to omit a vital part of the directions. So he called them again, and they called us again. Then the courier repeated the cycle a third time to ask whether we had a dangerous dog. When he eventually arrived, we asked whether it would not have been simpler and less aggravating to everyone if he had called us directly from the roadside telephone booth where he had been parked. "I can't do that," he said, "because they won't refund any money I spend." "But it's only pennies!" I exclaimed. "I know," he said, "but that only shows how little they trust us!"[25]

At first glance, it would appear that the story simply epitomizes the lack of empowerment and trust granted to the hapless courier: Don't ask questions, Do as you're told![26] However, implicit in this scenario is also the message that learning, information sharing, adaptation, decision making, and so on are *not* shared throughout the organization. In contrast to this admittedly rather extreme case, leading-edge organizations recognize the importance of having everyone involved in the process of actively learning and adapting. As noted by today's leading expert on learning organizations, MIT's Peter Senge, the days when Henry Ford, Alfred Sloan, and Tom Watson *"learned **for** the organization"* are gone.

> In an increasingly dynamic, interdependent, and unpredictable world, it is simply no longer possible for anyone to "figure it all out at the top." The old model, "the top thinks and the local acts," must now give way to integrating thinking and acting at all levels. While the challenge is great, so is the potential payoff. "The person who figures out how to harness the collective genius of the people in his or her organization," according to former Citibank CEO Walter Wriston, "is going to blow the competition away."[27]

Learning and change typically involve the ongoing questioning of an organization's status quo or method of procedure. This means that all individuals throughout the organization—not just those at the top—must reflect. Although this seems simple enough, it is easy to ignore. After all, organizations, especially successful ones, are so caught up in carrying out their day-to-day work that they rarely, if ever, stop to think objectively about themselves and their businesses. They often fail to ask the probing questions that might lead them to call into question their basic assumptions, to refresh their strategies, or to reengineer their work processes. According to Michael

Hammer and Steven Stanton, the pioneer consultants who touched off the reengineering movement:

> Reflection entails awareness of self, of competitors, of customers. It means thinking without preconception. It means questioning cherished assumptions and replacing them with new approaches. It is the only way in which a winning company can maintain its leadership position, by which a company with great assets can ensure that they continue to be well deployed.[28]

Successful learning organizations create a proactive, creative approach to the unknown, actively solicit the involvement of employees at all levels, and enable all employees to use their intelligence and apply their imagination. Higher-level skills are required of everyone, not just those at the top. A learning environment involves organizationwide commitment to change, an action orientation, and applicable tools and methods.[29] It must be viewed by everyone as a guiding philosophy and not simply as another change program that is often derisively labeled the new "flavor of the month."

A critical requirement of all learning organizations is that everyone feels and supports a compelling purpose. In the words of William O'Brien, CEO of Hanover Insurance, "Before there can be meaningful participation, people must share certain values and pictures about where we are trying to go. We discovered that people have a real need to feel that they're part of an enabling mission."[30]

Inspiring and motivating people with a mission or purpose is a necessary but not sufficient condition for developing an organization that can learn and adapt to a rapidly changing, complex, and interconnected environment. In the next four sections, we'll address four other critical ongoing processes of learning organizations:

- Empowering employees at all levels.
- Accumulating and sharing internal knowledge.
- Gathering and integrating external information.
- Challenging the status quo and enabling creativity.

Empowering Employees at All Levels

"The great leader is a great servant," asserted Ken Melrose, CEO of Toro Company and author of *Making the Grass Greener on Your Side*.[31] A manager's role becomes one of creating an environment where employees can achieve their potential as they help move the organization toward its goals. Instead of viewing themselves as resource controllers and power brokers, leaders must truly envision themselves as flexible resources willing to assume numerous (and perhaps unaccustomed) roles as coaches, information providers, teachers, decision makers, facilitators, supporters, or listeners, depending on the needs of their employees.

The central key to empowerment is effective leadership. Empowerment can't occur in a leadership vacuum. According to Melrose, "I came to understand that you best lead by serving the needs of your people. You don't do their jobs for them; you enable them to learn and progress on the job." In their article in *Organizational Dynamics*, Robert Quinn and Gretchen Spreitzer made an interesting point regarding what may be viewed as two diametrically opposite perspectives on empowerment.[32] In the top-down perspective, empowerment is about delegation and accountability—senior management has developed a clear vision and has communicated specific plans to the rest of the organization. This strategy for empowerment encompasses the following:

- Start at the top.
- Clarify the organization's mission, vision, and values.

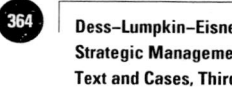

- Clearly specify the tasks, roles, and rewards for employees.
- Delegate responsibility.
- Hold people accountable for results.

By contrast, the bottom-up view looks at empowerment as concerned with risk taking, growth, and change. It involves trusting people to "do the right thing" and having a tolerance for failure. It encourages employees to act with a sense of ownership and typically "ask for forgiveness rather than permission." Here the salient elements of empowerment are:

- Start at the bottom by understanding the needs of employees.
- Teach employees self-management skills and model desired behavior.
- Build teams to encourage cooperative behavior.
- Encourage intelligent risk taking.
- Trust people to perform.

Clearly, these two perspectives draw a sharp contrast in assumptions that people make about trust and control. Interestingly, Quinn and Spreitzer recently shared these contrasting views of empowerment with a senior management team. After an initial heavy silence, someone from the first group voiced a concern about the second group's perspective, "We can't afford loose cannons around here." A person in the second group retorted, "When was the last time you saw a cannon of any kind around here?"

Many leading-edge organizations are moving in the direction of the second perspective—recognizing the need for trust, cultural control, and expertise (at all levels) instead of the extensive and cumbersome rules and regulations inherent in hierarchical control.[33] Some have argued that too often organizations fall prey to the "heroes-and-drones syndrome," wherein the value of those in powerful positions is exalted and the value of those who fail to achieve top rank is diminished. Such an attitude is implicit in phrases such as "Lead, follow, or get out of the way" or, even less appealing, "Unless you're the lead horse, the view never changes." Of course, few will ever reach the top hierarchical positions in organizations, but in the information economy, the strongest organizations are those that effectively use the talents of all the players on the team. Strategy Spotlight 11.6 illustrates how one company, Chaparral Steel, empowers its employees.

Accumulating and Sharing Internal Knowledge

Effective organizations must also *redistribute information, knowledge* (i.e., skills to act on the information), and *rewards*.[34] For example, a company might give frontline employees the power to act as "customer advocates," doing whatever is necessary to please the customers. Employees, however, also need to have the appropriate training to act as businesspeople. The company needs to disseminate information by sharing customer expectations and feedback as well as financial information. The employees need to know about the goals and objectives of the business as well as how key value-creating activities in the organization are related to each other. Finally, organizations should allocate rewards on the basis of how effectively employees use information, knowledge, and power to improve customer service quality and the company's financial performance.

Jack Stack is the president and CEO of Springfield ReManufacturing Corporation (SRC) in Springfield, Missouri, and author of *The Great Game of Business*. He is generally considered the pioneer of "open book" management—an innovative way to gather and disseminate internal information. Implementing this system involves three core activities.[35] First, numbers are generated daily for each of the company's employees, reflecting his or her work performance and production costs. Second, this information is aggregated once

11.6 STRATEGY SPOTLIGHT

Employee Empowerment at Chaparral Steel

Managers at Chaparral Steel, a steel minimill in Midlothian, Texas, are convinced that employee ownership empowers workers to act in the best interests of the company. They believe that ownership is not composed solely of the firm's equity but also of its knowledge. By sharing financial and knowledge resources with employees, Chaparral Steel is a model of employee empowerment—90 percent of its employees own company stock and everyone is salaried, wears the same white hard hats, drinks the same free coffee, and has access to the knowledge that goes into the innovative processes at the firm's manufacturing plants.

Rather than using managers as buffers between customers and line workers, Chaparral directly involves employees with customers. Customer concerns are routed directly to the line workers responsible for manufacturing a customer's specific products. "Everyone here is part of the sales department," president and CEO Gordon Forward said. "They carry their own business cards. If they visit a customer, we want them to come back and look at their own process differently. This helps employees from all levels to view operations from the customer's perspective." Forward believes that "if a melt shop crew understands why a customer needs a particular grade of steel, it will make sure the customer gets that exact grade."

This encourages employees to think beyond traditional functional boundaries and find ways to improve the organization's processes. By integrating the customer's perspective into their efforts, employees at Chaparral Steel become more than just salaried workers; they feel responsible to the firm as if each production process was their own creation and responsibility.

Sources: Johnson, D. 1998. Catching the third wave: How to succeed in business when it's changing at the speed of light. *Futurist*, March: 32–38; Petry, C. 1997. Chaparral poised on the brink of breakthrough: Chaparral Steel developing integrated automobile shredder-separation facility. *American Metal Market*, September 10: 18; Leonard-Barton, D. 1992. The factory as a learning laboratory. *Sloan Management Review*, 34: 23–38; and TXI Chaparral Steel Midlothian registered to ISO 2002. Chaparral Steel press release, July 8, 2001.

---

a week and shared with all of the company's people from secretaries to top management. Third, employees receive extensive training in how to use and interpret the numbers—how to understand balance sheets as well as cash flows and income statements.

In explaining why SRC embraces open book management, Stack provided an insightful counterperspective to the old adage "Information is power."

> We are building a company in which everyone tells the truth every day—not because everyone is honest but because everyone has access to the same information: operating metrics, financial data, valuation estimates. The more people understand what's really going on in their company, the more eager they are to help solve its problems. Information isn't power. It's a burden. Share information, and you share the burdens of leadership as well.

These perspectives help to point out both the motivational and utilitarian uses of sharing company information. It can apply to organizations of all sizes. Let's look at a very small company—Leonhardt Plating Company, a $1.5 million company that makes steel plating.

> Its CEO, Daniel Leonhardt, became an accidental progressive, so to speak. Recently, instead of trying to replace his polishing foreman, he resorted to a desperate, if cutting-edge, strategy. He decided to let the polishing department rule itself by committee.
>
> The results? Revenues have risen 25 percent in the past year. After employees had access to company information such as material prices, their decisions began paying off for the whole firm. Says Leonhardt: "The workers are showing more interest in the company as a whole." Not surprisingly, he plans to introduce committee rule to other departments.[36]

Additional benefits of management sharing company information can be gleaned from a look at Whole Foods Market, Inc., the largest natural foods grocer in the United States.[37] An important benefit of the sharing of internal information at Whole Foods becomes the active process of *internal benchmarking*. Competition is intense at Whole Foods. Teams compete against their own goals for sales, growth, and productivity; they compete against different teams in their stores; and they compete against similar teams at different stores and regions. Similarly, there is an elaborate system of peer reviews through which teams benchmark each other. The "Store Tour" is the most intense. On a periodic schedule, each Whole Foods store is toured by a group of as many as 40 visitors from another region. The tour is a mix of social interaction, reviews, performance audits, and structured feedback sessions. Lateral learning—discovering what your colleagues are doing right and carrying those practices into your organization—has become a driving force at Whole Foods.

In addition to enhancing the sharing of company information both up and down as well as across the organization, leaders also have to develop means to tap into some of the more informal sources of internal information. In a recent survey of presidents, CEOs, board members, and top executives in a variety of nonprofit organizations, respondents were asked what differentiated the successful candidates for promotion. The consensus: The executive was seen as a person who listens. According to Peter Meyer, the author of the study, "The value of listening is clear: You cannot succeed in running a company if you do not hear what your people, customers, and suppliers are telling you. Poor listeners do not survive. Listening and understanding well are key to making good decisions."[38]

John Chambers, president and CEO of Cisco Systems, the networking giant, also uses an effective vehicle for getting candid feedback from employees and for discovering potential problems.[39] Every year during their birthday month, employees at Cisco's corporate headquarters in San Jose, California, receive an e-mail invitation to a "birthday breakfast" with Chambers. Each month, several dozen of the employees fire some pretty tough questions, including bruising queries about partnering strategy and stark assessments of perceived management failings. Any question is fair game, and directors and vice presidents are strongly discouraged from attending.

Although not always pleasant, Chambers believes it is an indispensable hour of unmediated interaction. At times, he finds there is inconsistency between what his executives say they are doing and what is actually happening. For example, at one quarterly meeting with 500 managers, Chambers asked how many managers required potential hires to have five interviews. When all raised their hands, he retorted, "I have a problem, because at the past three birthday breakfasts, I asked the new hires how many had interviewed that way, and only half raised their hands. You've got to fix it." His take on the birthday breakfasts: "I'm not there for the cake."

Strategy Spotlight 11.7 discusses how Intel Corporation effectively shares information through a unique mentoring program.

Gathering and Integrating External Information

Recognizing opportunities, as well as threats, in the external environment is vital to a firm's success. Focusing exclusively on the efficiency of internal operations may result in a firm becoming, in effect, the world's most efficient producer of manual typewriters or leisure suits—hardly an enviable position! As organizations *and* environments become more complex and evolve rapidly, it is far more critical for employees and managers to become more aware of environmental trends and events—both general and industry-specific—and more knowledgeable about their firm's competitors and customers. Next, we will discuss some ideas on how to do it.

First, the Internet has dramatically accelerated the speed with which anyone can track down useful information or locate people who might have useful information. Prior to the Net, locating someone who used to work at a company—always a good source of

11.7 STRATEGY SPOTLIGHT

Information Sharing through Mentoring Relationships at Intel

Intel veteran Ann Otero seems to be an unlikely mentor. She is neither a star engineer nor a fast-track sales executive. She has, however, been with the company for the past 12 years and is currently a senior administrative assistant. Ann is part of Intel's new wedge—an innovative new mentoring movement that matches people not by job title or years of service but by specific skills that are in demand. The program uses an intranet-based questionnaire to match partners with the right mentor, creating relationships that stretch across state lines and national boundaries. The system works by having potential mentors list their top skills at Circuit, Intel's internal employee site. Partners click on topics they want to master, then an algorithm computes all of the variables and the database

hashes out a list of possible matches. Once a match is made, an automatic e-mail goes to the mentor asking her to set up a time to meet and talk. The mentor and partner learn and follow some simple guidelines:

1. The partner controls the relationship.
2. A mentoring contract is drawn up about what needs to be accomplished by the end of the mentoring.
3. Both the partner and the mentor decide what to talk about.

Unlike many corporations, Intel does not use its mentoring for career advancement. Its style is all about learning and sharing the knowledge pool of someone whom you have probably never met.

Sources: www.intel.com/jobs/news/news.htm; Warner, F. 2002. Inside Intel's mentoring movement. *Fast Company*, April: 67–69.

information—was quite a challenge. However, today people post their résumés on the Web; they participate in discussion groups and talk openly about where they work. It is pretty straightforward.

An example of the effective use of the Internet is provided by Marc Friedman, manager of market research at Andrew Corporation, a fast-growing manufacturer of wireless communications products with annual revenues of nearly $1 billion.[40] One of Friedman's preferred sites to visit is Corptech's Web site, which provides information on 45,000 high-tech companies and more than 170,000 executives. One of his firm's product lines consisted of antennae for air-traffic control systems. He got a request to provide a country-by-country breakdown of upgrade plans for various airports. Although he knew nothing about air-traffic control at the time, he found a site on the Internet for the International Civil Aviation Organization. Fortunately, it had a great deal of useful data, including several research companies working in his area of interest.

Second, in addition to the Internet, company employees at all levels can use "garden variety" traditional sources to acquire external information. Much can be gleaned by reading trade and professional journals, books, and popular business magazines such as *BusinessWeek, Forbes, Fortune,* and *Fast Company.* (Some professional journals might have an extremely narrow focus and, while they could prove to be very useful, they are not fireside reading for the general public.) Other venues for gathering external information include membership in professional or trade organizations and attendance at meetings and conventions. Networking among colleagues inside and outside of your industry is also very useful. Intel's Andy Grove, for example, gathers information from people like DreamWorks SKG's Steven Spielberg and Tele-Communications Inc.'s John Malone.[41] He believes that such interaction provides insights into how to make personal computers more entertaining and better at communicating. Internally, Grove spends time with the young "propeller-heads" who run Intel Architecture labs, an Oregon-based facility that Grove hopes will become the de facto R&D lab for the entire PC industry.

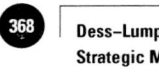

Third, benchmarking can be a useful means of employing external information. Here managers seek out the best examples of a particular practice as part of an ongoing effort to improve the corresponding practice in their own organization.[42] There are two primary types of benchmarking. *Competitive benchmarking* restricts the search for best practices to competitors, while *functional benchmarking* endeavors to determine best practices regardless of industry. Industry-specific standards (e.g., response times required to repair power outages in the electric utility industry) are typically best handled through competitive benchmarking, whereas more generic processes (e.g., answering 1-800 calls) lend themselves to functional benchmarking because the function is essentially the same in any industry.

Ford Motor Company benefited from benchmarking by studying Mazda's accounts payable operations.[43] Its initial goal of a 20 percent cut in its 500-employee accounts payable staff was ratcheted up to 75 percent—and met. Ford's benchmarkers found that staff spent most of their time trying to match often conflicting data in a mass of paper, including purchase orders, invoices, and receipts. Following Mazda's example, Ford created an "invoiceless system" in which invoices no longer trigger payments to suppliers. The receipt does the job.

Fourth, focus directly on customers for information. For example, William McKnight, head of 3M's Chicago sales office, required that salesmen of abrasives products talk directly to the workers in the shop to find out what they needed, instead of calling on only front-office executives.[44] This was very innovative at the time—1909! But it illustrates the need to get to the end user of a product or service. (McKnight went on to become 3M's president from 1929 to 1949 and chairman from 1949 to 1969.) More recently, James Taylor, senior vice president for global marketing at Gateway 2000, discussed the value of customer input in reducing response time, a critical success factor in the PC industry.

> We talk to 100,000 people a day—people calling to order a computer, shopping around, looking for tech support. Our Web site gets 1.1 million hits per day. The time it takes for an idea to enter this organization, get processed, and then go to customers for feedback is down to minutes. We've designed the company around speed and feedback.[45]

Challenging the Status Quo and Enabling Creativity

Earlier in this chapter we discussed some of the barriers that leaders face when trying to bring about change in an organization. These included vested interests in the status quo, systemic barriers, behavioral barriers, political barriers, and personal time constraints. For a firm to become a "learning organization," it must overcome such barriers in order to foster creativity and enable it to permeate the firm. This becomes quite a challenge, of course, if the firm is entrenched in a status quo mentality.

Perhaps the primary means to directly challenge the status quo is for the leader to forcefully create a sense of urgency. For example, Tom Kasten, vice president of Levi Strauss, has a direct approach to initiating change. He is charged with leading the campaign to transform the company for the 21st century.

> You create a compelling picture of the risks of *not* changing. We let our people hear directly from customers. We videotaped interviews with customers and played excerpts. One big customer said, "We trust many of your competitors implicitly. We sample their deliveries. We open *all* Levi's deliveries." Another said, "Your lead times are the worst. If you weren't Levi's, you'd be gone." It was powerful. I wish we had done more of it.[46]

Such initiative—if sincere and credible—establishes a shared mission and the need for major transformations. If effective, it can channel energies to bring about both change and creative endeavors.

Establishing a "culture of dissent" can be another effective means of questioning the status quo and serving as a spur toward creativity. Here norms are established whereby dissenters can openly question a superior's perspective without fear of retaliation or retribution. Consider the perspective of Steven Balmer, Microsoft's CEO.

> Bill [Gates] brings to the company the idea that conflict can be a good thing. . . . Bill knows it's important to avoid that gentle civility that keeps you from getting to the heart of an issue quickly. He likes it when anyone, even a junior employee, challenges him, and you know he respects you when he starts shouting back.[47]

Motorola has, in effect, gone a step further and institutionalized its culture of dissent.[48] By filing a "minority report," an employee can go above his or her immediate supervisor's head and officially lodge a different point of view on a business decision. According to former CEO George Fisher, "I'd call it a healthy spirit of discontent and a freedom by and large to express your discontent around here or to disagree with whoever it is in the company, me or anybody else."

Closely related to the culture of dissent is the fostering of a culture that encourages risk taking. "If you're not making mistakes, you're not taking risks, and that means you're not going anywhere," claimed John Holt, coauthor of *Celebrate Your Mistakes*.[49] "The key is to make errors faster than the competition, so you have more chances to learn and win."

Companies that cultivate cultures of experimentation and curiosity make sure that *failure* is not, in essence, an obscene word. People who stretch the envelope and ruffle feathers are protected. More importantly, they encourage mistakes as a key part of their competitive advantage. Wood Dickinson, CEO of the Kansas City–based Dickinson movie theater chain, told his property managers that he wanted to see them committing "intelligent failures in the pursuit of service excellence."[50] This philosophy was shared by Stan Shih, CEO of Acer, a Taiwan-based computer company. If a manager at Acer took an intelligent risk and made a mistake—even a costly one—Shih wrote off the loss as tuition payment for the manager's education. Such a culture must permeate the entire organization. As a high-tech executive told us during an interview: "Every person has a freedom to fail."

Strategy Spotlight 11.8 provides examples of how failures led to highly successful innovations.

>>Creating an Ethical Organization

What is ethics?[51] Ethics may be defined as a system of right and wrong. Ethics assists individuals in deciding when an act is moral or immoral, socially desirable or not. There are many sources for an individual's ethics. These include religious beliefs, national and ethnic heritage, family practices, community standards and expectations, educational experiences, and friends and neighbors. Business ethics is the application of ethical standards to commercial enterprise.

Individual Ethics versus Organizational Ethics

Many leaders may think of ethics as a question of personal scruples, a confidential matter between employees and their consciences. Such leaders are quick to describe any wrongdoing as an isolated incident, the work of a rogue employee. They assume the company should not bear any responsibility for an individual's misdeeds—it may not ever even enter their minds. After all, in their view, ethics has nothing to do with leadership.

In fact, ethics has everything to do with leadership. Seldom does the character flaw of a lone actor completely explain corporate misconduct. Instead, unethical business practices typically involve the tacit, if not explicit, cooperation of others and reflect the values,

STRATEGY SPOTLIGHT 11.8

Failures That Led to Later Successes

Experimentation can often fail. At times, such failures can be the seeds that lead to very successful products. As the famous writer James Joyce once said, "Mistakes are the portals for discovery." Below, we summarize three failures that evolved into remarkable innovations.

W. L. Gore & Associates is the well-known company that produces such innovative products as Gore-Tex, the material that is used in many outdoor clothing products to help keep out moisture, and Glide, a dental floss. It also has become the second-leading manufacturer in the $100 million stringed-instrument business—largely as the result of a failed product.

In 1997, a team at Gore was testing a material for the cables that control puppets at Disney's theme parks. The prototype failed. But it was the beginning of a successful product. "We gave it to guitar players to try out, and they were amazed that it didn't go dead," explains Steve Young, who now heads Gore's Elixir business.

It turned out that Gore's strings lasted up to five times longer than most others then available. However, they cost twice as much. How did they market the new product? Gore went straight to the musicians. It bought magazine subscriber lists and showed up at festivals, giving out

samples and building some buzz. It hired musically trained sales reps to develop relationships with retailers and got Taylor Guitars, a leading acoustical manufacturer, to install Elixir on all of its guitars. Today, Elixir Strings are sold by more than half the music stores in the United States.

Rubber shortages during World War II prompted the U.S. government to try to develop a synthetic rubber. It seemed to make sense to make this substitute out of something that was very plentiful. Silicone seemed to be the logical solution. An inventor at General Electric added a little boric acid to silicone oil and developed a gooey, bouncy substance.

Although the substance failed as a substitute for rubber, after the war it became a very popular toy—Silly Putty. Apollo 8 astronauts later used it to stabilize their tools in zero gravity. (The astronauts carried their Silly Putty in sterling silver eggs.) Today Binney & Smith produces about 20,000 eggs' worth of Silly Putty a day.

Wilson Greatbatch, a medical researcher, was working on a device to record irregular heartbeats. He accidentally inserted a resistor of the wrong size and he noticed that the circuit pulsed, stopped, and pulsed again—just like a human heart. After two years of tinkering, Greatbatch developed the first implantable pacemaker. He later invented a corrosion-free lithium battery to power it. Millions have benefited from his efforts.

Sources: Sacks, D. 2003. The Gore-Tex of guitar strings. *Fast Company*, December: 46; Jones, C. 1994. *Mistakes that worked*. New York: Random House; and Brokenbrough, M. 2005. *The greatest mistakes of all time*. encarta. msn.com, January 8: np.

attitudes, and behavior patterns that define an organization's operating culture. Clearly, ethics is as much an organizational as a personal issue. Leaders who fail to provide proper leadership to institute proper systems and controls that facilitate ethical conduct share responsibility with those who conceive, execute, and knowingly benefit from corporate misdeeds.

The ethical orientation of a leader is generally considered to be a key factor in promoting ethical behavior among employees. Ethical leaders must take personal, ethical responsibility for their actions and decision making. Leaders who exhibit high ethical standards become role models for others in the organization and raise its overall level of ethical behavior. In essence, ethical behavior must start with the leader before the employees can be expected to perform accordingly.

Over the last few decades, there has been a growing interest in corporate ethical performance. Perhaps some reasons for this trend may be the increasing lack of confidence regarding corporate activities, the growing emphasis on quality of life issues, and a spate of recent corporate scandals at such firms as Enron and Tyco. Clearly, concerns about protecting the environment, fair employment practices, and the distribution of unsafe products have served to create powerful regulatory agencies such as the Environmental Protection Agency, the Equal Opportunity Commission, and the Federal Drug Administration. Recently, however, other concerns are becoming salient, such as problems associated with fetal tissue for research, disproportionate executive pay levels, corporate crises such as the Firestone/Ford Explorer tire fiasco, race debacles at Texaco and at Denny's Restaurants, the *Exxon Valdez* oil spill, and the practices of major financial services institutions in the wake of the dot-com crash. Merely adhering to the minimum regulatory standards may not be enough to remain competitive in a world that is becoming more socially conscious.

Without a strong ethical culture, the chance of ethical crises occurring is enhanced. Ethical crises can be very expensive—both in terms of financial costs and in the erosion of human capital and overall firm reputation. Consider, for example, Texaco's class-action discrimination lawsuit.

> In 1994 a senior financial analyst, Bari-Ellen Roberts, and one of her co-workers, Sil Chambers, filed a class-action discrimination suit against Texaco after enduring racial slurs and being passed over for promotion on several occasions. The discrimination suit charged Texaco with using an "old boys network" to systematically discriminate against African Americans.
>
> Roberts remembers, "The hardest part of the suit was deciding to do it. I'd worked so hard to get where I was, and I had to risk all of that. Then I had to deal with loneliness and isolation. Even some of the other African Americans viewed me as a troublemaker. When you're standing up and calling for change, it makes people fear for their own security."
>
> Two years later, in 1996, Texaco settled the suit, paying $141 million to its African-American workers. This was followed with an additional $35 million to remove discriminatory practices.[52]

Please note that the financial cost alone of $176 million was certainly not the proverbial "drop in the bucket." This amount represented nearly 10 percent of Texaco Inc.'s entire net income for 1996.

As we are all aware, the past several years have been characterized by numerous examples of unethical and illegal behavior by many top-level corporate executives. These include executives of firms such as Enron, Tyco, Worldcom, Inc., Adelphia, and Healthsouth Corp., who were all forced to resign and are facing (or have been convicted of) criminal charges. Exhibit 11.4 briefly summarizes the unethical and/or illegal activities of other well-known corporate leaders.

The ethical organization is characterized by a conception of ethical values and integrity as a driving force of the enterprise.[53] Ethical values shape the search for opportunities, the design of organizational systems, and the decision-making process used by individuals and groups. They provide a common frame of reference that serves as a unifying force across different functions, lines of business, and employee groups. Organizational ethics helps to define what a company is and what it stands for.

There are many potential benefits of an ethical organization, but they are often indirect. The research literature in organizational behavior has found somewhat inconsistent results concerning the overall relationship between ethical performance and measures of financial performance.[54] However, positive relationships have generally been found between ethical performance and strong organizational culture, increased employee efforts, lower turnover, higher organizational commitment, and enhanced social responsibility.

Clearly, the advantages of a strong ethical orientation can have a positive effect on employee commitment and motivation to excel. This is particularly important in today's knowledge-intensive organizations, where human capital is critical in creating value and competitive advantages. As we discussed in Chapter 4, positive, constructive relationships among individuals (i.e., social capital) are vital in leveraging human capital and other resources in an organization. However, there are many other potential benefits as well. Drawing on the concept of stakeholder management that we discussed in Chapter 1, an ethically sound organization can also strengthen its bonds among its suppliers,

Exhibit 11.4

Unethical and Illegal Behavior by Top-Level Corporate Executives

Martha Stewart, CEO Martha Stewart Living Omnimedia	In December 2001, Stewart sold over one-quarter million dollars' worth of ImClone Systems stock prior to the stock's subsequent plunge. Her defense claimed that she had discussed selling the large sum of stock since the stock had dropped below $60 per share. However, it was later revealed that she and her broker were guilty of insider trading based on inside information from ImClone Systems' CEO Sam Waksal (who also was found guilty of the same felony and is now serving six years in a Pennsylvania prison camp). On July 16, 2004, Stewart was sentenced to five months in federal prison and five months house arrest and was fined $30,000.
Harry C. Stonecipher, CEO Boeing Co.	There are ethical dilemmas, of course, that fall outside the more recent focus on corrupt financial behavior. Boeing's Stonecipher engaged in an extramarital affair with fellow executive, Deborah Peabody. This raised a particularly difficult decision for Boeing's board of directors. In only 15 months on the job, Stonecipher had helped the company recover from ethical credibility problems created by a Pentagon scandal that landed two of its executives in prison. During Stonecipher's brief time at the top, the company's market valuation had climbed 50 percent. On February 28, 2005, Boeing's board requested that he cease his relationship with Peabody. The 68-year-old Stonecipher, ignoring the shareholder consequences of his questionable image, declined this request. The board responded with a demand for his resignation.
Maurice Greenberg, CEO American Insurance Group (AIG)	The Greenberg family may show that unethical behavior can be hereditary. In September 2004, New York Attorney General Eliot Spitzer insisted that the son of AIG's CEO Maurice "Hank" Greenberg, Jeffrey Greenberg, CEO of the world's largest insurance broker, Marsh & McLennan, resign due to account fixing and bid rigging charges. In Marsh's case, the defense attempted to plead that Jeffrey Greenberg "did not understand how the insurance business operated." In November 2004, AIG paid an $80 million fine to the U.S. Department of Justice to settle complaints concerning the crooked sale of insurance products. In April 2005, AIG's board requested that Maurice Greenberg, 79, step down from his position in the face of similar scandals associated with rigging bids of nontraditional insurance products that were pitched to the heads of other companies.

Sources: Kahn, J. 2004. Why CEOs should hope Martha walks. *Fortune,* February 9: 24–25; Sellers, P. 2004. Why Martha may choose jail now. *Fortune,* August 9: 36; Revell, J. 2004. Martha gets 5 to 20; Investors get life. *Fortune,* March 22: 40; Holmes, S. 2005. Why Boeing's culture breeds turmoil. *BusinessWeek,* March 21: 34–36; Henry, D., France, M., & Lavelle, Louis. 2005. The boss on the sidelines. April 25: 86–96; Elkind, P., & Devin, L. 2005. More bad news for AIG's Greenberg? *Fortune,* March 7: 28; Condon, B., & Coolidge, C. 2005. When gray becomes black-and-white. *Forbes,* May 9: 90–92; and http://www.insurancejournal.com/news/national/2004/10/15/46937.htm.

11.9 STRATEGY SPOTLIGHT

Procter & Gamble: Using Ethics to "Build the Spirit of the Place"

John Pepper, former CEO and chairman of Procter & Gamble Company, shares his perspective on ethics.

> Let me start by saying that while ethics may seem like a soft concept—not as hard, say, as strategy or budgeting or operations—it is, in fact, a very hard concept. It is tangible. It is crucial . . . it is good for business.
>
> There are several reasons for this. First, a company's values have a tremendous impact on who is attracted to your company and who will stay with it. We only have one life to live. All of us want to live it as part of an institution committed to high goals and high-sighted means of reaching these goals. This is true everywhere I've been. In our most mature countries and our newest.
>
> Strong corporate values greatly simplify decision making. It is important to know the things you won't even think about doing. Diluting a product. Paying a bribe. Not being fair to a customer or an employee.

Source: Pepper, J. E. 1997. The boa principle: Operating ethically in today's business environment. Speech presented at Florida A&M University, Tallahassee, January 30.

> Strong values earn the respect of customers and suppliers and governments and other companies, too. This is absolutely crucial over the long term.
>
> A company which pays bribes in a foreign market becomes an open target for more bribes when the word gets out. It never stops.
>
> A company which is seen to be offering different trade terms to different customers based on how big they are or how hard they push will forever be beset by requests for special terms.
>
> A company which is seen by a government as having weak or varying standards will not be respected by that government.
>
> And more positively, governments and other companies really do want to deal with companies they feel are pursuing sound values because in many, if not most, cases, they believe it will be good for them.
>
> One final but very fundamental reason for operating ethically is that strong values create trust and pride among employees. Simply put, they build the spirit of the place.

customers, and governmental agencies. John E. Pepper, former chairman of Procter & Gamble, addresses such a perspective in Strategy Spotlight 11.9.

Integrity-Based versus Compliance-Based Approaches to Organizational Ethics

Before discussing the key elements for building an ethical organization, it is important to understand the essential links between organizational integrity and the personal integrity of an organization's members.[55] There cannot be high-integrity organizations without high-integrity individuals. At the same time, individual integrity is rarely self-sustaining. Even good people can lose their bearings when faced with pressures, temptations, and heightened performance expectations in the absence of organizational support systems and ethical boundaries. Organizational integrity, on the other hand, is beyond personal integrity. It rests on a concept of purpose, responsibility, and ideals for an organization as a whole. An important responsibility of leadership in building organizational integrity is to create this ethical framework and develop the organizational capabilities to make it operational.

It is also important to know the approaches or strategies organizations take in dealing with ethics. Lynn Paine, a researcher at Harvard, identifies two such approaches: the compliance-based approach and the integrity-based approach. (See Exhibit 11.5 for a comparison of compliance-based and integrity-based strategies.) Faced with the prospect of litigation, several organizations reactively implement compliance-based ethics programs. Such programs are typically designed by a corporate counsel with the goal of preventing, detecting, and punishing legal violations. But being ethical is much more

422   Part 3   Strategic Implementation

Characteristics	Compliance-Based Approach	Integrity-Based Approach
Ethos	Conformity with externally imposed standards	Self-governance according to chosen standards
Objective	Prevent criminal misconduct	Enable responsible conduct
Leadership	Lawyer-driven	Management-driven with aid of lawyers, HR, and others
Methods	Education, reduced discretion, auditing and controls, penalties	Education, leadership, accountability, organizational systems and decision processes, auditing and controls, penalties
Behavioral Assumptions	Autonomous beings guided by material self-interest	Social beings guided by material self-interest, values, ideals, peers

Source: Paine, L. S. 1994. Managing for organizational integrity. *Harvard Business Review*, 72(2): 113 (with permission).

Exhibit 11.5

Approaches to Ethics Management

than being legal, and an integrity-based approach addresses the issue of ethics in a more comprehensive manner.

An integrity-based approach to ethics management combines a concern for law with an emphasis on managerial responsibility for ethical behavior. This approach is broader, deeper, and more demanding than a legal compliance initiative. It is broader in that it seeks to enable responsible conduct. It is deeper in that it cuts to the ethos and operating systems of an organization and its members, their core guiding values, thoughts, and actions. And it is more demanding because it requires an active effort to define the responsibilities and aspirations that constitute an organization's ethical compass. Most importantly, in this approach, organizational ethics is seen as the work of management. A corporate counsel may play a role in designing and implementing integrity strategies, but it is managers at all levels and across all functions that are involved in the process. Once integrated into the day-to-day operations of an organization, such strategies can help prevent damaging ethical lapses, while tapping into powerful human impulses for moral thought and action. Ethics then become the governing ethos of an organization and not burdensome constraints to be adhered to. Here is an example of an organization that goes beyond mere compliance to laws in building an ethical organization:

> In teaching ethics to its employees, Texas Instruments, the $8 billion chip and electronics manufacturer, asks them to run an issue through the following steps: Is it legal? Is it consistent with the company's stated values? Will the employee feel bad doing it? What will the public think if the action is reported in the press? Does the employee think it is wrong? Further, if the employees are not sure of the ethicality of the issue, they are encouraged to ask someone until they are clear about it. In the process, employees can approach high-level personnel and even the company's lawyers. As can be clearly noted, at Texas Instruments, the question of ethics goes much beyond merely being legal. It is no surprise, therefore, that this company is a benchmark for corporate ethics and has been a recipient of three ethics awards: the David C. Lincoln Award for Ethics and Excellence in Business, American Business Ethics Award, and Bentley College Center for Business Ethics Award.[56]

To sum up, compliance-based approaches are externally motivated—that is, based on the fear of punishment for doing something unlawful. On the other hand, integrity-based approaches are driven by a personal and organizational commitment to ethical behavior.

A firm must have several key elements before it can become a highly ethical organization. These elements must be both present and constantly reinforced in order for the firm to be successful:

- Role models.
- Corporate credos and codes of conduct.
- Reward and evaluation systems.
- Policies and procedures.

These elements are highly interrelated. For example, reward structures and policies will be useless if leaders throughout the organization are not sound role models. That is, leaders who implicitly say, "Do as I say, not as I do," will quickly have their credibility eroded and such actions will, in effect, sabotage other elements that are essential to building an ethical organization.

Role Models

For good or for bad, leaders are role models in their organizations. As we noted in Chapter 9, leaders must "walk the talk"; that is, they must be consistent in their words and deeds. The values as well as the character of leaders become transparent to an organization's employees through their behaviors. In addition, when leaders do not believe in the ethical standards that they are trying to inspire, they will not be effective as good role models. Being an effective leader often includes taking responsibility for ethical lapses within the organization—even though the executives themselves are not directly involved. Consider, for example, the perspective of Dennis Bakke, CEO of AES, the $8 billion global electricity company based in Arlington, Virginia.

> There was a major breach (in 1992) of the AES values. Nine members of the water treatment team in Oklahoma lied to the EPA about water quality at the plant. There was no environmental damage, but they lied about the test results. A new, young chemist at the plant discovered it, and she told a team leader, and, of course, we then were notified. Now, you could argue that the people who lied were responsible and were accountable, but the senior management team also took responsibility by taking pay cuts. My reduction was about 30 percent.[57]

Such action enhances the loyalty and commitment of employees throughout the organization. Many would believe that it would have been much easier (and personally less expensive!) for Bakke and his management team to merely take strong punitive action against the nine individuals who were acting contrary to the behavior expected in AES's ethical culture. However, by taking responsibility for the misdeeds, the top executives—through their highly visible action—made it very clear that responsibility and penalties for ethical lapses go well beyond the "guilty" parties. Such courageous behavior by leaders helps to strengthen an organization's ethical environment.

Corporate Credos and Codes of Conduct

Corporate credos or codes of conduct are another important element of an ethical organization. Such mechanisms provide a statement and guidelines for norms and beliefs as well as guidelines for decision making. They provide employees with a clear understanding of the organization's position regarding employee behavior. Such guidelines also provide the basis for employees to refuse to commit unethical acts and help to make them aware of issues before they are faced with the situation. For such codes to be truly effective, organization members must be aware of them and what behavioral guidelines they contain.[58]

Large corporations are not the only ones to develop and use codes of conduct. Consider the example of Wetherill Associates (WAI), a small, privately held supplier of electrical parts to the automotive market.

> Rather than a conventional code of conduct, WAI has a Quality Assurance Manual—a combination of philosophy text, conduct guide, technical manual, and company profile—that describes the company's commitment to honesty, ethical action, and integrity.
>
> Interestingly, WAI doesn't have a corporate ethics officer, because the company's corporate ethics officer is top management. Marie Bothe, WAI's chief executive officer, sees her main function as keeping the 350-employee company on the path of ethical behavior and looking for opportunities to help the community. She delegates the "technical" aspects of the business—marketing, finance, personnel, and operations—to other members of the organization.[59]

Perhaps the best-known credo, a statement describing a firm's commitment to certain standards, is that of Johnson & Johnson (J&J). It is reprinted in Exhibit 11.6. The credo stresses honesty, integrity, superior products, and putting people before profits. What

Exhibit 11.6
Johnson & Johnson's Credo

We believe our first responsibility is to the doctors, nurses and patients, to mothers and fathers and all others who use our products and services. In meeting their needs everything we do must be of high quality. We must constantly strive to reduce our costs in order to maintain reasonable prices. Customers' orders must be serviced promptly and accurately. Our suppliers and distributors must have an opportunity to make a fair profit.

We are responsible to our employees, the men and women who work with us throughout the world. Everyone must be considered as an individual. We must respect their dignity and recognize their merit. They must have a sense of security in their jobs. Compensation must be fair and adequate, and working conditions clean, orderly, and safe. We must be mindful of ways to help our employees fulfill their family responsibilities. Employees must feel free to make suggestions and complaints. There must be equal opportunity for employment, development, and advancement for those qualified. We must provide competent management, and their actions must be just and ethical.

We are responsible to the communities in which we live and work and to the world community as well. We must be good citizens—support good works and charities and bear our fair share of taxes. We must encourage civic improvements and better health and education. We must maintain in good order the property we are privileged to use, protecting the environment and natural resources.

Our final responsibility is to our stockholders. Business must make a sound profit. We must experiment with new ideas. Research must be carried on, innovative programs developed, and mistakes paid for. New equipment must be purchased, new facilities provided, and new products launched. Reserves must be created to provide for adverse times. When we operate according to these principles, the stockholders should realize a fair return.

Source: Reprinted with permission of Johnson & Johnson Co.

distinguishes the J&J credo from those of other firms is the amount of energy the company's top managers devote to ensuring that employees live by its precepts.

Over a three-year period, Johnson & Johnson undertook a massive effort to assure that its original credo, already decades old, was still valid. More than 1,200 managers attended two-day seminars in groups of 25, with explicit instructions to challenge the credo. The president or CEO of the firm personally presided over each session. In the end, the company came out of the process believing that its original document was still valid. However, the questioning process continues. Such "challenge meetings" are still replicated every other year for all new managers. These efforts force J&J to question, internalize, and then implement its credo. Such investments have paid off handsomely many times—most notably in 1982, when eight people died from swallowing capsules of Tylenol, one of its flagship products, that someone had laced with cyanide. Leaders such as James Burke, who without hesitation made an across-the-board recall of the product even though it affected only a limited number of untraceable units, send a strong message throughout their organization.

Reward and Evaluation Systems

It is entirely possible for a highly ethical leader to preside over an organization that commits several unethical acts. How? It may reflect a flaw in the organization's reward structure. A reward and evaluation system may inadvertently cause individuals to act in an inappropriate manner if rewards are seen as being distributed on the basis of outcomes instead of the means by which goals and objectives are achieved.[60]

Consider the example of Sears, Roebuck & Co.'s automotive operations. Here, unethical behavior, rooted in a faulty reward system, took place primarily at the operations level: its automobile repair facilities.[61]

> In 1992 Sears was flooded with complaints about its automotive service business. Consumers and attorneys general in more than 40 states accused the firm of misleading customers and selling them unnecessary parts and services, from brake jobs to front-end alignments. What were the causes?
>
> In the face of declining revenues and eroding market share, Sears's management attempted to spur the performance of its auto centers by introducing new goals and incentives for mechanics. Automotive service advisers were given product-specific quotas for a variety of parts and repairs. Failure to meet the quotas could lead to transfers and reduced hours. Many employees spoke of "pressure, pressure, pressure" to bring in sales.
>
> Not too surprisingly, the judgment of many employees suffered. In essence, employees were left to chart their own course, given the lack of management guidance and customer ignorance. The bottom line: In settling the spate of lawsuits, Sears offered coupons to customers who had purchased certain auto services over the most recent two-year period. The total cost of the settlement, including potential customer refunds, was estimated to be $60 million. The cost in terms of damaged reputation? Difficult to assess, but certainly not trivial.

The Sears automotive example makes two important points. First, inappropriate reward systems may cause individuals at all levels throughout an organization to commit unethical acts that they might not otherwise commit. Second, the penalties in terms of damage to reputations, human capital erosion, and financial loss—in the short run and long run—are typically much higher than any gains that could be obtained through such unethical behavior.

Policies and Procedures

Many situations that a firm faces have regular, identifiable patterns. Typically, leaders tend to handle such routine by establishing a policy or procedure to be followed that can

378

Dess–Lumpkin–Eisner:
Strategic Management:
Text and Cases, Third

III. Strategic
Implementation

11. Strategic Leadership:
Creating a Learning
Organization and an

© The McGraw–Hill
Companies, 2007

STRATEGY SPOTLIGHT

11.10

No More Whistleblowing Woes!

The landmark Sarbanes-Oxley Act of 2002 gives those who expose corporate misconduct strong legal protection. Henceforth, an executive who retaliates against the corporate whistleblower can be held criminally liable and imprisoned for up to 10 years. That's the same sentence a mafia don gets for threatening a witness. The Labor Department can order a company to rehire an employee without going to court. If the fired workers feel their case is moving too slowly, they can request a federal jury after six months.

Companies need to revisit their current policies, including nondisclosure pacts. They may no longer be able to enforce rules requiring employees to get permission to speak to the media or lawyers. Even layoffs should be planned in advance, lest they seem retaliatory.

Sources: www.sarbanes-oxley.com/pcaob.php/level=2&pub_id=Sarbanes-Oxley&chap_id=PCAOB11; Dwyer, P., Carney, D., Borrus, A., Woellert, L., & Palmeri, C. 2002. Year of the WhistleBlower. *BusinessWeek*, December 16: 107–109; and www.buchalter.com/FSL5CS/articles/articles204.asp.

Employees of publicly traded companies are now the most protected whistleblowers. Provisions coauthored by Senator Grassley in the Sarbanes-Oxley corporate-reform law:

- Make it unlawful to "discharge, demote, suspend or threaten, harass, or in any manner discriminate against" a whistleblower.

- Establish criminal penalties of up to 10 years in jail for executives who retaliate against whistleblowers.

- Require board audit committees to establish procedures for hearing whistleblower complaints.

- Allow the secretary of labor to order a company to rehire a terminated whistleblower with no court hearings whatsoever.

- Give a whistleblower a right to jury trial, bypassing months or years of cumbersome administrative hearings.

be applied rather uniformly to each occurrence. As we noted in Chapter 9, such guidelines can be useful in specifying the proper relationships with a firm's customers and suppliers. For example, Levi Strauss has developed stringent global sourcing guidelines and Chemical Bank (now part of J. P. Morgan Chase Bank) has a policy of forbidding any review that would determine whether or not suppliers are Chemical customers when the bank awards contracts.

Clearly, it is important to carefully develop policies and procedures to guide behavior so that all employees will be encouraged to behave in an ethical manner. However, it is not enough merely to have policies and procedures "on the books." Rather, they must be reinforced with effective communication, enforcement, and monitoring, as well as sound corporate governance practices. Strategy Spotlight 11.10 describes how the recently enacted Sarbanes-Oxley Act provides considerable legal protection to employees of publicly traded companies who report unethical or illegal practices.

Summary

Strategic leadership is vital in ensuring that strategies are formulated and implemented in an effective manner. Leaders must play a central role in performing three critical and interdependent activities: setting the direction, designing the organization, and nurturing a culture committed to excellence and ethical behavior. In the chapter we provided the imagery of these three activities as a "three-legged stool." If leaders ignore or are ineffective at performing any one of the three, the organization will not be very successful. Leaders must also use power effectively to overcome barriers to change.

For leaders to effectively fulfill their activities, emotional intelligence (EI) is very important. Five elements that contribute to EI are self-awareness, self-regulation, motivation, empathy, and social skill. The first three elements pertain to self-management skills, whereas the last two are associated with a person's ability to manage relationships with others. We also addressed some of the potential drawbacks from the ineffective use of EI. These include the dysfunctional use of power as well as a tendency to become overly empathetic, which may result in unreasonably lowered performance expectations.

Leaders must also play a central role in creating a learning organization. Gone are the days when the top-level managers "think" and everyone else in the organization "does." With the rapidly changing, unpredictable, and complex competitive environments that characterize most industries, leaders must engage everyone in the ideas and energies of people throughout the organization. Great ideas can come from anywhere in the organization—from the executive suite to the factory floor. The five elements that we discussed as central to a learning organization are inspiring and motivating people with a mission or purpose, empowering people at all levels throughout the organization, accumulating and sharing internal knowledge, gathering external information, and challenging the status quo to stimulate creativity.

In the final section of the chapter, we addressed a leader's central role in instilling ethical behavior in the organization. We discussed the enormous costs that firms face when ethical crises arise—costs in terms of financial and reputational loss as well as the erosion of human capital and relationships with suppliers, customers, society at large, and governmental agencies. And, as we would expect, the benefits of having a strong ethical organization are also numerous. We contrasted compliance-based and integrity-based approaches to organizational ethics. Compliance-based approaches are largely externally motivated; that is, they are motivated by the fear of punishment for doing something that is unlawful. Integrity-based approaches, on the other hand, are driven by a personal and organizational commitment to ethical behavior. We also addressed the four key elements of an ethical organization: role models, corporate credos and codes of conduct, reward and evaluation systems, and policies and procedures.

Summary Review Questions

1. Three key activities—setting a direction, designing the organization, and nurturing a culture and ethics—are all part of what effective leaders do on a regular basis. Explain how these three activities are interrelated.

2. Define emotional intelligence (EI). What are the key elements of EI? Why is EI so important to successful strategic leadership?

3. The knowledge a firm possesses can be a source of competitive advantage. Describe ways that a firm can continuously learn to maintain its competitive position.

4. How can the five central elements of "learning organizations" be incorporated into global companies?

5. What are the benefits to firms and their shareholders of conducting business in an ethical manner?

6. Firms that fail to behave in an ethical manner can incur high costs. What are these costs and what is their source?

7. What are the most important differences between an "integrity organization" and a "compliance organization" in a firm's approach to organizational ethics?

8. What are some of the important mechanisms for promoting ethics in a firm?

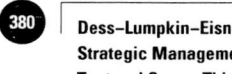
428   Part 3   Strategic Implementation

Experiential Exercise

Select two well-known business leaders—one you admire and one you do not. Evaluate each of them on the five characteristics of emotional intelligence.

Emotional Intelligence Characteristics	Admired Leader	Leader Not Admired
Self-awareness		
Self-regulation		
Motivation		
Empathy		
Social skills		

Application Questions Exercises

1. Identify two CEOs whose leadership you admire. What is it about their skills, attributes, and effective use of power that causes you to admire them?

2. Founders have an important role in developing their organization's culture and values. At times, their influence persists for many years. Identify and describe two organizations in which the cultures and values established by the founder(s) continue to flourish. You may find research on the Internet helpful in answering these questions.

3. Some leaders place a great emphasis on developing superior human capital. In what ways does this help a firm to develop and sustain competitive advantages?

4. In this chapter we discussed the five elements of a "learning organization." Select a firm with which you are familiar and discuss whether or not it epitomizes some (or all) of these elements.

Ethics Questions

1. Sometimes organizations must go outside the firm to hire talent, thus bypassing employees already working for the firm. Are there conditions under which this might raise ethical considerations?

2. Ethical crises can occur in virtually any organization. Describe some of the systems, procedures, and processes that can help to prevent such crises.

References

1. Gagnier, M. 2005. Kremed again. *BusinessWeek,* January 17:40; Anonymous. 2005. Worst managers. *BusinessWeek,* January 10: 74–77; Stires, D. 2004. Krispy Kreme is in the hole—again. *Fortune,* November 11: 42–43; and, McGowan, W. P. 2005. Krispy Kreme: A recipe for business failure. *Canyon News,* 19: 23.

2. Charan, R., & Colvin, G. 1999. Why CEOs fail. *Fortune,* June 21: 68–78.

3. These three activities and our discussion draw from Kotter, J. P. 1990. What leaders really do. *Harvard Business Review,* 68(3): 103–111; Pearson, A. E. 1990. Six basics for general managers. *Harvard Business Review,* 67(4): 94–101; and Covey, S. R. 1996. Three roles of the leader in the new paradigm. In *The leader of the future:* 149–160. Hesselbein, F., Goldsmith, M., & Beckhard, R. (Eds.). San Francisco: Jossey-Bass. Some of the discussion of each of the three leadership activity concepts draws on Dess, G. G., & Miller, A. 1993. *Strategic management:* 320–325. New York: McGraw-Hill.

4. Day, C., Jr., & LaBarre, P. 1994. GE: Just your average everyday $60 billion family grocery store. *Industry Week,* May 2: 13–18.

5. The best (& worst) managers of the year. 2003. *Business-Week,* January 13: 63.

6. Johnson, C. 2005. Lay, Skilling go on trial in January. *Washington Post,* February 25: E3.

7. Watkins, S. 2003. Former Enron vice president Sherron Watkins on the Enron collapse. *Academy of Management Executive,* 17(4): 119–125. Ms. Watkins has been widely recognized as a "whistleblower" and for her courage in bringing the Enron scandal to light. For example, she was one of three individuals to be recognized as *Time* magazine's Persons of the Year in 2002. She also received the Scales of Justice Award, Everyday Hero's Award, Women Mean Business Award, and the Academy of Management's 2003 Distinguished Executive Speaker.

8. In January 2004, Fastow agreed to serve a 10-year sentence, pay a $23 million fine, and cooperate with the U.S. government's continuing investigation. He had been charged with 78 counts of fraud, money laundering, and conspiracy.

9. For insightful perspectives on escalation, refer to Brockner, J. 1992. The escalation of commitment to a failing course of action. *Academy of Management Review,* 17(1): 39–61; and Staw, B. M. 1976. Knee-deep in the big muddy: A study of commitment to a chosen course of action. *Organizational Behavior and Human Decision Processes.* 16: 27–44. The discussion of systemic, behavioral, and political barriers draws on Lorange, P., & Murphy, D. 1984. Considerations in implementing strategic control. *Journal of Business Strategy.* 5: 27–35. In a similar vein, Noel M. Tichy has addressed three types of resistance to change in the context of General Electric: technical resistance, political resistance, and cultural resistance. See Tichy, N. M. 1993. Revolutionalize your company. *Fortune,* December 13: 114–118. Examples draw from O'Reilly, B. 1997. The secrets of America's most admired corporations: New ideas and new products. *Fortune.* March 3: 60–64.

10. This section draws on Champoux, J. E. 2000. *Organizational behavior: Essential tenets for a new millennium.* London: South-Western; and The mature use of power in organizations. 2003. *RHR International-Executive Insights,* May 29, 12.19.168.197/execinsights/8-3.htm.

11. An insightful perspective on the role of power and politics in organizations is provided in Ciampa, K. 2005. Almost ready: How leaders move up. *Harvard Business Review,* 83(1): 46–53.

12. A discussion of the importance of persuasion in bringing about change can be found in Garvin, D. A., & Roberto, M. A. 2005. Change through persuasion. *Harvard Business Review.* 83(4): 104–113.

13. Lorsch, J. W., & Tierney, T. J. 2002. *Aligning the stars: How to succeed when professionals drive results.* Boston: Harvard Business School Press.

14. For a review of this literature, see Daft, R. 1999. *Leadership: Theory and practice.* Fort Worth, TX: Dryden Press.

15. This section draws on Luthans, F. 2002. Positive organizational behavior: Developing and managing psychological strengths. *Academy of Management Executive,* 16(1): 57–72; and Goleman, D. 1998. What makes a leader? *Harvard Business Review,* 76(6): 92–105.

16. EI has its roots in the concept of "social intelligence" that was first identified by E. L. Thorndike in 1920 (Intelligence and its uses. *Harper's Magazine,* 140: 227–235). Psychologists have been uncovering other intelligences for some time now and have grouped them into such clusters as abstract intelligence (the ability to understand and manipulate verbal and mathematical symbols), concrete intelligence (the ability to understand and manipulate objects), and social intelligence (the ability to understand and relate to people). See Ruisel, I. 1992. Social intelligence: Conception and methodological problems. *Studia Psychologica,* 34(4–5): 281–296. Refer to trochim.human.cornell.edu/gallery.

17. See, for example, Luthans, op. cit.; Mayer, J. D., Salvoney, P., & Caruso, D. 2000. Models of emotional intelligence. In Sternberg, R. J. (Ed.). *Handbook of intelligence.* Cambridge, UK: Cambridge University Press; and Cameron, K. 1999. Developing emotional intelligence at the Weatherhead School of Management. *Strategy: The Magazine of the Weatherhead School of Management,* Winter: 2–3.

18. An insightful perspective on leadership, which involves discovering, developing and celebrating what is unique about each individual, is found in Buckingham, M. 2005. What great managers do. *Harvard Business Review*, 83(3): 70–79.

19. Goleman, op. cit.: 102.

20. This section draws upon Klemp. G. 2005. *Emotional intelligence and leadership: What really matters*. Cambria Consulting, Inc., www.cambriaconsulting.com.

21. Mayer, J. D. et al. 2004. Leading by feel. *Harvard Business Review*, 82(1): 27–37.

22. Heifetz, R. 2004. Question authority. *Harvard Business Review*, 82(1): 37.

23. Ibid.

24. For another insightful perspective, refer to Goleman, D., Boyztzis, R., & McKee, A. 2002. *Primal leadership: Realizing the power of emotional Intelligence*. Boston: Harvard Business School. In particular, this book addresses the advantages and drawbacks of six leadership styles that draw upon the EI concept.

25. Handy, C. 1995. Trust and the virtual organization. *Harvard Business Review*, 73(3): 40–50.

26. This section draws upon Dess, G. G., & Picken, J. C. 1999. *Beyond productivity*. New York: AMACOM. The elements of the learning organization in this section are consistent with the work of Dorothy Leonard-Barton. See, for example, Leonard-Barton, D. 1992. The factory as a learning laboratory. *Sloan Management Review*, 11: 23–38.

27. Senge, P. M. 1990. The leader's new work: Building learning organizations. *Sloan Management Review*, 32(1): 7–23.

28. Hammer, M., & Stanton, S. A. 1997. The power of reflection. *Fortune*, November 24: 291–296.

29. For some guidance on how to effectively bring about change in organizations, refer to Wall, S. J. 2005. The protean organization: Learning to love change. *Organizational Dynamics*, 34(1): 37–46.

30. Covey, S. R. 1989. *The seven habits of highly effective people: Powerful lessons in personal change*. New York: Simon & Schuster.

31. Melrose, K. 1995. *Making the grass greener on your side: A CEO's journey to leading by servicing*. San Francisco: Barrett-Koehler.

32. Quinn, R. C., & Spreitzer, G. M. 1997. The road to empowerment: Seven questions every leader should consider. *Organizational Dynamics*, 25: 37–49.

33. Helgesen, S. 1996. Leading from the grass roots. In *Leader of the future*: 19–24 Hesselbein et al.

34. Bowen, D. E., & Lawler, E. E., III. 1995. Empowering service employees. *Sloan Management Review*, 37: 73–84.

35. Stack, J. 1992. *The great game of business*. New York: Doubleday/Currency.

36. Lubove, S. 1998. New age capitalist. *Forbes*, April 6: 42–43.

37. Schafer, S. 1997. Battling a labor shortage? It's all in your imagination. *Inc.*, August: 24.

38. Meyer, P. 1998. So you want the president's job . . . . *Business Horizons*, January–February: 2–8.

39. Goldberg, M. 1998. Cisco's most important meal of the day. *Fast Company*, February–March: 56.

40. Imperato, G. 1998. Competitive intelligence: Get smart! *Fast Company*, May: 268–279.

41. Novicki, C. 1998. The best brains in business. *Fast Company*, April: 125.

42. The introductory discussion of benchmarking draws on Miller, A. 1998. *Strategic management*: 142–143. New York: McGraw-Hill.

43. Port, O., & Smith, G. 1992. Beg, borrow—and benchmark. *BusinessWeek*, November 30: 74–75.

44. Main, J. 1992. How to steal the best ideas around. *Fortune*, October 19: 102–106.

45. Taylor, J. T. 1997. What happens after what comes next? *Fast Company*, December–January: 84–85.

46. Sheff, D. 1996. Levi's changes everything. *Fast Company*, June–July: 65–74.

47. Isaacson, W. 1997. In search of the real Bill Gates. *Time*, January 13: 44–57.

48. Baatz, E. B. 1993. Motorola's secret weapon. *Electronic Business*, April: 51–53.

49. Holt, J. W. 1996. *Celebrate your mistakes*. New York: McGraw-Hill.

50. Harari, O. 1997. Flood your organization with knowledge. *Management Review*, November: 33–37.

51. This opening discussion draws upon Conley, J. H. 2000. Ethics in business. In Helms, M. M. (Ed.). *Encyclopedia of management* (4th ed.): 281–285; Farmington Hills, MI: Gale Group; Paine, L. S. 1994. Managing for organizational integrity. *Harvard Business Review*, 72(2): 106–117; and Carlson, D. S., & Perrewe, P. L. 1995. Institutionalization of organizational ethics through transformational leadership. *Journal of Business Ethics*, 14: 829–838.

52. Kiger, P. J. 2001. Truth and consequences. *Working Woman*, May: 57–61.

53. Soule, E. 2002. Managerial moral strategies—in search of a few good principles. *Academy of Management Review*, 27(1): 114–124.

54. Carlson & Perrewe, op. cit.

55. This discussion is based upon Paine. Managing for organizational integrity; Paine, L. S. 1997. *Cases in leadership, ethics, and organizational integrity: A Strategic approach*. Burr Ridge, IL: Irwin; and Fontrodona, J. 2002. Business ethics across the Atlantic. Business Ethics Direct, www.ethicsa.org/BED_art_fontrodone.html.

56. www.ti.com/corp/docs/company/citizen/ethics/benchmark. shtml; and www.ti.com/corp/docs/company/citizen/ethics/ quicktest.shtml.

57. Wetlaufer, S. 1999. Organizing for empowerment: An interview with AES's Roger Sant and Dennis Bakke. *Harvard Business Review,* 77(1): 110–126.

58. For an insightful, academic perspective on the impact of ethics codes on executive decision making, refer to Stevens, J. M., Steensma, H. K., Harrison, D. A., & Cochran, P. S. 2005. Symbolic or substantive document? The influence of ethics code on financial executives' decisions. *Strategic Management Journal,* 26(2): 181–195.

59. Paine. Managing for organizational integrity.

60. For a recent study on the effects of goal setting on unethical behavior, read Schweitzer, M. E., Ordonez, L., & Douma, B. 2004. Goal setting as a motivator of unethical behavior. *Academy of Management Journal,* 47(3): 422–432.

61. Paine. Managing for organizational integrity.

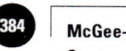

Chapter 19

Knowledge, information and innovation strategy

Introduction

A theme evident in Chapter 18 discussion of the balanced scorecard approach was the strategist's need to balance short-term and long-term performance. In order to create value in the long term, managers must commit current resources in an uncertain environment in order to create a sustainable future for the organization. They must gather the appropriate information and use judgement feedback and intuition from the accumulated knowledge and experience base in order to innovate, i.e. to develop new ideas, products, markets and business relationships that will facilitate expansion of existing markets or create entirely new markets.

In the strategy field there is increasing interest in the nature of 'knowledge', for example, how it is generated and fed back to

Chapter contents

individuals to improve strategies and to organizational members to facilitate organizational learning. New areas of strategy and organizational science such as knowledge management (Nonaka 1994), organizational learning (de Geus 1997) and the knowledge-based view of strategy (Grant 1996; Spender 1996) have mushroomed and have, in turn, posed critical questions about processes of innovation and the meaning of knowledge.

In this chapter we discuss the literature on innovation and technological change and introduce a number of competing concepts including 'disruptive innovations and the innovator's dilemma' (Christensen 1997), 'innovation as revolution' (Hamel 2000), and 'value innovation' (Kim and Mauborgne 1999). We try to define key terms such as knowledge, technology, innovation and core competences as a basis for examining four different perspectives on knowledge: knowledge as assets, knowledge through innovation, knowledge embedded in routines, and knowledge through learning. We then try to present the elements of the knowledge-based view of strategy and provide insights about how to foster organizational commitment to innovation and to structure the organization to achieve growth through innovation.

19.1 Concepts of knowledge and innovation

In their path-breaking book *The Knowledge-creating Company* (1995), Professors Nonaka and Takeuchi have stressed clearly the proposition that the *systemic knowledge* ingrained in the firm, its processes and its people is the single most important resource for the firm. This systemic knowledge is slowly developed, is distinctive and unique to the firm, is not easily transferable to others and may be protected by intellectual property regulations or other competitive barriers. The ease with which the knowledge is capitalized by the firm depends in part on how the knowledge is managed internally in the firm and transferred and replicated easily throughout the organization. Wal-Mart's inventory management and replenishment systems and McDonald's knowledge transfer of restaurant technology throughout its restaurant system are prime examples of good knowledge management and transfer in successful organizations. We define knowledge management as follows:

> *The process of identifying, extracting and managing the information, intellectual property and accumulated knowledge that exists within a company and the minds of its employees.*

Strategists such as Cooper and Schendel (1976) point out the nature of strategic responses to technological threats and indicate that incremental technological changes (competence-enhancing changes) reinforce the competitive positions of established firms in the industry, whereas more radical technological innovations (competence-destroying changes) may pressure existing incumbent firms to develop new competences, skills and capabilities. Dussauge, Hart and Ramanantsoa (1996, p. 14) emphasize the distinction

Table 19.1 Product innovators and winners

Product	Innovator	Product winner (follower)
Jet plane	British Aerospace: Comet	Boeing (707)
CT scanner	EMI	GE
Video-cassette recorder	Ampex	Sony/Matsushita
Video games	Atari	Nintendo/Sega
Photocopier	Xerox	Canon
Office P/C	Xerox	IBM

Source: D.J. Teece, 1987; P Anderson and M. Tushman, 1990.

between 'incremental' innovations (refining and improving existing products or processes) and 'radical' innovations (introducing totally new concepts). Innovation may involve the development of new technologies, such as bio-engineering and genetic engineering which define new industries, or the application of existing technologies to create new products, such as PCs, or to enhance existing products, such as digital cameras versus 35mm cameras. Generally, new products such as the CT scanner or the PC are new product configurations which link existing technologies and components in a new way. In these cases of new innovations (arising from *inventions* that create new products from new knowledge or distinctive combinations of existing knowledge) the product innovator is often not the eventual product winner. For example, Table 19.1 shows a range of innovative products for which the innovator is not the product winner. From a British viewpoint Sir Geoffrey Household of EMI won the Nobel Prize for the CT scanner yet the innovation was capitalized by GE. As a counter-example, however, Pilkington Glass of the UK was the innovator for float glass and also the winner in the marketplace despite US competition from Corning.

19.1.1 Disruptive technologies

Christensen (1997) focuses very closely on what he calls the innovators' dilemma in confronting different innovation types. He distinguishes between sustaining technologies, which foster improved product performance among existing firms and disruptive technologies, which result in worse near-term product performance and which precipitate the leading firm's failure. The dilemma for incumbent leading firms is that any adoption of disruptive breakthrough technologies requires cannibalization of purchases of existing products by current mainstream customers. This loss of revenue can lead these firms to go slow on implementing breakthrough technologies. Their mainstream customer focus, and associated market research, can then prevent leading firms from new product development, new markets and new customers in the future. This strategic weakness can allow entrepreneurial firms to exploit the new product pathway left open by the incumbent, leading firms.

Table 19.2 shows a list of the impacts of such disruptive innovations on the economic performance of leading incumbent firms.

19.1.2 Value innovation

Writers such as Kim and Mauborgne (1999) extend the concept of technological innovation to value innovation. They point out that while an innovator such as Ampex failed to capture the rents from inventing the VCR, their inventions nevertheless benefited the economy because later value innovators such as Sony and Matsushita made a success of the Ampex innovation. Value innovation places emphasis on the buyer as the centre of strategic thinking. To *value innovate*, companies must ask two questions:

1   Are we offering customers radically superior value?

Table 19.2 Examples of disruptive technologies (innovations)

Company	Disruptive innovation	Firms disrupted	Prior industry leader
DEC (Digital Equipment Corporation)	Mini computer	Mainframe computer manufacturers	IBM
HMOs e.g. Kaiser Permanente	Health maintenance organizations	Conventional health insurance	Blue Cross/Blue Shield
Compaq	Personal computer CPC	Mini-computer manufacturers	IBM, DEC
Dell	Direct order, customized PCs	Retail stores	Compaq
Charles Schwab	Discount trading/ broking	Investment banks	Merrill Lynch
Ford	Model T	Specialized car makers	Many
Toyota	Small cars and lean manufacturing	Large-volume car manufacturers	GM, Ford
Canon	Desk top photocopiers	High-speed photo-copying manufactuers (IBM, Kodak, Xerox)	Xerox
Wal-Mart	Discount retailing	Department stores	Macy's
Sony	Portable radios, TVs	Vacuum tube-based electronic products	RCA, Zenith

Source: Christensen, 1997.

2   Is our price level accessible to the mass of buyers in our target market?

As a consequence, the major inputs for value innovation are knowledge and ideas, new product concepts etc., which reject competitive strategies based on imitation but do not necessarily require new technology in order to succeed.

Table 19.3 shows a range of examples of value innovation given by Kim and Mauborgne (1999). It is instructive to note that in virtually all the cases given, the innovation shown is generally not a new 'technology' of a technical kind, but really a new product concept or a new way of framing a business opportunity using existing technologies and knowledge.

19.1.3 Revolutionary innovators

In his book *Leading the Revolution* (2000), Gary Hamel also stresses the importance of innovation as the engine to sustain corporate growth. Like Kim and Mauborgne, he believes that imitative strategies based on competitive strategy analysis have no basis in today's marketplace. He believes that the time has passed for strategies based on efficiency models (e.g. productive efficiency or benchmarking 'best practices' in competitors or the

Table 19.3 Example of value innovation

Company	Innovation
Callaway Golf – 'Big Bertha'	– made playing golf less difficult and more fun
SWATCH	– a price-competitive watch as a fashion accessory
Starbucks	– good coffee in a 'coffee bar'
Wal-Mart	– discount retailing
Charles Schwab	– investment and brokerage account management
CNN	– innovation in news broadcasting (24-hour news)
IKEA	– fashion home products and furniture retailing
SAP	– business applications software
Barnes & Noble	– book retailing
Southwest Airlines	– short-haul
Body Shop	– organic cosmetic retailing
Home Depot (B&Q)	– home improvement retail
Virgin Atlantic	– 'Upper class' – first-class service at a business-class price

Note: In virtually all these cases, with perhaps the exception of SAP, the concept is not a patentable innovation i.e. a scientifically excludable innovation.
Source: Kim and Mauborgne, 1999.

best-run companies). Senior managers must recognize the clear differences between innovation and imitation. Imitative approaches to the market mean that companies act reactively and try to emulate existing competitive strategies. In so doing, they misunderstand the customer demands and buyer needs in emerging mass markets.

Table 19.4 gives a few examples of companies seen as revolutionary innovators by Hamel.

Again, many of the ideas here rely on creative ideas and product concepts, and creative reconfigurations of existing technologies. New economy strategies are different and are discussed in Chapter 12.

The chapter now takes us systematically through four perspectives on knowledge which encompass economic concepts discussed earlier (for example, the resource-based view of the firm), alternative definitions of innovation (for example, radical, incremental, disruptive or value-based) and organizational approaches based on organizational evolution, routines and organization learning.

The traditional economic approach treats knowledge as an entity which affects the nature of the economic equilibrium, like so many other variables, but does not feature as a central player with regularity of effects on the competitive outcome. As we move towards placing knowledge at the centre of strategy theory we argue that there are four distinct approaches of how knowledge works. The first is the resource-based view (RBV) that provides us with the 'knowledge as asset' metaphor. A second view is Schumpeterian (Schumpeter 1934) in origin, picturing knowledge as innovation and as an essential element in the general theme of creative destruction of existing technological/knowledge bases. Third, evolutionary economics[1] moves away from a decision orientation towards a focus on the internal organization

Table 19.4 Hamel's revolutionary innovators (Hamel, 2000)

Company	Innovatory idea
SWATCH	Small objects of desire – combines Swiss watch making with Lego plastics
easyJet/Ryanair	Reinvented basic economics of airline business – real value to customers
Dell	Reinvented product cycle and cost structure of PCs
Nokia	Understood youth culture and its linkage to mobile phones

Source: Hamel, 2000.

[1] Nelson and Winter (1982) are most commonly identified with evolutionary economics. But the roots run deeper: *see* Veblen, 1898, on cumulative change; Marshall, 1920, on 'economic biology' and his well-known appreciation of dynamic analysis, and Alchian, 1950, 1953, on the implications of selection for the economic system.

of the firm and the role of organizational routines. The use of a Darwinian natural selection process coupled with adaptive feedback mechanisms explains the nature of organizational routines in large organizations. Such routines and their adaptation over time require embedded knowledge, acquisition of knowledge and transfer and integration of knowledge within organizations. Finally, the Teece, Pisano and Shuen (1997) approach to dynamic capabilities adds the elements of learning and other dynamics to the RBV and suggest paths by which both RBV and evolutionary approaches can take place in practice. The writers of these approaches did not place knowledge per se at the centre of their writing so, to a large degree, what follows is a reinterpretation of existing theory in terms of our view of knowledge and the role of knowledge in the processes of competitive strategy formulation and strategy development.

Case box: What do we know about the knowledge economy?

Pundits and politicians are forever proclaiming that we live in a knowledge economy, where success depends increasingly on brains not brawn. Yet little is actually known about the knowledge economy. An OECD study in 1999 made a start at filling in the picture – and debunks some myths.

For starters, Germany, not America, tops the OECD's knowledge-economy table. Knowledge-based industries accounted for 58.6% of German business output in 1996, compared with 55.3% in second-placed America (see chart). Japan is third, with Britain and France close behind, and Italy a notable laggard. In the OECD as a whole, knowledge-based industries accounted for over half of rich-country business output in the mid-1990s, up from around 45% in 1985.

The OECD's definition of the knowledge economy is pretty broad. As well as high-technology industries, such as computing and telecoms, the Paris-based think-tank counts sectors with a highly skilled workforce, such as finance and education. One reason that Germany is ahead of America is because of its big car, chemicals and machinery industries. Yet even in high-tech industries, where America is widely thought to be streets ahead, the United States comes behind Japan and Britain. High-tech industries produce 3.7% of Japan's business output and 3.3% of Britain's, but only 3% of America's. The United States is level-pegging with France, and only a bit ahead of Germany.

Growth in knowledge-based industries requires investment in knowledge as well as in physical capital. Such intangible investment is pretty hard to measure. By adding together spending on research and development (R&D), investment in software and public spending on education, the OECD puts it at 8% of rich-country GDP. Throwing in incomplete data on private education spending brings the total up to 10% of GDP, compared with physical investment in plant and machinery of 20% of GDP.

Sweden is the keenest investor in knowledge. Its investment in intangibles came to 10.6% of GDP in 1995; it spends far more of its national output on R&D than other countries.

708   CHAPTER 19   KNOWLEDGE, INFORMATION AND INNOVATION STRATEGY

France ranks second, thanks to its generously financed public-education system. America lags behind, because its government spends so little on schools. Japan, which spends a whopping 28.5% of GDP on physical investment, invests a puny 6.6% in intangibles.

Another myth that the new study pokes holes in is that the service sector, unlike manufacturing, does not innovate. Admittedly, R&D spending in services has traditionally been low. But in most countries it is now rising faster in services than in manufacturing. In 1980 services accounted for only 4.1% of business R&D in America; by 1996 its share had risen to 19.5%.

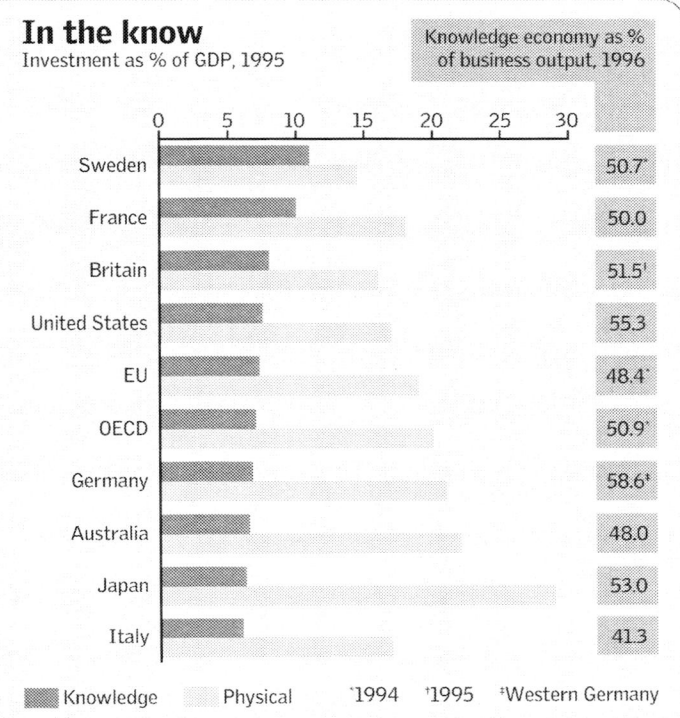

In the know
Investment as % of GDP, 1995

Knowledge economy as % of business output, 1996

	Knowledge economy as %
Sweden	50.7*
France	50.0
Britain	51.5‡
United States	55.3
EU	48.4*
OECD	50.9*
Germany	58.6‡
Australia	48.0
Japan	53.0
Italy	41.3

■ Knowledge   Physical   *1994   †1995   ‡Western Germany

Moreover, spending on R&D is only a fraction of total business spending on innovation. According to new evidence from business surveys compiled by the OECD, service industries spend far more on innovation than previously thought. Indeed, in Britain, spending on innovation in services is higher, at 4.02% of business sales in 1996, than in manufacturing, at 3.16%.

There are inevitably many gaps and flaws in the OECD's study. Its definition of the knowledge economy is far from perfect. It lumps together investment banking, a high-tech and pretty high-skill business, with estate agents, where knaves with badly written brochures still prosper. Another problem is that it includes many unskilled workers who work in knowledge industries. So, for example, hospital cleaners are counted as knowledge workers. But despite these shortcomings, the new report sheds new light on the knowledge economy.

Source: 'Knowledge gap', *The Economist*, 14 October 1999.
© The Economist Newspaper Limited, London (14 October 1999).

Questions for discussion

1   How would you define the 'knowledge economy'?

2   What are 'knowledge workers' and how are they different from other workers?

3   How do you expect the knowledge economy to develop over the next 10 years? 20 years? What implications does your answer have?

19.2 Knowledge as assets

Figure 19.1 portrays the market-based view commonly found in economic models in resource-based terms. The internals of the firm are here fleshed out in terms of resources and capabilities, the conventional description that permits discrimination between assets based on knowing and skills based on experience and actions. We do not summarize the key elements of the resource-based view here. They are familiar enough (see Wernerfelt 1984, Barney 1991; Grant (1991) and presented in depth in Chapter 7. Instead we suggest some conclusions in the language of *core competences*.

First, core competences can have a very significant impact by their effect on firm scope (boundaries), and by the (long) time scales over which they exist and change. They arise typically through collective learning – very much in the economics tradition of objectified knowledge (Spender 1996). Also, their impact is to create a framework through which we can view competition. This view is about contests for the acquisition of distinctive skills, in which competition in product markets is a 'superficial expression' of the more fundamental competition over competences. Therefore, the dynamics of the strategic theory of the firm focus on the process of core competence acquisition and collective learning because it occurs logically prior to product market evolution.

Figure 19.2 is a simple expansion of the range and nature of asset positions that are implied in Figure 19.1.[2] The broad categories give some idea of the differing demands on internal processes and on the challenge for integration of these different positions through some form of *corporate glue*, which integrates and binds these diverse asset positions for corporate value maximization. Many authors have provided classifications and explanations of the language of resources, assets, capabilities and competences. Grant (1991), for example, distinguishes between resources and capabilities, viewing resources as inputs and capabilities as those intermediate processes derived within the production function that are

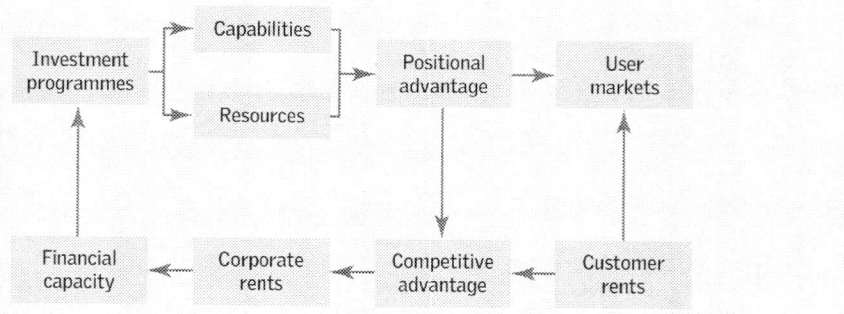

Figure 19.1 Resource-based view

---

[2] See the teaching notes in De Wit and Meyer (1994) for a practical illustration. Also see Barney (1991) and Grant (1991) for similar deconstructions of resources.

the main source of competitive advantage (refer back to the discussion in Chapter 7). Both are hard to define objectively and indeed Grant goes as far as to say that capabilities are organizational routines. Amit and Schoemaker (1993) (first discussed in Chapter 7) also deploy the language of resources and capabilities but seek to draw links with the industry analysis framework. Resources for them are intermediate goods (in contrast to Grant), and capabilities are '*based on developing, caring and exchanging information through the firm's human capital*'. They are built by combining physical, human and technological resources at the corporate level. The link with industry (or product market) arises when certain resources and capabilities become the prime determinant of economic rents and value. This can only occur if these resources and capabilities are subject to market failure and their possessions can therefore be firm-specific. Amit and Schoemaker refer to these as 'strategic assets'. This enables a distinction to be drawn between those resources and capabilities that are generally attainable and those that are asymmetrically distributed between firms, and difficult to trade and imitate.

Prahalad and Hamel (1990) (also first introduced in Chapter 7) have made famous the language of core competence and avoid using the language of resources and capabilities. For them, '*core competences are the collective learning in the organization, especially how to co-ordinate diverse production skills and integrate multiple streams of technologies*'.

Just as Amit and Schoemaker extend their notion of strategic assets towards product markets with a concept of strategic industry factors, so also do Prahalad and Hamel in making core competences the foundation for core products. For them the insight is not what is a core competence and how to build one, but a view of the strategic architecture

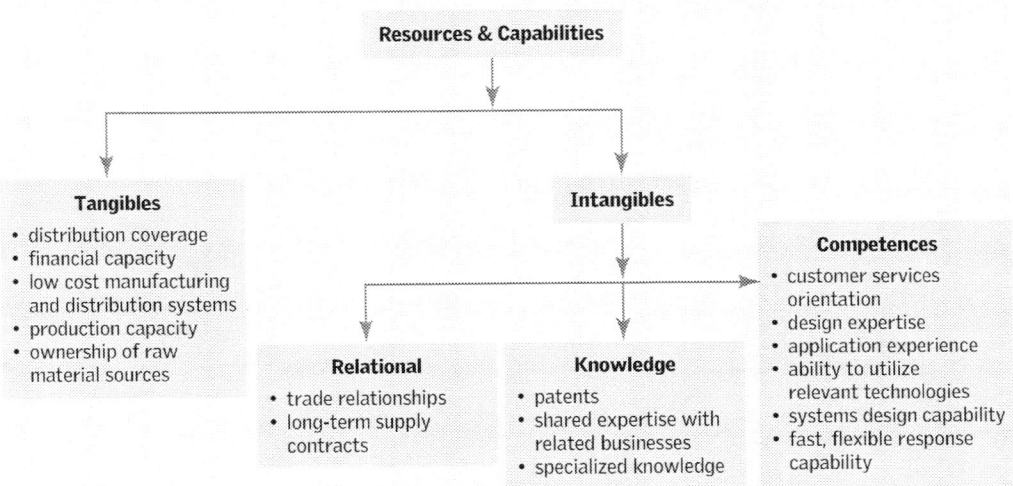

Figure 19.2 Resource positions (expanded)

of the firm, by which they mean '*a road map of the future that identifies which core competences to build and their constituent technologies*'. For these and other authors writing in the same vein, the common characteristic is the appeal to economic reasoning in the form of asymmetric distribution of assets to support economic rents and value. But the mainspring of firm-specific resources can lie anywhere between inputs and outputs with alternative scenarios about the contributory roles of organization structure and process, and managerial culture.

Our own approach in Figure 19.2 is more modest in intent. We seek only to distinguish between some categories or resources and capabilities so that we can see more clearly the different roles that knowledge can play. The distinction between tangible and intangible assets occurs prior to any distinction between resources and capabilities. We divide intangibles into three parts. The first companies those assets that are relational in character and involve the relationship of the organization with the outside world. The second is more explicitly concerned with knowledge and know-how. Although some entries under this heading suggest explicit knowledge (such as patents) they are surrounded by or produced by know-how that is essentially tacit. In the third part, our term competences can be used interchangeably with capabilities without any loss of meaning. There are, following Grant, intermediate processes, some of which are explicit in their design but many are likely to display characteristics of organizational routines.

19.3 Knowledge as innovation

The resource-based view provides a theory of protection and sustainability of competitive advantage. For an understanding of the genesis of advantage we have to turn elsewhere. The Schumpeterian approach (Schumpeter 1937) offers innovation as the medium through which creative destruction of existing technologies and knowledge bases takes place (see Box 1, Chapter 8). The element of destruction depicts intuitively and vividly but also convincingly how the old is replaced by the new. But it also sets these mechanisms in waves and floods of change, suggesting that a calculation of the benefits of change and innovation is overwhelmed by the magnitude of the opportunities on offer. Thus, Schumpeter suggested there were patterns of change and ferment (radical innovation) interspersed with stability (incremental innovation). In this way Schumpeter emphasized dynamic efficiency above static efficiency. Some recent writings clearly have their origins in Schumpeter. See, for example, d'Aveni's (1994) approach to hypercompetition, where he argues that the sources of competitive advantage are being created and destroyed at an increasingly rapid rate. Hamel and Prahalad (1993) use the language of dominance to assert a doctrine of strategic intent and define the gap between ambition and resources as strategic stretch. But the Schumpeterian world of enormous opportunity is not the only context for innovation. Firms may wish to create their own shocks or, more modestly, may seek to calculate finer pieces of sustainable advantage.

19.3.1 Innovation competition

But who innovates? Economists such as Kenneth Arrow have formulated models to explain whether new entrants have advantages over incumbents, whether monopoly can innovate more readily than competitive markets, and whether potential entrants can outwit monopolists. Of course, the answers depend on the situation but there is good reason for thinking that incomers often provide the wellspring of innovation – eventually. The behaviour to be explained is not that of the innovator who rationally examines the balance between costs and revenues in the light of prevailing competition and makes innovations when the return–risk ratio looks promising. The more difficult behaviour to explain is the reluctance of incumbents to refrain from innovating in the light of expected innovation from new entrants (*see* also Christensen 1997). The two rational economic reasons for this are the sunk cost effect and the replacement effect. The former arises when the incumbent assesses his existing technology by comparing its contribution margin to no new costs of investment beyond that of simple replacement. By contrast a new technology has a stiffer hurdle because the contribution margin (assuming for simplicity the same revenue stream from both technologies) has to cover new investment as well (*see* Besanko *et al.* 2000, pp. 488–9). The replacement effect was first formulated by Arrow (1962) in considering who has the greater propensity to invest, the monopolist or the new entrant. The incentive for the monopolist to invest in a radical new technology requires a comparison of the new stream of monopoly profits with the existing stream. However, for the new entrant who, if successful, will become the new monopolist, the incentive is simply the new stream of monopoly profits.

Through innovation an entrant can replace a monopolist but a monopolist can only replace itself, hence this is called the replacement effect. Thus, established firms under this thinking are less willing to stretch themselves to innovate. However, where the monopolist anticipates that new entry is likely then the incentives reverse to favour the monopolist. The incentive for the monopolist to innovate in the teeth of potential competitive intrusion is that of retaining monopoly profits from successful innovation versus sharing the market with a new entrant as a duopoly within which prices will be lower due to competition. This is greater than that of the new entrant who, expecting the monopolist to defend by innovation, can only anticipate the profit streams from sharing a competitive duopoly. Arrow called this the efficiency effect. The balance between these three effects depends on the probability of successful innovation by potential entrants. Where this is low, the sunk cost and replacement cost effects will dominate and the monopolists will prefer to maintain their existing cash flows. Where the probability is high then the efficiency motives will dominate and monopolists will seek to maintain their market position even if it is less favourable in absolute terms.

Case box: Outsource your innovations

When Frito-Lay added a little curl to its snacks, the company's sales improved. Of such seemingly modest innovations are great fortunes made. Next month Gillette will launch the successor to its sensationally successful Mach3 razor. Much as the company would like it to be as revolutionary as the Mach3 was in its day, the battery-operated vibrating beard-remover is unlikely to be more than evolutionary. That may not, however, prevent it from making a sizeable contribution to Gillette's profits.

Big firms still aspire to make truly great breakthrough inventions – products that will underwrite their profits for at least a decade. They are, however, coming up with such inventions less and less often, even though many industries, notably pharmaceuticals, continue to spend vast sums trying. Indeed, for most of industrial history, small firms have been responsible for the bulk of breakthrough products. America's Small Business Administration claims that the pacemaker, the personal computer, the Polaroid camera and pre-stressed concrete all emerged from small entrepreneurial outfits, and those are taken only from the list of items beginning with the letter P.

Big firms are better at less eye-catching forms of innovation – for example, Frito-Lay adding a little curl to its snacks, the clever twist allowing consumers to scoop up their guacamole or salsa dip and place relatively more of it in their mouths and less on their rugs, and generally improving the ways in which products invented elsewhere are manufactured, marketed and continually enhanced. Henry Ford did not invent the automobile. He 'merely' invented a far superior way to manufacture it – namely, the mass-production assembly line. And on that was built an industrial empire that has thrived for almost a century. Likewise, in the past few decades most of the companies that have created truly extraordinary amounts of wealth have done so by inventing great processes, not great products. Dell, Toyota and Wal-Mart, for example, have risen to the top of their respective industries by coming up with amazingly efficient ways of getting quite ordinary products into the hands of consumers more cheaply than their rivals.

Does this mean that big firms should sack all their scientists and leave inventing to others? In practice, more and more are doing just that. For some time, the computer industry has, in effect, relied for much of its research and development on small firms backed by venture capital, and the telecoms industry is outsourcing more and more research to smaller firms in India and elsewhere. Without their own in-house labs, however, big firms fear that they will be taken by surprise by what a Harvard professor, Clayton Christensen, famously described as a 'disruptive technology', an innovation so revolutionary that it will enable an upstart outsider to crush them, much as the PC did to the mainframe-computer business.

But, as history has shown time and time again, a bevy of in-house scientists gives no guarantee that their output will protect their employer from technological change. Xerox, AT&T and IBM spent billions on research but all failed to exploit much of what came out of their labs, and all ended up being caught out by new technologies. It is far better if big firms' managers keep their binoculars well trained on the outside world and their minds open to any new ideas they spot there. They can then buy them and do what they do best: find innovative ways to bring them to market.

Source: 'Less glamour, more profit', *The Economist*, 22 April 2004.
© The Economist Newspaper Limited, London (22 April 2004).

Questions for discussion

1   If in-house R&D is so risky, what are the arguments for doing it?

2   What are the arguments for outsourcing R&D?

19.3.2   Technology races

This analysis of innovation competition focuses on the pay-offs to innovation. There is also a literature on choosing the right levels of R&D under market uncertainty and under uncertainty about the response of rivals. The analysis of first mover advantage is well known. It asserts that the first mover gains advantage by establishing explicit knowledge protected by patents and trademarks and goes on to build advantages of scale, experience and scope so that later movers can never erode the early advantage (*see* the discussion in Chapter 6 of Ghemawat's 1997 analysis of Du Pont in titanium dioxide). There is also an interesting empirical literature on technology races and patent races (Gottinger 2003). These races describe the battles between firms to complete a successful R&D programme and to be the first to market with an innovation with all the benefits of first mover advantage. A race is an interactive pattern of competition characterized by firms constantly trying to get ahead of their rivals, or trying not to fall too far behind. Like the dominant design literature,[3] racing behaviour is also a dynamic story of how technology unfolds in an industry recognizing the fundamental importance of strategic interactions between competing firms. A simple race between two firms might involve the following. The leader may consider further investment to outdistance its rival and get to the winning post first. But it is aware of the diminishing marginal productivity of research for itself and the uncertainty of innovation for its rival. It therefore has to balance the risks and expenditures associated with pressing on with the benefits of delay in terms of consolidating its own knowledge and the difficulty for its rival of catching up. By contrast the follower is faced with the need to catch up, but has the same concerns about the productivity of research offset to some degree by at least some knowledge about the successful path followed by its rival. The leader has considerable incentives

---

[3]   Dominant design can be defined as 'after a technological innovation and a subsequent era of ferment in an industry, a basic architecture of product or process that becomes the accepted market standard', from Abernathy and Utterback 1978, cited by Anderson and Tushman 1990. Dominant designs may not be better than alternatives, nor innovative. They have the benchmark features to which subsequent designs are compared. Examples include the IBM 360 computer series and Ford's Model T automobile, and the IBM PC.

to be cautious, whereas the follower might be more inclined to plunge ahead. Clearly the variables are many and imponderable given the uncertainty of success in R&D and the difficulty of predicting the responses of rivals. Gottinger summarizes the implications:

> At one level, racing behaviour has implications for understanding technology strategy at the level of the individual firm and for understanding the impact of policies that aim to spur technological innovation. At another level, racing behaviour embodies both traditions that previous writings have attempted to synthesize: the 'demand-pull' side emphasized by economic theorists and the 'technology-push' emphasized by the autonomous technological innovation school. (Gottinger 2003, pp. 37–8)

Gottinger observes from his research on telecommunications and computer industries the apparent inability of technology-oriented companies to maintain leadership in fields that they pioneered (op. cit. p. 51). These failures might be due to agency problems or other suboptimal managerial behaviour. But of more interest to our thesis here is the existence of market asymmetries that affect racing behaviour: (i) risk-driven and (ii) resource-driven asymmetries. The latter are clearly linked to the replacement effect (above). All this literature (Abramowitz 1986; Gottinger 1998 and 2001; Lerner 1997; and Scherer 1991) carries implications for knowledge in terms of its creation, how it is accessed, transferred and integrated, and who has the incentives for these activities.

Case box: Does IT matter?

Nicholas Carr has foisted an existentialist debate on the mighty information-technology industry

His argument is simple, powerful and yet also subtle. He is not, in fact, denying that IT has the potential to transform entire societies and economies. On the contrary, his argument is based on the assumption that IT resembles the steam engine, the railway, the electricity grid, the telegraph, the telephone, the highway system and other technologies that proved revolutionary in the past. For commerce as a whole, Mr Carr is insistent, IT matters very much indeed.

But this often has highly ironic implications for individual companies, thinks Mr Carr. Electricity, for instance, became revolutionary for society only when it ceased to be a proprietary technology, owned or used by one or two factories here and there, and instead became an infrastructure – ubiquitous, and shared by all. Only in the early days, and only for the few firms that found proprietary uses for it, was electricity a source of strategic – i.e., more or less lasting – advantage. Once it became available to all firms, however, it became a commodity, a factor of production just like office supplies or raw materials, a cost to be managed rather than an edge over rivals, a risk (during black-outs) rather than an opportunity.

McGee–Thomas–Wilson:
Strategy: Analysis and
Practice, Text and Cases

19. Knowledge, information
and innovation strategy

Text

© The McGraw–Hill
Companies, 2006

399

Computer hardware and software, Mr Carr argues, have been following the same progression from proprietary technology to infrastructure. In the past, American Airlines, for example, gained a strategic advantage for a decade or two after it rolled out a proprietary computerised reservation system in 1962, called Sabre. In time, however, its rivals replicated the system, or even leap-frogged to better ones. Today, the edge that a computer system can give a firm is fleeting at best. IT, in other words, has now joined history's other revolutionary technologies by becoming an infrastructure, not a differentiator. In that sense, and from the point of view of individual firms, 'IT no longer matters.'

And what's IT all about?

Surely though, Mr Carr's critics counter, IT is different from electricity or steam engines. Even if hardware tends to become a commodity over time, software seems, like music or poetry, to have infinite potential for innovation and malleability. True, it may have, answers Mr Carr, but what matters is not whether a nifty programmer can still come up with new and cool code, but how quickly any such program can be replicated by rival companies. Besides, today's reality in the software industry has nothing to do with poetry or music. Many companies are furious about the bug-ridden, pricey and over-engineered systems that they bought during the bubble era and are doing their best to switch to simple, off-the-shelf software, offered in 'enterprise-resource planning' packages and the like. If there is any customisation at all, it tends to be done by outside consultants, who are likely to share their favours with other clients.

But surely Mr Carr does not appreciate the impressive pipeline of new technologies that is about to hit the market – the wireless gadgets, the billions of tiny radio-frequency identity tags that will turn Aspirin bottles, shirt collars, refrigerator doors and almost everything else into smart machines, and so on? Those are impressive indeed, says Mr Carr. But again, the issue is whether they will be proprietary technologies or open infrastructures. And everything points to the latter.

This is not a debate for the ivory tower. Since IT can no longer be a source of strategic advantage, Mr Carr urges CIOs to spend less on their data-centres, to opt for cheaper commodity equipment wherever possible, to follow their rivals rather than trying to outdo them with fancy new systems, and to focus more on IT's vulnerabilities, from viruses to data theft, than on its opportunities. As it happens, CIOs have been taking exactly this approach for the past three years, and their bosses like it that way.

Source: 'Does IT matter?', *The Economist*, 1 April 2004.
© The Economist Newspaper limited, London (1 April 2004).

Questions for discussion

1 If all innovations are destined to become commodities, what is the incentive to innovate?

2 What is it about knowledge that makes it 'strategic' for the economy and for society but a mere commodity for firms?

3 How might a firm resist the move towards commoditization of its intellectual property?

19.4 Knowledge embedded in routines[4]

Recently the strategy literature has paid attention to the organizational processes that form the basis for the development of the firm's strategy (Teece *et al.* 1997; Eisenhardt and Martin 2000). These scholars, along with others, focus on the routines, competences and capabilities of the firm that shape its development in the long run. This approach shifts the focus of attention from the market-positioning view (described earlier) to a more micro-analytic approach that aims to go even deeper than the resource-based view, aiming to understand the way in which competitive advantage is actually developed (Johnson and Bowman 1999). Our interest here is in the routinized elements of strategy making. This is well grounded in the literature (March and Simon 1958; Nelson and Winter 1982; Cyert and March 1963; and Teece *et al.* 1997).

Less well known and certainly less commonly cited alongside the above scholars is the long-standing preoccupation of economists with evolution.[5] Veblen (1898, p. 397) talks about *the process of cumulative change*. Marshall used the term *economic biology* and argued that the 'the key-note is that of dynamics rather than statics' (Marshall 1920, p. xiv). These represent early arguments about economic evolution. Although economists have spent considerable time developing the neoclassical theory of the firm (a misnomer for a theory of markets), the notion of *evolutionary economics* has gained considerable momentum. Some of the impetus for this derived from the long controversies about *marginalism*.[6] This led to the breaking open of the black box that was the firm in traditional microeconomics and the onset of the new theory of the firm. The essence of this is to throw light on the internal organization of the firm. Whereas the traditional theory is concerned with prices and output, the new theory is interested in how transactions are organized. The intellectual progress of this strand of economics is marked by Coase's (1937, 1988) path-breaking paper on the nature of the firm, new approaches to understanding the nature of ownership bringing in property rights (Alchian and Demsetz 1972) and agency costs (Jensen and Meckling 1976), and Williamson's transaction cost economics (1985, 1987). Coase anticipated all of this in pointing out that the essential differentiating feature of intrafirm transactions, as opposed to interfirm transactions, is authority and hierarchy. This stream of thinking does reinforce the idea of 'efficiency management' – Williamson expressed it as the strategy of *economizing* (1981), and this has strong resonance with the idea of cost minimization from neoclassical theory. But, more important than this, it opens the door to ideas about the evolution of efficient organizational forms. Vronen (1995, p. 2) maintains that evolutionary economics is inspired by the new institutional economics. This examines

[4] The approach adopted in this section owes much to Menuhin (2001) and Menuhin and McGee (2003).

[5] This is described and analysed in great detail by Vronen (1995).

[6] See, for example, the anti-marginalist critique exemplified by the Oxford Research Group in the 1930s, especially Hall and Hitch (1939) and the American economist Lester (1946).

processes through which institutions evolve (Langlois 1986). Similarly, the sociologist Granovetter (1985, p. 488) argues that:

> *social institutions and arrangements previously thought to be the adventitious result of legal, historical, social or political forces are better viewed as the efficient solution to certain economic problems.*

The central part of evolutionary theory is the selection proposition that argues that competitive markets select for the most efficient organizational forms. Although there are considerable debates about the precise forms and implications of this process, the selection argument is the hard core of evolutionary theory. Evolution is a form of organizational ecology where firms engage in behaviour that is routine rather than purposive. Adaptation takes place by mimicking the survivors which are accidentally well adapted. Managers get little credit in this view. Scholars such as James Brian Quinn have argued for processes that are typically fragmented, evolutionary and intuitive. He describes this as *logical incrementalism* (Quinn, 1978) in which minor changes in strategy take place as a response to changes in the external environment in an evolutionary and adaptive manner.

Nelson and Winter's (1982) approach (drawing heavily on Winter, 1964) is a sustained argument that selection is not an ad hoc or involuntary response, but is systematic and purposeful firm behaviour. They – famously – argued for collections of routines based on tacit knowledge supplemented by organized search behaviour for modifications or substitutes. This allowed, in our view, for the evolution of economic thinking (over many decades) to map on to the newer thinking from management theorists attempting to understand and map organizational processes. The essential link is the purposive behaviour of managers and we shall argue that this is characterized by asset and knowledge accumulation and by learning processes that allow knowledge to be transformed from a tacit to an explicit form (a distinction also offered by Nonaka and Takeuchi 1995). Thus we see Burgelman (1983) arguing that the intellectual basis for activist and explicit roles for top managers is based on complex organizations that are subject to both evolutionary and planned processes.

Nelson and Winter introduced us to evolutionary economics but much is owed to Simon (1955, 1959) with his seminal concepts of *satisficing* and *bounded rationality* and Penrose's (1959) theory of the growth of the firm. Although Nelson and Winter's tone is somewhat hostile to traditional economics, their approach can be seen as a rehabilitation of the theory of the firm by providing (far more) realistic assumptions. They shift attention away from an overarching organizational decision calculus (how can one continually make these complex trade-offs about everything?) to internal organization where organizational routines regularly and automatically make 'decisions' based on the knowledge and best practice embedded in those routines. The argument for routines that make 'good decisions' is based on two points: one, a Darwinian natural selection process at an organizational level that ensures that only the 'best' routines are kept in operation and, two, on an adaptive feedback mechanism at the individual level that permits new knowledge to be accessed and then diffused through the organization to be eventually embedded in routines. Routines are thus embodiments of organizational memory – better called organizational genetics.

The evolutionary approach is saved from ecological sterility by the learning process (based on Simon). Through this we can see the essential elements and characteristics of a knowledge-based view (KBV) starting to take shape: tacit versus explicit knowledge; relative roles of individuals, groups and organizations; sourcing and accessing of knowledge, transfer and integration of knowledge (note the classic formulation by Nonaka and Takeuchi 1995).

19.5 Knowledge as learning

Nelson and Winter's second set of routines are those that determine the long-run changes in the firm's stock of capital – hence they are called *strategizing routines*. Attention has been paid to the contribution of planning and budgeting processes to the accumulation of fixed assets over time. But more central to our argument are the product and technology development processes. For example, Henderson and Clark (1990) developed the concept of *architectural knowledge* explaining how the dominant organizational design '*incorporates a range of choices about the design that are not revisited in every subsequent design*' (1990, p. 15). They go on to link this architectural knowledge to the development of innovation processes.

Strategizing routines contribute to strategy and strategy making as they store the firm's experience in such a way that it can be used in a new context (for example, consultants such as McKinsey and Bain discuss how they develop experience libraries of problems and problem solutions through their ongoing consulting activities). They channel the structure of decision-making processes into the type of behaviour that has brought success in the past. But such routines have a negative side. Over time, as the environment changes, new forms of organization become appropriate and gaps emerge between environmental requirements and existing capabilities. These gaps cause routines to become dysfunctional (Teece *et al.* 1997; Leonard-Barton 1992) and inhibit future development of the firm (Levitt and March 1988; Henderson and Clark 1990; Leonard-Barton 1992; Teece *et al.* 1997). This leads to the processes of organizational learning by which routines are modified over time.

The literature makes many references to types of organizational learning. Cyert and March's (1963) view of organizations as complex adaptive systems suggest *modes of learning*. Levitt and March (1988) refer to change processes at several *nested levels*. Cohen and Baclayan (1994) illustrate the role of *experimental learning*. Bettis and Prahalad (1995) suggest that firms *unlearn* ineffective routines. Hedberg (1981, p. 18) suggests that unlearning is 'a process through which *learners discard knowledge*'. All of these notions build on the idea that routines flow from history and serve as the organizational memory in which knowledge about best practice is stored. The propositions about learning fall into two camps. The cognitivists (e.g. Porac, Thomas, and Baden Fuller 1989; Porac and

720 CHAPTER 19 KNOWLEDGE, INFORMATION AND INNOVATION STRATEGY

Thomas 2002) focus on learning at the individual level and on individual mental maps. Structuralists suggest that learning is an organizational phenomenon based on the firm's routines and that these routines are subject to formal change processes. Nonaka and Takeuchi (1995) combine these two views into their knowledge-creation spiral. This begins with a distinction between tacit and explicit knowledge and maps how tacit knowledge starts with the individual and proceeds through socialization and integration processes so that knowledge becomes a key ingredient in the organization's capital stock (see Figure 19.5 which is shown later in this chapter). More generally, such learning can be described as a *sense-making process* (Weick 1979, 1995) through which the members of an organization construct a *common reality* that influences the way they seek to achieve an *objective economic reality*.

Teece, Pisano and Shuen (1997) in their well-known paper on dynamic capabilities may have intended to add primarily to the RBV but they also provide a sense of the internal mechanisms by which learning and adaptation may actually take place. Their definition of dynamic capabilities is '*the sub-set of the competences and capabilities which allow the firm to create new products and processes and respond to changing market circumstances*' (1997, p. 270). In some ways this is a restatement of Nelson and Winter's strategizing routines but inherent in their discussion is recognition of learning. They identify three characteristics that permit learning. The first is the nature of the internal processes: co-ordination/integration (a static notion), learning (dynamic), and reconfiguration (a renewal or transformational concept). Second, they are specific about the variety of resource positions that might need to be addressed. Finally, they pay attention to the paths by which developments can take place. It has to be said that these concepts can be very slippery. Path dependency, for example, is celebrated only as an idea. However, they are on more firm

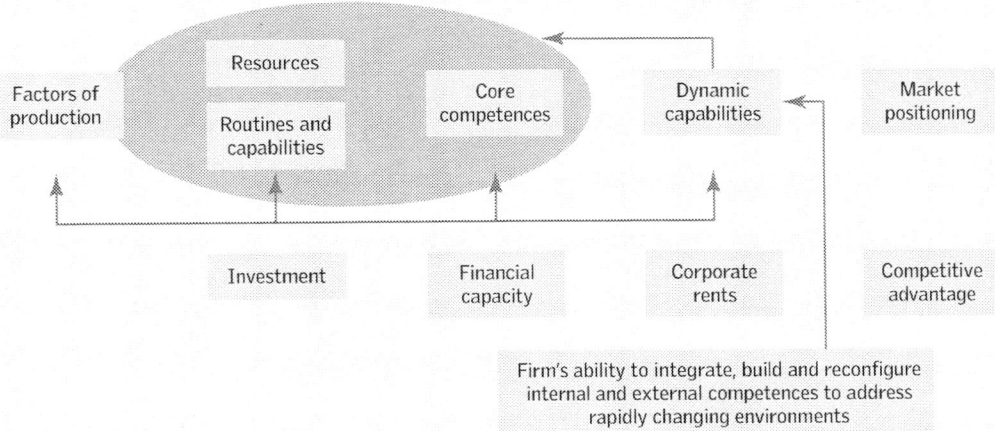

Figure 19.3 Dynamic capabilities view

ground in outlining the ways in which technological opportunity can shape the future. The hints they provide on the nature of increasing returns are suggested here.

We revisit our schematic again in the form of Figure 19.3. This time the resource side is further elaborated by the inclusion of learning and dynamics (feedback loops). Note, however, that the resource (knowledge) element defies construction in linear form – we begin here to see it as an interconnected whole (via the multiple arrows). Learning, moreover, creates multiple feedback effects.

19.6 Towards a knowledge-based view

We have reviewed four different perspectives on knowledge in strategy and in strategy making: knowledge as assets for protection, knowledge through innovation, knowledge embedded in routines, and knowledge through learning. In doing this we have touched on a wide variety of themes in strategic management, competitive advantage, the resource-based view, strategy making, and strategizing routines. We have also commented on developments in economic thinking ranging from neoclassical theory, through Schumpeter to evolutionary economics, with a hint also of institutional economics. Thus we have progressed from market positioning and the firm as a black box to serious consideration of internal organization and those processes that underpin competitive advantage. Knowledge makes its entry as an asset, albeit largely invisible, that protects competitive position. But we have moved to a more subtle position where knowledge is embedded in individuals and by complex processes is socialized and reintegrated into the organization at large. Do these various perspectives on knowledge enable us to articulate a *knowledge-based view of strategy* whose implications allow us to draw inferences about strategy and strategy making that are either absent from other theories or in contradiction to them? What are the essential ingredients of the knowledge-based view?

19.6.1 Organizational knowledge

Grant and Spender in a Special issue of the *Strategic Management Journal* in 1996 have two much quoted papers that step outside conventional economic approaches. Grant sees the firm as an institution for integrating knowledge, where knowledge is individually held and is typically tacit. The organization's role is to access, transfer and integrate that tacit knowledge within and throughout the organization. His approach is very similar to that of Nonaka and Takeuchi (see below). In Grant's view, the firm is a co-ordinating mechanism with implications for organizational design and for the nature of organizational process. Spender sees knowledge as too contentious a concept to easily bear the weight of a theory. The biggest problem, he sees, is the multitude of types and definitions. He therefore argues (as Grant does implicitly) for a pluralistic viewpoint and advances the idea of interplay between explicit and tacit knowledge, and between different units within the organization (from individuals through to collectives). This leads to a set of ideal types (see Figure 19.4). He moves from this to knowledge as activity and argues eventually for a Penrosian view – a historical, path-dependent process in which the individual rather than organizational machine bureaucracies are the important strategists. It is useful to start with Spender's view that our concepts of knowledge are highly varied and in many ways inconsistent or incapable of being interrelated:

> Knowledge is a highly contentious concept, far too problematic to bear the weight of a useful theory of the firm without a clear statement of the epistemology which gives it meaning (Spender 1996, p. 48).

He then proceeds by making three points.

1   Knowledge is interplay between the *tacit/implicit* and the *explicit*, the vertical dimension in Figure 19.4.

2   This distinction allows for several different *adaptation mechanisms* – for example, Nelson and Winter's own use of adaptive feedback mechanisms where the interplay between tacit and explicit takes place through individual choices that are eventually embedded in organizational routines ('organizational genetics').

3   Many theorists, starting with Polanyi (1966) and famously in Nonaka and Takeuchi (1995), see the origin of all knowledge in individual intuition. So the third element is the transformation and communication of what is known tacitly by individuals into collective or social knowledge. Hence the second, horizontal dimension in Figure 19.4.

Therefore, Spender advances four ideal types connected by an adaptation mechanism. He observes that the organizational intent is to transform tacit, individual knowledge into collectively owned, objectifiable knowledge – this is the world of standards, procedures, practices, patents, science, training, but still recognizably a world that remains dependent on the knowledge held by individuals although, in this diagram, the adaptation mechanisms of transformation and conversion process operate in silence. Given different types of knowledge, are there different types of knowledge-based theory, Spender asks. A theory of *conscious* knowledge would have to solve agency problems – how can inventors be persuaded to pass on their codified knowledge to an organization? A theory based on *automatic* knowledge also has agency problems where the brilliant man must be persuaded to stay with the firm (cf work-out clauses for entrepreneurs when they sell their businesses).

	Individual	Social
Explicit	Conscious	Objectified
Implicit	Automatic	Collective

Figure 19.4 Different types of organizational knowledge
Source: Spender, 1996.

A theory of *objectified* knowledge raises problems of imitability in a world where knowledge is explicit. A theory based on inherently immobile *collective* knowledge (this is where Nonaka and Takeuchi would wish to take us and where Nelson and Winter go with their extra-rational learning processes) leads to a conclusion that this is the most secure and strategically significant kind of organizational knowledge.

Nonaka and Takeuchi's knowledge spiral (Figure 19.5) predates Spender by some three years. Their arena (matrix) has become a standard framework of its kind. Their focus is on a *knowledge spiral*, an adaptation mechanism through which knowledge is converted and then transferred between the tacit and the explicit (it can go either way) and among individuals, groups and the whole organization. *Socialization* is the sharing of experiences so that tacit knowledge is shared between individuals, from individuals to the organization through the development of culture and shared mental models, and from the organization to individuals. *Externalization* is the conversion of tacit into explicit knowledge through its articulation and systematization within the organization. *Combination* involves the conversion of explicit knowledge held by individuals and groups into explicit knowledge at the organizational level, and subsequent conversion of organizational knowledge back to the individual in different form. This is the key role of information systems within the firm. *Internalization* is conversion of explicit knowledge back into tacit knowledge in the form of individual know-how and organizational routines. The *knowledge spiral* is the dynamic process by which knowledge is translated through separate but related stages, through socialization to combination and externalization, and back to internalization.

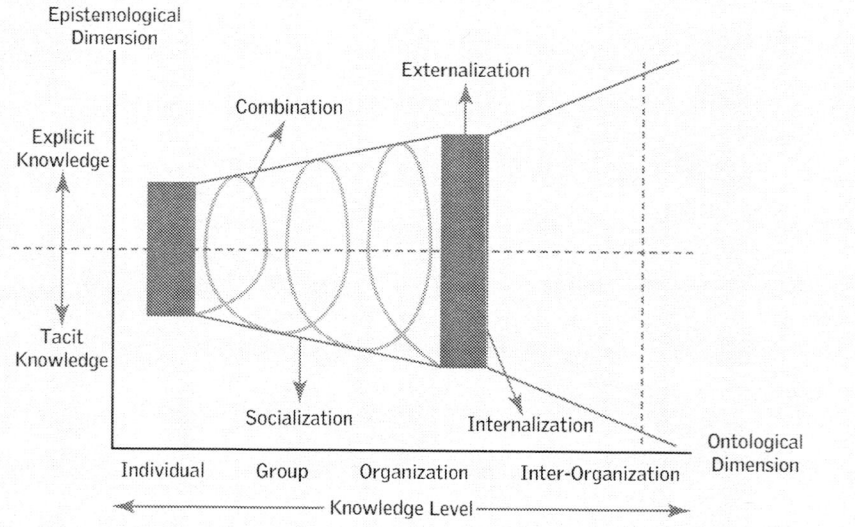

Figure 19.5 Spiral of organizational knowledge creation
Source: I Nonaka 'On a knowledge creating organization', Paper presented at AIF National Congress, Posma, October 1993.

Thus, individual creativity can be linked to the growth of collective knowledge.[7] Spender's contribution relates to the different types of organizational knowledge whereas Takeuchi and Nonaka use the same intellectual space to portray the adaptation mechanisms that organizations can use to convert and transfer various kinds of knowledge to inimitable and therefore rent-earning organizational knowledge.

19.6.2 From value chain to value web

The value chain, popular for its simple and robust character, can be restated firstly in the language of core competences and the RBV but more fundamentally in this language of knowledge. This characterization restates the linear chain of activities as a similar chain of core competences. The activities of the value chain might be dispersed across different owners but in any event they are controlled in economic terms through the operation of core competences. Thus economic power is operated through the conjunction and interaction of core competences. However, the linearity of the chain metaphor is uncomfortable where the empirical record suggests knowledge is multifaceted and capable of being attached to other pieces of knowledge in a variety of expected and unexpected ways, particularly as interface standards are developed and 'knowledge as Lego' becomes more and more possible.

The notion of a web is intuitively appealing (Figure 19.6). At the centre is the *corporate glue* (McGee 2003), that is, the organizationally held tacit knowledge that cannot readily be imitated – the *collective knowledge* according to Spender, and the *knowledge architecture* according to Henderson and Clark. This is characteristically a collective concept but also a tacit and sticky concept, meaning that the organization can be readily and sustainably differentiated by it. This corporate glue supports and is supported by a set of core competences within which elements of objectifiable knowledge may be evident.[8] These are buttressed by closely held partnerships with other organizations where the ability to control the agency costs becomes really important. More remotely managed are the subcontract relationships where market contracting suffices. The value of the web is a framework within which the *activity sets* formerly given pride of place in the value chain are now replaced by *knowledge concepts*.

Inherent in a knowledge-based view of strategy (and also in an economist's concept of a knowledge production function) are three key linkages between:

1   knowledge as assets;

2   knowledge embedded in processes; and

3   the pathways to competitive advantage.

---

[7] We are indebted to Rob Grant for this articulation of Nonaka and Takeuchi's model.

[8] An alternative description would be to describe the corporate glue as supported by elements of objectifiable knowledge and the conjunction of the two being core competence. This has the merit of defining core competence explicitly in terms of knowledge concepts.

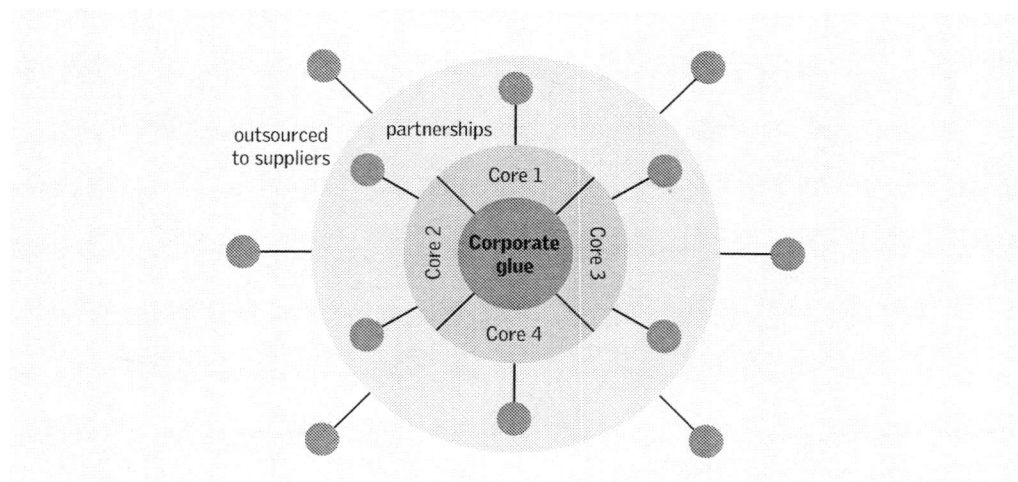

Figure 19.6 The knowledge web
Source: McGee, 2003.

According to the Teece *et al.* (1997) discussion of dynamic capabilities, there are four knowledge processes:

1 entrepreneurial (creative);

2 coordinative and integrative (static);

3 learning (dynamic); and

4 reconfigurational (transformational).

In asset or resource terms we see knowledge as embedded in many different classes of assets such as technology, complementary, financial, reputational, structural, institutional, and market structure. For example, Amit and Schoemaker (1993) provide an excellent description (see Chapter 7) of strategic assets and their linkage to organizational rent (competitive advantage). Following but not replicating Teece *et al.* (1997), we express the linkages to competitive advantage in terms of *dynamic pathways*. Whereas Amit and Schoemaker (1993) and Peteraf (1993) only assert that assets create profit possibilities, in this approach the dynamic pathways are defined in terms of path dependency (which allows us to call on an evolutionary perspective) and technological opportunities (which allows for returns to scale,[9] first/early mover advantage, and oligopolistic gaming). The strength of this approach lies in its organizational inclusivity, ranging from internal process to asset positions, linked over time through management of the pathways. Empirical evidence here is patchy but attracting research interest as we speak. In summary, this approach includes entrepreneurial (creative)

---

[9] Especially network externalities where 'winner takes all' strategies are possible; McGee and Sammut-Bonnici (2002, 2003), summarized in Chapter 12.

processes and a more explicit characterization of linkages of knowledge to
competitive advantage as dynamic pathways.

19.6.3 A knowledge-based view of strategy?

This approach enables us to see that there
are elements of knowledge that can be
related to sustainable competitive advantage. These knowledge concepts lie deeply
embedded behind the well-known notions
of strategic positioning and the resource-
based view and are powerful in that they, in a
fundamental sense, are the drivers behind core
competences and competitive advantage. So, is it
possible to draw this thinking together into a perspective that we might call the knowledge-based
view of strategy? Our approach is to suggest three
categories (Figure 19.7) called specific knowledge,
organizational knowledge, and the knowledge
web.[10]

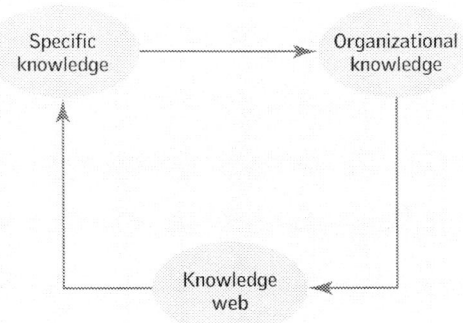

Figure 19.7 Elements of the knowledge-based view

Specific knowledge (Figure 19.8) relates to the
knowledge production function and draws links
between knowledge, production, access to knowledge, knowledge diffusion, connections between
elements of knowledge, and knowledge renewal
(including the discarding of knowledge). The

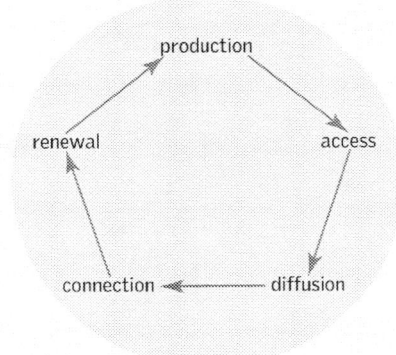

Figure 19.8 Elements of specific knowledge

foundations of this are highly dispersed throughout the academic literature. There is a considerable economic literature on innovation competition and on R&D. There is a
considerable scientific and social science literature on innovation processes. There is also
some considerable mystery about creativity, usually captured under the heading of
serendipity.

Organizational knowledge (Figure 19.9) is the process by which various elements of specific
knowledge are taken into the organization, transformed into social/collective knowledge
and, through dynamic pathways, linked into other organizational activities. The key
elements are characterized as types of organization knowledge, the knowledge creation

---

[10] Alternatively knowledge in action.

process, and dynamic pathways. The inheritance from such writers as Spender, Takeuchi and Nonaka, and Teece *et al.* is self-evident.

The knowledge web (*see* Figure 19.6) represents the way in which specific knowledge and organizational knowledge is captured into value-creating activities within the firm (discussed above) (*see* also Winter 1987 for an earlier exposition of this point). Both specific and organizational knowledge feed into the knowledge web. The notion of corporate glue or knowledge architecture stems directly from the conjunction of tacit and social knowledge. But specific knowledge is also evident from its role within core competences and within the core competences of strategic partners. The knowledge web is also dynamic in that incentives to innovate and to create new linkages between knowledge components are created here and therefore provide the link back to the knowledge production function that is captured within the category of specific knowledge.

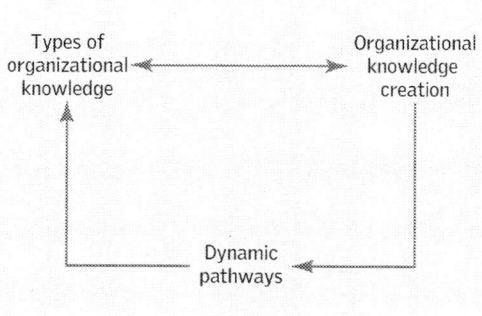

Figure 19.9 Organizational knowledge

This approach allows us to connect three strands. The first concerns the ways in which knowledge is produced, accessed, diffused, renewed and discarded. The second concerns the notion of organizational knowledge as an essentially invisible asset fostered and conditioned by visible and defined organizational routines and ad hoc processes. The third is a strategic theory of the firm in which positioning and resource-based approaches are recast in the form of knowledge.[11] Again, knowledge is the invisible asset but captured here in the form of specific activities on which management focuses attention. This does not answer all the questions but perhaps does allow us to define the arena of interesting questions and permit the formation of some conjectures. We suggest the following list.

1   *How is knowledge produced and accessed?* This includes the imponderable of 'knowledge creation' as well as 'knowledge conversion' (a word used by Grant (1996) and by Nonaka (1994) and has a parallel to the economists' idea of a production function). We know more about the processes of innovation and we also know quite a lot about the economic analysis of new technology decisions.

2   *How does knowledge fit into supply chain and value chain thinking* – in other words, how does it link and co-ordinate with the other activities of the firm to produce competitive advantage? The knowledge web is a useful framework but much needs to be done to identify the specifics in actual cases and applications.

[11] A link here could be made with Rumelt (1984) by developing the argument that our use of knowledge as corporate glue is directly analogous to his use of isolating mechanisms.

3 *How do pieces of knowledge connect up?* How do they change the nature of the corporate 'glue' – the integrative strategic architecture? The burgeoning function of knowledge management within knowledge-intensive organizations reflects these considerations.

4 *What difference does any of this make for the analysis of strategic decisions such as diversification and acquisition?* Does this have anything to contribute to economists' thinking about increasing returns industries – another arena where the 'new economy' appears to be challenging basic assumptions behind traditional thinking (*see* McGee and Sammut-Bonnici 2002, 2003, and the discussion in Chapter 12)? These are not simply criteria for shaping and assessing a theory but they are also conjectures. They are conjectures about the nature of knowledge itself, whether such a multi-faceted concept can be marshalled into the constraints inherent in a normative, organizationally focused theory.

Case box: Patient money at Corning Glass

Some companies prosper by making continuous improvements to their business practices. Others grow by using their market clout to acquire rivals for the skills and markets they covet. A few thrive by making patient investments in far-sighted ideas of their own that can take decades to pay off. Rarely does any company attempt to do all three things at once.

Corning, a glass maker that was founded 150 years ago, is one of those rare manufacturing enterprises that has managed to cling to its innovative roots. Apart from the upheaval of the 1970s and 1980s, which affected many American companies that had grown fat in the decades after the second world war, Corning has been remarkably consistent in giving full rein to the ingenuity of its researchers while pursuing total mastery over its process technologies.

Its reputation for continuous innovation over a century and a half is unrivalled anywhere. Without Corning's ribbon machine, electric light bulbs, vacuum flasks and cathode ray tubes would have been far costlier and more fragile affairs. Without its patented borosilicate glasses, there would have been no Pyrex ovenware. The glass ceramics called Pyroceram, which the company developed originally for missile nose cones, has not quite made Corning a household name. By contrast, its Corelle line became one of the world's most popular brands of tableware.

The firm's successful casting of the 200-inch (five-metre) mirror for the Hale telescope on Mount Palomar in 1934, a feat that even the mighty General Electric had attempted but failed to achieve, reinforced the company's reputation in the scientific world. Its patented vacuum-deposition processes, secretly used for years in the optics aboard American spy satellites, have made Corning the mirror maker of choice for optical astronomers everywhere since the end of the cold war. Corning's invention of ceramic substrates for catalytic converters made the firm the darling of Detroit. And then there was the optical waveguide – the invention, better known as optical fibre, that has transformed telecommunications the world over.

'Patient money' was the principle that guided the Houghton family when it first invested in a small glass company in Somerville, Massachusetts, in 1851. (The firm moved to the city of Corning, New York in 1868.) And the Houghton dynasty has influenced the company according to that principle ever since. Lacking access to the cheap immigrant labour, raw materials and exploding markets that rival glass makers enjoyed across the Alleghenies in the Ohio valley, to the west, the Houghtons also insisted that their fledgling corporation should focus exclusively on the specialist end of the business and use inventiveness as its principal competitive weapon. Producing me-too products was out of the question, so Corning's only choice was to be endlessly unorthodox – and so, for the most part, it has remained.

Central to Corning's success in turning unorthodoxy into a winning way has been the management's profound understanding of the value of the company's intellectual property, and its willingness to protect that at any cost. This has meant investing in research and development at a rate almost double that of the rest of the industry. It has also meant refusing to blink when bigger companies with deeper pockets infringed Corning's patents and sought to outspend it in the law courts, as when, one by one, wealthy corporations tried to muscle their way into Corning's optical fibre business. Even giants such as ITT in America and Sumitomo in Japan found to their cost that the feisty little glass maker from upstate New York refused to roll over and play dead. Today, Corning has 40% of the market for optical fibre – nearly three times more than its nearest rival. But it took Corning 15 years of patient investment in optical-fibre technology to make a profit.

Only once has Corning stumbled badly. The 20-odd acquisitions the company made building its MetPath business into the largest medical-testing organization in the world smacked of impatient money. Yet in the end, this helped the company rediscover its innovative roots. Once again, the Houghtons, still around and still influential, were there to help nudge Corning back to its 150-year-old formula for patient innovation.

Source: 'Patient money', *The Economist*, 5 July 2001.
© The Economist Newspaper Limited, London (5 July 2001).

Questions for discussion

1 Why should Corning Glass have succeeded in its close control of intellectual property when so many others (see the case box on the knowledge economy) have outsourced their R&D?

2 What risks did Corning take and how did it manage them?

3 Use the 'knowledge spiral' (Nonaka and Takeuchi) to describe and classify Corning's approach to intellectual property.

McGee–Thomas–Wilson:
Strategy: Analysis and
Practice, Text and Cases

19. Knowledge, information
and innovation strategy

Text

© The McGraw–Hill
Companies, 2006

413

19.7 Summary

Having taken a reasonably broad view of the writings in and around knowledge and strategy we have made a number of observations about current thinking:

1 Whereas knowledge is only implicit in the market-based view it is a central element of the resource-based view.

2 Dynamic theories of the firm cannot operate without some clear and operational concepts of knowledge. For example: (i) tacit and explicit and (ii) a knowledge production function incorporating innovating, accessing, transferring, integrating, and codifying.

3 However, we sympathize with assertions that knowledge is a highly contentious concept. For example: know-how vs know-what; explicit vs. implicit; individual vs collective; knowledge as knowing, as learning, as activity etc.

4 Nevertheless, our conjectures about the applicability of knowledge as a significant explanatory variable may be supported empirically; for example, see the wide range of citations in Eisenhardt and Santos (2001).

5 The writing on organizational knowledge has shown it as the lynchpin between internal organizational structures and processes and the capture of economic rents.

6 More controversially, there is a case for an evolutionary theory incorporating dynamic pathways as the external manifestation of organizational knowledge.

Our own approach to this has not been to attempt to provide 'a unified theory of absolutely everything'.[12] Rather, we have attempted to find a way of incorporating knowledge variables into the explanation of the long-run performance of firms, their long-run sustainable competitive advantages. To do this we offer a simple categorization that links three types of literature: on specific knowledge (a very dispersed literature), on organizational knowledge (which made considerable progress in the 1990s), and on the strategic theory of the firm. These strands we suggest are mutually reinforcing and interconnected. In particular, from a managerial perspective we can see how knowledge issues have a very direct economic content via the knowledge production/diffusion function, and a very organizational and individual element through analysis of organizational knowledge. These do not stand, however, as separable issues although elements of the problem can be treated in isolation. Rather, the system-wide characteristics of knowledge are evident particularly in the knowledge web through which value creation activities are composed.

We would also offer the final organizational observation that the knowledge web is a framework that allows firms to monitor threats. It should allow managers to question

---

[12] See the debates that have taken place in theoretical physics on just this issue.

the adequacy of existing business models and to analyse the unconventional responses that new entrants and innovators may be 'cooking up' to attack the entrenched positions of leading firms. In fact we believe that many leading firms fail to innovate because they act like hierarchies, not markets. They allocate resources for bureaucratic, political but not economic reasons. Too few of them make their organizational processes and routines receptive to idea and value innovation. Unfortunately they do not see innovation, learning and knowledge acquisition as key elements of the corporate DNA.

Key terms

Disruptive technologies *703*	Objectified knowledge *709*
Dominant design *714*	Replacement effect *712*
Efficiency effect *712*	Sunk cost effect *712*
Innovation *702*	Sustaining technologies *703*
Knowledge-based view *719*	Tacit knowledge *718*
Knowledge web *726*	Value innovation *704*

Recap questions and assignments

1   Compare the discussion of the knowledge economy in this chapter with the discussion of the new economy in Chapter 12. Identify the common elements and their effect on strategic discussions.

2   Consider also the discussion of risk in Chapter 14. What does a knowledge-based view of strategy imply for strategic risk and strategic decision-making?

3   Compare the action of disruptive technologies in this chapter with Schumpeter's 'Creative destruction' explained in Chapter 8. What role does tacit knowledge play in these ideas?

When you have read this chapter, log on to the Online Learning Centre website at www.mcgraw-hill.co.uk/textbooks/mcgee to explore chapter-by-chapter test questions, further reading and more online study tools for strategy.

Case 1 Procter & Gamble: Jager's gamble

Durk Jager, Procter & Gamble's new chief executive, wants to turn it into an innovative company. Easier said than done

A few years back, scientists at Procter & Gamble hit upon a big idea. Combining know-how in absorbent paper with a new 'dry-weave' polyethylene mesh, they came up with a thin, highly absorbent sanitary towel, the first breakthrough in feminine hygiene in 50 years. Today, P&G's 'Always' pads, now jazzed up with wings and even thinner, are sold in 80 countries, and are the mainstay of a product family that generates around $1.6 billion in annual sales.

This is just the kind of innovation that Durk Jager, who took over at P&G in January, sees as essential to rekindling growth at the world's largest consumer-products group. As its latest move, P&G announced on October 26th that it is prepared to give away or license any of its 25,000 patents, including those used in established brands. Chuck Hong, the firm's director of R&D for corporate innovations, thinks this will 'force us to continually invent'.

But why must P&G be forced to invent? Surely a firm with $38 billion in sales, more than 300 brands and 110,000 employees in 70 countries, with patents spanning fats and oils, plant fibres, surfactants and calcium, with vast marketing and financial resources, ought to be churning out exciting new products all the time? The trouble is, the new sanitary towel, which Mr Jager himself admits was the company's last big innovation, was launched away back in 1983. The story at P&G is not so much 'Always' as 'almost never'.

Mr Jager blames the consumer-product industry's problems on its failure to innovate. It has, he told this month's annual meeting in Cincinnati, 'led to commodity products and pricing pressure'. P&G has done worse than most. It has lost some 10% of its global market share in the past five years. Volumes this year will grow by 2% at best.

Turning a marketer into an innovator requires money, ideas and a nimble culture. P&G's problem has never been a lack of money or even ideas. Last year it was America's 21st-largest investor in research and development, spending $1.7 billion. Its R&D budget has grown from 2.9% to 4.5% of net sales over the past decade – still well below the 15% typical in the pharmaceuticals industry, but double that of Gillette. That spending has, however, yielded little. Less than 10% of P&G's thousands of patents are used in its hundreds of brands.

The fault lies with the culture. The firm has stifled innovation and prevented new ideas from getting to market quickly. Years after P&G developed its tissue-towel products, they have only just started to be rolled out globally. 'We're slower than my great-grandma,' says one executive.

Mr Jager is trying to change all that. In June he announced a big internal shake-up, sacking 13% of the workforce to streamline management and speed up decision-making. He is tying strategy and global profit targets to the performance of brands, rather than countries, and handing responsibility for new ideas to new business managers, not ones steeped in existing businesses. He has set up innovation teams to shoot promising ideas rapidly around the company and rush the best to market. And P&G plans to take more risks, cutting pre-market laboratory testing and putting products on sale earlier.

Spiffy Swiffer

P&G has had some success with the recent launch of products, including Swiffer, a dry mop that traps dust, Febreze spray to eliminate smells in fabric and Dryel, a home dry-cleaning kit, all of which he says are 'new-to-the-world' products, not just variants of old ones. Febreze, which was introduced in June last year, is already America's fifth-most successful new packaged product, with sales of $230m in its first year. And whereas Febreze took forever to be launched, Mr Jager boasts that Swiffer went from test marketing to global roll-out in a record 18 months.

P&G has even started looking outside for new ideas. To develop 'NutriDelight', a fortified orange powdered drink unveiled at the annual meeting, P&G worked with Unicef and licensed in the technology that lets iron exist with iodine and vitamin A in a stable form, helping undernourished children put on weight. And the group recently bought Iams Petfoods, admired for a scientific approach to pet health that includes low-calcium nosh for big dogs prone to overgrown bones, and oil and mineral formulas for 'senior' pets with bad joints.

Mr Jager is getting on the Internet, too. In November P&G will launch its majority-owned venture, reflect.com, an Internet-only range of 50,000 beauty products sold direct to consumers. Nathan Estruth, who helps run reflect.com, calls the venture 'heresy' for a mass-market company that has always sold through retailers.

Yet turning a marketing giant into a nippy innovator will be hard. P&G's line managers and country chiefs are trained to squeeze the last drop of sales out of existing products, not back risky new ones. Sam Stern, a professor at Oregon State University who has written a book on creativity in consumer-goods companies, points out that new ideas threaten the status quo.

However esoteric they sound, most consumer-goods technologies are unlikely to fend off imitators for long. A drug's effect is tied closely to its complex technology. Having gone through rigorous approval and lengthy clinical trials, patent challenges on drugs are rare. By contrast, Gillette's patent on a new toothbrush may specify with utmost precision how bristles are laid out; but there are lots of different 'technologies' that can clean teeth just as well. Lynn Dornblaser, director of the Global New Products Database, estimates that only 10% of the 55,000 brand new products that were launched globally last year are really innovative.

Even when consumer-products companies do come up with something novel, competitors catch up fast. 'Always' went unchallenged for ten years. Now, only one year after the launch of Febreze, Johnson & Johnson, Clorox and others have launched their own improved versions – mainly because Febreze was in pre-market testing for two years.

Similarly, Gillette took ten years and spent $1 billion developing its Mach3 triple-blade razor, launched last year. Within a few months, Asda, a British supermarket, rushed in with its own product, Tri-Flex, claiming that it was just as good and 40% cheaper.

What is more, packaged-goods companies not only have to develop the product, but also try to get jaded consumers to think they need it. That sometimes works. Upbeat marketing turned a very ordinary orange drink, Sunny Delight, into one of P&G's best brands.

But few new products are so successful. Information Resources, which researches packaged goods in America, finds that less than 1% of products launched in 1998 achieved $100m of sales in their first year. More than two-thirds flop in their first year. Hence, many managers in consumer-goods firms associate innovation with failure. Mr Jager has to persuade them that it is a condition for success.

Source: 'Jager's gamble', *The Economist*, 28 October 1999.
© The Economist Newspaper Limited, London (28 October 1999).

Case Questions

1 Why must P&G 'be forced to invent'? (p. 733)

2 Describe the incentives to innovate and the rewards and risks of innovation in terms of this P&G experience.

Further reading and references

Abramowitz, M (1986) 'Catching up, forging ahead, and falling behind', *Journal of Economic History,* **66**, pp. 385–406.

Alchian, AA (1950) 'Uncertainty, Evolution and Economic Theory', *Journal of Political Economy,* **58**, pp. 211–21.

Alchian, AA (1953) 'Biological Analogues in the Theory of the Firm: Comment', *American Economic Review,* **43**, pp. 600–3.

Alchian, AA and Demsetz, H (1972) 'Production, information costs, and economic organisation', *American Economic Review,* **62**, pp. 777–95.

Amit, R and Schoemaker, PJ (1993) 'Strategic assets and organisational rent', *Strategic Management Journal,* **14**, pp. 33–46.

Anderson, P and Tushman, ML (1990) 'Technological Discontinuities and Dominant Designs', *Administrative Science Quarterly,* **35**, pp. 604–33.

Argyris, C and Schon, D (1978) *Organisational Learning: A Theory in Action Perspective,* Addison-Wesley, Reading, MA.

Arrow, K (1962) 'Economic Welfare and the Allocation of Resources for Inventions,' in RR Nelson (ed.) *The Rate and Direction of Economic Activity,* Princeton University Press, Princeton, NJ.

Barney, J (1991) 'Firm resources and sustained competitive advantage', *Journal of Management,* **17**, pp. 99–120.

Besanko, D, Dranove, D and Shanley, M (2000) *Economics of Strategy,* 2nd edition, John Wiley & Sons, New York.

Bettis, RA and Prahalad, CK (1995) 'The dominant logic: retrospective and extension', *Strategic Management Journal,* **16**, **1**, pp. 5–15.

Brandenburger, AM and Nalebuff, BJ (1995) *Co-opetition,* Doubleday, New York.

Brown, JS and Duguid, P (1991) 'Organisational learning and communities of practice: Toward a unified view of working, learning and innovation', *Organization Science,* **2**, pp. 40–57.

Burgelman, RA (1983) 'A model of the interaction of strategic behaviour, corporate context, and the concept of strategy', *The Academy of Management Review,* **8**, **1**, pp. 61–70.

Chandler, AD Jr (1990) *Scale and Scope: The Economics of Industrial Competition,* Harvard University Press, Cambridge, MA.

Christensen, CM (1997) *The Innovator's Dilemma,* HBS Press, Boston, MA.

Coase, R (1937) 'The nature of the firm', *Economica,* **4**, pp. 386–405.

Coase, R (1988) 'Lecture on the nature of the firm, III', *Journal of Law, Economics and Organisation,* **4**, pp. 33–47.

Cohen, MD and Baclayan, P (1994) 'Organisational routines are stored as procedural memory: evidence from a laboratory study', *Organisation Science*, **5**, **4**, pp. 554–68.

Cooper, AC and Schendel, DE (1976) 'Strategic Response to Technological Threats', *Business Horizons*, **19**.

Cyert, RM and March, JG (1963) *A Behavioral Theory of the Firm*, Prentice-Hall, Englewood Cliffs, NJ.

D'Aveni, RA (1994) *Hypercompetition: Managing the Dynamics of Strategic Manoeuvring*, Free Press, New York.

De Geus, A (1976) *The Living Company*, HBS Press, Boston, MA.

De Wit, R and Meyer, R (1994) *Strategy: Process, Context, and Content*, West, St Paul, MN.

Dussage, P, Hart, S and Ramanantsoa (1996) *Strategic Technology Management*, Wiley, New York.

Eisenhardt, KM and Martin, JA (2000) 'Dynamic capabilities: what are they?' *Strategic Management Journal*, Special issue, pp. 1105–21.

Eisenhardt, KM and Santos, FM (2002) 'Knowledge-based view: a new theory of strategy?' in AM Pettigrew, H Thomas, and R Whittington (eds) *The Handbook of Strategy and Management*, Sage Publications, London.

Evans, P and Wurster, T (1997) 'Strategy and the New Economics of Information', *Harvard Business Review*, Sept/Oct, **75**, **5**, pp. 70–82.

Evans, P and Wurster, T (1999) *Blown to Bits: How the New Economics of Information Transforms Strategy*, Harvard Business School Press.

Ghemawat, P (1984) 'Capacity expansion in the titanium dioxide industry', *Journal of Industrial Economics*, **32**, pp. 145–63.

Ghemawat, P (1991) *Commitment: The Dynamics of Strategy*, Free Press, New York.

Ghemawat, P (1997) *Strategy and the Business Landscape*, Addison-Wesley, Reading MA.

Gottinger, H-W (1998) 'Technological races', *Annual Review of Economics* (Japan), **38**, 1–9.

Gottinger, H-W (2001) 'Stochastic innovation races', *Technological Forecasting and Social Change*, **68**, pp. 1–18.

Gottinger, H-W (2003) *Economics of Network Industries*, Routledge, London.

Granovetter, M (1985) 'Economic action and social structures', *American Journal of Sociology*, **91**, pp. 481–510.

Grant, RM (1991) 'The resource based theory of competitive advantage: implications for strategy formulation', *California Management Review*, Spring, pp. 119–45.

Grant, RM (1996) 'Toward a knowledge-based theory of the firm', *Strategic Management Journal*, 17 (Winter Special Issue), pp. 109–22.

Hall, RL and Hitch, CJ (1939) 'Price theory and business behaviour', *Oxford Economic*

Papers, 2, reprinted in T Wilson and PWS Andrews (eds) (1951) *Oxford Studies in the Price Mechanism*, Clarendon Press, Oxford.

Hamel, G (2000) *Leading the Revolution*, HBS Press, Boston, MA.

Hamel, G and Prahalad, CK (1993) 'Strategy as stretch and leverage', *Harvard Business Review*, March/April.

Hedberg, BLT (1981) 'How organisations learn and unlearn', in PC Nystrom and WH Starbuck (eds) *Handbook of Organisational Design*, Volume 1, pp. 2–27, Oxford University Press, New York.

Henderson, RM and Clark, KB (1990) 'Architectural innovation: the reconfiguration of existing technologies and the failure of established firms', *Administrative Science Quarterly*, **35, 1**, pp. 9–30.

Huff, AS (1994) 'Mapping strategic thought', in AS Huff (ed.) *Mapping Strategic Thought*, 2nd edition, pp. 11–52, John Wiley & Sons, Chichester.

Jensen, MC and Meckling, W (1976) 'Theory of the firm: managerial behaviour, agency costs, and ownership structure', *Journal of Financial Economics*, **3**, pp. 305–60.

Johnson, G and Huff, AS (1998) 'Everyday innovation/everyday strategy', in G Hamel, CK Prahalad and H Thomas (eds) *Strategic Flexibility: Managing in a Turbulent Economy*, John Wiley & Sons, Chichester.

Johnson, G and Bowman, C (1999) 'Strategy and everyday reality: the case for study of micro-strategy', working paper, 15th EGOS Colloquium.

Kim, W Chan and Mauborgne, R (1999) 'Strategy, Value Innovation and the Knowledge Economy', *Sloan Management Review*, **40, 3**, Spring, pp. 41–54.

Kogut, B and Zander, U (1992) 'Knowledge of the firm, combinative capabilities, and the replication of technology', *Organisation Science*, **3**, pp. 383–97.

Langlois, RN (1986) 'Rationality, institutions, and explanation', in RN Langlois (ed.) *Economics as a Process: Essays in the New Institutional Economics*: Cambridge University Press Cambridge, pp. 225–55.

Leonard-Barton, D (1992) 'Core capabilities and core rigidities: a paradox in managing new product development', *Strategic Management Journal*, **13** (Special Issue), pp. 111–26.

Lerner, J (1997) 'An empirical exploration of a technology race', *The Rand Journal of Economics*, **28, 2**, pp. 228–34.

Lester, RA (1946) 'Shortcomings of marginal analysis for wage-employment problems', *American Economic Review*, **36**, pp. 63–82.

Levitt, B and March, JG (1988) 'Organisational learning', *Annual Review of Sociology*, **14**, pp. 319–40

March, JG and Simon, HA (1958) *Organisations*, John Wiley, New York.

Marshall, A (1920) *Principles of Economics*, 8th edition, Macmillan Press, London.

McGee, J (2003) 'Strategy as Orchestrating Knowledge', in D Wilson and S Cummings (eds) *Images of Strategy*, Basil Blackwell, Oxford.

McGee, J and Sammut-Bonnici, T (2002) 'Network Industries in the New Economy', *European Business Journal*, **14**, **3**, September, pp. 116–32.

McGee, J and Sammut-Bonnici, T (2002) 'Network Strategies for the New Economy: Emerging Strategies for New Industry Structures', *European Business Journal*, **14**, **4**, December, pp. 174–85.

Menuhin, J (2001) *Strategising Routines: The Emergence of Strategic Initiatives*, unpublished PhD thesis, University of Warwick.

Menuhin, J and McGee, J (2003) 'Strategising routines in HSBC (UK)', unpublished working paper, University of Warwick, Warwick Business School.

Nelson, RR and Winter, SG (1982) *An Evolutionary Theory of Economic Change*, Belknap Press, Cambridge, MA.

Nonaka, I and Takeuchi, H (1995) *The Knowledge-creating Company: How Japanese Companies Create the Dynamics of Innovation*, Oxford University Press, New York.

Nonaka, I (1994) 'A dynamic theory of knowledge creation', *Organization Science*, **5**, pp. 14–37.

Penrose, KT (1959) *The Theory of the Growth of the Firm*, Basil Blackwell, Oxford.

Peteraf, MA (1993) 'The cornerstones of competitive advantage: a resource-based view', *Strategic Management Journal*, **14**, **3**, pp. 179–91.

Porac, JF, Thomas, H and Baden Fuller, C (1989) 'Competitive groups as cognitive communities: the case of the Scottish knitwear manufacturers', *Journal of Management Studies*, **26**, pp. 397–416.

Porac, JF and Thomas, H (2002) 'Managing Cognition and Strategy: Issues, Trends and Future Directions', in AM Pettigrew, H Thomas and R Whittington (eds) *Handbook of Strategy and Management*, Sage Publications, London.

Polanyi, M (1966) *The Tacit Dimension*, Anchor Day Books, New York.

Porter, ME (1980) *Competitive Strategy*, Free Press, New York.

Porter, ME (1982) *Competitive Advantage*, Free Press, New York.

Prahalad, CK and Hamel, G (1990) 'The core competence of the corporation', *Harvard Business Review*, May/June, pp. 79–81.

Quinn, JB (1978) 'Strategic Change: Logical Incrementalism', *Sloan Management Review*, (Fall).

Rumelt, RP (1984) 'Towards a Strategic Theory of the Firm', in Robert Boyden Lamb (ed.) *Competitive Strategic Management*, Prentice-Hall, Englewood Cliffs, NJ.

Scherer, F (1991) 'International R&D races: theory and evidence', in L-G Mattsson and B Stymme (eds) *Corporate and Industry Strategies for Europe*, Elsevier Science Publishers, New York.

Schumpeter, J (1934) *The Theory of Economic Development*, Harvard University Press, Cambridge, MA (first published in 1911, republished 1968).

Simon, HA (1955) 'A behavioural model of rational choice', *Quarterly Journal of Economics*, **69**, pp. 99–118.

Simon, HA (1959) 'Theories of decision-making in economics and behavioural science', *American Economic Review*, **49**, pp. 253–83.

Spender, J-C (1996) 'Making knowledge the basis of a dynamic theory of the firm', *Strategic Management Journal*, 17 (Winter Special Issue), pp. 45–62.

Teece, DJ (1980) 'Economics of scope and the scope of the enterprise', *Journal of Economic Behaviour and Organisation*, **1**, pp. 223–47.

Teece, DJ (ed.) (1987) *The Competitive Challenge: Strategies for Industrial Innovation and Renewal*, Ballinger, Cambridge, MA.

Teece, DJ, Pisano, G and Shuen, A (1997) 'Dynamic capabilities and strategic management', *Strategic Management Journal*, **18**, **7**, pp. 509–33.

Tsoukas, H (1996) 'The firm as a distributed knowledge system: a constructionist approach', *Strategic Management Journal*, **17**, Winter Special Issue, pp. 11–25.

Veblen, T (1898) 'Why economics is evolutionary science', *Quarterly Journal of Economics*, **12**, pp. 373–97.

Vronen, J (1995) *Economic Evolution*, Routledge, London.

Weick, KE (1979) *The Social Psychology of Organising*, McGraw-Hill, New York.

Weick, KE (1995) *Sense making in Organisations*, Sage, Thousand Oaks, CA.

Wernerfelt, B (1984) 'A resource-based view of the firm', *Strategic Management Journal*, **5**, **2**, pp. 171–80.

Williamson, OE (1981) 'Strategizing, economizing, and economic organization', *Strategic Management Journal*, **12**, Winter Special Issue, pp. 75–94.

Williamson, OE (1985) *The Economic Institutions of Capitalism*, Free Press, New York.

Williamson, OE (1987) 'Transactions costs economics', *Journal of Economic Behaviour and Organisation* **8**, pp. 617–25.

Winter, SG (1964) 'Economic "natural selection" and the theory of the firm', *Yale Economic Essays*, **4**, pp. 225–72.

Winter, SG (1987) 'Knowledge and competence as strategic assets', in DJ Teece (ed.) *Competitive Challenge – Strategies for Industrial Innovation and Renewal*, Ballinger, Cambridge, MA.

Chapter 21

Managing business value as a system: value creation from a systems perspective

Introduction

The term 'value' has been contested terrain for a number of years. For example, it has been used to describe business value (Parker and Harcourt 1969), social value (Carroll 1979) and as a term to replace the much maligned word 'profit' (Glautier and Underdown 2001). As we have seen in previous chapters of this book, over the past two decades, as a result of the globalization of trade and capital markets and the information technology revolution, the strategic attention of many leading companies has focused on the principle of generating and maximizing shareholder value for strategy evaluation and performance measurement. From this perspective, the primary task of senior managers is to act as agents for the shareholders and to maximize shareholder value (SVA) in

Chapter contents

financial terms, typically using an SVA discounted cash flow criterion. This allows shareholders to assess the value of their investment over time, using the rate of interest as the method of assessing the *time value* of money. For example, if the rate of interest is 10 per cent per annum, €1 invested now at 10 per cent will amount to €1.10 in a year. Or, conversely, the *value* of €1.10 a year hence is €1 now. Following Day and Fahey (1990), the SVA model can be depicted as:

- Purpose of strategy   ——➤   Maximize returns to shareholders
- Reference group   ——➤   Shareholders and proxies
- Decision variables   ——➤   Revenues, costs, investments and capital structure
- Level of analysis   ——➤   Company and strategic business unit
- Basis of measurement   ——➤   Share prices, market/book ratios and net present value of cash flows

Doyle (2000) argues that the adoption of SVA has eliminated much of the excess and inefficiency of capitalism in the decades of the 1960s and 1970s. We shall explore this claim later in this chapter.

While economists such as Friedman (1970) and Friedman and Friedman (1980) have stressed that business is in business to make profits and should not be expected and, indeed, is not best suited to do anything other than this, nevertheless, there is increasing recognition in today's environment that businesses cannot exist solely to make a profit. Henry Ford's much earlier statement is important here:

> *Business must be run at a profit, else it will die. But when anyone tries to run a business solely for profit . . . then also the business must die, for it no longer has a reason for existence.*

Many writers (e.g. Freeman 1984) have noted that the actions of business affect not only themselves but also other stakeholders, with sometimes contradictory expectations, such as employees, managers, customers, suppliers, investors, governments and communities. They argue, therefore, that business must recognize its responsibility to those stakeholders and society as a whole. In essence, they suggest that there is a strong mutual interdependence between business and society. The responsibility of a business to society is to build and improve conditions for wealth creation through such things as commercializing new innovations, investing in new plants and facilities, creating new job opportunities, paying corporate taxes and minimizing negative social or environmental externalities. In turn, business depends on society to create and foster an environment in which business can fulfil its goals of wealth creation (AACSB 2003).

It is clear that the challenges for business, and its corporate strategists, go far beyond simple bottom-line profitability goals. Writers from MIT's Innovation Project (such as Malone *et al.* 1996) also point out some of the critical issues in managing and inventing organizations in the future. They include the need to understand how to tap into the complex sources of competitive advantage in the new economy, in environments where new skills, new sources of continuous innovation and increasing impacts of information technology create new ways of working and constant strategic change.

In consequence, arguably richer conceptions and theories of the firm are now emerging that encompass both the social and economic context of the firm and that seek to balance the 'doing well' and 'doing good' aspects of a firm's performance (Elkington 1997). In the end (*see*, for example, Kay 1995), the success of a company depends on how it meets and balances the often incommensurable and incompatible objectives demanded by its various stakeholders. Kay argues that the purpose of companies is to produce, in their own distinctive fields of capability, goods and services we want as individuals and as a society. The distinctive capabilities (*see* earlier chapters on the resource-based view of the firm) of companies are, in turn, embedded in their relationships with the social and commercial environments in which they operate. The argument is that organizations can succeed only by managing the totality of these relationships.

Kay's views prompt many of the arguments in this chapter. We seek to explore new theories and concepts of the firm from the perspective of the systems viewpoint – the 'web' of relationships, internal and external to the organization, which must be managed in order to create sustainable advantage and long-term wealth creation. Note that the strategy framework used in this book is a systems model and this discussion provides the overarching strategic systems model which links the various elements of the strategic plan together (*see* Figure 1.6). This chapter explores the following:

- The strategic systems framework as a lens for managing value as a system.
- Stakeholder theories of the firm.
- Learning theories of the firm.
- Adaptive theories of the 'living company'.
- Common issues such as trust, accountability and reputation that drive the firm's purpose.
- The role of intangible assets in creating value.
- The concept of managing value from a systems viewpoint.

21.1 The strategic systems perspective

> *How do we use the information gleaned about the parts to build up a theory of the whole? The deep difficulty here lies in the fact that the complex whole may exhibit properties that are not readily explained by understanding the parts.*[1] *The complex whole, in a completely non-mystical sense, can often exhibit collective properties, 'emergent' features that are lawful in their own right.* (Kauffman 1995)

---

[1] See, for example, the case study 'Microworld' at the end of Chapter 16.

As we outlined in Chapters 1 and 2, a *system* is a collection of parts that interact to function as a whole. The behaviour of a system depends on its entire structure, the relative strengths of the many connections among its parts at any point in time, and the manner and degree to which these connections change over time. Systems theory involves the study of living systems as integrated wholes whose visible properties cannot be reduced to those of smaller sub-units. Viewed from a systems perspective, the world consists of relationships and integration. Instead of concentrating on basic building blocks to learn about the properties of the larger system, the systems approach emphasizes basic principles of organization – how the parts are interrelated and co-ordinated into a unified whole. From that viewpoint, value-creating strategies emerge through learning about the system and can only be understood by analysing the system conditions that give rise to success and strategy innovation. We firmly believe that today's strategist should frame strategic thinking from a 'strategic systems' perspective (Bell *et al.* 1997).

From the systems theorist's perspective, a living system interacts with its environment through structural coupling – recurring interactions, each of which triggers structural changes in the system, such as when a cell membrane infuses substances from its environment into its metabolic processes, or when an organism's central nervous system changes its connectivity after receiving information. A structurally coupled system is a learning system. The structure of such a system continually changes in response to its environment. Consequently, adaptation, learning and development are key characteristics of the behaviour of living systems.

At the company level, organizations exhibit emergent behaviour – that is, they behave quite differently from how they would behave if their sub-units were independent of each other. According to Kees van der Heijden, retired executive from Royal Dutch Shell, who headed its Business Environment Division and was in charge of scenario planning:

> *Emergent behaviour is the outside behavioural manifestation of the internal mediating processes. In systems terms, it implies a hierarchical organisation, with the upper level guiding and constraining the actions at the lower. It is the constraints on the lower level members that creates the emergent behaviour at the higher level ... If such constraints did not exist, lower level members would carry on as if they were independent and there would be no emergent behaviour and, therefore, no identity for the larger system.* (Van der Heijden 1996, p. 39)

The level of complexity inherent in an organization is a characteristic of the system's structure and is affected by the total number of its individual sub-units, the number of different layers in the structural hierarchy, the number of different business processes that perform business activities and the number and strengths of connections among all of these sub-units and between these sub-units and outside economic agents.

Beer (1981) has studied and written extensively about how to model the dynamics of complex systems such as today's business organizations calling such systems' perspectives 'exceedingly complex' (see Chapter 2 for a summary of Beer's five-level structure).

According to Richardson (1991, p. 187):

> *In Beer's view, every viable system is organised in such a hierarchy of five systems. Furthermore, complex viable systems are composed of viable sub-systems that again have this five-level structure. To be viable, a division of a firm should be organised this way. The entire firm as a set of inter-related divisions should also have the same sort of structure. A viable sector of an economy should have the same structure. Naturally, an entire national economy, to be viable, should be similarly organised. Viewed from the elevated level of the national economy, in the hierarchy an individual firm or sector operates at the level of systems one, two and three. The functions of its own high-level systems four and five are seen as part of the autonomic processes of the more aggregate system.*

To gain the appropriate level of understanding of a firm's business, industry and wider environment for the purpose of conducting a strategic analysis, we argue that strategists should direct their attention to the firm's systems dynamics – its strategic positioning within its environment; its emergent behaviours that impact its attained level of performance; the strength of its connections, or structural couplings, to outside economic agents; the nature and impact of any symbiotic alliances; the specific interrelationships and internal process interactions that dominate its performance; and potential changes in other reaches of the vast economic and social web that might threaten the viability of the client's strategies and niches. These systemic properties determine the strategic competencies and capabilities that enhance the value of the organization and that promote *changes in that value* over time.

Figure 21.1 depicts a firm as a complex web of interrelationships embedded within a broader complex economic web.[2] This complex web is what the strategist sees when looking through the strategic-systems lens. The strengths of the many interrelationships comprising this broader economic web reflect the extent of the organization's ability to manage its environment and therefore to create value and generate the cash flow needed to sustain growth. A fundamental understanding of the strengths of these connections provides a basis for development of expectations about the quality and creativity of the entity's strategies and its attained level of performance.

An example illustrates how, in an adaptive system, the relevance and strength of the interconnections changes over time (and how, in turn, value can be created or lost). Assume that the organization depicted in Figure 21.1 is a retail bookseller (such as Barnes & Noble or Borders in the USA or WH Smith or Waterstones in the UK) with a heavy capital investment in retail facilities located around the country. Now, assume that a new market niche emerges, involving the use of the World Wide Web in lieu of retail outlets to market and sell books.

---

[2] Figure 1.4 in Chapter 1 provides a simple picture and Chapters 3 and 4 provide a detailed description, of this complex economic web.

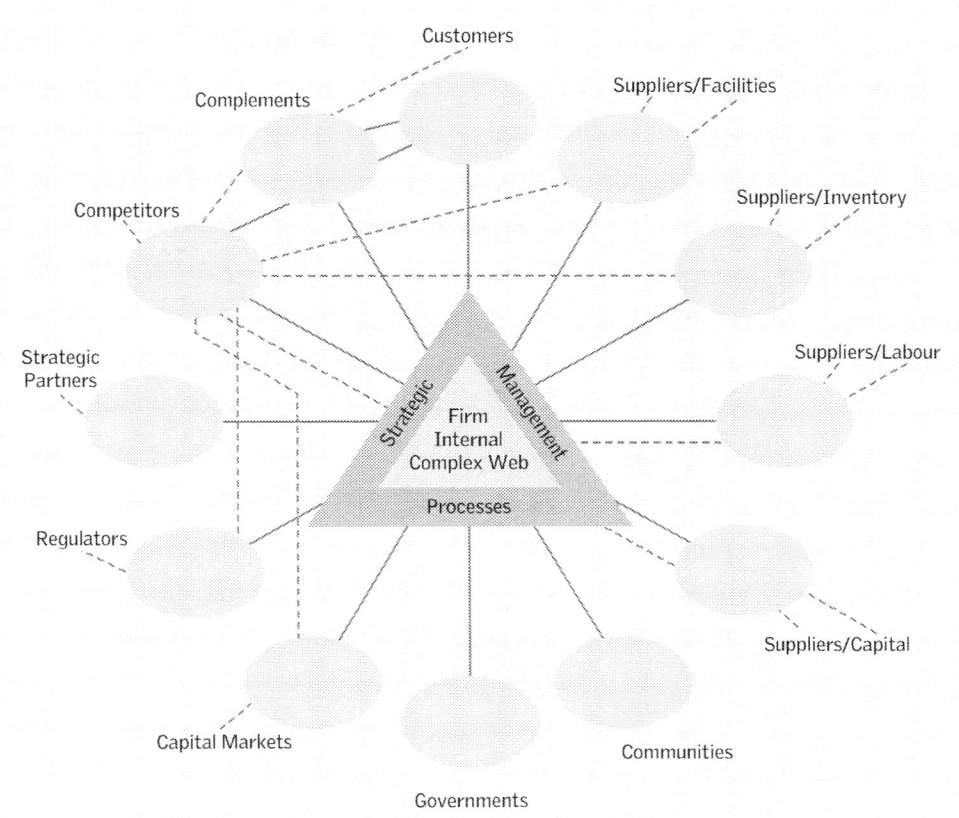

Figure 21.1 Viewing the organization as a complex web of interrelationships

New competitors such as Amazon.com occupying this niche offer access to much larger inventories than any retail outlet can stock, and can price their books at a substantial discount because of lower overhead costs. In addition, consumers can search these massive inventories using search engines provided by the new competitors and can access book reviews by other consumers available through these competitors' websites.

As the number of consumers connected to the World Wide Web grows over time, the connections between customers and competitors occupying this new niche are likely to increase in number. And, in turn, unless it adapts its own operation by moving into this new niche, the strength of connections between the original retailer and most of the other economic agents depicted in Figure 21.1 will diminish. For example, as the original retailer experiences a drop in demand, it will respond by reducing its own demand for facilities, inventory, labour and capital from suppliers.

21.2 The stakeholder management perspective

A particular example of a systems-type model is Freeman's stakeholder theory. Many of the stakeholders that have the potential to be most important to organizations are shown in Figure 21.2.

By definition, these stakeholders are individuals or organizations that have an interest in, or some kind of stake in, the firm's ongoing activities. Stakeholder analysis (Freeman 1984) is the process of identifying, understanding and prioritizing the needs of key stakeholders so that the question of which groups of stakeholders deserve management attention is addressed. The knowledge from this analysis is absorbed into the strategic framework, direction and management of the organization.

Clearly, the needs and goals of these stakeholders are sometimes in conflict with each other but stakeholder management is a never-ending task of balancing and integrating multiple relationships and multiple objectives (Freeman and McVea 2001). Some of the alternative stakeholder viewpoints are outlined in the following sections.

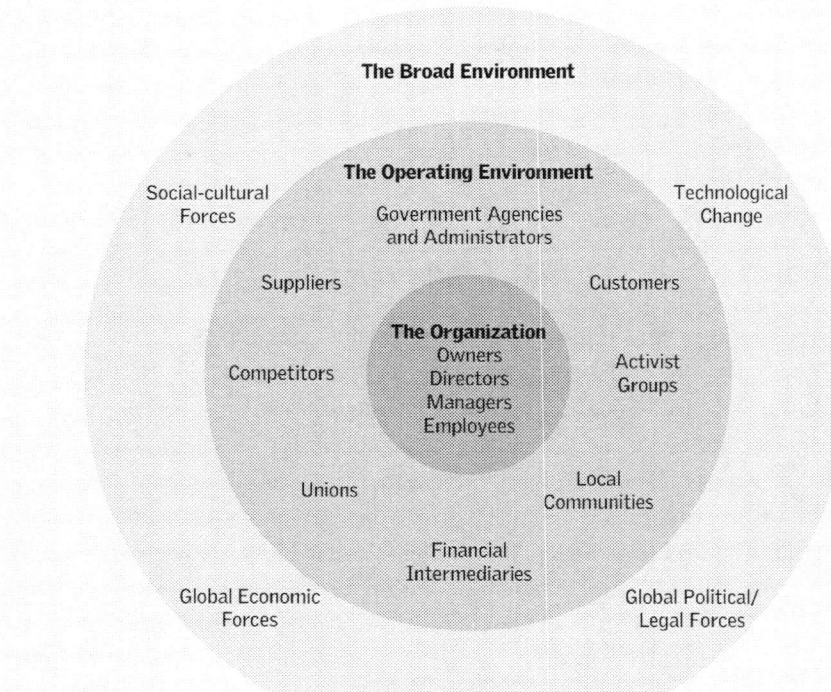

Figure 21.2 The organization and its primary stakeholders
Source: adapted from Harrison and St John, 1998.

Governments and local communities

Emerging conceptual frameworks that reflect changing societal expectations about the role of business in society can be seen in the following areas:

* Socially responsible investment.
* Corporate social responsibility (e.g. negative impacts arising from pollution and environmental damage – e.g. the *Exxon-Valdez* case and the Union Carbide Bhopal crisis).
* Corporate citizenship.
* Corporate governance.
* Sustainability and the 'triple bottom line'.

Local communities, governments and non-governmental organizations try to ensure that organizations act in a socially responsible manner to maintain such things as a 'green' environment, ethical investing and a sustainable level of national resources.

Customers

Without an appropriate level of customer value and satisfaction, there is unlikely to be shareholder value. However, attempting to achieve superior product quality, choice and lower prices may conflict with the attainment of shareholder value if the cost of providing superior quality and choice exceeds the price paid by the customer for the product. Customers can also influence product purchase considerably through questioning corporations about their global sourcing and investments. Nike, for example, suffered adverse publicity and financial consequences from consumers, arising from the sourcing of its running shoes in 'sweat shops' with poor environmental conditions in the Far East.

Employees

Sometimes there is a strategic gap between statements such as 'employees are our most valued asset' and subsequent corporate actions which threaten job security and satisfaction through downsizing employees following shortfalls in demand in rapidly changing markets. Empirical evidence suggests, however, that there is a strong correlation between a loyal, committed, happy workforce and financial performance.

Suppliers and partners

Key companies are nowadays often networked organizations, which are heavily dependent upon their network of suppliers. Trust and social capital are necessary in sourcing such relationships, and suppliers in such networks value long-term contract predictability, security and reasonable margins from companies. Changing technologies and customer needs, however, may from time to time require companies to change suppliers.

These changes will create conflicts in relationships with suppliers that value network stability and corporate commitments but are also in competition with other supplier networks.

Shareholders

Shareholders are often depicted as a somewhat isolated but wealthy group of individuals who act in their own self-interest. However, through the activities of financial institutions and pension funds, most individuals in Western countries own shares in companies and have a very clear interest in ensuring that stock prices and shareholder value continue to rise in order to protect their future pension and social security provision. The rise in shareholder activism (e.g. CALPERS, the California State Pension Fund in the US, and Anthony Bolton of Fidelity in the UK) is probably more due to reaction to financial underperformance by firms than concern about their ethical or corporate responsibility activities, despite such recent corporate failures as Enron, WorldCom and Parmalat.

Freeman (1984) provides a model, a stakeholder grid, shown in Table 21.1, which classifies stakeholders on two dimensions: first, the nature of their stakes in the organization; and, second, the behavioural influence or power they have on the organization.

Businesses (e.g. Nike in shoe manufacture and Toyota in car manufacture) are already moving to organize themselves into networked form (see Chapter 12) and, in doing so, become the hub of a web or nexus of contracts enacted with many of the entities shown in the web of Figure 21. 2 and the stakeholder grid of Table 21.1. Clearly, the effective

Table 21.2 Freeman's stakeholder grid

STAKE	Equity	Internal stakeholders Directors Minority interests	External shareholders	
	Economic	Outside directors Alliance partners Tax authorities	Customers Employees Suppliers Competitors Creditors	Local communities Local governments Unions Foreign governments
	Social	Regulatory or government agencies	Financial institutions and financial community	National government Activist, lobbying groups Trade associations
		Formal or Voting (Contractual or Regulatory)	Economic	Political

POWER OR INFLUENCE ON BEHAVIOUR

Source: adapted from Freeman, 1984, p. 63.

management of the web of stakeholders is critical to wealth and value creation. Research evidence (see, for example, Mohr and Spekman 1994) suggests that effective partnerships are associated with the following:

* Strong quality of communication
* Joint problem solving
* Commitment
* Co-ordination
* Trust

Weak partnerships tend to adversely affect the hub organization's image and reputation in the marketplace.

Writers such as Senge (1998) stress and emphasize the role of processes of learning and adaptability in organizations with regard to understanding the pace of strategic change and in providing new ways of conceptualizing the business environment. Thus, strategists can frame strategic issues in terms of the web of customers, stakeholders, etc. in order to manage the business better (create more value). In the next section we examine the processes of building learning organizations that can create value.

21.3 Learning theories of the firm and value creation

Senge emphasizes the importance of what he calls 'adaptive learning' and 'generative learning' in organizations. Adaptive learning is similar to what Argyris and Schon (1978) call 'single-loop' learning in which individuals, groups and organizations adjust their behaviour according to fixed organizational goals, norms and assumptions. Generative learning, on the other hand, is akin to 'double-loop' learning, in which organizational goals, norms and assumptions as well as behaviour are all open to change. In Senge's terms:

> Increasing adaptiveness is only the first stage in moving towards learning organisations. The impulse to learn in children goes deeper than desires to respond and adapt more effectively to environmental change. The impulse to learn, at its heart, is an impulse to be generative, to expand our capability. This is why leading corporations are focusing on generative learning, which is about creating, as well as adaptive learning, which is about coping.

Therefore, Senge is wedded to the idea of the firm both as a system and a social and knowledge web, which is conceptually very close to de Geus's framing of the firm as the 'living company' (1997). This 'living company' survives over the long term through such concrete factors as financial strength and stability, environmental sensitivity and adaptation to change, and a strong culture, identity and value system which enables it to become a systematic, living organism that continually grows and reinvents itself. Leaders of such organizations are 'systems thinkers' who see the 'big picture' and focus more on understanding the underlying reasons and forces that contribute to change. Important skills for such leaders include:

* The ability to see the interrelationships and processes in systemic change.

* The recognition that problems in change result from poorly designed systems.

* The ability to recognize and understand the dynamic complexity of system problems, i.e. when the cause and effect of strategic problems are distant in time and space, and when the consequences of interventions over time are subtle.

* The ability to focus on areas of high leverage, i.e. systems thinking shows that small, well-focused actions can produce significant enduring improvements if they are in the right place.

* The avoidance of symptomatic solutions, i.e. 'quick fixes' or so-called 'band-aid solutions'. The best solutions rely on the ability to analyse the system and, thus, find enduring solutions. Enduring solutions create value.

21.4 Trust, accountability, reputation and value

From these perspectives, it seems that strategists must make a paradigmatic (or at least ideological) choice. This choice is between whether we should adopt the multiple objective goals of stakeholder and/or learning views of the firm, or adopt the primacy of shareholder value maximization (SVA) for optimizing the value of the firm as a system. The key argument against shareholder value maximization is that it ignores an organization's social responsibilities and fails to balance the different stakeholder interests. Doyle (2000, p. 23) and Sunderam and Inkpen (2004, p. 353) offer spirited arguments for the primacy of shareholder value maximization as the preferred corporate goal or objective. Sunderam and Inkpen summarize their arguments as follows:

* The goal of maximizing shareholder value is pro-stakeholder.

* Maximizing shareholder value creates appropriate incentives for managers to assume entrepreneurial risks.

* Having more than one objective function will make governing difficult, if not impossible.

* It is easier to make shareholders out of stakeholders than vice-versa.

* In the event of contract or trust, stakeholders, compared with shareholders, have protection (or can seek remedies) through contracts and the legal system.

Doyle's fundamental argument (2000, p. 24) mirrors much of the above reasoning. He argues stridently that social responsibilities are not the job of business. He notes that, in a market-based economy, the only social responsibility of business is to create shareholder value legally and with integrity. He believes that there are strong market-based incentives for value-maximizing firms to take into account stakeholder interests. They include:

* The need to attract, retain and motivate key 'knowledge workers' and employees to ensure long-term competitiveness. This means paying competitive salaries to employees and offering safe and attractive workplace conditions.

* The need to satisfy customers through new product development, quality and customer service.

* The need to build trust, reputation and image with customers and society as a whole.

* The requirement to undertake investments to create wealth and value and avoid investments undertaken to 'balance other stakeholder interests' for reasons of prestige and public relations, but not value creation.

* The recognition that shareholders are generally pension funds, financial institutions and other societal institutions that require value-producing investments to meet their fiduciary obligations.

The alternative paradigm emphasizes the social role of organizations in society and argues that value emerges from conducting business in a socially responsible way. Such a perspective has many labels (such as corporate accountability or corporate citizenship) and in this chapter we will use the term corporate social responsibility (CSR) to cover the social and ethical roles of business organizations in society. In a basic way, laws already exist for some factors which affect the social good. Organizations are liable in law in many countries for the escape of dangerous substances, failing to provide adequate health and safety cover for employees and for rules about the manner in which accountability of business firms to investors and employees is met. CSR extends beyond this regulatory level. Originating in social and political theories, CSR argues three main points:

* Organizational decisions should be centrally concerned with socially responsible alternatives.

* The implementation of such decisions will help maximize profit (value) since customers will prefer to buy goods and services from ethical and responsible organizations.

* Trust, reputation and image will be enhanced more by ethical and socially responsible strategic decisions than by maximizing shareholder value.

Carroll (1979) argues that organizations should be socially responsive since they are created by and sustained by society. Drucker (1993) argues that organizations should be given rights and duties in society in much the same way as individual citizens are (hence the term corporate citizenship). Increased image and reputation for the organization will help create value. As Rosenfeld and Wilson (1999, p. 353) point out, such value creation from the point of view of ecological responsibility is big business. Since the establishment of an international standard for 'green-ness' (ISO 14001) organizations have quickly recognized the value of being accredited. Shell and Xerox were accredited early and many other firms have publicly announced pro-environmental strategies (e.g. Elf, Union Carbide, Interplan, The Body Shop).

There are some enduring problems with the CSR value-creating perspective. First, it is theoretically very difficult to establish exactly what CSR is and what it is not. There is no agreed (or generally accepted) definition of what CSR is – other than organizations and decision makers should weigh the impact of their actions upon others. Second, the scope of CSR is difficult to determine. Should it apply to every organizational action and operation or to a selection of activities? Third, unless strategists are able to determine a clear view of what are societies' preferences and ethical priorities, then much of what is classed as socially desirable will remain either guesswork or subjective judgement. Arrow's (1963) 'general impossibility theorem' captures this neatly. He argues that if we exclude the possibility of interpersonal comparisons of utility, then the only method of transferring from individual tastes to broad social preferences that will be satisfactory (and defined for a wide set of individual rankings) will either be imposed or dictated by definition.

Nevertheless, the impact of CSR has been substantial and the 'triple bottom line' has reinforced the value-creating aspects of socially responsible performance by organizations. Aware of possible paradigm incommensurability between the SVA and the CSR perspectives, we suggest that, at least in some key aspects (intangible assets), a systems perspective can begin to integrate some aspects of CSR and SVA to create value. We explore this argument in the next section.

21.5 Intangible assets and value creation

Given the theoretical approach we have adopted in this book, we would suggest a marriage to shareholder value maximization and the strategic systems lens offers the strategist the best opportunity for managing the business system from a value-based perspective. Such a marriage will require close attention for the 'embedded firm' to maximize value from the system resources available to it. We regard the following three issues as critical intangible assets to the implementation of a systems model for value maximization – trust, accountability and reputation/image/identity.

Trust

This involves creating a strong sense of mission and values. Collins and Porras (1996) note that core values are enduring, essential tenets for those inside the organization. The core ideology consists of core values and core purpose, where core purpose is the 'raison d'etre' – the reason for being. Core ideology has to be authentic and is the 'glue' that holds the organization together over time. It is a consistent identity that all stakeholders learn to trust over time. For example, Hewlett Packard's core ideology was a code of ethics called the 'HP way'. It includes:

* A deep respect for the individual.
* A dedication to affordable quality and reliability.
* A commitment to community responsibility.
* HP exists to make technical contributions for the advancement and welfare of humanity.

A good example of trust in practice is shown in the following case box.

Case box: Johnson & Johnson and Tylenol

In 1982, Johnson & Johnson (J&J) found itself facing a corporate nightmare when bottles of its best-selling Tylenol were tampered with, resulting in several deaths. The corporation's immediate response was to pull all Tylenol off the shelves of retail outlets. Thirty-one million capsules were destroyed, even though they were tested and found safe. Although the immediate cost was significant, no other action was possible, given the firm's Credo. Authored almost forty years earlier by president Robert Ward Johnson, Johnson & Johnson's Credo states that permanent success is possible only when modern industry realizes that:

* service to its customers comes first;
* service to its employees and management comes second;
* service to its stockholders, last.

Source: adapted from Senge, 1998.

As Senge notes, such credo statements may look like 'motherhood and apple pie' to those who have not seen how a clear core ideology can affect key business decisions. Johnson & Johnson's crisis management action in this case was based on the credo. It was simple, right and it worked.

Collins and Porras (1996, p. 67) quote Ralph Larsen, a former CEO of Johnson & Johnson, who puts it this way: 'The core values embodied in our credo might be a competitive advantage, but that is not *why* we have them. We have them because they define for us what we stand for, and we would hold them, even if they become a competitive *dis*advantage in certain situations.'

Accountability

A company must have in place 'systems' of accountability to measure performance outcomes for all relevant stakeholders in the system web of its corporate relationships and linkages. SVA on its own measures 'shareholder value', whereas the balanced scorecard approach (Kaplan and Norton 1996, 2001) in Chapter 18 introduces the viewpoint that firms need to develop performance measures along four dimensions – financial, customers, internal processes, and learning and growth – in order to achieve enduringly strong and balanced results along those multiple objectives and manage a strategy-focused organization.

More recently, Kaplan and Norton (2004) have added the notion of a 'strategy map' – a systems view of the organization – which maps the strategy, uncovers problems, monitors progress, identifies critical issues and communicates the strategy both internally to managers and employees and externally to investors, media, local and government communities. Critically, the strategy map incorporates a model to fit intangible assets: human capital readiness (e.g. skills), information capital readiness (e.g. databases) and organizational capital readiness (e.g. teamwork) into the balanced strategy approach. Ultimately, this is a strong attempt to provide a 'systemic' approach to discussing and investigating organizational strategy.

Reputation, image and identity

> 'Reputation, reputation, reputation – the one immortal part of man' (Shakespeare, from Othello).

The modern resource-based theory of the firm (RBV), discussed in Chapter 7, identifies a range of intangible assets including technology, patents, skills, etc. which, when combined with human and organizational resources, define the firm's core dynamic capabilities. A key set of intangible assets are the firm's reputational assets and these include the company name, its identity, brands, brand image and customer-based loyalty, the reputation of the firm's products and services, and the integrity of its relationships with the complex web or customers, suppliers, communities and governments. Many of the world's top brands (Coca-Cola, Microsoft, IBM, GE, Intel, Nescafe, etc.) are household names and help to develop a strong relationship of value, trust and goodwill with the customer. As we have recently seen, however, in the accounting industry, with the demise of Arthur Andersen, a hard-won reputation was easily dissipated and lost by the unethical and illegal behaviour of its employees. Therefore, a strong corporate reputation is a key strategic asset in managing value as a system.

21.6 Managing value as a system

What is critical from the strategic systems perspective is the ability to manage the organization strategically to maximize value. This requires:

* Strategy co-ordination – the strategy-focused organization.
* A clear objective of value creation and maximization.
* The ability to balance assets (e.g. trust, reputation, goodwill, etc.).
* The ability to balance financial measures.

◆ The ability to co-ordinate organization, operations and stakeholders so that the complex web of relationships works effectively.

As we have seen in this chapter, determining who the relevant business stakeholders and constituencies are requires a well-balanced understanding of the business system using, perhaps, Kaplan and Norton's concept of a strategy map. Value for customers results from customer satisfaction associated with product quality, choice and price. For shareholders and investors, SVA measures are appropriate. For employees, value may comprise such things as salaries, on-the-job training, stock options and job satisfaction. For suppliers, value may emanate from long-term corporate relationships and access to new technology and processes, as well as fair prices for their products. For governments and communities, value is measured by good corporate citizenship and social responsibility.

In addressing all these components of value – business strategy, customers, asset portfolios, organization and operations, learning and knowledge growth, supplier relationships, employees, local and government communities – the key skill is to treat them as a system and understand their context through the strategy map. In other words, by examining their interrelationships and treating the components of value concurrently and systematically, strategic decisions are examined relative to their impact on the other value components using SVA and balanced scorecard approaches. The strategy map, or systems diagram, then enables the manager to monitor and adapt strategy, develop organizational learning and growth and provide socially and financially responsible outcomes.

21.7 Summary and other issues in managing value

We continue to argue that the preferred objective for the corporation is the 'maximization of shareholder value', i.e. if an organization maximizes shareholder wealth in the long term, it will maximize firm value and enlarge the pie for all stakeholders. We recognize, however, that, as stated by Sundaram and Inkpen (2004, p. 371), 'All of us seek a path to a promised land in which accountable firms managed by ethical decision-makers create the greatest value for the greatest number of stakeholders'. This may occur using a shareholder value model, as we advocate, or through the development of a well-developed stakeholder theory, which is empirically supported (Freeman *et al.* 2004). In time, we may see such a theory developed but, in the meantime, some or all of the following issues are important in the process of managing the value of the business system:

◆ Would a company-wide ethical orientation (such as, for example, The Body Shop) or a strong commitment to corporate social responsibility constitute a key strategic resource in terms of the resource-based view of the firm? (*See* Wernerfelt 1984; Barney 1991.) In other words, is an ethical and socially responsible stance a non-imitable, unique source of sustainable long-term competitive advantage for the firm?

- Similarly, would strong organizational trust (Barney and Hansen 1994) create a long-term source of competitive advantage for the firm?

- Would core competencies and capabilities in business–government relations, such as the relationship between an ethical pharmaceutical company and the Federal Drug Administration in the drug-approval process, create a source of sustainable competitive advantage through effective management of the regulatory processes?

- Can a strong organizational identity or core ideology (e.g. Johnson & Johnson's credo) create an identity management competence for long-term sustainable competitive advantage?

- Managing value as a system requires a clear business model or 'Theory of the Business' (Drucker 1994). Drucker identifies four specifications about a valid theory of business:
  - The assumptions about environment, mission and core competencies must fit reality.
  - The assumptions in all three areas have to fit one another.
  - The theory of the business must be known throughout the organization.
  - The theory of the business has to be tested constantly.

    Throughout, Drucker has a systems-oriented view. He states 'when a theory shows the first signs of becoming obsolete, it is time to start thinking again.'

- As Yoffie (1988) points out, companies can strengthen their competitive advantage by forging closer ties with government. A political strategy may offer creative strategic choices in newly opened markets, such as in the dynamics of deregulated markets (e.g. rail, bus and utility companies in the UK).

In conclusion, we offer a couple of quotes and a case example from the challenging and controversial entrepreneur Anita Roddick, drawn from her book *Business as Unusual* (2000). Her stance on business challenges us all to examine the core values that drive business as a system and which create value.

> *One of our greatest frustrations at The Body Shop is that we are still judged by the media and the City by our profits, by the amount of product we sell, whereas we want, and have always wanted, to be judged by our activities in the larger world, by the positive difference we make. The shaping force for us from the start has not been our products but our principles.*

> *In terms of power and influence, you can forget the church, forget politics. There is no more powerful institution in society than business – I believe it is more important than ever before for business to assume a moral leadership. The business of business should not be about money, it should be about responsibility. It should be about public good, not private greed.*

Key terms

Business value *775*

Complexity *778*

Corporate social responsibility *786*

Create value *779*

Freeman's stakeholder theory *781*

Reputational assets *789*

Shareholder value *775*

Social value *775*

Structural coupling *778*

Systems theory *778*

Value *779*

Recap questions and assignments

1   What are the implications of the systems perspective for the work of a board of directors and the top management team? (refer back to the discussion on corporate governance in Chapter 17).

2   Does competition make it more or less difficult to apply a systems perspective? (refer back to the discussion in the previous chapter, pp. 760–2).

Online
LearningCentre

When you have read this chapter, log on to the Online Learning Centre website at www.mcgraw-hill.co.uk/textbooks/mcgee to explore chapter-by-chapter test questions, further reading and more online study tools for strategy.

Case 1 Oh, the joy of the journey!

I guess you'd call it one of those defining moments. The year was 1987. The Body Shop was still in its protoplasmic period, but the Confederation of British Industry had chosen us as Company of the Year. Which meant I had to pick up the award.

There, they sat, the captains of industry, the bankers, the analysts, the journalists, just about the entire British financial establishment, all lined up and holding their collective breath as I mounted the podium.

It was irresistible. Every provocative bone in my body was aching to act up. I'd prepared what I hoped would be a mildly inflammatory speech. When I showed it to my husband, Gordon, he advised me to challenge them all. I also showed it to Jilly Forster, a close friend who also happened to be our PR person. She told me I had to say what I'd written. As I started to speak, the tension was such that I could see tears streaming down her face. I could also see our brokers, sitting stoney-faced on either side of her.

What did I say? I stood up for entrepreneurs against the big corporations. I told these business titans they were stuck in the past. (I believe the phrase I used was 'dinosaurs in pin-striped suits'.) What else could I do? 'I've never met a captain of industry who made my blood sing', I declared – at which point I looked up to see Robert Maxwell walking out. For all I know he had another appointment, but still I felt a surge of pride. My blood did sing, thanks, indirectly, to Cap'n Bob.

That speech was a watershed for me. I had the optimistic sensation that The Body Shop way of doing business was the inescapable future.

In the decade or so that followed, the story got a lot more complex – 'richer', but darker too. History did 1800 flips. The Wall came down (so did Robert Maxwell for that matter). The maximalism of the 1980s surrendered to the minimalism of the 1990s. All the while, The Body Shop was growing into one of the most successful retailers in the world. And I found myself on an extraordinary journey, a journey which made me even more passionate about the urgent need for a new model of business. It was also a journey through a minefield, with every explosion a reminder – as if I needed one – of how fragile were the goals we'd set ourselves. That journey is the subject matter of this book.

Looking back from the vantage point of a new century, I can trace how the path I've taken has radicalized me. Whether it was a sally into the forests of Sarawak to photograph illegal logging or up the Amazon to set up the first direct trading link with the Kayapo, it gave me a glimpse of the way in which global corporations threaten to engulf life, not just in our society but also in the communities where businesspeople simply never go. The outrage I felt was no abstract emotion. It grew stronger the more I travelled, the more I met people forced to eke out a bare existence on the margins of the world, denied their fundamental human rights by the fickle voracity of the global business juggernaut.

I'd always known I was in uncharted territory, but sometimes the landscape I found myself in was so alien that the people I thought were friends were actually enemies – and vice versa. Talk about a recipe for paranoia. Life in a minefield isn't easy. There have been many dents in my optimism and challenges to my convictions – our libel action, our mistakes in the American market, that relationship with the Kayapo I mentioned – but this was ultimately a good thing. When you've had some years when everyone – including the stock market – says you can do no wrong, it's good to be reminded that you're running the same race as the rest of the world. What doesn't kill you makes you stronger.

Yet that sentiment is actually too harsh. Be kind, Harvey Keitel writes on Kate Winslet's forehead in the movie Holy Smoke. That's what I wanted to do to the business world – nurture a revolution in kindness. But underlying that ambition has been the recurring theme of my role in the company I founded, now that it has grown into such a huge and complicated organization. So this book actually has another subject as well. It is the story of how I managed to maintain some intimate part of myself – the original core, if you like – in a business gone global. I have had to constantly reinvent the role of the founder entrepreneur. That's tough when your natural tendency is towards a gleeful anarchy. There are no road-maps, no instruction manuals. Passion is your guide. Instinct tells you where to go when a challenge arises.

So this book is more than a chronicle of a decade at The Body Shop, more than a condensed manual for the wannabe business radical. It is also about one individual's attempt to marry the often impersonal wants of a successful business with the very personal needs of a successful businessperson. Despite the enormous constraints of a global company, despite the general intractability of life, I need to find new ways to push the limits of business, to change its language, to make it a force for positive change. **That's what I mean by business as unusual**.

Source: Anita Roddick (2000) *Business as Unusual: The Journey of Anita Roddick and The Body Shop*, Thorsons, London.

Case Questions

1   Discuss Anita Roddick's conception of a responsible business.

2   How do her guiding principles and values allow the business to grow?

3   What is the role of the founder-entrepreneur in the growth of a successful business?

Further reading and references

AACSB (2003) *Ethics Education in Business Schools*, St. Louis, AACSB International.

Argyris, C and Schon, D (1978) *Organisational Learning: A Theory-in-Action Perspective*, Reading, MA, Addison-Wesley.

Arrow, KJ (1963) *Social Choice and Individual Values*, Yale, Yale University Press.

Barney, JB (1991) 'Firm resources and sustained competitive advantage', *Journal of Management*, **17**, pp. 99–120.

Barney, JB and Hansen, MH (1994) 'Trustworthiness as a source of competitive advantage', *Strategic Management Journal*, **15**, pp. 175–90.

Beer, S (1981) *Brain of the Firm: The Managerial Cybernetics of Organisation*, Chichester, John Wiley & Sons.

Bell, T, Marrs, F, Solomon, I and Thomas, H (1997) *Auditing Organisations Through a Strategic-Systems Lens*, Montvale, NJ, KPMG Publications.

Carroll, AB (1979) 'A Three-Dimensional Conceptual Model of Corporate Performance', *Academy of Business Review*, **4**, pp. 497–505.

Collins, JC and Porras, JI (1996) 'Building Your Company's Vision', *Harvard Business Review*, **74**, September/October, pp. 64–77.

Day, GS and Fahey, L (1990) 'Putting Strategy into Shareholder Value Analysis', *Harvard Business Review*, **68**, March/April, pp.156–63.

De Geus, AP (1988) 'Planning as Learning', *Harvard Business Review*, **66**, March/April, pp. 70–5.

Doyle, P (2000) *Value-based Marketing*, Chichester and New York, Wiley.

Drucker, PF (1993) *Post-Capitalist Society*, Oxford, Butterworth-Heinemann.

Drucker, PF (1994) 'The Theory of the Business', *Harvard Business Review*, **72**, Sept/Oct, pp. 95–104.

Elkington, J (1997) *Cannibals with Forks: The Triple Bottom Line of 21st Century Business*, Oxford, Capstone.

Freeman, RE (1984) *Strategic Management: A Stakeholder Perspective*, London, Pitman.

Freeman, RE and McVea, J, (2001) 'A Stakeholder Approach to Strategic Management', in M Hitt, E Freeman and J Harrison (eds) *Handbook of Strategic Management*, Oxford, Blackwell, pp. 189–207.

Friedman, M (1970) 'The Social Responsibility of Business is to Increase its Profits', *New York Time Magazine*, September, pp. 32–3.

Friedman, M and Friedman, R (1980) *Free to Choose: A Personal Statement*, London, Secker & Warburg.

Glautier, MWE and Underdown, B (2001) *Accounting Theory and Practice*, New York, Prentice-Hall.

Grant, RM (1997) *Contemporary Strategy Analysis*, 3rd edition, Oxford, Blackwell.

Harrison, JS and St John, CH (1998) *Strategic Management of Organisations and Stakeholders*, 2nd edition, Cincinnati, Ohio, South Western Publishing.

Kaplan, RS and Norton, DP (2004) 'Measuring the Strategic Readiness of Intangible Assets', *Harvard Business Review*, **82**, **2**, February, pp. 52–64.

Kaplan, RS and Norton, DP (1996) *The Balanced Scorecard*, Cambridge, HBS Press.

Kauffman, S (1995) *At Home in the Universe: The Search for Laws of Self-Organisation and Complexity*, Oxford, Oxford University Press.

Kay, J (1995) *Why Firms Succeed*, Oxford, Oxford University Press.

Magretta, J (2003) *What Management Is*, London, Profile Books.

Malone, TW, Scott-Morton, MS and Halperin, RR (1996) 'Organising for the 21st Century', *Strategy and Leadership*, **24**, July/August, pp. 6–11.

Mintzberg, H (1987) 'Crafting Strategy', *Harvard Business Review*, **65**, July/August, pp. 66–76.

Mohr, J and Spekman, R (1994) 'Characteristics of Partnership Success: Partnership Attributes Communication Behaviour and Conflict Resolution Techniques', *Strategic Management Journal*, **15**, pp. 135–52.

Parker, RH and Harcourt, GC (1969) *Readings in the Concept and Management of Income*, Cambridge, Cambridge University Press.

Richardson, GP (1991) *Feedback Thought in Social Science and Systems Theory*, Philadelphia, University of Philadelphia Press.

Roddick, A (2000) *Business as Unusual*, London, Thorsons.

Rosenfeld, R and Wilson, DC (1999) *Managing Organizations: Text Readings and Cases*, Maidenhead, McGraw-Hill.

Senge, P (1998) 'The leader's new work: Building learning organisations', in S Segal-Horn (ed.) *The Strategy Reader*, Oxford, Blackwell, pp. 296–312.

Sundaram, AK and Inkpen, AC (2004) 'The Corporate Objective Revisited', *Organisation Science*, **15**, **3**, May/June, pp. 350–63.

Van der Heijden, K (1996) *Scenarios: The Art of Strategic Conversation*, Chichester, John Wiley & Sons.

Wernerfelt, B (1984) 'A resource-based view of the firm', *Strategic Management Journal*, **5**, pp. 171–80.

Yoffie, DB (1988) 'How an Industry Builds Political Advantage', *Harvard Business Review*, **66**, May/June, pp. 82–90.

ISSUE 4

Should Corporations Adopt Policies of Corporate Social Responsibility?

YES: Robert D. Hay and Edmund R. Gray, from "Introduction to Social Responsibility," in David Keller, man. ed., *Ethics and Values: Basic Readings in Theory and Practice* (Pearson Custom Publishing, 2002)

NO: Milton Friedman, from "The Social Responsibility of Business Is to Increase Its Profits," in Thomas Donaldson and Patricia H. Werhane, eds., *Ethical Issues in Business: A Philosophical Approach,* 4th ed. (Prentice Hall, 1993)

ISSUE SUMMARY

YES: Robert D. Hay, professor of management at the University of Arkansas, and Edmund R. Gray, professor and chair of the Department of Management at Loyola Marymount University, argue that in the long run, businesses will only be successful if they are directed to the needs of the society. If they choose to ignore that advice, government regulation is likely to fill the gap between business operations and the welfare of the people the government is sworn to protect.

NO: In this classic defense of *laissez-faire*, Paul Snowden Russell Distinguished Service Professor Emeritus of Economics at the University of Chicago Milton Friedman states that businesses have neither the right, in law or morals, nor the ability to meddle with "social responsibility." Customers, employees, and the general public, he concludes, are best served when the company simply does its job with maximum efficiency.

Should a company think past the bottom line and try to do good (or at least avoid evil)? This question, probably the first one asked in the infant discipline of business ethics a quarter of a century ago, has received many answers along the spectrum between yes and no; this spectrum is one of the arcs along which the political pendulum swings. In the 1950s Milton Friedman's arguments were taken as gospel truth. Those who agreed with Robert D. Hay and Edmund R. Gray were regarded as "do-gooders" who understood nothing of business. During the 1970s, in a very rapid switch brought on by the consumer movements of the 1960s, the pendulum moved to Hay and Gray's position. By the 1970s, when he wrote the article reproduced here, Friedman was regarded as an interesting dinosaur. During the Reagan-Bush administrations, the pendulum swung back, to the point where at present Friedman is regarded as a prophet and Hay and Gray's orientation a "variant perspective." Many agree that in this debate, nothing is certain, save that the pendulum will eventually swing the other way.

And so it should. There are widely differing opinions on the costs and benefits of an economic regime oriented to liberty rather than protection, but the American consensus has always been, following Smith, that the free market is good, individual liberty to pursue self-interest in economic matters is good, and that if everyone pursues self-interest exclusively—if business increases profits, to the exclusion of all other goals—in the end we will all, even the poorest of us, be better off. Whenever possible, Americans adhere to the free-market ideology. Many insist that it must be balanced by a strong legal regime prohibiting the uses of force and fraud, banning toxins and other dangers invisible to the consumer, and actively intervening in the endemic tendency of businesses to create monopolies—designed to thwart the market for the greater profit of the combiners. When that regime fails, businesses turn into predators, citizens are robbed, poisoned, and impoverished; and citizens eventually become outraged. Then the government is re-empowered to defeat—through arrest, jail, fines, or banishment—the "malefactors of great wealth," and a period of protection and rehabilitation of the poor succeeds the period of liberty for the corporations. It has happened often, and many predict that it will happen again, with the only change being the sophistication of the technology.

Underneath the political pendulum is a fixed structure of partnership. Society retains the right to seek the maximum happiness—without leaving the poor behind. Nor would it be in accordance with justice to abandon the U.S. economy to businesses: after all, the public granted the rights that the corporations have exercised to make their profits, protected their operations at taxpayer expense, and created and maintained the infrastructures (e.g., roads, water, power, and sanitation) upon which corporations depend.

Ask yourself, as you read these selections, what balance between the freedom of the entrepreneur and the protection of the rest of the citizenry would be appropriate for a free and affluent society. How much of the responsibility for the citizenry should be taken on by corporations?

Robert D. Hay and
Edmund R. Gray

 **YES**

Introduction to Social Responsibility

It was Jeremy Bentham, late eighteenth century English philosopher, who espoused the social, political, and economic goal of society to be "the greatest happiness for the greatest number." His cardinal principle was written into the Declaration of Independence as "the pursuit of happiness," which became a societal goal of the American colonists. Bentham's principle was also incorporated into the Constitution of the United States in the preamble where the goal was stated "to promote the general welfare."

The economic-political system through which we in America strive to achieve this societal goal emphasizes the economic and political freedom to pursue individual interests. Adam Smith, another English political economist of the late eighteenth century, stated that the best way to achieve social goals was as follows:

> Every individual is continually exerting himself to find out the most advantageous employment for whatever capital he can command. It is his own advantage, indeed, and not that of the society, which he has in view. But the study of his own advantage naturally, or rather necessarily, leads him to prefer that employment which is most advantageous to the society. . . .
>
> As every individual, therefore, endeavors as much as he can both to employ his capital in the support of domestic industry, and so to direct that industry that its produce may be of the greatest value, every individual necessarily labours to render the annual revenue of the society as great as he can. He generally, indeed, neither intends to promote the public interest, nor knows how much he is promoting it By preferring the support of domestic to that of foreign industry, he intends only his own security; and by directing that industry in such a manner as its produce may be of the greatest value, he intends only his own gain, and he is in this, as in many other cases, led by an invisible hand to promote an end which was not part of his intention. Nor is it always the worse for the society that it was no part of it. By pursuing his own interest he frequently promotes that of the society more effectually than when he really intends to promote it. I have never known much good done by those who affected to trade for the

YES / Hay and Gray   **79**

public good. It is an affectation, indeed, not very common among merchants, and very few words need be employed in dissuading them from it.

Adam Smith's economic values have had an important influence on American business thinking. As a result, most business people for the first hundred and fifty years of our history embraced the theory that social goals could be achieved by pursuing individual interests.

By 1930 American values were beginning to change from that of the individual owner ethic to that of the group or social ethic. As part of this changing mood, it was felt that Smith's emphasis on owner's interests was too predominant at the expense of other contributors to a business organization. Consequently, a new philosophy of management took shape which stated that the social goals could be achieved by balancing the interests of several groups of people who had an interest in a business. It was stated by Charles H. Percy, then president of Bell and Howell, in the 1950s as follows:

> There are over 64 million gainfully employed people in the United States. One half of these work directly for American corporations, and the other half are vitally affected by business directly or indirectly. Our entire economy, therefore, is dependent upon the type of business management we have. Business management is therefore in many respects a public trust charged with the responsibility of keeping America economically sound. We at Bell & Howell can best do this by keeping our own company's program on a firm foundation and by having a growing group of management leaders to direct the activities of the company.
>
> Management's role in a free society is, among other things, to prove that the real principles of a free society can work within a business organization.
>
> Our basic objective is the development of individuals. In our own present program we are doing everything conceivable to encourage, guide, and assist, and provide an opportunity to everyone to improve their abilities and skills, thus becoming more valuable to the company and enabling the company to improve the rewards paid to the individual for such additional efforts.
>
> Our company has based its entire program for the future on the development of the individual and also upon the building of an outstanding management group. This is why we have emphasized so strongly the supervisory training program recently completed by all Bell & Howell supervisors, and why we are now offering this program to others in the organization training for future management responsibilities.
>
> But a company must also have a creed to which its management is dedicated. I hope that we can all agree to the following:
>
> We believe that our company must develop and produce outstanding products that will perform a great service or fill a need for our customers.
>
> We believe that our business must be run at an adequate profit and that the services and products that we offer must be better than those offered by competitors.
>
> We believe that management must serve employees, stockholders, and customers, but that we cannot serve the interests of any one group at the undue expense of the other two. A proper and fair balance must be preserved.

80   ISSUE 4 / Should Corporations Adopt Policies of Responsibility?

We believe that our business must provide stability of employment and job security for all those who depend on our company for their livelihood.

We believe that we are failing in our responsibility if our wages are not sufficiently high to not only meet the necessities of life but provide some of the luxuries as well. Wherever possible, we also believe that bonus earning should be paid for performance and output "beyond the call of duty."

We believe that every individual in the company should have an opportunity for advancement and growth with the organization. There should be no dead-end streets any place in an organization.

We believe in the necessity for constantly increasing productivity and output. Higher wages and greater benefits can never be "given" by management. Management can only see that they are paid out when "earned."

We believe in labor-saving machinery. We do not think human beings should perform operations that can be done by mechanical or electronic means. We believe in this because we believe in the human dignity and creative ability of the individual. We are more interested in the intellect, goodwill, initiative, enthusiasm, and cooperativeness of the individual than we are in his muscular energy.

We believe that every person in the company has a right to be treated with the respect and courtesy that is due a human being. It is for this reason that we have individual merit ratings, individual pay increases, job evaluation, and incentive pay; and it is why we keep every individual fully informed—through The Finder, through our annual report, through Family Night, and through individual letters—about the present program of the company and also about our future objectives.

We believe that our business must be conducted with the utmost integrity. We may fight the principle of confiscatory taxation, but we will pay our full share. We will observe every governmental law and regulation, local, state, and national. We will deal fairly with our customers, we will advertise our product truthfully, and we will make every attempt to maintain a friendly relationship with our competitors while at the same time waging the battle of free competition.

Some business leaders, on the one hand, preach the virtues of the free enterprise, democratic system and, on the other hand, run their own business in accordance with autocratic principles—all authority stemming from the top with little delegation of responsibility to individuals within the organization. We believe in democracy—in government and in our business.

We hope that every principle we believe in is right and is actually being practiced throughout the company as it affects every individual.

Then in the late 1960s American business leaders began to take another look at the problems of society in light of the goal of "the greatest happiness for the greatest number." How could people be happy if they have to breathe foul air, drink polluted water, live in crowded cities, use very unsafe products, be misled by untruthful advertising, be deprived of a job because of race, and face many other problems? Thus, another philosophy of management emerged. It was voiced by several American business leaders:

Business must learn to look upon its social responsibilities as inseparable from its economic function. If it fails to do so, it leaves a void that will quickly be filled by others—usually by the government. (George Champion, Chase National Bank, 1966.)

I believe there is one basic principle that needs to be emphasized more than ever before. It is the recognition that business is successful in the long term only when it is directed toward the needs of the society. (Robert F. Hansberger, Boise Cascade, 1971.)

The actions of the great corporations have so profound an influence that the public has come to judge them not only by their profit-making record, but by the contribution of their work to society as a whole. Under a political democracy such as ours, if the corporation fails to perceive itself and govern its action in essentially the same manner as the public at large, it may find itself in serious trouble. (Louis B. Lundborg, Bank of America, 1971.)

With these remarks we can see that there has been a shift in managerial emphasis from owners' interests to group interests, and finally, to society's interests. Managers of some American businesses have come to recognize that they have a social responsibility.

Historical Perspective of Social Responsibility

The concept of the social responsibility of business managers has in recent years become a popular subject of discussion and debate within both business and academic circles. Although the term itself is of relatively recent origin, the underlying concept has existed as long as there have been business organizations. It rests on the logical assumption that because the firm is a creation of society, it has a responsibility to aid in the accomplishment of society's goals. In the United States concepts of social responsibility have moved from three distinct phases which may be labeled Phases I, II, and III.

Phase I—Profit Maximizing Management

The Phase I concept was based on the belief that business managers have but one single objective—maximize profits. The only constraint on this pursuit was the legal framework within which the firm operated. The origin of this view may be found in Adam Smith's *Wealth of Nations*. As previously noted, Smith believed that individual business people acting in their own selfish interest would be guided by an "invisible hand" to promote the public good. In other words, the individual's drive for maximum profits and the regulation of the competitive marketplace would interact to create the greatest aggregate wealth for a nation and therefore the maximum public good. In the United States this view was universally accepted throughout the nineteenth century and the early part of the twentieth century. Its acceptance rested not only on economic logic but also on the goals and values of society. America in the nineteenth and first half of the twentieth centuries was a society of economic scarcity; therefore, economic growth and the accumulation of aggregate wealth were primary goals. The business system with its emphasis on maximum profit was seen as a vehicle for eliminating economic scarcity. In the process employee abuses such as child labor, starvation wages, and unsafe

Newton–Ford: Taking
Sides: Issues in Business
Ethics and Society, Ninth
Edition

I. Capitalism and the
Corporation

4. Should Corporations
Adopt Policies of
Corporate Social
Responsibility?

© The McGraw–Hill
Companies, 2006

82   ISSUE 4 / Should Corporations Adopt Policies of Responsibility?

working conditions could be tolerated. No questions were raised with regard to using up the natural resources and polluting streams and land. Nor was anyone really concerned about urban problems, unethical advertising, unsafe products, and poverty problems of minority groups.

The profit maximization view of social responsibility also complemented the Calvinistic philosophy which pervaded nineteenth and twentieth century American thinking. Calvinism stressed that the road to salvation was through hard work and the accumulation of wealth. It then logically followed that a business person could demonstrate diligence (and thus godliness) and accumulate a maximum amount of wealth by adhering to the discipline of profit maximization.

Phase II—Trusteeship Management

Phase II, which may be labeled the "trusteeship" concept, emerged in the 1920s and 30s. It resulted from structural changes in both business institutions and in society. According to this concept, corporate managers were responsible not simply for maximizing the stockholders' wealth but rather for maintaining an equitable balance among the competing claims of customers, employees, suppliers, creditors, and the community. In this view the manager was seen as "trustee" for the various contributor groups to the firm rather than simply an agent of the owners.

The two structural trends largely responsible for the emergence of this newer view of social responsibility were: (1) the increasing diffusion of ownership of the shares of American corporations, and (2) the development of a pluralistic society. The extent of the diffusion of stock ownership may be highlighted by the fact that by the early 1930s the largest stockholders in corporations such as American Telephone and Telegraph, United States Steel, and the Pennsylvania Railroad owned less than one percent of the total shares outstanding of these companies. Similar dispersion of stock ownership existed in most other large corporations. In such situations management typically was firmly in control of the corporation. Except in rare circumstances, the top executives were able to perpetuate themselves in office through the proxy mechanism. If an individual shareholder was not satisfied with the performance of the firm, there was little recourse other than to sell the stock. Hence, although the stockholder's legal position was that of an owner—and thus a principal-agent relationship existed between the stockholder and the managers—the stockholder's actual position was more akin to bondholders and other creditors of the firm. Given such a situation it was only natural to ask, "To whom is management responsible?" The "trusteeship" concept provided an answer. Management was responsible to all the contributors to the firm—that is, stockholders, workers, customers, suppliers, creditors, and the community.

The emergence of a largely pluralistic society reinforced the logic of the "trusteeship" concept. A pluralistic society has been defined as "one which has many semi-autonomous and autonomous groups through which power is diffused. No one group has overwhelming power over all others, and each has direct or indirect impact on all others. From the perspective of business firms this translated into the fact that exogenous groups had considerable impact

Newton–Ford: Taking
Sides: Issues in Business
Ethics and Society, Ninth
Edition

I. Capitalism and the
Corporation

4. Should Corporations
Adopt Policies of
Corporate Social
Responsibility?

© The McGraw–Hill
Companies, 2006

455

YES / Hay and Gray **83**

upon and influence over them. In the 1930s the major groups exerting significant pressure on business were labor unions and the federal government. Today the list has grown to include numerous minority, environmental, and consumer groups among others. Clearly, one logical approach to such a situation is to consider that the firm has a responsibility to each interested group and that management's task is to reconcile and balance the claims of the various groups.

Phase III—Quality of Life Management

Phase III, which may be called the "quality of life" concept of social responsibility, has become popular in recent years. The primary reason for the emergence of this concept is the very significant metamorphosis in societal goals which this nation is experiencing. Up to the middle part of this century, society's principal goal was to raise the standard of living of the American people, which could be achieved by producing more goods and services. The fact that the U.S. had become the wealthiest nation in the world was testimony to the success of business in meeting this expectation.

In this process, however, the U.S. has become what John Kenneth Galbraith calls an "affluent society" in which the aggregate scarcity of basic goods and services is no longer the fundamental problem. Other social problems have developed as direct and indirect results of economic success. Thus, there are pockets of poverty in a nation of plenty, deteriorating cities, air and water pollution, defacement of the landscape, and a disregard for consumers to mention only a few of the prominent social problems. The mood of the country seems to be that things have gotten out of balance—the economic abundance in the midst of a declining social and physical environment does not make sense. As a result, a new set of national priorities which stress the "Quality of life" appear to be emerging.

Concomitant with the new priorities, societal consensus seems to be demanding that business, with its technological and managerial skills and its financial resources, assume broader responsibilities—responsibilities that extend beyond the traditional economic realm of the Phase I concept or the mere balancing of the competing demands of the sundry contributors and pressure groups of the Phase II concept. The socially responsible firm under Phase III reasoning is one that becomes deeply involved in the solution of society's major problems.

Personal Values of the Three Styles of Managers

Values are the beliefs and attitudes which form one's frame of reference and help to determine the behavior which an individual displays. All managers have a set of values which affect their decisions, but the values are not the same for each manager; however, once values are ingrained in a manager, they do not change except over a period of time. It is possible to group these values into a general pattern of behavior which characterizes three styles of managers—the profit-maximizing style, the trusteeship style, and the "quality of life" style of management.

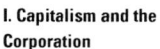
84   ISSUE 4 / Should Corporations Adopt Policies of Responsibility?

Phase I Managers

Phase I, profit-maximizing managers have a personal set of values which reflects their economic thinking. They believe that raw self-interest should prevail in society, and their values dictate that "What's good for me is good for my country." Therefore, Phase I managers rationalize that making as much profit as is possible would be good for society. They make every effort to become as efficient as possible and to make as much money as they can. To them money and wealth are the most important goals of their lives.

In the pursuit of maximum profit the actions of Phase I managers toward customers are reflected in a *caveat emptor* philosophy. "Let the buyer beware" characterizes decisions and actions in dealing with customers. They are not necessarily concerned with product quality or safety, or with sufficient and/or truthful information about products and services. A profit-maximizing manager's view toward employees can be stated as, "Labor is a commodity to be bought and sold in the marketplace." Thus, chief accountability lies with the owners of the business, and usually the Phase I manager is the owner or part owner of the organization.

To profit maximizers technology is very important. Machines and equipment rank high on their scale of values, therefore, materialism characterizes their philosophy.

Social values do not predominate the thinking of Phase I managers. In fact, they believe that employee problems should be left at home. Economics should be separate from societal or family concerns. A Phase I manager's leadership style is one of the rugged individualist—"I'm my own boss, and I'll manage my business as I please." Values about minority groups dictate that such groups are inferior, so they must be treated accordingly.

Political values are based on the doctrine of laissez faire. "That government is best which governs the least" characterizes the thinking of Phase I managers. As a result anything dealing with politicians and governments is foreign and distasteful to them.

Their beliefs about the environment can be stated, "The natural environment controls one's destiny; therefore, use it to protect your interests before it destroys you. Don't worry about the physical environment because there are plenty of natural resources which you can use."

Aesthetic values to the profit maximizer are minimal. In fact, Phase I managers would say, "Aesthetic values? What are they?" They have very little concern for the arts and cultural aspects of life. They hold musicians, artists, entertainers, and social scientists in low regard.

The values that a profit-maximizing manager holds were commonly accepted in the economic textbooks of the 1800s and early 1900s although they obviously did not apply to all managers of those times. It is easy to see how they conflict with the values of the other two styles of management.

Phase II Managers

Phase II, trusteeship managers have a somewhat different set of values. They recognize that self-interest plays a large role in their actions, but they also

YES / Hay and Gray **85**

recognize the interests of those people who contribute to the organization—the customers, employees, suppliers, owners, creditors, government, and community. In other words, they operate with self-interest plus the interests of other groups. They believe that "What is good for my company is good for the country." They balance profits of the owners and the organization with wages for employees, taxes for the government, interest for the creditors, and so forth. Money is important to them but so are people, because their values tells them that satisfying people's needs is a better goal than just making money.

In balancing the needs of the various contributors to the organization, Phase II managers deal with customers as the chief providers of revenue to the firm. Their values tell them not to cheat the customers because cheating is not good for the firm.

They are concerned with providing sufficient quantities of goods as well as sufficient quality for customer satisfaction. They view employees as having certain rights which must be recognized and that employees are more than mere commodities to be traded in the marketplace. Their accountability as managers is to owners as well as to customers, employees, suppliers, creditors, government, and the community.

To the trusteeship-style manager, technology is important, but so are people. Innovation of technology is to be commended because new machines, equipment, and products are useful to people to create a high standard of living. Materialism is important, but so is humanism.

The social values held by trusteeship managers are more liberal than those held by profit maximizers. They recognize that employees have several needs beyond their economic needs. Employees have a desire for security and a sense of belonging as well as recognition. Phase II managers see themselves as individualists, but they also appreciate the value of group participation in managing the business. They view minority groups as having their place in society. But, a trusteeship manager would add: "Their place is usually inferior to mine; they are usually not qualified to hold their jobs but that's not my fault."

The political values of Phase II managers are reflected in recognizing that government and politics are important, but they view government and politics as necessary evils. They distrust both, recognizing that government serves as a threat to their existence if their firms do not live up to the laws passed since the 1930s.

The environmental beliefs of trusteeship managers are stated as follows: "People can control and manipulate their environment. Therefore, let them do it for their own benefit and incidentally for society's benefit."

Aesthetic values are all right to the trusteeship manager, but "they are not for our firm although someone has to support the arts and cultural values."

Phase III Managers

In contrast to profit maximizers and trustee managers, "quality of life" managers believe in enlightened self-interest. They agree that selfishness and group interests are important, but that society's interests are also important in making decisions. "What's good for society is good for our company" is their opinion.

86   ISSUE 4 / Should Corporations Adopt Policies of Responsibility?

They agree that profit is essential for the firm, but that profit in and of itself is not the end objective of the firm. As far as money and wealth are concerned, their set of values tells them that money is important but people are more important than money.

In sharp contrast to *caveat emptor* in dealings with customers, the philosophy of Phase II managers is *caveat venditor*, that is, let the seller beware. The company should bear the responsibility for producing and distributing products and services in sufficient quantities at the right time and place with the necessary quality, information, and services necessary to satisfy customers' needs. Their views about employees are to recognize the dignity of each, not treating them as a commodity to be bought and sold. Their accountability as managers is to the owners, to the other contributors of the business, and to society in general.

Technological values are important but people are held in higher esteem than machines, equipment, computers, and esoteric products. A "quality of life" manager is a humanist rather than a materialist.

The social values of "quality of life" managers dictate that a person cannot be separated into an economic being or family being. Their philosophy is, "We hire the whole person including any problems that person might have." Phase III managers recognize that group participation rather than rugged individualism is a determining factor in an organization's success. Their values about minority groups are different from the other managers. Their view is that "A member of a minority group needs support and guidance like any other person."

The political values of "quality of life" managers dictate that government and politicians are necessary contributors to a quality of life. Rather than resisting government, they believe that business and government must cooperate to solve society's problems.

Their environmental beliefs are stated as, "A person must preserve the environment, not for the environment's sake alone, but for the benefit of people who want to lead a quality life."

As far as aesthetic values are concerned, Phase III managers recognize that the arts and cultural values reflect the lives of people whom they hold in high regard. Their actions support aesthetic values by committing resources to their preservation and presentation.

NO

Milton Friedman

The Social Responsibility of Business Is to Increase Its Profits

When I hear businessmen speak eloquently about the "social responsibilities of business in a free-enterprise system," I am reminded of the wonderful line about the Frenchman who discovered at the age of 70 that he had been speaking prose all his life. The businessmen believe that they are defending free enterprise when they declaim that business is not concerned "merely" with profit but also with promoting desirable "social" ends; that business has a "social conscience" and takes seriously its responsibilities for providing employment, eliminating discrimination, avoiding pollution and whatever else may be the catchwords of the contemporary crop of reformers. In fact they are—or would be if they or anyone else took them seriously—preaching pure and unadulterated socialism. Businessmen who talk this way are unwitting puppets of the intellectual forces that have been undermining the basis of a free society these past decades.

The discussions of the "social responsibilities of business" are notable for their analytical looseness and lack of rigor. What does it mean to say that "business" has responsibilities? Only people can have responsibilities. A corporation is an artificial person and in this sense may have artificial responsibilities, but "business" as a whole cannot be said to have responsibilities, even in this vague sense. The first step toward clarity in examining the doctrine of the social responsibility of business is to ask precisely what it implies for whom.

Presumably, the individuals who are to be responsible are businessmen, which means individual proprietors or corporate executives. Most of the discussion of social responsibility is directed at corporations, so in what follows I shall mostly neglect the individual proprietors and speak of corporate executives.

In a free-enterprise, private-property system, a corporate executive is an employee of the owners of the business. He has direct responsibility to his employers. That responsibility is to conduct the business in accordance with their desires, which generally will be to make as much money as possible while conforming to the basic rules of the society, both those embodied in law and those embodied in ethical custom. Of course, in some cases his employers may have a different objective. A group of persons might establish a corporation for

From Milton Friedman, "The Social Responsibility of Business Is to Increase Its Profits," in Thomas Donaldson and Patricia H. Werhane, eds., *Ethical Issues in Business: A Philosophical Approach,* 4th ed. (Prentice Hall, 1993). Reprinted from *The New York Times Magazine* (September 13, 1970). Copyright © 1970 by Milton Friedman. Reprinted by permission of The New York Times Syndication Sales Corp.

88   ISSUE 4 / Should Corporations Adopt Policies of Responsibility?

an eleemosynary purpose—for example, a hospital or a school. The manager of such a corporation will not have money profit as his objective but the rendering of certain services.

In either case, the key point is that, in his capacity as a corporate executive, the manager is the agent of the individuals who own the corporation or establish the eleemosynary institution, and his primary responsibility is to them.

Needless to say, this does not mean that it is easy to judge how well he is performing his task. But at least the criterion of performance is straightforward, and the persons among whom a voluntary contractual arrangement exists are clearly defined.

Of course, the corporate executive is also a person in his own right. As a person, he may have many other responsibilities that he recognizes or assumes voluntarily—to his family, his conscience, his feelings of charity, his church, his clubs, his city, his country. He may feel impelled by these responsibilities to devote part of his income to causes he regards as worthy, to refuse to work for particular corporations, even to leave his job, for example, to join his country's armed forces. If we wish, we may refer to some of these responsibilities as "social responsibilities." But in these respects he is acting as a principal, not an agent; he is spending his own money or time or energy, not the money of his employers or the time or energy he has contracted to devote to their purposes. If these are "social responsibilities," they are the social responsibilities of individuals, not of business.

What does it mean to say that the corporate executive has a "social responsibility" in his capacity as businessman? If this statement is not pure rhetoric, it must mean that he is to act in some way that is not in the interest of his employers. For example, that he is to refrain from increasing the price of the product in order to contribute to the social objective of preventing inflation, even though a price increase would be in the best interests of the corporation. Or that he is to make expenditures on reducing pollution beyond the amount that is in the best interests of the corporation or that is required by law in order to contribute to the social objective of improving the environment. Or that, at the expense of corporate profits, he is to hire "hardcore" unemployed instead of better qualified available workmen to contribute to the social objective of reducing poverty.

In each of these cases, the corporate executive would be spending someone else's money for a general social interest. Insofar as his actions in accord with his "social responsibility" reduce returns to stockholders, he is spending their money. Insofar as his actions raise the price to customers, he is spending the customers' money. Insofar as his actions lower the wages of some employees, he is spending their money.

The stockholders or the customers or the employees could separately spend their own money on the particular action if they wished to do so. The executive is exercising a distinct "social responsibility," rather than serving as an agent of the stockholders or the customers or the employees, only if he spends the money in a different way than they would have spent it.

But if he does this, he is in effect imposing taxes, on the one hand, and deciding how the tax proceeds shall be spent, on the other.

NO / Milton Friedman   **89**

This process raises political questions on two levels: principle and consequences. On the level of political principle, the imposition of taxes and the expenditure of tax proceeds are governmental functions. We have established elaborate constitutional, parliamentary and judicial provisions to control these functions, to assure that taxes are imposed so far as possible in accordance with the preferences and desires of the public—after all, "taxation without representation" was one of the battle cries of the American Revolution. We have a system of checks and balances to separate the legislative function of imposing taxes and enacting expenditures from the executive function of collecting taxes and administering expenditure programs and from the judicial function of mediating disputes and interpreting the law.

Here the businessman—self-selected or appointed directly or indirectly by stockholders—is to be simultaneously legislator, executive and jurist. He is to decide whom to tax by how much and for what purpose, and he is to spend the proceeds—all this guided only by general exhortations from on high to restrain inflation, improve the environment, fight poverty and so on and on.

The whole justification for permitting the corporate executive to be selected by the stockholders is that the executive is an agent serving the interests of his principal. This justification disappears when the corporate executive imposes taxes and spends the proceeds for "social" purposes. He becomes in effect a public employee, a civil servant, even though he remains in name an employee of a private enterprise. On grounds of political principle, it is intolerable that such civil servants—insofar as their actions in the name of social responsibility are real and not just window dressing—should be selected as they are now. If they are to be civil servants, then they must be elected through a political process. If they are to impose taxes and make expenditures to foster "social" objectives, then political machinery must be set up to make the assessment of taxes and to determine through a political process the objectives to be served.

This is the basic reason why the doctrine of "social responsibility" involves the acceptance of the socialist view that political mechanisms, not market mechanisms, are the appropriate way to determine the allocation of scarce resources to alternative uses.

On the grounds of consequences, can the corporate executive in fact discharge his alleged "social responsibilities"? On the other hand, suppose he could get away with spending the stockholders' or customers' or employees' money. How is he to know how to spend it? He is told that he must contribute to fighting inflation. How is he to know what action of his will contribute to that end? He is presumably an expert in running his company—in producing a product or selling it or financing it. But nothing about his selection makes him an expert on inflation. Will his holding down the price of his product reduce inflationary pressure? Or, by leaving more spending power in the hands of his customers, simply divert it elsewhere? Or, by forcing him to produce less because of the lower price, will it simply contribute to shortages? Even if he could answer these questions, how much cost is he justified in imposing on his stockholders, customers and employees for this social purpose? What is his appropriate share and what is the appropriate share of others?

90   ISSUE 4 / Should Corporations Adopt Policies of Responsibility?

And, whether he wants to or not, can he get away with spending his stockholders', customers' or employees' money? Will not the stockholders fire him? (Either the present ones or those who take over when his actions in the name of social responsibility have reduced the corporation's profits and the price of its stock.) His customers and his employees can desert him for other producers and employers less scrupulous in exercising their social responsibilities.

This facet of "social responsibility" doctrine is brought into sharp relief when the doctrine is used to justify wage restraint by trade unions. The conflict of interest is naked and clear when union officials are asked to subordinate the interest of their members to some more general purpose. If the union officials try to enforce wage restraint, the consequence is likely to be wildcat strikes, rank-and-file revolts and the emergence of strong competitors for their jobs. We thus have the ironic phenomenon that union leaders—at least in the U.S.—have objected to Government interference with the market far more consistently and courageously than have business leaders.

The difficulty of exercising "social responsibility" illustrates, of course, the great virtue of private competitive enterprise—it forces people to be responsible for their own actions and makes it difficult for them to "exploit" other people for either selfish or unselfish purposes. They can do good—but only at their own expense.

Many a reader who has followed the argument this far may be tempted to remonstrate that it is all well and good to speak of Government's having the responsibility to impose taxes and determine expenditures for such "social" purposes as controlling pollution or training the hard-core unemployed, but that the problems are too urgent to wait on the slow course of political processes, that the exercise of social responsibility by businessmen is a quicker and surer way to solve pressing current problems.

Aside from the question of fact—I share Adam Smith's skepticism about the benefits that can be expected from "those who affect to trade for the public good"—this argument must be rejected on grounds of principle. What it amounts to is an assertion that those who favor the taxes and expenditures in question have failed to persuade a majority of their fellow citizens to be of like mind and that they are seeking to attain by undemocratic procedures what they cannot attain by democratic procedures. In a free society, it is hard for "evil" people to do "evil," especially since one man's good is another's evil.

I have, for simplicity, concentrated on the special case of the corporate executive, except only for the brief digression on trade unions. But precisely the same argument applies to the newer phenomenon of calling upon stockholders to require corporations to exercise social responsibility (the recent G.M. crusade for example). In most of these cases, what is in effect involved is some stockholders trying to get other stockholders (or customers or employees) to contribute against their will to "social" causes favored by the activists. Insofar as they succeed, they are again imposing taxes and spending the proceeds.

The situation of the individual proprietor is somewhat different. If he acts to reduce the returns of his enterprise in order to exercise his "social responsibility," he is spending his own money, not someone else's. If he wishes to spend his

NO / Milton Friedman **91**

money on such purposes, that is his right, and I cannot see that there is any objection to his doing so. In the process, he, too, may impose costs on employees and customers. However, because he is far less likely than a large corporation or union to have monopolistic power, any such side effects will tend to be minor.

Of course, in practice the doctrine of social responsibility is frequently a cloak for actions that are justified on other grounds rather than a reason for those actions.

To illustrate, it may well be in the long-run interest of a corporation that is a major employer in a small community to devote resources to providing amenities to that community or to improving its government. That may make it easier to attract desirable employees, it may reduce the wage bill or lessen losses from pilferage and sabotage or have other worthwhile effects. Or it may be that, given the laws about the deductibility of corporate charitable contributions, the stockholders can contribute more to charities they favor by having the corporation make the gift than by doing it themselves, since they can in that way contribute an amount that would otherwise have been paid as corporate taxes.

In each of these—and many similar—cases, there is a strong temptation to rationalize these actions as an exercise of "social responsibility." In the present climate of opinion, with its widespread aversion to "capitalism," "profits," the "soulless corporation" and so on, this is one way for a corporation to generate goodwill as a by-product of expenditures that are entirely justified in its own self-interest.

It would be inconsistent of me to call on corporate executives to refrain from this hypocritical window-dressing because it harms the foundations of a free society. That would be to call on them to exercise a "social responsibility"! If our institutions, and the attitudes of the public make it in their self-interest to cloak their actions in this way, I cannot summon much indignation to denounce them. At the same time, I can express admiration for those individual proprietors or owners of closely held corporations or stockholders of more broadly held corporations who disdain such tactics as approaching fraud.

Whether blameworthy or not, the use of the cloak of social responsibility, and the nonsense spoken in its name by influential and prestigious businessmen, does clearly harm the foundations of a free society. I have been impressed time and again by the schizophrenic character of many businessmen. They are capable of being extremely far-sighted and clearheaded in matters that are internal to their businesses. They are incredibly short-sighted and muddle-headed in matters that are outside their businesses but affect the possible survival of business in general. This short-sightedness is strikingly exemplified in the calls from many businessmen for wage and price guidelines or controls or income policies. There is nothing that could do more in a brief period to destroy a market system and replace it by a centrally controlled system than effective governmental control of prices and wages.

The short-sightedness is also exemplified in speeches by businessmen on social responsibility. This may gain them kudos in the short run. But it helps to strengthen the already too prevalent view that the pursuit of profits is wicked and immoral and must be curbed and controlled by external forces. Once this view is adopted, the external forces that curb the market will not be the social

92   ISSUE 4 / Should Corporations Adopt Policies of Responsibility?

consciences, however highly developed, of the pontificating executives; it will be the iron fist of Government bureaucrats. Here, as with price and wage controls, businessmen seem to me to reveal a suicidal impulse.

The political principle that underlies the market mechanism is unanimity. In an ideal free market resting on private property, no individual can coerce any other, all cooperation is voluntary, all parties to such cooperation benefit or they need not participate. There are no values, no "social" responsibilities in any sense other than the shared values and responsibilities of individuals. Society is a collection of individuals and of the various groups they voluntarily form.

The political principle that underlies the political mechanism is conformity. The individual must serve a more general social interest—whether that be determined by a church or a dictator or a majority. The individual may have a vote and say in what is to be done, but if he is overruled, he must conform. It is appropriate for some to require others to contribute to a general social purpose whether they wish to or not.

Unfortunately, unanimity is not always feasible. There are some respects in which conformity appears unavoidable, so I do not see how one can avoid the use of the political mechanism altogether.

But the doctrine of "social responsibility" taken seriously would extend the scope of the political mechanism to every human activity. It does not differ in philosophy from the most explicitly collectivist doctrine. It differs only by professing to believe that collectivist ends can be attained without collectivist means. That is why, in my book *Capitalism and Freedom*, I have called it a "fundamentally subversive doctrine" in a free society, and have said that in such a society, "there is one and only one social responsibility of business—to use its resources and engage in activities designed to increase its profits so long as it stays within the rules of the game, which is to say, engages in open and free competition without deception or fraud."

POSTSCRIPT

Should Corporations Adopt Policies of Corporate Social Responsibility?

Why should a business be moral? This question is different from the original question of ethics, which is, why should any human being be moral? Many argue that we should be moral as individuals because we are social animals, and we cannot fulfill our nature unless we recognize, honor, and work to protect the community that enfolds us. The corporation is different. It is an artificial entity, chartered by the state, for the sole purpose of enriching its owners. Corporations, then, have no interest but self-interest; in that respect, they are solitary animals, and they violate their nature if they try to live for others. As the selections by Hay and Gray and Friedman demonstrate, the essential. difference between the social-responsibility theorist and the increase-profit theorist is one of long-range or short-range planning. The intelligent corporate officer knows that in the long run, government, customers, and the press will make life intolerable for the company unless he or she takes care of the community's needs as conscientiously as he or she does the corporation's.

Suggested Readings

John K. Galbraith, *The Affluent Society* (Random House, 1971).

George A. Steiner, *Business and Society* (Random House, 1971).

Manuel G. Velasquez, *Business Ethics* (Prentice-Hall, 1982).

Peter A. French, *Collective and Corporate Responsibility* (Columbia University Press, 1984).

R. Edward Freeman, "Fixing the Ethics Crisis in Corporate America," *Miller Center Report* (Fall 2002).

Bennett Daviss, *The Futurist* (March 1999).

Adam Smith, *The Wealth of Nations* (Clarendon Press, 1976).

Thomas Donaldson and L. E. Preston, "The Stakeholder Theory of the Corporation: Concepts, Evidence, and Implications," *Academy of Management Review* (vol. 20).

On the Internet . . .

STAT-USA/Internet

This site, a service of the U.S. Department of Commerce, provides one-stop Internet browsing for business, trade, and economic information. It contains daily economic news, frequently requested statistical releases, information on export and international trade, domestic economic news and statistical series, and databases.

http://www.stat-usa.gov/stat-usa.html

PhRMA: America's Pharmaceutical Companies

PhRMA membership represents approximately 100 U.S. pharmaceutical companies that have a primary commitment to pharmaceutical research. Information on the effects of pharmaceutical price controls on research spending is one of the many topics covered at this site.

http://www.phrma.org

NumaWeb

This Numa Financial Systems site calls itself "the Internet's home page for financial derivatives." This site includes a reference index, a discussion forum, and links to many related sites.

http://www.numa.com/index.htm

Newton–Ford: Taking
Sides: Issues in Business
Ethics and Society, Ninth
Edition

II. Current Issues in
Business

7. Is Wal–Mart a Good
Model for Retail Sales?

© The McGraw–Hill
Companies, 2006

467

ISSUE 7

Is Wal-Mart a Good Model for Retail Sales?

YES: Sam Walton with John Huey, from *Made in America* (Doubleday, 1992)

NO: Silvia Ribeiro, from "The Costs of 'Walmartization,'" http://www.zmag.org/content/showarticle.cfm:SectionID (January 16, 2005)

ISSUE SUMMARY

YES: America loves Wal-Mart, and no one loved it better than Sam Walton, who founded it with a very clear idea of what the American consumer wanted and what had to be done to get a disparate workforce working together. His book is the best place to catch the spirit that informs the company, and the best argument for Wal-Mart's determination to get affordable goods into the hands of the American consumer.

NO: Silvia Ribeiro argues that this consumer heaven is achieved at a very high cost to the workers and to the community. As a megamonopoly, Wal-Mart is now the nineteenth most powerful economy in the world (only 49 of the top 100 are countries!), and in the long run, its monopolistic practices cheat even the consumer.

In 1945, as World War II drew to a close, Sam Walton bought a variety store that wasn't making any money and figured out how to cut costs until it did. Then he bought another store and did the same thing. For the most part, he wasn't very cagey about what he was doing; he set up his corporate headquarters in the least expensive part of the least expensive state in the union, he scouted all over the country and the world to find saleable goods at the lowest possible price, and he didn't mark them up very much; he put his new "big-box" stores out in the country where the other stores didn't bother to go but where he knew that there was a commodity-hungry customer base; he paid his workers subsistence wages and didn't bother to supply benefits (although the workers could buy health insurance if they were independently wealthy). Customers reacted positively: They flocked in for the lower prices, they loved the staff, which was trained to be really helpful and cheerful, and the huge volume made a huge profit. Were Sam still alive (he died in 1992), he'd be the richest person in the world, with double the wealth of Bill Gates. As it is, his family controls billions of dollars in wealth.

But the effect on all the other stakeholders in the enterprise is not as cheerful. Those smiling workers are glad enough to have jobs, which they will not have if they do not smile; but their pay contributes very little to the local economy. Worse, the "big-box" stores, huge islands in a sea of parking lot, destroy the country soils and forest, blocking off watercourses and causing other environmental damage, and they draw off what remains of downtown business. As downtown collapses, the landlords collapse, and there is no revenue for the school district. Most of Wal-Mart's revenue finds its way out of state; there are few ways that it can be redirected to the local community. (Note: Before arriving in town, Wal-Mart had negotiated tax holidays, so its own revenues yield little in the way of taxes.) As in the new free trade administration, Wal-Mart imports most of its merchandise from low-cost export platforms in Mexico and (increasingly) China, which has to pay very little for its labor because much of it is in prison, while off-shoring its accounting to India—jobs leave the United States and do not come back. Meanwhile, Wal-Mart workers, clinging to the only jobs left, protest that they are underpaid, have no benefits or job security, and are often locked into the building on the night shift to prevent theft and slacking.

What are *you:* a consumer, a worker, or a citizen? Which is more valuable to you, to be able to hold a dignified job, to be able to buy commodities at a very low price, or to support your community? Your answer to that question will determine your position on the next Wal-Mart fight in your backyard!

YES

Sam Walton with John Huey

Made in America

Hello, friends, I'm Sam Walton, founder and chairman of Wal-Mart Stores. By now I hope you've shopped in one of our stores, or maybe bought some stock in our company. If you have, you probably already know how proud I am of what is simply the miracle that all these Wal-Mart associates of mine have accomplished in the thirty years since we opened our first Wal-Mart here in northwest Arkansas, which Wal-Mart and I still call home. As hard as it is to believe sometimes, we've grown from that one little store into what is now the largest retailing outfit in the world. And we've really had a heck of a time along the way.

I realize we have been through something amazing here at Wal-Mart, something special that we ought to share more of with all the folks who've been so loyal to our stores and to our company. That's one thing we never did much of while we were building Wal-Mart, talk about ourselves or do a whole lot of bragging outside the Wal-Mart family—except when we had to convince some banker or some Wall Street financier that we intended to amount to something someday, that we were worth taking a chance on. When folks have asked me, "How did Wal-Mart do it?" I've usually been flip about answering them. "Friend, we just got after it and stayed after it," I'd say. We have always pretty much kept to ourselves, and we've had good reasons for it; we've been very protective of our business dealings and our home lives, and we still like it that way.

But as a result, a whole lot of misinformation and myth and half-truths have gotten around over the years about me and about Wal-Mart. And I think there's been way too much attention paid to my personal finances, attention that has caused me and my family a lot of extra trouble in our lives—though I've just ignored it and pretty much gone about my life and the business of Wal-Mart as best I could.

None of this has really changed. But I've been fighting cancer for a while now, and I'm not getting any younger anyway. And lately a lot of folks—including Helen and the kids, some of our executives here at the company, and even some of the associates in our stores—have been fussing at me that I'm really the best person to tell the Wal-Mart tale, and that—like it or not—my life is all wrapped up in Wal-Mart, and I should get it down right while I still can. So I'm going to try to tell this story the best I'm able to, as close to the

126   ISSUE 7 / Is Wal-Mart a Good Model for Retail Sales?

way it all came about, and I hope it will be almost as interesting and fun and exciting as it's been for all of us, and that it can capture for you at least something of the spirit we've all felt in building this company. More than anything, though, I want to get across once and for all just how important Wal-Mart's associates have been to its success.

This is a funny thing to do, this looking back on your life trying to figure out how all the pieces came together. I guess anybody would find it a little strange, but it's really odd for somebody like me because I've never been a very reflective fellow, never been one to dwell in the past. But if I had to single out one element in my life that has made a difference for me, it would be a passion to compete. That passion has pretty much kept me on the go, looking ahead to the next store visit, or the next store opening, or the next merchandising item I personally wanted to promote out in those stores—like a minnow bucket or a Thermos bottle or a mattress pad or a big bag of candy.

As I look back though, I realize that ours is a story about the kinds of traditional principles that made America great in the first place. It is a story about entrepreneurship, and risk, and hard work, and knowing where you want to go and being willing to do what it takes to get there. It's a story about believing in your idea even when maybe some other folks don't, and about sticking to your guns. But I think more than anything it proves there's absolutely no limit to what plain, ordinary working people can accomplish if they're given the opportunity and the encouragement and the incentive to do their best. Because that's how Wal-Mart became Wal-Mart: ordinary people joined together to accomplish extraordinary things. At first, we amazed ourselves. And before too long, we amazed everybody else, especially folks who thought America was just too complicated and sophisticated a place for this sort of thing to work anymore.

The Wal-Mart story is unique: nothing quite like it has been done before. So maybe by telling it the way it really happened, we can help some other folks down the line take these same principles and apply them to their dreams and make them come true.

⁓⁕⁓

. . . For all my confidence, I hadn't had a day's experience in running a variety store, so Butler Brothers sent me for two weeks' training to the Ben Franklin in Arkadelphia, Arkansas. After that, I was on my own, and we opened for business on September 1, 1945. Our store was a typical old variety store, 50 feet wide and 100 feet deep, facing Front Street, in the heart of town, looking out on the railroad tracks. Back then, those stores had cash registers and clerk aisles behind each counter throughout the store, and the clerks would wait on the customers. Self-service hadn't been thought of yet.

It was a real blessing for me to be so green and ignorant, because it was from that experience that I learned a lesson which has stuck with me all through the years: you can learn from everybody. I didn't just learn from reading every retail publication I could get my hands on, I probably learned the most from studying what John Dunham was doing across the street. . . .

YES / Walton with Huey   **127**

I learned a tremendous amount from running a store in the Ben Franklin franchise program. They had an excellent operating program for their independent stores, sort of a canned course in how to run a store. It was an education in itself. They had their own accounting system, with manuals telling you what to do, when and how. They had merchandise statements, they had accounts-payable sheets, they had profit-and-loss sheets, they had little ledger books called Beat Yesterday books, in which you could compare this year's sales with last year's on a day-by-day basis. They had all the tools that an independent merchant needed to run a controlled operation. I had no previous experience in accounting—and I wasn't all that great at accounting in college—so I just did it according to their book. In fact, I used their accounting system long after I'd started breaking their rules on everything else. I even used it for the first or six Wal-Marts.

As helpful as that franchise program was to an eager-to-learn twenty-seven-year-old kid, Butler Brothers wanted us to do things literally by the book—their book. They really didn't allow their franchisees much discretion. The merchandise was assembled in Chicago, St. Louis, or Kansas City. They told me what merchandise to sell, how much to sell it for, and how much they would sell it to me for. They told me that their selection of merchandise was what the customers expected. They also told me I had to buy at least 80 percent of my merchandise from them, and if I did, I would get a rebate at year-end. If I wanted to make a 6 or 7 percent net profit, they told me I would have to hire so much help and do so much advertising. This is how most franchises work.

At the very beginning, I went along and ran my store by their book because I really didn't know any better. But it didn't take me long to start experimenting—that's just the way I am and always have been. Pretty soon I was laying on promotional programs of my own, and then I started buying merchandise directly from manufacturers. I had lots of arguments with manufacturers. I would say, "I want to buy these ribbons and bows direct. I don't want you to sell them to Butler Brothers and then I have to pay Butler Brothers 25 percent more for them. I want it direct." Most of the time, they didn't want to make Butler Brothers mad so they turned me down. Every now and then, though, I would find one who would cross over and do it my way.

That was the start of a lot of the practices and philosophies that still prevail at Wal-Mart today. I was always looking for offbeat suppliers or sources. I started driving over to Tennessee to some fellows I found who would give me special buys at prices way below what Ben Franklin was charging me. One I remember was Wright Merchandising Co. in Union City, which would sell to small businesses like mine at good wholesale prices. I'd work in the store all day, then take off around closing and drive that windy road over to the Mississippi River ferry at Cottonwood Point, Missouri, and then into Tennessee with an old homemade trailer hitched to my car. I'd stuff that car and trailer with whatever I could get good deals on—usually on softlines: ladies' panties and nylons, men's shirts—and I'd bring them back, price them low, and just blow that stuff out the store.

128   ISSUE 7 / Is Wal-Mart a Good Model for Retail Sales?

I've got to tell you, it drove the Ben Franklin folks crazy. Not only were they not getting their percentages, they couldn't compete with the prices I was buying at. Then I started branching out further than Tennessee. Somehow or another, I got in touch by letter with a manufacturer's agent out of New York named Harry Weiner. He ran Weiner Buying Services at 505 Seventh Avenue. That guy ran a very simple business. He would go to all these different manufacturers and then list what they had for sale. When somebody like me sent him an order, he would take maybe 5 percent for himself and then send the order on to the factory, which would ship it to us. That 5 percent seemed like a pretty reasonable cut to me, compared to 25 percent for Ben Franklin.

I'll never forget one of Harry's deals, one of the best items I ever had and an early lesson in pricing. It first got me thinking in the direction of what eventually became the foundation of Wal-Mart's philosophy. If you're interested in "how Wal-Mart did it," this is one story you've got to sit up and pay close attention to. Harry was selling ladies' panties—two-barred, tricot satin panties with an elastic waist—for $2.00 a dozen. We'd been buying similar panties from Ben Franklin for $2.50 a dozen and selling them at three pair for $1.00. Well, at Harry's price of $2.00, we could put them out at four for $1.00 and make a great promotion for our store.

Here's the simple lesson we learned—which others were learning at the same time and which eventually changed the way retailers sell and customers buy all across America: say I bought an item for 80 cents. I found that by pricing it at $1.00 I could sell three times more of it than by pricing it at $1.20. I might make only half the profit per item, but because I was selling three times as many, the overall profit was much greater. Simple enough. But this is really the essence of discounting: by cutting your price, you can boost your sales to a point where you earn far more at the cheaper retail price than you would have by selling the item at the higher price. I retailer language, you can lower your markup but earn more because of the increased volume.

I began to mull this idea in Newport, but it would be another ten years before I took it seriously. I couldn't follow up on it in Newport because the Ben Franklin program was too cut-and-dried to permit it. And despite my dealings with the likes of Harry Weiner, I still had that contract saying I was supposed to buy at least 80 percent of my merchandise from Ben Franklin. If I missed that target, I didn't get my year-end rebate. The fact of the matter is I stretched that contract every way I could. I would buy as much as I could on the outside and still try to meet the 80 percent. Charlie Baum—who was then one of the field men for Ben Franklin—would say we were only at 70 percent, and I would foam at the mouth and rant and rave about it. I guess the only reason Butler Brothers didn't give me a harder time about it all is that our store had quickly gone from being a laggard to one of the top performers in our district.

Things began to clip along pretty good in Newport in a very short time. After only two and a half years we had paid back the $20,000 Helen's father loaned us, and I felt mighty good about that. It meant the business had taken off on its own, and I figured we were really on our way now.

We tried a lot of promotional things that worked really well. First, we put a popcorn machine out on the sidewalk, and we sold that stuff like crazy. So I thought and thought about it and finally decided what we needed was a soft ice cream machine out there too. I screwed my courage up and went down to the bank and borrowed what at the time seemed like the astronomical sum of $1,800 to buy that thing. That was the first money I ever borrowed from a bank. Then we rolled the ice cream machine out there on the sidewalk next to the popcorn machine, and I mean we attracted some attention with those two. It was new and different—another experiment—and we really turned a profit on it. I paid off that $1,800 note in two or three years, and I felt great about it. I really didn't want to be remembered as the guy who lost his shirt on some crazy ice cream machine. . . .

*

Not many companies out there gather several hundred of their executives, managers, and associates together every Saturday morning at seven-thirty to talk about business. Even fewer would begin such a meeting by having their chairman call the Hogs. That's one of my favorite ways to wake everybody up, by doing the University of Arkansas's Razorback cheer, real early on a Saturday. You probably have to be there to appreciate the full effect, but it goes like this:

> Whooooooooooooooooooooo Pig. Sooey!
> Whooooooooooooooooooooooooooo Pig. Sooey!
> Whooooooooooooooooooooooooooooooo Pig. Sooey!
> RAZORBACKS!!!!!

And if I'm leading the cheer, you'd better believe we do it loud. I have another cheer I lead whenever I visit a store: our own Wal-Mart cheer. The associates did it for President and Mrs. Bush when they were here in Bentonville not long ago, and you could see by the look on their faces that they weren't used to this kind of enthusiasm. For those of you who don't know, it goes like this:

> Give Me a W!
> Give Me an A!
> Give Me an L!
> Give Me a Squiggly!
> (Here, everybody sort of does the twist.)
> Give Me an M!
> Give Me an A!
> Give Me an R!
> Give Me a T!
> What's that spell?
> Wal-Mart!
> What's that spell?
> Wal-Mart!

130   ISSUE 7 / Is Wal-Mart a Good Model for Retail Sales?

Who's number one?

THE CUSTOMER!

I know most companies don't have cheers, and most board chairmen probably wouldn't lead them even if they did. But then most companies don't have folks like Mike "Possum" Johnson, who entertained us one Saturday morning back when he was safety director by taking on challengers in a no-holds-barred persimmon-seed-spitting contest, using Robert Rhoads, our company general counsel, as the official target. Most companies also don't have a gospel group called the Singing Truck Drivers, or a management singing group called Jimmy Walker and the Accountants.

My feeling is that just because we work so hard, we don't have to go around with long faces all the time, taking ourselves seriously, pretending we're lost in thought over weighty problems. At Wal-Mart, if you have some important business problem on your mind, you should be bringing it out in the open at a Friday morning session called the merchandising meeting or at the Saturday morning meeting, so we can all try to solve it together. But while we're doing all this work, we like to have a good time. It's sort of a "whistle while you work" philosophy, and we not only have a heck of a good time with it, we work better because of it. We build spirit and excitement. We capture the attention of our folks and keep them interested, simply because they never know what's coming next. We break down barriers, which helps us communicate better with one another. And we make our people feel part of a family in which no one is too important or too puffed up to lead a cheer or be the butt of a joke—or the target in a persimmon-seed-spitting contest.

We don't pretend to have invented the idea of a strong corporate culture, and we've been aware of a lot of the others that have come before us. In the early days of IBM, some of the things Tom Watson did with his slogans and group activities weren't all that different from the things we do. And, as I've said, we've certainly borrowed every good idea we've come across. Helen and I picked up several ideas on a trip we took to Korea and Japan in 1975. A lot of the things they do over there are very easy to apply to doing business over here. Culturally, things seem so different—like sitting on the floor eating eels and snails—but people are people, and what motivates one group generally will motivate another. . . .

Back in 1984, people outside the company began to realize just how different we folks at Wal-Mart are. That was the year I lost a bet to David Glass and had to pay up by wearing a grass skirt and doing the hula on Wall Street. I thought I would slip down there and dance, and David would videotape it so he could prove to everyone back at the Saturday morning meeting that I really did it, but when we got there, it turned out David had hired a truckload of real hula dancers and ukulele players—and he had alerted the newspapers and TV networks. We had all kinds of trouble with the police about permits, and the dancers' union wouldn't let them dance without heaters because it was so cold, and we finally had to get permission from the head of Merrill Lynch to dance on his steps. Eventually, though, I slipped on the grass skirt and the Hawaiian shirt and the leis over my suit and did what I think was a

YES / Walton with Huey   **131**

pretty fair hula. It was too good a picture to pass up, I guess—this crazy chairman of the board from Arkansas in this silly costume—and it ran everywhere. It was one of the few times one of our company stunts really embarrassed me. But at Wal-Mart, when you make a bet like I did—that we couldn't possibly produce a pretax profit of more than 8 percent—you always pay up. Doing the hula was nothing compared to wrestling a bear, which is what Bob Schneider, once a warehouse manager in Palestine, Texas, had to do after he lost a bet with his crew that they couldn't beat a production record.

Most folks probably thought we just had a wacky chairman who was pulling a pretty primitive publicity stunt. What they didn't realize is that this sort of stuff goes on all the time at Wal-Mart. It's part of our culture, and it runs through everything we do. Whether it's Saturday morning meetings or stockholders' meetings or store openings or just normal days, we always have tried to make life as interesting and as unpredictable as we can, and to make Wal-Mart a fun proposition. We're constantly doing crazy things to capture the attention of our folks and lead them to think up surprises of their own. We like to see them do wild things in the stores that are fun for the customers and fun for the associates. If you're committed to the Wal-Mart partnership and its core values, the culture encourages you to think up all sorts of ideas that break the mold and fight monotony. . . .

Silvia Ribeiro  **NO**

The Costs of "Walmartization"

For the first time in history, demarcating the beginning of the 21st century, the biggest company in the world was not an oil concern or an automobile manufacturer, but Wal-Mart, a supermarket chain. The symbolic value of this fact weighs as much as its crushing implications: it is the "triumph" of the anonymous, the substitution of the traditional way of acquiring what we need to feed ourselves, take care of our houses, tools and even medicine, traditionally involving interpersonal relationships, for a new one which is standardized, "mercantilized," and where we know progressively less about who, where and how or under which conditions what we buy is produced. Now, we can theoretically buy everything under the same roof, and even though goods seem cheaper, which actually is an illusion, the whole paradigm can end up being very expensive. To buy today at Wal-Mart may mean losing one's own job or contributing to the loss of somebody else's in your family or community sometime down the line.

Wal-Mart's policy of low prices is maintained while there are other places to shop in the same community. When the other shops go under, not able to compete, nothing prevents Wal-Mart from raising their prices, which the company invariably ends up doing. Wal-Mart has had a devastating influence in those communities where it showed up, and according to Wal-Mart Watch, an organization of citizens affected by the company's policies, for every two jobs that are created when it moves into a community, three are lost.

Wal-Mart is 19th among the 100 most powerful economies in the world, only 49 of which are now countries. Sam Walton's widow and their four sons control 38 percent of its shares. In 2004 they were sixth among the richest people in the world, with about 20 billion dollars each. If Sam Walton was alive he would be twice as rich as Bill Gates, who is number one on the list with 46 billion. Both are a clear expression of the modern megamonopoly and the control that they exert over consumers. These monopolies are of course intent on increasing their control. Wal-Mart, it could be argued, has the biggest impact, as it sells such a wide range of products and it wields tremendous power over suppliers and politicians.

It is the biggest chain of direct sales to the consumer in North America. In the U.S. it has over three thousand Wal-Mart stores and 550 Sam's Club outfits.

Newton–Ford: Taking
Sides: Issues in Business
Ethics and Society, Ninth
Edition

II. Current Issues in
Business

7. Is Wal–Mart a Good
Model for Retail Sales?

© The McGraw–Hill
Companies, 2006

477

NO / Silvia Ribeiro   **133**

In Mexico it already possesses 54 percent of the market, with 687 stores in 71 cities, including Wal-Mart, Sam's Club, Bodegas Aurrera, Superama and Suburbia, aside from the restaurant chains Vips, El Porton and Ragazzi. It already controls very large sectors of the market in Canada, Great Britain, Brazil, Germany and Puerto Rico, and its influence is on the rise in many others, Japan, for example.

It is the biggest private employer in the United States and Mexico. In the few decades it has been in existence it has accumulated an amazing history of being sued for many reasons, including illegally preventing the unionizing of its workers, and just about every other imaginable violation of workers' rights: discrimination against the disabled, sexual discrimination, child labor, lack of health care coverage, and unpaid overtime. In the U.S., 38 percent of its workers are without health care, and the salaries it pays are, on average, 26 percent lower than the industry norm. In December 2003 there were 39 class action lawsuits pending against the company in 30 different states in the U.S. for violations of overtime laws. In a round up in October, 2003 the government found 250 undocumented foreign workers, who of course were operating in even worse conditions. In June 2004 Wal-Mart lost the largest class action lawsuit in history, where 1,600,000 women proved that they suffered gender discrimination as employees of the company since 1998.

But the company's low prices are not based only in the exploitation of its workers in the countries where it operates directly. The prices are the direct result of the systematic use of "maquiladoras" in conditions of extreme exploitation. A worker in one of these, located in Bangladesh, told the Los Angeles Times in 2003 that her normal workday was from 8 am to 3 am, 10 or 15 days in a row. This is what it took to be able to survive given the wages she was getting paid. But in the same article, the manager of the plant complained that they had to become even more efficient, as Wal-Mart was threatening to move the production to China, where it could obtain lower prices.

Though absolutely terrible, labor exploitation is not the only "Wal-Mart" effect. There are many others, including the use of new technologies to track people's purchases even after leaving the supermarket. Control seems to be the name of the game in the "Walmartization" of the world.

Feeding Big Brother

Supermarkets are the segment of the food chain that moves the most capital. According to certain analysts, their influence towers over and could devour every other previous link in the chain, such as food and beverage producers, distributors, and agricultural suppliers, and producers. Whether they end up getting involved in these parts of the chain will depend on the economics of the game, so that if it is cheaper to allow other companies to compete amongst themselves, they will not get involved. The effect, nevertheless, is the same: the concentration of control and power in fewer and fewer hands. This is not limited to Wal-Mart but also includes other giants such as Carrefour, Ahold, Costco or Tesco.

But Wal-Mart stands out particularly because, besides being the biggest company in the world, its income is four times that of its largest competitor,

478

Newton–Ford: Taking
Sides: Issues in Business
Ethics and Society, Ninth
Edition

II. Current Issues in
Business

7. Is Wal–Mart a Good
Model for Retail Sales?

© The McGraw–Hill
Companies, 2006

134   ISSUE 7 / Is Wal-Mart a Good Model for Retail Sales?

and larger than the next four combined. Because it is the biggest seller of food products on a global level, it has tremendous influence over what and how food gets produced. It's already dabbling, for example, in agriculture by contract directly with the agricultural producers. It also is third in sales in medicines.

As if it was not enough to be such an economic power, largely due to its growing monopoly, Wal-Mart is beginning, as mentioned earlier, to utilize new technologies to obtain information over people's buying patterns. It is already testing, in three cities in the US, the substitution of bar codes for identification systems through radio frequency. This is a "labeling" system utilizing an electronic chip, no bigger than a grain of rice and potentially much smaller, containing information about the product, which is transmitted wirelessly to a computer. This chip is capable of storing much more information than the bar code. The problem is that its signal follows the purchaser outside of the supermarket doors. According to Wal-Mart, the consumer would have the choice of asking at the checkout that the chip be turned off, except it has no plans to advertise this possibility.

It has already experimented using products from Gillete and Procter & Gamble, and others such as Coca Cola, Kodak, Nestle and many others.

At the beginning of 2004, Wal-Mart told its 100 principal suppliers that they would have to be ready to provide this technology in January, 2005.

The system would start, at the beginning, only as a means to track wholesale shipments, that is to say, not necessarily directly related to the packaging that the consumer takes home. In November it announced that the majority of suppliers, plus an extra 37 added to the original list, would be ready. It is now only a matter of time until the cost of the chips goes down sufficiently before it is included in everything a consumer buys.

In practice, this means, for example, that consumers who register their credit cards on entering the store could conceivably pay for their purchase without having to go through a cashier, as the products would automatically register when exiting. But Wal-Mart and the others using the technology would have exact information regarding who, what, when, how much and where the products are used.

Though Wal-Mart is not the only one testing the technology—there's Tesco in Great Britain, and Metro, Carrefour and Home Depot in other places—it is the biggest force behind its development. It is important to know that the technology was first developed and implemented by the U.S. Defense Department.

Orwell must be spinning in his grave. These tiny systems of control, "little brothers," if you will, will go much further than the Big Brother he envisioned.

The paradigm of Walmartization towards a "happy world" trumpeted by the transnational companies needs our ignorance and passive indifference to succeed. Paradoxically, those remaining without access to credit or debit cards—in other words, the majority of the planet's inhabitants—will remain out of the reach of this control system. With all its power, Wal-Mart and the transnational needs us to survive. We don't need them.

POSTSCRIPT

Is Wal-Mart a Good Model for Retail Sales?

America is not the land that it used to be. A largely agrarian society in origin, we were a nation of small towns where people were born, lived, worked, worshipped, and died, where all the businesses were independently owned by residents who were full participants in the community. Now we move away, and leave the little towns, in pursuit of the advantages of the "mass society," commuting to work, traveling to entertainment, and picking our homes from all over the country—all over the world, actually. Why should we object to mass society's favorite retail chains displacing the small shops of the past, while our delightfully low prices are financed by slave labor in China? Part of our problem is that we want our world to stand still while we move freely through it. The next decades will confront us with many serious choices about our homes and our work. It may be time to learn Chinese.

If the topic of the patterns and forces of jobs and sales in the globalized economy continues to interest you, you may be interested in the following works: Barbara Ehrenrich, *Nickel and Dimed On (Not) Getting by in America* (Metropolitan/Owl Book, Henry Holt and Company, 2001); Tracie Rozhon, "Teaching Wal-Mart New Tricks—Retailing's Goliath Learns to Listen," *New York Times* (May 8, 2005, section 3, p. 1); David Hest, "Is Walmartization Ahead?" *Farm Industry News,* http://www.farmindustrynews.com/mag/farming_walmartization_ahead (September 1, 2004).